THE

COMPLETE WORKS

OF

SAMUEL TAYLOR COLERIDGE.

WITH AN INTRODUCTORY ESSAY

UPON HIS

PHILOSOPHICAL AND THEOLOGICAL OPINIONS.

EDITED BY

PROFESSOR SHEDD.

IN SEVEN VOLUMES.

VOL. I.

NEW YORK:
HARPER & BROTHERS, PUBLISHERS,
Nos. 329 AND 331 PEARL STREET,
FRANKLIN SQUARE.
1853.

THE

COMPLETE WORKS

OF

SAMUEL TAYLOR COLERIDGE,

VOL. I.

AIDS TO REFLECTION.

STATESMAN'S MANUAL.

NEW YORK:
HARPER & BROTHERS.
1853.

PUBLISHERS' ADVERTISEMENT.

THIS collection of Coleridge's Works contains all the productions of this author that have appeared in England, with the exception of his newspaper articles, which have been recently republished under the title of *Essays on his own Times.* It has not been deemed advisable to include these in this series, on account of the ephemeral character of most of them, and because the author's social, political and ethical philosophy is much more fully and clearly presented in the Essays of *The Friend.* The English editions of several of the treatises are accompanied with introductory and supplementary essays by the editors, which have generally been omitted, because of their prevailing reference to topics and controversies of local and temporary interest.

The purchaser of this edition, therefore, will, with the above-mentioned exception, possess the *entire and unabridged* works of S. T. Coleridge.

CONTENTS.

INTRODUCTORY ESSAY.

In presenting the public with a complete edition of the works of Samuel Taylor Coleridge, it seems proper to preface it with some remarks upon their general spirit and tendency. At first sight this may seem to be a superfluous attempt, because from the very first appearance of this author before the world, down to the present moment, he has been the subject of analysis and criticism, both offensive and defensive, to an extent unparalleled in the case of any other literary man, within the same length of time. Yet a second look will enable any one to see, that notwithstanding all this remark upon Coleridge, it is still difficult to form an estimate of his mind, and of his real worth as a Thinker. Critics themselves have been embarrassed by the remarkable universality of his genius, and the wonderful variety of his productions, and have generally confined themselves to one side of his mind, and one class of his works. The result is that one gift of the man has been extolled to the depreciation of another. Those, and they are the great majority, who have been impressed by the rich and exhaustless Imagination of Coleridge, and by his contributions to the lighter and more beautiful forms of Literature, have lamented that so much of the power and vigor of his intellect, should have been enlisted in Philosophy; while the lesser number who have been stimulated and strengthened by his profound speculations, as they have been by no contemporaneous English writer, have regretted that the poetic nature prevented that singleness of aim and unity of pursuit, which might have left as the record of his life, a philosophic system, to be placed beside those of Plato and Kant. With the exception of the clear and masterly Essay, prefixed to his edition of the *Aids to Reflection*, by the late Dr. Marsh, whose premature decease, in the full vigor of his powers, and the full maturity of his discipline and scholarship, is the greatest loss American

Philosophy has yet been called to meet, we call to mind no thoroughly elaborated, and truly profound estimate, of the philosophical opinions of Coleridge. There are two reasons for this. In the first place, the speculative opinions of Coleridge were a slow formation, and although they finally came to have a fixed and determined character, yet during the first half of his literary career, he was undoubtedly not clear in his own mind. The consequence therefore is, that the philosophy of Coleridge must be *gathered* from his writings rather than *quoted* from them, and hence the difficulty for the critic, which does not exist in the instance of a rounded and finished treatise, to determine the real form and matter of his system. In the second place, the literary world has not been interested in the department of Philosophy. Those problems relating to the nature of man, the universe, and God, which in some ages of the world have swallowed up in their living vortex all the best thinking of the human mind, and which in reality have been the root whence have sprung all the loftiest growths of the human intellect, have been displaced by other and slighter themes, and hence the English Philosopher of this age has been a lonely and solitary thinker. There have been ages when the striking expression of Hazlitt, would apply with literal truth to the majority of the literary class :—" Sir, I am a metaphysician, and nothing makes an impression upon me but abstract ideas." But the age in which one of the most subtile and profound of English minds made his appearance and cast his bread upon all waters, was the least abstract in its way of thinking, the most concrete and outward in its method and tendency, of any. These two causes combined, will account, perhaps, for the fact that while the poetical and strictly literary productions of Coleridge have on the whole met with a genial reception and an appreciative criticism, his philosophical and theological opinions have been at the best, imperfectly understood, and more often, much misunderstood and misrepresented. While therefore Coleridge has done more than any other man, with the exception of Wordsworth, to form the poetic taste of the age and to impart style and tone to the rising generation of English Poets, and as a literary man has done more by far than any other one, to revolutionize the criticism of the age—while in this way " he has been melted into the rising literatures of England and America" —Coleridge as a Thinker has accomplished far less.

And yet it is our belief, that in this latter character—in the capacity of a Philosopher and Theologian—Coleridge is to exert his greatest and best influence. After his immediate influence upon Poetry and Belles Lettres shall have disappeared in that most vital and therefore most shifting of all processes—the ever-evolving development of a national Literature—the direction and impulse which his speculative opinions have given to the English thinking of the nineteenth century, will for a long time to come, be as distinct and unmistakable as the Gulf-Stream in the Atlantic. It is for this reason that we shall, in this introductory essay, confine our remarks to the philosophical and theological opinions of Coleridge; and it will be our aim, as fully as our limits will permit, to contemplate him as a Thinker, the main tendency of whose thinking is in the right direction, and the general spirit and influence of whose system is profound and salutary. It will be our object to justify to the general mind that respectful regard for Coleridge's philosophical and theological views, and that confidence in their general soundness, which is so marked a characteristic of that lesser but increasing public who have been swayed by him for the last twenty years. In doing this, however, we mean not to appear as the mere passive recipient of his opinions, or as the blind adherent of each and every one of them. How far we are disposed to look upon Coleridge as an original thinker, in the sense in which the phrase is applied to the Platos and Aristotles, the Leibnitzes and Kants of the race, and to what extent we think he may be regarded as the author of a system, and as the head of a school in Philosophy, will appear in the course of our remarks.

And we would here in the outset direct attention to the manner in which the opinions of Coleridge originated. It is unfortunate that no biography at all worthy of the man is in existence, his own most interesting but most fragmentary *Biographia Literaria*, still being the best account of his intellectual and moral history yet given to the world. With the aid, however, to be derived from the biographical materials now before the world, a careful study of his writings themselves will enable the discerning student, not only to gather the general system finally adopted, and to some extent developed, by Coleridge, but also to trace the origin and growth of it. A full account, however, of the inward as well as outward life of Coleridge, by a congenial mind, would be, in many respects, the richest contribution to psychology that could be made.

For the mental development of Coleridge was eminently an historic process. He did not, as do the majority of men, even literary men, begin with the same general system and method of thinking, with which he ended, but like the age in which he lived and upon which he impressed himself, he passed by a slow but most thorough process from a sensuous to a spiritual system of speculation. Bred up in the reigning empirical philosophy of the eighteenth century, it was only gradually, and as we think, through the intermediate stage of Pantheism, that he finally came out, in the maturity of his powers, upon the high ground of a rational and Christian Theism. In like manner, and parallel with this, he went through a great theological change. Beginning with the Socinianism, which, at the close of the last century, existed not merely in an independent and avowed form of dissent from the Established Church of England, but also to some extent in the clergy of this church itself, Coleridge, partly from the change in his philosophic views, and still more as we believe from severe inward struggles, and a change in his own religious experience, in the end, embraced the Christian system with a depth and sincerity, a humility and docility of spirit rarely to be found in the history of philosophers and poets, of whom "few are called." And finally the same revolution, the same change for the better, and growth, appears in his political opinions. Embracing with "proud precipitance of soul" the cause of a false freedom, he gradually moderated his views, grew conservative, and in the end settled down upon the principles of the majority of cultivated Englishmen, and rested in them.

Now this peculiarity in the origin and formation of the system of opinions finally adopted by Coleridge, and by which he ought to be known, and will be known to posterity, deserves serious and candid attention for several reasons. In the first place, the student will thereby be saved from the errors into which many individuals, and to some extent the age itself, have fallen, of attributing to Coleridge, as the ultimate and fixed view of his mind, opinions which had but an early and transient existence in it, and which sustain about the same relation to his final system, that the pang and the throe do to the living birth. The question for the student in relation to Coleridge is not:—What did he believe and teach on this point, and on that point, in the year 1800—but what did he teach and believe in the fulness of his development and in the maturity of his ripened reason. The question is not :—What can be logically deduced, and still less what can be twisted and tortured, out of this or that passage in his writings, but what is unquestionably the strong drift and general spirit of them as a whole. No writer more needs, or is more deserving of a generous and large-minded criticism than this one. Without reserve he has communicated himself to the world, in all the phases of experience and varieties of opinion through which he passed—in all his weaknesses and in all his strength—and such an exposure as this, surely ought not to be subjected to the same remorseless inference as that to which we of right subject the single treatise on a single doctrine, of a mind made up.

Again, this recognition of the manner in which the opinions of Coleridge were formed will, at the very same time that it opens the eye to all that is true and sound in them, also open it to whatever is defective or erroneous. How much there is of the latter is a point upon which each mind must judge for itself, and such freedom of judgment is one of the plainest lessons and most natural fruits of the general system contained in these volumes. Provided only the judgment be intelligent and free from bigotry, we believe Coleridge will suffer no more than the finite human mind must suffer, when it allows itself to expatiate in all regions of inquiry, and attempts to construct a system of universal knowledge. If we remember the immense range of Coleridge's studies and the vastness of his schemes, and also remember that though he had not the constructive ability of an Aristotle or a Hegel, and did not fairly and fully realize a single one of his many plans, he yet has left on record some expression of his mind, upon nearly or quite all the more serious and important subjects that come before the human understanding, we shall not be surprised to find some misconceptions and errors in his multifarious productions. But these mistakes and deficiencies themselves will be the most unerringly detected, and the most effectually guarded against, by him who is able to view and criticize them from the very vantage-ground itself, to which his mind has been lifted by the principles of the general system of Coleridge. Having made these "the fountain-light of all his day, the master-light of all his seeing," the inquirer after truth will be able to detect the errors to which the human mind is always liable, and which in the present instance are, as we verily believe, the excrescences merely.

But however it may have been with Coleridge himself, it is plain that this slow process of renunciation of erroneous systems and reception of more correct ones, is one of increased interest and worth for the inquirer. Like the *Retractions* of Augustine, the retractions of Coleridge, if we may call them such, have a negative worth almost equal to that of the positive statements to which they lead. This rise of the mind through doubts and prejudices to a higher and more rectified position—this nearing the centre of absolute truth, by these corrections—is always one of the most instructive passages in literary history. And especially is it so in the case of Coleridge. We see here one of the most capacious and powerfully-endowed minds of the race, after a slow and toilsome course, first through the less profound, and lastly through the most profound of the two erroneous systems of speculation, in which many of the most gifted intellects, contemporaneous with him, were caught and stopped, ultimately and with a deep and clear consciousness finding rest in Christianity as the eternal ground not only of life but also of truth, not only of religion but also of philosophy. Coleridge lived contemporaneously with that most wonderful, and for the speculating intellect most overmastering, of all mental processes, the pantheistic movement in the German mind. But while he was at one period of his life—the heyday of hope and aspiration—involved in it so far as to say that his head was with Spinoza, we find him freeing himself from it at an after-period when the whole continental mind was drawn within reach of its tremendous sweep as within the circles of a maelstrom. He worked his way through and out of a system the most stupendous for its logical consistence, and the most fascinating for the imagination of any that the world has yet seen, and undoubtedly stablished and settled his own mind, whether he may have done the same for others or not, in the Christian Theism, at a time when the speculation and philosophizing of his day were fast departing from the centre of truth, and drawing nearly all the inquiring intellect of Germany and France with them. During the last quarter of his life, as matter of fact, Coleridge was the resort and the teacher for many minds who were seeking rest and finding none in the sphere of philosophy, and whether he relieved their doubts and cleared up their difficulties or not, no one of them ever seems to have doubted that he was clear and settled in his own mind, and that though he might not succeed in refuting the positions of Atheism and Pantheism, he was himself impregnable to them. But there is reason to believe that many minds were strengthened and armed by him, and that the philosophy and theology of England is at this very moment very different from what it would have been had the thinking of Coleridge not been working like leaven in it.* It is a remark of Goethe that our own faith is wonderfully increased on learning that another mind shares it with us; and perhaps one of the strongest reasons for a wavering soul, for believing in the highest truths of philosophy and religion, and for rejecting the skepticism of the human understanding, lies in such examples as that of Coleridge. His belief was not hereditary and passive. He was not ignorant of the arguments and gigantic schemes which the speculative reason has constructed in opposition to the truth. He had painfully felt in his own being the difficulties and doubts to which man is liable, and to which the acutest intellects have too often succumbed. He had been over the whole ground from Pyrrho to Hegel, and after all his investigation saw his way clear into the region of Christian Revelation and rested there. Surely such an example is an argument and an authority for the doubting mind. All that Burke† says of the relation of the culture of Montesquieu to the Constitution of England, in that splendid passage, at once the most magnificent rhetoric and the strongest logic, applies with fuller and far deeper force, to the relation of an endowment, a discipline, and an acquisition, like that of Coleridge, to Philosophy and Christianity.

It is in reference to this historical formation and enunciation of the opinions of Coleridge that this, so far as we know, first *complete* collection of his works finds its justification and recommendation. It has been said in respect to the publication of such portions of his writings as the *Table Talk* and the *Lit-*

* Even the recent picture of Coleridge by Carlyle, unconsciously betrays his sense of the superiority of this intellect, in reference to the deeper problems of man's existence and destiny, while poor Sterling seems to have derived from the oracle at Highgate, most of that little faith in a personal God and in man's freedom and immortality, which throws such a sadly-pleasing air over his biography.

† Appeal from the New to the Old Whigs, *sub fine.*

erary Remains, that their extremely fragmentary character ought to exclude them from a permanent collection of a great writer's works, and that at least they should be subjected to a revision that would strike out the less important matter, the sometimes hastily conceived and rashly uttered remark. But in the light of what has been said, the value of every jot and tittle of what Coleridge, and his friends, for him, have ever printed, is clearly apparent. Not that every thing he has left on record has high intrinsic worth—not that every thing he has written can be regarded as the pure product of his own brain—not that every thing contained in these volumes is to be received as truth by the reader—but each and every thing here, has value and interest, if for nothing else, as exhibiting the course and development of his intellect. In this reference the volumes containing the *Table Talk* and *Literary Remains* are of the highest value not only for the wonderful pregnancy and suggestiveness of his remarks upon all things human or divine, but for the acquaintance they give the reader with the interior process and change going on within him. A careful perusal of these *in connection with the dates*, throws great light upon the history of Coleridge's mind. Aside however from the value of these productions in this respect, they have great intrinsic worth. Besides the profound and piercing glances into the highest truths of metaphysical philosophy, scattered throughout the *Literary Remains*, unquestionably the best philosophy of Art and of Criticism, and the very best actual criticism upon the great creative minds in Literature, that is accessible to the merely English reader, are to be found in this same miscellany.

It is of course impossible in an introductory essay, to attempt a criticism in detail upon all the principal topics upon which Coleridge has philosophized, even if we were competent to the task, and we shall therefore confine ourselves to a few points, which we think are deserving of consideration, and which will tend to place their author in a just and fair light as a thinker.

1. And in the first place, we think this author is to be recommended and confided in, as the foremost and ablest English opponent of Pantheism. We do not speak of formal opposition to this, the most powerful and successful of all systems of false philosophy, for Coleridge has left on record no professed and finished refutation of Spinoza or Schelling, but we allude to the whole

plan and structure of the philosophy which he finally adopted and defended, as in its own nature the most effectual preventive of the adoption of Pantheism, and the best positive remedy for it when adopted, to be found out of that country, which has furnished both, the most virulent bane, and the most powerful antidote. The distinctions lying at the foundation of his whole system, if recognized and received, render it impossible for the recipient to be diverted from the true method of thinking, into one so illegitimate and abnormal, as the pantheistic, to say nothing of their incompatibility with the fundamental positions of Pantheism. No ingenuity whatever, *e. g.* can amalgamate the doctrine of which Coleridge makes so much, of an *essential* distinction between Nature and Spirit, with the doctrine of the *substantia una et unica.* If the Natural is of one substance, and the Spiritual is of another—if the distinction is not merely formal but substantial, and no possible heightening and clarification of the former can result in the latter—then there is a gulf between Nature and Spirit, between Matter and Mind, which can not be filled up. This distinction, moreover, not only permits, but naturally conducts to, the conceptions of an uncreated and a created essence—conceptions which are precluded by the assumption, which the pantheist supposes he must make in order to introduce unity into the system of the universe, that there is ultimately only one substance, uncreated, infinite, and eternal. The very moment that the materialism, which is to be found in ideal Pantheism notwithstanding its boast of spirituality, as really as in material Pantheism, is eliminated and refuted and precluded, by the recognition of a difference *in kind* between Nature and Spirit, the inquirer is left alone with the self-determined, *personal* Spirit; the contrary and antithesis of Nature and of Matter, with its Reason and its Conscience, and thereafter may be safely left to answer the questions :—Is there an uncreated personal God ? am I a created and accountable being ? am I destined to a conscious immortality of existence ? But if this distinction is denied, and Nature and Spirit, Matter and Mind, the World and God, are all one essence and substance, and the distinctions denoted by these terms are merely formal, subjective and phenomenal, then such questions as the above are absurd and impossible.

We are aware that in these pantheistic systems the terms, Nature and Spirit, the World and God, are as freely employed as in theistic systems, and that in the last and most remarkable of them all, Philosophy itself is divided into the Philosophy of Nature and the Philosophy of Spirit. But on the hypothesis of a one sole substance, the subject-matter of each must be one and the same, and the inquirer in the latter department is only investigating a mere *modification* of the same thing which he has just investigated in the former. He has risen into no *essentially* higher sphere of being or of knowing, by passing from the philosophy of Nature to that of Spirit, as he understands and employs these terms, because he has not passed into any *essentially* different sphere. The vice of the whole system is in the fatal error—the pantheistic postulate—at the outset. There is, and can be, but one substance, and notwithstanding all the modification it may undergo in infinite space and everlasting time, it remains but one substance still. But this vice is impossible in any system of philosophy or in any method of thinking, that starts with the fundamental hypothesis of a difference *in kind* between the substance of the Natural and the substance of the Spiritual, or between Matter and Mind.*

Now the earnestness and force with which this distinction, so fundamental to Theism and preclusive of Pantheism, is insisted upon by Coleridge, particularly in the *Aids to Reflection*, the most complete and self-consistent of his strictly philosophic writings, will strike every reflecting reader. It is not merely formally laid down, but it enters so thoroughly into his whole method of philosophizing, that it can be eliminated from it only as oxygen can from atmospheric air, by decomposition and destruction. And especially are all pantheistic conceptions and tendencies excluded by the distinction in question, when it is further considered that the constituent element in the Spiritual, is freedom, as that of the Natural is necessity. In Nature, as distinguished from Spirit, there is no absolute beginning, no first start, consequently no self-motion, and consequently no responsibility. Nature, says Coleridge, is an endless line, in constant and continuous evolution. To be in the middle of an endless series, is the characteristic of a thing of Nature, says Jacobi,† between whose

* We use Matter in a somewhat loose way in this connection, in order to illustrate the strict use of the word Nature as the contrary of Spirit, and not because it contains all that is meant by Nature.

† Werke, Bd. 3, S. 401. Leipsic Ed. 1816.

statements regarding this general distinction, in the last part of his *Von Göttlichen Dingen,* and those of Coleridge in the *Aids,* there is a striking coincidence. In the Spirit and the Spiritual realm, on the contrary, this law, and process, of continuity, by which we are hurried back from the effect to its foregoing cause, and from this foregoing cause to *its* foregoing cause, and so backward endlessly into an infinite inane, and can never reach a point where a movement has no antecedent, because it really *begins,* by *self*-movement—that point where a *responsible* movement is first found, and which is to be reached, not by a gradual ascent within the sphere of the Natural, to the highest degree of the same kind, but by a leap over the gulf which divides the two great domains from each other—this law of continuous cause and effect, we say, is excluded from the sphere of the Spiritual by virtue of its differing *in kind* from the Natural; by virtue of its being of *another substance,* and consequently, of having an essentially different function and operation, from Nature and Matter. It is true that we speak of a continuous evolution and development, and properly too, within the realm of Spirit as well as of Nature, but the continuity in this instance is not continuity without beginning and without ending, or the continuity of the law of cause and effect which is the only law in the Natural world, but continuity that has a true beginning or first start, or the continuity of self-determination. Development in the Spiritual world—that of the human Will for example—begins with the creation of the Will, and proceeds freely and responsibly so long as the Will exists. The development or movement, in this instance, is not like that of a movement in Nature, a mere and pure effect. If it were, a cause must be found for it antecedent to, and other than, it; and this would bring the process out of the sphere of the Spiritual or *self*-moved, into the sphere of Nature, and make it a dependent unit in an endless series of processes, to the destruction of all responsibility. But we have no disposition to repeat what has been so clearly expressed by Coleridge on this point, and re-affirmed and explained by Dr. Marsh in his preliminary Essay to the *Aids.* The distinction itself, never more important than at this time when Naturalism is so rife, can not, after all, be taught in words, so well as it can be thought out. It is a matter of direct perception, if perceived at all, as must be the case with all *à priori* and fundamental positions. The contradiction which clings to the idea of *self*-motion, when we attempt to express it through the imperfect medium of language is merely verbal, and will weigh nothing with the mind that has once *seen* the distinction.

Now on the pantheistic system there is really nothing but Nature. The one Substance, of which all things are modifications and developments, is nothing but a single infinite Nature. From eternity to eternity the process of emanation and evolution goes on, and the result is, all that was, is, and is to come. Though the terms God and Man, Spirit and Nature, Mind and Matter, may be employed, yet the objects denoted by them are of one and the same substance, and therefore have the same primary attributes. The history of the universe is the history of a single Being, and of one, merely Natural, necessitated process, slowly and blindly evolving from that dark ground of all existence, the one aboriginal substance. There is no creation out of nothing, of a new and secondary substance, but merely the shaping of the eternal and only substance. There is, except in a phenomenal and scenic way, no finite being. The All is One and infinite. The self-consciousness of the finite subject which the pantheist recognizes does not help the matter. This consciousness itself is but a mockery, by which a modification of the one and only Being is made to suppose for a little time that it has a truly individual and responsible existence. The only *reality* on this scheme is a single universal Nature with its innumerable processes, and all the personal self-consciousness which is recognized by it is a deceptive and transitory phenomenon, for the reason, that there is, in an essence which is not simply beneath and through all things, but IS all things, no basis for distinct personality, free self-determination and permanent self-consciousness either in God or man. For there must be coherence between attributes and their substance, and it is absurd to endow with the attributes of freedom and responsibility, a substance, or a subjective modification of a substance, whose whole history is in fact a necessitated and blind evolution. In order to an infinite Personality there must be an infinite personal Essence or Being. In order to finite Personality there must be a finite personal Essence or Being. And these two can not be or become one Essence or Being, without destroying the peculiar basis for the peculiar consciousness belonging to each. Pantheism has, therefore, no right to the terms of Theism, for the simple reason that the objects denoted by them, are not recognized by it as metaphysically and scientifically real. Pantheism is but a Philosophy of Nature, and as matter of fact it has accomplished more, or rather has done least injury to the cause of truth and true philosophy, when, as in the case of the earlier system of Schelling, it has been confined mainly to the sphere of Nature. It would be unjust to deny that the Pantheism of Schelling has done something toward destroying the mechanical theory and view of Nature and Natural Science, while the fact that he proceeded no farther with it in its application to the Philosophy of Spirit and of Intelligence, and is understood to have renounced it in his late attempt to construct a system that will solve the problems of Intellectual and Spiritual existence, seems to corroborate the position here taken, that Pantheism can never at any time, or under any of its forms, rise out of the sphere of Nature, because it, in reality, recognizes the existence of nothing but Nature.

It has been asserted, we are aware, and perhaps it is still to some extent believed, that the philosophy of Coleridge is itself liable to the charge of Pantheism. The warm admiration with which he regarded Schelling, and the reception at one time of Schelling's doctrine of the original identity of Subject and Object, have given some ground for the assertion and belief. We shall, therefore, dwell briefly upon this point of Coleridge's relation to Schelling, because while we are clear that the earlier system of this philosopher, whatever his later system shall prove to be, is nothing but Spinozism, we are equally clear that Coleridge freed himself from it, as decidedly as he did from the mechanical philosophy of his youthful days.

After all the study and reflection which Coleridge expended upon the systems of speculation that sprang up in Germany after that of Kant, it is very evident that his closest and longest continued study was applied to Kant himself. After all his wide study of philosophy, ancient and modern, the two minds who did most toward the formation of Coleridge's philosophic opinions were Plato and Kant. From the Greek he derived the doctrine of Ideas, and fully sympathized with his warmly-glowing and poetic utterance of philosophic truths. From the German he derived the more strictly scientific part of his system—the fundamental distinctions between the Understanding and the Reason (with the sub-distinction of the latter into Speculative and Practical), and between Nature and Spirit. With him also he sympathized in that deep conviction of the absolute nature and validity of the great ideas of God, Freedom and Immortality—of the binding obligation of Conscience—and generally of the supremacy of the Moral and Practical over the purely Speculative. Indeed any one who goes to the study of Kant, after having made himself acquainted with the writings of Coleridge, will be impressed by the spontaneous and vital concurrence of the latter with the former—the heartiness and entireness with which the Englishman enters into the method and system, of this, in many respects, greatest philosopher of the modern world. For to say that Coleridge was the originator of the distinctions above-mentioned, in the sense that Kant was, is to claim for him what will never be granted by the scholar; and on the other hand to say that Coleridge was a mere vulgar plagiary, copying for the mere sake of gratifying vanity, is not to be thought of for a moment. The plagiary is always a copyist and never an imitator, to use a distinction of Kant,* also naturalized among us by Coleridge. There is no surer test of plagiarism therefore than a dry, mechanical, and dead method, by which the material handled becomes a mere *caput mortuum*. But who would charge such a method upon Coleridge? Whatever else may be laid to his charge, there is no lack of life, and life, too, that organizes and vitalizes. Much of that obscurity charged upon him is owing to an excess of life; the warm stream gushes out with such ebullience that it can not be confined to a channel, but spreads out on all sides like an inundation. Had there been less play of living power in his mind, he would have been a more distinct thinker for the common mind, and as we believe, less exposed to the charge of plagiarism. This power of sympathy with the great minds of the race in all departments of mental effort—this opulence and exuberance of endowment, coupled with an immense range of reading and a brooding contemplation that instantaneously assimilated every thing brought into his mind—put him *unconsciously, and in spite of himself*, into communication with all the best thinking of the race; and hence it is, that while the beginner in philosophy finds the writings of Coleridge full to bursting, with principles, and germs of truth, freshly presented and entirely new to him, his

* Urtheilskraft, § 32.

after-study of the great thinkers of ancient and of modern times, compels him to deduct from Coleridge's merits on the score of absolute discovery and invention, though not an iota from them on the score of originality, in the sense of original treatment. It is for this reason that the writings of this author are the very best preparatory exercise for the student, before he launches out upon the "mighty and mooned sea" of general philosophy. One who has thoroughly studied them, is well prepared to begin his philosophical studies; and, we may add, no one who has once mastered this author can possibly stop with him, but is urged on to the study of the greatest and choicest philosophic systems themselves.

But returning to the relation of Coleridge to Schelling, we think that it is very evident that his reception of the doctrine of the identity of Subject and Object, of which he gives an account in the *Biographia Literaria*, that is mainly a transfusion from Schelling, was temporary. In the year 1834, we find him speaking thus of this account, "The metaphysical disquisition at the end of the first volume of the *Biographia Literaria*, is unformed and immature; it contains the fragments of the truth, but it is not fully thought out."* This, taken in connection with the general drift of Coleridge's annotations upon Schelling, contained in the latest edition of the *Biographia Literaria*,† we think is nearly

* Table Talk, Works, VI. p. 520.

† At the end of Schelling's *Denkmal der Schrift von den göttlichen Dingen, &c., des Jacobi*, Coleridge has written:

"Spite of all the superior airs of the *Natur-Philosophie*, I confess that in the perusal of Kant I breathe the air of good sense and logical understanding with the light of reason shining in it and through it: while in the Physics of Schelling, I am amused with happy conjectures, and in his Theology I am bewildered by positions which in their first sense are transcendental (über fliegend), and in their literal sense scandalous."—*Biog. Lit. Appen.*, III. p. 709.

P. 54, and then pp. 59–62. "The *Spinozism* of Schelling's system first betrays itself."—*Biog. Lit. Appendix*, III. p. 707.

"Strange that Fichte and Schelling both hold that the very object which is the condition of self-consciousness, is nothing but the self itself by an act of free self-limitation.

"P.S. The above I wrote a year ago; but the more I reflect, the more convinced I am of the gross materialism which lies under the whole system." —*Biog. Lit. Appendix*, III. p. 701.

This last is a note, it deserves to be noticed, upon Schelling's *Briefe über Dogmatismus und Criticismus*, or attack upon the Critical Philosophy; and equivalent to a distinct verbal renunciation of the theory in question. At any rate his rejection of the system of Spinoza is expressed often and with emphasis in his writings,* although in common with all who have made themselves acquainted with the works of this remarkable mind, he expresses himself in terms of the highest admiration, respecting the loftiness and grandeur of many of his sentiments and reflections, even on subjects pertaining to ethics and religion. But what is Schelling's identity of Subject and Object in their ultimate ground, but the reappearance of the one Substance of Spinoza with its two modifications Thought and Extension? The theory which teaches that the Subject contemplating and the Object contemplated are in reality but one substance, and that the consciousness we have of things without us "is not only coherent, but identical and one and the same thing, with our own immediate self-consciousness,"† plainly does not differ in matter, however it may in form, from the theory of the *substantia una et unica.* What is gained by saying that Spinoza started with an unthinking substance, but that the system of Identity starts with a thinking subject,‡ when the position that *One is All, and All is One*, is the fundamental postulate of both systems alike? This position, common to both, renders both systems alike pantheistic, because it precludes that duality —that difference in substance between God and the World, and that distinction between an uncreated and a created Essence or Being—which must be recognized by a truly theistic philosophy. The only difference between the two systems is adjective: Spinozism being material, and the system of Identity ideal, Pantheism. If the postulate in question were limited in its application to the sphere of the finite alone, there might be a shadow of reason for saying that the doctrine of Identity does not annihilate the Deity, as other than the World. If an identity of substance were affirmed only between the human mind and the created universe, a supramundane Deity, other than and above all this finite unity might still be affirmed without self-contradiction; though even in this

the earnestness with which Coleridge in these notes generally, sides with this latter system, shows that neither his head nor his heart was with the system of Identity at the time he wrote these annotations.

* Aids to Reflection, Works, I. p. 211. Table Talk, Works, VI. pp. 301, 302

† Biog. Lit. chapter xii.

‡ Hegel's Phänomenologie, S. 14.

case this limited annihilation of the essential distinction between Nature and Spirit would result in its universal and absolute annihilation, so soon as it became apparent that the finite Spirit though not of the *same*, is yet of *similar* substance with the Infinite Spirit. But there is no limitation of this sort in the system, neither can there be, for it is its boast that it reduces the All to a One. It is the *universal* Subject and the *universal* Object between which an identity of substance is affirmed.*

But we lay much stress upon the indirect evidence in the case. It is perfectly plain, as we have already remarked, that the philosophy of Kant is the modern system with which Coleridge finally and most fully sympathized. If he is to be called after any one of the great founders of philosophical systems among the moderns, Coleridge was a Kantean. Not that he pushed his inquiries no further than Kant had gone, for there is abundant evidence on many a page of the *Literary Remains*, that the highest problems of Christianity, during the last period of his life, were themes constantly present to his deep and brooding reflection, and that whatever it shall be found that he actually accomplished, in the way of distinct statement, in the unfinished work which was to put the crown upon his literary life, he did satisfy his own mind upon these subjects, and was himself convinced of the absolute rationality of the highest mysteries of the Christian Faith. Yet the groundwork of all these processes—the psychology and metaphysics from which they all started—was unquestionably the theistic method of Kant, and not the pantheistic method of his successors. Even supposing that Coleridge at one time may have gone so far as to regard the system of Schelling, (with the still more remarkable one of Hegel, he does not seem to have been acquainted, for we do not recall any allusion to him throughout the whole of his works) as a positive and natural advance upon that of Kant, there is sufficient reason for saying, that he saw the error, and fell back upon the old position of Kant, as the farthest point yet reached in the line of a true philosophic progress, regarding the systems that sprang up afterward as an illegitimate progeny. And in so doing, he only exhibited in an individual, the very same process that has gone on, and is still going on in the Germanic mind itself. There was a time, when even the serious theist was inclined to regard with favor at least, that wondrous evolution of the theoretic brain—the three systems

* See Biog. Lit., Works, III. pp. 270, 271 (Note).

of Fichte, Schelling and Hegel—as a natural and normal development from Kanteanism, and so to regard the four systems as being in one and the same straight line of advance. It is true that at the very time when these later systems were rising into existence "like an exhalation," a man like Jacobi was found, to protest against the deviation and error, and to proclaim, with a serious and deep-toned eloquence that will ever endear him and his opinions to every serious-minded scholar who feels that his own mental repose, with that of the reflecting mind generally, is bound up in the Ideas of Theism, that these later systems were not genuine offshoots from Kant, but wild grafts into him. But at the time, the national mind was caught in the process, and it was not until the speculative enthusiasm had cooled down, and the utter barrenness of this method of philosophizing, so far as all the deeper and more interesting problems of Philosophy and Religion are concerned, had revealed itself, that men began to see that all the movement had been off and away from the line of true progress, and that the thinker who would make real advance, must join on where Kant, and not Hegel, left off.

In thus siding ultimately with the Critical Philosophy rather than with the system of Identity that succeeded it, Coleridge had much in common with Jacobi. Indeed it seems to us that speaking generally, Coleridge stands in nearly the same relation to English Philosophy, that Jacobi does to that of Germany, and Pascal to that of France. Neither of these three remarkably rich and genial thinkers has left a strictly scientific and finished system of philosophy, but the function of each was rather an awakening and suggestive one. The resemblance between Coleridge and Jacobi is very striking. Each has the same estimate of instinctive feelings, and the same religious sense of the preeminence of the Moral and Spiritual over the merely Intellectual and Speculative. Each clings, with the same firm and lofty spirit, to the Ideas of Theism, and plants himself with the same moral firmness, upon the imperative decisions of Conscience and the Moral Reason. But in no respect do they harmonize more than in their thorough rejection of the pantheistic view of things —of that mere Naturalism which swallows up all personality, and thereby, all morality and religion. In reading Jacobi's *Von göttlichen Dingen* one is struck with the great similarity in conception, and often in statement, with remarks and trains of discussion in the *Aids to Reflection.* The coincidence in this case, it is very plain to the reader, does not arise, as in the case of Coleridge's coincidence with Schelling, from a previous study and mastery of a predecessor, but from sustaining a similar relation to Kant, together with a deep sense of the vital importance and absolute truth of Theism in philosophy. The coincidence in this case is not a mere genial reception, and fresh transfusion, of the thought of another mind, but an independent and original shoot, in common with others, from the one great stock, the general system of Theism. Add to this, that both Coleridge and Jacobi were close students of Plato, and by mental constitution, were alike predisposed to the moulding influence of this greatest philosophic mind of the Pagan world, and we have still another ground and cause for the resemblance between the two.

Now in this resemblance with Jacobi, we find still another indirect proof of the position, that Coleridge's adoption of the system of Schelling was temporary, and that he returned, with still deeper faith and clearer insight, to the theistic system. For no mind of the age in which he lived, or of any age, was more decidedly and determinedly theistic, than Jacobi. His *Letters to Mendelssohn upon the system of Spinoza*, and still more, because more regularly constructed, his treatise on *Divine Things and their Revelation*, are among the most genial certainly, and we think among the most impressive, and practically effective, of all attacks upon the pantheistic Naturalism. We know that it was fashionable, especially when the hard logical processes of Hegelianism were more influential and authoritative as models than they now are, to decry the method of Jacobi as unscientific, and to endeavor to weaken the force of his views, by the assertion, that his is the mere "philosophy of feeling." But there is reason to believe, that this same thinker, though deficient as must be acknowledged in the logical and systematizing ability of Kant and Hegel, has done a giant's work, in aiding to bring the German mind back to the position of Theism in philosophy. His influence, healthful and fruitful, is to be traced through the whole of the spiritual school of theologians. If there is any one of the many philosophers of Germany, who is regarded with admiration and veneration by this class of reflecting men—a class which shares largely in the disposition of its great head Schleiermacher, to establish theology upon an independent basis, and thereby divorce it altogether from philosophy—it is Jacobi; and this, principally on the ground of his earnest religious abhorrence of that speculation of the mere understanding, which under the name of philosophy, has so invariably ended in the overthrow of the foundations of Ethics and Religion.

We have dwelt the longer upon this point of Coleridge's relation to Schelling, because we believe it to be the fact that the philosophic system which he finally adopted, and which is the prominent one in these volumes, is irreconcilable with the system of Identity, and if so, that it is of the highest importance that the fact be known and acknowledged. Moreover the establishment of the position we have taken, acquires some additional interest, in relation to the charge of plagiarism which has of late been frequently urged. This charge becomes of little importance, so far as the question of Coleridge's original power as a philosopher is concerned, so soon as it appears that this reception of the views of Schelling, was only one feature in the temporary pantheistic stage of his mental history, and of still less importance, when it is further considered, that Schelling himself is entitled to but small credit on the score of absolute invention;—the philosophy of Spinoza being "the rock and the quarry," on and out of which the whole system of Identity was constructed. Indeed, in leaving this system, Coleridge has been imitated by Schelling himself, if, as there is reason to believe, the later system of this philosopher is a renunciation of his earlier, and not a mere development of it. How far either of these two minds possessed that highest, and most truly original, philosophic power—the power of forming an era in the history of philosophy, by carrying the philosophic mind onward through another stadium in its *normal* course and development—remains yet to be seen. This point can not be settled until the publication of the *Logosophia* of Coleridge, and the recent system of Schelling.

The influence, however, of this pantheistic system upon Coleridge, was for a time undoubtedly great, harmonizing as it did with the imaginative side of his nature, and promising, as it always has done, to reduce all knowledge to a unity—that promise always so impressive and fascinating for the human intellect, and which moreover addresses, though in this instance by a false method, one of the necessary and organic wants of reason itself. Besides the disquisition in the *Biographia*

Literaria, there are statements respecting the mutual relations of Nature and the Mind of man, and trains of reflection, here and there in these volumes,* which spring, as it seems to us, from the pantheistic intuition, and which, run out to their legitimate consequences, would end in a mere Naturalism, of which all Coleridge's more matured, and more strictly scientific views are a profound and powerful refutation, and against which, his own moral and spiritual consciousness, certainly for the last twenty years of his life, was one loud and solemn protest.

In this connection, also, it may be proper to speak of the objection made to the system of Kant himself, that it is essentially skeptical. This objection is founded upon the fact, that the Critical philosophy denies the possibility, within a certain sphere, of an absolute knowledge on the part of the human mind, because its knowledge is conformed to forms and modes of cognition, that pertain to the human understanding, and are peculiar to it. The thing *in itself* is not known, but only the thing as it *appears* to the finite intelligence. An absolute knowledge, true intrinsically, and irrespective of the subjective laws of human intelligence, is therefore impossible within this sphere.

If this theory were to be extended over the whole domain of knowledge, Spiritual as well as Natural, it is plain that it would end in universal skepticism. If for instance the knowledge which the human mind has of right and wrong, of its own freedom and immortality, of the divine attributes and the Dread One in whom they inhere, is no real and absolute knowledge, but is merely subjective, the foundations of all morals and religion would sink out of sight immediately, and the human mind would be afloat upon the sea of doubt, conjecture, and denial. This was the identical skepticism against which Socrates and Plato waged such serious and successful war. But Kant, as it seems to us, by his distinction of the Speculative and Practical reason, intended to confine, and actually does confine, this doctrine of a subjective and conditional knowledge to the sphere of the Natural and the Sensuous. Within this sphere there *is* no absolute knowledge, for the good reason that there is no absolute object to be known. The absolutely and necessarily true, is not within the domain of Nature, but above it altogether, in the domain of Spirit.† The

* See Essays X. and XI. of The Friend, Works, II. pp. 448–472.

† See Cudworth's Immutable Morality, *passim*.

things that are sensuous, are in continual flux, and even in regard to the immaterial principles beneath them, even in regard to the laws of Nature themselves, we can not conceive of their being of such a necessary and immutable character, as we can not but conceive moral and spiritual realities to be. For they are creations, and as such, are only one, out of the infinitely various manners in which the divine Mind can express itself in a material universe. The whole domain of Nature and of Matter is itself but a means to an end, and therefore can not, like the domain of the Spiritual, which is an end, have absolute and necessary characteristics, and therefore can not be the object of an absolute knowledge. All this domain of the Conditional, therefore, legitimately comes before the Understanding, with its subjective forms of knowing.

But there is another and a higher realm than that of Nature; of another substance, and therefore not merely a higher development of the Natural. The moral and Spiritual world, as it is not subject, in its functions and operations, to the law of cause and effect, but is the sphere of freedom, so it is not cognizable under the forms of the Understanding, but by the direct intuitions of Reason. It is no mere afterthought therefore, as has been charged, but a most strictly philosophic procedure in the system of Kant, by which, after the whole domain of the Natural and the Conditional has been legitimately brought within the ken of the rationalized Understanding, the domain of the Spiritual and the Absolute is assigned to a higher, even the very highest, faculty of the soul, as the proper organ and inlet of knowledge regarding it. It is because such an object of knowledge as God, *e. g.*, can not be truly known, by being brought within the limitations of time and space, and under the categories of quantity, quality, &c. &c., that Kant affirmed the existence of a power in man, not hampered by these forms of the Understanding, through which by an act of direct spiritual contemplation, this highest of all objects is known. Not *fully* and *completely* known, as some have falsely asserted that he taught, for the object in question is infinite, and reason in man is finite; but truly and absolutely known so far as the cognition does extend. Kant never claimed, for the finite reason of man, that *plenitude* of knowledge, which belongs only to the infinite reason, but he did affirm, that so far as the reason in man does have any knowledge of God, and of spiritual objects generally, it has an absolute and reliable knowledge. God is not thus, for one man's reason, and thus, for another man's, as a color is thus, for the sense of one man, and thus, for the sense of another; but so far as His infinite fulness *is* known by the finite reason, it is known *as it really is*, and is therefore known in the same way by all rational beings, and is the same to all. The same is true of all the ideas and objects of the Spiritual, as distinguished from the Natural world. In the former, the human mind has an absolute, *i. e.* unconditionally true knowledge, so far as it has any at all (for there may be no development of reason, and no use of the faculty at all), while in the latter, its knowledge is merely subjective and conditional. Hence the prominence, the supremacy, assigned in Kant's system to the Moral or Practical Reason. This is reason in its highest and substantive form, and no decisions of any other faculty of the human soul, have such absolute authority as those of this faculty. It stands over against the moral and spiritual world, precisely as the five senses stand over against the world of sense, and there is the same *immediateness* of knowledge, in the one case, as in the other. In the phrase of Jacobi, reason, *i. e.* the Moral Reason—is the *sense* for the supernatural,* and therefore we have in fact the same kind of evidence for the reality of spiritual objects, that we have for that of objects of sense—the evidence of a sense; the evidence of a direct intuition.

There is therefore no room for skepticism on this system within the only sphere in which the philosopher and the theologian have any *vital* interest in keeping it out—the sphere of the Moral and Spiritual. However subjective and relative may be our knowledge of the Natural, coming to us as it does through the mechanism of the understanding, and shaped by it, into conformity with our subjective structure, as creatures of sense and time, our knowledge of the supernatural, so far as we have any at all, is absolute and unconditional. We may doubt in regard to the real nature of matter, but we can not doubt in regard to the real nature of right and wrong. We may grant that our knowledge of an object of sense is conditional, and not absolutely reliable, but we may not grant that our knowledge of a moral attribute of God, is conditional and not absolutely reliable. The skepticism of the human mind, on this system, is confined to the lower and

* Von den göttlichen Dingen. Beilage A.

less important sphere of Nature, while the "confidence of reason," the faith that is insight, and the insight that is faith—can exist only in relation to the Moral and Spiritual world; only in relation to Moral and Spiritual objects.

Kant's treatise on the Practical Reason therefore, though from the very nature of the subject—(it being that Reason which is freest from the complexity of logical forms—) not so artificially constructed as that upon the Theoretic Reason, and seemingly occupying a humbler place in his general system, should be regarded as the sincere and serious expression of his real views upon the highest form of reason, and upon the very highest themes of reflection. Certainly no one can peruse those lofty and ennobling enunciations, respecting the great practical ideas, of God, Freedom, and Immortality, and those grand and swelling sentiments, regarding the nature of duty and the moral law, that are contained in this treatise, without a deep conviction that this part of Kant's system, was by no means an afterthought, or contrivance to save himself from universal skepticism. If the cold and passionless intellect of the sage of Königsberg ever rises into the sphere of feeling, and ever exhibits any thing of that real enthusiasm, by which a *living* knowledge is always accompanied and manifested, it is in this, the most practical and serious-toned of all his productions. And if it is objected, as it has been, that this knowledge of the Spiritual is rather a belief, than a knowledge, and that the function of this so-called Practical Reason, is that of feeling, rather than scientific cognition, the objection must be acknowledged to have force, provided that that only is scientific, which is the result of logical deductions, and that alone is knowledge, which comes mediately into the mind by processes of comparison and generalization. But on the other hand, if it is proper to call that, knowledge, which by virtue of its *immediateness* in the rational consciousness, is a most original and intimate union of *both* knowing and feeling, of *both* reason and faith, of *both* the scientific and the moral, then the knowledge in question is the absolutely highest of all, for it contains the elements of both varieties of knowing, and is the most essentially scientific of all, because, in the form of first principles, it lies at the foundation of all the processes of logic, and all the structures of science.

But whatever may have been the relative position of the Practical Reason and its correspondent Ideas, in the general system of Kant, or in Kant's own mind, no reader of Coleridge can doubt that for him, and his system, this form of Reason and these Ideas are paramount. Coleridge had an interest in developing this part of philosophy, and establishing an absolute validity for the decisions of the moral Reason and Conscience, superadded to that which actuated Kant. The former had received into his soul the peculiar doctrines of Christianity, while the latter, so far as we have had the means of judging, stood upon the position of the serious-minded Deist, and was impelled to the defence of the foundations of Ethics and Natural Religion, by no other motives than such as actuated minds like the Emperor Marcus Aurelius and Lord Herbert of Cherbury. Coleridge had more than a merely moral interest in saving the fundamental principles of Ethics and Religion from an all-destroying Skepticism, or an all-absorbing Naturalism, in philosophy. And hence the positiveness and in the best sense of the word, the dogmatism, with which he iterates and reiterates his affirmation that "religion as both the corner-stone and the key-stone of morality, must have a *moral* origin : so far at least, that the evidence of its doctrines can not, like the truths of abstract science, be wholly independent of the *Will*."*

Now as the defender and interpreter of this decidedly and profoundly theistic system of philosophy, we regard the works of Coleridge as of great and growing worth, in the present state of the educated and thinking world. It is not to be disguised that Pantheism is the most formidable opponent which truth has to encounter in the cultivated and reflecting classes. We do not here allude to the formal reception and logical defence of the system, so much as to that pantheistic way of thinking, which is unconsciously stealing into the lighter and more imaginative species of modern literature, and from them is passing over into the principles and opinions of men at large. This popularized Naturalism—this Naturalism of polite literature and of literary society—is seen in the lack of that depth and strength of tone, and that heartiness and robustness of temper, which characterize a mind into which the personality of God, and the responsibility of man, cut sharply, and which does not cowardly shrink from a severe and salutary moral consciousness. There

* Biographia Literaria, Works, III. p. 297.

is no remedy for this error of the brain and of the heart, but in that resolute and positive affirmation (worthy of the name of *Virtue* wherever found) of the existence of a distinction in essence, between the Natural and the Spiritual, with its implication of a Supreme and Infinite Spirit, the first cause and last end of both the finitely Spiritual, and the Natural. For all philosophy, false as well as true, must begin with an affirmation —a postulate upon which all else rests, and which is itself unsusceptible of proof, because it is the ground of proof for all other affirmations. Pantheism itself starts in Dogmatism—starts with postulating, not proving, the existence of its one only Substance. It has an interest in so doing. The evidence of this its so-called first truth " is not altogether independent of the *Will*." Here too, the voluntary and the theoretic, the practical and the speculative, are, though illegitimately, in one act of the understanding. In respect therefore to the logical necessity—the compulsory necessity—of its first position, we see not the advantage which it boasts of having, over a Theism which does not pretend to reject all aid from the moral side of the human soul, or to regard all evidence as not truly scientific and absolute, which is not of the nature of mathematical. Since, then, there must be a postulate to start from, in either or any case, let the individual mind imitate that justifiable Positivity—that rational Dogmatism —of the general human mind (which the soundly philosophizing mind only repeats with a fuller and distincter consciousness of the meaning and contents of the affirmation) by which the absolute existence of a personal supra-mundane God, is affirmed. This Being styles Himself the I AM—the self-affirmed self-existence ; and what is left for the human Reason but to imitate this positive affirmation, and steadfastly to assert that " HE IS, and is the rewarder of them that diligently seek him."

In driving the hesitating mind over its hesitancy, and urging it up to that moral resoluteness, which is at the same time the most rational freedom, whereby it takes sides with the instincts of Reason and the convictions of Conscience, rather than with the figments and fictions of the speculative Understanding and the immoral deductions from them, we regard these volumes of Coleridge to be of great worth. Apart from the influence of the example of this most learned and most contemplative mind, the clearness and profundity with which the doctrines of Theism are enunciated, and their mutual relation and dependence explained, is admirably fitted to propagate the living process of insight and of faith into the mind of the student. For it is one great merit of this author, that when his views are once mastered, they become inward and germinant. The consciousness of the teacher becomes that of the pupil. "You may," he says with perfect truth, "you may not understand my system, or any given part of it—or by a determined act of wilfulness, you may, even without perceiving a ray of light, reject it, in anger and disgust. But this I will say—that if you once master it, or any part of it, you can not hesitate to acknowledge it as the truth. You can not be skeptical about it."* And we appeal with confidence to those who have had opportunities for observing, whether as matter of fact those minds, and especially those young minds (ever most liable to be misled by the imposing pretensions of a false and miscalled spiritualism in philosophy) who have once come fairly and continuously under the influence of the opinions of Coleridge, have not been, not only shielded from error, but also, fortified in the truth. Are those who have been educated and trained in this general method of philosophizing, liable to be drawn aside from it? Does not the method itself, beget and nurture a determined strength of philosophic character, which obstinately refuses to receive the brilliant and specious theories that are continually arising in the speculating world?

This self-conscious and determined spirit in the recipient of the general system promulgated by Coleridge, springs naturally from its predominantly moral and practical character. The staple and stuff of this philosophy, are the great moral Ideas, and the faculties of the human soul most honored and developed by it, are the moral Reason, the Conscience, and the Will. The purely speculative *materiël* of philosophy, is made to hold its proper subordinate place, and the merely speculative and dialectic faculty, is also subordinated along with it. By recognizing the absolute authority of Conscience, not only within the domain of Religion but also of Philosophy, and by affirming that the Will itself, being the inmost centre of the man, and ideally, conjoint and one with Reason, ought not to stand entirely aloof, while by a compulsory logical process, the first truths of Philosophy and Religion are attempted to be forced upon the mind, with the same passivity

* Table Talk, Works, VI. pp. 519, 520.

and indifference, with which its belief of abstract axioms is *necessitated*—by regarding, in short, the moral Reason and the Free-Will, in their living synthesis, as the dominant faculty and seat of authority in the human soul, this system of philosophy not only secures a belief in the truths of Theism, but at the same time builds up and strengthens the human mind. Mental belief, in this system, has the element of Will in it. The doctrine of the Divine existence *e. g.* is believed not merely passively and from the mere mechanic structure of the intellect, as the axioms of Geometry are, but to a certain extent by free self-determination. The individual believes in the essential difference between Right and Wrong, partly because he *will* believe it, and not because it is impossible to sophisticate himself into the disbelief of it. On this theory man becomes responsible for his belief, even in respect to the first principles of Morals and Religion, and thus feels all the stimulation of a free and therefore hazardous position.

And this brings us back again to the intensely theistic character of this philosophy. It is rooted and grounded in the Personal and the Spiritual, and not in the least in the Impersonal and the Natural. Drawing in the outset, as we have remarked above, a distinct and broad line between these two realms, it keeps them apart from each other, by affirming a difference in essence, and steadfastly resists any, and every, attempt to amalgamate them into one sole substance. The doctrine of Creation, and not of emanation or of modification, is the doctrine by which it constructs its theory of the Universe, and the doctrine of responsible self-determination and not of irresponsible natural development, is the doctrine by which it constructs its systems of Philosophy and Religion.

2. In the second place, we think that this author is worthy of study, for his general method of Theologizing, and as an able defender and expounder of the doctrines of Christianity, on grounds of reason and philosophy.

In treating of this point, we shall be led to speak of Coleridge, in his other principal character of a Theologian. In regard to his general merits under this head, there is, both in this country and in Great Britain, more difference of opinion than in regard to his general merits as a Philosopher. We are inclined to the belief, however, that there is a growing confidence in the substantial orthodoxy of his theological opinions, and that it is coming to be the belief, even of those who do not sympathize with his philosophical opinions, and of course not, therefore, with his method of unfolding and defending the truths of Christianity, that the name of Coleridge deserves to be associated with those of the great English Divines of the seventeenth century, and that his views do not differ fundamentally from that body of Christian doctrine, which had its first systematic origin in the head and heart of Augustine. We are ourselves firm in the belief, that the theology of Coleridge, notwithstanding variations on some points, of which we shall speak hereafter, and which we are by no means disposed to regard as insignificant, is yet heartily and fully on the Augustinian side of that controversy, which after all, makes up the pith and substance of dogmatic church history. Even in relation to the difference between the Calvinistic and Arminian schemes,—schemes which, though essentially the same with the Augustinian and Pelagian, yet have a narrower sweep, and therefore allow their adherents less latitude of movement,—even in relation to these two schemes, respecting which there is such a shrinking in the English clergy, notwithstanding the strongly-pronounced tone of the Thirty-nine Articles, from a clear expression of opinion, Coleridge has not hesitated to say, that "Calvinism (Archbishop Leighton's for example), compared with Jeremy Taylor's Arminianism, is as the lamb in the wolf's skin, to the wolf in the lamb's skin: the one is cruel in phrases, the other in the doctrine."*

If the reader will peruse the Confession of Faith drawn up by Coleridge, as far back as 1816,† he will find that he expresses his solemn belief in the Personality and Tri-unity of God, the free and guilty Fall of man, the Redemption of man by the incarnation and death of the Son of God, and the Regeneration of the human soul by the Holy Spirit; and if he will further peruse the development of Coleridge's views, in the *Aids to Reflection* especially, on these cardinal doctrines of Christianity, he will find that, with the exception of that part of the subject of Redemption technically denominated Justification, Coleridge did not shrink from the most thorough-going statements. No divine—not even Calvin himself—ever expressed himself more decidedly than this author, in regard to such points as the Divinity of Christ, the depth and totality of man's apostasy, and the utter bondage and

* Lit. Rem., Works, V. p. 200.

† Lit. Rem., Works, V. p. 15.

helplessness of the fallen will: and the mere novice in theology knows that profound and thorough views of Sin, lie at the foundation of all depth, comprehensiveness, and correctness, in a general theological system.

It is rare, very rare, in the history of literature, to find a mind so deeply interested in the pursuits of Philosophy and Poetry as was that of Coleridge, at the same time deeply and increasingly interested in theological studies and speculations: and still more rare to find the Philosopher and the Poet so thoroughly committed to the *distinguishing* doctrines of the Scriptures. Compare Coleridge, for example, with his learned and able contemporary in Philosophy, Sir James Mackintosh, and observe the wide difference between the two men, in respect to the relation of each to the so-called Evangelical system. Compare him again with his contemporary and friend, the poet Southey, and notice the same wide difference, in the same respect. Neither Mackintosh nor Southey seem to have had that profound and living consciousness of the truth of such doctrines, as those of Sin and Redemption, which imparts so much of the theological character to Coleridge, and which would justify his being placed among the Divines of England, were not Theology, in this as in too many other instances, thrown into the shade by the less noble but more imposing departments of Philosophy and Poetry. He tells us that he was drawn off from Poetry by the study of Philosophy; and the account we gather of his studies and reflections during the last quarter of his life, shows that he was drawn off—so far as the nature of the case permits this—from Philosophy itself by Theology; or rather that the one passed over into the other.

Now it seems to us that this mind, having received such a profound discipline in Philosophy, and that too a spiritual and theistic Philosophy, and being led both by its original tendency and the operation of Divine Grace, to the study and defence of the truths of the Christian religion, on grounds of reason, is eminently fitted to be a guide and aid to reflection in this direction. We do not recommend Coleridge to the student as the author of a theological system, but rather as the defender and expounder of a general method of inquiry and reflection upon theological doctrines, in the highest degree fruitful and sound. Indeed, what we have said of Coleridge's lack of systematizing and constructive ability in the department of Philosophy, applies with still more force to him as a Theologian. The longest and most continuous statements, that Coleridge has made upon the doctrines of Christianity, are to be found in the *Aids to Reflection*, and yet the general character of this the most elaborate and valuable of his prose productions, is aphoristic. The aphoristic method is obviously not the best by which to convey opinions upon so intrinsically systematic and systematized themes as the doctrines of Christianity: much less therefore can this method be employed successfully, in constructing a whole theological system. Still as an *aid* to reflection, as inducing a general style of thinking, and manner of unfolding and defending truth, this method has some decided advantages over that of the connected treatise. It allows of more mental freedom on the part of the pupil, and fosters original reflection more, than a work finished in all its parts and details. "For," says Lord Bacon, "as young men, when they knit and shape perfectly, do seldom grow to a further stature, so knowledge, while it is in aphorisms and observations, it is in growth; but when it is once comprehended in exact methods, it may perchance be further polished and illustrated, and accommodated for use and practice; but it increaseth no more in bulk and substance."*

We regard the general method of Theologizing induced by the reflections of Coleridge upon theological doctrines as eminently profound and comprehensive. It leads the student to prize first of all, depth, breadth, and certainty, in his own views, in this department of knowledge. It does this by teaching as its first and great lesson, that "the scheme of Christianity though not discov-

* Advancement of Learning, Book I.

Consonant with this are the following remarks of *Schleiermacher*:—

Denn erinnert euch nur, wie wenige von denen, welche auf einem eigenen Wege in das innre der Natur und des Geistes eingedrungen sind und deren gegenseites Verhaltnisz und innere Harmonie in einem eigenen Lichte angeschaut und dargestellt haben, wie dennoch nur wenige von ihnen gleich ein System ihres Erkennens hingestellt, sondern vielmehr fast alle in einer zarteren, sollte es auch sein zerbrechlicheren, Form ihre Entdeckkungen mitgetheilt haben. Und wenn Ihr dagegen auf die Systeme seht in allen Schulen; wie oft diese nicht anders sind als der Sitz und die Pflanzstätte des todten Buchstabens, weil namlich mit seltenen Ausnahmen, der selbstbildende Geist der hohen Betrachtung zu flüchtig ist und zu frei für die strengen Formen. *Reden Ueber die Religion. Erste Rede*

erable by human reason, is yet in accordance with it,"* and that all reflection upon the truths of Scripture ought therefore to carry the mind down into deeper and deeper depths of its own being, and result in the most absolute and unassailable conviction that Divine Revelation is likewise Divine Reason. The influence of Coleridge's speculations is to produce and establish the belief that there is no inward and necessary contradiction between Faith and Reason, but that when both are traced to their ultimate and central unity, Faith, in the phrase of Heinroth,† will be seen to be undeveloped and unconscious Reason, and Reason again, this same Faith, developed, self-conscious, and self-intelligent: in other words, that when the believer shall have been raised by the highest grade of Christian consciousness to the highest grade of Christian knowledge, he will see that the unquestioning and childlike docility with which he trusted and rested in the truths and mysteries of Christianity, was the most rational of all mental acts, and the most philosophic of all mental processes. That this absolute consciousness can be perfectly reached, even by the most profound and holiest soul while in the flesh, we for one deny; for the same reason that, within the sphere of life and practice, we deny the doctrine of spiritual perfection here on earth. But that this knowledge, this insight into the identity of the revelation of God, with the reason of God, is a reality, and may be striven after, and that in its perfect completeness it will be attained by the human spirit when it has ceased to see through a glass darkly, has been the steadfast belief of the holy and the wise, in all ages of the Christian church. There is a point, a final centre, where faith and insight meet, even in regard to the mysteries of Christianity, and to this point the earnest straining eye of Christian speculation, has in all ages steadily turned. This point is at once the mysterious power that attracts, and the goal where the whole mighty tendency is to come to a rest. Only on the hypothesis that the problem is not in its own nature absurd and insoluble, but that by a legitimate method, Christian Philosophy may draw nearer and nearer its solution, even here in space and time, can we account for the existence of a Christian Theology at all. How far Coleridge has contributed in the employment of this method to the scientific statement and philosophical defence of the doctrines of Christianity, and generally what his

* Biographia Literaria sub fine.

† Anthropologie, S. 219.

positive merits are in respect to this relation of Philosophy to Revelation, is a question to which we would devote a short space.

In respect to the doctrine of *The Trinity*, upon which his thoughts seem to have centered during his latter life, the position which he took, that this doctrine, though mysterious is yet rational, and is therefore a legitimate object of investigation for a rational mind, at first sight seems to extend the sphere of Christian speculation beyond its proper limits. For the last two centuries it has been customary among English and American theologians to receive the doctrine of the Trinity purely on the ground of its being revealed in Scripture, and attempts to establish its rationality and intrinsic necessity, have, in the main, been deprecated. It has not always been so. In some ages the doctrine of the Triunity of the Divine Being, was the battle-ground of the church, and we are inclined to think that the Christian mind has never reached a deeper depth in metaphysical philosophy, than that to which it was compelled to sink, by the acute objections of Arianism and Sabellianism. Let any one thoughtfully peruse the creeds that had their origin in these controversies, and see with what masterly care and ability, the orthodox mind, in spite of all the imperfections of human language, strove to express the idea with which it was laboring, so as to avoid the Arian, the Sabellian and Tritheistic ideas of the Divine Nature, and then ask himself if there is not something of the mental, something of the national, in the doctrine of the Trinity, by virtue of which it becomes a legitimate object of contemplation for the human mind, and to some extent a guide to its inquiry. How could a man like Athanasius, for example, contend so earnestly, and with such truth of counter-statement, *against* a false idea, unless he had the true Idea somewhat clear in his own mind to contend *for*. And if it be said that this was derived from the bare letter of the Scriptures, and that the whole controversy between the contending parties hinged upon the citation of proof texts, the question arises:—how came Athanasius to see such a different truth in these texts from that which his opponents saw in them? Suppose a transfer of consciousness—suppose that the inward convictions and notions, upon the subject of the Trinity, possessed by Arius, could have been carried over into the mind of Athanasius, would the letter of these proof-texts have contained the same spirit or meaning for him, that they actually did? For it must be recollected that the Scriptures do not furnish ready-formed, a systematic and scientific statement of the doctrine in question. How then came the orthodox mind to derive its own sharply-defined dogma from the Scriptures, and the hetorodox mind its own equally sharply-defined dogma from the very same Scriptures, unless each brought an antecedent interpreting Idea into the controversy? We do not by any means suppose that this orthodox Idea of the Trinity, sprang up in the orthodox mind at this particular instant in the history of the church, and entirely independent of the Scriptures. It was a slow formation, and had come down from the beginning, as the joint product of Scriptural teaching and rational reflection, but was brought out, by this controversy, into a greater clearness and fulness than it had ever before appeared in, outside of the circle of inspired minds. But that the doctrine of the Trinity was now *an Idea in the mind of the church*, and therefore contained a mental element by virtue of which, it was a legitimate object of rational contemplation, and not a mere letter upon the page of Scripture, is the point we wished to bring out.

Now we think it a return to an older and better view of the subject, and not a mere novelty, that Coleridge was disposed to affirm, that whether it can be distinctly and fully shown or not, the doctrine of the Trinity *is* a rational doctrine, and is not, therefore, a theme altogether forbidden to the theologian because it stands in no sort of relation to a human intelligence. We believe that the position, taken by him in common with the spiritual school of theologians in Germany, between whose general views in theology, and those of Coleridge there is much affinity, that the doctrine of the Trinity contains the only adequate and final answer to the standing objection of Pantheism :—viz. that an Infinite Being can not be personal, because all personal self-consciousness implies limitation—is a valuable one for both Philosophy and Theology. It proposes a high aim for both of these sciences, and provided the investigation be conducted in the light of Scripture and of the Christian consciousness, and for the very purpose of destroying the pantheistic conception of the Deity, into which such abstruse and recondite speculation we confess is very apt to run,* we have little fear, that the cause of true philosophy and religion will suffer from the attempt. Whether the attempt

* The Trinity of Hegel is an example.

be successful or not, surely it is honoring Divine Revelation, and that body of systematic knowledge which has sprung up out of it, to affirm with Julius Müller, that "the Christian Religion as it lies in the New Testament, contains the fundamental elements of a perfect system of philosophy in itself—that there can not be a real reconciliation between Philosophy and Christianity, if such reconciliation must come in from without, and that such a reconciliation is possible only as it is merely an unfolding of that which is already contained by implication in Christianity : and hence that it must be possible to find, from the immediate contents of the Christian Religion, *as its metaphysical complement, ultimate and absolutely scientific statements* relative to the existence of God and the world, and their mutual relations, in such way as that they shall of themselves constitute a system of Christian Philosophy."*

Furthermore, whether the attempt to construct the doctrine of the Trinity philosophically, succeed or not, the mere recognition of the fact that it is grounded in reason, and the necessity of the Divine Nature, cuts the root of the doctrine of a merely modal Trinity: a heresy which was revived by the contemplative Schleiermacher. If the doctrine of a Trinity has a rational necessity, *i. e.* a necessity in the Divine Essence itself—if God, *in order to be personal and self-conscious*, and not merely that He may manifest Himself, must be Triune—then it follows that a mere Trinity of manifestation, whatever it may do for other beings than the Deity, leaves the Deity himself destitute of self-consciousness. The position of the Christian Theology is, that irrespective of His manifestation in the universe, antecedent to the Creation, and in the solitude of His own eternity, God is personally self-conscious and therefore Triune—absolutely self-sufficient and therefore needing to undergo no process of development and manifestation, in order to absolute plenitude and perfection of existence. By affirming that the doctrine of the Trinity is an absolutely rational and necessary one, because the Trinity is grounded in the Divine Essence, the doctrine of a relative and modal Trinity is logically precluded.

So far as concerns the speculations themselves, of Coleridge, upon this doctrine, he undoubtedly received the theological statement of it, contained in the Nicene Creed, as the truth, and en-

* Lehre von der Sünde, Bd. i. SS. 7, 8, 9.

deavored, from this as a point of departure, to originate a corresponding philosophical determination of the doctrine. How much he has actually contributed to the scientific solution of the problem, each reader will decide for himself. We are free to say for ourselves, that we think Coleridge committed an error in leaving the scheme of the Triad for that of the Tetrad, in his construction. The symbols of the Church, and the Christian mind, proceed upon the hypothesis of a simple Triad, which is *also* a Monad, and hence teach a Trinity *in* Unity and a Unity *in* Trinity. Coleridge, on the other hand, proceeds upon the scheme of the Pagan Trinity, of which hints are to be found in Plato, and which can be traced back as far as Pythagoras—the scheme namely of a Monad logically anterior to, and other than, the Triad—of a Monad which originally *is* not a Triad, but *becomes* one—whereby four factors are introduced into the problem. The error in this scheme consists in this its assumption of an aboriginal Unity existing primarily by itself, and in the order of nature, *before* a Trinity—of a *ground* for the Trinity, or, in Coleridge's phrase, a *prothesis,* which is not in its own nature either triune or personal, but is merely the impersonal base from which the Trinity proper is evolved. In this way, we think, a process of development is introduced into the Godhead which is incompatible with its immutable perfection, and with that golden position of the schoolmen that God is *actus purissimus sine ulla potentialitate.* There is no latency in the Divine Being. He is the same yesterday, to-day, and forever. We think we see in this scheme of Coleridge, the influence of the pantheistic conception of potentiality, instead of the theistic conception of self-completeness, and that if he had taken the distinct and full personality of the finite spirit, as the image and likeness of the Infinite Personality, and having steadfastly contemplated the necessary conditions of self-consciousness in man, had merely freed them from the limitations of the Finite—of time and degree—he would have been more successful, certainly more continuous and progressive. While we say this, however, we are far from believing that Coleridge's practical faith as a Christian in the Trinity, was in the least affected by this tendency to modalism in his speculative construction of the doctrine—a modalism, too, which, as we have remarked above, is logically, and ought actually to have been, precluded by the position which he heartily adopted, of the intrinsic rationality and necessity of the doctrine. Few minds in the whole history of the Christian Church, as we believe, have had more awful and adoring views of the Triune God, or have bowed down in more absolute and lowly worship before the Father, Son, and Holy Ghost.

The reflections of Coleridge upon the great and important doctrine of *Sin*, we regard as of the highest worth both in a practical and speculative respect. Indeed a profound consciousness of Sin in the heart, and a correspondingly profound theory of it in the head, are fundamental to all depth and soundness of view in the general domain of Theology. Coleridge speaks in several places of his renunciation of Socinianism and reception of Trinitarianism as resulting from a change in his philosophical opinions: of a Spiritual Philosophy as the means of bringing him to a Spiritual Religion. Without denying the co-operation of this influence, we are yet inclined to the belief, that in his case, as in that of Augustine and of men of a strongly contemplative bent, generally, the change from error to truth had its first and deepest source in that profound and bitter experience of an evil nature, which every child of Adam must pass through before reaching peace of soul, and which more than any other experience, carries the mind down into the depths of both the nature of man and of God. The biographical materials for forming an estimate of the spirituality, and religious experience, of Coleridge, are exceedingly meagre, but there is full reason for believing, from the gushes of tender devotional feeling that burst up spontaneously, and with the utmost unconsciousness, on the slightest hint or occasion,* that a most profound Christian experience lay warm and tremulous under the whole of his culture and character. We think we can see plainly in those most touching expressions of a sense of bondage which sometimes escape from him, that Coleridge in common with the wise and the holy of all ages, was slowly but triumphantly fighting through that great fight between the flesh and the spirit, which, far more than the richness of a merely human endowment, is the secret of that lofty and melancholy interest with which, even if personally unacquainted with the struggle, every truly noble and thoughtful mind, contemplates the lives of those elect spirits whom God's grace has chosen as its distinguished organs of manifesta-

* See Table Talk, Works, VI. pp. 323 (Note), 327 (Note), 478 (Note), 527; and Lit. Rem., Works, V. pp. 19–21, 368, 372, 290.

tion—that unearthly contest which, more than all else, is the secret of that superior charm, which sets the *Confessions* of Augustine as high above the *Confessions* of Rousseau, as the heavens are above the earth. In this connection we believe that the opium-eating of Coleridge, about which so much has been said in a pharisaic spirit by those who had small if any knowledge of that publican-like humility and lowly self-despair which is the heart and kernel of a Christian, as distinguished from a merely pagan or ethnic, character, was the occasion, as are all evil habits in the regenerate soul, of this deep and continually deepening religious consciousness: and that if that peculiarity, which resulted from this struggle with an evil habit, were to be taken out of Coleridge's experience as a Christian, it would lose much of its depth, expanse, and true elevation. We have not the slightest doubt that when told, "the tale of his long and passionate struggle with, and final victory over, the habit, will form one of the brightest, as well as most interesting traits of the moral and religious being of this humble, this exalted, Christian."* The pious-minded believer who finds an analogy in his own experience to this struggle with the relics of an evil nature, and the truly philosophic inquirer who traces the Christian life to its hidden and lowest springs, are both of them alike, far better qualified to be judges and censors over such a frailty and sin, as the one in question, than those moralists, who are precluded, as of old, from both the reception and the apprehension of an evangelical spirit, by their self-righteousness, and whose so-called religion is that merely negative thing, which owes its origin not to the conflict of grace with sin, but to an excess of lymph in the blood.

Coleridge's view of Sin, which is to be found the most fully expressed in the *Aids to Reflection,* is so intimately connected with his view of the Will, that it is necessary to direct attention to the nature and functions of this important faculty. The place which the Will holds in his system of philosophy was briefly alluded to under that head. As the Spiritual, *i. e.* self-determined, principle in man, it stands over against all that is strictly and merely Natural in him, in the sharpest opposition. In the idea and plan of the human soul it was intended to control and subject to its own rational self-determination all the functions and

* H. N. Coleridge's Preface to the Table Talk, Works, VI. p. 252.

operations, all the appetencies and tendencies of a Nature which, unallied with such a higher Spiritual power, would be as irresponsible, because as necessitated in its development, in man, as we find it to be in the brute. All *radical* deterioration, therefore, in the human soul, must begin in the *self*-determined part of it, for this is the only point at which a *radical*, *responsible* change can be introduced, and from which it can evolve. A mere Nature, as in the case of irrational and irresponsible existences, is not capable of either a radical deterioration or a radical improvement. It must develop itself in the main, and substantially, in accordance with what has been inlaid in it. There are, therefore, in the world of Nature as distinguished from that of Spirit, no *radical* changes—no terrible catastrophes like the fall of the Will, no glorious recoveries like its renovation. There is, and must be, within the realm of the strictly Natural, only one uniform evolution, in one continuous and endless line, because the development can not, by a free act, go behind itself, and alter the basis from which it proceeds.

Sin, therefore, as involving a radical change in the character, development, and history of the human soul originates in the Will. If man were a mere creature of Nature, his development would go on with the same necessary uniformity with which a crystal or a tree is built up in accordance with the law of Nature. But he is also a Spiritual, *i. e. self*-determined, creature, and hence that possibility of sinning which has become a dreadful actuality. By virtue of this power, man is capable of throwing himself out of the normal line of development prescribed for him by his Creator, and of beginning by an absolute beginning, a character, a course, and career, the precise contrary to the right and ideal one.

Without going into further detail in regard to Sin as originating within the sphere of freedom—a point upon which there is no controversy among those who hold to the existence of Sin at all —we wish to allude as concisely as possible to the idea of the Will itself as held by Coleridge, and as it is found generally, we think, in the Platonic as distinguished from the Locke Calvinism. For the doctrine of Sin assumes a very different form, and is accompanied with totally different results, both in speculative and practical theology, according as the idea of the Will is capacious, deep, and exhaustive, or the contrary. If the Will is regarded as merely the faculty of single choices, or particular volitions, the Sin that has its origin in it, must necessarily be atomic—a mere series of single and isolated acts, or in the technics of theology, actual and conscious transgressions. If, on the other hand, the Will is regarded as the power of determining the *whole soul, and the soul as a whole*, to an ultimate end of living, the Sin that has its origin in it, is dynamic—an immanent process or *state* of the Will, having the unity, depth, and totality of a nature, and in theological phraseology, is an evil nature, from which all actual and volitionary transgressions proceed. This distinction between the volitionary and the voluntary power—a distinction plainly marked by the Latin *arbitrium* and *voluntas*, and equally plainly by the German *Willkühr* and *Wille*—is important, not only intrinsically, but, in order to an apprehension of Coleridge's view of the doctrine of Original Sin, which we think does not differ materially from that of Augustine and the Reformers. For although Coleridge insists earnestly and at length upon the doctrine of free self-determination, he is equally earnest and decided in affirming the absolute bondage and helplessness of the fallen human Will. According to him, the Will is capable of absolutely originating its states—its holy state only in concurrence with, and aided by, the One Holy Will which is the ground and support of all finite holiness, and its sinful state without any aid or concurrence, on the part of the Infinite Will—but when the evil moral state has once been originated, and the Will has once responsibly formed its sinful character and nature, a central radical change in the direction and tendency of this faculty is, from the very nature of the case, then out of its power. For the Will is not the surface-faculty of single volitions, over which the individual has arbitrary control, but that central and inmost active principle, into which all the powers of knowing and feeling are grafted, as into the very core and substance of the personality itself. So that when the Will, in this full and adequate sense of the word, puts forth its self-movement, it takes the whole soul along with it, from centre to circumference, leaving no remainder of power in reserve, by which the existing direction of its movement can be reversed. The fall of the Will, therefore, though a free and self-moved procedure, brings this faculty into such a relation to holiness, that it is utterly impossible for it to recover itself back into its primitive state: it being a contradiction, to attribute a power of being holy, to a faculty, the *whole* of whose power is already absorbed in an unintermittent determination to be evil. The Will as thus conceived, is a unit and a unity, and having once freely set itself in the direction of evil, it thereby, and in the same proportion, becomes powerless in respect to a contrary direction : not because, be it observed, of any compulsion from without, but because of the obstinate energy and overmastering momentum within. It is an impossibility, for Satan to cast out Satan, because it is an incompatibility.

Coleridge, in short, while holding to the doctrine of free self-determination with the serious earnestness of a philosopher who well knew the vital importance of it in a system of Theism—the doctrine of responsible and personal free-will being the very and only corrosive of all pantheistic Naturalism—at the same time agreed with the oldest and soundest theology of the Christian Church, in not affirming the existence of positive and efficient power in the fallen Will, either to recover itself, or to maintain itself in holiness, after recovery. "The difference," he says, "between a Calvinist and a Priestleyan Materialist-Necessitarian consists in this :—the former not only believes a Will, but that it is equivalent to the *ego ipse*, to the actual self, in every moral agent; though he believes that in human nature, it is an enslaved, because a corrupt Will. In denying free-Will to the unregenerate, he no more denies Will, than in asserting the poor negroes in the West Indies to be slaves, I deny them to be men. Now the latter, the Priestleyan, uses the word Will—not for any distinct correspondent power, but—for the mere result and aggregate of fibres, motions, and sensations; in short it is a mere generic term with him, just as when we say, the main current of a river."* In fine the fallen Will in relation to a holy state—in relation to the "new heart" of the Scriptures—is a capability and not an ability, a recipiency and not a self-sufficient power, because the decided and positive energy of the faculty, its actual and actuating power, is entirely enlisted and swallowed up in the process of a sinful self-determination. This sinful self-determination, involving the whole soul into itself, and implicating all the tendencies of the inward being of man, with itself, constitutes that evil ground and nature below the range of distinct consciousness, from

* Literary Remains, Works, V. p. 448; compare also Aids to Reflection: Comment on Aphorism x., Works, I. pp. 271–291.

which all conscious transgression proceeds, and of which it is the phenomenal manifestation. In this way Sin is seen to be a single indivisible nature, or disposition, and not merely an innumerable series of isolated acts, and this nature again is seen to be essential guilt, because as originated in a Will and by a Will, it is self-originated and self-determined. In the phrase of Coleridge man "receives a nature into his Will, which by this very act becomes a corrupt Will; and *vice versâ* this Will becomes his nature and thus a corrupt nature;" and bearing in mind the distinguishing characteristics of Nature and Spirit, the reader will see the truth of the further position of this author, "that a nature in a Will is as inconsistent with freedom, as free choice with an incapacity of choosing aught but evil; and that a free power in a nature to fulfil a law above nature is a startling paradox to the reason."*

Respecting the doctrine of Original Sin, therefore, we think there is a substantial agreement between Coleridge and that form of doctrine which has come down in the Christian Church, as the best expression of both the Christian experience and the Christian reflection upon this momentous subject; and as we have already remarked, a profound view of Sin is the deep and strong soil from which all sound, healthy, and healing growths in theological speculation, shoot up. Depth and truth of theory here, is the very best preventive of errors and misconceptions elsewhere, and the very best mitigation, and remedy for them, if they exist.

We have thus far spoken of the soundness and fruitfulness of Coleridge's general method of Theologizing; of his profound belief in the inward harmony of Reason and Revelation, and of that instinctive and irresistible desire, which he shared with the profoundest theologians of all ages, to exhibit and establish this harmony. We have also dwelt upon his views upon the fundamental doctrines of the Trinity and the Fall of man, selecting these out of the great circle of Christian doctrines, because they are fundamental, and in their implication contain the whole Christian system. It is impossible, however, within the space of an essay, and it is not perhaps desirable, to pursue the opinions of this author through the whole series of individual doctrines, and having, as we think, shown his substantial agreement, so far

* Aids to Reflection, Works, I. p. 281 (Note). See also Notes on Jeremy Taylor's Unum Necessarium. Literary Remains, Works, V. p. 195.

as the general type and character of his Theology is concerned, with the Augustinian, we pass now to a brief consideration of some erroneous and defective views that cling to it.

Notwithstanding Coleridge's earnest advocacy of the doctrine of the self-determining power of the human Will, whereby the origin of Sin is taken out of the course of Nature and merely Natural processes, and brought within the sphere of freedom and amenability to justice, we think that the idea of Guilt, though by no means denied, or unrecognized, either in his personal experience or his speculations, was not sufficiently deep, clear, and impressive, for him. Sin, for him, as for many contemplative minds in the Christian Church—as it was for Origen in the early Church, for the Mystical Theology of the Middle Ages, for the school of Schleiermacher at the present time—was too disproportionately the corruption and disharmony of the human soul, and not sufficiently its guilt. Now the strongest motive which the Theologian, as distinguished from the Philosopher, has for maintaining the doctrine of Free Will, is to find an adequate and rational ground for the responsibility and criminality of the human soul as fallen and corrupt. He is not so anxious, if he is thoughtful and wise, to establish the doctrine of self-determination in reference to the origin of holiness (though in this reference the doctrine is important) as in reference to the origin of Sin: knowing that while there is little hazard in attributing too much to the Divine agency, in the production of moral good, there is the greatest of hazard, in implicating the Deity in the origin of moral evil. It would seem, therefore, that so determined an advocate of the doctrine of human freedom as Coleridge was, should have not only seen that the very essence of Sin, as self-willed, and thereby distinguished from all other forms of evil, consists in its ill-desert and penality, and that therefore its first and most important relation is to Law and Justice, but should especially have allowed this view to have moulded and shaped in a proper degree his theory of Redemption. But the scheme which Coleridge presents in the *Aids to Reflection* is defective in not insisting with emphasis upon the truth, that as the *essential* nature of sin (by virtue of which it is different in kind from all other forms of evil, and becomes, strictly speaking, *the only evil per se*) is *guilt*, so an *essential* element in any remedial plan must be atonement or expiation. The correlate to guilt is atonement, and to attempt to satisfy those specific wants of the sinful soul, which spring out of remorse of conscience, which is the *felt* and *living* relation of sin to law and justice, by a mere provision for spiritual sanctification, however needed and necessary this may be, in its own place, must be like the attempt to satisfy thirst with food. Coleridge was repelled from the doctrine of vicarious atonement, by some of the mechanical schemes and forms under which it has been exhibited, but if, as the best theology of the church has generally done, he had looked at it from the view-point of the *absolute nature of justice*, and had brought it under the category of want and correlate—one of the most vital of all, and one with which Coleridge's own mind was thoroughly familiar—it seems to us that he would have seen, that although the terms *ransom* and *payment of a debt*, when applied to the agency of the Redeemer, are indeed metaphorical, the term *sacrificial expiation*, is not.* If he had steadfastly contemplated the subjective wants of the human soul, while filled with the consciousness of guilt, and before that sense of corruption and those yearnings for holiness of heart, which are the consequent rather than antecedent of regeneration, have sprung up in it, and then had gone still farther and contemplated the dread objective ground of this remorseful and guilty conscience, in the Divine justice, which through this finite medium, reveals itself against all unrighteousness, he would have seen as the Augustines, the Anselms, the Calvins, and the Howes have seen, that there is a rational necessity for the expiation of guilt—a necessity founded secondarily, in the rational nature and moral wants of man, and therefore primarily, in the nature and attributes of that infinitely Holy Being, who made man in His own image and after His own likeness.

* See *Aids to Reflection*, Aph. xix.: Comment, Works, I. pp. 306–321. We never read this ardent but merely analogical argument against substituted penal suffering within the Spiritual sphere of justice, based upon the merely Natural, and wholly unjudicial, relation of a son to his mother, without thinking of the words in Wallenstein,

"O thou art *blind*, with thy deep-seeing eyes."

There is no inward and real analogy between the two spheres. There can be no legitimate arguing from a sphere, from which the *retributive* is altogether excluded, such as that of the mother and child, over into a sphere in which the *retributive* is the sole element, such as that of God the just, and man the guilty. It is *μετάβασις ἐις ἀλλο γένος*.

Moreover, in taking the position which he does—viz., that the real and absolute relation of the Passion of the Redeemer to the Divine attributes, is a mystery, in such sense that nothing can be affirmed concerning it, that can be intelligible to the human intellect, or edifying to the human heart (for this is said, when it is said that the subjective consequences in the redeemed, are *all* that can be known upon the subject), Coleridge stands in remarkable inconsistency with himself. We have seen that even the Trinity was not by him regarded as a mystery, in this modern, but really improper, sense, of standing in no sort of relation to a rational intelligence; in this sense of containing no element of the rational and mental, upon which the human mind can seize as a point of union and communion. And yet one whole side of the work of Redemption—that side too which stands in the very closest connection with the deepest and most awful sense in the human soul—the sense of guilt—and ministers to the deepest and most awful craving that ever emerges into the horizon of consciousness—the craving for a deliverance from guilt *on real grounds, i. e. on grounds of justice:* (a craving that lies at the bottom of the whole system of sacrifices, Pagan as well as Jewish, and is both their rational justification and explanation)—this whole side of the work of Redemption is thrown utterly out of, and beyond the range of the human mind, so that although its consequences in the redeemed may be known, its own inward nature—the ground and origin of these very consequences—is as utterly unknown and unknowable as that of a "gorgon or chimæra dire!" But aside from this inconsistency it is a fatal objection to this theory, that these consequences themselves—this Christian peace of conscience and sense of reconciliation with a Holy Lawgiver—can not come into existence through such an ignorant and blind faith as the soul is shut up to on this scheme. Such effects can not proceed from such a cause. Here, if anywhere in the whole field of the Christian consciousness, there must be the union of faith with insight. There must be some knowledge of the *purpose* and *purport* of the death of the Son of God—some knowledge of the inward and real relation which the substituted sufferings of Christ sustain to divine justice—before the guilt-stricken spirit looking about instinctively, but despairingly, for an atonement of guilt, can confidently and calmly rest in them for purposes of justification. At the very least their intrinsic *adaptation* to the end proposed and desired—their *adequacy*—must be recognized by the mind, and what is such recognition but a species and a grade of knowledge respecting their nature, fitness and rational necessity ? The faith of the common Christian contains the *rationale* of the doctrine of Atonement, for the origin and existence of this faith itself, is explicable only on the hypothesis that there is reason in the doctrine ; and if it is rational it is apprehensible.

While, however, we are noticing this defect in Coleridge's statement of the doctrine of Redemption, it ought at the same time to be observed, that he was not impelled to the view he took, by a morbid and feeble moral sentiment, or from any disposition to merge all the Divine attributes into an irrational and blind Benevolence. It was an intellectual, more than a moral defect, with him, for when he is himself opposing Socinianism—and few minds have been more heartily opposed to it than his—we find him employing the very same objections to a scheme of salvation that makes no provision for the guilt of man and the Justice of God, which the orthodox mind has urged in all ages. "Socinianism," he says, "is not a religion, but a theory, and that too, a very pernicious, or a very unsatisfactory theory. Pernicious—for it excludes all our deep and awful ideas of the perfect holiness of God, His justice and His mercy, and thereby makes the voice of conscience a delusion, as having no correspondent in the character of the legislator ; regarding God as merely a good-natured pleasure-giver, so happiness is produced, indifferent as to the means :—unsatisfactory, for it promises forgiveness, without any solution of *the difficulty of the compatibility of this, with the Justice of God*."*

In other places,† on the other hand, we find him expressing himself, respecting the more mechanical view of this doctrine, with an impatience and rashness, which a deeper, calmer, and more truly philosophic insight into it, would have precluded. For he who has meditated profoundly upon the Divine Being, and has thoughtfully asked himself the question :—Has the Deity affections in any sense, and what solid meaning have such terms as *Anger* and *Propitiation*, when applied to Him?—will not be in haste to condemn even the most inadequate statement upon this "abyssmal subject," provided he sees that its general meaning

* Lit. Rem., Works, V. pp. 552, 553, and compare V. pp. 447, 448.

† Lit. Rem., Works, V. p. 74, *e. g.*

and purport is on the right side of the great controversy. That Coleridge had not speculatively reached the bottom of this doctrine, and acquired a view of it as profound and comprehensive as that of *Anselm*, *e. g.* in his *Cur Deus homo?* or as that to which a tract, like *Owen's*, on the *absolute* nature of Divine Justice, leads, is evident from the irresolution of his mind, and the unsteadiness of his attitude.* In fine, as we remarked at the outset, the defect in Coleridge's view of this subject is traceable to a deficiency in his theoretic view of Sin in one of its two main aspects. The Idea was not full. And perhaps the cause of this speculative deficiency was a practical one at bottom. Like many other contemplative spirits, Coleridge came into Christianity gradually, and not through a violent inward crisis, and hence his experimental consciousness of Sin, though not by any means entirely lacking the element of remorse, was yet predominantly a sense of bondage and corruption. We doubt not that Coleridge's exposition of the doctrine of Redemption (as would that of Schleiermacher) would have been different from what it now is, by a very important modification, had his own Christian consciousness been the result of such an inward conflict with Guilt, as Luther's was, or of such a keen insight into the nature of Law and Justice, as Calvin had, instead of being, as it was, the result of a comparatively quiet transition into Christianity and growth therein; in which process the yearning after holiness and purity, instead of the craving after atonement for agonizing Guilt in the conscience, was the predominant, *though not sole*, feeling,

In respect to the views of Coleridge upon the subject of *Inspiration*, it is not our purpose to enter into any detail, but simply to notice the defect in the general principle adopted by him. This principle, to state it in a word, is as follows:—In determining the absolute truth and authority of the Scriptures, the Objective generally, is subordinate to the Subjective. With the exception of those particular cases, in which the Objective Revelation explicitly claims a paramount superiority to the Subjective Intelligence, by asserting a direct dictation or revelation from God, the

* When himself attacking Socinianism, Coleridge employs the phraseology of the Calvinist, and seems thereby to reserve the attacking of Calvinism as a *peculium* of his own: as Johnson allowed no one to abuse Goldsmith but himself. See Lit. Rem., passim, and observe the general *animus* of the notes on *Jeremy Taylor*, and on *A Barrister's Hints.*

former has intrinsic authority or validity, only so far as it *acquires* it before the bar of the individual judgment. The Subjective Reason, with the exception specified, is placed first, as the fixed and absolute norm or rule to which the Objective Reason is to be brought up and conformed. Now the strongest objection to this theory of Revelation is to be derived from the principles of the philosophy adopted, as we have endeavored to show, by Coleridge himself. But even if we should regard him as an adherent of the later German philosophy, the absolute and fixed truth would not lie in the Subject alone, but in the *identity* of the Subject and the Object—in a common ground that contains *both* factors. And even this position would be more sound and less objectionable when applied to the mutual relations of the individual mind and Divine Revelation than the one which we have mentioned above, and which is really tenable only by an adherent of Fichte's system, in which the truth is laid in the Subject wholly. Even on the principles of the philosophy of Identity, the truth would not be wholly and ultimately in the Subjective, nor would the Objective Revelation be so passively exposed to the fluctuations of an individual consciousness, because, at the very least, there would be room for action and *re*action, of correction and *counter*-correction.

But we think it has been made out, that Coleridge, on this point of the relation of the Subject to the Object, ultimately adopted the views of the Critical philosophy, substantially those of all theistic systems, which explains the possibility of knowledge, by a preconformity of the Subject to the Object, instead of an identity of substance between them. On this system there is a dualism between the Object and the Subject. Of the two, the former is the unlimited and the universal, and stands over against the latter as the limited and particular. It is the *Objective*, therefore, which possesses the fixed and uniform character (in this instance, the infallibility) to which the Subjective comes up with its pre-conformed powers of apprehension, and the function of the latter consequently, is a recipient instead of an originant or creative one, as in the system of Fichte, or a self-developing one, as in the system of Schelling and Hegel.

We are aware that Coleridge believed that the Scriptures are, as matter of fact, true on all primary points, and that those Christian doctrines which he, in common with the Christian

Church, regarded as *vital* to human salvation, are all plainly revealed in them. This ought to be noticed, because this of itself separates him heaven-wide, from a mere Rationalist, and places him in the same general class with the evangelical school of theologians in Germany, in respect to this doctrine of Inspiration. Still we regard it an error in him, and in them, that the Canon is not contemplated as a complete whole in and by itself, having a *common* origin in the Divine Mind, in such sense, that as a body of information it is infallibly correct on all the subjects that come within its scope and purpose. There must be truth somewhere, in regard to all, even the most unimportant particulars of history, biography, and geography, that enter into the subject matter of the Sacred Canon, and it seems to us altogether the most rational, in accordance with the general principle enounced above, to presume and assume that it lies in the Canon itself—in the outward Revelation considered as a finished whole, and an infallible unit and unity. These secondary matters are always an important, and sometimes vital, part* of the great whole, and as they are so integrated into the solid doctrinal substance of the Scriptures, that they can not be taken out of it, any more than the blue veins can be from the solid marble, why is it not rational to believe, that they had the same *common* origin with the doctrines and fundamental truths themselves, which are encrusted and crystallized in them—in other words, that the Divine Mind, whether as positively revealing, or inspiring, or superintending, is the ultimate Author of the whole? There are but two objections to this position. The first is—that the inspired writers become thereby, mere amanuenses and automata. This objection has no force for one who believes that the Divine can, and does, dwell and work in the Human, in the most real and absolute manner, without in the least mutilating or suppressing the

* In *some* instances at least, a *vital* part; as *e. g.* the biographic memoirs of the Redeemer by the Evangelists. If these are not infallible as history, then the whole Christian Religion instantaneously disappears:—for the Personage in whom it centres and rests can not be proved to have had an existence in space and time, and the forecasting intimations which the human soul (of a Plato, *e. g.*) has had of a Redeemer to come, would not save it from skepticism and despair. Hence the four gospels, in the late contest between Rationalism and Supernaturalism in Germany, have been the hottest part of the battle-field.

Human, and ought not to be urged by one who believes in the indwelling of the Holy Ghost in the regenerate soul. As in this instance, the Human can not be separated from the Divine, in the individual consciousness, and all "the fruits of the Spirit" seem to be the very spontaneity of the human soul itself, so in the instance of the origination of the body of Holy Writ, while all, even the minutest, parts have the flexibility, freshness, and naturalness of purely human productions, there is yet in and through them all, the unerring agency of the Supreme Mind. In other words, the Supreme Intelligence is *the organizing principle* of that outstanding body of information which is called the Bible, and working like any other organizing principle, *with thoroughness*, produces a whole, that is characterized by its own characteristic—perfection of knowledge—even as life in the natural world diffuses itself and produces all the characteristic marks of life, out to the rim of the tiniest leaf. The second objection, and a fatal one, if it can be maintained, is—that there are actual errors in the Scriptures, on points, in regard to which, they profess to teach the truth. Let this be shown, if it can be, but until it has been shown, without possibility of contradiction, the Christian mind is certainly rational, in continuing to assume and affirm the infallibility of the Written Word. We say this with confidence, because out of the great number of alleged errors and contradictions that have been urged against the plenary inspiration of the Scriptures, there is not a single one established as such on grounds that render it absurd for a defender of the doctrine to take the opposite side. There is no list of conceded errors in the Scriptures. There are many difficulties still remaining, we grant, but while there is not a single case in which the absolute and unappealable settlement has resulted in establishing the fact of undoubted error, there are many in which it has resulted in favor of the doctrine of plenary inspiration. No one acquainted with the results of the severe and skeptical criticism to which the Canon has been subjected for the last half-century in Germany, will deny that the number of apparent contradictions and errors is much smaller now, than it was at the beginning of this period, and that the remainder of the series is diminishing. And had Coleridge himself kept up with the progress of Biblical Criticism in that country where the foundation of his views on this subject seems to have been laid, he would undoubtedly have seen reasons for rejecting some erroneous hypotheses, which, though exploded in the land of their birth, clung to him till the end of his life. He seems in regard to such an important point, as the inspiration and canonical authority of the *Christopædia** in both Matthew's and Luke's gospels, *e. g.* not to have made any advance upon the general views of the brilliant but superficial Eichorn, who was his teacher in 1799.

This whole subject of Inspiration, a most important, and a most difficult one, in some respects, turns upon the true relation of the Subjective to the Objective, and particularly of the Human to the Divine Reason. We can not but regard the theory of Inspiration set forth by Coleridge, in common with that spiritual school of theologians in Germany, which is destined to exert a great, and we believe, on the whole, salutary influence upon the theology of this country and Great Britain, for some time to come, as in direct opposition to that sober and rational philosophy which regards the Objective as fixed, reliable, and absolute, and conceives of the Subjective as designed to receive this into itself with intelligence and freedom, and as really free from fluctuation and error only so far as it partakes of the fixedness and truth of the Objective. The finite Reason is rather a recipiency than a self-subsistent power, according to Kant and Jacobi, and there are passages in these volumes that endorse this. The Human Mind is rather a capacity, than a self-sufficing fulness like the Divine Mind; and therefore the only rational attitude of the Subjective Intelligence towards an Objective Revelation, and towards all Revelation of the Supreme Reason, is that of intelligent and living recipiency. The Christian consciousness itself can not safely be left to its own independent movement, without any moulding and modifying influence of the Written Word. The outward, fixed, and self-included Revelation, must go down, through all the ages and changes of the Christian experience and Christian doctrine, as the absolute norm by which the whole process of practical and speculative development is to be protected from deviations to the right hand and to the left. The Canon is to steady and solidify that living process of thinking and of feeling which is embodied and manifested in the Christian Church, and keep it from the extremes on either hand, to which a finite mind and a living process are ever liable. Neither the practical nor the

* Lit. Remains, Works, V. pp. 76, 78, 79, 532.

scientific form of a particular doctrine, or of Christian Theology generally, may be sought for in the Christian consciousness, except as it has been rectified and purified by the Scriptures—in this Subjective, except as it has been rectified from its errors, and purified from its foreign elements by the conscious reception into itself of this Objective, which is absolutely free from both. There would be more weight in the doctrine of the authority of the finite Reason, and the Christian consciousness, than there now is, if all the processes of the human soul—even the regenerate human soul—were *normal* processes. But he has studied the history of even Christian Speculation, to little purpose, who has not learned from it, the need of an objective and fixed authority for the *fallen* human mind. Taken as a whole, the thinking of the human mind has never been nearer the central line of truth, than while it has been under the influence and guidance of Christianity. Christian Philosophy is far nearer this centre than the best schools of merely Pagan philosophy. And yet how fluctuating has been the movement, and what constant need there has been of an absolute standard by which to determine and correct the aberrations of the human mind! We think that in his strong belief that Christianity is absolutely rational, and in his earnest desire to exhibit it as such, Coleridge was led, at times certainly, to attribute a greater power of origination to the finite Reason than it really possesses, and to forget that as an endowment superinduced, and not as the whole essence of the finite mind, Reason in man, though the same in kind with the Supreme Reason, is not that infinite *plenitude* of Wisdom, which is incommunicable to a created Spirit.

We have been the more free and full, in speaking of the views of Coleridge upon the two topics of *Vicarious Atonement*, and *Inspiration*, because we believe that the defect in them originated not so much from a moral as from a speculative source. We have already spoken of the manner in which he identifies himself with the orthodox feeling and view, in relation to the doctrine of Atonement, when himself opposing Socinianism, and any one, who will carefully peruse the expressions of reverence and awe for the Scriptures, which spontaneously break from him, and bear in mind that whatever may be the actual *influence*, the serious and solemn *purpose*, of his little tract, was to strengthen the Bible in its claims upon the human mind, as the source of religious knowledge, can not doubt that Coleridge was induced to reject the common theory of Inspiration from a conviction that it really defeated its own end, and not because he wished to weaken in the least, the belief of Christendom in the Divine Oracles. While therefore we have distinctly expressed our convictions upon these points, we wish at the same time to remind the reader that these defects, though important, are not the substance and staple of the theological opinions of this author. Notwithstanding a partial disagreement with the Christian Mind upon these subjects, there is a positive and profound agreement with it, on all the other important doctrines of Christianity; and it should be remembered that in a fundamental agreement with such a body of truth as the Christian Religion, a basis is laid for the ultimate correction of views and opinions not in consonance with it. When a mind has once received into itself the substance of Christianity, it is its tendency, to deepen and widen its own religious consciousness, and in this process, foreign and contradictory elements are finally cast out of it, by its own saliency and vitality. In the case of Coleridge, it should moreover be observed, that he was compelled to clear himself of systems of philosophy and religion, inimical to a theistic Philosophy and a spiritual Christianity, in and during the development of his positive and final opinions; and hence, that it is not to be wondered at, that these latter should, here and there, exhibit the vanishing hues of the former. It is not to be wondered at, that some particles of the chaotic slime should have cleaved to him, compelled as he was, to paw himself out of ground, like the first lion.*

We have now as briefly as possible, touched upon the leading points in the Philosophy and Theology of Coleridge, thereby to show what is the general drift and spirit of his speculations in these two highest departments of knowledge. We have not been anxious to defend this Author upon each and every one of the various topics on which he has given the world his thoughts, believing that on some of them he is indefensible. At the same

* * * * * now half appeared
The tawny lion, pawing to get free
His hinder parts; then springs, as broke from bonds,
And rampant shakes his brinded mane. *Par. Lost*, B. VII.

time we have expressed a decided opinion, that in respect generally to the highest problems of Philosophy and Theology, the opinions of Coleridge are every way worthy of being classed with those of the master minds of the race. We are confident that these volumes contain, after subtracting the subtrahend, a body of thought upon the highest themes of reflection, well worthy of the study of every mind that is seeking a deep, clear, and expanded development of itself. Into the great variety of philosophical theories, and the great diversity in the ways and methods of thinking, characteristic of this age, we think the speculations of Coleridge deserve to be cast, and believe that just in proportion as they are thoroughly apprehended, and thereby enter vitally into the thinking world, will they allay the furious fermentation that is going on, and introduce unity, order, serenity, and health, into the mental processes of the times. We believe that they will do still more than this. We believe that they will help to fortify the minds of the rising generation of educated men, in that Platonic method of philosophizing, which has come down through all the mutations in the philosophic world, which has survived them all, which, more than any other method, has shown an affinity with Religion—natural and revealed—and which, through its doctrine of seminal and germinant Ideas, has been the fertile root of all the finest growths and fruitage of the human mind.

AIDS TO REFLECTION.

BY

SAMUEL TAYLOR COLERIDGE.

WITH A PRELIMINARY ESSAY BY

JAMES MARSH, D.D.

EDITED BY

HENRY NELSON COLERIDGE.

NEW YORK:
HARPER & BROTHERS.
1853.

THIS MAKES, THAT WHATSOEVER HERE BEFALLS,
YOU IN THE REGION OF YOURSELF REMAIN
NEIGHB'RING ON HEAVEN; AND THAT NO FOREIGN LAND.

DANIEL.

ADVERTISEMENT TO THE FOURTH EDITION.

THIS corrected Edition of the Aids to Reflection is commended to Christian readers, in the hope and the trust that the power which the book has already exercised over hundreds, it may, by God's furtherance, hereafter exercise over thousands. No age, since Christianity had a name, has more pointedly needed the mental discipline taught in this work than that in which we now live; when, in the Author's own words, all the great ideas or verities of religion seem in danger of being condensed into idols, or evaporated into metaphors. Between the encroachments, on the one hand, of those who so magnify means that they practically impeach the supremacy of the ends which those means were meant to subserve; and of those, on the other hand, who, engrossed in the contemplation of the great Redemptive Act, rashly disregard or depreciate the appointed ordinances of grace; —between those who, confounding the sensuous Understanding, varying in every individual, with the universal Reason, the image of God, the same in all men, inculcate a so-called faith, having no demonstrated harmony with the attributes of God, or the essential laws of humanity, and being sometimes inconsistent with both; and those again who requiring a logical proof of that which, though not contradicting, does in its very kind, transcend, our reason, virtually deny the existence of true faith altogether;—between these almost equal enemies of the truth, Coleridge,—in all his works, but pre-eminently in this—has kindled an inextinguishable beacon of warning and of guidance. In so doing, he has taken his stand on the sure word of Scripture, and is supported by the authority of almost every one of our great divines, before the prevalence of that system of philosophy (Locke's), which no consistent reasoner can possibly reconcile with the undoubted meaning of the Articles and Formularies of the English Church :—

In causaque valet, causamque juvantibus armis.

The Editor had intended to offer to the reader a few words by way of introduction to some of the leading points of philosophy contained in this Volume. But he has been delighted to find the work already done to his hand, in a manner superior to anything he could have hoped to accomplish himself, by an affectionate disciple of Coleridge on the other side of the Atlantic. The following Essay was written by the Rev. James Marsh, President of the University of Vermont, United States of America, and prefixed by him to his Edition of the Aids to Reflection, published at Burlington in 1829. The Editor has printed this Essay entire ;—as well out of respect for its author, as believing that the few paragraphs in it, having a more special reference to the state of opinion in America, will not be altogether without an interest of their own to the attentive observers of the progress of Truth in this or any other country.

25th April, 1836.

PRELIMINARY ESSAY.

BY THE REV. JAMES MARSH. D.D.

WHETHER the present state of religious feeling, and the prevailing topics of theological inquiry among us, are particularly favorable to the success of the Work herewith offered to the Public can be determined only by the result. The question, however, has not been left unconsidered ; and however that may be, it is not a work, the value of which depends essentially upon its relation to the passing controversies of the day. Unless I distrust my own feelings and convictions altogether, I must suppose, that for some, I hope for many, minds, it will have a deep and enduring interest. Of those classes, for whose use it is more especially designated in the Author's Preface, I trust there are many also in this country, who will justly appreciate the object at which it aims, and avail themselves of its instruction and assistance. I could wish it might be received, by all who concern themselves in religious inquiries and instruction especially, in the spirit which seems to me to have animated its great and admirable author ; and I hesitate not to say, that to all of every class, who shall so receive it, and peruse it with the attention and thoughtfulness, which it demands and deserves, it will be found by experience to furnish, what its title imports, "AIDS TO REFLECTION" on subjects, upon which every man is bound to reflect deeply and in earnest.

What the specific objects of the Work are, and for whom it is written, may be learned in few words from the Preface of the Author. From this, too, it will be seen to be professedly didactic. It is designed to aid those who wish for instruction, or assistance in the instruction of others. The plan and composition of the Work will to most readers probably appear somewhat anomalous ; but reflection upon the nature of the objects aimed at, and some little experience of its results, may convince them that the method adopted is not without its advantages. It is important to observe, that it is designed, as its general characteristic, to aid REFLECTION, and for the most part upon subjects which can be learned and understood only by the exercise of reflection in the strict and proper sense of that term. It was not so much to teach a speculative system of doctrines built upon established premisses, for which a different method would have been obviously preferable, as to turn the mind continually back upon the premisses themselves—upon the inherent grounds of truth and error in its own being. The only way in which it is possible for any one to learn the science of words, which is one of the objects to be sought in the present Work, and the true import of those words especially, which most concern us as rational and accountable beings, is by reflecting upon and bringing forth into distinct consciousness, those mental acts, which the words are intended to designate. We must discover and distinctly apprehend different meanings, before we can appropriate to each a several word, or understand the words so appropriated by others. Now it is not too much to say, that most men, and even a large proportion of educated men, do not reflect sufficiently upon their own inward being, upon the constituent laws of their own understanding, upon the mysterious powers and agencies of reason, and conscience, and will, to apprehend with much distinctness the objects to be named, or of course to refer the names with correctness to their several objects. Hence the necessity of associating the study of words with the study of morals and religion; and that is the most effectual method of instruction, which enables the teacher most especially to fix the attention upon a definite meaning, that is, in these studies, upon a particular act, or process, or law of the mind—to call it into distinct consciousness, and assign to it its proper name, so that the name shall thenceforth have for the learner a distinct, definite, and intelligible sense. To impress upon the reader the importance of this, and to exemplify it in the particular subjects taken up in the Work, is a leading aim of the Author throughout; and it is obviously the only possible way by which we can arrive at any satisfactory and conclusive results on subjects of philosophy, morals, and religion. The first principles, the ultimate grounds, of these, so far as they are possible objects of knowledge for us, must be sought and found in the laws of our being, or they are not found at all. The knowledge of these, terminates in the knowledge of ourselves, of our rational and personal being, of our proper and distinctive humanity, and of that Divine Being, in whose image we are created. "We must retire inward," says St. Bernard, "if we would ascend upward." It is by self-inspection, by reflecting upon the mysterious grounds of our own being, that we can alone arrive at any rational knowledge of the central and absolute ground of all being. It is by this only, that we can discover that principle of unity and consistency, which reason instinctively seeks after, which shall reduce to an harmonious system all our views of truth and of being, and destitute of which all the knowledge that comes to us from without is fragmentary, and in its relation to our highest interests as rational beings but the patch-work of vanity.

Now, of necessity, the only method, by which another can aid our efforts in the work of reflection, is by first reflecting himself, and so pointing out the process and marking the result by words, that we can repeat it, and try the conclusions by our own consciousness. If he have reflected aright, if he have excluded all causes of self-deception, and directed his thoughts by those principles of truth and reason, and by those laws of the understanding, which belong in common to all men, his conclusions must be true for all. We have only to repeat the process, impartially to reflect ourselves, unbiassed by received opinions, and undeceived by the idols of our own understandings, and we shall find the same truths in the depths of our own self-consciousness. I am persuaded that such, for the most part, will be found to be the case with regard to the principles developed in the present Work, and that those who, with serious reflection and an unbiassed love of truth, will refer them to the laws of thought in their own minds, to the requirements of their own reason, will find there a witness to their truth.

Viewing the Work in this manner, therefore, as an instructive and safe guide to the knowledge of what it concerns all men to know, I can not but consider it in itself as a work of great and permanent value to any Christian community. Whatever indeed tends to awaken and cherish the power and to form the habit, of reflection upon the great constituent principles of our own permanent being and proper humanity, and upon the abiding laws of truth and duty, as revealed in our reason and conscience, can not but promote our highest interests as moral and rational beings. Even if the particular conclusions, to which the Author has arrived, should prove erroneous, the evil is comparatively of little importance, if he have at the same time communicated to our minds such powers of thought, as will enable us to detect his errors, and attain by our own efforts to a more perfect knowledge of the truth. That some of his views may not be erroneous, or that they are to be received on his authority, the Author, I presume, would be the last to affirm ; and although in the nature of the case it was impossible for him to aid reflection without anticipating, and in some measure influencing, the results, yet the primary tendency and design of the Work is, not to establish this or that system, but to cultivate in every mind the power and the will to seek earnestly and steadfastly for the truth in the only direction, in which it can ever be found. The work is no further controversial, than every work must be, " that is writ with freedom and reason" upon subjects of the same kind ; and if it be found at variance with existing opinions and modes of philosophizing, it is not necessarily to be considered the fault of the writer.

In republishing the Work in this country, I could wish that it might be received by all, for whose instruction it was designed, simply as a didactic work, on its own merits, and without controversy. I must not, however, be supposed ignorant of its bearing upon those questions, which have so often been, and still are, the prevailing topics of theological controversy among us. It was indeed incumbent on me, before inviting the attention of the religious community to the Work, to consider its relation to existing opinions, and its probable influence on the progress of truth. This I have done with as severe thought as I am capable of bestowing upon any subject, and I trust too with no want of deference and conscientious regard to the feelings and opinions of others. I have not attempted to disguise from myself, nor do I wish to disguise from the readers of the Work, the inconsistency of some of its leading principles with much that is taught and received in our theological circles. Should it gain much of the public attention in any way, it will become, as it ought, an object of special and deep interest to all, who would contend for the truth, and labor to establish it upon a permanent basis. I venture to assure such, even those of them who are most capable of comprehending the philosophical grounds of truth in our speculative systems of theology, that in its relation to this whole subject they will find it to be a Work of great depth and power, and, whether right or wrong, eminently deserving their attention. It is not to be supposed that all who read, or even all who comprehend it, will be convinced of the soundness of its views, or be prepared to abandon those which they have long considered essential to the truth. To those, whose understandings by long habit have become limited in their powers of apprehension, and as it were identified with certain schemes of doctrine, certain modes of contemplating all that pertains to religious truth, it may appear novel, strange, and unintelligible, or even dangerous in its tendency, and be to them an occasion of offence. But I have no fear that any earnest and single-hearted lover of the truth as it is in Jesus, who will free his mind from the idols of preconceived opinion, and give himself time and opportunity to understand the Work by such reflection as the nature of the subject renders unavoidable, will find in it any cause of offence, or any source of alarm. If the Work become the occasion of controversy at all, I should expect it from those, who, instead of reflecting deeply upon the first principles of truth in their own reason and conscience and in the word of God, are more accustomed to speculate—that is, from premisses given or assumed, but considered unquestionable, as the constituted point of observation, to look abroad upon the whole field of their intellectual vision, and thence to decide upon the true form and dimensions of all which meets their view. To such I would say with deference, that the merits of this Work can not be determined by the merely relative aspect of its doctrines, as seen from the high ground of any prevailing metaphysical or theological system. Those on the contrary who will seek to comprehend it by reflection, to learn the true meaning of the whole and of all its parts, by retiring into their own minds and finding there the true point of observation for each, will not be in haste to question the truth or the tendency of its principles. I make these remarks because I am anxious, as far as may be, to anticipate the causeless fears of all, who earnestly pray and labor for the promotion of the truth, and to preclude that unprofitable controversy, which might arise from hasty or prejudiced views of a Work like this. At the same time

I should be far from deprecating any discussion which might tend to unfold more fully the principles which it teaches, or to exhibit more distinctly its true bearing upon the interests of theological science and of spiritual religion. It is to promote this object, indeed, that I am induced in the remarks which follow to offer some of my own thoughts on these subjects, imperfect I am well aware, and such as, for that reason, as well as others, worldly prudence might require me to suppress. If, however, I may induce reflecting men, and those who are engaged in theological inquiries especially, to indulge a suspicion that all truth, which it is important for them to know, is not contained in the systems of doctrine usually taught, and that this Work may be worthy of their serious and reflecting perusal, my chief object will be accomplished. I shall of course not need to anticipate in detail the contents of the Work itself, but shall aim simply to point out what I consider its distinguishing and essential character and tendency, and then direct the attention of my readers to some of those general feelings and views on the subjects of religious truth, and of those particulars in the prevailing philosophy of the age, which seem to me to be exerting an injurious influence on the cause of theological science and of spiritual religion, and not only to furnish a fit occasion, but to create an imperious demand, for a Work like that which is here offered to the public.

In regard then to the distinguishing character and tendency of the Work itself, it has already been stated to be didactic, and designed to aid reflection on the principles and grounds of truth in our own being; but in another point of view, and with reference to my present object, it might rather be denominated A PHILOSOPHICAL STATEMENT AND VINDICATION OF THE DISTINCTIVELY SPIRITUAL AND PECULIAR DOCTRINES OF THE CHRISTIAN SYSTEM. In order to understand more clearly the import of this statement, and the relation of the Author's views to those exhibited in other systems, the reader is requested to examine in the first place, what he considers the *peculiar doctrines of Christianity*, and what he means by the terms *spirit* and *spiritual*. A synoptical view of what he considers peculiar to Christianity as a revelation is given in Aph. vii. on Spiritual Religion, and, if I mistake not, will be found essentially to coincide, though not perhaps in the language employed, with what among us are termed the Evangelical doctrines of religion. Those who are anxious to examine further into the orthodoxy of the Work in connection with this statement, may consult the articles on ORIGINAL SIN and REDEMPTION, though I must forewarn them that it will require much study in connection with the other parts of the Work, before one unaccustomed to the Author's language, and unacquainted with his views, can fully appreciate the merit of what may be peculiar in his mode of treating those subjects. With regard to the term *spiritual*, it may be sufficient to remark here, that he regards it as having a specific import, and maintains that in the sense of the New Testament, *spiritual* and *natural* are contradistinguished, so that what is spiritual is different in kind from that which is natural, and is in fact *super*-natural. So, too, while morality is something more than prudence, religion, the spiritual life, is something more than morality.

In vindicating the peculiar doctrines of the Christian system so stated, and a faith in the reality of agencies and modes of being essentially spiritual or supernatural, he aims to show their consistency with reason and with the true principles of philosophy, and that indeed, so far from being irrational, CHRISTIAN FAITH IS THE PERFECTION OF HUMAN REASON. By reflection upon the subjective grounds of knowledge and faith in the human mind itself, and by an analysis of its faculties, he develops the distinguishing characteristics and necessary relations of the natural and the spiritual in our modes of being and knowing, and the all-important fact, that although the former does not comprehend the latter, yet neither does it preclude its existence. He proves, that "the scheme of Christianity, though not discoverable by reason, is yet in accordance with it—that link follows link by necessary consequence—that religion passes out of the ken of reason only where the eye of reason has reached its own horizon—and that faith is then but its continuation."* Instead of adopting, like the popular metaphysicians of the day, a system of philosophy at war with religion, and which tends inevitably to undermine our belief in the reality of any thing spiritual in the only proper sense of that word, and then coldly and ambiguously referring us for the support of our faith to the authority of Revelation, he boldly asserts the reality of something distinctively spiritual in man, and the futility of all those modes of philosophizing, in which this is not recognized, or which are incompatible with it. He considers

* *Biographia Literaria*, Works III. p. 594.—*S. C.*

it the highest and most rational purpose of any system of philosophy, at least of one professing to be Christian, to investigate those higher and peculiar attributes, which distinguish us from the brutes that perish—which are the image of God in us, and constitute our proper humanity. It is in his view the proper business and the duty of the Christian philosopher to remove all appearance of contradiction between the several manifestations of the one Divine Word, to reconcile reason with revelation, and thus to justify the ways of God to man. The methods by which he accomplishes this, either in regard to the terms in which he enunciates the great doctrines of the Gospel, or the peculiar views of philosophy by which he reconciles them with the subjective grounds of faith in the universal reason of man, need not be stated here. I will merely observe, that the key to his system will be found in the distinctions, which he makes and illustrates between *nature* and *free-will*, and between the *understanding* and *reason*. It may meet the prejudices of some to remark farther, that in philosophizing on the grounds of our faith he does not profess or aim to solve all mysteries, and to bring all truth within the comprehension of the understanding. A truth may be mysterious, and the primary ground of all truth and reality must be so. But though we may believe what *passeth all understanding*, we *can not* believe what is *absurd*, or contradictory to *reason*.

Whether the Work be well executed, according to the idea of it, as now given, or whether the Author have accomplished his purpose, must be determined by those who are capable of judging, when they shall have examined and reflected upon the whole as it deserves. The inquiry which I have now to propose to my readers is, whether the idea itself be a rational one, and whether the purpose of the Author be one which a wise man and a Christian ought to aim at, or which in the present state of our religious interests, and of our theological science, specially needs to be accomplished.

No one, who has had occasion to observe the general feelings and views of our religious community for a few years past, can be ignorant, that a strong prejudice exists against the introduction of philosophy, in any form, in the discussion of theological subjects. The terms *philosophy* and *metaphysics*, even *reason* and *rational*, seem, in the minds of those most devoted to the support of religious truth, to have forfeited their original, and to have acquired a new import, especially in their relation to matters of faith. By a philosophical view of religious truth would generally be understood a view, not only varying from the religion of the Bible in the form and manner of presenting it, but at war with it; and a rational religion is supposed to be of course something diverse from revealed religion. A philosophical and rational system of religious truth would by most readers among us, if I mistake not, be supposed a system deriving its doctrines not from revelation, but from the speculative reason of men, or at least relying on that only for their credibility. That these terms have been used to designate such systems, and that the prejudice against reason and philosophy so employed is not, therefore, without cause, I need not deny; nor would any friend of revealed truth be less disposed to give credence to such systems, than the Author of the Work before us.

But, on the other hand, a moment's reflection only can be necessary to convince any man, attentive to the use of language, that we do at the same time employ these terms in relation to truth generally in a better and much higher sense. *Rational*, as contradistinguished from *irrational* and *absurd*, certainly denotes a quality, which every man would be disposed to claim, not only for himself, but for his religious opinions. Now, the adjective *reasonable* having acquired a different use and signification, the word *rational* is the adjective corresponding in sense to the substantive *reason*, and signifies what is conformed to reason. In one sense, then, all men would appeal to reason in behalf of their religious faith; they would deny that it was irrational or absurd. If we do not in this sense adhere to reason, we forfeit our prerogative as rational beings, and our faith is no better than the bewildered dream of a man who has lost his reason. Nay, I maintain that when we use the term in this higher sense, it is impossible for us to believe on any authority what is directly contradictory to reason and seen to be so. No evidence from another source, and no authority could convince us, that a proposition in geometry, for example, is false, which our reason intuitively discovers to be true. Now if we suppose (and we may at least suppose this), that reason has the same power of intuitive insight in relation to certain moral and spiritual truths, as in relation to the truths of geometry, then it would be equally impossible to divest us of our belief of those truths.

Furthermore, we are not only unable to believe the same proposition to be false, which our reason sees to be true, but we can not believe another proposition, which by the exercise of the same rational faculty we see to be incompatible with the former, or to contradict it. We may, and probably often do, receive with a certain kind and degree of credence opinions, which reflection would show to be incompatible. But when we have reflected, and discovered the inconsistency, we can not retain both. We can not believe two contradictory propositions, knowing them to be such. It would be irrational to do so.

Again, we can not conceive it possible, that what by the same power of intuition we see to be universally and necessarily true should appear otherwise to any other rational being. We can not, for example, but consider the propositions of geometry as necessarily true for all rational beings. So, too, a little reflection, I think, will convince any one, that we attribute the same necessity of reason to the principles of moral rectitude. What in the clear daylight of our reason, and after mature reflection, we see to be right, we can not believe to be wrong in the view of other rational beings in the distinct exercise of their reason. Nay, in regard to those truths, which are clearly submitted to the view of our reason, and which we behold with distinct and steadfast intuitions, we necessarily attribute to the Supreme Reason, to the Divine Mind, views the same, or coincident, with those of our own reason. We can not (I say it with reverence and I trust with some apprehension of the importance of the assertion), we *can not* believe that to be right in the view of the Supreme Reason, which is clearly and decidedly wrong in the view of our own. It would be contradictory to reason, it would be irrational, to believe it, and therefore we can not do so, till we lose our reason, or cease to exercise it.

I would ask, now, whether this be not an authorized use of the words reason and rational, and whether so used they do not mean something. If it be so—and I appeal to the mind of every man capable of reflection, and of understanding the use of language, if it be not—then there is meaning in the terms *universal reason,* and *unity of reason,* as used in this Work. There is, and can be, in this highest sense of the word, but one reason, and whatever contradicts that reason, being seen to do so, can not be received as matter either of knowledge or faith. To reconcile religion with reason used in this sense, therefore, and to justify the ways of God to man, or in the view of reason, is so far from being irrational, that reason imperatively demands it of us. We can not, as rational beings, believe a proposition on the grounds of reason, and deny it on the authority of revelation. We can not believe a proposition in philosophy, and deny the same proposition in theology: nor can we believe two incompatible propositions on the different grounds of reason and revelation. So far as we compare our thoughts, the objects of our knowledge and faith, and by reflection refer them to their common measure in the universal laws of reason, so far the instinct of reason impels us to reject whatever is contradictory and absurd, and to bring unity and consistency into all our views of truth. Thus, in the language of the Author of this Work, though "the word *rational* has been strangely abused of late times, this must not disincline us to the weighty consideration, that thoughtfulness, and a desire to rest all our convictions on grounds of right reason, are inseparable from the character of a Christian."

But I beg the reader to observe, that in relation to the doctrines of spiritual religion—to all that he considers the peculiar doctrines of the Christian revelation, the Author assigns to reason only a negative validity. It does not teach us what those doctrines are, or what they are not, except that they are not, and can not be, such as contradict the clear convictions of right reason. But his views on this point are fully stated in the Work, and the general office of reason in relation to all that is proposed for our belief, is given with philosophical precision in other parts of his Works.*

If then it be our prerogative, as rational beings, and our duty as Christians, to think, as well as to act, *rationally*,—to see that our convictions of truth rest on the grounds of right reason; and if it be one of the clearest dictates of reason, that we should endeavor to shun, and on discovery should reject, whatever is contradictory to the universal laws of thought, or to doctrines already established, I know not by what means we are to avoid the application of philosophy, at least to some extent, in the study of theology. For to determine what *are* the grounds of right reason, what are those ultimate truths, and those universal laws of

* See Statesman's Manual, Appendix (B.), p. 258, 2d. edit.—*Ed.*

thought, which we can not rationally contradict, and by reflection to compare with these whatever is proposed for our belief, is in fact to philosophize; and whoever does this to a greater or less extent, is so far a philosopher in the best and highest sense of the word. To this extent we are bound to philosophize in theology, as well as in every other science. For what is not rational in theology, is, of course, irrational, and can not be of the household of faith; and to determine whether it be rational in the sense already explained or not, is the province of philosophy. It is in this sense that the Work before us is to be considered a philosophical work, namely, that it proves the doctrines of the Christian Faith to be rational, and exhibits philosophical grounds for the *possibility* of a truly spiritual religion. The *reality* of those experiences, or states of being, which constitute experimental or spiritual religion, rests on other grounds. It is incumbent on the philosopher to free them from the contradictions of reason, and nothing more; and who will deny, that to do this is a purpose worthy of the ablest philosopher and the most devoted Christian? Is it not desirable to convince all men that the doctrines, which we affirm to be revealed in the Gospel, are not contradictory to the requirements of reason and conscience? Is it not, on the other hand, vastly important to the cause of religious truth, and even to the practical influence of religion on our own minds, and the minds of the community at large, that we should attain and exhibit views of philosophy and doctrines in metaphysics, which are at least compatible with, if they do not specially favor, those views of religion, which, on other grounds, we find it our duty to believe and maintain? For, I beg it may be observed, as a point of great moment, that it is not the method of the genuine philosopher to separate his philosophy and religion, and adopting his principles independently in each, to leave them to be reconciled or not, as the case may be. He has, and can have, rationally but one system, in which his philosophy becomes religious, and his religion philosophical. Nor am I disposed in compliance with popular opinion to limit the application of this remark, as is usually done, to the mere external evidences of revelation. The philosophy which we adopt will and must influence not only our decision of the question, whether a book be of divine authority, but our views also of its meaning.

But this is a subject, on which, if possible, I would avoid being misunderstood, and must, therefore, exhibit it more fully, even at the risk of repeating what was said before, or is elsewhere found in the Work. It has been already, I believe, distinctly enough stated, that reason and philosophy ought to prevent our reception of doctrines claiming the authority of revelation only so far as the very necessities of our rational being require. However mysterious the thing affirmed may be, though *it passeth all understanding*, if it can not be shown to contradict the unchangeable principles of right reason, its being incomprehensible to our understandings is not an obstacle to our faith. If it contradict reason, we can not believe it, but must conclude, either that the writing is not of divine authority, or that the language has been misinterpreted. So far it seems to me, that our philosophy ought to modify our views of theological doctrines, and our mode of interpreting the language of an inspired writer. But then we must be cautious, that we philosophize rightly, and "do not call *that* reason which is not so. Otherwise we may be led by the supposed requirements of reason to interpret metaphorically, what ought to be received literally, and evacuate the Scriptures of their most important doctrines." But what I mean to say here is, that we can not avoid the application of our philosophy in the interpretation of the language of Scripture, and in the explanation of the doctrines of religion generally. We can not avoid incurring the danger just alluded to of philosophizing erroneously, even to the extent of rejecting as irrational that which tends to the perfection of reason itself. And hence I maintain, that instead of pretending to exclude philosophy from our religious inquiries, it is very important that we philosophize in earnest—that we should endeavor by profound reflection to learn the real requirements of reason, and attain a true knowledge of ourselves.

If any dispute the necessity of thus combining the study of philosophy with that of religion, I would beg them to point out the age since that of the Apostle's, in which the prevailing metaphysical opinions have not distinctly manifested themselves in the prevailing views of religion; and if, as I fully believe will be the case, they fail to discover a single system of theology, a single volume on the subject of the Christian religion, in which the author's views are not modified by the metaphysical opinions of the age or of the individual, it would be desirable to ascertain, whether this influence be accidental or necessary. The metaphysician analyzes the faculties and operations of the human mind, and teaches us to arrange, to classify, and to name them, according to his views of their various distinctions. The language of the Scriptures, at least to a great extent, speaks of subjects that can be understood only by a reference to those same powers and processes of thought and feeling, which we have learned to think of, and to name, according to our particular system of metaphysics. How is it possible then to avoid interpreting the one by the other? Let us suppose, for example, that a man has studied and adopted the philosophy of Brown, is it possible for him to interpret the 8th chapter of Romans, without having his views of its meaning influenced by his philosophy? Would he not unavoidably interpret the language and explain the doctrines, which it contains, differently from one, who should have adopted such views of the human mind as are taught in this Work? I know it is customary to disclaim the influence of philosophy in the business of interpretation, and every writer now-a-days on such subjects will assure us, that he has nothing to do with metaphysics, but is guided only by common sense and the laws of interpretation. But I should like to know how a man comes by any common sense in relation to the movements and laws of his intellectual and moral being without metaphysics. What is the common sense of a Hottentot on subjects of this sort? I have no hesitation in saying, that from the very nature of the case, it is nearly, if not quite, impossible for any man entirely to separate his philosophical views of the human mind from his reflections on religious subjects. Probably no man has endeavored more faithfully to do this, perhaps no one has succeeded better in giving the truth of Scripture free from the glosses of metaphysics, than Professor Stuart. Yet, I should risk little in saying that a reader deeply versed in the language of metaphysics, extensively acquainted with the philosophy of different ages, and the peculiar phraseology of different schools, might ascertain his metaphysical system from many a passage of his Commentary on the Epistle to the Hebrews. What then, let me ask, is the possible use to the cause of truth and of religion, from thus perpetually decrying philosophy in theological inquiries, when we can not avoid it if we would? Every man, who has reflected at all, has his metaphysics; and if he reads on religious subjects, he interprets and understands the language, which he employs, by the help of his metaphysics. He can not do otherwise.—And the proper inquiry is, not whether we admit our philosophy into our theological and religious investigations, but whether our philosophy be right and true. For myself, I am fully convinced that we can have no right views of theology, till we have right views of the human mind; and that these are to be acquired only by laborious and persevering reflection. My belief is, that the distinctions unfolded in this Work will place us in the way to truth, and relieve us from numerous perplexities, in which we are involved by the philosophy which we have so long taken for our guide. For we are greatly deceived, if we suppose for a moment that the systems of theology which have been received among us, or even the theoretical views which are now most popular, are free from the entanglements of worldly wisdom. The readers of this Work will be able to see, I think, more clearly the import of this remark, and the true bearing of the received views of philosophy on our theological inquiries. Those who study the Work without prejudice, and adopt its principles to any considerable extent, will understand too how deeply an age may be ensnared in the metaphysical webs of its own weaving, or entangled in the net which the speculations of a former generation have thrown over it, and yet suppose itself blessed with a perfect immunity from the dreaded evils of metaphysics.

But before I proceed to remark on those particulars, in which our prevailing philosophy seems to be dangerous in its tendency, and unfriendly to the cause of spiritual religion, I must beg leave to guard myself and the Work from misapprehension on another point of great importance in its relations to the whole subject While it is maintained that reason and philosophy, in their true character, *ought* to have a certain degree and extent of influence in the formation of our religious system, and that our metaphysical opinions, whatever they may be, *will* almost unavoidably, modify more or less our theoretical views of religious truth *generally*, it is yet a special object of the Author of the Work to show that the spiritual life, or what among us is termed experimental religion, is, in itself, and in its own proper growth and development, essentially distinct from the forms and processes of the understanding; and that, although a true faith can not contradict any universal principle of speculative reason, it is yet in a certain sense independent of the discursions of philosophy, and in its proper nature beyond the reach "of positive science and theoretical *insight.*" "Christianity is not a *theory* or a *speculation;* but a *life.* Not a *philosophy* of life, but a life and a living process." It is not, therefore, so properly a species of knowledge, as a form of being. And although the theoretical views of the understanding, and the motives of prudence which it presents, may be, to a certain extent, connected with the development of the spiritual principle of religious life in the Christian, yet a true and living faith is not incompatible with at least some degree of speculative error. As the acquisition of merely speculative knowledge can not of itself communicate the principle of spiritual life, so neither does that principle, and the living process of its growth, depend wholly, at least, upon the degree of speculative knowledge with which it co-exists. That religion, of which our blessed Saviour is himself the essential Form and the living Word, and to which he imparts the actuating Spirit, has a principle of unity and consistency in itself distinct from the unity and consistency of our theoretical views. Of this we have evidence in every day's observation of Christian character; for how often do we see and acknowledge the power of religion, and the growth of a spiritual life in minds but little gifted with speculative knowledge, and little versed in the forms of logic or philosophy! How obviously, too, does the living principle of religion manifest the same specific character, the same essential form, amidst all the diversities of condition, of talents, of education, and natural disposition, with which it is associated; everywhere rising above nature, and the powers of the natural man, and unlimited in its goings on by the forms in which the understanding seeks to comprehend and confine its spiritual energies. *There are diversities of gifts, but the same Spirit;* and it is no less true now than in the age of the Apostles, that in all lands, and in every variety of circumstances, the manifestations of spiritual life are essentially the same; and all who truly believe in heart, however diverse in natural condition, in the character of their understandings, and even in their theoretical views of truth, are *one* in *Christ Jesus.* The essential faith is not to be found in the understanding or the speculative theory, but "the *life*, the *substance*, the *hope*, the *love*—in one word, the *faith*—these are derivatives from the practical, moral, and spiritual nature and being of man."

Speculative systems of theology indeed have often had little connection with the essential spirit of religion, and are usually little more than schemes resulting from the strivings of the finite understanding to comprehend and exhibit under its own forms and conditions a mode of being and spiritual truths essentially diverse from their proper objects, and with which they are incommensurate.

This I am aware is an imperfect, and I fear may be an unintelligible, view of a subject exceedingly difficult of apprehension at the best. If so, I must beg the reader's indulgence, and request him to suspend his judgment, as to the absolute intelligibility of it, till he becomes acquainted with the language and sentiments of the Work itself. It will, however, I hope, be so far understood, at least, as to answer the purpose for which it was introduced—of precluding the supposition that, in the remarks which preceded, or in those which follow, any suspicion was intended to be expressed, with regard to the religious principles or the essential faith of those who hold the opinions in question. According to this view of the inherent and essential nature of Spiritual Religion, as existing in the *practical reason* of man, we may not only admit, but can better understand the possibility of what every charitable Christian will acknowledge to be a fact, so far as human observation can determine facts of this sort—that a man may be truly religious, and essentially a believer at heart, while his understanding is sadly bewildered with the attempt to comprehend and express philosophically, what yet he feels and knows spiritually. It is indeed impossible for us to tell how far the understanding may impose upon itself by partial views and false disguises, without perverting the will, or estranging it from the laws and the authority of reason and the divine word. We can not say to what extent a false system of philosophy and metaphysical opinions, which in their natural and uncounteracted tendency would go to destroy all religion, may be received in a Christian community, and yet the power of spiritual religion retain its hold and its efficacy in the hearts of the people. We may perhaps believe that in opposition to all the might of false philosophy, so long as the great body of the people have the Bible in their hands, and are taught to reverence and receive its heavenly instructions, though the Church may suffer injury from unwise and unfruitful speculations, it will yet be preserved;

and that the spiritual seed of the divine word, though mingled with many tares of worldly wisdom and philosophy falsely so-called, will yet spring up, and bear fruit unto everlasting life.

But though we may hope and believe this, we can not avoid believing, at the same time, that injury must result from an unsuspecting confidence in metaphysical opinions, which are essentially at variance with the doctrines of Revelation. Especially must the effect be injurious, where those opinions lead gradually to alter our views of religion itself, and of all that is peculiar in the Christian system. The great mass of the community, who know little of metaphysics, and whose faith in revelation is not so readily influenced by speculations not immediately connected with it, may, indeed, for a time, escape the evil, and continue to *receive with meekness the ingrafted word.* But in the minds of the better educated, especially those who think and follow out their conclusions with resolute independence of thought, the result must be either a loss of confidence in the opinions themselves, or a rejection of all those parts of the Christian system which are at variance with them. Under particular circumstances, indeed, where both the metaphysical errors, and the great doctrines of the Christian Faith, have a strong hold upon the minds of a community, a protracted struggle may take place, and earnest and long-continued efforts may be made to reconcile opinions which we are resolved to maintain, with a faith which our consciences will not permit us to abandon. But so long as the effort continues and such opinions retain their hold upon our confidence, it must be with some diminution of the fulness and simplicity of our faith. To a greater or less degree, according to the education and habits of thought in different individuals, the word of God is received with doubt, or with such glozing modifications as enervate its power. Thus the light from heaven is intercepted, and we are left to a shadow-fight of metaphysical schemes and metaphorical interpretations. While one party, with conscientious and earnest endeavors, and at great expense of talent and ingenuity, contends for the Faith, and among the possible shapings of the received metaphysical system, seeks that which will best comport with the simplicity of the Gospel,—another more boldly interprets the language of the Gospel itself in conformity with those views of religion to which their philosophy seems obviously to conduct them. The substantial being and the living energy of the Word, which is not only the light but the life of men, is either misapprehended or denied by all parties; and even those who contend for what they conceive the literal import of the Gospel, do it—as they must to avoid too glaring absurdity—with such explanations of its import as to make it to become, in no small degree, the *words of man's wisdom*, rather than a simple *demonstration of the Spirit and of power.* Hence, although such as have experienced the spiritual and life-giving power of the Divine Word, may be able, through the promised aids of the Spirit, to overcome the natural tendency of speculative error, and, by *the law of the spirit of life* which is in them, may at length be made *free from the law of sin and death*, yet who can tell how much they may lose of the blessings of the Gospel, and be retarded in their spiritual growth when they are but too often fed with the lifeless and starveling products of the human understanding, instead of that *living bread which came down from heaven?* Who can tell, moreover, how many, through the prevalence of such philosophical errors as lead to misconceptions of the truth or create a prejudice against it, and thus tend to intercept the light from heaven, may continue in their ignorance, *alienated from the life of God*, and groping in the darkness of their own understandings?

But however that may be, enlightened Christians, and especially Christian instructors, know it to be their duty, as far as possible, to prepare the way for the full and unobstructed influence of the Gospel, to do all in their power to remove those natural prejudices, and those errors of the understanding, which are obstacles to the truth, that the word of God may find access to the heart, and conscience, and reason of every man, that it may have *free course, and run, and be glorified.* My own belief, that such obstacles to the influence of truth exist in the speculative and metaphysical opinions generally adopted in this country, and that the present Work is in some measure at least calculated to remove them, is pretty clearly indicated by the remarks which I have already made. But, to be perfectly explicit on the subject I do not hesitate to express my conviction, that the natural tendency of some of the leading principles of our prevailing system of metaphysics, and those which must unavoidably have more or less influence on our theoretical views of religion, are of an injurious and dangerous tendency, and that so long as we retain them, however we may profess to exclude their influence from our theological inquiries, and from the interpretation of Scripture, we can maintain no consistent system of Scriptural theology, nor clearly and distinctly apprehend the spiritual import of the Scripture language. The grounds of this conviction I shall proceed to exhibit, though only in a very partial manner, as I could not do more without anticipating the contents of the Work itself, instead of merely preparing the reader to peruse them with attention. I am aware, too, that some of the language, which I have already employed, and shall be obliged to employ, will not convey its full import to the reader, till he becomes acquainted with some of the leading principles and distinctions unfolded in the Work. But this also is an evil which I saw no means of avoiding without incurring a greater, and writing a book instead of a brief essay.

Let it be understood, then, without further preface, that by the prevailing system of metaphysics, I mean the system, of which in modern times Locke is the reputed author, and the leading principles of which, with various modifications, more or less important, but not altering its essential character, have been almost universally received in this country. It should be observed, too, that the causes enumerated by the Author, as having elevated it to its "pride of place" in Europe, have been aided by other favoring circumstances here. In the minds of our religious community, especially, some of its most important doctrines have become associated with names justly loved and revered among ourselves, and so connected with all our theoretical views of religion, that a man can hardly hope to question their validity without hazarding his reputation, not only for orthodoxy, but even for common sense. To controvert, for example, the prevailing doctrines with regard to the freedom of the will, the sources of our knowledge, the nature of the understanding as containing the controlling principles of our whole being, and the universality of the law of cause and effect, even in connection with the arguments and the authority of the most powerful intellect of the age, may even now be worse than in vain. Yet I have reasons for believing there are some among us, and that their number is fast increasing, who are willing to revise their opinions on these subjects, and who will contemplate the views presented in this Work with a liberal, and something of a prepared feeling of curiosity. The difficulties in which men find themselves involved by the received doctrines on these subjects, in their most anxious efforts to explain and defend the peculiar doctrines of spiritual religion, have led many to suspect that there must be some lurking error in the premises. It is not that these principles lead us to mysteries which we can not comprehend; they are found, or believed at least by many, to involve us in absurdities which we can comprehend. It is necessary indeed only to form some notion of the distinctive and appropriate import of the term spiritual, as opposed to natural in the New Testament, and then to look at the writings, or hear the discussions, in which the doctrines of the Spirit and of spiritual influences are taught and defended, to see the insurmountable nature of the obstacles, which these metaphysical dogmas throw in the way of the most powerful minds. To those who shall read this Work with any degree of reflection, it must, I think, be obvious, that something more is implied in the continual opposition of these terms in the New Testament, than can be explained consistently with the prevailing opinions on the subjects above enumerated; and that through their influence our highest notions of that distinction have been rendered confused, contradictory, and inadequate. I have already directed the attention of the reader to those parts of the Work, where this distinction is unfolded; and had I no other grounds than the arguments and views there exhibited, I should be convinced that so long as we hold the doctrines of Locke and the Scotch metaphysicians respecting power, cause and effect, motives, and the freedom of the will, we not only can make and defend no essential distinction between that which is *natural*, and that which is *spiritual*, but we can not even find rational grounds for the feeling of *moral obligation*, and the distinction between *regret* and *remorse*.

According to the system of these authors, as nearly and distinctly as my limits will permit me to state it, the same law of cause and effect is the law of the universe. It extends to the moral and spiritual—if in courtesy these terms may still be used—no less than to the properly natural powers and agencies of our being. The acts of the free-will are pre-determined by a cause *out of the will*, according to the same law of cause and effect which controls the changes in the physical world. We have no notion of power but uniformity of antecedent and consequent. The notion of a power in the will to act freely is therefore nothing more than an inherent capacity of being acted upon, agreeably to its nature, and according to a fixed law, by the motives which are present in the understanding. I feel authorized to take this statement partly from Brown's Philosophy, because that work has been decidedly approved by our highest theological authorities; and indeed it would not be essentially varied, if expressed in the precise terms used by any of the writers most usually quoted in reference to these subjects.

I am aware that variations may be found in the mode of stating these doctrines; but I think every candid reader, who is acquainted with the metaphysics and theology of this country, will admit the above to be a fair representation of the form in which they are generally received. I am aware, too, that much has been said and written to make out, consistently with these general principles, a distinction between natural and moral causes, natural and moral ability, and inability, and the like. But I beg all lovers of sound and rational philosophy to look carefully at the general principles, and see whether there be, in fact, ground left for any such distinctions of this kind as are worth contending for. My first step in arguing with a defender of these principles, and of the distinctions in question, as connected with them, would be to ask for his definition of nature and *natural*. And when he had arrived at a distinctive general notion of the import of these, it would appear, if I mistake not, that he had first subjected our whole being to the law of nature, and then contended for the existence of something which is not nature. For in their relation to the law of moral rectitude, and to the feeling of moral responsibility, what difference is there, and what difference can there be, between what are called natural and those which are called moral powers and affections, if they are all under the control of the same universal *law* of cause and effect? If it still be a mere nature, and the determinations of our will be controlled by causes out of the will, according to our nature, then I maintain that a moral nature has no more to do with the feeling of responsibility than any other nature.

Perhaps the difficulty may be made more obvious in this way. It will be admitted that brutes are possessed of various natures, some innocent or useful, otherwise noxious, but all alike irresponsible in a moral point of view. But why? Simply because they act in accordance with their natures. They possess, each according to its proper nature, certain appetites and susceptibilities which are stimulated and acted upon by their appropriate objects in the world of the senses; and the relation—the law of action and reaction—subsisting between these specific susceptibilities and their corresponding outward objects, constitutes their nature. They have a power of selecting and choosing in the world of sense the objects appropriate to the wants of their nature; but that nature is the sole law of their being. Their power of choice is but a part of it, instrumental in accomplishing its ends, but not capable of rising above it, of controlling its impulses, and of determining itself with reference to a purely ideal law, distinct from their nature. They act in accordance with the law of cause and effect, which constitutes their several natures, and can not do otherwise. They are, therefore, not responsible—not capable of guilt, or of remorse.

Now let us suppose another being, possessing, in addition to the susceptibilities of the brute, certain other specific susceptibilities with their correlative objects, either in the sensible world, or in a future world, but that these are subjected, like the other, to the same binding and inalienable law of cause and effect. What, I ask, is the amount of the difference thus supposed between this being and the brute? The supposed addition, it is to be understood, is merely an addition to its nature; and the only power of will belonging to it is, as in the case of the brute, only a capacity of choosing and acting uniformly in accordance with its nature. These additional susceptibilities still act but as they are acted upon; and the will is determined accordingly. What advantage is gained in this case by calling these supposed additions moral affections, and their correlative stimulants moral causes? Do we thereby find any rational ground for the feeling of moral responsibility, for conscience, for remorse? The being acts according to its nature, and why is it blameworthy more than the brute? If the moral law existing out of the will be a power or cause which, in its relation to the specific susceptibility of the moral being, produces under the same circumstances uniformly the same result, according to the law of cause and effect; if the acts of the will be subject to the same law, as mere links in the chain of antecedents and consequents, and thus a part of our nature, what is gained, I ask again, by the distinction of a moral and a physical nature? It is still only a nature under the law of cause and effect, and the liberty of the moral being is under the same condition with the liberty of the brute. Both are free to follow and fulfil the law of their nature, and both are alike bound by that law, as by an adamantine chain. The very conditions of the law preclude the possibility of a power to act otherwise than according to their nature. They preclude the very idea of a free-will, and render the feeling of moral responsibility not an enigma merely, not a mystery, but a self-contradiction and an absurdity.

Turn the matter as we will—call these correlatives, namely, the inherent susceptibilities and the causes acting on them from without, natural, or moral, or spiritual—so long as their action and reaction, or the law of reciprocity, which constitutes their specific natures, is considered as the controlling law of our whole being, so long as we refuse to admit the existence in the will of a power capable of rising above this law, and controlling its operation by an act of absolute self-determination, so long as we shall be involved in perplexities both in morals and religion. At all events, the only method of avoiding them will be to adopt the creed of the Necessitarians entire, to give man over to an irresponsible nature as a better sort of animal, and resolve the will of the Supreme Reason into a blind and irrational fate.

I am well aware of the objections that will be made to this statement, and especially the demonstrated incomprehensibleness of a self-determining power. To this I may be permitted to answer, that, although the power to originate an act or state of mind may be beyond the capacity of our understandings to comprehend, it is still not contradictory to reason; and that I find it more easy to believe the existence of that, which is simply incomprehensible to my understanding, than of that which involves an absurdity for my reason. I venture to affirm, moreover, that however we may bring our understandings into bondage to the more comprehensible doctrine, simply because it is comprehensible under the forms of the understanding, every man does, in fact, believe himself possessed of freedom in the higher sense of self-determination. Every man's conscience commands him to believe it, whenever for a moment he indulges the feeling of moral self-approbation, or of remorse. Nor can we on any other grounds justify the ways of God to man upon the supposition that he inflicts or will inflict any other punishment than that which is simply remedial or disciplinary. But this subject will be found more fully explained in the course of the Work. My present object is merely to show the necessity of some system in relation to these subjects different from the received one.

It may perhaps be thought, that the language used above is too strong and too positive. But I venture to ask every candid man, at least every one who has not committed himself by writing and publishing on the subject, whether in considering the great questions connected with moral accountability and the doctrine of rewards and punishments, he has not felt himself pressed with such difficulties as those above stated ; and whether he has ever been able fully to satisfy his reason, that there was not a lurking contradiction in the idea of a being created and placed under the law of its nature, and possessing at the same time a feeling of moral obligation to fulfil a law above its nature. That many have been in this state of mind I know. I know, too, that some whose moral and religious feelings had led them to a full belief in the doctrines of spiritual religion, but who at the same time had been taught to receive the prevailing opinions in metaphysics, have found these opinions carrying them unavoidably, if they would be consequent in their reasonings, and not do violence to their reason, to adopt a system of religion which does not profess to be spiritual, and thus have been compelled to choose between their philosophy and their religion. In most cases indeed, where men reflect at all, I am satisfied that it requires all the force of authority, and all the influence of education, to carry the mind over these difficulties ; and that then it is only by a vague belief that, though we can not see how, there must be some method of reconciling what seems to be so contradictory.

If examples were wanting to prove that serious and trying difficulties are felt to exist here, enough may be found, as it has appeared to me, in the controversy respecting the nature and origin of sin, which is at this moment interesting the public mind. Let any impartial observer trace the progress of that discussion, and after examining the distinctions which are made or attempted to be made, decide whether the subject, as there presented, be not involved in difficulties, which can not be solved on the principles to which, hitherto, both parties have adhered; whether, holding as they do the same premisses in regard to the freedom of the will, they can avoid coming to the same conclusion in regard to the nature and origin of sin; whether in fact the distinctions aimed at must not prove merely verbal distinctions, and the controversy a fruitless one. But in the September number of the Christian Spectator, the reader will find remarks on this subject, to which I beg leave to refer him, and which I could wish him attentively to consider in connection with the remarks which I have made. I allude to the correspondence with the editors near the end of the number. The letter there inserted is said to be, and obviously is, from the pen of a very learned and able writer; and I confess it has been no small gratification and encouragement to me, while laboring to bring this Work and this subject before the public, to find such a state of feeling expressed, concerning the great question at issue, by such a writer. It will be seen by reference to p. 545, of the C. S., that he places the "*nucleus* of the dispute" just where it is placed in this Work and in the above remarks. It will be seen, too, that by throwing authorities aside, and studying his own mind, he has "come seriously to doubt," whether the received opinions with regard to *motives*, the law of *cause and effect*, and the *freedom of the will*, may not be erroneous. They appear to him "to be bordering on fatalism, if not actually embracing it." He doubts whether the mind may not have within itself the adequate cause of its own acts; whether indeed it have not a self-determining power, "for the power in question involves the idea of originating volition. Less than this it can not be conceived to involve, and yet be *free* agency." Now this is just the view offered in the present Work; and, as it seems to me, these are just the doubts and conclusions which every one will entertain, who lays aside authority, and reflects upon the goings on of his own mind, and the dictates of his own reason and conscience.

But let us look for a moment at the remarks of the editors in reply to the letter above quoted. They maintain, in relation to original sin and the perversion of the will, that from either the *original* or the *acquired* strength of certain natural appetites, principles of self-love, &c., "left to themselves," the corruption of the heart will certainly follow. "In every instance the will does, in fact, yield to the demands of these. But whenever it thus yielded, *there was power to the contrary;* otherwise there could be no freedom of moral action." Now I beg leave to place my finger on the phrase in italics, and ask the editors what they mean by it. If they hold the common doctrines with regard to the relation of cause and effect, and with regard to power as connected with that relation, and apply these to the acts of the will, I can see no more possibility of conceiving a *power to the contrary* in this case, than of conceiving such a power in the current of a river. But if they mean to assert the existence in the will of an *actual* power to rise above the demands of appetite, &c., above the law of nature and to decide *arbitrarily*, whether to yield or not to yield, then they admit that the will is not determined *absolutely* by the extraneous *cause*, but is in fact *self*-determined. They agree with the letter-writer ; and the question for them is at rest. Thus, whatever distinctions may be attempted here, there can be no real distinction but between an irresponsible nature and a will that is self-determined. The reader will find a few additional remarks on this topic in a note, and for the general views of the Work is again referred to a former note and the references there made. To the subject of that note, and to the great distinction between nature and the will, between the natural and the spiritual, as unfolded in the Work, I must beg leave, also, again to request the special and candid attention of the reader. I must beg, too, the unprejudiced attention of every reader, friendly to the cause of practical and spiritual religion, to the tendency of this part of the Author's system, and of the remarks hazarded above.

I can not but be aware, that the views of the Will here exhibited will meet with strong prejudices in a large portion, at least, of our religious community. I could wish that all such would carefully distinguish between the Author's views of the doctrines of religion and the philosophical grounds on which he supposes those doctrines are to be defended. If no one disputes, and I trust no one will dispute, the substantial orthodoxy of the Work, without first carefully examining what has been the orthodoxy of the Church in general, and of the great body of the Reformers, then I should hope it may be wisely considered, whether, as a question of philosophy, the metaphysical principles of this Work are not in themselves more in accordance with the doctrines of a spiritual religion, and better suited to their explanation and defence, than those above treated of. If on examination it can not be disputed that they are, then, if not before, I trust the two systems may be compared without undue impartiality, and the simple question of the truth of each may be determined by that calm and persevering reflection, which alone can determine questions of this sort.

If the system here taught be true, then it will follow, not, be it observed, that our religion is necessarily wrong, or our essential faith erroneous, but that the *philosophical grounds*, on which we are accustomed to defend our faith, are unsafe, and that their *natural tendency* is to error. If the spirit of the Gospel still exert its influence; if a truly spiritual religion be maintained, it is in *opposition* to our philosophy, and not at all by its aid. I know it will be said, that the practical results of our peculiar forms of doctrine are at variance with these remarks. But this I am not prepared to admit. True, religion and religious institutions have flourished: the Gospel, in many parts of our country, has been affectionately and faithfully preached by great and good men; the word and the Spirit of God have been communicated to us in rich abundance; and I rejoice with heartfelt joy and thanksgiving, in the belief, that thereby multitudes have been regenerated to a new and spiritual life. But so were equal or greater effects produced under the preaching of Baxter, and Howe, and other good and faithful men of the same age, with none of the peculiarities of our theological systems. Neither reason nor experience indeed furnish any ground for believing that the living and life-giving power of the Divine Word has ever derived any portion of its efficacy, in the conversion of the heart to God, from the forms of metaphysical theology, with which the human understanding has invested it. It requires, moreover, but little knowledge of the history of philosophy, and of the writings of the 16th and 17th centuries to know, that the opinions of the Reformers, and of all the great divines of that period, on subjects of this sort, were far different from those of Mr. Locke and his followers, and were in fact essentially the same with those taught in this Work. This last remark applies not only to the views entertained by the eminent philosophers and divines of that period on the particular subject above discussed, but to the distinctions made, and the language employed by them, with reference to other points of no less importance in the constitution of our being.

It must have been observed by the reader of the foregoing

pages, that I have used several words, especially *understanding* and *reason*, in a sense somewhat diverse from their present acceptation; and the occasion of this I suppose would be partly understood from my having already directed the attention of the reader to the distinction exhibited between these words in the Work, and from the remarks made on the ambiguity of the word "reason" in its common use. I now proceed to remark, that the ambiguity spoken of, and the consequent perplexity in regard to the use and authority of reason, have arisen from the habit of using, since the time of Locke, the terms understanding and reason indiscriminately, and thus confounding a distinction clearly marked in the philosophy and in the language of the older writers. Alas! had the *terms* only been confounded, or had we suffered only an inconvenient ambiguity of language, there would be comparatively little cause for earnestness upon the subject; or had our views of the things signified by these terms been only partially confused, and had we still retained correct notions of our prerogative, as rational and spiritual beings, the consequences might have been less deplorable. But the misfortune is, that the powers of understanding and reason have not merely been blended and confounded in the view of our philosophy;—the higher and far more characteristic, as an essential constituent of our proper humanity, has been as it were obscured and hidden from our observation in the inferior power, which belongs to us in common with the brutes which perish. According to the old, the more spiritual, and genuine philosophy, the distinguishing attributes of our humanity—that *image of* God in which man alone was created of all the dwellers upon earth, and in virtue of which he was placed at the head of this lower world, was said to be found in the *reason* and *free-will*. But understanding these in their strict and proper sense, and according to the true *ideas* of them, as contemplated by the older metaphysicians, we have literally, if the system of Locke and the popular philosophy of the day be true, neither the one nor the other of these—neither reason nor free-will. What they esteemed the image of God in the soul, and considered as distinguishing us specifically, and so vastly too, above each and all of the irrational animals, is found, according to this system, to have in fact no real existence. The reality neither of the free-will, nor of any of those laws or ideas, which spring from, or rather constitute reason, can be authenticated by the sort of proof which is demanded, and we must therefore relinquish our prerogative, and take our place with becoming humility among our more unpretending companions. In the ascending series of powers, enumerated by Milton, with so much philosophical truth, as well as beauty of language, in the fifth book of Paradise Lost, he mentions

> *Fancy* and *understanding*, whence the soul
> REASON receives. And reason is her *being*,
> Discursive or intuitive.

But the highest power here, that which is the being of the soul, considered as any thing differing in kind from the understanding, has no place in our popular metaphysics. Thus we have only the *understanding*, "the faculty judging according to sense," a faculty of abstracting and generalizing, of contrivance and forecast, as the highest of our intellectual powers; and this we are expressly taught belongs to us in common with brutes. Nay, these views of our essential being, consequences and all, are adopted by men, whom one would suppose religion, if not philosophy, should have taught their utter inadequateness to the true and essential constituents of our humanity. Dr. Paley tells us in his Natural Theology, that only "CONTRIVANCE," a power obviously and professedly belonging to brutes, is necessary to constitute *personality*. His whole system both of theology and morals neither teaches, nor implies, the existence of any specific difference either between the understanding and reason, or between nature and the will. It does not imply the existence of any power in man, which does not obviously belong, in a greater or less degree, to irrational animals. Dr. Fleming, another reverend prelate in the English Church, in his "Philosophy of Zoology," maintains in express terms, that we have no faculties differing in kind from those which belong to brutes. How many other learned, and reverend, and wise men adopt the same opinions, I know not: though these are obviously not the peculiar views of the individuals, but conclusions resulting from the essential principles of their system. If, then, there is no better *system*, if this be the genuine philosophy, and founded in the nature of things, there is no help for us, and we must believe it—*if we can.* But most certainly it will follow, that we ought, as fast as the prejudices of education will permit, to rid ourselves of certain notions of prerogative, and certain feelings of our own superiority, which somehow have been strangely prevalent among our race. For though we have indeed, according to this system, a little *more* understanding than other animals—can abstract and generalize and forecast events, and the consequences of our actions, and compare motives *more* skilfully than they; though we have thus *more* knowledge and can circumvent them; though we have *more* power and can subdue them; yet, as to any *distinctive* and *peculiar* characteristic—as to any inherent and essential *worth*, we are after all but little better—though we may be better off—than our dogs and horses. There is no essential difference, and we may rationally doubt—at least we might do so, if by the supposition we were rational beings—whether our fellow animals of the kennel and the stall are not unjustly deprived of certain *personal rights*, and whether a dog charged with trespass may not *rationally* claim to be tried by a jury of his *peers*. Now however trifling and ridiculous this may appear, I would ask in truth and soberness, if it be not a fair and legitimate inference from the premisses, and whether the *absurdity* of the one does not *demonstrate* the utter falsity of the other. And where, I would beg to know, shall we look, according to the popular system of philosophy, for that *image of God* in which we are created? Is it a thing of *degrees?* And is it simply because we have something *more* of the same faculties which belong to brutes, that we become the objects of God's special and fatherly care, the *distinguished* objects of his Providence, and the *sole* objects of his Grace?—*Doth God take care for oxen?* But why not?

I assure my readers, that I have no desire to treat with disrespect and contumely the opinions of great or good men; but the distinction in question, and the assertion and exhibition of the higher prerogatives of reason, as an essential constituent of our being, are so vitally important, in my apprehension, to the formation and support of any rational system of philosophy, and—no less than the distinction before treated of—so pregnant of consequences to the interests of truth, in morals, and religion, and indeed of all truth, that mere opinion and the authority of names may well be disregarded. The discussion, moreover, relates to facts, and to such facts, too, as are not to be learned from the instruction, or received on the authority, of any man. They must be ascertained by every man for himself, by reflection upon the processes and laws of his own inward being, or they are not learned at all to any valuable purpose. We do indeed find in ourselves then, as no one will deny, certain powers of intelligence, which we have abundant reason to believe the brutes possess in common with us in a greater or less degree. The functions of the understanding, as treated of in the popular systems of metaphysics, its faculties of attention, of abstraction, of generalization, the power of forethought and contrivance, of adapting means to ends, and the law of association, may be, so far as we can judge, severally represented more or less adequately in the instinctive intelligence of the higher orders of brutes. But, not to anticipate too far a topic treated of in the Work, do these, or any and all the faculties which we discover in irrational animals, satisfactorily account to a reflecting mind for all the *phenomena* which are presented to our observation in our own consciousness? Would any supposable addition to the *degree* merely of those powers which we ascribe to brutes, render them *rational* beings, and remove the sacred distinction, which law and reason have sanctioned, between things and persons? Will any such addition account for our having—what the brute is not supposed to have—the pure *ideas* of the geometrician, the power of ideal construction, the intuition of geometrical or other necessary and universal truths? Would it give rise, in irrational animals, to a *law of moral rectitude* and *to conscience*—to the feelings of moral *responsibility* and *remorse?* Would it awaken them to a reflective self-consciousness, and lead them to form and contemplate the *ideas* of the *soul*, of *free-will*, of *immortality*, and of God? It seems to me, that we have only to reflect for a serious hour upon what we mean by these, and then to compare them with our notion of what belongs to a brute, its inherent powers and their correlative objects, to feel that they are utterly incompatible—that in the blessing of these we enjoy a prerogative, which we can not disclaim without a violation of reason, and a voluntary abasement of ourselves—and that we must therefore be possessed of some *peculiar* powers—of some source of ideas *distinct* from the understanding, differing *in kind* from any and all of those which belong to us in common with inferior and irrational animals.

But what these powers are, or what is the precise nature of the distinction between the understanding and reason, it is not my province, nor have I undertaken, to show. My object is merely to illustrate its necessity, and the palpable obscurity, vagueness and deficiency, in this respect, of the mode of philosophizing, which is held in so high honor among us. The distinction itself will be found illustrated with some of its important bearings in the Work, and in the notes and Appendix attached to it; and can not be too carefully studied—in connection with that between nature and the will—by the student who would acquire distinct and intelligible notions of what constitutes the truly spiritual in our being, or find rational grounds for the possibility of a truly spiritual religion. Indeed, could I succeed in fixing the attention of the reader upon this distinction, in such a way as to secure his candid and reflecting perusal of the Work, I should consider any personal effort or sacrifice abundantly recompensed. Nor am I alone in this view of its importance. A literary friend, whose opinion on this subject would be valued by all who knew the soundness of his scholarship, says in a letter just now received,—"If you can get the attention of thinking men fixed on his distinction between the reason and the understanding, you will have done enough to reward the labor of a life. As prominent a place as it holds in the writings of Coleridge, he seems to me far enough from making too much of it." No person of serious and philosophical mind, I am confident, can reflect upon the subject, enough to understand it in its various aspects, without arriving at the same views of the importance of the distinction, whatever may be his conviction with regard to its truth.

But indeed the only grounds, which I find, to apprehend that the reality of the distinction and the importance of the consequences resulting from it, will be much longer denied and rejected among us, is in the overweening assurance, which prevails with regard to the adequateness and perfection of the system of philosophy which is already received. It is taken for granted, as a fact undisputed and indisputable, that this is the most enlightened age of the world, not only with regard to the more general diffusion of certain points of practical knowledge; in which, probably, it may be so, but *in all respects;* that our whole system of the philosophy of mind as derived from Lord Bacon, especially, is the only one, which has any claims to common sense; and that all distinctions not recognized in that are consequently unworthy of our regard. What those Reformers, to whose transcendent powers of mind, and to whose characters as truly spiritual divines, we are accustomed to look with feelings of so much general regard, might find to say in favor of their philosophy, few take the pains to inquire. Neither they nor the great philosophers with whom they held communion on subjects of this sort, can appear among us to speak in their own defence; and even the huge folios and quartos, in which, though dead, they yet speak—and ought to be heard—have seldom strayed to this side of the Atlantic. All our information respecting their philosophical opinions, and the grounds on which they defended them, has been received from writers, who were confessedly advocating a system of recent growth, at open war with every thing more ancient, and who, in the great abundance of their self-complacency, have represented their own discoveries as containing the sum and substance of all philosophy, and the accumulated treasures of ancient wisdom as unworthy the attention of "this enlightened age." Be it so—yet the *foolishness* of antiquity, if it be *of God*, may prove *wiser than men*. It may be found that the philosophy of the Reformers and their religion are essentially connected, and must stand or fall together. It may at length be discovered, that a system of religion essentially spiritual, and a system of philosophy which excludes the very idea of all spiritual power and agency, in their only distinctive and proper character, can not be consistently associated together.

It is our peculiar misfortune in this country, that while the philosophy of Locke and the Scottish writers has been received in full faith, as the only rational system, and its leading principles especially passed off as unquestionable, the strong attachment to religion, and the fondness for speculation, by both of which we are strongly characterized, have led us to combine and associate these principles, such as they are, with our religious interests and opinions, so variously and so intimately, that by most persons they are considered as necessary parts of the same system; and from being so long contemplated together, the rejection of one seems impossible without doing violence to the other. Yet how much evidence might not an impartial observer find in examining the theological discussions which have prevailed, the speculative systems which have been formed and arrayed against each other, for the last seventy years, to convince him that there must be some discordance in the elements, some principle of secret but irreconcilable hostility between a philosophy and a religion, which, under every ingenious variety of form and shaping, still stand aloof from each other and refuse to cohere. For is it not a fact, that in regard to every speculative system which has been formed on these philosophical principles,—to every new shaping of theory which has been devised and has gained adherents among us,—is it not a fact, I ask, that, to all, except those adherents, the *system*—the philosophical *theory*—has seemed dangerous in its tendency, and at war with orthodox views of religion—perhaps even with the attributes of God? Nay, to bring the matter still nearer and more plainly to view, I ask, whether at this moment the organs and particular friends of our leading theological seminaries in New England, both devotedly attached to an orthodox and spiritual system of religion, and expressing mutual confidence as to the *essentials* of their mutual faith, do not each consider the other as holding a philosophical *theory* subversive of orthodoxy? If I am not misinformed, this is the simple fact.

Now, if these things be so, I would ask again with all earnestness, and out of regard to the interests of truth alone, whether serious and reflecting men may not be permitted, without the charge of heresy in RELIGION, to stand in doubt of this PHILOSOPHY *altogether*; whether these facts which will not be disputed, do not furnish just grounds for suspicion, that the principles of our philosophy may be erroneous, or at least induce us to look with candor and impartiality at the claims of another and a different system?

What are the claims of the system, to which the attention of the public is invited in this Work, can be understood fully, only by a careful and reflecting examination of its principles in connection with the conscious wants of our inward being—the requirements of our own reason and consciences. Its purpose and tendency, I have endeavored in some measure to exhibit; and if the influence of authority, which the prevailing system furnishes against it, can and must be counteracted by any thing of a like kind—(and whatever professions we may make, the influence of authority produces at least a predisposing effect upon our minds)—the remark which I have made, will show, that the principles here taught are not wholly unauthorized by men, whom we have been taught to reverence among the great and good. I can not but add, as a matter of simple justice to the question, that however our prevailing system of philosophizing may have appealed to the authority of Lord Bacon, it needs but a candid examination of his writings, especially the first part of his *Novum Organum*, to be convinced that such an appeal is without grounds; and that in fact the fundamental principles of his philosophy are the same with those taught in this work. The great distinction especially, between the understanding and the reason, is fully and clearly recognized; and as a philosopher he would be far more properly associated with Plato, or even Aristotle, than with the modern philosophers, who have miscalled their systems by his name. For further remarks on this point, the reader is requested to refer to the notes. In our own times, moreover, there is abundant evidence, whatever may be thought of the principles of this Work here, that the same general views of philosophy are regaining their ascendency elsewhere. In Great Britain there are not few, who begin to believe that the deep-toned and sublime eloquence of Coleridge on these great subjects may have something to claim their attention besides a few peculiarities of language. In Paris, the doctrines of a rational and spiritual system of philosophy are taught to listening and admiring thousands by one of the most learned and eloquent philosophers of the age; and in Germany, if I mistake not, the same general views are adopted by the serious friends of religious truth among her great and learned men.

Such—as I have no doubt—must be the case, wherever thinking men can be brought distinctly and impartially to examine their claims; and indeed to those who shall study and comprehend the general history of philosophy, it must always be matter of special wonder, that in the Christian community, anxiously striving to explain and defend the doctrines of Christianity in their spiritual sense, there should have been a long-continued and tenacious adherence to philosophical principles, so subversive of their faith in every thing distinctively spiritual; while those of an opposite tendency, and claiming a near relationship and correspondence with the truly spiritual in the Christian system, and the mysteries of its sublime faith, were looked upon with suspicion and jealousy, as unintelligible or dangerous metaphysics.

And here I must be allowed to add a few remarks with regard

to the popular objections against the system of philosophy, the claims of which I am urging, especially against the writings of the Author, under whose name it appears in the present Work. These are various and often contradictory, but usually have reference either to his peculiarities of language, or to the depth—whether apparent or real,—and the unintelligibleness, of his thoughts.

To the first of these it seems to me a sufficient answer, for a mind that would deal honestly and frankly by itself, to suggest that in the very nature of things it is impossible for a writer to express by a single word any truth, or to mark any distinction, not recognized in the language of his day, unless he adopts a word entirely new, or gives to one already in use a new and more peculiar sense. Now in communicating truths, which the writer deems of great and fundamental importance, shall he thus appropriate a single word old or new, or trust to the vagueness of perpetual circumlocution? Admitting for example, the existence of the important distinction, for which this writer contends, between the understanding and reason, and that this distinction when recognized at all is confounded in the common use of language by employing the words indiscriminately, shall he still use these words indiscriminately, and either invent a new word, or mark the distinction by descriptive circumlocutions, or shall he assign a more distinctive and precise meaning to the words already used? It seems to me obviously more in accordance with the laws and genius of language to take the course which he has adopted. But in this case and in many others, where his language seems peculiar, it can not be denied that the words had already been employed in the same sense, and the same distinctions recognized, by the older and many of the most distinguished writers in the language. But the reader will find the Author's own views of the subject in the Work.

With regard to the more important objection, that the *thoughts* of Coleridge are *unintelligible*, if it be intended to imply, that his language is not in itself expressive of an intelligible meaning, or that he affects the appearance of depth and mystery, while his thoughts are common-place, it is an objection, which no one who has read his Works attentively, and acquired a feeling of interest for them, will treat their Author with so much disrespect as to answer at all. Every such reader *knows* that he uses words uniformly with astonishing precision, and that language becomes, in his use of it—in a degree, of which few writers can give us a conception—a living power, "consubstantial" with the power of thought, that gave birth to it, and awakening and calling into action a corresponding energy in our own minds. There is little encouragement, moreover, to answer the objections of any man, who will permit himself to be incurably prejudiced against an Author by a few peculiarities of language, or an apparent difficulty of being understood, and without inquiring into the cause of that difficulty, where at the same time he can not but see and acknowledge the presence of great intellectual and moral power.

But if it be intended by the objection to say simply, that the thoughts of the Author are often difficult to be apprehended—that he makes large demands not only upon the attention, but upon the reflecting and thinking powers, of his readers, the fact is not, and need not be, denied: and it will only remain to be decided, whether the instruction offered, as the reward, will repay us for the expenditure of thought required, or can be obtained for less. I know it is customary in this country, as well as in Great Britain—and that too among men from whom different language might be expected—to affect either contempt or modesty, in regard to all that is more than common-place in philosophy, and especially "Coleridge's Metaphysics," as "too deep for them." Now it may not be every man's duty, or in every man's power, to devote to such studies the time and thought necessary to understand the deep things of philosophy. But for one who professes to be a scholar, and to cherish a manly love of truth for the truth's sake, to object to a system of metaphysics because it is "too *deep* for him," must be either a disingenuous insinuation, that its depths are not worth exploring—which is more than the objector knows—or a confession that—with all his professed love of truth and knowledge—he prefers to "sleep after dinner." The misfortune is, that men have been cheated into a belief, that all philosophy and metaphysics worth knowing are contained in a few volumes, which can be understood with little expense of thought; and that they may very well spare themselves the vexation of trying to comprehend the depths of "Coleridge's Metaphysics." According to the popular notions of the day, it is a very easy matter to understand the philosophy of mind. A new work on philosophy is as easy to read as the last new novel; and superficial, would-be scholars, who have a very sensible horror at the thought of studying Algebra, or the doctrine of fluxions, can yet go through a course of moral sciences, and know all about the philosophy of the mind.

Now why will not men of sense, and men who have any just pretensions to scholarship, see that there must of necessity be gross sophistry somewhere in any system of metaphysics, which pretends to give us an adequate and scientific self-knowledge—to render comprehensive to us the mysterious laws of our own inward being, with less manly and persevering effort of thought on our part, than is confessedly required to comprehend the simplest of those sciences, all of which are but some of the *phænomena*, from which the laws in question are to be inferred?—Why will they not see and acknowledge—what one would suppose a moment's reflection would teach them—that to attain true self-knowledge by reflection upon the objects of our inward consciousness—not merely to understand the motives of our conduct as conscientious Christians, but to know ourselves scientifically as philosophers—must, of necessity, be the most deep and difficult of all our attainments in knowledge? I trust that what I have already said will be sufficient to expose the absurdity of objections against metaphysics in general, and do something towards showing, that we are in actual and urgent need of a system somewhat deeper than those, the contradictions of which have not without reason made the name of philosophy a terror to the friends of truth and of religion. "False metaphysics can be effectually counteracted by true metaphysics alone; and if the reasoning be clear, solid, and pertinent, the truth deduced can never be the less valuable on account of the depth from which it may have been drawn." It is a fact, too, of great importance to be kept in mind, in relation to this subject, that in the study of ourselves—in attaining a knowledge of our own being,—there are truths of vast concernment, and living at a great depth, which yet no man can draw for another. However the depth may have been fathomed, and the same truth brought up by others, for a light and a joy to their own minds, it must still remain, and be sought for by us, each for himself, at the bottom of the well.

The system of philosophy here taught does not profess to make men philosophers, or—which ought to mean the same thing—to guide them to the knowledge of themselves, without the labor both of attention and of severe thinking. If it did so, it would have, like the more popular works of philosophy, far less affinity than it now has, with the mysteries of religion, and those profound truths concerning our spiritual being and destiny, which are revealed in the *things hard to be understood* of St. Paul and of the beloved disciple. For I can not but remind my readers again, that the Author does not undertake to teach us the philosophy of the human mind, with the exclusion of the truth and influences of religion. He would not undertake to philosophize respecting the being and character of man, and at the same time exclude from his view the very principle which constitutes his proper humanity : he would not, in teaching the doctrine of the solar system, omit to mention the sun, and the law of gravitation. He professes to investigate and unfold the being of man *as man*, in his higher, his peculiar, and distinguishing attributes. These it is, which are hard to be understood, and to apprehend which requires the exercise of deep reflection and exhausting thought. Nor in aiming at this object would he consider it very philosophical to reject the aid and instruction of eminent writers on the subject of religion, or even of the volume of Revelation itself. He would consider St. Augustine as none the less a philosopher, because he became a Christian. The Apostles John and Paul were, in the view of this system of philosophy, the most rational of all writers, and the New Testament the most philosophical of all books. They are so because they unfold more fully, than any other, the true and essential principles of our being; because they give us a clearer and deeper insight into those constituent laws of our humanity, which as men, and therefore as philosophers, we are most concerned to know. Not only to those, who seek the practical self-knowledge of the humble, spiritually-minded Christian, but to those also, who are impelled by the "heaven descended *γνῶθι σεαυτόν*" to study themselves as philosophers, and to make self-knowledge a science, the truths of Scripture are a light and a revelation. The more earnestly we reflect upon these and refer them, whether as Christians or as philosophers, to the movements of our inward being—to the laws which reveal themselves in our own consciousness, the more fully shall we understand, not only the language of Scripture, but all that most demands and excites the curiosity of the genuine philosopher in the mysterious character of man. It is by this guiding light, that we can best search into and apprehend the constitution of that "marvellous microcosm," which, the more it has been known, has awakened more deeply the wonder and admiration of the true philosopher in every age.

Nor would the Author of this Work, or those who have imbibed the spirit of his system, join with the philosophers of the day in throwing aside and treating with a contempt, as ignorant as it is arrogant, the treasures of ancient wisdom. *He*, says the son of Sirach, *that giveth his mind to the law of the Most High, and is occupied in the meditation thereof, will seek out the wisdom of all the ancient.* In the estimation of the true philosopher, the case should not be greatly altered in the present day; and now that two thousand years have added such rich and manifold abundance to those ancient "sayings of the wise," he will still approach them with reverence, and receive their instruction with gladness of heart. In seeking to explore and unfold these deeper and more solemn mysteries of our being, which inspire us with awe, while they baffle our comprehension, he will especially beware of trusting to his own understanding, or of contradicting, in compliance with the self-flattering inventions of a single age, the universal faith and consciousness of the human race. On such subjects, though he would call no man master, yet neither would he willingly forego the aids to be derived, in the search after truth, from those great oracles of human wisdom—those giants in intellectual power, who from generation to generation were admired and venerated by the great and good. Much less could he think it becoming, or consistent with his duty to hazard the publication of his own thoughts on subjects of the deepest concernment, and on which minds of greatest depth and power had been occupied in former ages, while confessedly ignorant alike of their doctrines and of the arguments by which they are sustained.

It is in this spirit, that the Author of the work here offered to the public has prepared himself to deserve the candid and even confiding attention of his readers, with reference to the great subject of which he treats.

And although the claims of the Work upon our attention, as of every other work, must depend more upon its inherent and essential character, than upon the worth and authority of its Author, it may yet be of service to the reader to know, that he is no hasty or unfurnished adventurer in the department of authorship, to which the Work belongs. The discriminating reader of this Work can not fail to discover his profound knowledge of the philosophy of language, the principles of its construction, and the laws of its interpretation. In others of his works, perhaps more fully than in this, there is evidence of an unrivalled mastery over all that pertains both to logic and philology. It has been already intimated, that he is no contemner of the great writers of antiquity and of their wise sentences; and probably few English scholars, even in those days when there were giants of learning in Great Britain, and minds more richly furnished with the treasures of ancient lore. But especially will the reader of this Work observe with admiration the profoundness of his philosophical attainments, and his thorough and intimate knowledge, not only of the works and systems of Plato and Aristotle, and of the celebrated philosophers of modern times, but of those too much neglected writings of the Greek and Roman Fathers, and of the great leaders of the Reformation, which more particularly qualified him for discussing the subjects of the present Work. If these qualifications, and—with all these, and above all—a disposition professed and made evident seriously to value them, chiefly as they enable him more fully and clearly to comprehend and illustrate the truths of the Christian system,—if these, I say, can give an Author a claim to serious and thoughtful attention, then may the Work here offered urge its claim upon the reader. My own regard for the cause of truth, for the interests of philosophy, of reason, and of religion, lead me to hope that they may not be urged in vain.

Of his general claims to our regard, whether from exalted personal and moral worth, or from the magnificence of his intellectual powers, and the vast extent and variety of his accumulated stores of knowledge, I shall not venture to speak. If it be true indeed that a really great mind can be worthily commended only by those who adequately both appreciate and *comprehend* its greatness, there are few who should undertake to estimate, and set forth in appropriate terms, the intellectual power and moral worth of Samuel Taylor Coleridge. Neither he, nor the public, would be benefited by such commendations as I could bestow.

The few among us who have read his works with the attention which they deserve, are at no loss what rank to assign him among the writers of the present age; to those who have not, any language, which I might use, would appear hyperbolical and extravagant. The character and influence of his principles as a philosopher, a moralist, and a Christian, and of the writings by which he is enforcing them, do not ultimately depend upon the estimation in which they may now be held; and to posterity he may safely intrust those "productive ideas" and "living words"—those

> —— truths that wake
> To perish never,

the possession of which will be for their benefit, and connected with which, in the language of the Son of Sirach,—*His own memorial shall not depart away, and his name shall live from generation to generation.*

J. M.

THE AUTHOR'S ADDRESS TO THE READER.

FELLOW-CHRISTIAN! the wish to be admired as a fine writer held a very subordinate place in my thoughts and feelings in the composition of this Volume. Let then its comparative merits and demerits, in respect of style and stimulancy, possess a proportional weight, and no more, in determining your judgment for or against its contents. Read it through: then compare the state of your mind with the state in which your mind was when you first opened the book. Has it led you to reflect? Has it supplied or suggested fresh subjects for reflection? Has it given you any new information? Has it removed any obstacle to a lively conviction of your responsibility as a moral agent? Has it solved any difficulties, which had impeded your faith as a Christian? Lastly, has it increased your power of thinking connectedly—especially on the scheme and purpose of the Redemption by Christ? If it have done none of these things, condemn it aloud as worthless: and strive to compensate for your own loss of time, by preventing others from wasting theirs. But if your conscience dictates an affirmative answer to all or any of the preceding questions, declare this too aloud, and endeavor to extend my utility.

Οὕτως πάντα πρὸς ἑαυτὴν ἐπάγουσα, καὶ συνηθροισμένη ψυχη, αὐτὴ εἰς αὑτὴν, ῥαῖστα καὶ μάλα βεβαίως μακαρίζεταὶ. MARINUS.

*Omnis divinæ atque humanæ eruditionis elementa tria, Nosse, Velle, Posse; quorum principium unum Mens; cujus oculus Ratio; cui lumen * * præbet Deus.* VICO.

Naturam hominis hanc Deus ipse voluit, ut duarum rerum cupidus et appetens esset, religionis et sapientiæ. Sed homines ideo falluntur, quod aut religionem suscipiunt omissa sapientia; aut sapientiæ soli student omissa religione; cum alterum sine altero esse non possit verum.

LACTANTIUS.

THE AUTHOR'S PREFACE.

An Author has three points to settle: to what sort his work belongs, for what description of readers it is intended, and the specific end or object, which it is to answer. There is indeed a preliminary question respecting the end which the writer himself has in view, whether the number of purchasers, or the benefit of the readers. But this may be safely passed by; since where the book itself or the known principles of the writer do not supersede the question, there will seldom be sufficient strength of character for good or for evil to afford much chance of its being either distinctly put or fairly answered.

I shall proceed therefore to state as briefly as possible the intentions of the present Volume in reference to the three first-mentioned points, namely, What? For whom? For what?

I. What? The answer is contained in the title-page. It belongs to the class of didactic works. Consequently, those who neither wish instruction for themselves, nor assistance in instructing others, have no interest in its contents.

Sis sus, sis Divus: sum caltha, et non tibi spiro!

II. For whom? Generally, for as many in all classes as wish for aid in disciplining their minds to habits of reflection; for all, who desirous of building up a manly character in the light of distinct consciousness, are content to study the principles of moral architecture on the several grounds of prudence, morality, and religion. And lastly, for all who feel an interest in the position which I have undertaken to defend, this, namely, that the Christian Faith is the perfection of human intelligence,—an interest sufficiently strong to insure a patient attention to the arguments brought in its support.

But if I am to mention any particular class or description of readers, who were prominent in my thought during the composition of the volume, my reply must be; that it was especially designed for the studious young at the close of their education or on their first entrance into the duties of manhood and the rights of self-government. And of these, again, in thought and wish I destined the work (the latter and larger portion. at least) yet more particularly to students intended for the ministry; first, as in duty bound, to the members of our Universities: secondly (but only in respect of this mental precedency second), to all alike of whatever name, who have dedicated their future lives to the cultivation of their race, as pastors, preachers, missionaries, or instructors of youth.

III. For what? The worth of an author is estimated by the ends, the attainment of which he proposed to himself by the particular work; while the value of the work depends on its fitness, as the means. The objects of the present volume are the following, arranged in the order of their comparative importance.

1. To direct the reader's attention to the value of the science of words, their use and abuse, and the incalculable advantages attached to the habit of using them appropriately, and with a distinct knowledge of their primary, derivative, and metaphorical senses. And in furtherance of this object I have neglected no occasion of enforcing the maxim, that to expose a sophism and to detect the equivocal or double meaning of a word is, in the great majority of cases, one and the same thing. Horne Tooke entitled his celebrated work, *Ἔπεα πτερόεντα*, winged words: or language, not only the vehicle of thought but the wheels. With my convictions and views, for ἔπεα I should substitute λόγοι, that is, words select and determinate, and for πτερόεντα ζώοντες, that is, living words. The wheels of the intellect I admit them to be: but such as Ezekiel beheld in *the visions of God* as he sate among the captives by the river of Chebar. *Whithersoever the Spirit was to go, the wheels went, and thither was their Spirit to go; for the Spirit of the living creature was in the wheels also.*

2. To establish the distinct characters of prudence, morality, and religion: and to impress the conviction, that though the second requires the first, and the third contains and supposes both the former; yet still moral goodness is other and more than prudence on the principle of expediency; and religion more and higher than morality. For this distinction the better Schools even of Pagan Philosophy contended.

3. To substantiate and set forth at large the momentous distinction between reason and understanding. Whatever is achievable by the understanding for the purposes of worldly interest, private or public, has in the present age been pursued with an activity and a success beyond all former experience, and to an extent which equally demands my admiration and excites my wonder. But likewise it is, and long has been, my conviction, that in no age since the first dawning of science and philosophy in this island have the truths, interests, and studies which especially belong to the reason, contemplative or practical, sunk into such utter neglect, not to say contempt, as during the last century. It is therefore one main object of this volume to establish the position, that whoever transfers to the understanding the primacy due to the *reason*, loses the one and spoils the other.

4. To exhibit a full and consistent scheme of the Christian Dispensation, and more largely of all the peculiar doctrines of the Christian Faith; and to answer all the objections to the same, which do not originate in a corrupt will rather than an erring judgment; and to do this in a manner intelligible for all who, possessing the ordinary advantages of education, do in good earnest desire to form their religious creed in the light of their own convictions, and to have a reason for the faith which they profess. There are indeed mysteries, in evidence of which no reasons can be brought. But it has been my endeavor to show, that the true solution of this problem is, that these mysteries are reason, reason in its highest form of self-affirmation.

Such are the special objects of these Aids to Reflection. Concerning the general character of the work, let me be permitted to add the few following sentences. St. Augustine, in one of his Sermons, discoursing on a high point of theology, tells his auditors—*Sic accipite, ut mereamini intelligere. Fides enim debet præcedere intellectum, ut sit intellectus fidei præmium.* Now without a certain portion of gratuitous and (as it were) experimentative faith in the writer, a reader will scarcely give that degree of continued attention, without which no didactic work worth reading can be read to any wise or profitable purpose. In this sense, therefore, and to this extent, every author, who is competent to the office he has undertaken, may without arrogance repeat St. Augustine's words in his own right, and advance a similar claim on similar grounds. But I venture no further than to intimate the sentiment at a humble distance, by avowing my belief that he, who seeks instruction in the following pages, will not fail to find entertainment likewise; but that whoever seeks entertainment only will find neither.

Reader!—You have been bred in a land abounding with men, able in arts, learning, and knowledges manifold, this man in one, this in another, few in many, none in all. But there is one art, of which every man should be master, the art of reflection. If you are not a thinking man, to what purpose are you a man at all? In like manner, there is one knowledge, which it is every man's interest and duty to acquire, namely, self-knowledge; or to what end was man alone, of all animals, endued by the Creator with the faculty of self-consciousness? Truly said the Pagan moralist,

e cœlo descendit, Γνῶθι σέαυτον.

But you are likewise born in a Christian land: and Revelation has provided for you new subjects for reflection, and new treasures of knowledge, never to be unlocked by him who remains self-ignorant. Self-knowledge is the key to this casket; and by reflection alone can it be obtained. Reflect on your own thoughts, actions, circumstances, and—which will be of especial aid to you in forming a habit of reflection,—accustom yourself to reflect on the words you use, hear, or read, their birth, derivation and history. For if words are not things, they are living powers, by which the things of most importance to mankind are actuated, combined, and humanized. Finally, by reflection you may draw from the fleeting facts of your worldly trade, art, or profession, a science permanent as your immortal soul; and make even these subsidiary and preparative to the reception of spiritual truth, "doing as the dyers do, who having first dipt their silks in colors of less value, then give them the last tincture of crimson in grain."

AIDS TO REFLECTION.

INTRODUCTORY APHORISMS.

APHORISM I.

In philosophy equally as in poetry, it is the highest and most useful prerogative of genius to produce the strongest impressions of novelty, while it rescues admitted truths from the neglect caused by the very circumstance of their universal admission. Extremes meet. Truths, of all others the most awful and interesting, are too often considered as so true, that they lose all the power of truth, and lie bed-ridden in the dormitory of the soul, side by side with the most despised and exploded errors.

APHORISM II.

There is one sure way of giving freshness and importance to the most common-place maxims—that of reflecting on them in direct reference to our own state and conduct, to our own past and future being.

APHORISM III.

To restore a common-place truth to its first uncommon lustre, you need only translate it into action. But to do this, you must have reflected on its truth.

APHORISM IV.

Leighton and Coleridge.

It is the advice of the wise man, "Dwell at home," or, with yourself; and though there are very few that do this, yet it is surprising that the greatest part of mankind can not be prevailed upon, at least to visit themselves sometimes; but, according to the saying of the wise Solomon, *The eyes of the fool are in the ends of the earth.*

A reflecting mind, says an ancient writer, is the spring and source of every good thing. "*Omnis boni principium intellectus cogitabundus.*" It is at once the disgrace and the misery of men, that they live without fore-thought. Suppose yourself fronting a mirror. Now what the objects behind you are to their images at the same apparent distance before you, such is reflection to fore-thought. As a man without fore-thought scarcely deserves the name of a man, so fore-thought without reflection is but a metaphorical phrase for the instinct of a beast.

APHORISM V.

As a fruit-tree is more valuable than any one of its fruits singly, or even than all its fruits of a single season, so the noblest object of reflection is the mind itself, by which we reflect:

And as the blossoms, the green and the ripe fruit of an orange-tree are more beautiful to behold when on the tree and seen as one with it, than the same growth detached and seen successively, after their importation into another country and different clime; so it is with the manifold objects of reflection, when they are considered principally in reference to the reflective power, and as part and parcel of the same. No object, of whatever value our passions may represent it, but becomes foreign to us as soon as it is altogether unconnected with our intellectual, moral, and spiritual life. To be ours, it must be referred to the mind, either as a motive, or consequence, or symptom.

APHORISM VI.

Leighton.

He who teaches men the principles and precepts of spiritual wisdom, before their minds are called off from foreign objects, and turned inward upon themselves, might as well write his instructions, as the Sibyl wrote her prophecies, on the loose leaves of trees, and commit them to the mercy of the inconstant winds.

APHORISM VII.

In order to learn, we must attend: in order to profit by what we have learnt, we must think—that is, reflect. He only thinks who reflects.*

APHORISM VIII.

Leighton and Coleridge.

It is a matter of great difficulty, and requires no ordinary skill and address, to fix the attention of men on the world within them, to induce them to study the processes and superintend the works which they are themselves carrying on in their own minds; in short, to awaken in them both the faculty of thought† and the inclination to exercise it. For, alas! the largest part of mankind are nowhere greater strangers than at home.

APHORISM IX.

Life is the one universal soul, which by virtue of the enlivening Breath, and the informing Word, all organized bodies have in common, each after its kind. This, therefore, all animals possess, and man as an animal. But, in addition to this, God transfused into man a higher gift, and specially imbreathed;—even a living (that is, self-subsisting) soul, a soul having its life in itself. *And*

* The indisposition, nay, the angry aversion to think, even in persons who are most willing to attend, and on the subjects to which they are giving studious attention, as political economy, Biblical theology, classical antiquities, and the like,—is the fact that forces itself on my notice afresh, every time I enter into the society of persons in the higher ranks. To assign a feeling and a determination of will, as a satisfactory reason for embracing or rejecting this or that opinion or belief, is of ordinary occurrence, and sure to obtain the sympathy and the suffrages of the company. And yet to me this seems little less irrational than to apply the nose to a picture, and to decide on its genuineness by the sense of smell.

† Distinction between Thought and Attention.—By Thought is here meant the voluntary reproduction in our minds of those states of consciousness, to which, as to his best and most authentic documents, the teacher of moral or religious truth refers us. In attention, we keep the mind passive: in thought, we rouse it into activity. In the former, we submit to an impression—we keep the mind steady, in order to receive the stamp. In the latter, we seek to imitate the artist, while we ourselves make a copy or duplicate of his work. We may learn arithmetic or the elements of geometry by continued attention alone; but self-knowledge, or an insight into the laws and constitution of the human mind and the grounds of religion and true morality, in addition to the effort of attention, requires the energy of thought.

man became a living soul. He did not merely possess it, he became it. It was his proper being, his truest self, the man in the man. None then, not one of human kind, so poor and destitute, but there is provided for him, even in his present state, *a house not built with hands;* ay, and spite of the philosophy (falsely so called) which mistakes the causes, the conditions, and the occasions of our becoming conscious of certain truths and realities for the truths and realities themselves—a house gloriously furnished. Nothing is wanted but the eye, which is the light of this house, the light which is the eye of this soul. This seeing light, this enlightening eye, is reflection.* It is more, indeed, than is ordinarily meant by that word; but it is what a Christian ought to mean by it, and to know too, whence it first came, and still continues to come—of what light even this light is but a reflection. This, too, is thought; and all thought is but unthinking that does not flow out of this, or tend towards it.

APHORISM X.

Self-Superintendence! that any thing should overlook itself! Is not this a paradox, and hard to understand? It is, indeed, difficult, and to the imbruted sensualist a direct contradiction: and yet most truly does the poet exclaim,

—— Unless above himself he can
Erect himself, how mean a thing is man!

APHORISM XI.

An hour of solitude passed in sincere and earnest prayer, or the conflict with, and conquest over a single passion or 'subtle bosom sin,' will teach us more of thought, will more effectually awaken the faculty, and form the habit, of reflection, than a year's study in the Schools without them.

APHORISM XII.

In a world, the opinions of which are drawn from outside shows, many things may be paradoxical (that is, contrary to the

* The διάνοια of St. John i. v. 20, inadequately rendered *understanding* in our translation. To exhibit the full force of the Greek word, we must say, a *power of discernment by reason.*

common notion), and nevertheless true : nay, because they are true. How should it be otherwise, as long as the imagination of the worldling is wholly occupied by surfaces, while the Christian's thoughts are fixed on the substance, that which is and abides, and which, because it is the substance,* the outward senses can not recognize. Tertullian had good reason for his assertion, that the simplest Christian (if indeed a Christian) knows more than the most accomplished irreligious philosopher.

COMMENT.

Let it not, however, be forgotten, that the powers of the understanding and the intellectual graces are precious gifts of God; and that every Christian, according to the opportunities vouchsafed to him, is bound to cultivate the one and to acquire the other. Indeed, he is scarcely a Christian who wilfully neglects so to do. What says the Apostle ? Add to your faith knowledge, and to knowledge manly energy,—ἀρέτη.†

APHORISM XIII.

Never yet did there exist a full faith in the Divine Word (by whom light, as well as immortality, was brought into the world), which did not expand the intellect, while it purified the heart ;—which did not multiply the aims and objects of the understanding, while it fixed and simplified those of the desires and passions.‡

* *Quod stat subtus*, that which stands beneath, and (as it were) supports, the appearance. In a language like ours, so many words of which are derived from other languages, there are few modes of instruction more useful or more amusing than that of accustoming young people to seek for the etymology, or primary meaning of the words they use. There are cases, in which more knowledge of more value may be conveyed by the history of a word, than by the history of a campaign.

† 2 Pet. i. 5.—*Ed.*

‡ The effects of a zealous ministry on the intellects and acquirements of the laboring classes are not only attested by Baxter, and the Presbyterian divines, but admitted by Bishop Burnet, who during his mission in the west of Scotland, was 'amazed to find a poor commonalty so able to argue,' &c. But we need not go to a sister church for proof or example. The diffusion of light and knowledge through this kingdom, by the exertions of the bishops and clergy, by Episcopalians and Puritans, from Edward VI. to the Restoration, was as wonderful as it is praiseworthy, and may be justly placed among the most remarkable facts in history

COMMENT.

If acquiescence without insight; if warmth without light; if an immunity from doubt, given and guaranteed by a resolute ignorance; if the habit of taking for granted the words of a catechism, remembered or forgotten; if a mere sensation of positiveness substituted—I will not say for the sense of certainty, but—for that calm assurance, the very means and conditions of which it supersedes; if a belief that seeks the darkness, and yet strikes no root, immovable as the limpet from the rock, and, like the limpet, fixed there by mere force of adhesion:—if these suffice to make men Christians, in what sense could the Apostle affirm that believers receive, not indeed worldly wisdom, which comes to naught, but the wisdom of God, *that we might know and comprehend* the things that are freely given to us of God? On what grounds could he denounce the sincerest fervor of spirit as defective, where it does not likewise bring forth fruits in the understanding?

APHORISM XIV.

In our present state, it is little less than impossible that the affections should be kept constant to an object which gives no employment to the understanding, and yet can not be made manifest to the senses. The exercise of the reasoning and reflecting powers, increasing insight, and enlarging views, are requisite to keep alive the substantial faith in the heart.

APHORISM XV.

In the state of perfection, perhaps, all other faculties may be swallowed up in love, or superseded by immediate vision; but it is on the wings of the cherubim, that is (according to the interpretation of the ancient Hebrew doctors), the intellectual powers and energies, that we must first be borne up to the "pure empyrean." It must be seraphs, and not the hearts of imperfect mortals, that can burn unfuelled and self-fed. *Give me understanding* (is the prayer of the Royal Psalmist), *and I shall observe thy law with my whole heart.—Thy law is exceeding broad*—that is, comprehensive, pregnant, containing far more than the apparent import of the words on a first perusal. *It is my meditation all the day.**

COMMENT.

It is worthy of special observation, that the Scriptures are distinguished from all other writings pretending to inspiration, by the strong and frequent recommendations of knowledge, and a spirit of inquiry. Without reflection, it is evident that neither the one can be acquired nor the other exercised.

APHORISM XVI.

The word rational has been strangely abused of late times. This must not, however, disincline us to the weighty consideration, that thoughtfulness, and a desire to bottom all our convictions on grounds of right reason, are inseparable from the character of a Christian.

APHORISM XVII.

A reflecting mind is not a flower that grows wild, or comes up of its own accord. The difficulty is indeed greater than many, who mistake quick recollection for thought, are disposed to admit; but how much less than it would be, had we not been born and bred in a Christian and Protestant land, few of us are sufficiently aware. Truly may we, and thankfully ought we to, exclaim with the Psalmist: *The entrance of thy words giveth light; it giveth understanding to the simple.*†

APHORISM XVIII.

Examine the journals of our zealous missionaries, I will not say among the Hottentots or Esquimaux, but in the highly civilized, though fearfully uncultivated, inhabitants of ancient India. How often, and how feelingly, do they describe the difficulty of rendering the simplest chain of thought intelligible to the ordinary natives, the rapid exhaustion of their whole power of attention, and with what distressful effort it is exerted while it lasts! Yet it is among these that the hideous practices of self-torture chiefly prevail. O if folly were no easier than wisdom, it

* Ps. cxix.—*Ed.*

† Ps. cxix.—*Ed.*

being often so very much more grievous, how certainly might these unhappy slaves of superstition be converted to Christianity! But, alas! to swing by hooks passed through the back, or to walk in shoes with nails of iron pointed upwards through the soles—all this is so much less difficult, demands so much less exertion of the will than to reflect, and by reflection to gain knowledge and tranquillity!

COMMENT.

It is not true that ignorant persons have no notion of the advantages of truth and knowledge. They confess, they see and bear witness to these advantages, in the conduct, the immunities, and the superior powers of the possessors. Were they attainable by pilgrimages the most toilsome, or penances the most painful, we should assuredly have as many pilgrims and self-tormentors in the service of true religion, as now exist under the tyranny of Papal or Brahmin superstition.

APHORISM XIX.

In countries enlightened by the Gospel, however, the most formidable and (it is to be feared) the most frequent impediment to men's turning their minds inwards upon themselves, is that they are afraid of what they shall find there. There is an aching hollowness in the bosom, a dark cold speck at the heart, an obscure and boding sense of a somewhat, that must be kept out of sight of the conscience: some secret lodger, whom they can neither resolve to eject or retain.*

* The following Sonnet from Herbert's Temple, may serve as a forcible comment on the words in the text:

Graces vouchsafed in a Christian land.

Lord! with what care hast thou begirt us round!
Parents first season us. Then schoolmasters
Deliver us to laws. They send us bound
To rules of reason. Holy messengers;
Pulpits and Sundays; sorrow dogging sin;
Afflictions sorted; anguish of all sizes;
Fine nets and stratagems to catch us in;
Bibles laid open; millions of surprises;
Blessings beforehand; ties of gratefulness;
The sound of glory ringing in our ears;

COMMENT.

Few are so obdurate, few have sufficient strength of character, to be able to draw forth an evil tendency or immoral practice into distinct consciousness, without bringing it in the same moment before an awaking conscience. But for this very reason it becomes a duty of conscience to form the mind to a habit of distinct consciousness. An unreflecting Christian walks in twilight among snares and pitfalls! He entreats the heavenly Father not to lead him into temptation, and yet places himself on the very edge of it, because he will not kindle the torch which his Father had given into his hands, as a mean of prevention, and lest he should pray too late.

APHORISM XX.

Among the various undertakings of men, can there be mentioned one more important, can there be conceived one more sublime, than an intention to form the human mind anew after the Divine Image? The very intention, if it be sincere, is a ray of its dawning. The requisites for the execution of this high intent may be comprised under three heads; the prudential, the moral, and the spiritual.

APHORISM XXI.

First, Religious Prudence.—What this is, will be best explained by its effects and operations. Prudence, in the service of religion, consists in the prevention or abatement of hindrances and distractions; and consequently in avoiding, or removing, all such circumstances as, by diverting the attention of the workman, retard the progress and hazard the safety of the work. It is likewise (I deny not) a part of this unworldly prudence, to place ourselves as much and as often as it is in our power so to do, in circumstances directly favorable to our great design; and to avail ourselves of all the positive helps and furtherances which these circumstances afford. But neither dare we, as Christians,

---

Without, our shame; within, our consciences
Angels and grace; eternal hopes and fears!
Yet all these fences, and their whole array,
One cunning bosom sin blows quite away.

forget whose and under what dominion the things are, *quæ nos circumstant*, that is, which stand around us. We are to remember, that it is the world that constitutes our outward circumstances; that in the form of the world, which is evermore at variance with the divine form or idea, they are cast and moulded; and that of the means and measures which prudence requires in the forming anew of the divine image in the soul, the greatest part supposes the world at enmity with our design. We are to avoid its snares, to repel its attacks, to suspect its aids and succors, and even when compelled to receive them as allies within our trenches, yet to commit the outworks alone to their charge, and to keep them at a jealous distance from the citadel. The powers of the world are often christened, but seldom Christianized. They are but proselytes of the outer gate; or, like the Saxons of old, enter the land as auxiliaries, and remain in it as conquerors and lords.

APHORISM XXII.

The rules of prudence in general, like the laws of the stone tables, are for the most part prohibitive. *Thou shalt not* is their characteristic *formula*: and it is an especial part of Christian prudence that it should be so. Nor would it be difficult to bring under this head all the social obligations that arise out of the relations of the present life, which the sensual understanding (τὸ φρόνημα τῆς σαρκὸς, *Rom.* viii. 6), is of itself able to discover, and the performance of which, under favorable circumstances, the merest worldly self-interest, without love or faith, is sufficient to enforce; but which Christian prudence enlivens by a higher principle, and renders symbolic and sacramental. (*Eph.* v. 32.)

COMMENT.

This then, under the appellation of prudential requisites, comes first under consideration: and may be regarded as the shrine and frame-work for the divine image, into which the worldly human is to be transformed. We are next to bring out the divine portrait itself, the distinct features of its countenance, as a sojourner among men; its benign aspect turned towards its fellow-pilgrims, the extended arm, and the hand that blesseth and healeth.

APHORISM XXIII.

The outward service (θρησκεία*) of ancient religion, the rites, ceremonies and ceremonial vestments of the old law, had morality for their substance. They were the letter, of which morality was the spirit; the enigma, of which morality was the meaning. But morality itself is the service and ceremonial (*cultus exterior*, θρησκεία) of the Christian religion. The scheme of grace and truth that became† through Jesus Christ, the faith that looks‡ down into the perfect law of liberty, has *light for its garment;* its very *robe is righteousness.*

* See the epistle of St. James, i. 26, 27, where, in the authorized version, the Greek word θρησκεία is rendered *religion.* This is, or at all events, for the English reader of our times, has the effect of an erroneous translation. It not only obscures the connection of the passage, and weakens the peculiar force and sublimity of the thought, rendering it comparatively flat and trivial, almost indeed tautological, but has occasioned this particular verse to be perverted into a support of a very dangerous error: and the whole epistle to be considered as a set-off against the epistles and declarations of St. Paul, instead of (what in fact it is) a masterly comment and confirmation of the same. I need not inform the reader, that *James* i. 27, is the favorite text and most boasted authority of those divines who represent the Redeemer of the world as little more than a moral reformer, and the Christian faith as a code of ethics, differing from the moral system of Moses and the Prophets by an additional motive, or rather by the additional strength and clearness which the historical fact of the resurrection has given to the same motive.

† The Greek word ἐγένετο unites in itself the two senses of *began to exist* and *was made to exist.* It exemplifies the force of the middle voice, in distinction from the verb reflex. The same word is used in the same sense by Aristophanes in that famous parody on the cosmogonies of the mythic poets, or the creation of the finite, as delivered, or supposed to be delivered, in the Cabiric or Samothracian mysteries, in the Comedy of the Birds.

———γένετ Οὐρανος 'Ωκεανός τε
Καὶ Γῆ.

‡ *James* i. 25. 'Ο δὲ παρακύψας εἰς νόμον τέλειον τὸν τῆς ἐλευθερίας. Παρακύψας signifies the incurvation or bending of the body in the act of *looking down into;* as, for instance, in the endeavor to see the reflected image of a star in the water at the bottom of a well. A more happy or forcible word could not have been chosen to express the nature and ultimate object of reflexion, and to enforce the necessity of it, in order to discover the living fountain and spring-head of the evidence of the Christian faith in the believer himself, and at the same time to point out the seat and region

COMMENT.

Herein the Apostle places the pre-eminence, the peculiar and distinguishing excellence, of the Christian religion. The ritual is of the same kind (*ὁμοούσιον*) though not of the same order, with the religion itself—not arbitrary or conventional, as types and hieroglyphics are in relation to the things expressed by them; but inseparable, consubstantiated (as it were), and partaking therefore of the same life, permanence, and intrinsic worth with its spirit and principle.

APHORISM XXIV.

Morality is the body, of which the faith in Christ is the soul—so far indeed its earthly body, as it is adapted to its state of warfare on earth, and the appointed form and instrument of its communion with the present world; yet not '*terrestrial*,' nor of the world, but a celestial body, and capable of being transfigured from glory to glory, in accordance with the varying circumstances and outward relations of its moving and informing spirit.

APHORISM XXV.

Woe to the man, who will believe neither power, freedom, nor morality, because he nowhere finds either entire, or unmixed with sin, thraldom and infirmity. In the natural and intellectual realms, we distinguish what we can not separate; and in the moral world, we must distinguish in order to separate. Yea,

where alone it is to be found. *Quantum sumus scimus.* That which we find within ourselves, which is more than ourselves, and yet the ground of whatever is good and permanent therein, is the substance and life of all other knowledge.

N. B. The Familists of the sixteenth century, and similar enthusiasts of later date, overlooked the essential point, that it was a law, and a law that involved its own end (*τέλος*), a perfect law (*τέλειος*) or law that perfects or completes itself; and therefore its obligations are called, in reference to human statutes, imperfect duties, that is, incoercible from without. They overlooked that it was a law that portions out (*νόμος from νέμω to allot, or make division of*) to each man the sphere and limits, within which it is to be exercised—which, as St. Peter notices of certain profound passages in the writings of St. Paul (2 *Pet.* iii. 16), *οἱ ἀμαθεῖς καὶ ἀστήρικτοι στρεβλοῦσιν, ὡς καὶ τὰς λοίπας γραφὰς, πρὸς τὴν ἰδίαν αὐτῶν ἀπώλειαν.*

in the clear distinction of good from evil the process of separation commences.

COMMENT.

It was customary with religious men in former times, to make a rule of taking every morning some text, or aphorism,* for their occasional meditation during the day, and thus to fill up the intervals of their attention to business. I do not point it out for imitation, as knowing too well, how apt these self-imposed rules are to degenerate into superstition or hollowness ; otherwise I would have recommended the following as the first exercise.

APHORISM XXVI.

It is a dull and obtuse mind, that must divide in order to distinguish ; but it is a still worse, that distinguishes in order to divide. In the former, we may contemplate the source of superstition and idolatry ;† in the latter, of schism, heresy, and a seditious and sectarian spirit.‡

APHORISM XXVII.

Exclusively of the abstract sciences, the largest and worthiest portion of our knowledge consists of aphorisms : and the greatest and best of men is but an aphorism.

* *Aphorism*, determinate position, from *ἀφορίζειν*, to bound, or limit; whence our horizon.—In order to get the full sense of a word, we should first present to our minds the visual image that forms its primary meaning. Draw lines of different colors round the different counties of England, and then cut out each separately, as in the common play-maps that children take to pieces and put together—so that each district can be contemplated apart from the rest, as a whole in itself. This twofold act of circumscribing, and detaching, when it is exerted by the mind on subjects of reflection and reason, is to aphorize, and the result an aphorism.

† Τὸ *νόητον διῃρήκασιν εἰς πολλῶν θεῶν ἰδιοτήτας.—Damasc. de Myst. Egypt;* that is, They divided the intelligible into many and several individualities.

‡ I mean these words in their large and philosophic sense in relation to the spirit, or originating temper and tendency, and not to any one mode under which, or to any one class in or by which, it may be displayed. A seditious spirit may (it is possible, though not probable) exist in the council-chamber of a palace as strongly as in a mob in Palace-Yard; and a sectarian spirit in a cathedral, no less than in a conventicle.

APHORISM XXVIII.

On the prudential influence which the fear or foresight of the consequences of his actions, in respect of his own loss or gain, may exert on a newly converted believer.

PRECAUTIONARY REMARK.

I meddle not with the dispute respecting conversion, whether, and in what sense, necessary in all Christians. It is sufficient for my purpose, that a very large number of men, even in Christian countries, need to be converted, and that not a few, I trust, have been. The tenet becomes fanatical and dangerous, only when rare and extraordinary exceptions are made to be the general rule;—when what was vouchsafed to the Apostle of the Gentiles by especial grace, and for an especial purpose, namely, a conversion* begun and completed in the same moment, is demanded or expected of all men, as a necessary sign and pledge of their election. Late observations have shown, that under many circumstances the magnetic needle, even after the disturbing influence has been removed, will continue wavering, and require many days before it points aright, and remains steady to the pole. So is it ordinarily with the soul, after it has begun to free itself from the disturbing forces of the flesh, and the world, and to convert† itself towards God.

APHORISM XXIX.

Awakened by the cock-crow—(a sermon, a calamity, a sick-bed, or a providential escape)—the Christian pilgrim sets out in the morning twilight, while yet the truth (the νόμος τέλειος ὁ τῆς

* "In this sense, especially, doth St. Paul call himself *abortivum*, a person born out of season, that whereas Christ's other disciples and apostles had a breeding under him, and came first *ad discipulatum*, and then, *ad apostolatum*, first to be disciples, and after to be apostles, St. Paul was born a man, an apostle: not carved out as the rest, in time, but a fusile apostle, an apostle poured out and cast in a mould. As Adam was a perfect man in an instant, so was St. Paul an apostle as soon as Christ took him in hand." *Donne's Serm.* (vol. ii. p. 299. Alford's edit. *Ed.*) The same spirit was the lightning that melted, and the mould that received and shaped him.

† That is, by an act of the will to turn towards the true pole, at the same time that the understanding is convinced and made aware of its existence and direction.

ἐλευθερίας) is below the horizon. Certain necessary consequences of his past life and his present undertaking will be seen by the refraction of its light: more will be apprehended and conjectured. The phantasms, that had predominated during the long hours of darkness, are still busy. Though they no longer present themselves as distinct forms, they yet remain as formative motions in the pilgrim's soul, unconscious of its own activity and over-mastered by its own workmanship. Things take the signature of thought. The shapes of the recent dream become a mould for the objects in the distance, and these again give an outwardness and sensation of reality to the shapings of the dream. The bodings inspired by the long habit of selfishness, and self-seeking cunning, though they are now commencing the process of their purification into that fear which is the beginning of wisdom, and which, as such, is ordained to be our guide and safeguard, till the sun of love, the perfect law of liberty, is fully arisen—these bodings will set the fancy at work, and haply, for a time, transform the mists of dim and imperfect knowledge into determinate superstitions. But in either case, whether seen clearly or dimly, whether beholden or only imagined, the consequences contemplated in their bearing on the individual's inherent* desire of happiness and dread of pain become motives;

* The following extract from the second of Leighton's Theological Lectures may serve as a comment on this sentence:

"Yet the human mind, however stunned and weakened by so dreadful a fall, still retains some faint idea, some confused and obscure notions, of the good it has lost, and some remaining seeds of its heavenly original. It has also still remaining a kind of languid sense of its misery and indigence, with affections suitable to those obscure notions. This at least is beyond all doubt and indisputable, that all men wish well to themselves; nor can the mind of man divest itself of this propensity, without divesting itself of its being. This is what the Schoolmen mean when in their manner of expression they say, that 'the will (*voluntas* not *arbitrium*) is carried towards happiness, not simply as will, but as nature.'"

I venture to remark that this position, if not more certainly, would be more evidently, true, if instead of *beatitudo*, the word *indolentia* (that is, freedom from pain, negative happiness) had been used. But this depends on the exact meaning attached to the term self, of which more in another place. One conclusion, however, follows inevitably from the preceding position; namely, that this propensity can never be legitimately made the principle of morality, even because it is no part or appurtenance of the moral will; and because the proper object of the moral principle is to limit

and, unless all distinction in the words be done away with, and either prudence or virtue be reduced to a superfluous synonyme, a redundancy in all the languages of the civilized world, these motives and the acts and forbearances directly proceeding from them fall under the head of Prudence, as belonging to one or other of its four very distinct species.

I. It may be prudence, that stands in opposition to a higher moral life, and tends to preclude it, and to prevent the soul from ever arriving at the hatred of sin for its own exceeding sinfulness (*Rom.* vii. 13) : and this is an evil prudence.

II. Or it may be a neutral prudence, not incompatible with spiritual growth : and to this we may, with especial propriety, apply the words of our Lord, *What is not against us is for us.* It is therefore an innocent, and (being such) a proper, and commendable prudence.

III. Or it may lead and be subservient to a higher principle than itself. The mind and conscience of the individual may be reconciled to it, in the foreknowledge of the higher principle, and with yearning towards it that implies a foretaste of future freedom. The enfeebled convalescent is reconciled to his crutches, and thankfully makes use of them, not only because they are necessary for his immediate support, but likewise, because they are the means and conditions of exercise, and by exercise, of establishing, *gradatim paulatim*, that strength, flexibility, and almost spontaneous obedience of the muscles, which the idea and cheering presentiment of health hold out to him. He finds their value in their present necessity, and their worth as they are the instruments of finally superseding it. This is a faithful, a wise prudence, having, indeed, its birth-place in the world, and the wisdom of this world for its father ; but naturalized in a better land, and having the wisdom from above for its sponsor and spiritual parents. To steal a dropt feather from the spicy nest of the phœnix (the fond humor, I mean, of the mystic divines and allegorizers of Holy Writ)—it is the *son of Terah from Ur of the Chaldees*, who gives a tithe of all to the King of Right-

and control this propensity, and to determine in what it may be, and what it ought to be, gratified ; while it is the business of philosophy to instruct the understanding, and the office of religion to convince the whole man, that otherwise than as a regulated, and of course therefore subordinate, end, this propensity, innate and inalienable though it be, can never be realized or fulfilled.

eousness, without father, without mother, without descent (νόμος αὐτόνομος), and receives a blessing on the remainder.

IV. Lastly, there is a prudence that co-exists with morality, as morality co-exists with the spiritual life : a prudence that is the organ of both, as the understanding is to the reason and the will, or as the lungs are to the heart and brain. This is a holy prudence, the steward faithful and discreet (οἰκονόμος πιστὸς καὶ φρόνιμος, *Luke* xii. 42) the *eldest servant* in the family of faith, born in the house, and *made the ruler over his lord's household.*

Let not then, I entreat you, my purpose be misunderstood ; as if, in distinguishing virtue from prudenc, I wished to divide the one from the other. True morality is hostile to that prudence only, which is preclusive of true morality. The teacher, who subordinates prudence to virtue, can not be supposed to dispense with virtue ; and he, who teaches the proper connection of the one with the other, does not depreciate the lower in any sense ; while by making it a link of the same chain with the higher, and receiving the same influence, he raises it.

In general, morality may be compared to the consonant ; prudence to the vowel. The former can not be uttered (reduced to practice) but by means of the latter.

APHORISM XXX.

WHAT the duties of morality are, the Apostle instructs the believer in full, comprising them under the two heads of negative and positive ; negative, to keep himself pure from the world ; and positive, beneficence from loving-kindness, that is, love of his fellow-men (his kind) as himself.

APHORISM XXXI.

LAST and highest come the spiritual, comprising all the truths, acts, and duties, that have an especial reference to the timeless, the permanent, the eternal, to the sincere love of the true as truth, of the good as good, and of God as both in one. It comprehends the whole ascent from uprightness (morality, virtue, inward rectitude) to godlikeness, with all the acts, exercises, and disciplines of mind, will, and affection, that are requisite or conducive to the great design of our redemption from the form of the evil One, and of our second creation or birth in the divine image.*

APHORISM XXXII.

It may be an additional aid to reflection, to distinguish the three kinds severally, according to the faculty to which each corresponds, the part of our human nature which is more particularly its organ. Thus: the prudential corresponds to the sense and the understanding; the moral to the heart and the conscience; the spiritual to the will and the reason, that is, to the finite will reduced to harmony with, and in subordination to, the reason, as a ray from that true light which is both reason and will, universal reason, and will absolute.

* It is worthy of observation, and may furnish a fruitful subject for future reflection, how nearly this Scriptural division coincides with the Platonic, which commencing with the prudential or the habit of act and purpose proceeding from enlightened self-interest [*qui animi imperio, corporis servitio, rerum auxilio, in proprium sui commodum et sibi providus utitur, hunc esse prudentem statuimus*], ascends to the moral, that is, to the purifying and remedial virtues; and seeks its summit in the imitation of the divine nature. In this last division, answering to that which we have called the spiritual, Plato includes all those inward acts and aspirations, waitings, and watchings, which have a growth in godlikeness for their immediate purpose, and the union of the human soul with the supreme good as their ultimate object. Nor was it altogether without grounds that several of the Fathers ventured to believe that Plato had some dim conception of the necessity of a divine Mediator;—whether through some indistinct echo of the Patriarchal faith, or some rays of light refracted from the Hebrew Prophets through the Phœnician medium (to which he may possibly have referred in his phrase *θεοπαραδότος σοφία*, the wisdom delivered from God), or by his own sense of the mysterious contradiction in human nature between the will and the reason, the natural appetences and the not less innate law of conscience (*Romans* ii. 14, 15), we shall in vain attempt to determine. It is not impossible that all three may have co-operated in partially unveiling these awful truths to this plank from the wreck of Paradise thrown on the shores of idolatrous Greece, to this divine philosopher,

Che'n quella schiera andó più presso al segno
Al qual aggiunge, a chi dal cielo è dato.

Petrarch. Trionfo della Fama, *cap.* iii. 5, 6.

REFLECTIONS

INTRODUCTORY TO

MORAL AND RELIGIOUS APHORISMS.

ON SENSIBILITY.

If Prudence, though practically inseparable from morality, is not to be confounded with the moral principle; still less may Sensibility, that is, a constitutional quickness of sympathy with pain and pleasure, and a keen sense of the gratifications that accompany social intercourse, mutual endearments, and reciprocal preferences, be mistaken, or deemed a substitute, for either. Sensibility is not even a sure pledge of a good heart, though among the most common meanings of that many-meaning and too commonly misapplied expression.

So far from being either morality, or one with the moral principle, it ought not even to be placed in the same rank with prudence. For prudence is at least an offspring of the understanding; but sensibility (the sensibility, I mean, here spoken of), is for the greater part a quality of the nerves, and a result of individual bodily temperament.

Prudence is an active principle, and implies a sacrifice of self, though only to the same self projected, as it were, to a distance. But the very term sensibility marks its passive nature; and in its mere self, apart from choice and reflection, it proves little more than the coincidence or contagion of pleasurable or painful sensations in different persons.

Alas! how many are there in this over-stimulated age,—in which the occurrence of excessive and unhealthy sensitiveness is so frequent, as even to have reversed the current meaning of the word, nervous,—how many are there whose sensibility prompts them to remove those evils alone, which by hideous spectacle or clamorous outcry are present to their senses and disturb their selfish enjoyments! Provided the dunghill is not before their parlor window, they are well contented to know that it exists, and perhaps as the hotbed on which their own luxuries ary reared. Sensibility is not necessarily benevolence. Nay, be rendering us tremblingly alive to trifling misfortunes, it frequently prevents it, and induces an effeminate selfishness instead,

———pampering the coward heart
With feelings all too delicate for use.

Sweet are the tears, that from a Howard's eye
Drop on the cheek of one, he lifts from earth:
And he, who works me good with unmoved face,
Does it but half: he chills me, while he aids,
My benefactor, not my brother man.
But even this, this cold benevolence,
Seems worth, seems manhood, when there rise before me
The sluggard pity's vision-weaving tribe,
Who sigh for wretchedness yet shun the wretched,
Nursing in some delicious solitude
Their slothful loves and dainty sympathies.*

Where virtue is, sensibility is the ornament and becoming attire of virtue. On certain occasions it may almost be said to become† virtue. But sensibility and all the amiable qualities may likewise become, and too often have become, the pandars of vice, and the instruments of seduction.

So must it needs be with all qualities that have their rise only in parts and fragments of our nature. A man of warm passions may sacrifice half his estate to rescue a friend from prison; for he is naturally sympathetic, and the more social part of his nature happened to be uppermost. The same man shall afterwards ex-

* Poet. Works, VII. p. 150.—*Ed.*

† There sometimes occurs an apparent play on words, which not only to the moralizer, but even to the philosophical etymologist, appears more than a mere play. Thus in the double sense of the word, *become.* I have known persons so anxious to have their dress become them, as to convert it at length into their proper self, and thus actually to become the dress. Such a one (safeliest spoken of by the neuter pronoun), I consider as but a suit of live finery. It is indifferent whether we say—it becomes he, or, he becomes it.

hibit the same disregard of money in an attempt to seduce that friend's wife or daughter.

All the evil achieved by Hobbes and the whole school of materialists will appear inconsiderable if it be compared with the mischief effected and occasioned by the sentimental philosophy of Sterne, and his numerous imitators. The vilest appetites and the most remorseless inconstancy towards their objects, acquired the titles of the *heart, the irresistible feelings, the too tender sensibility:* and if the frosts of prudence, the icy chains of human law thawed and vanished at the genial warmth of human nature, who could help it? It was an amiable weakness!

About this time, too, the profanation of the word, Love, rose to its height. The French naturalists, Buffon and others, borrowed it from the sentimental novelists: the Swedish and English philosophers took the contagion; and the Muse of science condescended to seek admission into the saloons of fashion and frivolity, rouged like a harlot, and with the harlot's wanton leer. I know not how the annals of guilt could be better forced into the service of virtue, than by such a comment on the present paragraph, as would be afforded by a selection from the sentimental correspondence produced in courts of justice within the last thirty years, fairly translated into the true meaning of the words, and the actual object and purpose of the infamous writers.

Do you in good earnest aim at dignity of character? By all the treasures of a peaceful mind, by all the charms of an open countenance, I conjure you, O youth! turn away from those who live in the twilight between vice and virtue. Are not reason, discrimination, law, and deliberate choice, the distinguishing characters of humanity? Can aught then worthy of a human being proceed from a habit of soul, which would exclude all these and (to borrow a metaphor from paganism) prefer the den of Trophonius to the temple and oracles of the God of light? Can any thing manly, I say, proceed from those, who for law and light would substitute shapeless feelings, sentiments, impulses, which as far as they differ from the vital workings in the brute animals owe the difference to their former connection with the proper virtues of humanity; as dendrites derive the outlines, that constitute their value above other clay-stones, from the casual neighborhood and pressure of the plants, the names of which they assume. Remember, that love itself in its highest earthly bearing, as the ground of the marriage union,* becomes love by an inward fiat of the will, by a completing and sealing act of moral election, and lays claim to permanence only under the form of duty.†

* It might be a mean of preventing many unhappy marriages, if the youth of both sexes had it early impressed on their minds, that marriage contracted between Christians is a true and perfect symbol or mystery; that is, the actualizing faith being supposed to exist in the receivers, it is an outward sign co-essential with that which it signifies, or a living part of that, the whole of which it represents. Marriage, therefore, in the Christian sense (*Ephesians* v. 22, 23), as symbolical of the union of the soul with Christ the Mediator, and with God through Christ, is perfectly a sacramental ordinance, and not retained at the Reformation as one of the sacraments, for two reasons: first, that the sign is not distinctive of the Church of Christ, and the ordinance not peculiar, nor owing its origin to the Gospel dispensation; secondly, that it is not of universal obligation, nor a means of grace enjoined on all Christians. In other and plainer words, marriage does not contain in itself an open profession of Christ, and it is not a sacrament of the Church, but only of certain individual members of the Church. It is evident, however, that neither of these reasons affects or diminishes the religious nature and dedicative force of the marriage vow, or detracts from the solemnity in the Apostolic declaration: *This is a great mystery.*

The interest, which the State has in the appropriation of one woman to one man, and the civil obligations therefrom resulting, form an altogether distinct consideration. When I meditate on the words of the Apostle, confirmed and illustrated as they are, by so many harmonies in the spiritual structure of our proper humanity—(in the image of God, male and female created he the man),—and then reflect how little claim so large a number of legal cohabitations have to the name of Christian marriages—I feel inclined to doubt, whether the plan of celebrating marriages universally by the civil magistrate, in the first instance, and leaving the religious covenant and sacramental pledge to the election of the parties themselves, adopted during the Commonwealth in England, and in our own times by the French legislature, was not in fact, whatever it might be in intention, reverential to Christianity. At all events, it was their own act and choice, if the parties made bad worse by the profanation of a Gospel mystery.

† See the beautiful passages Poet. Works, VII. pp. 302, 306.—*Ed.*

PRUDENTIAL APHORISMS.

APHORISM I.

Leighton and Coleridge.

WITH respect to any final aim or end, the greater part of mankind live at hazard. They have no certain harbor in view, nor direct their course by any fixed star. But to him that knoweth not the port to which he is bound, no wind can be favorable; neither can he, who has not yet determined at what mark he is to shoot, direct his arrow aright.

It is not, however, the less true that there is a proper object to aim at; and if this object be meant by the term happiness (though I think that not the most appropriate term for a state, the perfection of which consists in the exclusion of all hap, that is, chance), I assert that there is such a thing as human happiness, a *summum bonum*, or ultimate good. What this is, the Bible alone shows clearly and certainly, and points out the way that leads to the attainment of it. This is that which prevailed with St. Augustine to study the Scriptures, and engaged his affection to them. 'In Cicero, and Plato, and other such writers,' says he, 'I meet with many things acutely said, and things that excite a certain warmth of emotion, but in none of them do I find these words, *Come unto me, all ye that labor, and are heavy laden, and I will give you rest.**

COMMENT.

Felicity, in its proper sense, is but another word for fortunateness, or happiness; and I can see no advantage in the improper

* *Apud Ciceronem et Platonem, aliosque ejusmodi scriptores, multa sunt acute dicta, et leniter calentia, sed in iis omnibus hoc non invenio, Venite ad me, &c.* [*Matt.* xi. 28.] (See *Confess.* vii. xxi. 27.—*Ed.*)

use of words, when proper terms are to be found, but, on the contrary, much mischief. For, by familiarizing the mind to equivocal expressions, that is, such as may be taken in two or more different meanings, we introduce confusion of thought, and furnish the sophist with his best and handiest tools. For the juggle of sophistry consists, for the greater part, in using a word in one sense in the premiss, and in another sense in the conclusion. We should accustom ourselves to think, and reason in precise and steadfast terms, even when custom, or the deficiency, or the corruption of the language will not permit the same strictness in speaking. The mathematician finds this so necessary to the truths which he is seeking, that his science begins with, and is founded on, the definition of his terms. The botanist, the chemist, the anatomist, feel and submit to this necessity at all costs, even at the risk of exposing their several pursuits to the ridicule of the many, by technical terms, hard to be remembered, and alike quarrelsome to the ear and the tongue. In the business of moral and religious reflection, in the acquisition of clear and distinct conceptions of our duties, and of the relations in which we stand to God, our neighbor, and ourselves, no such difficulties occur. At the utmost we have only to rescue words, already existing and familiar, from the false or vague meanings imposed on them by carelessness, or by the clipping and debasing misusage of the market. And surely happiness, duty, faith, truth, and final blessedness, are matters of deeper and dearer interest for all men, than circles to the geometrician, or the characters of plants to the botanist, or the affinities and combining principle of the elements of bodies to the chemist, or even than the mechanism (fearful and wonderful though it be!) of the perishable tabernacle of the soul can be to the anatomist. Among the aids to reflection, place the following maxim prominent: let distinctness in expression advance side by side with distinction in thought. For one useless subtlety in our elder divines and moralists, I will produce ten sophisms of equivocation in the writings of our modern preceptors: and for one error resulting from excess in distinguishing the indifferent, I could show ten mischievous delusions from the habit of confounding the diverse.

Whether you are reflecting for yourself, or reasoning with another, make it a rule to ask yourself the precise meaning of the word, on which the point in question appears to turn; and if it may be (that is, by writers of authority has been) used in several senses, then ask which of these the word is at present intended to convey. By this mean, and scarcely without it, you will at length acquire a facility in detecting the *quid pro quo*. And believe me, in so doing you will enable yourself to disarm and expose four-fifths of the main arguments of our most renowned irreligious philosophers, ancient and modern. For the *quid pro quo* is at once the rock and quarry, on and with which the strongholds of disbelief, materialism, and (more pernicious still) Epicurean morality, are built.

APHORISM II.

Leighton.

If we seriously consider what religion is, we shall find the saying of the wise king Solomon to be unexceptionably true: *Her ways are ways of pleasantness, and all her paths are peace.**

Doth religion require any thing of us more than that we live *soberly, righteously, and godly in this present world?* Now what, I pray, can be more pleasant or peaceable than these? Temperance is always at leisure, luxury always in a hurry; the latter weakens the body and pollutes the soul; the former is the sanctity, purity, and sound state of both. It is one of Epicurus's fixed maxims, 'That life can never be pleasant without virtue.'

COMMENT.

In the works of moralists, both Christian and Pagan, it is often asserted—(indeed there are few common-places of more frequent recurrence)—that the happiness even of this life consists solely, or principally, in virtue; that virtue is the only happiness of this life; that virtue is the truest pleasure, and the like.

I doubt not that the meaning, which the writers intended to convey by these and the like expressions, was true and wise. But I deem it safer to say, that in all the outward relations of this life, in all our outward conduct and actions, both in what we should do, and in what we should abstain from, the dictates of virtue are the very same with those of self-interest; tending to, though they do not proceed from, the same point. For the outward object of virtue being the greatest producible sum of happiness of all men, it must needs include the object of an intelligent

* Prov. iii. 17.—*Ed.*

self-love, which is the greatest possible happiness of one individual; for what is true of all must be true of each. Hence, you can not become better, that is, more virtuous, but you will become happier: and you can not become worse, that is, more vicious, without an increase of misery, or at the best a proportional loss of enjoyment as the consequence. If the thing were not inconsistent with our well-being, and known to be so, it would not have been classed as a vice. Thus what in an enfeebled and disordered mind is called prudence, is the voice of nature in a healthful state: as is proved by the known fact, that the prudential duties, that is, those actions which are commanded by virtue because they are prescribed by prudence, brute animals fulfil by natural instinct.

The pleasure that accompanies or depends on a healthy and vigorous body will be the consequence and reward of a temperate life and habits of active industry, whether this pleasure were or were not the chief or only determining motive thereto. Virtue may, possibly, add to the pleasure a good of another kind, a higher good, perhaps, than the worldly mind is capable of understanding, a spiritual complacency, of which in your present sensualized state you can form no idea. It may add, I say, but it can not detract from it. Thus the reflected rays of the sun that give light, distinction, and endless multiformity to the mind, give at the same time the pleasurable sensation of warmth to the body.

If then the time has not yet come for any thing higher, act on the maxim of seeking the most pleasure with the least pain: and, if only you do not seek where you yourself know it will not be found, this very pleasure and this freedom from the disquietude of pain may produce in you a state of being directly and indirectly favorable to the germination and up-spring of a nobler seed. If it be true, that men are miserable because they are wicked, it is likewise true, that many are wicked because they are miserable. Health, cheerfulness, and easy circumstances, the ordinary consequences of temperance and industry, will at least leave the field clear and open, will tend to preserve the scales of the judgment even: while the consciousness of possessing the esteem, respect, and sympathy of your neighbors, and the sense of your own increasing power and influence, can scarcely fail to give a tone of dignity to your mind, and incline you to hope nobly of your own being. And thus they may prepare and predispose you to the sense and acknowledgment of a principle differing, not merely in degree but in kind, from the faculties and instincts of the higher and more intelligent species of animals (the ant, the beaver, the elephant), and which principle is therefore your proper humanity. And on this account and with this view alone may certain modes of pleasurable or agreeable sensation, without confusion of terms, be honored with the title of refined, intellectual, ennobling pleasures. For pleasure—(and happiness in its proper sense is but the continuity and sum total of the pleasure which is allotted or happens to a man, and hence by the Greeks called εὐτυχία, that is, good hap, or more religiously, εὐδαιμονία, that is, favorable providence)—pleasure, I say, consists in the harmony between the specific excitability of a living creature, and the exciting causes correspondent thereto. Considered therefore exclusively in and for itself, the only question is *quantum*, not *quale?* How much on the whole? the contrary, that is, the painful and disagreeable, having been subtracted. The quality is a matter of taste: *et de gustibus non est disputandum.* No man can judge for another.

This, I repeat, appears to me a safer language than the sentences quoted above—(that virtue alone is happiness: that happiness consists in virtue, and the like)—sayings which I find it hard to reconcile with other positions of still more frequent occurrence in the same divines, or with the declaration of St. Paul: *If in this life only we have hope, we are of all men most miserable.**

At all events, I should rely far more confidently on the converse, namely, that to be vicious is to be miserable. Few men are so utterly reprobate, so imbruted by their vices, as not to have some lucid, or at least quiet and sober, intervals; and in such a moment *dum desæviunt iræ*, few can stand up unshaken against the appeal to their own experience—What have been the wages of sin? What has the devil done for you? What sort of master have you found him? Then let us in befitting detail, and by a series of questions that ask so loud, and are secure against any false answer, urge home the proof of the position, that to be vicious is to be wretched; adding the fearful corollary, that if even in the body, which as long as life is in it can never be wholly bereaved of pleasurable sensations, vice is found to be misery,

* 1 Cor. xv. 19.—*Ed.*

what must it not be in the world to come? There, where even the crime is no longer possible, much less the gratifications that once attended it;—where nothing of vice remains but its guilt and its misery—vice must be misery itself; all and utter misery So best, if I err not, may the motives of prudence be held forth, and the impulses of self-love be awakened, in alliance with truth, and free from the danger of confounding things—(the laws of duty, I mean, and the maxims of interest)—which it deeply concerns us to keep distinct; inasmuch as this distinction and the faith therein are essential to our moral nature, and this again the ground-work and pre-condition of the spiritual state, in which the humanity strives after godliness, and in the name and power, and through the prevenient and assisting grace, of the Mediator, will not strive in vain.

The advantages of a life passed in conformity with the precepts of virtue and religion, and in how many and various respects they recommend virtue and religion even on grounds of prudence, form a delightful subject of meditation, and a source of refreshing thought to good and pious men. Nor is it strange if, transported with the view, such persons should sometimes discourse on the charm of forms and colors to men whose eyes are not yet couched; or that they occasionally seem to invert the relations of cause and effect, and forget that there are acts and determinations of the will and affections, the consequences of which may be plainly foreseen, and yet can not be made our proper and primary motives for such acts and determinations, without destroying or entirely altering the distinct nature and character of the latter. Sophron is well informed that wealth and extensive patronage will be the consequence of his obtaining the love and esteem of Constantia. But if the foreknowledge of this consequence were, and were found out to be, Sophron's main and determining motive for seeking this love and esteem; and if Constantia were a woman that merited, or was capable of feeling, either the one or the other; would not Sophron find (and deservedly too) aversion and contempt in their stead? Wherein, if not in this, differs the friendship of worldlings from true friendship? Without kind offices and useful services, wherever the power and opportunity occur, love would be a hollow pretence. Yet what noble mind would not be offended, if he were thought to value the love for the sake of the services, and not rather the services for the sake of the love?

APHORISM III.

Though prudence in itself is neither virtue nor spiritual holiness, yet without prudence, or in opposition to it, neither virtue nor holiness can exist.

APHORISM IV.

Art thou under the tyranny of sin—a slave to vicious habits—at enmity with God, and a skulking fugitive from thine own conscience? O, how idle the dispute, whether the listening to the dictates of prudence from prudential and self-interested motives be virtue or merit, when the not listening is guilt, misery, madness, and despair! The best, the most Christianlike, pity thou canst show, is to take pity on thy own soul. The best and most acceptable service thou canst render, is to do justice and show mercy to thyself.

MORAL AND RELIGIOUS APHORISMS.

APHORISM I.

Leighton.

WHAT the Apostles were in an extraordinary way, befitting the first annunciation of a religion for all mankind, this all teachers of moral truth, who aim to prepare for its reception by calling the attention of men to the law in their own hearts, may, without presumption, consider themselves to be under ordinary gifts and circumstances: namely, ambassadors for the greatest of kings, and upon no mean employment, the great treaty of peace and reconcilement betwixt him and mankind.

APHORISM II.

OF THE FEELINGS NATURAL TO INGENUOUS MINDS TOWARDS THOSE WHO HAVE FIRST LED THEM TO REFLECT.

Leighton.

Though divine truths are to be received equally from every minister alike, yet it must be acknowledged that there is something (we know not what to call it) of a more acceptable reception of those which at first were the means of bringing men to God, than of others; like the opinion some have of physicians whom they love.

APHORISM III.

Leighton and Coleridge.

The worth and value of knowledge is in proportion to the worth and value of its object. What, then, is the best knowledge?

The exactest knowledge of things is, to know them in their causes; it is then an excellent thing, and worthy of their endeavors who are most desirous of knowledge, to know the best things in their highest causes ; and the happiest way of attaining to this knowledge is, to possess those things, and to know them in experiece.

APHORISM IV.

Leighton.

It is one main point of happiness, that he that is happy doth know and judge himself to be so. This being the peculiar good of a reasonable creature, it is to be enjoyed in a reasonable way. It is not as the dull resting of a stone, or any other natural body in its natural place ; but the knowledge and consideration of it is the fruition of it, the very relishing and tasting of its sweetness.

REMARK.

As in a Christian land we receive the lessons of morality in connection with the doctrines of revealed religion, we can not too early free the mind from prejudices widely spread, in part through the abuse, but far more from ignorance, of the true meaning of doctrinal terms, which, however they may have been perverted to the purposes of fanaticism, are not only Scriptural, but of too frequent occurrence in Scripture to be overlooked or passed by in silence. The following extract, therefore, deserves attention, as clearing the doctrine of salvation, in connection with the divine foreknowledge, from all objections on the score of morality, by the just and impressive view which the Archbishop here gives of those occasional revolutionary moments, that turn of the tide in the mind and character of certain individuals, which (taking a religious course, and referred immediately to the Author of all good) were in his day, more generally than at present, entitled Effectual Calling. The theological interpretation, and the philosophic validity of this Apostolic triad, election, salvation, and effectual calling (the latter being the intermediate), will be found among the comments on the Aphorisms of spiritual import. For my present purpose it will be sufficient if only I prove that the doctrines are in themselves innocuous, and may be both holden and taught without any practical ill consequences, and without detriment to the moral frame.

APHORISM V.

Leighton.

Two links of the chain (namely, Election and Salvation) are up in heaven in God's own hand; but this middle one (that is, Effectual Calling) is let down to earth, into the hearts of his children, and they laying hold on it, have sure hold on the other two: for no power can sever them. If, therefore, they can read the characters of God's image in their own souls, those are the counterpart of the golden characters of his love, in which their names are written in the book of life. Their believing writes their names under the promises of the revealed book of life (the Scriptures) and thus ascertains them, that the same names are in the secret book of life which God hath by himself from eternity. So that finding the stream of grace in their hearts, though they see not the fountain whence it flows, nor the ocean into which it returns, yet they know that it hath its source in their eternal election, and shall empty itself into the ocean of their eternal salvation.

If Election, Effectual Calling, and Salvation, be inseparably linked together, then, by any one of them a man may lay hold upon all the rest, and may know that his hold is sure; and this is the way wherein we may attain, and ought to seek, the comfortable assurance of the love of God. Therefore, *make your calling sure,* and by that your *election;* for that being done, this follows of itself. We are not to pry immediately into the decree, but to read it in the performance. Though the mariner sees not the pole-star, yet the needle of the compass which points to it, tells him which way he sails: thus the heart that is touched with the loadstone of divine love, trembling with godly fear, and yet still looking towards God by fixed believing, interprets the fear by the love in the fear, and tells the soul that its course is heavenward, towards the haven of eternal rest. He that loves, may be sure he was loved first; and he that chooses God for his delight and portion, may conclude confidently, that God hath chosen him to be one of those that shall enjoy him, and be happy in him forever: for that our love and electing of him is but the return and repercussion of the beams of his love shining upon us.

Although from present unsanctification, a man can not infer

that he is not elected ; for the decree may, for the part of a man's life, run (as it were) underground ; yet this is sure, that that estate leads to death, and unless it be broken, will prove the black line of reprobation. A man hath no portion amongst the children of God, nor can read one word of comfort in all the promises that belong to them, while he remains unholy.

REMARK.

In addition to the preceding, I select the following paragraphs, as having nowhere seen the terms, Spirit, the Gifts of the Spirit, and the like, so effectually vindicated from the sneers of the sciolist on the one hand, and protected from the perversions of the fanatic on the other. In these paragraphs the Archbishop at once shatters and precipitates the only drawbridge between the fanatical and the orthodox doctrine of grace, and the gifts of the Spirit. In Scripture the term Spirit, as a power or property seated in the human soul, never stands singly, but is always specified by a genitive case following ; this being a Hebraism instead of the adjective which the writer would have used if he had thought, as well as written, in Greek. It is *the spirit of meekness* (a meek spirit), or *the spirit of chastity*, and the like. The moral result, the specific form and character in which the Spirit manifests its presence, is the only sure pledge and token of its presence ; which is to be, and which safely may be, inferred from its practical effects, but of which an immediate knowledge or consciousness is impossible ; and every pretence to such knowledge is either hypocrisy or fanatical delusion.

APHORISM VI.

Leighton.

If any pretend that they have the Spirit, and so turn away from the straight rule of the Holy Scriptures, they have a spirit indeed, but it is a fanatical spirit, the spirit of delusion and giddiness : but the Spirit of God, that leads his children in the way of truth, and is for that purpose sent them from heaven to guide them thither, squares their thoughts and ways to that rule whereof it is author, and that word which was inspired by it, and sanctifies them to obedience. *He that saith, I know him, and keepeth not his commandments, is a liar, and the truth is not in him.* (1 *John* ii. 4.)

Now this Spirit which sanctifieth, and sanctifieth to obedience, is within us the evidence of our election, and the earnest of our salvation. And whoso are not sanctified and led by this Spirit, the Apostle tells us what is their condition: *If any man have not the Spirit of Christ, he is none of his.** The stones which are appointed for that glorious temple above, are hewn, and polished, and prepared for it here; as the stones were wrought and prepared in the mountains, for building the temple at Jerusalem.

COMMENT.

There are many serious and sincere Christians who have not attained to a fulness of knowledge and insight, but are well and judiciously employed in preparing for it. Even these may study the master-works of our elder divines with safety and advantage, if they will accustom themselves to translate the theological terms into their moral equivalents; saying to themselves—This may not be all that is meant, but this is meant, and it is that portion of the meaning, which belongs to me in the present stage of my progress. For example: render the words, sanctification of the Spirit, or the sanctifying influences of the Spirit, by purity in life and action from a pure principle.

He needs only reflect on his own experience to be convinced, that the man makes the motive, and not the motive the man. What is a strong motive to one man, is no motive at all to another. If, then, the man determines the motive, what determines the man—to a good and worthy act, we will say, or a virtuous course of conduct? The intelligent will, or the self-determining power? True, in part it is: and therefore the will is pre-eminently, the spiritual constituent in our being. But will any reflecting man admit, that his own will is the only and sufficient determinant of all he is, and all he does? Is nothing to be attributed to the harmony of the system to which he belongs, and to the pre-established fitness of the objects and agents, known and unknown, that surround him, as acting on the will, though, doubtless, with it likewise?—a process, which the co-instantaneous yet reciprocal action of the air and the vital energy of the lungs in breathing, may help to render intelligible.

Again: in the world we see everywhere evidences of a unity,

* *Rom.* viii. 9.—*Ed.*

which the component parts are so far from explaining, that they necessarily pre-suppose it as the cause and condition of their existing as those parts; or even of their existing at all. This antecedent unity, or cause and principle of each union, it has since the time of Bacon and Kepler been customary to call a law. This crocus, for instance, or any other flower, the reader may have in sight, or choose to bring before his fancy. That the root, stem, leaves, petals, &c. cohere to one plant, is owing to an antecedent power or principle in the seed, which existed before a single particle of the matters that constitute the size and visibility of the crocus, had been attracted from the surrounding soil, air, and moisture. Shall we turn to the seed? Here too the same necessity meets us. An antecedent unity—(I speak not of the parent plant, but of an agency antecedent in the order of operance, yet remaining present as the conservative and reproductive power)—must here too be supposed. Analyze the seed with the finest tools, and let the solar microscope come in aid of your senses,—what do you find? Means and instruments, a wondrous fairy tale of nature, magazines of food, stores of various sorts, pipes, spiracles, defences—a house of many chambers, and the owner and inhabitant invisible! Reflect further on the countless millions of seeds of the same name, each more than numerically differenced from every other: and further yet, reflect on the requisite harmony of all surrounding things, each of which necessitates the same process of thought, and the coherence of all of which to a system, a world, demands its own adequate antecedentunity, which must therefore of necessity be present to all and in all, yet in no wise excluding or suspending the individual law or principle of union in each. Now, will reason, will common sense, endure the assumption, that it is highly reasonable to believe a universal power, as the cause and pre-condition of the harmony of all particular wholes, each of which involves the working principle of its own union—that it is reasonable, I say, to believe this respecting the aggregate of objects, which, without a subject (that is, a sentient and intelligent existence), would be purposeless; and yet unreasonable and even superstitious or enthusiastic to entertain a similar belief in relation to the system of intelligent and self-conscious beings, to the moral and personal world? But if in this too, in the great community of persons, it is rational to infer a one universal presence, a one present to all and in all, is it not most irrational to suppose that a finite will can exclude it?

Whenever, therefore, the man is determined (that is, impelled and directed) to act in harmony of inter-communion, must not something be attributed to this all-present power as acting in the will? And by what fitter names can we call this than THE LAW, as empowering; THE WORD, as informing; and THE SPIRIT, as actuating?

What has been here said amounts, I am aware, only to a negative conception; but this is all that is required for a mind at that period of its growth which we are now supposing, and as long as religion is contemplated under the form of morality. A positive insight belongs to a more advanced stage: for spiritual truths can only spiritually be discerned. This we know from revelation, and (the existence of spiritual truths being granted) philosophy is compelled to draw the same conclusion. But though merely negative, it is sufficient to render the union of religion and morality conceivable; sufficient to satisfy an unprejudiced inquirer, that the spiritual doctrines of the Christian religion are not at war with the reasoning faculty, and that if they do not run on the same line, or *radius*, with the understanding yet neither do they cut or cross it. It is sufficient, in short, to prove, that some distinct and consistent meaning may be attached to the assertion of the learned and philosophic Apostle, that *the Spirit beareth witness with our spirit*,* that is, with the will, as the supernatural in man and the principle of our personality—of that, I mean, by which we are responsible agents; persons, and not merely living things.†

It will suffice to satisfy a reflecting mind, that even at the porch and threshold of revealed truth there is a great and worthy sense in which we may believe the Apostle's assurance, that not

* *Rom.* viii. 16.—*Ed.*

† Whatever is comprised in the chain and mechanism of cause and effect, of course necessitated, and having its necessity in some other thing, antecedent or concurrent—this is said to be natural; and the aggregate and system of all such things is NATURE. It is, therefore, a contradiction in terms to include in this the free-will, of which the verbal definition is—that which originates an act or state of being. In this sense, therefore, which is the sense of St. Paul, and indeed of the New Testament throughout, spiritual and supernatural are synonymous.

only doth *the Spirit help our infirmities;** that is, act on the will by a predisposing influence from without, as it were, though in a spiritual manner, and without suspending or destroying its freedom—(the possibility of which is proved to us in the influences of education, providential occurrences, and, above all, of example)—but that in regenerate souls it may act in the will; that uniting and becoming one† with our will or spirit it may *make intercession for us*:‡ nay, in this intimate union taking upon itself the form of our infirmities, may intercede for us *with groanings that can not be uttered.*§ Nor is there any danger of fanaticism or enthusiasm as the consequence of such a belief, if only the attention be carefully and earnestly drawn to the concluding words of the sentence; if only the due force and the full import be given to the term *unutterable* or incommunicable,—ἀλαλήτοις—in St. Paul's use of it. In this the strictest and most proper use of the term, it signifies that the subject, of which it is predicated, is something which I can not, which from the nature of the thing it is impossible that I should, communicate to any human mind (even of a person under the same conditions with myself) so as to make it in itself the object of his direct and immediate consciousness. It can not be the object of my own direct and immediate consciousness; but must be inferred. Inferred it may be from its workings; it can not be perceived in them. And thanks to God! in all points in which the knowledge is of high and necessary concern to our moral and religious welfare, from the effects it may safely be inferred by us, from the workings it may be assuredly known; and the Scriptures furnish the clear and unfailing rules for directing the inquiry, and for drawing the conclusion.

If any reflecting mind be surprised that the aids of the Divine Spirit should be deeper than our consciousness can reach, it must arise from the not having attended sufficiently to the nature and necessary limits of human consciousness. For the same impossi-

* *Rom.* viii. 26.—*Ed.*

† Some distant and faint similitude of this, that merely as a similitude may be innocently used to quiet the fancy, provided it be not imposed on the understanding as an analogous fact, or as identical in kind, is presented to us in the power of the magnet to awaken and strengthen the magnetic power in a bar of iron, and (in the instance of the compound magnet) of its acting in and with the latter.

‡ *Rom.* viii. 26.—*Ed.* § *Ibid.*

bility exists as to the first acts and movements of our own will;—the farthest distance our recollection can follow back the traces never leads us to the first foot-mark; the lowest depth that the light of our consciousness can visit even with a doubtful glimmering, is still at an unknown distance from the ground: and so, indeed, must it be with all truths, and all modes of being, that can neither be counted, colored, nor delineated. Before and after, when applied to such subjects, are but allegories, which the sense or imagination supplies to the understanding. The position of the Aristoteleans, *nihil in intellectu quod non prius in sensu*, on which Locke's Essay is grounded, is irrefragable: Locke erred only in taking half the truth for a whole truth. Conception is consequent on perception. What we can not imagine, we can not, in the proper sense of the word, conceive.

I have already given one definition of Nature. Another, and differing from the former in words only, is this: Whatever is representable in the forms of time and space, is Nature. But whatever is comprehended in time and space, is included in the mechanism of cause and effect. And conversely, whatever, by whatever means, has its principle in itself, so far as to originate its actions, can not be contemplated in any of the forms of space and time; it must, therefore, be considered as spirit or spiritual by a mind in that stage of its development which is here supposed, and which we have agreed to understand under the name of morality or the moral state: for in this stage we are concerned only with the forming of negative conceptions, negative convictions; and by spiritual I do not pretend to determine what the will is, but what it is not—namely, that it is not nature. And as no man who admits a will at all (for we may safely presume that no man, not meaning to speak figuratively, would call the shifting current of a stream the will* of the river), can suppose it below nature, we may safely add, that it is supernatural; and this without the least pretence to any positive notion or insight.

Now Morality accompanied with convictions like these, I have ventured to call Religious Morality. Of the importance I attach

* "The river glideth at his own sweet will."

Wordsworth's exquisite Sonnet on Westminster Bridge at sunrise.

But who does not see that here the poetic charm arises from the known and felt impropriety of the expression, in the technical sense of the word, impropriety, among grammarians?

to the state of mind implied in these convictions, for its own sake, and as the natural preparation for a yet higher state and a more substantive knowledge, proof more than sufficient, perhaps, has been given in the length and minuteness of this introductory discussion, and in the foreseen risk which I run of exposing the Volume at large to the censure which every work, or rather which every writer, must be prepared to undergo, who, treating of subjects that can not be seen, touched, or in any other way made matters of outward sense, is yet anxious to convey a distinct meaning by the words he makes use of—the censure of being dry, abstract, and—(of all qualities most scaring and opprobrious to the ears of the present generation)—metaphysical: though how it is possible that a work not physical, that is, employed on objects known or believed on the evidence of senses, should be other than metaphysical, that is, treating on subjects, the evidence of which is not derived from the senses, is a problem which critics of this order find it convenient to leave unsolved.

I shall, indeed, have reason to think myself fortunate, if this be all the charge. How many smart quotations, which (duly cemented by personal allusions to the author's supposed pursuits, attachments, and infirmities) would of themselves make up a review of this Volume, might be supplied from the works of Butler, Swift, and Warburton! For instance: 'It may not be amiss to inform the public, that the compiler of the Aids to Reflection, and commenter on a Scotch Bishop's Platonico-Calvinistic commentary on St. Peter, belongs to the sect of the Æolists, whose fruitful imaginations led them into certain notions, which although in appearance very unaccountable, are not without their mysteries and their meanings: furnishing plenty of matter for such, whose converting imaginations dispose them to reduce all things into types; who can make shadows, no thanks to the sun; and then mould them into substances, no thanks to philosophy; whose peculiar talent lies in fixing tropes and allegories to the letter, and refining what is literal into figure and mystery.'

And would it were my lot to meet with a critic, who, in the might of his own convictions, and with arms of equal point and efficiency from his own forge, would come forth as my assailant; or who, as a friend to my purpose, would set forth the objections to the matter and pervading spirit of these Aphorisms, and the accompanying elucidations. Were it my task to form the mind of a young man of talent, desirous to establish his belief on solid principles, and in the light of distinct understanding, I would commence his theological studies, or, at least, that most important part of them respecting the aid which religion promises in our attempts to realize the ideas of morality, by bringing together all the passages scattered throughout the writings of Swift and Butler, that bear on enthusiasm, spiritual operations, and pretences to the gifts of the spirit, with the whole train of new lights, raptures, experiences, and the like. For all that the richest wit, in intimate union with profound sense and steady observation, can supply on these topics, is to be found in the works of these satirists; though unhappily alloyed with much that can only tend to pollute the imagination.

Without stopping to estimate the degree of caricature in the portraits sketched by these bold masters, and without attempting to determine in how many of the enthusiasts brought forward by them in proof of the influence of false doctrines, a constitutional insanity, that would probably have shown itself in some other form, would be the truer solution, I would direct my pupil's attention to one feature common to the whole group—the pretence, namely, of possessing, or a belief and expectation grounded on other men's assurances of their possessing, an immediate consciousness, a sensible experience, of the Spirit in and during its operation on the soul. It is not enough that you grant them a consciousness of the gifts and graces infused, or an assurance of the spiritual origin of the same, grounded on their correspondence to the Scripture promises, and their conformity with the idea of the divine Giver. No! they all alike, it will be found, lay claim, or at least look forward, to an inward perception of the Spirit itself and of its operating.

Whatever must be misrepresented in order to be ridiculed, is in fact not ridiculed; but the thing substituted for it. It is a satire on something else, coupled with a lie on the part of the satirist, who knowing, or having the means of knowing the truth, chose to call one thing by the name of another. The pretensions to the supernatural, pilloried by Butler, sent to Bedlam by Swift, and (on their re-appearance in public) gibbeted by Warburton, and anatomized by Bishop Lavington,* one and

* "A Comparison between the enthusiasm of Methodists and of Papists."—*Ed.*

all, have this for their essential character, that the Spirit is made the immediate object of sense or sensation. Whether the spiritual presence and agency are supposed cognizable by indescribable feeling or unimaginable vision by some specific visual energy; whether seen or heard, or touched, smelt, and tasted—for in those vast store-houses of fanatical assertion,—the volumes of ecclesiastical history and religious auto-biography,—instances are not wanting even of the three latter extravagancies;—this variety in the mode may render the several pretensions more or less offensive to the taste; but with the same absurdity for the reason, this being derived from a contradiction in terms common and radical to them all alike,—the assumption of a something essentially supersensual, which is nevertheless the object of sense, that is not supersensual.

Well then!—for let me be allowed still to suppose the Reader present to me, and that I am addressing him in the character of companion and guide—the positions recommended for your examination not only do not involve, but exclude, this inconsistency. And for aught that hitherto appears, we may see with complacency the arrows of satire feathered with wit, weighted with sense, and discharged by a strong arm, fly home to their mark. Our conceptions of a possible spiritual communion, though they are but negative, and only preparatory to a faith in its actual existence, stand neither in the level nor the direction of the shafts.

If it be objected that Swift and Warburton did not choose openly to set up the interpretations of later and more rational divines against the decisions of their own Church, and from prudential considerations did not attack the doctrine *in toto:* that is their concern (I would answer), and it is more charitable to think otherwise. But we are in the silent school of reflection, in the secret confessional of thought. Should we *lie for God*, and that to our own thoughts?—They, indeed, who dare do the one, will soon be able to do the other. So did the comforters of Job: and to the divines, who resemble Job's comforters, we will leave both attempts.

But, it may be said, a possible conception is not necessarily a true one; nor even a probable one, where the facts can be otherwise explained. In the name of the supposed pupil I would reply—That is the very question I am preparing myself to examine; and am now seeking the vantage-ground where I may best command the facts. In my own person, I would ask the objector, whether he counted the declarations of Scripture among the facts to be explained. But both for myself and my pupil, and in behalf of all rational inquiry, I would demand that the decision should not be such, in itself or in its effects, as would prevent our becoming acquainted with the most important of these facts; nay, such as would for the mind of the decider, preclude their very existence. *Unless ye believe*, says the prophet, *ye can not understand.* Suppose (what is at least possible) that the facts should be consequent on the belief, it is clear that without the belief the materials, on which the understanding is to exert itself, would be wanting.

The reflections that naturally arise out of this last remark, are those that best suit the stage at which we last halted, and from which we now recommence our progress—the state of a moral man, who has already welcomed certain truths of religion, and is inquiring after other and more special doctrines: still, however, as a moralist, desirous, indeed, to receive them into combination with morality, but to receive them as its aid, not as its substitute. Now, to such a man I say;—Before you reject the opinions and doctrines asserted and enforced in the following extract from Leighton, and before you give way to the emotions of distaste or ridicule, which the prejudices of the circle in which you move, or your own familiarity with the mad perversions of the doctrine by fanatics in all ages, have connected with the very words, spirit, grace, gifts, operations, and the like, re-examine the arguments advanced in the first pages of this introductory comment, and the simple and sober view of the doctrine, contemplated in the first instance as a mere idea of the reason, flowing naturally from the admission of an infinite omnipresent mind as the ground of the universe. Reflect again and again, and be sure that you understand the doctrine before you determine on rejecting it. That no false judgments, no extravagant conceits, no practical ill-consequences need arise out of the belief of the Spirit, and its possible communion with the spiritual principle in man, or can arise out of the right belief, or are compatible with the doctrine truly and Scripturally explained, Leighton, and almost every single period in the passage here transcribed from him, will suffice to convince you.

On the other hand, reflect on the consequences of rejecting it. For surely it is not the act of a reflecting mind, nor the part of a man of sense, to disown and cast out one tenet, and yet persevere in admitting and clinging to another that has neither sense nor purpose, but what supposes and rests on the truth and reality of the former. If you have resolved that all belief of a divine Comforter present to our inmost being and aiding our infirmities, is fond and fanatical,—if the Scriptures promising and asserting such communion are to be explained away into the action of circumstances, and the necessary movements of the vast machine, in one of the circulating chains of which the human will is a petty link;—in what better light can prayer appear to you, than the groans of a wounded lion in his solitary den, or the howl of a dog with his eyes on the moon? At the best, you can regard it only as a transient bewilderment of the social instinct, as a social habit misapplied. Unless, indeed, you should adopt the theory which I remember to have read in the writings of the late Bishop Jebb, and for some supposed beneficial re-action of praying on the prayer's own mind, should practise it as a species of animal-magnetism to be brought about by a wilful eclipse of the reason, and a temporary make-believe on the part of the self-magnetizer!

At all events, do not pre-judge a doctrine, the utter rejection of which must oppose a formidable obstacle to your acceptance of Christianity itself, when the books, from which alone we can learn what Christianity is and what it teaches, are so strangely written, that in a series of the most concerning points, including (historical facts excepted) all the peculiar tenets of the religion, the plain and obvious meaning of the words, that in which they were understood by learned and simple, for at least sixteen centuries, during the larger part of which the language was a living language, is no sufficient guide to their actual sense or to the writer's own meaning! And this too, where the literal and received sense involves nothing impossible, or immoral, or contrary to reason. With such a persuasion, Deism would be a more consistent creed. But, alas! even this will fail you. The utter rejection of all present and living communion with the universal Spirit impoverishes Deism itself, and renders it as cheerless as Atheism, from which indeed it would differ only by an obscure impersonation of what the atheist receives unpersonified under the name of Fate or Nature.

APHORISM VII

Leighton and Coleridge.

The proper and natural effect, and in the absence of all disturbing or intercepting forces, the certain and sensible accompaniment of peace or reconcilement with God, is our own inward peace, a calm and quiet temper of mind. And where there is a consciousness of earnestly desiring, and of having sincerely striven after the former, the latter may be considered as a sense of its presence. In this case, I say, and for a soul watchful and under the discipline of the Gospel, the peace with a man's self may be the medium or organ through which the assurance of his peace with God is conveyed. We will not, therefore, condemn this mode of speaking, though we dare not greatly recommend it. Be it, that there is, truly and in sobriety of speech, enough of just analogy in the subjects meant, to make this use of the words, if less than proper, yet something more than metaphorical; still we must be cautious not to transfer to the object the defects or the deficiency of the organ, which must needs partake of the imperfections of the imperfect beings to whom it belongs. Not without the co-assurance of other senses and of the same sense in other men, dare we affirm that what our eye beholds is verily there to be beholden. Much less may we conclude negatively, and from the inadequacy, or the suspension, or from any other affection of sight infer the non-existence, or departure, or changes of the thing itself. The chameleon darkens in the shade of him that bends over it to ascertain its colors. In like manner, but with yet greater caution, ought we to think respecting a tranquil habit of the inward life, considered as a spiritual sense,—a medial organ in and by which our peace with God, and the lively working of his grace on our spirit, are perceived by us. This peace which we have with God in Christ is inviolable; but because the sense and persuasion of it may be interrupted, the soul that is truly at peace with God may for a time be disquieted in itself, through weakness of faith, or the strength of temptation, or the darkness of desertion, losing sight of that grace, that love and light of God's countenance, on which its tranquillity and joy depend. *Thou didst hide thy face*, saith David, *and I was troubled*. But when these eclipses are over, the soul is revived with new consolation, as the face of the earth is renewed and made to smile with the return of the sun in the spring; and this ought always to uphold Christians in the saddest times, namely, that the grace and love of God towards them depend not on their sense, nor upon any thing in them, but is still in itself, incapable of the smallest alteration.

A holy heart that gladly entertains grace, shall find that it and peace can not dwell asunder; while an ungodly man may sleep to death in the lethargy of carnal presumption and impenitency; but a true, lively, solid peace, he can not have. *There is no peace, saith my God, to the wicked.* Isa. lvii. 21.

APHORISM VIII.

WORLDLY HOPES.

Leighton.

Worldly hopes are not living, but lying hopes; they die often before us, and we live to bury them, and see our own folly and infelicity in trusting to them; but at the utmost, they die with us when we die, and can accompany us no further. But the lively hope, which is the Christian's portion, answers expectation to the full, and much beyond it, and deceives no way but in that happy way of far exceeding it.

A living hope, living in death itself! The world dares say no more for its device, than *Dum spiro spero;* but the children of God can add, by virtue of this living hope, *Dum exspiro spero.*

APHORISM IX.

THE WORLDLING'S FEAR.

Leighton.

It is a fearful thing when a man and all his hopes die together. Thus saith Solomon of the wicked, *Prov.* xi. 7,—When he dieth, then die his hopes (many of them before, but at the utmost then, all of them); but *the righteous hath hope in his death. Prov.* xiv. 32.*

* One of the numerous proofs against those who, with a strange inconsistency, hold the Old Testament to have been inspired throughout, and yet deny that the doctrine of a future state is taught therein.

APHORISM X.

WORLDLY MIRTH.

Leighton and Coleridge.

As he that taketh away a garment in cold weather, and as vinegar upon nitre, so is he that singeth songs to a heavy heart. Prov. xxv. 20. Worldly mirth is so far from curing spiritual grief, that even worldly grief, where it is great and takes deep root, is not allayed but increased by it. A man who is full of inward heaviness, the more he is encompassed about with mirth, it exasperates and enrages his grief the more; like ineffectual weak physic, which removes not the humor, but stirs it and makes it more unquiet. But spiritual joy is seasonable for all estates; in prosperity, it is pertinent to crown and sanctify all other enjoyments, with this which so far surpasses them; and in distress, it is the only *Nepenthe*, the cordial of fainting spirits: so *Psal.* iv. 7, *He hath put joy into my heart.* This mirth makes way for itself, which other mirth can not do. These songs are sweetest in the night of distress.

There is something exquisitely beautiful and touching in the first of these similes: and the second, though less pleasing to the imagination, has the charm of propriety, and expresses the translation with equal force and liveliness. A grief of recent birth is a sick infant that must have its medicine administered in its milk, and sad thoughts are the sorrowful heart's natural food. This is a complaint that is not to be cured by opposites, which for the most part only reverse the symptoms while they exasperate the disease—or like a rock in the mid channel of a river swollen by a sudden rain-flush from the mountain, which only detains the excess of waters from their proper outlet, and makes them foam, roar, and eddy. The soul in her desolation hugs the sorrow close to her, as her sole remaining garment: and this must be drawn off so gradually, and the garment to be put in its stead so gradually slipt on and feel so like the former, that the sufferer shall be sensible of the change only by the refreshment. The true spirit of consolation is well content to detain the tear in the eye, and finds a surer pledge of its success in the smile of resignation that dawns through that, than in the liveliest shows of a forced and alien exhilaration.

APHORISM XI.

Leighton.

Plotinus thanked God, that his soul was not tied to an immortal body.

APHORISM XII.

Leighton and Coleridge.

What a full confession do we make of our dissatisfaction with the objects of our bodily senses, that in our attempts to express what we conceive the best of beings, and the greatest of felicities to be, we describe by the exact contraries of all that we experience here—the one as infinite, incomprehensible, immutable; the other as incorruptible, undefiled, and that passeth not away. At all events, this coincidence, say rather, identity of attributes, is sufficient to apprize us, that to be inheritors of bliss, we must become the children of God.

This remark of Leighton's is ingenious and startling. Another, and more fruitful, perhaps more solid, inference from the fact would be, that there is something in the human mind which makes it know (as soon as it is sufficiently awakened to reflect on its own thoughts and notices), that in all finite quantity there is an infinite, in all measure of time an eternal; that the latter are the basis, the substance, the true and abiding reality of the former; and that as we truly are, only as far as God is with us, so neither can we truly possess—that is, enjoy—our being or any other real good, but by living in the sense of his holy presence.

A life of wickedness is a life of lies; and an evil being, or the being of evil, the last and darkest mystery.

APHORISM XIII.

THE WISEST USE OF THE IMAGINATION.

Leighton.

It is not altogether unprofitable,—yea, it is great wisdom in Christians to be arming themselves against such temptations as may befall them hereafter, though they have not as yet met with them; to labor to overcome them beforehand, to suppose the hardest things that may be incident to them, and to put on the strongest resolutions they can attain unto. Yet all that is but an imaginary effort; and therefore there is no assurance that the victory is any more than imaginary too, till it come to action, and then, they that have spoken and thought very confidently, may prove but (as one said of the Athenians) *fortes in tabula*, patient and courageous in picture or fancy; and, notwithstanding all their arms, and dexterity in handling them by way of exercise, may be foully defeated when they are to fight in earnest.

APHORISM XIV.

THE LANGUAGE OF SCRIPTURE.

The word of God speaks to men, and therefore it speaks the language of the children of men. This just and pregnant thought was suggested to Leighton by *Gen.* xxii. 12. The same text has led me to unfold and expand the remark.—On moral subjects, the Scriptures speak in the language of the affections which they excite in us; on sensible objects, neither metaphysically, as they are known by superior intelligences; nor theoretically, as they would be seen by us were we placed in the sun; but as they are represented by our human senses in our present relative position. Lastly, from no vain, or worse than vain, ambition of seeming *to walk on the sea* of mystery in my way to truth, but in the hope of removing a difficulty that presses heavily on the minds of many who in heart and desire are believers, and which long pressed on my own mind, I venture to add: that on spiritual things, and allusively to the mysterious union or conspiration of the divine with the human in the spirits of the just, spoken of in *Rom.* viii. 27, the word of God attributes the language of the spirit sanctified to the Holy One, the Sanctifier.

Now the spirit in man (that is, the will, knows its own state in and by its acts alone: even as in geometrical reasoning the mind knows its constructive faculty in the act of constructing, and contemplates the act in the product (that is, the mental figure or diagram) which is inseparable from the act and coinstantaneous.

Let the reader join these two positions: first, that the divine Spirit acting in the human will is described as one with the will so filled and actuated: secondly, that our actions are the means, by which alone the will becomes assured of its own state: and he will understand, though he may not perhaps adopt my suggestion, that the verse, in which God speaking of himself, says to Abraham, *Now I know that thou fearest God, seeing thou hast not withheld thy son, thy only son, from me*—may be more than merely figurative. An accommodation I grant; but in the thing expressed, and not altogether in the expressions. In arguing with infidels, or with the weak in faith, it is a part of religious prudence, no less than of religious morality, to avoid whatever looks like an evasion. To retain the literal sense, wherever the harmony of Scripture permits, and reason does not forbid, is ever the honester, and, nine times in ten, the more rational and pregnant interpretation. The contrary plan is an easy and approved way of getting rid of a difficulty; but nine times in ten a bad way of solving it. But alas! there have been too many commentators who are content not to understand a text themselves, if only they can make the reader believe they do.

Of the figures of speech in the sacred Volume, that are only figures of speech, the one of most frequent occurrence is that which describes an effect by the name of its most usual and best known cause: the passages, for instance, in which grief, fury, repentance, and the like, are attributed to the Deity. But these are far enough from justifying the (I had almost said, dishonest) fashion of metaphorical glosses, in as well as out of the Church; and which our fashionable divines have carried to such an extent, as in the doctrinal part of their creed, to leave little else but metaphors.

APHORISM XV.

THE CHRISTIAN NO STOIC.

Leighton and Coleridge.

Seek not altogether to dry up the stream of sorrow, but to bound it and keep it within its banks. Religion doth not destroy the life of nature, but adds to it a life more excellent; yea, it doth not only permit, but requires some feeling of afflictions. Instead of patience, there is in some men an affected pride of spirit, suitable only to the doctrine of the Stoics as it is usually taken. They strive not to feel at all the afflictions that are on them; but where there is no feeling at all, there can be no patience.

Of the sects of ancient philosophy the Stoic is, perhaps, the nearest to Christianity. Yet even to this sect Christianity is fundamentally opposite. For the Stoic attaches the highest honor (or rather attaches honor solely) to the person that acts virtuously in spite of his feelings, or who has raised himself above the conflict by their extinction; while Christianity instructs us to place small reliance on a virtue that does not begin by bringing the feelings to a conformity with the commands of the conscience. Its especial aim, its characteristic operation, is to moralize the affections. The feelings, that oppose a right act, must be wrong feelings. The act, indeed, whatever the agent's feelings might be, Christianity would command: and under certain circumstances would both command and commend it—commend it, as a healthful symptom in a sick patient; and command it, as one of the ways and means of changing the feelings, or displacing them by calling up the opposite.

COROLLARIES TO APHORISM XV.

I. The more consciousness in our thoughts and words, and the less in our impulses and general actions, the better and more healthful the state both of head and heart. As the flowers from an orange-tree in its time of blossoming, that burgeon forth, expand, fall, and are momently replaced, such is the sequence of hourly and momently charities in a pure and gracious soul. The modern fiction which depictures the son of Cytherea with a bandage round his eyes, is not without a spiritual meaning. There is a sweet and holy blindness in Christian love even as there is a blindness of life, yea, and of genius too, in the moment of productive energy.

II. Motives are symptoms of weakness, and supplements for the deficient energy of the living principle, the law within us. Let them then be reserved for those momentous acts and duties in which the strongest and best balanced natures must feel themselves deficient, and where humility, no less than prudence, prescribes deliberation. We find a similitude of this, I had almost said a remote analogy, in organized bodies. The lowest class of animals or *protozoa*, the *polypi* for instance, have neither brain nor nerves. Their motive powers are all from without. The sun, light, the warmth, the air are their nerves and brain. As life ascends, nerves appear; but still only as the conductors of an external influence; next are seen the knots or ganglions, as so many *foci* of instinctive agency, which imperfectly imitate the yet wanting centre. And now the promise and token of a true individuality are disclosed; both the reservoir of sensibility and the imitative power that actuates the organs of motion, (the muscles) with the network of conductors, are all taken inward and appropriated; the spontaneous rises into the voluntary, and finally after various steps and long ascent, the material and animal means and conditions are prepared for the manifestations of a free will, having its law within itself, and its motive in the law—and thus bound to originate its own acts, not only without, but even against, alien stimulants. That in our present state we have only the dawning of this inward sun (the perfect law of liberty) will sufficiently limit and qualify the preceding position, if only it have been allowed to produce its two-fold consequence—the excitement of hope and the repression of vanity.*

APHORISM XVI.

Leighton.

As excessive eating or drinking both makes the body sickly and lazy, fit for nothing but sleep, and besots the mind, as it clogs up with crudities the way through which the spirits should pass,† bemiring them, and making them move heavily, as a coach in a deep way; thus doth all immoderate use of the world and its delights wrong the soul in its spiritual condition, makes it sickly and feeble, full of spiritual distempers and inactivity, benumbs the graces of the Spirit, and fills the soul with sleepy vapors, makes it grow secure and heavy in spiritual exercises, and obstructs the way and motion of the Spirit of God in the soul. Therefore, if you would be spiritual, healthful and vigorous, and enjcy much of the consolations of Heaven, be sparing and sober in those of the earth, and what you abate of the one, shall be certainly made up in the other.

* The reader is referred, upon the subject of this remarkable paragraph, to Mr. Joseph Henry Green's Recapitulatory Lecture, p. 110, *Vital Dynamics*, 1840;—a volume of singular worth and importance.—*Ed.*

† Technical phrases of an obsolete system will yet retain their places, nay, acquire universal currency, and become sterling in the language, when they at once represent the feelings, and give an apparent solution of them by visual images easily managed by the fancy. Such are many terms and phrases from the humoral physiology long exploded, but which are far more popular than any description would be from the theory that has taken its place.

APHORISM XVII.

INCONSISTENCY.

Leighton and Coleridge.

It is a most unseemly and unpleasant thing, to see a man's life full of ups and downs, one step like a Christian, and another like a worldling; it can not choose but both pain himself and mar the edification of others.

The same sentiment, only with a special application to the maxims and measures of our cabinet statesmen, has been finely expressed by a sage poet of the preceding generation, in lines which no generation will find inapplicable or superannuated.

God and the world we worship both together,
  Draw not our laws to Him, but His to ours;
Untrue to both, so prosperous in neither,
  The imperfect will brings forth but barren flowers!

Unwise as all distracted interests be,
  Strangers to God, fools in humanity:
Too good for great things, and too great for good,
  While still "I dare not" waits upon "I wou'd."

APHORISM XVII. CONTINUED.

THE ORDINARY MOTIVE TO INCONSISTENCY.

Leighton.

What though the polite man count thy fashion a little odd and too precise, it is because he knows nothing above that model of goodness which he hath set himself, and therefore approves of nothing beyond it: he knows not God, and therefore doth not discern and esteem what is most like Him. When courtiers come down into the country, the common home-bred people possibly think their habit strange; but they care not for that, it is the fashion at court. What need, then, that Christians should be so tender foreheaded, as to be put out of countenance because the world looks on holiness as a singularity; it is the only fashion in the highest court, yea, of the King of kings himself.

APHORISM XVIII.

SUPERFICIAL RECONCILIATIONS, AND SELF-DECEIT IN FORGIVING.

Leighton.

When, after variances, men are brought to an agreement, they are much subject to this, rather to cover their remaining malices with superficial verbal forgiveness, than to dislodge them and free the heart of them. This is a poor self-deceit. As the philosopher said to him, who being ashamed that he was espied by him in a tavern in the outer room, withdrew himself to the inner, 'That is not the way out; the more you go that way, you will be the further in:'—so when hatreds are upon admonition not thrown out, but retire inward to hide themselves, they grow deeper and stronger than before; and those constrained semblances of reconcilement are but a false healing, do but skin the wound over, and therefore it usually breaks forth worse again.

APHORISM XIX.

OF THE WORTH AND THE DUTIES OF THE PREACHER.

Leighton.

The stream of custom and our profession bring us to the preaching of the Word, and we sit out our hour under the sound; but how few consider and prize it as the great ordinance of God for the salvation of souls, the beginner and the sustainer of the divine life of grace within us! And certainly, until we have these thoughts of it, and seek to feel it thus ourselves, although we hear it most frequently, and let slip no occasion, yea, hear it with attention, and some present delight, yet still we miss the right use of it, and turn it from its true end, while we take it not as *that ingrafted word which is able to save our souls.* (Jas. i. 21.)

Thus ought they who preach to speak the word; to endeavor their utmost to accommodate it to this end, that sinners may be converted, begotten again, and believers nourished and strengthened in their spiritual life; to regard no lower end, but aim steadily at that mark. Their hearts and tongues ought to be set on fire with holy zeal for God and love to souls, kindled by the Holy Ghost, that came down on the Apostles in the shape of fiery tongues.

And those that hear should remember this as the end of their hearing, that they may receive spiritual life and strength by the word. For though it seems a poor despicable business, that a frail sinful man like yourselves should speak a few words in your hearing, yet, look upon it as the way wherein God communicates happiness to those who believe, and works that believing unto happiness, alters the whole frame of the soul, and makes a new creation as it begets it again to the inheritance of glory,—consider it thus, which is its true notion; and then what can be so precious!

APHORISM XX.

Leighton.

The difference is great in our natural life, in some persons especially; that they who in infancy were so feeble, and wrapped up as others in swaddling-clothes, yet afterwards come to excel in wisdom and in the knowledge of sciences, or to be commanders of great armies, or to be kings: but the distance is far greater and more admirable betwixt the small beginnings of grace, and our after perfection, that fulness of knowledge that we look for, and that crown of immortality, which all they are born to who are born to God.

But as in the faces or actions of some children, characters and presages of their after-greatness have appeared—as a singular beauty in Moses' face, as they write of him, and as Cyrus was made king among the shepherds' children with whom he was brought up,—so also, certainly, in these children of God, there be some characters and evidences that they are born for Heaven by their new birth. That holiness and meekness, that patience and faith which shine in the actions and sufferings of the saints, are characters of their Father's image, and show their high original, and foretell their glory to come; such a glory as doth not only surpass the world's thoughts, but the thoughts of the children of God themselves. 1 *John* iii. 2.

COMMENT.

This Aphorism would, it may seem, have been placed more fitly in the Chapter following. In placing it here, I have been determined by the following convictions: 1. Every state, and consequently that which we have described as the state of religious morality, which is not progressive, is dead or retrograde. 2. As a pledge of this progression, or, at least, as the form in which the propulsive tendency shows itself, there are certain hopes, aspirations, yearnings, that with more or less of consciousness rise and stir in the heart of true morality as naturally as the sap in the full-formed stem of a rose flows towards the bud, within which the flower is maturing. 3. No one, whose own experience authorizes him to confirm the truth of this statement, can have been conversant with the volumes of religious biography, can have perused for instance the lives of Cranmer, Ridley, Latimer, Wishart, Sir Thomas More, Bernard Gilpin, Bishop Bedel, or of Egede, Swartz, and the missionaries of the frozen world, without an occasional conviction, that these men lived under extraordinary influences, which in each instance and in all ages of the Christian æra bear the same characters, and both in the accompaniments and the results evidently refer to a common origin. And what can this be ? is the question that must needs force itself on the mind in the first moment of reflection on a fact so interesting and apparently so anomalous. The answer is as necessarily contained in one or the other of two assumptions. These influences are either the product of delusion—*insania amabilis*, and the reaction of disordered nerves—or they argue the existence of a relation to some real agency, distinct from what is experienced or acknowledged by the world at large, for which as not merely natural on the one hand, and yet not assumed to be miraculous* on the other, we have no apter name than spiritual. Now, if neither analogy justifies, nor the moral feelings permit, the former assumption, and we decide therefore in favor of the reality of a state other and higher than the mere moral man, whose religion† consists in morality, has attained under these convictions; can the existence of a transitional state appear other than probable ; or that these very convictions, when ac-

* In check of fanatical pretensions, it is expedient to confine the term miraculous, to cases where the senses are appealed to, in proof of something that transcends the experience derived from the senses.

† For let it not be forgotten, that Morality, as distinguished from Prudence, implying (it matters not under what name, whether of honor, or duty, or conscience, still, I say, implying), and being grounded in, an awe of the invisible and a confidence therein beyond (nay, occasionally in apparent contradiction to) the inductions of outward experience, is essentially religious.

companied by correspondent dispositions and stirrings of the heart, are among the marks and indications of such a state? And thinking it not unlikely that among the readers of this Volume, there may be found some individuals, whose inward state, though disquieted by doubts and oftener still perhaps by blank misgivings, may, nevertheless, betoken the commencement of a transition from a not irreligious morality to a spiritual religion,—with a view to their interests I placed this Aphorism under the present head.

APHORISM XXI.

Leighton.

The most approved teachers of wisdom, in a human way, have required of their scholars, that to the end their minds might be capable of it, they should be purified from vice and wickedness. And it was Socrates' custom, when any one asked him a question, seeking to be informed by him, before he would answer them, he asked them concerning their own qualities and course of life.

APHORISM XXII.

KNOWLEDGE NOT THE ULTIMATE END OF RELIGIOUS PURSUITS.

Leighton and Coleridge.

The hearing and reading of the word, under which I comprise theological studies generally, are alike defective when pursued without increase of knowledge, and when pursued chiefly for increase of knowledge. To seek no more than a present delight, that evanishes with the sound of the words that die in the air, is not to desire the word as meat, but as music, as God tells the prophet Ezekiel of his people, *Ezek.* xxxiii. 32. *And lo, thou art unto them as a very lovely song of one that hath a pleasant voice, and can play well upon an instrument; for they hear thy words, and they do them not.* To desire the word for the increase of knowledge, although this is necessary and commendable, and, being rightly qualified, is a part of spiritual accretion, yet, take it as going no further, it is not the true end of the word. Nor is the venting of that knowledge in speech and frequent discourse of the word and the divine truths that are in it; which, where it is governed with Christian prudence, is not to be despised, but commended; yet, certainly, the highest knowledge, and the most frequent and skilful speaking of the word severed from the growth here mentioned, misses the true end of the word. If any one's head or tongue should grow apace, and all the rest stand at a stay, it would certainly make him a monster; and they are no other, who are knowing and discoursing Christians, and grow daily in that respect, but not at all in holiness of heart and life, which is the proper growth of the children of God. Apposite to their case is Epictetus's comparison of the sheep; they return not what they eat in grass, but in wool.

APHORISM XXIII.

THE SUM OF CHURCH HISTORY.

Leighton.

In times of peace, the Church may dilate more, and build as it were into breadth, but in times of trouble, it arises more in height; it is then built upwards; as in cities where men are straightened, they build usually higher than in the country.

APHORISM XXIV.

WORTHY TO BE FRAMED AND HUNG UP IN THE LIBRARY OE EVERY THEOLOGICAL STUDENT.

Leighton and Coleridge.

Where there is a great deal of smoke and no clear flame, it argues much moisture in the matter, yet it witnesseth certainly that there is fire there; and therefore dubious questioning is a much better evidence, than that senseless deadness which most take for believing. Men that know nothing in sciences, have no doubts. He never truly believed, who was not made first sensible and convinced of unbelief.

Never be afraid to doubt, if only you have the disposition to believe, and doubt in order that you may end in believing the truth. I will venture to add in my own name and from my own conviction the following:

APHORISM XXV.

He, who begins by loving Christianity better than truth, will proceed by loving his own sect or church better than Christianity, and end in loving himself better than all.

APHORISM XXVI.

THE ABSENCE OF DISPUTES, AND A GENERAL AVERSION TO RELIGIOUS CONTROVERSIES NO PROOF OF TRUE UNANIMITY.

Leighton and Coleridge.

The boasted peaceableness about questions of faith too often proceeds from a superficial temper, and not seldom from a supercilious disdain of whatever has no marketable use or value, and from indifference to religion itself. Toleration is a herb of spontaneous growth in the soil of indifference; but the weed has none of the virtues of the medicinal plant, reared by humility in the garden of zeal. Those who regard religions as matters of taste, may consistently include all religious differences in the old adage, *De gustibus non est disputandum.* And many there be among these of Gallio's temper, who *care for none of these things*, and who account all questions in religion, as he did, but matter of words and names. And by this all religions may agree together. But that were not a natural union produced by the active heat of the spirit, but a confusion rather, arising from the want of it; not a knitting together, but a freezing together, as cold congregates all bodies how heterogeneous soever, sticks, stones and water; but heat makes first a separation of different things, and then unites those that are of the same nature.

Much of our common union of minds, I fear, proceeds from no other than the aforementioned causes, want of knowledge, and want of affection to religion. You that boast you live conformably to the appointments of the Church, and that no one hears of your noise, we may thank the ignorance of your minds for that kind of quietness.

The preceding extract is particularly entitled to our serious reflections, as in a tenfold degree more applicable to the present times than to the age in which it was written. We all know, that lovers are apt to take offence and wrangle on occasions that perhaps are but trifles, and which assuredly would appear such to those who regard love itself as folly. These quarrels may, indeed, be no proof of wisdom; but still, in the imperfect state of our nature the entire absence of the same, and this too on far more serious provocations, would excite a strong suspicion of a comparative indifference in the parties who can love so coolly where they profess to love so well. I shall believe our present religious tolerancy to proceed from the abundance of our charity and good sense, when I see proofs that we are equally cool and forbearing as litigants and political partisans.

APHORISM XXVII.

THE INFLUENCE OF WORLDLY VIEWS (OR WHAT ARE CALLED A MAN'S PROSPECTS IN LIFE), THE BANE OF THE CHRISTIAN MINISTRY.

Leighton.

It is a base, poor thing for a man to seek himself: far below that royal dignity that is here put upon Christians, and that priesthood joined with it. Under the law, those who were squint-eyed were incapable of the priesthood: truly, this squinting toward our own interests, the looking aside to that, in God's affairs especially, so deforms the face of the soul, that it makes it altogether unworthy the honor of this spiritual priesthood. Oh! this is a large task, an infinite task. The several creatures bear their part in this; the sun says somewhat, and moon and stars, yea, the lowest have some share in it; the very plants and herbs of the field speak of God; and yet, the very highest and best, yea all of them together, the whole concert of heaven and earth can not show forth all His praise to the full. No, it is but a part, the smallest part of that glory, which they can reach.

APHORISM XXVIII.

DESPISE NONE: DESPAIR OF NONE.

Leighton.

The Jews would not willingly tread upon the smallest piece of paper in their way, but took it up: for possibly, said they, the name of God may be on it. Though there was a little superstition in this, yet truly there is nothing but good religion in it, if we apply it to men. Trample not on any; there may be some work of grace there, that thou knowest not of. The name of God may be written upon that soul thou treadest on; it may be a soul that Christ thought so much of, as to give his precious blood for it; therefore despise it not.

APHORISM XXIX.

MEN OF LEAST MERIT MOST APT TO BE CONTEMPTUOUS BECAUSE MOST IGNORANT AND MOST OVERWEENING OF THEMSELVES.

Leighton.

Too many take the ready course to deceive themselves; for they look with both eyes on the failings and defects of others, and scarcely give their good qualities half an eye, while, on the contrary, in themselves, they study to the full their own advantages, and their weaknesses and defects (as one says), they skip over, as children do their hard words in their lesson, that are troublesome to read: and making this uneven parallel, what wonder if the result be a gross mistake of themselves!

APHORISM XXX.

VANITY MAY STRUT IN RAGS, AND HUMILITY BE ARRAYED IN PURPLE AND FINE LINEN.

Leighton.

It is not impossible that there may be in some an affected pride in the meanness of apparel, and in others, under either neat or rich attire, a very humble unaffected mind: using it upon some of the aforementioned engagements, or such like, and yet, the heart not at all upon it. *Magnus qui fictilibus utitur tanquam argento, nec ille minor qui argento tanquam fictilibus,* says Seneca: Great is he who enjoys his earthenware as if it were plate, and not less great is the man to whom all his plate is no more than earthenware.

APHORISM XXXI.

OF DETRACTION AMONG RELIGIOUS PROFESSORS.

Leighton and Coleridge.

They who have attained to a self-pleasing pitch of civility or formal religion, have usually that point of presumption with it, that they make their own size the model and rule to examine all by. What is below it, they condemn indeed as profane; but what is beyond it, they account needless and affected preciseness: and therefore are as ready as others to let fly invectives or bitter taunts against it, which are the keen and poisoned shafts of the tongue, and a persecution that shall be called to a strict account

The slanders, perchance, may not be altogether forged or untrue; they may be the implements, not the inventions, of malice. But they do not on this account escape the guilt of detraction. Rather, it is characteristic of the evil spirit in question, to work by the advantage of real faults; but these stretched and aggravated to the utmost. IT IS NOT EXPRESSIBLE HOW DEEP A WOUND A TONGUE SHARPENED TO THIS WORK WILL GIVE, WITH NO NOISE AND A VERY LITTLE WORD. This is the true white gunpowder, which the dreaming projectors of silent mischiefs and insensible poisons sought for in the laboratories of art and nature, in a world of good; but which was to be found in its most destructive form, in *the world of evil, the tongue.*

APHORISM XXXII.

THE REMEDY.

Leighton.

All true remedy must begin at the heart; otherwise it will be but a mountebank cure, a false imagined conquest. The weights and wheels are there, and the clock strikes according to their motion. Even he that speaks contrary to what is within him, guilefully contrary to his inward conviction and knowledge, yet speaks conformably to what is within him in the temper and frame of his heart, which is double, *a heart and a heart,* as the Psalmist hath it, *Psal.* xii. 2.

APHORISM XXXIII.

Leighton and Coleridge.

It is an argument of a candid ingenuous mind, to delight in the good name and commendations of others; to pass by their defects and take notice of their virtues; and to speak and hear of those willingly, and not endure either to speak or hear of the other; for in this indeed you may be little less guilty than the evil speaker, in taking pleasure in it, though you speak it not. He that willingly drinks in tales and calumnies, will, from the delight he hath in evil hearing, slide insensibly into the humor of evil speaking. It is strange how most persons dispense with themselves in this point, and that in scarcely any societies shall we find a hatred of this ill, but rather some tokens of taking pleasure in it; and until a Christian sets himself to an inward watchfulness over his heart, not suffering in it any thought that is uncharitable, or vain self-esteem, upon the slight of others' frailties, he will still be subject to somewhat of this, in the tongue or ear at least. So, then, as for the evil of guile in the tongue, a sincere heart, *truth in the inward parts*, powerfully redresses it; therefore it is expressed, *Psal.* xv. 2, *That speaketh the truth from his heart;* thence it flows. Seek much after this, to speak nothing with God, nor men, but what is the sense of a single unfeigned heart. O sweet truth! excellent but rare sincerity! He that *loves that truth within*, and who is Himself at once THE TRUTH and THE LIFE, He alone can work it there! Seek it of him.

It is characteristic of the Roman dignity and sobriety, that, in the Latin, *to favor with the* tongue (*favere lingua*) means, *to be silent.* We say, Hold your tongue! as if it were an injunction, that could not be carried into effect but by manual force, or the pincers of the forefinger and thumb! And verily—I blush to say it—it is not women and Frenchmen only that would rather have their tongues bitten than bitted, and feel their souls in a strait-waistcoat, when they are obliged to remain silent.

APHORISM XXXIV.

ON THE PASSION FOR NEW AND STRIKING THOUGHTS.

Leighton.

In conversation seek not so much either to vent thy knowledge, or to increase it, as to know more spiritually and effectually what thou dost know. And in this way those mean despised truths, that every one thinks he is sufficiently seen in, will have a new sweetness and use in them, which thou didst not so well perceive before—(for these flowers can not be sucked dry); and in this humble sincere way thou shalt *grow in grace and in knowledge* too.

APHORISM XXXV.

THE RADICAL DIFFERENCE BETWEEN THE GOOD MAN AND THE VICIOUS MAN.

Leighton and Coleridge.

The godly man hates the evil he possibly by temptation hath been drawn to do, and loves the good he is frustrated of, and, having intended, hath not attained to do. The sinner, who hath his denomination from sin as his course, hates the good which sometimes he is forced to do, and loves that sin which many times he does not, either wanting occasion and means, so that he can not do it, or through the check of an enlightened conscience possibly dares not do; and though so bound up from the act, as a dog in a chain, yet the habit, the natural inclination and desire in him is still the same, the strength of his affection is carried to sin. So in the weakest sincere Christian, there is that predominant sincerity and desire of holy walking, according to which he is called a righteous person: the Lord is pleased to give him that name, and account him so, being upright in heart though often failing.

Leighton adds, "There is a righteousness of a higher strain." I do not ask the reader's full assent to this position: I do not suppose him as yet prepared to yield it. But thus much he will readily admit, that here, if anywhere, we are to seek the fine line which, like stripes of light in light, distinguishes, not divides, the summit of religious morality from spiritual religion.

"A righteousness" Leighton continues, "that is not in him, but upon him. He is clothed with it." This, Reader! is the controverted doctrine, so warmly asserted and so bitterly decried under the name of IMPUTED RIGHTEOUSNESS. Our learned archbishop, you see, adopts it; and it is on this account principally, that by many of our leading churchmen his orthodoxy has been more than questioned, and his name put in the list of proscribed divines, as a Calvinist. That Leighton attached a definite sense to the words above quoted, it would be uncandid to doubt; and the general spirit of his writings leads me to presume that it was compatible with the eternal distinction between things and persons, and therefore opposed to modern Calvinism. But what it was, I have not, I own, been able to discover. The sense, however, in which I think he might have received this doctrine, and in which I avow myself a believer in it, I shall have an opportunity of showing in another place. My present object is to open out the road by the removal of prejudices, so far at least as to throw some disturbing doubts on the secure taking-for-granted, that the peculiar tenets of the Christian faith asserted in the Articles and Homilies of our national Church are in contradiction to the common sense of mankind. And with this view (and not in the arrogant expectation or wish, that a mere *ipse dixit* should be received for argument)—I here avow my conviction, that the doctrine of IMPUTED righteousness, rightly and Scripturally interpreted, is so far from being either irrational or immoral, that reason itself prescribes the idea in order to give a meaning and an ultimate object to morality; and that the moral law in the conscience demands its reception in order to give reality and substantive existence to the idea presented by the reason.

APHORISM XXXVI.

Leighton.

Your blessedness is not,—no, believe it, it is not where most of you seek it, in things below you. How can that be? It must be a higher good to make you happy.

COMMENT.

Every rank of creatures, as it ascends in the scale of creation, leaves death behind it or under it. The metal at its height of being seems a mute prophecy of the coming vegetation, into a mimic semblance of which it crystallizes. The blossom and flower, the acme of vegetable life, divides into correspondent organs with reciprocal functions, and by instinctive motions and approximations seems impatient of that fixure, by which it is differenced in kind from the flower-shaped Psyche, that flutters with free wing above it. And wonderfully in the insect realm doth the irritability, the proper seat of instinct, while yet the nascent sensibility is subordinated thereto—most wonderfully, I say, doth the muscular life in the insect, and the musco-arterial in the bird, imitate and typically rehearse the adaptive understanding, yea, and the moral affections and charities, of man. Let us carry ourselves back, in spirit, to the mysterious week, the teeming work-days of the Creator; as they rose in vision before the eye of the inspired historian of *the generations of the heavens and of the earth, in the day that the Lord God made the earth and the heavens.** And who that hath watched their ways with an understanding heart, could, as the vision evolving still advanced towards him, contemplate the filial and loyal Bee; the home-building, wedded, and divorceless Swallow; and above all

* Gen. ii. 4.—*Ed.*

the manifoldly intelligent* Ant tribes, with their commonwealths and confederacies, their warriors and miners, the husband-folk, that fold in their tiny flocks on the honeyed leaf, and the virgin sisters with the holy instincts of maternal love, detached and in selfless purity—and not say to himself, Behold the shadow of approaching humanity, the sun rising from behind, in the kindling morn of creation! Thus all lower natures find their highest good in semblances and seekings of that which is higher and better. All things strive to ascend, and ascend in their striving. And shall man alone stoop? Shall his pursuits and desires, the reflections of his inward life, be like the reflected image of a tree on the edge of a pool, that grows downward, and seeks a mock heaven in the unstable element beneath it, in neighborhood with the slim water-weeds and oozy bottom-grass that are yet better than itself and more noble, in as far as substances that appear as shadows are preferable to shadows mistaken for substance. No! it must be a higher good to make you happy. While you labor for any thing below your proper humanity, you seek a happy life in the region of death. Well saith the moral poet—

Unless above himself he can
Erect himself, how mean a thing is man!

APHORISM XXXVII.

Leighton.

There is an imitation of men that is impious and wicked, which consists in taking the copy of their sins. Again, there is an imitation which though not so grossly evil, yet is poor and servile, being in mean things, yea, sometimes descending to imitate the very imperfections of others, as fancying some comeliness in them: as some of Basil's scholars, who imitated his slow speaking, which he had a little in the extreme, and could not help. But this is always laudable, and worthy of the best minds, to be imitators of that which is good, wheresoever they find it; for that stays not in any man's person, as the ultimate pattern, but rises to the highest grace, being man's nearest likeness to God, His image and resemblance, bearing His stamp and superscription, and belonging peculiarly to Him, in what hand soever it be found, as carrying the mark of no other owner than Him.

* *See Huber on Bees, and on Ants.*

APHORISM XXXVIII.

Leighton.

Those who think themselves high-spirited, and will bear least, as they speak, are often, even by that, forced to bow most, or to burst under it; while humility and meekness escape many a burden, and many a blow, always keeping peace within, and often without too.

APHORISM XXXIX.

Leighton.

Our condition is universally exposed to fears and troubles, and no man is so stupid but he studies and projects for some fence against them, some bulwark to break the incursion of evils, and so to bring his mind to some ease, ridding it of the fear of them. Thus, men seek safety in the greatness, or multitude, or supposed faithfulness, of friends ; they seek by any means to be strongly underset this way, to have many, and powerful, and trustworthy friends. But wiser men, perceiving the unsafety and vanity of these and all external things, have cast about for some higher course. They see a necessity of withdrawing a man from externals, which do nothing but mock and deceive those most who trust most to them ; but they can not tell whither to direct him. The best of them bring him into himself, and think to quiet him so, but the truth is, he finds as little to support him there ; there is nothing truly strong enough within him, to hold out against the many sorrows and fears which still from without do assault him. So then, though it is well done, to call off a man from outward things, as moving sands, that he build not on them, yet this is not enough ; for his own spirit is as unsettled a piece as is in all the world, and must have some higher strength than its own, to fortify and fix it. This is the way that is here taught, *Fear not their fear, but sanctify the Lord your God in your hearts :* and if you can attain this latter, the former will follow of itself.

APHORISM XL.

WORLDLY TROUBLES IDOLS.

Leighton.

The too ardent love or self-willed desire of power, or wealth, or credit in the world, is (an Apostle has assured us) idolatry. Now among the words or synonymes for idols in the Hebrew language, there is one that in its primary sense signifies *troubles* (*tegirim*), other two that signify *terrors* (*miphletzeth* and *enim*). And so it is certainly. All our idols prove so to us. They fill us with nothing but anguish and troubles, with cares and fears, that are good for nothing but to be fit punishments of the folly, out of which they arise.

APHORISM XLI.

ON THE RIGHT TREATMENT OF INFIDELS.

Leighton and Coleridge.

A regardless contempt of infidel writings is usually the fittest answer: *Spreta vilescerent.* But where the holy profession of Christians is likely to receive either the main or the indirect blow, and a word of defence may do any thing to ward it off, there we ought not to spare to do it.

Christian prudence goes a great way in the regulating of this. Some are not capable of receiving rational answers, especially in divine things; they were not only lost upon them, but religion dishonored by the contest.

Of this sort are the vulgar railers at religion, the foul-mouthed beliers of the Christian faith and history. Impudently false and slanderous assertions can be met only by assertions of their impudent and slanderous falsehood: and Christians will not, must not, condescend to this. How can mere railing be answered by them who are forbidden to return a railing answer? Whether, or on what provocations, such offenders may be punished or coerced on the score of incivility, and ill-neighborhood, and for abatement of a nuisance, as in the case of other scolds and endangerers of the public peace, must be trusted to the discretion of the civil magistrate. Even then there is danger of giving them importance, and flattering their vanity, by attracting attention to their works, if the punishment be slight; and if severe, of spreading far and wide their reputation as martyrs, as the smell of a dead dog at a distance is said to change into that of musk. Experience hitherto seems to favor the plan of treating these *bêtes puantes* and *enfans de Diable*, as their four-footed brethren, the skink and squash, are treated* by American woodmen, who turn their backs

* "About the end of the same year," (says Kalm), "another of these animals (*Mephitis Americana*) crept into our cellar; but did not exhale the

upon the fetid intruder, and make appear not to see him, even at the cost of suffering him to regale on the favorite viand of these animals, the brains of a stray goose or crested *thraso* of the dunghill. At all events, it is degrading to the majesty, and injurious to the character, of religion, to make its safety the plea for their punishment, or at all to connect the name of Christianity with the castigation of indecencies that properly belong to the beadle, and the perpetrators of which would have equally deserved his lash, though the religion of their fellow-citizens, thus assailed by them, had been that of Fo or of Juggernaut.

On the other hand, we are to answer every one that inquires a reason, or an account; which supposes something receptive of it. We ought to judge ourselves engaged to give it, be it an enemy, if he will hear; if it gain him not, it may in part convince and cool him; much more, should it be one who ingenuously inquires for satisfaction, and possibly inclines to receive the truth, but has been prejudiced by misrepresentations of it.

APHORISM XLII.

PASSION NO FRIEND TO TRUTH.

Leighton.

Truth needs not the service of passion; yea, nothing so disserves it, as passion when set to serve it. The *Spirit of truth* is withal the *Spirit of meekness*. The Dove that rested on that great champion of truth, who is The Truth itself, is from Him derived to the lovers of truth, and they ought to seek the participation of it. Imprudence makes some kind of Christians lose much of their labor in speaking for religion, and drive those further off, whom they would draw into it.

The confidence that attends a Christian's belief makes the believer not fear men, to whom he answers, but still he fears his God, for whom he answers, and whose interest is chief in those things he speaks of. The soul that hath the deepest sense of

smallest scent, *because it was not disturbed. A foolish old woman, however, who perceived it at night, by the shining, and thought, I suppose, that it would set the world on fire, killed it; and at that moment its stench began to spread.*"

I recommend this anecdote to the consideration of sundry old women, on this side of the Atlantic, who, though they do not wear the appropriate garment, are worthy to sit in their committee-room, like Bickerstaff in the Tatler, under the canopy of their grandam's hoop-petticoat.

spiritual things, and the truest knowledge of God, is most afraid to miscarry in speaking of Him, most tender and wary how to acquit itself when engaged to speak of and for God.*

APHORISM XLIII.

ON THE CONSCIENCE.

Leighton.

It is a fruitless verbal debate, whether Conscience be a faculty or a habit. When all is examined, conscience will be found to be no other than the mind of a man, under the notion of a particular reference to himself and his own actions.

COMMENT.

I rather think that conscience is the ground and antecedent of human (or self-) consciousness, and not any modification of the latter. I have selected the preceding extract as an exercise for reflection; and because I think that in too closely following Thomas a Kempis, the Archbishop has strayed from his own judgment. The definition, for instance, seems to say all, and in fact says nothing; for if I asked, How do you define the human mind? the answer must at least contain, if not consist of, the words, "a mind capable of conscience." For conscience is no synonyme of consciousness, nor any mere expression of the same as modified by the particular object. On the contrary, a consciousness properly human (that is, self-consciousness), with the sense of moral responsibility, pre-supposes the conscience as its antecedent condition and ground.—Lastly, the sentence, "It is a fruitless verbal debate,"—is an assertion of the same complexion with the contemptuous sneers at verbal criticism by the contemporaries of Bentley. In questions of philosophy or divinity that

* To the same purpose are the two following sentences from Hilary:

Etiam quæ pro *religione dicimus, cum grandi metu et disciplina dicere debemus.*—Hilarius de Trinit. Lib. 7.

Non relictus est hominum eloquiis de Dei rebus alius quam Dei sermo.—Ib.

The latter, however, must be taken with certain qualifications and exceptions: as when any two or more texts are in apparent contradiction, and it is required to state a truth that comprehends and reconciles both, and which, of course, can not be expressed in the words of either:—for example, the Filial subordination (*My Father is greater than I*), in the equal Deity (*My Father and I are one*).

have occupied the learned and been the subjects of many successive controversies, for one instance of mere logomachy I could bring ten instances of logodædaly, or verbal legerdemain, which have perilously confirmed prejudices, and withstood the advancement of truth, in consequence of the neglect of verbal debate, that is, strict discussion of terms. In whatever sense, however, the term Conscience may be used, the following Aphorism is equally true and important. It is worth noticing, likewise, that Leighton himself in a following page, tells us, that a good conscience is the root of a good conversation: and then quotes from St. Paul a text, *Titus* i. 15, in which the Mind and the Conscience are expressly distinguished.

APHORISM XLIV.

THE LIGHT OF KNOWLEDGE A NECESSARY ACCOMPANIMENT OF A GOOD CONSCIENCE.

Leighton.

If you would have a good conscience, you must by all means have so much light, so much knowledge of the will of God, as may regulate you, and show you your way, may teach you how to do, and speak, and think, as in His presence.

APHORISM XLV.

YET THE KNOWLEDGE OF THE RULE, THOUGH ACCOMPANIED BY AN ENDEAVOR TO ACCOMMODATE OUR CONDUCT TO THIS RULE, WILL NOT OF ITSELF FORM A GOOD CONSCIENCE.

Leighton.

To set the outward actions right, though with an honest intention, and not so to regard and find out the inward disorder of the heart, whence that in the actions flows, is but to be still putting the index of a clock right with your finger, while it is foul or out of order within, which is a continual business and does no good. Oh! but a purified conscience, a soul renewed and refined in its temper and affections, will make things go right without, in all the duties and acts of our calling.

APHORISM XLVI.

THE DEPTH OF THE CONSCIENCE

How deeply seated the Conscience is in the human soul, is seen in the effect which sudden calamities produce on guilty men, even when unaided by any determinate notion or fears of punishment after death. The wretched criminal, as one rudely awakened from a long sleep, bewildered with the new light, and half recollecting, half striving to recollect, a fearful something, he knows not what, but which he will recognize as soon as he hears the name, already interprets the calamities into judgments, executions of a sentence passed by an invisible judge; as if the vast pyre of the last judgment were already kindled in an unknown distance, and some flashes of it, darting forth at intervals beyond the rest, were flying and lighting upon the face of his soul. The calamity may consist in the loss of fortune, or character, or reputation; but you hear no regrets from him. Remorse extinguishes all regret; and remorse is the implicit creed of the guilty.

APHORISM XLVII.

Leighton and Coleridge.

God hath suited every creature He hath made with a convenient good to which it tends, and in the obtainment of which it rests and is satisfied. Natural bodies have all their own natural place, whither, if not hindered, they move incessantly till they be in it; and they declare, by resting there, that they are (as I may say) where they would be. Sensitive creatures are carried to seek a sensitive good, as agreeable to their rank in being, and, attaining that, aim no further. Now in this is the excellency of man, that he is made capable of a communion with his Maker, and, because capable of it, is unsatisfied without it: the soul, being cut out (so to speak) to that largeness, can not be filled with less. Though he is fallen from his right to that good, and from all right desire of it, yet not from a capacity of it, no, nor from a necessity of it, for the answering and filling of his capacity.

Though the heart once gone from God turns continually further away from Him, and moves not towards Him till it be renewed, yet, even in that wandering, it retains that natural relation to God, as its centre, that it hath no true rest elsewhere, nor can by any means find it. It is made for Him, and is therefore still restless till it meet with Him.

It is true, the natural man takes much pains to quiet his heart by other things, and digests many vexations with hopes of contentment in the end and accomplishment of some design he hath: but still the heart misgives. Many times he attains not the thing he seeks; but if he do, yet he never attains the satisfaction he seeks and expects in it, but only learns from that to desire something further, and still hunts on after a fancy, drives his own shadow before him, and never overtakes it; and if he did, yet it is but a shadow. And so, in running from God, besides the sad end, he carries an interwoven punishment with his sin, the natural disquiet and vexation of his spirit, fluttering to and fro, and *finding no rest for the sole of his foot:* the *waters* of inconstancy and vanity *covering the whole face of the earth.*

These things are too gross and heavy. The soul, the immortal soul, descended from heaven, must either be more happy or remain miserable. The highest, the uncreated Spirit, is the proper good, *the Father of spirits,* that pure and full Good which raises the soul above itself; whereas all other things draw it down below itself. So, then, it is never well with the soul, but when it is near unto God, yea, in its union with Him, married to Him; mismatching itself elsewhere it hath never any thing but shame and sorrow. *All that forsake Thee shall be ashamed,* says the Prophet *Jer.* xvii. 13; and the Psalmist, *They that are far off from Thee shall perish. Psal.* lxxiii. 27. And this is indeed our natural miserable condition, and it is often expressed this way, by estrangedness and distance from God.

The same sentiments are to be found in the works of Pagan philosophers and moralists. Well then may they be made a subject of reflection in our days. And well may the pious Deist, if such a character now exists, reflect that Christianity alone both teaches the way, and provides the means, of fulfilling the obscure promises of this great instinct for all men, which the philosophy of boldest pretensions confined to the sacred few.

APHORISM XLVIII.

A CONTRACTED SPHERE, OR WHAT IS CALLED RETIRING FROM THE BUSINESS OF THE WORLD, NO SECURITY FROM THE SPIRIT OF THE WORLD.

Leighton.

The heart may be engaged in a little business as much, if thou watch it not, as in many and great affairs. A man may drown in a little brook or pool, as well as in a great river, if he be down and plunge himself into it, and put his head under water. Some care thou must have, that thou mayest not care. Those things that are thorns indeed, thou must make a hedge of them, to keep out those temptations that accompany sloth, and extreme want that waits on it; but let them be the hedge: suffer them not to grow within the garden.

APHORISM XLIX.

ON CHURCH-GOING, AS A PART OF RELIGIOUS MORALITY, WHEN NOT IN REFERENCE TO A SPIRITUAL RELIGION.

Leighton.

It is a strange folly in multitudes of us, to set ourselves no mark, to propound no end in the hearing of the Gospel. The merchant sails not merely that he may sail, but for traffic, and traffics that he may be rich. The husbandman plows not merely to keep himself busy, with no further end, but plows that he may sow, and sows that he may reap with advantage. And shall we do the most excellent and fruitful work fruitlessly—hear, only to hear, and look no further? This is indeed a great vanity and a great misery, to lose that labor, and gain nothing by it, which, duly used, would be of all others most advantageous and gainful; and yet all meetings are full of this!

APHORISM L.

ON THE HOPES AND SELF-SATISFACTION OF A RELIGIOUS MORALIST, INDEPENDENT OF A SPIRITUAL FAITH—ON WHAT ARE THEY GROUNDED?

Leighton.

There have been great disputes one way or another, about the merit of good works; but I truly think they who have laboriously engaged in them have been very idly, though very eagerly, employed about nothing, since the more sober of the Schoolmen themselves acknowledge there can be no such thing as meriting from the blessed God, in the human, or, to speak more accurately, in any created nature whatsoever; nay so far from any possibility of merit, there can be no room for reward any otherwise than of the sovereign pleasure and gracious kindness of God; and the more ancient writers, when they use the word merit, mean nothing by it but a certain correlate to that reward which God both promises and bestows of mere grace and benignity. Otherwise, in order to constitute what is properly called merit, many things must concur, which no man in his senses will presume to attribute to human works, though ever so excellent; particularly, that the thing done must not previously be matter of debt, and that it be entire, or our own act, unassisted by foreign aid; it must also be perfectly good, and it must bear an adequate proportion to the reward claimed in consequence of it. If all these things do not concur, the act can not possibly amount to merit. Whereas I think no one will venture to assert, that any one of these can take place in any human action whatever. But why should I enlarge here, when one single circumstance overthrows all those titles? The most righteous of mankind would not be able to stand, if his works were weighed in the balance of strict justice; how much less then could they deserve that immense glory which is now in question! Nor is this to be denied only concerning the unbeliever and the sinner, but concerning the righteous and pious believer, who is not only free from all the guilt of his former impenitence and rebellion, but endowed with the gift of the Spirit. *For the time is come that judgment must begin at the house of God; and if it first begin at us, what shall the end be of them that obey not the Gospel of God? And if the righteous scarcely be saved, where shall the ungodly and the sinner appear?* 1 Peter iv. 17, 18. The Apostle's interrogation expresses the most vehement negation, and signifies that no mortal, in whatever degree he is placed, if he be called to the strict examination of divine justice, without daily and repeated forgiveness, could be able to keep his standing, and much less could he arise to that glorious height. 'That merit,' says Bernard, 'on which my hope relies, consists in these three things; the love of adoption, the truth of the promise, and the power of its performance.' This is the three-fold cord which can not be broken.

COMMENT.

Often have I heard it said by advocates for the Socinian scheme—True! we are all sinners; but even in the Old Testament God has promised forgiveness on repentance. One of the Fathers (I forget which) supplies the retort—True! God has promised pardon on penitence; but has he promised penitence on sin?—He that repenteth shall be forgiven; but where is it said, He that sinneth shall repent? But repentance, perhaps, the repentance required in Scripture, the passing into a new and contrary principle of action, this METANOIA, is in the sinner's own power? at his own liking? He has but to open his eyes to the sin, and the tears are close at hand to wash it away?—Verily, the tenet of Transubstantiation is scarcely at greater variance with the common sense and experience of mankind, or borders more closely on a contradiction in terms, than this volunteer transmentation, this self-change, as the easy means of self-salvation! But the reflections of our evangelical Author on this subject will appropriately commence the Aphorisms relating to Spiritual Religion.

ELEMENTS OF RELIGIOUS PHILOSOPHY.

PRELIMINARY TO THE APHORISMS ON

SPIRITUAL RELIGION.

Philip saith unto him: Lord, show us the Father, and it sufficeth us. Jesus saith unto him, He that hath seen me hath seen the Father: and how sayest thou then, Show us the Father? Believest thou not that I am in the Father and the Father in me? And I will pray the Father and he shall give you another Comforter, even the Spirit of Truth: whom the world cannot receive, because it seeth him not, neither knoweth him. But ye know him, for he dwelleth with you and shall be in you. And in that day ye shall know that I am in my Father, and ye in me and I in you. John xiv. 8, 9, 10, 16, 17, 20.

PRELIMINARY.

If there be aught spiritual in man, the Will must be such.

If there be a Will, there must be a spirituality in man.

I suppose both positions granted. The Reader admits the reality of the power, agency, or mode of being expressed in the term, Spirit; and the actual existence of a Will. He sees clearly that the idea of the former is necessary to the conceivability of the latter; and that, *vice versa*, in asserting the fact of the latter he presumes and instances the truth of the former;—just as in our common and received systems of natural philosophy, the being of imponderable matter is assumed to render the lode-stone intelligible, and the fact of the lode-stone adduced to prove the reality of imponderable matter.

In short, I suppose the Reader, whom I now invite to the third and last division of this Work, already disposed to reject for himself and his human brethren the insidious title of "Nature's noblest animal," or to retort it as the unconscious irony of the Epicurean poet on the animalizing tendency of his own philosophy. I suppose him convinced, that there is more in man than can be rationally referred to the life of nature and the mechanism of organization; that he has a will not included in this mechanism; and that the will is in an especial and pre-eminent sense the spiritual part of our humanity.

Unless, then, we have some distinct notion of the Will, and some acquaintance with the prevalent errors respecting the same, an insight into the nature of spiritual religion is scarcely possible; and our reflections on the particular truths and evidences of a spiritual state will remain obscure, perplexed, and unsafe. To place my Reader on this requisite vantage-ground, is the purpose of the following exposition.

We have begun, as in geometry, with defining our terms; and we proceed, like the geometricians, with stating our postulates; the difference being, that the postulates of geometry no man can deny, those of moral science as such as no good man will deny. For it is not in our power to disclaim our nature as sentient beings; but it is in our power to disclaim our nature as moral beings. It is possible—(barely possible, I admit)—that a man may have remained ignorant or unconscious of the moral law within him; and a man need only persist in disobeying the law of conscience to make it possible for himself to deny its existence, or to reject and repel it as a phantom of superstition. Were it otherwise, the Creed would stand in the same relation to morality as the muliplication table.

This then is the distinction of moral philosophy—not that I begin with one or more assumptions; for this is common to all science; but—that I assume a something, the proof of which no man can give to another, yet every man may find for himself. If any man assert that he can not find it, I am bound to disbelieve him. I can not do otherwise without unsettling the very foundations of my own moral nature. For I either find it as an essential of the humanity common to him and me: or I have not found it at all, except as a hypochondriast finds glass legs. If, on the other hand, he will not find it, he excommunicates himself. He forfeits his personal rights, and becomes a thing: that is, one who may rightfully be employed or used, as* means to an end. against his will, and without regard to his interest.

* On this principle alone is it possible to justify capital or ignominious punishments, or indeed any punishment not having the reformation of the

All the significant objections of the Materialist and Necessitarian are contained in the term, Morality, all the objections of the Infidel in the term, Religion. The very terms, I say, imply a something granted, which the objection supposes not granted. The term presumes what the objection denies, and in denying presumes the contrary. For it is most important to observe, that the reasoners on both sides commence by taking something for granted, our assent to which they ask or demand: that is, both set off with an assumption in the form of a postulate. But the Epicurean assumes what according to himself he neither is nor can be under any obligation to assume, and demands what he can have no right to demand: for he denies the reality of all moral obligation, the existence of any right. If he use the words, right and obligation, he does it deceptively, and means only power and compulsion. To overthrow the faith in aught higher or other than nature and physical necessity, is the very purpose of his argument. He desires you only to take for granted, that all reality is included in nature, and he may then safely defy you to ward off his conclusion—that nothing is excluded!

But as he can not morally demand, neither can he rationally expect, your assent to this premiss: for he can not be ignorant, that the best and greatest of men have devoted their lives to the enforcement of the contrary; that the vast majority of the human race in all ages and in all nations have believed in the contrary; and that there is not a language on earth, in which he could argue, for ten minutes, in support of his scheme, without sliding into words and phrases that imply the contrary. It has been said, that the Arabic has a thousand names for a lion; but this would be a trifle compared with the number of superfluous words and useless synonymes that would be found in an *index expurgatorius* of any European dictionary, constructed on the principles of a consistent and strictly consequential Materialism.

criminal as one of its objects. Such punishments, like those inflicted on suicides, must be regarded as posthumous: the wilful extinction of the moral and personal life being, for the purposes of punitive justice, equivalent to a wilful destruction of the natural life. If the speech of Judge Burnet to the horse-stealer,—(You are not hanged for stealing a horse; but, that horses may not be stolen)—can be vindicated to all, it must be on this principle; and not on the all-unsettling scheme of expedience, which is the anarchy of morals.

The Christian likewise grounds his philosophy on assertions; but with the best of all reasons for making them—namely, that he ought so to do. He asserts what he can neither prove, nor account for, nor himself comprehend; but with the strongest inducements, that of understanding thereby whatever else it most concerns him to understand aright. And yet his assertions have nothing in them of theory or hypothesis; but are in immediate reference to three ultimate facts; namely, the reality of the law of CONSCIENCE; the existence of a responsible WILL, as the subject of that law; and lastly, the existence of EVIL—of evil essentially such, not by accident of outward circumstances, not derived from its physical consequences, nor from any cause out of itself. The first is a fact of consciousness; the second a fact of reason necessarily concluded from the first; and the third a fact of history interpreted by both.

Omnia exeunt in mysterium, says a Schoolman; that is, There is nothing, the absolute ground of which is not a mystery. The contrary were indeed a contradiction in terms: for how can that, which is to explain all things, be susceptible of an explanation? It would be to suppose the same thing first and second at the same time.

If I rested here, I should merely have placed my creed in direct opposition to that of the Necessitarians, who assume—(for observe, both parties begin in an assumption and can not do otherwise)—that motives act on the will, as bodies act on bodies; and that whether mind and matter are essentially the same, or essentially different, they are both alike under one and the same law of compulsory causation. But this is far from exhausting my intention. I mean at the same time to oppose the disciples of Shaftesbury and those who, substituting one faith for another, have been well called the pious Deists of the last century, in order to distinguish them from the infidels of the present age, who persuade themselves—(for the thing itself is not possible)—that they reject all faith. I declare my dissent from these too, because they imposed upon themselves an idea for a fact: a most sublime idea indeed, and so necessary to human nature, that without it no virtue is conceivable; but still an idea. In contradiction to their splendid but delusory tenets, I profess a deep conviction that man was and is a fallen creature, not by accidents of bodily constitution or any other cause, which human wisdom in a course of ages might be supposed capable of removing; but as diseased in his will, in that will which is the true and only strict synonyme of the word, I, or the intelligent Self. Thus at each of these two opposite roads (the philosophy of Hobbes and that of Shaftesbury), I have placed a directing post, informing my fellow-travellers, that on neither of these roads can they see the truths to which I would direct their attention.

But the place of starting was at the meeting of four roads, and one only was the right road. I proceed therefore to preclude the opinion of those likewise, who indeed agree with me as to the moral responsibility of man in opposition to Hobbes and the anti-moralists, and that he is a fallen creature, essentially diseased, in opposition to Shaftesbury and the misinterpreters of Plato; but who differ from me in exaggerating the diseased weakness of the will into an absolute privation of all freedom, thereby making moral responsibility, not a mystery above comprehension, but a direct contradiction, of which we do distinctly comprehend the absurdity. Among the consequences of this doctrine, is that direful one of swallowing up all the attributes of the Supreme Being in the one attribute of infinite power, and thence deducing that things are good and wise because they were created, and not created through wisdom and goodness. Thence too the awful attribute of justice is explained away into a mere right of absolute property; the sacred distinction between things and persons is erased; and the selection of persons for virtue and vice in this life, and for eternal happiness or misery in the next, is represented as the result of a mere will, acting in the blindness and solitude of its own infinity. The title of a work written by the great and pious Boyle is, "Of the awe which the human mind owes to the Supreme Reason." This, in the language of these gloomy doctors, must be translated into—"The horror, which a being capable of eternal pleasure or pain is compelled to feel at the idea of an Infinite Power, about to inflict the latter on an immense majority of human souls, without any power on their part either to prevent it or the actions which are (not indeed its causes but) its assigned signals, and preceding links of the same iron chain!"

Against these tenets I maintain, that a will conceived separately from intelligence is a nonentity, and a mere phantasm of abstraction; and that a will, the state of which does in no sense originate in its own act, is an absolute contradiction. It might be an instinct, an impulse, a plastic power, and, if accompanied with consciousness, a desire; but a will it could not be. And this every human being knows with equal clearness, though different minds may reflect on it with different degrees of distinctness; for who would not smile at the notion of a rose willing to put forth its buds and expand them into flowers? That such a phrase would be deemed a poetic license proves the difference in the things: for all metaphors are grounded on an apparent likeness of things essentially different. I utterly disclaim the notion, that any human intelligence, with whatever power it might manifest itself, is alone adequate to the office of restoring health to the will: but at the same time I deem it impious and absurd to hold that the Creator would have given us the faculty of reason, or that the Redeemer would in so many varied forms of argument and persuasion have appealed to it, if it had been either totally useless or wholly impotent. Lastly, I find all these several truths reconciled and united in the belief, that the imperfect human understanding can be effectually exerted only in subordination to, and in a dependent alliance with, the means and aidances supplied by the All-perfect and Supreme Reason; but that under these conditions it is not only an admissible, but a necessary instrument of bettering both ourselves and others.

We may now proceed to our reflections on the Spirit of Religion. The first three or four Aphorisms I have selected from the theological works of Dr. Henry More, a contemporary of Archbishop Leighton, and, like him, held in suspicion by the Calvinists of that time as a Latitudinarian and Platonizing divine, and who probably, like him, would have been arraigned as a Calvinist by the Latitudinarians (I can not say, Platonists) of this day, had the suspicion been equally groundless. One or two I have ventured to add from my own reflections. The purpose, however, is the same in all—that of declaring, in the first place, what spiritual religion is not, what is not a religious spirit, and what are not to be deemed influences of the Spirit. If after these disclaimers I shall without proof be charged by any with renewing or favoring the errors of the Familists, Vanists, Seekers, Behmenists, or by whatever other names Church history records the poor bewildered enthusiasts, who in the swarming time of our Republic, turned the facts of the Gospel into allegories, and superseded the written ordinances of Christ by a pretended teaching and sensible presence of the Spirit, I appeal against them to their own consciences as wilful slanderers. But if with proof, I have in these Aphorisms signed and sealed my own condemnation.

"These things I could not forbear to write. For the light within me, that is, my reason and conscience, does assure me, that the ancient and Apostolic faith, according to the historical meaning thereof, and in the literal sense of the Creed, is solid and true: and that Familism* in its fairest form and under whatever disguise, is a smooth tale to seduce the simple from their allegiance to Christ."

HENRY MORE.†

* The Family of Love, a sect founded by Henry Nicholas in Holland in 1555.—*Ed.*

† Myst. of Godliness, vi.—*Ed.*

APHORISMS ON SPIRITUAL RELIGION.

And here it will not be impertinent to observe, that what the eldest Greek philosophy entitled the Reason (ΝΟΥΣ) and ideas, the philosophic Apostle names *the Spirit* and *truths spiritually* discerned: while to those who, in the pride of learning or in the overweening meanness of modern metaphysics, decry the doctrine of the Spirit in man and its possible communion with the Holy Spirit as vulgar enthusiasm, I submit the following sentences from a Pagan philosopher, a nobleman and a minister of state—"*Ita dico, Lucili, sacer intra nos Spiritus sedet, malorum bonorumque nostrorum observator et custos. Hic prout a nobis tractatus est, ita nos ipse tractat. Bonus vir sine Deo nemo est.*" SENECA. Epist. xli.

APHORISM I.

H. More.

EVERY one is *to give a reason of his faith;* but priests and ministers more punctually than any, their province being to make good every sentence of the Bible to a rational inquirer into the truth of these oracles. Enthusiasts find it an easy thing to heat the fancies of unlearned and unreflecting hearers; but when a sober man would be satisfied of the grounds from whence they speak, he shall not have one syllable or the least tittle of a pertinent answer. Only they will talk big of the Spirit, and inveigh against reason with bitter reproaches, calling it carnal or fleshly, though it be indeed no soft flesh, but enduring and penetrant steel, even the sword of the Spirit, and such as pierces to the heart.

APHORISM II

H. More.

There are two very bad things in this resolving of men's faith and practice into the immediate suggestion of a Spirit not acting on our understandings, or rather into the illumination of such a Spirit as they can give no account of, such as does not enlighten their reason or enable them to render their doctrine intelligible to others. First, it defaces and makes useless that part of the image of God in us, which we call reason: and secondly, it takes away that advantage, which raises Christianity above all other religions, that she dares appeal to so solid a faculty.

APHORISM III.

It is the glory of the Gospel charter and the Christian constitution, that its author and head is the Spirit of truth, essential Reason as well as absolute and incomprehensible Will. Like a just monarch, he refers even his own causes to the judgment of his high courts.—He has his King's Bench in the reason, his Court of Equity in the conscience; that the representative of his majesty and universal justice, this the nearest to the king's heart, and the dispenser of his particular decrees. He has likewise his Court of Common Pleas in the understanding, his Court of Exchequer in the prudence. The laws are his laws. And though by signs and miracles he has mercifully condescended to interline here and there with his own hand the great statute-book, which he had dictated to his *amanuensis*, Nature; yet has he been graciously pleased to forbid our receiving as the king's mandates aught that is not stamped with the Great Seal of the Conscience, and countersigned by the Reason.

APHORISM IV.

ON AN UNLEARNED MINISTRY, UNDER PRETENCE OF A CALL OF THE SPIRIT, AND INWARD GRACES SUPERSEDING OUTWARD HELPS.

H. More.

Tell me, ye high-flown perfectionists, ye boasters of the light within you, could the highest perfection of your inward light ever show to you the history of past ages, the state of the world at present, the knowledge of arts and tongues, without books or teachers? How then can you understand the providence of God, or the age, the purpose, the fulfilment of prophecies, or distinguish such as have been fulfilled from those to the fulfilment of which we are to look forward? How can you judge concerning the authenticity and uncorruptedness of the Gospels, and the other sacred Scriptures? And how, without this knowledge, can you support the truth of Christianity? How can you either have, or give a reason for, the faith which you profess? This light within, that loves darkness, and would exclude those excellent gifts of God to mankind, knowledge and understanding, what is it but a sullen self-sufficiency within you, engendering contempt of superiors, pride and a spirit of division, and inducing you to reject for yourselves, and to undervalue in others, the helps without, which the grace of God has provided and appointed for his Church—nay, to make them grounds or pretexts of your dislike or suspicion of Christ's ministers who have fruitfully availed themselves of the helps afforded them?

APHORISM V.

H. More.

There are wanderers, whom neither pride nor a perverse humor have led astray; and whose condition is such, that I think few more worthy of a man's best directions. For the more imperious sects having put such unhandsome vizards on Christianity, and the *sincere milk of the word* having been everywhere so sophisticated by the humors and inventions of men, it has driven these anxious melancholists to seek for a teacher that can not deceive, the voice of the eternal Word within them; to which if they be faithful, they assure themselves it will be faithful to them in return. Nor would this be a groundless presumption, if they had sought this voice in the reason and the conscience, with the Scripture articulating the same, instead of giving heed to their fancy and mistaking bodily disturbances, and the vapors resulting therefrom, for inspiration and the teaching of the Spirit.

APHORISM VI.

Hacket.

When every man is his own end, all things will come to a bad end. Blessed were those days, when every man thought himself rich and fortunate by the good success of the public wealth and glory. We want public souls, we want them. I speak it with compassion: there is no sin and abuse in the world that affects my thought so much. Every man thinks, that he is a whole commonwealth in his private family. *Omnes quæ sua sunt quærunt.* All seek their own.

COMMENT.

Selfishness is common to all ages and countries. In all ages self-seeking is the rule, and self-sacrifice the exception. But if to seek our private advantage in harmony with, and by the furtherance of, the public prosperity, and to derive a portion of our happiness from sympathy with the prosperity of our fellow-men—if this be public spirit, it would be morose and querulous to pretend that there is any want of it in this country and at the present time. On the contrary, the number of "public souls" and the general readiness to contribute to the public good, in science and in religion, in patriotism and in philanthropy, stand prominent* among the characteristics of this and the preceding generation. The habit of referring actions and opinions to fixed laws; convictions rooted in principles; thought, insight, system;—these, had the good Bishop lived in our times, would have been his *desiderata*, and the theme of his complaints. "We want *thinking* souls, we want them."

This and the three preceding extracts will suffice as precautionary Aphorisms. And here, again, the Reader may exemplify the great advantages to be obtained from the habit of tracing the proper meaning and history of words. We need only recollect the common and idiomatic phrases in which the word "spirit" occurs in a physical or material sense (as, fruit has lost its *spirit* and flavor), to be convinced that its property is to improve, enliven, actuate some other thing, not constitute a thing in its own name.

* The very marked, positive as well as comparative, magnitude and prominence of the bump, entitled BENEVOLENCE (see Spurzheim's map of the human skull) on the head of the late Mr. John Thurtel, has wofully unsettled the faith of many ardent phrenologists, and strengthened the previous doubts of a still greater number into utter disbelief. On my mind this fact (for a fact it is) produced the directly contrary effect; and inclined me to suspect, for the first time, that there may be some truth in the Spurzheimian scheme. Whether future craniologists may not see cause to new-name this and one or two other of these convex gnomons, is quite a different question. At present, and according to the present use of words, any such change would be premature: and we must be content to say, that Mr. Thurtel's benevolence was insufficiently modified by the unprotrusive and unindicated convolutes of the brain, that secrete honesty and common sense. The organ of destructiveness was indirectly potentiated by the absence or imperfect development of the glands of reason and conscience, in this "*unfortunate gentleman!*"

The enthusiast may find one exception to this where the material itself is called spirit. And when he calls to mind, how this spirit acts when taken alone by the unhappy persons who in their first exultation will boast that it is meat, drink, fire, and clothing to them, all in one—when he reflects, that its properties are to inflame, intoxicate, madden, with exhaustion, lethargy, and atrophy for the sequels;—well for him, if in some lucid interval he should fairly put the question to his own mind, how far this is analogous to his own case, and whether the exception does not confirm the rule. The letter without the spirit killeth; but does it follow, that the spirit is to kill the letter? To kill that which it is its appropriate office to enliven?

However, where the ministry is not invaded, and the plain sense of the Scriptures is left undisturbed, and the believer looks for the suggestions of the Spirit only or chiefly in applying particular passages to his own individual case and exigencies; though in this there may be much weakness, some delusion and imminent danger of more, I can not but join with Henry More in avowing, that I feel knit to such a man in the bonds of a common faith far more closely, than to those who receive neither the letter nor the Spirit, turning the one into metaphor and oriental hyperbole, in order to explain away the other into the influence of motives suggested by their own understandings, and realized by their own strength.

APHORISMS

ON THAT WHICH IS INDEED SPIRITUAL RELIGION.

In the selection of the extracts that form the remainder of this Volume, and of the comments affixed, I had the following objects principally in view:—first, to exhibit the true and Scriptural meaning and intent of several articles of faith, that are rightly classed among the mysteries and peculiar doctrines of Christianity: —secondly, to show the perfect rationality of these doctrines, and their freedom from all just objection when examined by their proper organ, the reason and conscience of man:—lastly, to exhibit from the works of Leighton, who perhaps of all our learned Protestant theologians best deserves the title of a spiritual divine, as instructive and affecting picture of the contemplations, reflections, conflicts, consolations, and monitory experiences of a philosophic and richly-gifted mind, amply stored with all the knowledge that books and long intercourse with men of the most discordant characters could give, under the convictions, impressions, and habits of a spiritual religion.

To obviate a possible disappointment in any of my Readers, who may chance to be engaged in theological studies, it may be well to notice, that in vindicating the peculiar tenets of our Faith, I have not entered on the doctrine of the Trinity, or the still profounder mystery of the origin of moral Evil—and this for the reasons following. 1. These doctrines are not, in strictness, subjects of reflection, in the proper sense of this word: and both of them demand a power and persistency of abstraction, and a previous discipline in the highest forms of human thought, which it would be unwise, if not presumptuous, to expect from any, who require aids to reflection, or would be likely to seek them in the present

Work. 2. In my intercourse with men of various ranks and ages, I have found the far larger number of serious and inquiring persons little, if at all, disquieted by doubts respecting articles of faith simply above their comprehension. It is only where the belief required of them jars with their moral feelings; where a doctrine, in the sense in which they have been taught to receive it, appears to contradict their clear notions of right and wrong, or to be at variance with the divine attributes of goodness and justice, that these men are surprised, perplexed, and alas! not seldom offended and alienated. Such are the doctrines of arbitrary election and reprobation; the sentence to everlasting torment by an eternal and necessitating decree; vicarious atonement, and the necessity of the abasement, agony and ignominious death of a most holy and meritorious person, to appease the wrath of God. Now it is more especially for such persons, unwilling skeptics, who, believing earnestly, ask help for their unbelief, that this Volume was compiled, and the Comments written: and therefore, to the Scripture doctrines intended by the above-mentioned, my principal attention has been directed.

APHORISM I.

Leighton.

Where, if not in Christ, is the power that can persuade a sinner to return, that can *bring home a heart to God?*

Common mercies of God, though they have a leading faculty to repentance (*Rom.* ii. 4), yet the rebellious heart will not be led by them. The judgments of God, public or personal, though they ought to drive us to God, yet the heart, unchanged, runs the further from God. Do we not see it by ourselves and other sinners about us? They look not at all towards Him who smites, much less do they return; or if any more serious thoughts of returning arise upon the surprise of an affliction, how soon vanish they, either the stroke abating, or the heart, by time, growing hard and senseless under it! Leave Christ out, I say, and all other means work not this way; neither the works nor the word of God sounding daily in his ear, *Return, return.* Let the noise of the rod speak it too, and both join together to make the cry the louder, *yet the wicked will do wickedly.* Dan. xii. 10.

COMMENT.

By the phrase "in Christ," I understand all the supernatural aids vouchsafed and conditionally promised in the Christian dispensation: and among them the spirit of truth, which the world can not receive, were it only that the knowledge of spiritual truth is of necessity immediate and intuitive; and the world or natural man possesses no higher intuitions than those of the pure sense, which are the subjects of mathematical science. But aids, observe:—therefore, not by the will of man alone; but neither without the will. The doctrine of modern Calvinism, as laid down by Jonathan Edwards and the late Dr. Williams, which represents a will absolutely passive, clay in the hands of a potter, destroys all will, takes away its essence and definition, as effectually as in saying—This circle is square—I should deny the figure to be a circle at all. It was in strict consistency, therefore, that these writers supported the Necessitarian scheme, and made the relation of cause and effect the law of the universe, subjecting to its mechanism the moral world no less than the material or physical. It follows that all is nature. Thus, though few writers use the term Spirit more frequently, they in effect deny its existence, and evacuate the term of all its proper meaning. With such a system not the wit of man nor all the theodices ever framed by human ingenuity, before and since the attempt of the celebrated Leibnitz, can reconcile the sense of responsibility, nor the fact of the difference in kind between regret and remorse. The same compulsion of consequence drove the fathers of modern (or pseudo) Calvinism to the origination of holiness in power, of justice in right of property, and whatever other outrages on the common sense and moral feelings of mankind they have sought to cover under the fair name of Sovereign Grace.

I will not take on me to defend sundry harsh and inconvenient expressions in the works of Calvin. Phrases equally strong, and assertions not less rash and startling, are no rarities in the writings of Luther: for *catachresis* was the favorite figure of speech in that age. But let not the opinions of either on this most fundamental subject be confounded with the New-England system, now entitled Calvinistic. The fact is simply this. Luther considered the pretensions to free-will boastful, and better suited to the "budge doctors of the Stoic Fur," than to the preachers of the Gospel, whose great theme is the redemption of the will from slavery; the restoration of the will to perfect freedom being the end and consummation of the redemptive process, and the same with the entrance of the soul into glory, that is, its union with Christ: "*glory*" (John xvii. 5) being one of the names or tokens or symbols of the spiritual Messiah. Prospectively to this we are to understand the words of our Lord, *At that day ye shall know that I am in my Father, and ye in me* (John xiv. 20): the freedom of a finite will being possible under this condition only, that it has become one with the will of God. Now as the difference of a captive and enslaved will, and no will at all, such is the difference between the Lutheranism of Calvin and the Calvinism of Jonathan Edwards.

APHORISM II.

Leighton.

There is nothing in religion farther out of nature's reach, and more remote from the natural man's liking and believing, than the doctrine of redemption by a Saviour, and by a crucified Saviour. It is comparatively easy to persuade men of the necessity of an amendment of conduct; it is more difficult to make them see the necessity of repentance in the Gospel sense, the necessity of a change in the principle of action; but to convince men of the necessity of the death of Christ is the most difficult of all. And yet the first is but varnish and whitewash without the second; and the second but a barren notion without the last. Alas! of those who admit the doctrine in words, how large a number evade it in fact, and empty it of all its substance and efficacy, making the effect the efficient cause, or attributing their election to salvation to supposed foresight of their faith and obedience. But it is most vain to imagine a faith in such and such men, which, being foreseen by God, determined him to elect them for salvation: were it only that nothing at all is future, or can have this imagined futurition, but as it is decreed, and because it is decreed, by God so to be.

COMMENT.

No impartial person, competently acquainted with the history of the Reformation, and the works of the earlier Protestant divines at home and abroad, even to the close of Elizabeth's reign, will deny that the doctrines of Calvin on redemption and the natural state of fallen man, are in all essential points the same as those of Luther, Zuinglius, and the first Reformers collectively. These doctrines have, however, since the re-establishment of the Episcopal Church at the return of Charles II., been as generally* exchanged for what is commonly entitled Arminianism, but which, taken as a complete and explicit scheme of belief, it would be both historically and theologically more accurate to call Grotianism, or Christianity according to Grotius. The change was not, we may readily believe, effected without a struggle. In the Romish Church this latitudinarian system, patronized by the Jesuits, was manfully resisted by Jansenius, Arnauld, and Pascal; in our own Church by the Bishops Davenant, Sanderson, Hall, and the Archbishops Ussher and Leighton: and in the latter half of the preceding Aphorism the Reader has a specimen of the reasonings by which Leighton strove to invalidate or counterpoise the reasonings of the innovators.

* At a period in which Bishop Marsh and Dr. Wordsworth have, by the zealous on one side, been charged with Popish principles on account of their anti-bibliolatry, and, on the other, the sturdy adherents of the doctrines common to Luther and Calvin, and the literal interpreters of the Articles and Homilies, are—(I wish I could say, altogether without any fault of their own)—regarded by the Clergy generally as virtual schismatics, dividers of, though not from, the Church,—it is serving the cause of charity to assist in circulating the following instructive passage from the Life of Bishop Hacket, respecting the disputes between the Augustinians, or Luthero-Calvinistic divines, and the Grotians of his age: in which controversy (says his biographer) he, Hacket, "was ever very moderate."

"But having been bred under Bishop Davenant and Dr. Ward in Cambridge, he was addicted to their sentiments. Archbishop Ussher would say, that Davenant understood those controversies better than ever any man did since St. Augustine. But he (Bishop Hacket) used to say, that he was sure he had three excellent men of his opinion in this controversy; 1. Padre Paolo (Father Paul) whose letter is extant in Heinsius, *anno* 1604. 2. Thomas Aquinas. 3. St. Augustine. But besides and above them all, he believed in his conscience that St. Paul was of the same mind likewise. Yet at the same time he would profess that he disliked no Arminians but such as revile and defame every one who is not so: and he would often commend Arminius himself for his excellent wit and parts, but only tax his want of reading and knowledge in antiquity. And he ever held, it was the foolishest thing in the world to say the Arminians were Popishly inclined, when so many Dominicans and Jansenists were rigid followers of Augustine

Passages of this sort are, however, of rare occurrence in Leighton's works. Happily for thousands, he was more usefully employed in making his readers feel that the doctrines in question, Scripturally treated and taken as co-organized parts of a great organic whole, need no such reasonings. And better still would it have been, had he left them altogether for those, who, severally detaching the great features of Revelation from the living context of Scripture, do by that very act destroy their life and purpose. And then, like the eyes of the Indian spider,* they become clouded microscopes, to exaggerate and distort all the other parts and proportions. No offence then will be occasioned, I trust, by the frank avowal that I have given to the preceding passage a place among the spiritual Aphorisms for the sake of comment: the following remarks having been the first marginal note I had pencilled on Leighton's pages, and thus (remotely, at least), the occasion of the present Work.

Leighton, I observed, throughout his inestimable Work, avoids all metaphysical views of Election, relatively to God, and confines himself to the doctrine in its relation to man; and in that sense too, in which every Christian may judge of it who strives to be sincere with his own heart. The following may, I think, be taken as a safe and useful rule in religious inquiries. Ideas, that derive their origin and substance from the moral being, and to the reception of which as true objectively (that is, as corresponding to a reality out of the human mind) we are determined by a practical interest exclusively, may not, like theoretical positions, be pressed onward into all their logical consequences.†

in these points: and no less foolish to say that the Anti-Arminians were Puritans and Presbyterians, when Ward, and Davenant, and Prideaux, and Browning, those stout champions for Episcopacy, were decided Anti-Arminians: while Arminius himself was ever a Presbyterian. Therefore he greatly commended the moderation of our Church, which extended equal communion to both."

* *Aranea prodigiosa.* See Baker's Microscopic Experiments.

† Perhaps this rule may be expressed more intelligibly (to a mathematician at least) thus:—Reasoning from finite to finite on a basis of truth; also, reasoning from infinite to infinite on a basis of truth,—will always lead to truth as intelligibly as the basis on which such truths respectively rest. While reasoning from finite to infinite, or from infinite to finite, will lead to apparent absurdity although the basis be true: and is not such apparent absurdity, another expression for "truth unintelligible by a finite mind?"

The law of conscience, and not the canons of discursive reasoning, must decide in such cases. At least, the latter have no validity, which the single *veto* of the former is not sufficient to nullify. The most pious conclusion is here the most legitimate.

It is too seldom considered, though most worthy of consideration, how far even those ideas or theories of pure speculation, that bear the same name with the objects of religious faith, are indeed the same. Out of the principles necessarily presumed in all discursive thinking, and which being, in the first place, universal, and secondly, antecedent to every particular exercise of the understanding, are therefore referred to the reason, the human mind (wherever its powers are sufficiently developed, and its attention strongly directed to speculative or theoretical inquiries) forms certain essences, to which for its own purposes it gives a sort of notional subsistence. Hence they are called *entia rationalia:* the conversion of which into *entia realia,* or real objects, by aid of the imagination, has in all times been the fruitful stock of empty theories and mischievous superstitions, of surreptitious premisses and extravagant conclusions. For as these substantiated notions were in many instances expressed by the same terms as the objects of religious faith; as in most instances they were applied, though deceptively, to the explanation of real experiences; and lastly, from the gratifications which the pride and ambition of man received from the supposed extension of his knowledge and insight; it was too easily forgotten or overlooked, that the stablest and most indispensable of these notional beings were but the necessary forms of thinking, taken abstractedly: and that like the breadthless lines, depthless surfaces, and perfect circles of geometry, they subsist wholly and solely in and for the mind that contemplates them. Where the evidence of the senses fails us, and beyond the precincts of sensible experience, there is no reality attributable to any notion, but what is given to it by Revelation, or the law of conscience, or the necessary interests of morality.

Take an instance:

It is the office, and as it were, the instinct of reason, to bring a unity into all our conceptions and several knowledges. On this all system depends; and without this we could reflect connectedly neither on nature nor our own minds. Now this is possible only on the assumption or hypothesis of a One as the ground and cause of the universe, and which, in all succession and through all changes, is the subject neither of time nor change. The One must be contemplated as eternal and immutable.

Well! the idea, which is the basis of religion, commanded by the conscience and required by morality, contains the same truths, or at least truths that can be expressed in no other terms; but this idea presents itself to our mind with additional attributes, and those too not formed by mere abstraction and negation—with the attributes of holiness, providence, love, justice, and mercy. It comprehends, moreover, the independent (extra-mundane) existence and personality of the Supreme One, as our Creator, Lord, and Judge.

The hypothesis of a one ground and principle of the universe (necessary as an hypothesis, but having only a logical and conditional necessity), is thus raised into the idea of the Living God, the supreme object of our faith, love, fear, and adoration. Religion and morality do indeed constrain us to declare him eternal and immutable. But if from the eternity of the Supreme Being a reasoner should deduce the impossibility of a creation; or conclude with Aristotle, that the creation was co-eternal; or, like the later Platonists, should turn creation into emanation, and make the universe proceed from the Deity, as the sunbeams from the solar orb;—or if from the divine immutability he should infer that all prayer and supplication must be vain and superstitious; then however evident and logically necessary such conclusions may appear, it is scarcely worth our while to examine, whether they are so or not. The positions must be false. For were they true, the idea would lose the sole ground of its reality. It would be no longer the idea intended by the believer in his premiss—in the premiss, with which alone religion and morality are concerned. The very subject of the discussion would be changed. It would no longer be the God, in whom we believe; but a stoical Fate, or the superessential One of Plotinus, to whom neither intelligence, nor self-consciousness, nor life, nor even being can be attributed; or lastly, the World itself, the indivisible one and only substance (*substantia una et unica*) of Spinoza, of which all *phænomena*, all particular and individual things, lives, minds, thoughts, and actions are but modifications.

Let the believer never be alarmed by objections wholly speculative, however plausible on speculative grounds such objections may appear, if he can but satisfy himself, that the result is repugnant to the dictates of conscience, and irreconcilable with the interests of morality. For to baffle the objector we have only to demand of him, by what right and under what authority he converts a thought into a substance, or asserts the existence of a real somewhat corresponding to a notion not derived from the experience of his senses. It will be to no purpose for him to answer that it is a legitimate notion. The notion may have its mould in the understanding; but its realization must be the work of the fancy.

A reflecting reader will easily apply these remarks to the subject of Election, one of the stumbling stones in the ordinary conceptions of the Christian Faith, to which the Infidel points in scorn, and which far better men pass by in silent perplexity. Yet, surely, from mistaken conceptions of the doctrine. I suppose the person, with whom I am arguing, already so far a believer, as to have convinced himself, both that a state of enduring bliss is attainable under certain conditions; and that these conditions consist in his compliance with the directions given and rules prescribed in the Christian Scriptures. These rules he likewise admits to be such, that, by the very law and constitution of the human mind, a full and faithful compliance with them can not but have consequences of some sort or other. But these consequences are moreover distinctly described, enumerated, and promised in the same Scriptures, in which the conditions are recorded; and though some of them may be apparent to God only, yet the greater number of them are of such a nature that they can not exist unknown to the individual, in and for whom they exist. As little possible is it, that he should find these consequences in himself, and not find in them the sure marks and the safe pledges that he is at the time in the right road to the life promised under these conditions. Now I dare assert that no such man, however fervent his charity and however deep his humility may be, can peruse the records of history with a reflecting spirit, or look round the world with an observant eye, and not find himself compelled to admit, that *all* men are *not* on the right road. He can not help judging that even in Christian countries many,—a fearful many,—have not their faces turned toward it.

This then is a mere matter of fact. Now comes the question. Shall the believer, who thus hopes on the appointed grounds of hope, attribute this distinction exclusively to his own resolves and strivings,—or if not exclusively, yet primarily and principally? Shall he refer the first movements and preparations to his own will and understanding, and bottom his claim to the promises on his own comparative excellence? If not, if no man dare take this honor to himself, to whom shall he assign it, if not to that Being in whom the promise originated, and on whom its fulfilment depends? If he stop here, who shall blame him? By what argument shall his reasoning be invalidated, that might not be urged with equal force against any essential difference between obedient and disobedient, Christian and worldling;—that would not imply that both sorts alike are, in the sight of God, the sons of God by adoption? If he stop here, I say, who shall drive him from his position? For thus far he is practically concerned;—this the conscience requires; this the highest interests of morality demand. It is a question of facts, of the will and the deed, to argue against which on the abstract notions and possibilities of the speculative reason, is as unreasonable, as an attempt to decide a question of colors by pure geometry, or to unsettle the classes and specific characters of natural history by the doctrine of fluxions.

But if the self-examinant will abandon this position, and exchange the safe circle of religion and practical reason for the shifting sand-wastes and *mirages* of speculative theology; if instead of seeking after the marks of Election in himself, he undertakes to determine the ground and origin, the possibility and mode of Election itself in relation to God;—in this case, and whether he does it for the satisfaction of curiosity, or from the ambition of answering those, who would call God himself to account, why and by what right certain souls were born in Africa instead of England; or why—(seeing that it is against all reason and goodness to choose a worse, when, being omnipotent, He could have created a better)—God did not create beasts men, and men angels;—or why God created any men but with foreknowledge of their obedience, and left any occasion for Election;—In this case, I say, we can only regret that the inquirer had not been better instructed in the nature, the bounds, the true purposes and proper objects of his intellectual faculties, and that he had not previously asked himself, by what appropriate sense, or organ of knowledge, he hoped to secure an insight into a nature which was neither an object of his senses, nor a part of his self-consciousness; and so leave him to ward off shadowy spears with the shadow of a shield, and to retaliate the nonsense of blasphemy with the *abracadabra* of presumption. He that will fly without wings must fly in his dreams: and till he awakes, will not find out that to fly in a dream is but to dream of flying.

Thus then the doctrine of Election is in itself a necessary inference from an undeniable fact—necessary at least for all who hold that the best of men are what they are through the grace of God. In relation to the believer it is a hope, which if it spring out of Christian principles, be examined by the tests and nourished by the means prescribed in Scripture, will become a lively and an assured hope, but which can not in this life pass into knowledge, much less certainty of fore-knowledge. The contrary belief does indeed make the article of Election both tool and parcel of a mad and mischievous fanaticism. But with what force and clearness does not the Apostle confute, disclaim, and prohibit the pretence, treating it as a downright contradiction in terms! See *Rom.* viii. 24.

But though I hold the doctrine handled as Leighton handles it (that is practically, morally, humanly) rational, safe, and of essential importance, I see reasons* resulting from the peculiar circumstances, under which St. Paul preached and wrote, why a discreet minister of the Gospel should avoid the frequent use of the term, and express the meaning in other words perfectly equivalent and equally Scriptural; lest in saying truth he may convey error.

Had my purpose been confined to one particular tenet, an apol-

* For example: at the date of St. Paul's Epistles, the Roman world may be resembled to a mass in the furnace in the first moment of fusion, here a speck and there a spot of melted metal shining pure and brilliant amid the scum and dross. To have received the name of Christian was a privilege, a high and distinguishing favor. No wonder therefore, that in St. Paul's writings the words, Elect and Election often, nay, most often, mean the same as ἐκκαλούμενοι, *ecclesia*, that is, those who have been *called out* of the world: and it is a dangerous perversion of the Apostle's word to interpret it in the sense, in which it was used by our Lord, viz. in opposition to the called. (*Many are called but few chosen.*) In St. Paul's sense and at that time the believers collectively formed a small and select number; and every Christian, real or nominal, was one of the elect. Add too, that this ambiguity is increased by the accidental circumstance, that the *Kyriak, ædes Dominicæ*, Lord's House, *kirk;* and *ecclesia*, the sum total of the ἐκκαλούμενοι, *evocati*, *called out;* are both rendered by the same word, Church.

ogy might be required for so long a comment. But the Reader will, I trust, have already perceived, that my object has been to establish a general rule of interpretation and vindication applicable to all doctrinal tenets, and especially to the (so called) mysteries of the Christian Faith : to provide a safety-lamp for religious inquirers. Now this I find in the principle, that all revealed truths are to be judged of by us, so far only as they are possible subjects of human conception, or grounds of practice, or in some way connected with our moral and spiritual interests. In order to have a reason for forming a judgment on any given article, we must be sure that we possess a reason, by and according to which a judgment may be formed. Now in respect of all truths, to which a real independent existence is assigned, and which yet are not contained in, or to be imagined under, any form of space or time, it is strictly demonstrable, that the human reason, considered abstractly, as the source of positive science and theoretical insight, is not such a reason. At the utmost, it has only a negative voice. In other words, nothing can be allowed as true for the human mind, which directly contradicts this reason. But even here, before we admit the existence of any such contradiction, we must be careful to ascertain, that there is no equivocation in play, that two different subjects are not confounded under one and the same word. A striking instance of this has been adduced in the difference between the notional One of the Ontologists, and the idea of the living God.

But if not the abstract or speculative reason, and yet a reason there must be in order to a rational belief—then it must be the practical reason of man, comprehending the will, the conscience, the moral being with its inseparable interests and affections—that reason, namely, which is the organ of wisdom, and, as far as man is concerned, the source of living and actual truths.

From these premisses we may further deduce, that every doctrine is to be interpreted in reference to those, to whom it has been revealed, or who have or have had the means of knowing or hearing the same. For instance: the doctrine that *there is no name under heaven, by which a man can be saved, but the name of Jesus.* If the word here rendered *name*, may be understood—(as it well may, and as in other texts it must be)—as meaning the power, or originating cause, I see no objection on the part of the practical reason to our belief of the declaration in its whole extent. It is true universally or not true at all. If there be any redemptive power not contained in the power of Jesus, then Jesus is not the Redeemer: not the Redeemer of the world, not the Jesus, that is, Saviour of mankind. But if with Tertullian and Augustine we make the text assert the condemnation and misery of all who are not Christians by Baptism and explicit belief in the revelation of the New Covenant—then, I say, the doctrine is true to all intents and purposes. It is true, in every respect, in which any practical, moral, or spiritual interest or end can be connected with its truth. It is true in respect to every man who has had, or who might have had, the Gospel preached to him. It is true and obligatory for every Christian community and for every individual believer, wherever the opportunity is afforded of spreading the light of the Gospel, and making known the name of the only Saviour and Redeemer. For even though the uninformed Heathens should not perish, the guilt of their perishing will attach to those who not only had no certainty of their safety, but who are commanded to act on the supposition of the contrary. But if, on the other hand, a theological dogmatist should attempt to persuade me that this text was intended to give us an historical knowledge of God's future actions and dealings—and for the gratification of our curiosity to inform us, that Socrates and Phocion, together with all the savages in the woods and wilds of Africa and America, will be sent to keep company with the Devil and his angels in everlasting torments—I should remind him, that the purpose of Scripture was to teach us our duty, not to enable us to sit in judgment on the souls of our fellow-creatures.

One other instance will, I trust, prevent all misconception of my meaning. I am clearly convinced, that the Scriptural and only true* idea of God will, in its development, be found to involve the idea of the Triunity. But I am likewise convinced that previously to the promulgation of the Gospel the doctrine had no claim on the faith of mankind: though it might have been a legitimate contemplation for a speculative philosopher, a theorem in metaphysics valid in the Schools.

* Or, I may add, any idea which does not either identify the Creator with the creation; or else represent the Supreme Being as a mere impersonal Law or *ordo ordinans*, differing from the law of gravitation only by its universality.

I form a certain notion in my mind, and say: This is what I understand by the term, God. From books and conversation I find that the learned generally connect the same notion with the same word. I then apply the rules laid down by the masters of logic, for the involution and evolution of terms, and prove (to as many as agree with me in my premisses) that the notion, God, involves the notion, Trinity. I now pass out of the Schools, and enter into discourse with some friend or neighbor, unversed in the formal sciences, unused to the process of abstraction, neither logician nor metaphysician; but sensible and single-minded, *an Israelite indeed*, trusting in *the Lord God of his fathers, even the God of Abraham, of Isaac, and of Jacob.* If I speak of God to him, what will he understand me to be speaking of? What does he mean, and suppose me to mean, by the word? An accident or product of the reasoning faculty, or an abstraction which the human mind forms by reflecting on its own thoughts and forms of thinking? No. By God he understands me to mean an existing and self-subsisting reality,* a real and personal Being

* I have elsewhere remarked on the assistance which those that labor after distinct conceptions would receive from the reintroduction of the terms *objective* and *subjective*, *objective* and *subjective reality*, and the like, as substitutes for *real* and *notional*, and to the exclusion of the false *antithesis* between *real* and *ideal*. For the student in that noblest of the sciences, the *scire teipsum*, the advantage would be especially great. The few sentences that follow, in illustration of the terms here advocated, will not, I trust, be a waste of the reader's time.

The celebrated Euler having demonstrated certain properties of arches, adds: "All experience is in contradiction to this; but this is no reason for doubting its truth." The words sound paradoxical; but mean no more than this—that the mathematical properties of figure and space are not less certainly the properties of figure and space because they can never be perfectly realized, in wood, stone, or iron. Now this assertion of Euler's might be expressed at once, briefly and simply, by saying, that the properties in question were subjectively true, though not objectively—or that the mathematical arch possessed a subjective reality, though incapable of being realized objectively.

In like manner, if I had to express my conviction that space was not itself a thing, but a mode or form of perceiving, or the inward ground and condition in the percipient, in consequence of which things are seen as outward and co-existing, I convey this at once by the words:—Space is subjective, or space is real in and for the subject alone.

If I am asked, Why not say, in and for the mind, which every one would understand? I reply: We know indeed, that all minds are subjects; but

—even the Person, the I AM, who sent Moses to his forefathers in Egypt. Of the actual existence of this Divine Being he has the same historical assurance as of theirs; confirmed indeed by the book of Nature, as soon and as far as that stronger and better light has taught him to read and construe it—confirmed by it, I

are by no means certain that all subjects are minds. For a mind is a subject that knows itself, or a subject that is its own object. The inward principle of growth and individual form in every seed and plant is a subject, and without any exertion of poetic privilege, poets may speak of the soul of the flower. But the man would be a dreamer, who otherwise than poetically should speak of roses and lilies as self-conscious subjects. Lastly, by the assistance of the terms, Object and Subject, thus used as correspondent opposites, or as negative and positive in physics,—(for example, negative and positive electricity)—we may arrive at the distinct import and proper use of the strangely misused word, Idea. And as the forms of logic are all borrowed from geometry—(*ratiocinatio discursiva formas suas sive canonas recipit ab intuitu*)—I may be permitted thence to elucidate my present meaning. Every line may be, and by the ancient geometricians was, considered as a point produced, the two extremes being its poles, while the point itself remains in, or is at least represented by, the mid point, the indifference of the two poles, or correlative opposites. Logically applied, the two extremes or poles are named *thesis* and *antithesis*. Thus in the line,

I
T————————A

we have T=*thesis*, A=*antithesis*, and I=*punctum indifferens sive amphotericum*, which latter is to be conceived as both in as far as it may be either of the two former. Observe: not both at the same time in the same relation: for this would be the identity of T and A, not the indifference; but so, that relatively to A, I is equal to T, and relatively to T, it becomes= A. For the purposes of the universal Noetic, in which we require terms of most comprehension and least specific import, the Noetic Pentad might, perhaps, be,—

	1. *Prothesis.*	
2. *Thesis.*	4. *Mesothesis.*	3. *Antithesis.*
	5. *Synthesis.*	

	Prothesis.	
	Sum.	
Thesis.	*Mesothesis.*	*Antithesis.*
Res.	*Agere.*	*Ago, Patior.*
	Synthesis.	
	Agens.	

1. Verb substantive=*Prothesis*, as expressing the identity or co-inherence of act and being.

2. Substantive=*Thesis*, expressing being. 3. Verb=*Antithesis*, expressing act. 4. Infinitive=*Mesothesis*, as being either substantive or verb, or

say, but not derived from it. Now by what right can I require this man—(and of such men the great majority of serious believers consisted previously to the light of the Gospel)—to receive a notion of mine, wholly alien from his habits of thinking, because it may be logically deduced from another notion, with which he was almost as little acquainted, and not at all concern-

both at once, only in different relations. 5. Participle=*Synthesis.* Thus, in chemistry, sulphureted hydrogen is an acid relatively to the more powerful alkalis, and an alkali relatively to a powerful acid. Yet one other remark, and I pass to the question. In order to render the constructions of pure mathematics applicable to philosophy, the Pythagoreans, I imagine, represented the line as generated, or, as it were, radiated, by a point not contained in the line, but independent, and (in the language of that School) transcendent to all production, which it caused but did not partake in. *Facit, non patitur.* This was the *punctum invisibile et præsuppositum:* and in this way the Pythagoreans guarded against the error of Pantheism, into which the later Schools fell. The assumption of this point I call the logical *prothesis.* We have now therefore four relations of thought expressed: 1. *Prothesis,* or the identity of T and A, which is neither, because in it, as the transcendent of both, both are contained and exist as one. Taken absolutely, this finds its application in the Supreme Being alone, the Pythagorean *Tetractys;* the ineffable name, to which no image can be attached; the point, which has no (real) opposite or counterpoint. But relatively taken and inadequately, the germinal power of every seed might be generalized under the relation of Identity. 2. *Thesis,* or position. 3. *Antithesis,* or opposition. 4. Indifference. To which when we add the *Synthesis* or composition, in its several forms of *equilibrium,* as in quiescent electricity; of neutralization, as of oxygen and hydrogen in water; and of predominance, as of hydrogen and carbon, with hydrogen predominant, in pure alcohol; or of carbon and hydrogen, with the comparative predominance of the carbon, in oil; we complete the five most general forms or preconceptions of constructive logic.

And now for the answer to the question, what is an Idea, if it mean neither an impression on the senses, nor a definite conception, nor an abstract notion? (And if it does mean any one of these, the word is superfluous: and while it remains undetermined which of these is meant by the word, or whether it is not which you please, it is worse than superfluous.) But supposing the word to have a meaning of its own, what does it mean? What is an Idea? In answer to this I commence with the absolutely Real as the *prothesis:* the subjectively Real as the *thesis;* the objectively Real as the *antithesis;* and I affirm, that Idea is the indifference of the two—so namely, that if it be conceived as in the subject, the idea is an object, and possesses objective truth; but if in an object, it is then a subject, and is necessarily thought of as exercising the powers of a subject. Thus an idea conceived as subsisting in an object becomes a law: and a law contemplated subjectively in a mind is an idea.

ed? Grant for a moment, that the latter (that is, the notion, with which I first set out) as soon as it is combined with the assurance of a corresponding reality becomes identical with the true and effective Idea of God! Grant, that in thus realizing the notion I am warranted by revelation, the law of conscience, and the interests and necessities of my moral being! Yet by what authority, by what inducement, am I entitled to attach the same reality to a second notion, a notion drawn from a notion? It is evident, that if I have the same right, it must be on the same grounds. Revelation must have assured it, my conscience required it—or in some way or other I must have an interest in this belief. It must concern me, as a moral and responsible being. Now these grounds were first given in the redemption of mankind by Christ, the Saviour and Mediator: and by the utter incompatibility of these offices with a mere creature. On the doctrine of Redemption depends the faith, the duty, of believing in the divinity of our Lord. And this again is the strongest ground for the reality of that Idea, in which alone this divinity can be received without breach of the faith in the unity of the Godhead. But such is the Idea of the Trinity. Strong as the motives are that induce me to defer the full discussion of this great article of the Christian Creed, I can not withstand the request of several divines, whose situation and extensive services entitle them to the utmost deference, that I should so far deviate from my first intention as at least to indicate the point on which I stand, and to prevent the misconception of my purpose: as if I held the doctrine of the Trinity for a truth which men could be called on to believe by mere force of reasoning, independently of any positive Revelation. Now though it might be sufficient to say, that I regard the very phrase, "Revealed Religion," as a pleonasm, inasmuch as a religion not revealed is, in my judgment, no religion at all; I have no objection to announce more particularly and distinctly what I do and what I do not maintain on this point: provided that in the following paragraph, with this view inserted, the Reader will look for nothing more than a plain statement of my opinions. The grounds on which they rest, and the arguments by which they are to be vindicated, are for another place.

I hold then, it is true, that all the so called demonstrations of a God either prove too little, as that from the order and apparent purpose in nature; or too much, namely, that the World is itself God: or they clandestinely involve the conclusion in the premisses, passing off the mere analysis or explication of an assertion for the proof of it,—a species of logical legerdemain not unlike that of the jugglers at a fair, who putting into their mouths what seems to be a walnut, draw out a score yards of ribbon—as in the postulate of a First Cause. And lastly, in all these demonstrations the demonstrators presuppose the idea or a conception of a God without being able to authenticate it, that is, to give an account whence they obtained it. For it is clear, that the proof first mentioned and the most natural and convincing of all—(the cosmological, I mean, or that from the order in nature)—presupposes the ontological—that is, the proof of a God from the necessity and necessary objectivity of the Idea. If the latter can assure us of a God as an existing reality, the former will go far to prove his power, wisdom, and benevolence. All this I hold. But I also hold, that this truth, the hardest to demonstrate, is the one which of all others least needs to be demonstrated; that though there may be no conclusive demonstrations of a good, wise, living, and personal God, there are so many convincing reasons for it, within and without—a grain of sand sufficing, and a whole universe at hand to echo the decision!—that for every mind not devoid of all reason, and desperately conscience-proof, the truth which it is the least possible to prove, it is little less than impossible not to believe;—only indeed just so much short of impossible, as to leave some room for the will and the moral election, and thereby to keep it a truth of religion, and the possible subject of a commandment.*

* In a letter to a friend on the mathematical Atheists of the French Revolution, La Lande and others, or rather on a young man of distinguished abilities, but an avowed and proselyting partisan of their tenets, I concluded with these words: "The man who will believe nothing but by force of demonstrative evidence—(even though it is strictly demonstrable that the demonstrability required would countervene all the purposes of the truth in question, all that render the belief of the same desirable or obligatory)—is not in a state of mind to be reasoned with on any subject. But if he further denies the fact of the law of conscience, and the essential difference between right and wrong, I confess he puzzles me. I can not without gross inconsistency appeal to his conscience and moral sense, or I should admonish him that, as an honest man, he ought to advertise himself with a *Cavete omnes! Scelus sum.* And as an honest man myself, I dare not advise him on prudential grounds to keep his opinions secret, lest I should make myself his accomplice, and be helping him on with a wrap rascal."

On this account I do not demand of a Deist, that he should adopt the doctrine of the Trinity. For he might very well be justified in replying, that he rejected the doctrine *not* because it could not be *demonstrated*, nor yet on the score of any incomprehensibilities and seeming contradictions that might be objected to it, as knowing that these might be, and in fact had been, urged with equal force against a personal God under any form capable of love and veneration; but because he had not the same theoretical necessity, the same interests and instincts of reason for the one hypothesis as for the other. It is not enough, the Deist might justly say, that there is no cogent reason why I should *not* believe the Trinity; you must show me some cogent reason why I should.

But the case is quite different with a Christian, who accepts the Scriptures as the word of God, yet refuses his assent to the plainest declarations of these Scriptures, and explains away the most express texts into metaphor and hyperbole, because the literal and obvious interpretation is (according to his notions) absurd and contrary to reason. He is bound to show, that it is so in any sense, not equally applicable to the texts asserting the being, infinity, and personality of God the Father, the Eternal and Omnipresent One, who created the heaven and the earth. And the more is he bound to do this, and the greater is my right to demand it of him, because the doctrine of Redemption from sin supplies the Christian with motives and reasons for the divinity of the Redeemer far more concerning and coercive subjectively, that is, in the economy of his own soul, than are all the inducements that can influence the Deist objectively, that is, in the interpretation of nature.

Do I then utterly exclude the speculative reason from theology? No! It is its office and rightful privilege to determine on the negative truth of whatever we are required to believe. The doctrine must not contradict any universal principle: for this would be a doctrine that contradicted itself. Or philosophy? No. It may be and has been the servant and pioneer of faith by convincing the mind that a doctrine is cogitable, that the soul can present the idea to itself; and that if we determine to contemplate, or think of, the subject at all, so and in no other form can this be effected. So far are both logic and philosophy to be received and trusted. But the duty, and in some cases and for some persons even the right, of thinking on subjects beyond the bounds of sensible experience; the grounds of the real truth; the life, the substance, the hope, the love, in one word, the faith;—these are derivatives from the practical, moral, and spiritual nature and being of man.

APHORISM III.

Burnet and Coleridge.

That Religion is designed to improve the nature and faculties of man, in order to the right governing of our actions, to the securing the peace and progress, external and internal, of individuals and of communities, and lastly, to the rendering us capable of a more perfect state, entitled the kingdom of God, to which the present life is probationary—this is a truth, which all who have truth only in view, will receive on its own evidence. If such then be the main end of religion altogether (the improvement namely of our nature and faculties), it is plain, that every part of religion is to be judged by its relation to this main end. And since the Christian scheme is religion in its most perfect and effective form, a revealed religion, and, therefore, in a special sense proceeding from that Being who made us and knows what we are, of course therefore adapted to the needs and capabilities of human nature; nothing can be a part of this holy Faith that is not duly proportioned to this end.

COMMENT.

This Aphorism should be borne in mind, whenever a theological resolve is proposed to us as an article of faith. Take, for instance, the determinations passed at the Synod of Dort, concerning the absolute decrees of God in connection with his omniscience and foreknowledge. Or take the decision in the Council of Trent on Transubstantiation, founded on the difference between its two kinds; the one in which both the substance and the accidents are changed, the same matter remaining—as in the conversion of water into wine at Cana: the other, in which the matter and the substance are changed, the accidents remaining unaltered as in the Eucharist—this latter being Transubstantiation *par eminence*:*—and further that it is indispensable to a saving faith

* ——*ideo persuasum semper in Ecclesia Dei fuit, idque nunc denuo sancta hæc Synodus declarat, per consecrationem panis et vini conversionem*

carefully to distinguish the one kind from the other, and to believe both, and to believe the necessity of believing both in order to salvation! For each of these extra-Scriptural articles of faith the preceding Aphorism supplies a safe criterion. Will the belief tend to the improvement of any of my moral or intellectual faculties? But before I can be convinced that a faculty will be improved, I must be assured that it exists. On all these dark sayings, therefore, of Dort or Trent, it is quite sufficient to ask, by what faculty, organ, or inlet of knowledge, we are to assure ourselves that the words mean any thing, or correspond to any object out of our own mind or even in it: unless indeed the mere craving and striving to think on, after all the materials for thinking have been exhausted, can be called an object. When a number of trust-worthy persons assure me, that a portion of fluid which they saw to be water, by some change in the fluid itself or in their senses, suddenly acquired the color, taste, smell, and exhilarating property of wine, I perfectly understand what they tell me, and likewise by what faculties they might have come to the knowledge of the fact. But if any one of the number, not satisfied with my acquiescence in the fact, should insist on my believing that the matter remained the same, the substance and the accidents having been removed in order to make way for a different substance with different accidents, I must entreat his permission to wait till I can discover in myself any faculty, by which there can be presented to me a matter distinguishable from accidents, and a substance that is different from both. It is true, I have a faculty of articulation; but I do not see that it can be improved by my using it for the formation of words without

fieri totius substantiæ panis in substantiam corporis Christi Domini nostri, et totius substantiæ vini in substantiam sanguinis ejus.—Sess. xii. c. 4.

Totus—et integer Christus sub panis specie, et sub quavis ipsius speciei parte, totus item sub vini specie, et sub ejus partibus existit.—Ib. c. 3.

Si quis dixerit, in sacrosancto Eucharistiæ Sacramento remanere substantiam panis et vini una cum corpore et sanguine Domini nostri Jesu Christi, negaveritque mirabilem illam et singularem conversionem totius substantiæ panis in corpus, et totius substantiæ vini in sanguinem, manentibus duntaxat speciebus panis et vini; quam quidem conversionem Catholica Ecclesia Transsubstantiationem appellat—Anathema sit.—Ib. Can. 12.

Si quis negaverit, in venerabili Sacramento Eucharistiæ sub unaquaque specie, et sub singulis cujusque speciei partibus, separatione facta, totum Christum contineri—Anathema sit.—Ib. Can. 3.—Ed.

meaning, or at best, for the utterance of thoughts, that mean only the act of so thinking, or of trying so to think. But the end of religion is the improvement of our nature and faculties. I sum up the whole in one great practical maxim. The object of religious contemplation, and of a truly spiritual faith, is "the ways of God to man." Of the workings of the Godhead God himself has told us, *My ways are not as your ways, nor my thoughts as your thoughts.*

APHORISM IV.

THE CHARACTERISTIC DIFFERENCE BETWEEN THE DISCIPLINE OF THE ANCIENT PHILOSOPHERS AND THE DISPENSATION OF THE GOSPEL.

By undeceiving, enlarging, and informing the intellect, Philosophy sought to purify and to elevate the moral character. Of course, those alone could receive the latter and incomparably greater benefit, who by natural capacity and favorable contingencies of fortune were fit recipients of the former. How small the number, we scarcely need the evidence of history to assure us. Across the night of Paganism, Philosophy flitted on, like the lantern-fly of the Tropics, a light to itself, and an ornament, but alas! no more than an ornament, of the surrounding darkness.

Christianity reversed the order. By means accessible to all, by inducements operative on all, and by convictions, the grounds and materials of which all men might find in themselves, her first step was to cleanse the heart. But the benefit did not stop here. In preventing the rank vapors that steam up from the corrupt heart, Christianity restores the intellect likewise to its natural clearness. By relieving the mind from the distractions and importunities of the unruly passions, she improves the quality of the understanding: while at the same time she presents for its contemplations objects so great and so bright as can not but enlarge the organ, by which they are contemplated. The fears, the hopes, the remembrances, the anticipations, the inward and outward experience, the belief and the faith, of a Christian, form of themselves a philosophy and a sum of knowledge, which a life spent in the Grove of Academus, or the painted Porch, could not have attained or collected. The result is contained in the fact of a wide and still widening Christendom.

Yet I dare not say that the effects have been proportionate to the divine wisdom of the scheme. Too soon did the Doctors of the Church forget that the heart, the moral nature, was the beginning and the end: and that truth, knowledge, and insight were comprehended in its expansion. This was the true and first apostasy—when in council and synod the divine humanities of the Gospel gave way to speculative systems, and religion became a science of shadows under the name of theology, or at best a bare skeleton of truth, without life or interest, alike inaccessible and unintelligible to the majority of Christians. For these therefore there remained only rites and ceremonies and spectacles, shows and semblances. Thus among the learned *the substance of things hoped for* (Heb. xi. 1) passed off into notions; and for the unlearned the surfaces of things became* substance. The Christian world was for centuries divided into the many, that did not think at all, and the few who did nothing but think—both alike unreflecting, the one from defect of the act, the other from the absence of an object.

APHORISM V.

There is small chance of truth at the goal where there is not a child-like humility at the starting-post.

COMMENT.

Humility is the safest ground of docility, and docility the surest promise of docibility. Where there is no working of self-love in the heart that secures a leaning beforehand; where the great magnet of the planet is not overwhelmed or obscured by partial masses of iron in close neighborhood to the compass of the judgment though hidden or unnoticed; there will this great *desideratum* be found of a child-like humility. Do I then say, that I am to be influenced by no interest? Far from it! There is an interest of truth: or how could there be a love of truth? And that a love of truth for its own sake, and merely as truth, is possible, my soul bears witness to itself in its inmost recesses. But there are other interests—those of goodness; of beauty, of utility. It would be a sorry proof of the humility I am extolling, were I

* *Virium et proprietatum, quæ non nisi de substantibus prædicari possunt, formis superstantibus attributio, est Superstitio.*

to ask for angel's wings to overfly my own human nature. I exclude none of these. It is enough if the *lene clinamen*, the gentle bias, be given by no interest that concerns myself other than as I am a man, and included in the great family of mankind; but which does therefore especially concern me, because being a common interest of all men it must needs concern the very essentials of my being, and because these essentials, as existing in me, are especially intrusted to my particular charge.

Widely different from this social and truth-attracted bias, different both in its nature and its effects, is the interest connected with the desire of distinguishing yourself from other men, in order to be distinguished by them. Hoc revera *est inter* te et veritatem. This interest does indeed stand between thee and truth. I might add between thee and thy own soul. It is scarcely more at variance with the love of truth than it is unfriendly to the attainment of it. By your own act you have appointed the many as your judges and appraisers: for the anxiety to be admired is a loveless passion, ever strongest with regard to those by whom we are least known and least cared for, loud on the hustings, gay in the ball-room, mute and sullen at the family fireside. What you have acquired by patient thought and cautious discrimination, demands a portion of the same effort in those who are to receive it from you. But applause and preference are things of barter; and if you trade in them, experience will soon teach you that there are easier and less unsuitable ways to win golden judgments than by at once taxing the patience and humiliating the self-opinion of your judges. To obtain your end, your words must be as indefinite as their thoughts: and how vague and general these are even on objects of sense, the few who at a mature age have seriously set about the discipline of their faculties, and have honestly *taken stock*, best know by recollection of their own state. To be admired you must make your auditors believe at least that they understand what you say; which be assured, they never will, under such circumstances, if it be worth understanding, or if you understand your own soul. But while your prevailing motive is to be compared and appreciated, is it credible, is it possible, that you should in earnest seek for a knowledge which is and must remain a hidden light, a secret treasure? Have you children, or have you lived among children, and do you not know, that in all things, in food, in medicine, in all their doings and abstainings they must believe in order to acquire a reason for their belief? But so is it with religious truths for all men. These we must all learn as children. The ground of the prevailing error on this point is the ignorance, that in spiritual concernments to believe and to understand are not diverse things, but the same thing in different periods of its growth. Belief is the seed, received into the will, of which the understanding or knowledge is the flower, and the thing believed is the fruit. Unless ye believe ye can not understand: and unless ye be humble as children, ye not only will not, but ye can not believe. Of such therefore is the Kingdom of Heaven. Yea, blessed is the calamity that makes us humble: though so repugnant thereto is our nature, in our present state, that after a while, it is to be feared, a second and sharper calamity would be wanted to cure us of our pride in having become so humble.

Lastly, there are among us, though fewer and less in fashion than among our ancestors, persons who, like Shaftesbury, do not belong to "the herd of Epicurus," yet prefer a philosophic paganism to the morality of the Gospel. Now it would conduce, methinks, to the child-like humility we have been discoursing of, if the use of the term, virtue, in that high, comprehensive, and notional sense in which it was used by the ancient Stoics, were abandoned, as a relic of Paganism, to these modern Pagans: and if Christians restoring the word to its original import, namely, manhood or manliness, used it exclusively to express the quality of fortitude; strength of character in relation to the resistance opposed by nature and the irrational passions to the dictates of reason: energy of will in preserving the line of rectitude tense and firm against the warping forces and treacheries of temptation. Surely, it were far less unseemly to value ourselves on this moral strength than on strength of body, or even strength of intellect. But we will rather value *it* for ourselves: and bearing in mind the old query,—*Quis custodiet ipsos custodes?*—we will value it the more, yea, then only will we allow it true spiritual worth, when we possess it as a gift of grace, a boon of mercy undeserved, a fulfilment of a free promise (1 *Cor.* x. 13). What more is meant in this last paragraph, let the venerable Hooker say for me in the following:—

APHORISM VI.

Hooker.

What is virtue but a medicine, and vice but a wound? Yea, we have so often deeply wounded ourselves with medicine, that God hath been fain to make wounds medicinable; to secure by vice where virtue hath stricken; to suffer the just man to fall, that being raised he may be taught what power it was which upheld him standing. I am not afraid to affirm it boldly with St. Augustine, that men puffed up through a proud opinion of their own sanctity and holiness receive a benefit at the hands of God, and are assisted with his grace when with his grace they are *not* assisted, but permitted (and that grievously) to transgress. Whereby, as they were through overgreat liking of themselves supplanted (*tripped up*), so the dislike of that which did supplant them may establish them afterwards the surer. Ask the very soul of Peter, and it shall undoubtedly itself make you this answer: My eager protestations made in the glory of my spiritual strength I am ashamed of. But my shame and the tears, with which my presumption and my weakness were bewailed, recur in the songs of my thanksgiving. My strength had been my ruin, my fall hath proved my stay.

APHORISM VII.

The being and providence of One Living God, holy, gracious, merciful, the Creator and Preserver of all things, and a Father of the righteous; the Moral Law in its[1] utmost height, breadth and purity; a state of retribution after death; the[2] resurrection of the dead; and a day of Judgment—all these were known and received by the Jewish people, as established articles of the national Faith, at or before the proclaiming of Christ by the Baptist. They are the ground-work of Christianity, and essentials in the Christian Faith, but not its characteristic and peculiar doctrines: except indeed as they are confirmed, enlivened, realized and brought home to the whole being of man, head, heart, and spirit, by the truths and influences of the Gospel.

Peculiar to Christianity are:

I. The belief that a Mean of Salvation has been effected and provided for the human race by the incarnation of the Son of God in the person of Jesus Christ; and that his life on earth, his sufferings, death, and resurrection, are not only proofs and manifestations, but likewise essential and effective parts of the great redemptive act, whereby also the obstacle from the corruption of our nature is rendered no longer insurmountable.

II. The belief in the possible appropriation of this benefit by repentance and faith, including the aids that render an effective faith and repentance themselves possible.

III. The belief in the reception (by as many as *shall be heirs of salvation*) of a living and spiritual principle, a seed of life capable of surviving this natural life, and of existing in a divine and immortal state.

IV. The belief in the awakening of the spirit in them that truly believe, and in the communion of the spirit, thus awakened, with the Holy Spirit.

V. The belief in the accompanying and consequent gifts, graces, comforts, and privileges of the Spirit, which acting primarily on the heart and will can not but manifest themselves in suitable works of love and obedience, that is, in right acts with right affections, from right principles.

VI. Further, as Christians we are taught, that these Works are the appointed signs and evidences of our Faith ; and that, under limitation of the power, the means, and the opportunities afforded us individually, they are the rule and measure, by which we are bound and enabled to judge, of *what spirit we are*.

VII. All these, together with the doctrine of the Fathers reproclaimed in the everlasting Gospel, we receive in the full assurance, that God beholds and will finally judge us with a merciful consideration of our infirmities, a gracious acceptance of our sincere though imperfect strivings, a forgiveness of our defects, through the mediation, and a completion of our deficiencies by the perfect righteousness, of the Man Christ Jesus, even the Word that was in the beginning with God, and who, being God, became man for the redemption of mankind.

COMMENT.

I earnestly entreat the Reader to pause awhile, and to join with me in reflecting on the preceding Aphorism. It has been my aim throughout this Work to enforce two points : 1. That Morality arising out of the reason and conscience of men, and

Prudence, which in like manner flows out of the understanding and the natural wants and desires of the individual, are two distinct things. 2. That Morality with Prudence as its instrument has, considered abstractedly, not only a value but a worth in itself. Now the question is (and it is a question which every man must answer for himself)—From what you know of yourself; of your own heart and strength; and from what history and personal experience have led you to conclude of mankind generally; dare you *trust* to it? Dare *you* trust to it? To *it*, and to it alone? If so, well! It is at your own risk. I judge you not. Before Him, who can not be mocked, you stand or fall. But if not, if you have had too good reason to know that your heart is deceitful and your strength weakness: if you are disposed to exclaim with Paul—The Law indeed is holy, just, good, spiritual; but I am carnal, sold under sin: for that which I do, I allow not, and what I would, that I do not!—in this case, there is a Voice that says, *Come unto me: and I will give you rest.* This is the voice of Christ: and the conditions, under which the promise was given by him, are that you believe *in* him, and believe his words. And he has further assured you, that if you do so, you will obey him. You are, in short, to embrace the Christian Faith as your religion—those truths which St. Paul believed after his conversion, and not those only which he believed no less undoubtedly while he was persecuting Christ and an enemy of the Christian Religion. With what consistency could I offer you this Volume as aids to reflection, if I did not call on you to ascertain in the first instance what these truths are? But these I could not lay before you without first enumerating certain other points of belief, which though truths, indispensable truths, and truths comprehended or rather pre-supposed in the Christian scheme, are yet not *these* truths. (*John* i. 17.)

While doing this, I was aware that the positions, in the first paragraph of the preceding Aphorism, to which the numerical marks are affixed, will startle some of my readers. Let the following sentences serve for the notes corresponding to the marks:

[1] *Ye shall be holy; for I the Lord your God am holy.** *He hath showed thee, O man, what is good: and what doth the Lord require of thee, but to do justly, to love mercy, and walk humbly with thy God?*† To these summary passages from

* *Lev.* xix. 2.—*Ed.*

† *Micah* vi. 8.—*Ed.*

Moses and the Prophet (the first exhibiting the closed, the second the expanded, hand of the Moral Law) I might add the authorities of Grotius and other more orthodox and not less learned divines, for the opinion that the Lord's Prayer was a selection, and the famous passage [*The hour is coming, &c.* John v. 28, 29] a citation by our Lord from the Liturgy of the Jewish Church. But it will be sufficient to remind the reader, that the apparent difference between the prominent moral truths of the Old and those of the New Testament results from the latter having been written in Greek; while the conversations recorded by the Evangelists took place in Syro-Chaldaic or Aramaic. Hence it happened that where our Lord cited the original text, his biographers substituted the Septuagint Version, while our English Version is in both instances immediate and literal—in the Old Testament from the Hebrew Original, in the New Testament from the freer Greek translation. The text, *I give you a new commandment*, has no connection with the present subject.

There is a current mistake on this point likewise, though this article of the Jewish belief is not only asserted by St. Paul, but is elsewhere spoken of as common to the Twelve Tribes. The mistake consists in supposing the Pharisees to have been a distinct sect in doctrine, and in strangely over-rating the number of the Sadducees. The former were distinguished not by holding, as matters of religious belief, articles different from the Jewish Church at large: but by their pretences to a more rigid orthodoxy, a more scrupulous performance. They were the strict professors of the day. The latter, the Sadducees, whose opinions much more nearly resembled those of the Stoics than the Epicureans—(a remark that will appear paradoxical to those only who have abstracted their notions of the Stoic philosophy from Epictetus, Mark Antonine, and certain brilliant inconsistencies of Seneca),—were a handful of rich men, Romanized Jews, not more numerous than Infidels among us, and holden by the people at large in at least equal abhorrence. Their great argument was: that the belief of a future state of rewards and punishments injured or destroyed the purity of the Moral Law for the more enlightened classes, and weakened the influence of the laws of the land for the people, the vulgar multitude.

I will now suppose the reader to have thoughtfully reperused the paragraph containing the tenets peculiar to Christianity, and if he have his religious principles yet to form, I should expect to overhear a troubled murmur: How can I comprehend this? How is this to be proved? To the first question I should answer: Christianity is not a theory, or a speculation; but a life;—not a philosophy of life, but a life and a living process. To the second: TRY IT. It has been eighteen hundred years in existence: and has one individual left a record, like the following:—"I tried it, and it did not answer. I made the experiment faithfully according to the directions: and the result has been, a conviction of my own credulity?" Have you, in your own experience, met with any one in whose words you could place full confidence, and who has seriously affirmed:—"I have given Christianity a fair trial. I was aware, that its promises were made only conditionally. But my heart bears me witness, that I have to the utmost of my power complied with these conditions. Both outwardly and in the discipline of my inward acts and affections, I have performed the duties which it enjoins, and I have used the means which it prescribes. Yet my assurance of its truth has received no increase. Its promises have not been fulfilled: and I repent of my delusion?" If neither your own experience nor the history of almost two thousand years has presented a single testimony to this purport; and if you have read and heard of many who have lived and died bearing witness to the contrary: and if you have yourself met with some one, in whom on any other point you would place unqualified trust, who has on his own experience made report to you, that He is faithful who promised, and what He promised He has proved Himself able to perform: is it bigotry, if I fear that the unbelief, which prejudges and prevents the experiment, has its source elsewhere than in the uncorrupted judgment; that not the strong free mind, but the enslaved will, is the true original infidel in this instance? It would not be the first time, that a treacherous bosom-sin had suborned the understandings of men to bear false witness against its avowed enemy, the right though unreceived owner of the house, who had long warned that sin out, and waited only for its ejection to enter and take possession of the same.

I have elsewhere in the present Work explained the difference between the Understanding and the Reason, by reason meaning exclusively the speculative or scientific power so called, the νοῦς, or *mens* of the ancients. And wider still is the distinction between the understanding and the spiritual mind. But no gift of God does or can contradict any other gift, except by misuse or misdirection. Most readily therefore do I admit, that there can be no contrariety between revelation and the understanding; unless you call the fact, that the skin, though sensible of the warmth of the sun, can convey no notion of its figure or its joyous light, or of the colors which it impresses on the clouds, a contrariety between the skin and the eye; or infer that the cutaneous and the optic nerves contradict each other.

But we have grounds to believe, that there are yet other rays or effluences from the sun, which neither feeling nor sight can apprehend, but which are to be inferred from the effects. And were it even so with regard to the spiritual sun, how would this contradict the understanding or the reason? It is a sufficient proof of the contrary, that the mysteries in question are not in the direction of the understanding or the (speculative) reason. They do not move on the same line or plane with them, and therefore can not contradict them. But besides this, in the mystery that most immediately concerns the believer, that of the birth into a new and spiritual life, the common sense and experience of mankind come in aid of their faith. The analogous facts, which we know to be true, not only facilitate the apprehension of the facts promised to us, and expressed by the same words in conjunction with a distinctive epithet: but being confessedly not less incomprehensible, the certain knowledge of the one disposes us to the belief of the other. It removes at least all objections to the truth of the doctrine derived from the mysteriousness of its subject. The life, we seek after, is a mystery; but so both in itself and in its origin is the life we have. In order to meet this question, however, with minds duly prepared, there are two preliminary inquiries to be decided; the first respecting the purport, the second respecting the language of the Gospel.

First then, of the purport, namely, what the Gospel does not, and what it does profess to be. The Gospel is not a system of theology, nor a *syntagma* of theoretical propositions and conclusions for the enlargement of speculative knowledge, ethical or metaphysical. But it is a history, a series of facts and events related or announced. These do indeed involve, or rather I should say they at the same time are, most important doctrinal truths; but still facts and declaration of facts.

Secondly, of the language. This is a wide subject. But the point, to which I chiefly advert, is the necessity of thoroughly understanding the distinction between analogous and metaphorical language. Analogies are used in aid of conviction: metaphors, as means of illustration. The language is analogous, wherever a thing, power, or principle in a higher dignity is expressed by the same thing, power, or principle in a lower but more known form. Such, for instance, is the language of *John* iii. 6. *That which is born of the flesh, is flesh; that which is born of the Spirit, is Spirit.* The latter half of the verse contains the fact asserted; the former half the analogous fact, by which it is rendered intelligible. If any man choose to call this metaphorical or figurative, I ask him whether with Hobbes and Bolingbroke he applies the same rule to the moral attributes of the Deity? Whether he regards the divine justice, for instance, as a metaphorical term, a mere figure of speech? If he disclaims this, then I answer, neither do I regard the phrase *born again*, or spiritual life, as a figure or metaphor. I have only to add, that these analogies are the material, or (to speak chemically) the base, of symbols and symbolical expressions; the nature of which is always tautegorical, that is, expressing the same subject but with a difference, in contra-distinction from metaphors and similitudes, which are always allegorical, that is, expressing a different subject but with a resemblance.*

Of metaphorical language, on the other hand, let the following be taken as instance and illustration. I am speaking, we will suppose, of an act, which in its own nature, and as a producing and efficient cause, is transcendent; but which produces sundry effects, each of which is the same in kind with an effect produced by a cause well known and of ordinary occurrence. Now when I characterize or designate this transcendent act, in exclusive reference to these its effects, by a succession of names borrowed from their ordinary causes; not for the purpose of rendering the act itself, or the manner of the agency, conceivable, but in order to show the nature and magnitude of the benefits received from it, and thus to excite the due admiration, gratitude, and love in the receivers; in this case I should be rightly described as speak-

* See Works, I. p. 453, IV. p. 247, V. p. 224.—*Ed.*

ing metaphorically. And in this case to confound the similarity in respect of the effects relatively to the recipients, with an identity in respect of the causes or modes of causation relatively to the transcendent act or the Divine Agent, is a confusion of metaphor with analogy, and of figurative with literal; and has been and continues to be a fruitful source of superstition or enthusiasm in believers, and of objections and prejudices to infidels and skeptics. But each of these points is worthy of a separate consideration; and apt occasions will be found of reverting to them severally in the following Aphorisms, or the comments thereto attached.

APHORISM VIII.

Leighton.

Faith elevates the soul not only above sense and sensible things, but above reason itself. As reason corrects the errors which sense might occasion, so supernatural faith corrects the errors of natural reason judging according to sense.

COMMENT.

My remarks on this Aphorism from Leighton can not be better introduced, or their purport more distinctly announced, than by the following sentence from Harrington, with no other change than is necessary to make the words express, without aid of the context, what from the context it is evident was the writer's meaning. "The definition and proper character of man—that, namely, which should contra-distinguish him from other animals—is to be taken from his reason rather than from his understanding: in regard that in other creatures there may be something of understanding, but there is nothing of reason."

Sir Thomas Brown, in his *Religio Medici*, complains, that there are not impossibilities enough in religion for his active faith; and adopts by choice and in free preference such interpretations of certain texts and declarations of Holy Writ, as place them in irreconcilable contradiction to the demonstrations of science and the experience of mankind, because (says he) "I love to lose myself in a mystery, and 'tis my solitary recreation to pose my apprehension with those involved enigmas and riddles of the Trinity and Incarnation;"—and because he delights (as thinking it no vulgar part of faith) to believe a thing not only above but contrary to reason, and against the evidence of our proper senses.

For the worthy knight could answer all the objections of the Devil and reason "with the old resolution he had learnt of Tertullian: *Certum est quia impossibile est.* It is certainly true because it is quite impossible!" Now this I call Ultrafidianism.*

* There is this advantage in the occasional use of a newly minted term or title, expressing the doctrinal schemes of particular sects or parties, that it avoids the inconvenience that presses on either side, whether we adopt the name which the party itself has taken up by which to express its peculiar tenets, or that by which the same party is designated by its opponents. If we take the latter, it most often happens that either the persons are invidiously aimed at in the designation of the principles, or that the name implies some consequence or occasional accompaniment of the principles denied by the parties themselves, as applicable to them collectively. On the other hand, convinced as I am, that current appellations are never wholly indifferent or inert: and that, when employed to express the characteristic belief or object of a religious confederacy, they exert on the many a great and constant, though insensible, influence; I can not but fear that in adopting the former I may be sacrificing the interests of truth beyond what the duties of courtesy can demand or justify. I have elsewhere stated my objections to the word Unitarians, as a name which in its proper sense can belong only to the maintainers of the truth impugned by the persons, who have chosen it as their designation. For *unity* or unition, and indistinguishable *unicity* or sameness, are incompatible terms. We never speak of the unity of attraction, or the unity of repulsion; but of the unity of attraction and repulsion in each corpuscle. Indeed, the essential diversity of the conceptions, unity and sameness, was among the elementary principles of the old logicians; and Leibnitz, in his critique on Wissowatius, has ably exposed the sophisms grounded on the confusion of the two terms. But in the exclusive sense, in which the name, Unitarian, is appropriated by the Sect, and in which they mean it to be understood, it is a presumptuous boast and an uncharitable calumny. No one of the Churches to which they on this article of the Christian Faith stand opposed, Greek or Latin, ever adopted the term, Trini—or Tri-uni-tarians as their ordinary and proper name: and had it been otherwise, yet unity is assuredly no logical opposite to Tri-unity, which expressly includes it. The triple alliance is *à fortiori* an alliance. The true designation of their characteristic tenet, and which would simply and inoffensively express a fact admitted on all sides, is Psilanthropism, or the assertion of the mere humanity of Christ.*

I dare not hesitate to avow my regret that any scheme of doctrines or tenets should be the subject of penal law: though I can easily conceive, that any scheme, however excellent in itself, may be propagated, and however false or injurious, may be assailed, in a manner and by means that would make the advocate or assailant justly punishable. But then it is the manner, the means, that constitute the crime. The merit or demerit of the

* See the second Lay Sermon, Works, VI. p. 187.—*Ed.*

Again, there is a scheme constructed on the principle of retaining the social sympathies, that attend on the name of believer, at the least possible expenditure of belief; a scheme of picking and choosing Scripture texts for the support of doctrines, that have been learned beforehand from the higher oracle of common

opinions themselves depends on their originating and determining causes, which may differ in every different believer, and are certainly known to Him alone, who commanded us, *Judge not, lest ye be judged.* At all events, in the present state of the law, I do not see where we can begin, or where we can stop, without inconsistency and consequent hardship. Judging by all that we can pretend to know or are entitled to infer, who among us will take on himself to deny that the late Dr. Priestley was a good and benevolent man, as sincere in his love, as he was intrepid and indefatigable in his pursuit, of truth? Now let us construct three parallel tables, the first containing the articles of belief, moral and theological, maintained by the venerable Hooker, as the representative of the Established Church, each article being distinctly lined and numbered; the second the tenets and persuasions of Lord Herbert, as the representative of the Platonizing Deists; and the third, those of Dr. Priestley. Let the points, in which the second and third agree with or differ from the first, be considered as to the comparative number modified by the comparative weight and importance of the several points—and let any competent and upright man be appointed the arbiter, to decide according to his best judgment, without any reference to the truth of the opinions, which of the two differed from the first more widely. I say this, well aware that it would be abundantly more prudent to leave it unsaid. But I say it in the conviction, that the adoption of admitted misnomers in the naming of doctrinal systems, if only they have been negatively legalized, is but an equivocal proof of liberality towards the persons who dissent from us. On the contrary, I more than suspect that the former liberality does in too many men arise from a latent pre-disposition to transfer their reprobation and intolerance from the doctrines to the doctors, from the belief to the believers. Indecency, abuse, scoffing on subjects dear and awful to a multitude of our fellow-citizens, appeals to the vanity, appetites, and malignant passions of ignorant and incompetent judges—these are flagrant over-acts, condemned by the law written in the heart of every honest man, Jew, Turk, and Christian. These are points respecting which the humblest honest man feels it his duty to hold himself infallible, and dares not hesitate in giving utterance to the verdict of his conscience in the jury-box as fearlessly as by his fire-side. It is far otherwise with respect to matters of faith and inward conviction: and with respect to these I say—Tolerate no belief that you judge false and of injurious tendency: and arraign no believer. The man is more and other than his belief: and God only knows, how small or how large a part of him the belief in question may be, for good or for evil. Resist every false doctrine: and call no man heretic. The false doctrine does not necessarily make the man a heretic; but an evil heart can make any doctrine heretical.

sense; which, as applied to the truths of religion, means the popular part of the philosophy in fashion. Of course, the scheme differs at different times and in different individuals in the number of articles excluded; but, it may always be recognized by this permanent character, that its object is to draw religion down to the believer's intellect, instead of raising his intellect up to religion. And this extreme I call Minimi-fidianism.

Actuated by these principles, I have objected to a false and deceptive designation in the case of one system. Persuaded that the doctrines, enumerated in pp. 229, 30 are not only essential to the Christian religion, but those which contra-distinguish the religion as Christian, I merely repeat this persuasion in another form, when I assert, that (in my sense of the word, Christian) Unitarianism is not Christianity. But do I say, that those who call themselves Unitarians are not Christians? God forbid! I would not think, much less promulgate, a judgment at once so presumptuous and so uncharitable.* Let a friendly antagonist retort on my scheme of faith in the like manner: I shall respect him all the more for his consistency as a reasoner, and not confide the less in his kindness towards me as his neighbor and fellow-Christian. This latter and most endearing name I scarcely know how to withhold even from my friend, Hyman Hurwitz, as often as I read what every reverer of Holy Writ and of the English Bible ought to read, his admirable *Vindiciæ Hebraicæ.* It has trembled on the verge, as it were, of my lips, every time I have conversed with that pious, learned, strong-minded, and single-hearted Jew, an Israelite indeed, and without guile—

Cujus cura sequi naturam, legibus uti,
Et mentem vitiis, ora negare dolis;
Virtutes opibus, verum præponere falso,
Nil vacuum sensu dicere, nil facere.
Post obitum vivam secum,† secum requiescam,
Nec fiat melior sors mea sorte sua!

From a poem of Hildebert on his Master, the persecuted Berengarius.

Under the same feelings I conclude this aid to reflection by applying the principle to another misnomer not less inappropriate and far more influential. Of those, whom I have found most reason to respect and value, many have been members of the Church of Rome: and certainly I did not honor those the least, who scrupled even in common parlance to call our Church a reformed Church. A similar scruple would not, methinks, disgrace a Protestant as to the use of the words, Catholic or Roman Catholic; and if (tacitly at least, and in thought) he remembered that the Romish anti-Catholic Church would more truly express the fact. *Romish,* to mark that the corruptions in discipline, doctrine, and practice do, for the larger part,

* See Table Talk, Works VI. p. 387.—*Ed.*

† I do not answer for the corrupt Latin.

Now if there be one preventive of both these extremes more efficacious than another, and preliminary to all the rest, it is the being made fully aware of the diversity of Reason and the Understanding. And this is the more expedient, because though there is no want of authorities ancient and modern for the distinction of the faculties, and the distinct appropriation of the terms, yet our best writers too often confound the one with the other.

owe both their origin and perpetuation to the Romish Court, and the local tribunals of the City of Rome; and neither are nor ever have been Catholic, that is, universal, throughout the Roman Empire, or even in the whole Latin or Western Church—and anti-Catholic, because no other Church acts on so narrow and excommunicative a principle, or is characterized by such a jealous spirit of monopoly. Instead of a Catholic (universal) spirit, it may be truly described as a spirit of particularism counterfeiting Catholicity by a negative totality, and heretical self-circumscription—in the first instances cutting off, and since then cutting herself off from, all the other members of Christ's body. For the rest, I think as that man of true catholic spirit and apostolic zeal, Richard Baxter, thought; and my readers will thank me for conveying my reflections in his own words, in the following golden passage from his Life, "faithfully published from his own original MSS. by Matthew Silvester, 1696."

"My censures of the Papists do much differ from what they were at first. I then thought that their errors in the doctrines of faith were their most dangerous mistakes. But now I am assured that their misexpressions and misunderstanding of us, with our mistakings of them, and inconvenient expressing of our own opinions, have made the difference in most points appear much greater than it is; and that in some it is next to none at all. But the great and unreconcilable differences lie in their Church tyranny; in the usurpations of their hierarchy, and priesthood, under the name of spiritual authority exercising a temporal lordship; in their corruptions and abasement of God's worship; but above all in their systematic befriending of ignorance and vice.

"At first I thought that Mr. Perkins well proved that a Papist can not go beyond a reprobate; but now I doubt not that God hath many sanctified ones among them, who have received the true doctrine of Christianity so practically, that their contradictory errors prevail not against them, to hinder their love of God and their salvation: but that their errors are like a conquerable dose of poison, which a healthful nature doth overcome. *And I can never believe that a man may not be saved by that religion, which doth but bring him to a true love of God and to a heavenly mind and life: nor that God will ever cast a soul into hell that truly loveth him.* Also at first it would disgrace any doctrine with me, if I did but hear it called Popery and anti-Christian; but I have long learned to be more impartial, and to know that Satan can use even the names of Popery and Antichrist, to bring a truth into suspicion and discredit."—Baxter's *Life*, Part I. p. 131.

Even Lord Bacon himself, who in his *Novum Organum* has so incomparably set forth the nature of the difference, and the unfitness of the latter faculty for the objects of the former, does nevertheless in sundry places use the term reason where he means the understanding, and sometimes, though less frequently, understanding for reason.* In consequence of thus confounding the two terms, or rather of wasting both words for the expression of one and the same faculty, he left himself no appropriate term for the other and higher gift of reason, and was thus under the necessity of adopting fantastical and mystical phrases, for example, the dry light (*lumen siccum*), the lucific vision, and the like, meaning thereby nothing more than reason in contradistinction from the understanding. Thus too in the preceding Aphorism, by reason Leighton means the human understanding, the explanation annexed to it being (by a noticeable coincidence) word for word, the very definition which the founder of the Critical Philosophy gives of the understanding—namely, "the faculty judging according to sense."

ON THE DIFFERENCE IN KIND OF REASON AND THE UNDERSTANDING.

SCHEME OF THE ARGUMENT.

On the contrary, Reason is the power of universal and necessary convictions, the source and substance of truths above sense, and having their evidence in themselves. Its presence is always marked by the necessity of the position affirmed: this necessity being conditional, when a truth of reason is applied to facts of experience, or to the rules and maxims of the understanding; but absolute, when the subject matter is itself the growth or offspring of reason. Hence arises a distinction in reason itself, derived from the different mode of applying it, and from the objects to which it is directed: accordingly as we consider one and the same gift, now as the ground of formal principles, and now as the origin of ideas. Contemplated distinctively in reference to formal (or abstract) truth, it is the Speculative Reason; but in reference to actual (or moral) truth, as the fountain of ideas and

* See The Friend, II. pp. 146–150; Essays VIII. and IX., II. pp. 437–448.—*Ed.*

the light of the conscience, we name it the Practical Reason. Whenever by self-subjection to this universal light, the will of the individual, the particular will, has become a will of reason, the man is regenerate: and reason is then the spirit of the regenerated man, whereby the person is capable of a quickening intercommunion with the Divine Spirit. And herein consists the mystery of Redemption, that this has been rendered possible for us. *And so it is written; the first man Adam was made a living soul, the last Adam a quickening Spirit.* (1 Cor. xv. 45.) We need only compare the passages in the writings of the Apostles Paul and John, concerning the Spirit and spiritual gifts, with those in the Proverbs and in the Wisdom of Solomon respecting Reason, to be convinced that the terms are synonymous.* In this at once most comprehensive and most appropriate acceptation of the word, Reason is pre-eminently spiritual, and a spirit, even our spirit, through an effluence of the same grace by which we are privileged to say, Our Father!

On the other hand, the judgments of the Understanding are binding only in relation to the objects of our senses, which we reflect under the forms of the understanding. It is, as Leighton rightly defines it, "the faculty judging according to sense." Hence we add the epithet human without tautology: and speak of the human understanding in disjunction from that of beings higher or lower than man. But there is, in this sense, no human reason. There neither is nor can be but one reason, one and the same; even the light that lighteth every man's individual understanding (*discursus*), and thus maketh it a reasonable understanding, discourse of reason—*one only*, yet *manifold: it goeth through all understanding, and remaining in itself regenerateth all other powers.* The same writer calls it likewise *an influence from the Glory of the Almighty*, this being one of the names of the Messiah, as the *Logos*, or co-eternal Filial Word. And most noticeable for its coincidence is a fragment of Heraclitus, as I have indeed already noticed elsewhere;—"To discourse rationally it behooves us to derive strength from that which is common to all men: for all human understandings are nourished by the one Divine Word."

Beasts, I have said, partake of understanding. If any man deny this, there is a ready way of settling the question. Let

* See Wisd. of Sol. c. vii. 22, 23, 27.—*Ed.*

him give a careful perusal to Hüber's two small volumes on bees and ants (especially the latter), and to Kirby and Spence's Introduction to Entomology: and one or other of two things must follow. He will either change his opinion as irreconcilable with the facts; or he must deny the facts; which yet I can not suppose, inasmuch as the denial would be tantamount to the no less extravagant than uncharitable assertion, that Hüber, and the several eminent naturalists, French and English, Swiss, German, and Italian, by whom Hüber's observations and experiments have been repeated and confirmed, have all conspired to impose a series of falsehoods and fairy-tales on the world. I see no way, at least, by which he can get out of this dilemma, but by overleaping the admitted rules and fences of all legitimate discussion, and either transferring to the word, Understanding, the definition already appropriated to Reason, or defining understanding *in genere* by the specific and accessional perfections which the human understanding derives from its co-existence with reason and free-will in the same individual person; in plainer words, from its being exercised by a self-conscious and responsible creature. And, after all, the supporter of Harrington's position would have a right to ask him, by what other name he would designate the faculty in the instances referred to? If it be not understanding, what is it?

In no former part of this Volume have I felt the same anxiety to obtain a patient attention. For I do not hesitate to avow, that on my success in establishing the validity and importance of the distinction between Reason and the Understanding, rest my hopes of carrying the Reader along with me through all that is to follow. Let the student but clearly see and comprehend the diversity in the things themselves, and the expediency of a correspondent distinction and appropriation of the words will follow of itself. Turn back for a moment to the Aphorism, and having re-perused the first paragraph of this Comment thereon, regard the two following narratives as the illustration. I do not say proof: for I take these from a multitude of facts equally striking for the one only purpose of placing my meaning out of all doubt.

I. Hüber put a dozen humble-bees under a bell-glass along with a comb of about ten silken cocoons so unequal in height as not to be capable of standing steadily. To remedy this two or three of the humble-bees got upon the comb, stretched themselves over its edge, and with their heads downwards fixed their fore-feet on the table on which the comb stood, and so with their hind feet kept the comb from falling. When these were weary others took their places. In this constrained and painful posture, fresh bees relieving their comrades at intervals, and each working in its turn, did these affectionate little insects support the comb for nearly three days: at the end of which they had prepared sufficient wax to build pillars with. But these pillars having accidentally got displaccd, the bees had recourse again to the same manœuvre, till Hüber pitying their hard case, &c.

II. "I shall at present describe the operations of a single ant that I observed sufficiently long to satisfy my curiosity.

"One rainy day I observed a laborer digging the ground near the aperture which gave entrance to the ant-hill. It placed in a heap the several fragments it had scraped up, and formed them into small pellets, which it deposited here and there upon the nest. It returned constantly to the same place, and appeared to have a marked design, for it labored with ardor and perseverance. I remarked a slight furrow, excavated in the ground in a straight line, representing the plan of a path or gallery. The laborer, the whole of whose movements fell under my immediate observation, gave it greater depth and breadth, and cleared out its borders: and I saw at length, in which I could not be deceived, that it had the intention of establishing an avenue which was to lead from one of the stories to the underground chambers. This path, which was about two or three inches in length, and formed by a single ant, was opened above and bordered on each side by a buttress of earth; its concavity *en forme de goutière* was of the most perfect regularity, for the architect had not left an atom too much. The work of this ant was so well followed and understood, that I could almost to a certainty guess its next proceeding, and the very fragment it was about to remove. At the side of the opening where this path terminated, was a second opening to which it was necessary to arrive by some road. The same ant engaged in and executed alone this undertaking. It furrowed out and opened another path, parallel to the first, leaving between each a little wall of three or four lines in height. Those ants who lay the foundation of a wall, chamber, or gallery, from working separately occasion, now and then, a want of coincidence in the parts of the same or different objects. Such examples are of no unfrequent occurrence, but they by no means embarrass them. What follows proves that the workman, on discovering his error, knew how to rectify it. A wall had been erected with the view of sustaining a vaulted ceiling, still incomplete, that had been projected from the wall of the opposite chamber. The workman who began constructing it, had given it too little elevation to meet the opposite partition upon which it was to rest. Had it been continued on the original plan, it must infallibly have met the wall at about one half of its height, and this it was necessary to avoid. This state of things very forcibly claimed my attention, when one of the ants arriving at the place, and visiting the works, appeared to be struck by the difficulty which presented itself; but this it as soon obviated, by taking down the ceiling and raising the wall upon which it reposed. It then, in my presence, constructed a new ceiling with the fragments of the former one."—*Hüber's Natural History of Ants*, pp. 38–41.

Now I assert, that the faculty manifested in the acts here narrated does not differ *in kind* from understanding, and that it *does* so differ from reason. What I conceive the former to be, physiologically considered, will be shown hereafter. In this place I take the understanding as it exists in men, and in exclusive reference to its *intelligential* functions; and it is in this sense of the word that I am to prove the necessity of contra-distinguishing it from reason.

Premising then, that two or more subjects having the same essential characters are said to fall under the same general definition, I lay it down, as a self-evident truth—(it is, in fact, an identical proposition)—that whatever subjects fall under one and the same general definition are of one and the same kind: consequently, that which does *not* fall under this definition, must differ in kind from each and all of those that *do*. Difference in degree does indeed suppose sameness in kind; and difference in kind precludes distinction from difference of degree. *Heterogenea non comparari, ergo nec distingui, possunt.* The inattention to this rule gives rise to the numerous sophisms comprised by Aristotle under the head of *μετάβασις εἰς ἄλλο γένος*, that is, transition into a new kind, or the falsely applying to X what had been truly asserted of A, and might have been true of X, had it differed from

A in its degree only. The sophistry consists in the omission to notice what not being noticed will be supposed not to exist; and where the silence respecting the difference in kind is tantamount to an assertion that the difference is merely in degree. But the fraud is especially gross, where the heterogeneous subject, thus clandestinely slipt in, is in its own nature insusceptible of degree: such as, for instance, certainty or circularity, contrasted with strength, or magnitude.

To apply these remarks for our present purpose, we have only to describe Understanding and Reason, each by its characteristic qualities. The comparison will show the difference.

UNDERSTANDING.	REASON.
1. Understanding is discursive.	1. Reason is fixed.
2. The Understanding in all its judgments refers to some other faculty as its ultimate authority.	2. The Reason in all its decisions appeals to itself as the ground and *substance* of their truth. (*Heb.* vi. 13.)
3. Understanding is the faculty of reflection.	3. Reason of contemplation. Reason indeed is much nearer to Sense than to Understanding: for Reason (says our great Hooker) is a direct aspect of truth, an inward beholding, having a similar relation to the intelligible or spiritual, as Sense has to the material or phenomenal.

The result is, that neither falls under the definition of the other. They differ *in kind:* and had my object been confined to the establishment of this fact, the preceding columns would have superseded all further disquisition. But I have ever in view the especial interest of my youthful readers, whose reflective power is to be cultivated, as well as their particular reflections to be called forth and guided. Now the main chance of their reflecting on religious subjects aright, and of their attaining to the contemplation of spiritual truths at all, rests on their insight into the nature of this disparity still more than on their conviction of its existence. I now, therefore, proceed to a brief analysis of the Understanding, in elucidation of the definitions already given.

The Understanding then, considered exclusively as an organ of human intelligence, is the faculty by which we reflect and generalize. Take, for instance, any object consisting of many parts, a house, or a group of houses: and if it be contemplated, as a whole, that is, as many constituting a one, it forms what, in the technical language of psychology, is called a total impression. Among the various component parts of this, we direct our attention especially to such as we recollect to have noticed in other total impressions. Then, by a voluntary act, we withhold our attention from all the rest to reflect exclusively on these; and these we henceforward use as common characters, by virtue of which the several objects are referred to one and the same sort.* Thus, the whole process may be reduced to three acts, all depending on and supposing a previous impression on the senses: first, the appropriation of our attention; second (and in order to the continuance of the first) abstraction, or the voluntary withholding of the attention; and, third, generalization. And these are the proper functions of the Understanding: and the power of so doing, is what we mean, when we say we possess understanding, or are created with the faculty of understanding.†

* Accordingly as we attend more or less to the differences, the sort becomes, of course, more or less comprehensive. Hence there arises for the systematic naturalist the necessity of subdividing the sorts into orders, classes, families, &c.: all which, however, resolve themselves for the mere logician into the conception of *genus* and *species*, that is, the comprehending and the comprehended.

† It is obvious, that the third function includes the act of comparing one object with another. The act of comparing supposes in the comparing faculty certain inherent forms, that is, modes of reflecting not referable to the objects reflected on, but pre-determined by the constitution and mechanism of the understanding itself. And under some one or other of these forms, the resemblances and differences must be subsumed in order to be conceivable, and *à fortiori* therefore in order to be comparable. The senses do not compare, but merely furnish the materials for comparison.

Were it not so, how could the first comparison have been possible? It would involve the absurdity of measuring a thing by itself. But if we think on some one thing, the length of our own foot, or of our hand and arm from the elbow-joint, it is evident that in order to do this, we must have the conception of measure. Now these antecedent and most general conceptions are what is meant by the constituent forms of the understanding: we call them constituent because they are not acquired by the understanding, but

Now when a person speaking to us of any particular object or appearance refers it by means of some common character to a known class (which he does in giving it a name), we say, that we understand him; that is, we understand his words. The name of a thing, in the original sense of the word name (*nomen*,

are implied in its constitution. As rationally might a circle be said to acquire a centre and circumference, as the understanding to acquire these its inherent forms or ways of conceiving. This is what Leibnitz meant, when to the old adage of the Peripatetics, *Nihil in intellectu quod non prius in sensu*—there is nothing in the understanding not derived from the senses, or—there is nothing *con*ceived that was not previously *per*ceived,—he replied—*præter intellectum ipsum*, except the misunderstanding itself.

And here let me remark for once and all: whoever would reflect to any purpose—whoever is in earnest in his pursuit of self-knowledge, and of one of the principal means to this, an insight into the meaning of the words he uses, and the different meanings properly or improperly conveyed by one and the same word, accordingly as it is used in the schools or the market,—accordingly as the *kind* or a high *degree* is intended (for example, heat, weight, and the like, as employed scientifically, compared with the same word used popularly)—whoever, I say, seriously, proposes this as his object, must so far overcome his dislike of pedantry, and his dread of being sneered at as a pedant, as not to quarrel with an uncouth word or phrase, till he is quite sure that some other and more familiar one would not only have expressed the precise meaning with equal clearness, but have been as likely to draw attention to this meaning exclusively. The ordinary language of a philosopher in conversation or popular writings, compared with the language he uses in strict reasoning, is as his watch compared with the chronometer in his observatory. He sets the former by the town-clock, or even, perhaps, by the Dutch clock in his kitchen, not because he believes it right, but because his neighbors and his cook go by it. To afford the reader an opportunity for exercising the forbearance here recommended, I turn back to the phrase, "most general conceptions," and observe, that in strict and severe propriety of language, I should have said *generalific* or *generific* rather than general, and concipiences or conceptive acts rather than conceptions.

It is an old complaint, that a man of genius no sooner appears, but the host of dunces are up in arms to repel the invading alien. This observation would have made more converts to its truth, I suspect, had it been worded more dispassionately and with a less contemptuous antithesis. For "dunces," let us substitute "the many," or the "*οὐτος κόσμος*" (*this world*) of the Apostle, and we shall perhaps find no great difficulty in accounting for the fact. To arrive at the root, indeed, and last ground of the problem, it would be necessary to investigate the nature and effects of the sense of difference on the human mind where it is not holden in check by reason and reflection. We need not go to the savage tribes of North America, or the yet ruder natives of the Indian Isles, to learn how slight a degree of difference will, in

νοούμενον, τὸ *intelligible, id quod intelligitur*), expresses that which is *understood* in an appearance, that which we place (or make to *stand*) *under* it, as the condition of its real existence, and in proof that it is not an accident of the senses, or affection of the individual, not a phantom or apparition, that is, an appearance

uncultivated minds, call up a sense of diversity, and inward perplexity and contradiction, as if the strangers were, and yet were not, of the same kind with themselves. Who has not had occasion to observe the effect which the gesticulations and nasal tones of a Frenchman produce on our own vulgar? Here we may see the origin and primary import of our *unkindness*. It is a sense of *un*kind, and not the mere negation but the positive opposite of the sense of *kind*. Alienation, aggravated now by fear, now by contempt, and not seldom by a mixture of both, aversion, hatred, enmity, are so many successive shapes of its growth and *metamorphosis*. In application to the present case, it is sufficient to say, that Pindar's remark on sweet music holds equally true of genius: as many as are not delighted by it are disturbed, perplexed, irritated. The beholder either recognizes it as a projected form of his own being, that moves before him with a glory round its head, or recoils from it as from a spectre. But this speculation would lead me too far; I must be content with having referred to it as the ultimate ground of the fact, and pass to the more obvious and proximate causes. And as the first, I would rank the person's not understanding what yet he expects to understand, and as if he had a right to do so. An original mathematical work, or any other that requires peculiar and technical marks and symbols, will excite no uneasy feelings—not in the mind of a competent reader, for he understands it; and not with others, because they neither expect nor are expected to understand it. The second place we may assign to the misunderstanding, which is almost sure to follow in cases where the incompetent person, finding no outward marks (diagrams, arbitrary signs, and the like) to inform him at first sight, that the subject is one which he does not pretend to understand, and to be ignorant of which does not detract from his estimation as a man of abilities generally, will attach some meaning to what he hears or reads; and as he is out of humor with the author, it will most often be such a meaning as he can quarrel with and exhibit in a ridiculous or offensive point of view.

But above all, the whole world almost of minds, as far as we regard intellectual efforts, may be divided into two classes of the busy-indolent and lazy-indolent. To both alike all thinking is painful, and all attempts to rouse them to think, whether in the re-examination of their existing convictions, or for the reception of new light, are irritating. "It *may* all be very deep and clever; but really one ought to be quite sure of it before one wrenches one's brain to find out what it is. I take up a book as a companion, with whom I can have an easy cheerful chitchat on what we both know beforehand, or else matters of fact. In our leisure hours we have a right to relaxation and amusement."

Well! but in their *studious* hours, when their bow is to be bent, when

which is *only* an appearance. (See *Gen.* ii. 19, 20, and in *Psalm* xx. 1, and in many other places of the Bible, the identity of *nomen* with *numen*, that is, invisible power and presence, the *nomen substantivum* of all real objects, and the ground of their reality, independently of the affections of sense in the percipient.) In like manner, in a connected succession of names, as the speaker passes from one to the other, we say that we understand his *dis-*

they are *apud Musas*, or amidst the Muses? Alas! it is just the same. The same craving for *amusement*, that is, to be away from the Muses; for relaxation, that is, the unbending of a bow which in fact had never been strung? There are two ways of obtaining their applause. The first is: enable them to reconcile in one and the same occupation the love of sloth and the hatred of vacancy. Gratify indolence, and yet save them from *ennui* —in plain English, from themselves. For, spite of their antipathy to dry reading, the keeping company with themselves is, after all, the insufferable annoyance: and the true secret of their dislike to a work of thought and inquiry lies in its tendency to make them acquainted with their own permanent being. The other road to their favor is, to introduce to them their own thoughts and predilections, tricked out in the fine language, in which it would gratify their vanity to express them in their own conversation, and with which they can imagine themselves showing off: and this (as has been elsewhere remarked) is the characteristic difference between the second-rate writers of the last two or three generations, and the same class under Elizabeth and the Stuarts. In the latter we find the most far-fetched and singular thoughts in the simplest and most native language; in the former, the most obvious and common-place thoughts in the most far-fetched and motley language. But lastly, and as the *sine qua non* of their patronage, a sufficient arc must be left for the reader's mind to oscillate in—freedom of choice,

To make the shifting cloud be what you please,

save only where the attraction of curiosity determines the line of motion. The attention must not be fastened down: and this every work of genius, not simply narrative, must do before it can be justly appreciated.

In former times a popular work meant one that adapted the results of studious meditation or scientific research to the capacity of the people, presenting in the concrete, by instances and examples, what had been ascertained in the abstract and by discovery of the law. Now, on the other hand, that is a popular work which gives back to the people their own errors and prejudices, and flatters the many by creating them under the title of THE PUBLIC, into a supreme and inappellable tribunal of intellectual excellence.

P.S. In a continuous work, the frequent insertion and length of notes would need an apology: in a book like this, of aphorisms and detached comments, none is necessary, it being understood beforehand that the sauce and the garnish are to occupy the greater part of the dish.

course, discursio intellectus, discursus, his passing from one thing to another. Thus, in all instances, it is words, names, or, if images, yet images used as words or names, that are the only and exclusive subjects of understanding. In no instance do we understand a thing in itself; but only the name to which it is referred. Sometimes indeed, when several classes are recalled conjointly, we identify the words with the object—though by courtesy of idiom rather than in strict propriety of language. Thus we may say that we *understand* a rainbow, when recalling successively the several names for the several sorts of colors, we know that they are to be applied to one and the same *phænomenon,* at once distinctly and simultaneously; but even in common speech we should not say this of a single color. No one would say he understands red or blue. He *sees* the color, and had seen it before in a vast number and variety of objects; and he understands the *word* red, as referring his fancy or memory to this his collective experience.

If this be so, and so it most assuredly is—if the proper functions of the understanding be that of generalizing the notices received from the senses in order to the construction of names: of referring particular notices, that is, impressions or sensations, to their proper names; and, *vice versa,* names to their correspondent class or kind of notices—then it follows of necessity, that the Understanding is truly and accurately defined in the words of Leighton and Kant, a faculty judging according to sense.

Now whether in defining the speculative Reason,—(that is, the reason considered abstractedly as an intellective power)—we call it "the source of necessary and universal principles, according to which the notices of the senses are either affirmed or denied;" or describe it as "the power by which we are enabled to draw from particular and contingent appearances universal and necessary conclusions:"* it is equally evident that the two definitions

* Take a familiar illustration. My sight and touch convey to me a certain impression, to which my understanding applies its pre-conceptions (*conceptus antecedentes et generalissimi*) of quantity and relation, and thus refers it to the class and name of three-cornered bodies—we will suppose it the iron of a turf-spade. It compares the sides, and finds that any two measured as one are greater than the third; and according to a law of the imagination, there arises a presumption that in all other bodies of the same figure (that is, three-cornered and equilateral) the same proportion exists. After this, the senses have been directed successively to a number of three-

differ in their essential characters, and consequently the subjects differ in *kind*.

The dependence of the Understanding on the representations of the senses, and its consequent posteriority thereto, as contrasted with the independence and antecedency of Reason, are strikingly

cornered bodies of unequal sides—and in these too the same proportion has been found without exception, till at length it becomes a fact of experience, that in all triangles hitherto seen, the two sides together are greater than the third: and there will exist no ground or analogy for anticipating an exception to a rule, generalized from so vast a number of particular instances. So far and no farther could the understanding carry us: and as far as this "the faculty, judging according to sense," conducts many of the inferior animals, if not in the same, yet in instances analogous and fully equivalent.

The reason supersedes the whole process, and on the first conception presented by the understanding in consequence of the first sight of a triangular figure, of whatever sort it might chance to be, it affirms with an assurance incapable of future increase, with a perfect certainty, that in all possible triangles any two of the inclosing lines will and must be greater than the third. In short, understanding in its highest form of experience remains commensurate with the experimental notices of the senses from which it is generalized. Reason, on the other hand, either predetermines experience, or avails itself of a past experience to supersede its necessity in all future time; and affirms truths which no sense could perceive, nor experiment verify, nor experience confirm.

Yea, this is the test and character of a truth so affirmed, that in its own proper form it is inconceivable. For to conceive is a function of the understanding, which can be exercised only on subjects subordinate thereto. And yet to the forms of the understanding, all truth must be reduced, that is to be fixed as an object of reflection, and to be rendered expressible. And here we have a second test and sign of a truth so affirmed, that it can come forth out of the moulds of the understanding only in the disguise of two contradictory conceptions, each of which is partially true, and the conjunction of both conceptions becomes the representative or expression (the exponent) of a truth beyond conception and inexpressible. Examples: Before Abraham *was*, I *am*.—God is a circle, the centre of which is everywhere, and circumference nowhere. The soul is all in every part.

If this appear extravagant, it is an extravagance which no man can indeed learn from another, but which, (were this possible,) I might have learnt from Plato, Kepler, and Bacon; from Luther, Hooker, Pascal, Leibnitz, and Fenelon. But in this last paragraph I have, I see, unwittingly overstepped my purpose, according to which we were to take reason as a simply intellectual power. Yet even as such, and with all the disadvantage of a technical and arbitrary abstraction, it has been made evident:—1. that there is an intuition or *im*mediate beholding, accompanied by a conviction of the necessity and universality of the truth so beholden, not derived from the senses, which intuition, when it is construed by pure sense, gives birth to the

exemplified in the Ptolemaic system—that truly wonderful product and highest boast of the faculty, judging according to the senses—compared with the Newtonian, as the offspring of a yet higher power, arranging, correcting, and annulling the representations of the senses according to its own inherent laws and constitutive ideas.

science of mathematics, and when applied to objects supersensuous or spiritual is the organ of theology and philosophy:—and 2. that there is likewise a reflective and discursive faculty, or mediate apprehension which, taken by itself and uninfluenced by the former, depends on the senses for the materials on which it is exercised, and is contained within the sphere of the senses. And this faculty it is, which in generalizing the notices of the senses constitutes sensible experience, and gives rise to maxims or rules which may become more and more general, but can never be raised into universal verities, or beget a consciousness of absolute certainty; though they may be sufficient to extinguish all doubt. (Putting revelation out of view, take our first progenitor in the 50th or 100th year of his existence. His experience would probably have freed him from all doubt, as the sun sank in the horizon, that it would re-appear the next morning. But compare this state of assurance with that which the same man would have had of the 47th proposition of Euclid, supposing him like Pythagoras to have discovered the demonstration.) Now is it expedient, I ask, or conformable to the laws and purposes of language, to call two so altogether disparate subjects by one and the same name? Or, having two names in our language, should we call each of the two diverse subjects by both—that is, by either name, as caprice might dictate? If not, then as we have the two words, reason and understanding (as indeed what language of cultivated man has not?)—what should prevent us from appropriating the former to the power distinctive of humanity? We need only place the derivatives from the two terms in opposition (for example, "A and B are both rational beings; but there is no comparison between them in point of intelligence," or "She always concludes rationally, though not a woman of much understanding") to see that we can not reverse the order—that is, call the higher gift understanding, and the lower reason. What should prevent us? I asked. Alas! that which has prevented us—the cause of this confusion in the terms—is only too obvious; namely, inattention to the momentous distinction in the things, and generally, to the duty and habit recommended in the fifth introductory Aphorism of this Volume. But the cause of this, and of all its lamentable effects and subcauses, *false doctrine, blindness of heart, and contempt of the word,* is best declared by the philosophic Apostle: *they did not like to retain God in their knowledge* (Rom. i. 28), and though they could not extinguish *the light that lighteth every man,* and which *shone in the darkness:* yet because the darkness could not comprehend the light, they refused to bear witness of it and worshiped, instead, the shaping mist, which the light had drawn upward from the ground (that is, from the mere animal nature and instinct), and which that light alone had made visible, that is, by superinducing on the animal instinct the principle of self-consciousness.

APHORISM IX.

In wonder all philosophy began; in wonder it ends; and admiration fills up the interspace. But the first wonder is the offspring of ignorance: the last is the parent of adoration. The first is the birth-throe of our knowledge: the last is its euthanasy and *apotheosis*.

SEQUELÆ: OR THOUGHTS SUGGESTED BY THE PRECEDING APHORISM.

As in respect of the first wonder we are all on the same level, how comes it that the philosophic mind should, in all ages, be the privilege of a few? The most obvious reason is this. The wonder takes place before the period of reflection, and (with the great mass of mankind) long before the individual is capable of directing his attention freely and consciously to the feeling, or even to its exciting causes. Surprise (the form and dress which the wonder of ignorance usually puts on) is worn away, if not precluded, by custom and familiarity. So is it with the objects of the senses, and the ways and fashions of the world around us; even as with the beat of our own hearts, which we notice only in moments of fear and perturbation. But with regard to the concerns of our inward being, there is yet another cause that acts in concert with the power in custom to prevent a fair and equal exertion of reflective thought. The great fundamental truths and doctrines of religion, the existence and attributes of God and the life after death, are in Christian countries taught so early, under such circumstances, and in such close and vital association with whatever makes or marks reality for our infant minds, that the words ever after represent sensations, feelings, vital assurances, sense of reality—rather than thoughts, or any distinct conception. Associated, I had almost said identified, with the parental voice, look, touch, with the living warmth and pressure of the mother, on whose lap the child is first made to kneel, within whose palms its little hands are folded, and the motion of whose eyes *its* eyes follow and imitate—(yea, what the blue sky is to the mother, the mother's upraised eyes and brow are to the child, the type and symbol of an invisible heaven!)—from within and without these great first truths, these good and gracious tidings, these holy and humanizing spells, in the preconformity to which our very humanity may be said to consist, are so infused that it were but a tame and inadequate expression to say, we all take them for granted. At a later period, in youth or early manhood, most of us, indeed (in the higher and middle classes at least), read or hear certain proofs of these truths—which we commonly listen to, when we listen at all, with much the same feelings as a popular prince on his coronation day, in the centre of a fond and rejoicing nation, may be supposed to hear the champion's challenge to all the non-existents, that deny or dispute his rights and royalty. In fact, the order of proof is most often reversed or transposed. As far at least as I dare judge from the goings on in my own mind, when with keen delight I first read the works of Derham, Nieuwentiet, and Lyonet, I should say that the full and life-like conviction of a gracious Creator is the proof (at all events, performs the office and answers all the purposes of a proof) of the wisdom and benevolence in the construction of the creature.

Do I blame this? Do I wish it to be otherwise? God forbid! It is only one of its accidental, but too frequent, consequences, of which I complain, and against which I protest. I regret nothing that tends to make the light become the life of men, even as the life in the eternal Word is their only and single true light. But I do regret, that in after-years—when by occasion of some new dispute on some old heresy, or any other accident, the attention has for the first time been distinctly attracted to the superstructure raised on these fundamental truths, or to truths of later revelation supplemental of these and not less important—all the doubts and difficulties, that can not but arise where the understanding, *the mind of the flesh*, is made the measure of spiritual things; all the sense of strangeness and seeming contradiction in terms; all the marvel and the mystery, that belong equally to both, are first thought of and applied in objection exclusively to the latter. I would disturb no man's faith in the great articles of the (falsely so called) religion of nature. But before a man rejects, and calls on other men to reject, the revelations of the Gospel and the religion of all Christendom, I would have him place himself in the state and under all the privations of a Simonides, when in the fortieth day of his meditation the sage and philosophic poet abandoned the problem in despair. Ever and anon he seemed to have hold of the truth ; but when he asked himself what he meant by it, it escaped from him, or resolved itself into meanings, that destroyed each other. I would have the skeptic, while yet a skeptic only, seriously consider whether a doctrine, of the truth of which a Socrates could obtain no other assurance than what he derived from his strong wish that it should be true ; and which Plato found a mystery hard to discover, and when discovered, communicable only to the fewest of men ; can, consonantly with history or common sense, be classed among the articles, the belief of which is insured to all men by their mere common sense ? Whether without gross outrage to fact, they can be said to constitute a religion of nature, or a natural theology antecedent to revelation, or superseding its necessity ? Yes ! in prevention (for there is little chance, I fear, of a cure) of the pugnacious dogmatism of partial reflection, I would prescribe to every man who feels a commencing alienation from the Catholic faith, and whose studies and attainments authorize him to argue on the subject at all, a patient and thoughtful perusal of the arguments and representations which Bayle supposes to have passed through the mind of Simonides. Or I should be fully satisfied if I could induce these eschewers of mystery to give a patient, manly, and impartial perusal to the single treatise of Pomponatius, *De Fato*.*

When they have fairly and satisfactorily overthrown the objections and cleared away the difficulties urged by this sharp-witted Italian against the doctrines which they profess to retain, then let them commence their attack on those which they reject. As far as the supposed irrationality of the latter is the ground of argument, I am much deceived if, on reviewing their forces, they would not find the ranks wofully thinned by the success of their own fire in the preceding engagement—unless, indeed, by pure heat of controversy, and to storm the lines of their antagonists, they can bring to life again the arguments which they had themselves killed off in the defence of their own positions. In vain

* The philosopher, whom the Inquisition would have burnt alive as an atheist, had not Leo X. and Cardinal Bembo decided that the work might be formidable to those semi-pagan Christians who regarded revelation as a mere make-weight to their boasted religion of nature ; but contained nothing dangerous to the Catholic Church or offensive to a true believer. (He was born at Mantua in 1462 and died in 1525.—*Ed.*)

shall we seek for any other mode of meeting the broad facts of the scientific Epicurean, or the requisitions and queries of the all-analyzing Pyrrhonist, than by challenging the tribunal to which they appeal, as incompetent to try the question. In order to nonsuit the plaintiff, we must remove the cause from the faculty, that judges according to sense, and whose judgments, therefore, are valid only on objects of sense, to the superior courts of conscience and intuitive reason. *The words I speak unto you, are Spirit*, and such only *are life*, that is, have an inward and actual power abiding in them.

But the same truth is at once shield and bow. The shaft of Atheism glances aside from it to strike and pierce the breast-plate of the heretic. Well for the latter, if, plucking the weapon from the wound, he recognizes an arrow from his own quiver, and abandons a cause that connects him with such confederates! An insight into the proper functions and subaltern rank of the understanding may not, indeed, disarm the Psilanthropist of his metaphorical glosses, or of his versions fresh from the forge, with no other stamp than the private mark of the individual manufacturer; but it will deprive him of the only rational pretext for having recourse to tools so liable to abuse, and of such perilous example.

COMMENT.

Since the preceding pages were composed, and during an interim of depression and disqualification. I heard with a delight and an interest which I might without hyperbole call medicinal, that the contradistinction of the understanding from reason,—for which during twenty years I have been contending, *casting my bread upon the waters* with a perseverance which in the existing state of the public taste, nothing but the deepest conviction of its importance could have inspired—has been lately sanctioned by the present distinguished Professor of Anatomy, in the course of lectures given by him at the Royal College of Surgeons, on the zoological part of natural history; and, if I am rightly informed, in one of the eloquent and impressive introductory discourses.* In explaining the nature of Instinct, as deduced from the actions

* The allusion is to Mr. Green; and the passage to which the Author refers, will be found in an Appendix, reprinted from the "Vital Dynamics." —*Ed.*

and tendencies of animals successively presented to the observation of the comparative physiologist in the ascending scale of organic life—or rather, I should have said, in an attempt to determine that precise import of the term, which is required by the facts*—the Professor explained the nature of what I have elsewhere called the adaptive power, that is, the faculty of adapting means to a proximate end. I mean here a relative end—that which relatively to one thing is an end, though relatively to some other it is in itself a mean. It is to be regretted that we have no single word to express those ends, that are not *the* end: for the distinction between those and an end in the proper sense of the term, is an important one. The Professor, I say, not only explained, first, the nature of the adaptive power *in genere*, and, secondly, the distinct character of the same power as it exists specifically and exclusively in the human being, and acquires the name of understanding; but he did it in a way which gave the whole sum and substance of my convictions, of all I had so long wished, and so often, but with such imperfect success, attempted to convey, free from all semblance of paradoxy, and from all occasion of offence—*omnem offendiculi ansam præcidens.*† It is,

* The word, Instinct, brings together a number of facts into one class by the assertion of a common ground, the nature of which ground it determines negatively only,—that is, the word does not explain what this common ground is; but simply indicates that there is such a ground, and that it is different in kind from that in which the responsible and consciously voluntary actions of men originate. Thus, in its true and primary import, Instinct stands in antithesis to Reason; and the perplexity and contradictory statements into which so many meritorious naturalists and popular writers on natural history (Priscilla Wakefield, Kirby, Spence, Hüber, and even Reimarus) have fallen on this subject, arise wholly from their taking the word in opposition to Understanding. I notice this, because I would not lose any opportunity of impressing on the mind of my youthful readers the important truth that language, as the embodied and articulated spirit of the race, as the growth and emanation of a people, and not the work of any individual wit or will, is often inadequate, sometimes deficient, but never false or delusive. We have only to master the true origin and original import of any native and abiding word, to find in it, if not the solution of the facts expressed by it, yet a finger-mark pointing to the road on which this solution is to be sought.

† *Neque quicquam addubito, quin ea candidis omnibus faciat satis. Quid autem facias istis qui vel ob ingenii pertinaciam sibi satisfieri nolint vel stupidiores sint quam ut satisfactionem intelligant? Nam quemadmodum Simonides dixit, Thessalos hebetiores esse quam ut possint a se decipi, ita quos-*

indeed, for the fragmentary reader only that I have any scruple. In those who have had the patience to accompany me so far on the up-hill road to manly principles, I can have no reason to guard against that disposition to hasty offence from anticipation of consequences—that faithless and loveless spirit of fear which plunged Galileo into a prison;*—a spirit most unworthy of an educated man, who ought to have learnt that the mistakes of scientific men have never injured Christianity, while every new truth discovered by them has either added to its evidence, or prepared the mind for its reception

ON INSTINCT IN CONNECTION WITH THE UNDERSTANDING.

It is evident, that the definition of a *genus* or class is an adequate definition only of the lowest *species* of that *genus:* for each higher *species* is distinguished from the lower by some additional character, while the general definition includes only the characters common to all the *species.* Consequently it describes the lowest only. Now I distinguish a *genus* or kind of powers under

dam videas stupidiores quam ut placari queant. Adhuc non mirum est invenire quod calumnietur qui nihil aliud quærit nisi quod calumnietur. (Erasmi Epist. ad Dorpium.) At all events, the paragraph passing through the *medium* of my own prepossessions, if any fault be found with it, the fault probably, and the blame certainly, belongs to the reporter.

* And which (I may add) in a more enlightened age, and in a Protestant country, impelled more than one German University to anathematize Fr. Hoffman's discovery of carbonic acid gas, and of its effects on animal life, as hostile to religion, and tending to atheism! Three or four students at the University of Jena, in the attempt to raise a spirit for the discovery of a supposed hidden treasure, were strangled or poisoned by the fumes of the charcoal they had been burning in a close garden-house of a vineyard near Jena, while employed in their magic fumigations and charms. One only was restored to life: and from his account of the noises and spectres (in his ears and eyes) as he was losing his senses, it was taken for granted that the bad spirit had destroyed them. Frederick Hoffman admitted that it was a very bad spirit who had tempted them, the spirit of avarice and folly; and that a very noxious spirit (gas, or *Geist*) was the immediate cause of their death. But he contended that this latter spirit was the spirit of charcoal, which would have produced the same effect, had the young men been chanting psalms instead of incantations: and acquitted the Devil of all direct concern in the business. The theological faculty took the alarm: even physicians pretended to be horror-stricken at Hoffman's audacity. The controversy and its appendages embittered several years of this great and good man's life.

the name of adaptive power, and give as its generic definition—the power of selecting and adapting means to proximate ends; and as an instance of the lowest *species* of this *genus*, I take the stomach of a caterpillar. I ask myself, under what words I can generalize the action of this organ; and I see, that it selects and adapts the appropriate means (that is, the assimilable part of the vegetable *congesta*) to the proximate end, that is, the growth or reproduction of the insect's body. This we call Vital Power, or *vita propria* of the stomach; and this being the lowest *species*, its definition is the same with the definition of the kind.

Well! from the power of the stomach I pass to the power exerted by the whole animal. I trace it wandering from spot to spot, and plant to plant, till it finds the appropriate vegetable; and again on this chosen vegetable, I mark it seeking out and fixing on the part of the plant, bark, leaf, or petal, suited to its nourishment: or (should the animal have assumed the butterfly form), to the deposition of its eggs, and the sustentation of the future *larva*. Here I see a power of selecting and adapting means to proximate ends according to circumstances: and this higher species of adaptive power we call Instinct.

Lastly, I reflect on the facts narrated and described in the preceding extracts from Hüber, and see a power of selecting and adapting the proper means to the proximate ends, according to varying circumstances. And what shall we call this yet higher species? We name the former, Instinct: we must call this Instinctive Intelligence.

Here then we have three powers of the same kind; life, instinct, and instinctive intelligence: the essential characters that define the *genus* existing equally in all three. But in addition to these, I find one other character common to the highest and lowest: namely, that the purposes are all manifestly predetermined by the peculiar organization of the animals; and though it may not be possible to discover any such immediate dependency in all the actions, yet the actions being determined by the purposes, the result is equivalent: and both the actions and the purposes are all in a necessitated reference to the preservation and continuance of the particular animal or the progeny. There is selection, but not choice; volition rather than will. The possible knowledge of a thing, or the desire to have that thing representable by a distinct correspondent thought, does not, in the animal, suffice to render the thing an object, or the ground of a purpose. I select and adapt the proper means to the separation of a stone from a rock, which I neither can, nor desire to use for food, shelter, or ornament; because, perhaps, I wish to measure the angles of its primary crystals, or, perhaps, for no better reason than the apparent difficulty of loosening the stone—*sit pro ratione voluntas*—and thus make a motive out of the absence of all motive, and a reason out of the arbitrary will to act without any reason.

Now what is the conclusion from these premisses? Evidently this: that if I suppose the adaptive power in its highest *species*, or form of instinctive intelligence, to co-exist with reason, free-will, and self-consciousness, it instantly becomes Understanding: in other words, that understanding differs indeed from the noblest form of instinct, but not in itself or in its own essential properties, but in consequence of its co-existence with far higher powers of a diverse kind in one and the same subject. Instinct in a rational, responsible, and self-conscious animal, is Understanding.

Such I apprehend to be the true view and exposition of Instinct; and in confirmation of its truth, I would merely request my readers, from the numerous well-authenticated instances on record, to recall some one of the extraordinary actions of dogs for the preservation of their masters' lives, and even for the avenging of their deaths. In these instances we have the third *species* of the adaptive power in connection with an apparently moral end—with an end in the proper sense of the word. Here the adaptive power co-exists with a purpose apparently voluntary, and the action seems neither pre-determined by the organization of the animal, nor in any direct reference to his own preservation, nor to the continuance of his race. It is united with an imposing semblance of gratitude, fidelity, and disinterested love. We not only value the faithful brute; we attribute worth to him. This, I admit, is a problem, of which I have no solution to offer. One of the wisest of uninspired men has not hesitated to declare the dog a great mystery, on account of this dawning of a moral nature, unaccompanied by any the least evidence of reason, in whichever of the two senses we interpret the word—whether as the practical reason, that is, the power of proposing an ultimate end, the determinability of the will by ideas; or as the sciential reason, that is, the faculty of concluding universal and necessary truths from particular and contingent appearances. But in a question respecting the possession of reason, the absence of all proof is tantamount to a proof of the contrary. It is, however, by no means equally clear to me, that the dog may not possess an *analogon* of words, which I have elsewhere shown to be the proper objects of the "faculty, judging according to sense."

But to return to my purpose: I entreat the Reader to reflect on any one fact of this kind, whether occurring in his own experience, or selected from the numerous anecdotes of the Dog preserved in the writings of zoologists. I will then confidently appeal to him, whether it is in his power not to consider the faculty displayed in these actions as the same in kind with the understanding, however inferior in degree. Or should he even in these instances prefer calling it instinct, and this in *contra*-distinction from understanding, I call on him to point out the boundary between the two, the chasm or partition-wall that divides or separates the one from the other. If he can, he will have done what none before him have been able to do, though many and eminent men have tried hard for it: and my recantation shall be among the first trophies of his success. If he can not, I must infer that he is controlled by his dread of the consequences, by an apprehension of some injury resulting to religion or morality from this opinion; and I shall console myself with the hope, that in the sequel of this Work he will find proofs of the directly contrary tendency. Not only is this view of the Understanding, as differing in degree from Instinct, and in kind from Reason, innocent in its possible influences on the religious character, but it is an indispensable preliminary to the removal of the most formidable obstacles to an intelligent belief of the peculiar doctrines of the Gospel, of the characteristic articles of the Christian Faith, with which the advocates of the truth in Christ have to contend;—the evil heart of unbelief alone excepted.

REFLECTIONS INTRODUCTORY TO APHORISM X.

The most momentous question a man can ask is, Have I a Saviour? And yet as far as the individual querist is concerned, it is premature and to no purpose, unless another question has been previously put and answered, (alas! too generally put after the wounded conscience has already given the answer!)

namely, Have I any need of a Saviour? For him who needs none, (O bitter irony of the evil Spirit, whose whispers the proud soul takes for its own thoughts, and knows not how the tempter is scoffing the while!) there is none, as long as he feels no need. On the other hand, it is scarcely possible to have answered this question in the affirmative, and not ask—first, in what the necessity consists—secondly, whence it proceeded—and, thirdly, how far the answer to this second question is or is not contained in the answer to the first. I entreat the intelligent Reader, who has taken me as his temporary guide on the straight, but yet, from the number of cross roads, difficult way of religious inquiry, to halt a moment, and consider the main points which, in this last division of my Work, have been already offered for his reflection. I have attempted, then, to fix the proper meaning of the words, Nature and Spirit, the one being the *antithesis* to the other: so that the most general and negative definition of nature is, whatever is not spirit; and *vice versa* of spirit, that which is not comprehended in nature; or in the language of our elder divines, that which transcends nature. But Nature is the term in which we comprehend all things that are representable in the forms of time and space, and subjected to the relations of cause and effect: and the cause of the existence of which, therefore, is to be sought for perpetually in something antecedent. The word itself expresses this in the strongest manner possible: *Naturâ*, that which is about to be born, that which is always *becoming*. It follows, therefore, that whatever originates its own acts, or in any sense contains in itself the cause of its own state, must be spiritual, and consequently supernatural; yet not on that account necessarily miraculous. And such must the responsible Will in us be, if it be at all.

A prior step has been to remove all misconceptions from the subject; to show the reasonableness of a belief in the reality and real influence of a universal and divine Spirit; the compatibility and possible communion of such a spirit with the spiritual in principle; and the analogy offered by the most undeniable truths of natural philosophy.*

* It has in its consequences proved no trifling evil to the Christian world, that Aristotle's definitions of Nature are all grounded on the petty and rather rhetorical than philosophical *antithesis* of nature to art—a conception inadequate to the demands even of his philosophy. Hence in the prog-

These views of the Spirit, and of the Will as spiritual, form the ground-work of my scheme. Among the numerous corollaries or appendents, the first that presented itself respects the question;—whether there is any faculty in man by which a knowledge of spiritual truths, or of any truths not abstracted from nature, is rendered possible;—and an answer is attempted in the comment on Aphorism VIII. And here I beg leave to remark, that in this comment the only novelty, and if there be merit, the only merit is—that there being two very different meanings, and two different words, I have here and in former works appropriated one meaning to one of the words, and the other to the other—instead of using the words indifferently and by hap-hazard: a confusion, the ill effects of which in this instance are so great and of such frequent occurrence in the works of our ablest philosophers and divines, that I should select it before all others in proof of Hobbes' maxim: that it is a short downhill passage from errors in words or errors in things. The difference of the Reason from the Understanding, and the imperfection and limited sphere of the latter, have been asserted by many both before and since Lord Bacon;* but still the habit of using reason and understanding as syno-

ress of his reasoning, he confounds the *natura naturata* (that is, the sum total of the facts and *phænomena* of the senses) with an hypothetical *natura naturans*, a Goddess Nature, that has no better claim to a place in any sober system of natural philosophy than the Goddess *Multitudo;* yet to which Aristotle not rarely gives the name and attributes of the Supreme Being. The result was, that the idea of God thus identified with this hypothetical nature becomes itself but an *hypothesis*, or at best but a precarious inference from incommensurate premisses and on disputable principles: while in other passages, God is confounded with (and everywhere, in Aristotle's genuine works), included in the universe: which most grievous error it is the great and characteristic merit of Plato to have avoided and denounced.

* Take one passage among many from the Posthumous Tracts (1660) of John Smith, not the least star in that bright constellation of Cambridge men, the contemporaries of Jeremy Taylor. "While we reflect on our own idea of Reason, we know that our souls are not it, but only partake of it: and that we have it *κατὰ μέθεξιν* and not *κατ' οὐσιήν*. Neither can it be called a faculty, but far rather a light, which we enjoy, but the source of which is not in ourselves, nor rightly by any individual to be denominated *mine*." This pure intelligence he then proceeds to contrast with the discursive faculty, that is, the Understanding. (See the notes on this remarkable writer in the Author's "Literary Remains." V. p. 266.—*Ed.*)

Also see Cudworth's Immutable Morality, book iv. chap. 4, et passim.—*Am. Ed.*

nymes acted as a disturbing force. Some it led into mysticism, others it set on explaining away a clear difference in kind into a mere superiority in degree: and it partially eclipsed the truth for all.

In close connection with this, and therefore forming the comment on the Aphorism next following, is the subject of the legitimate exercise of the Understanding, and its limitation to objects of sense; with the errors both of unbelief and of misbelief, which result from its extension beyond the sphere of possible experience. Wherever the forms of reasoning appropriate only to the natural world are applied to spiritual realities, it may be truly said, that the more strictly logical the reasoning is in all its parts, the more irrational it is as a whole.

To the Reader thus armed and prepared, I now venture to present the so-called mysteries of Faith, that is, the peculiar tenets and especial constituents of Christianity, or religion in spirit and in truth. In right order I must have commenced with the articles of the Trinity and Apostasy, including the question respecting the origin of Evil, and the Incarnation of the WORD. And could I have followed this order, some difficulties that now press on me would have been obviated. But the limits of the present Volume render it alike impracticable and inexpedient; for the necessity of my argument would have called forth certain hard though most true sayings, respecting the hollowness and tricksy sophistry of the so-called "natural theology," "religion of nature," "light of nature," and the like, which a brief exposition could not save from innocent misconceptions, much less protect against plausible misinterpretation. And yet both reason and experience have convinced me, that in the greater number of our Alogi, who feed on the husks of Christianity, the disbelief of the Trinity, the divinity of Christ included, has its origin and support in the assumed self-evidence of this natural theology, and in their ignorance of the insurmountable difficulties which on the same mode of reasoning press upon the fundamental articles of their own remnant of a creed. But arguments, which would prove the falsehood of a known truth, must themselves be false, and can prove the falsehood of no other position in *eodem genere*.

This hint I have thrown out as a spark that may perhaps fall where it will kindle. And worthily might the wisest of men make inquisition into the three momentous points here spoken of, for the purposes of speculative insight, and for the formation of enlarged and systematic views of the destination of Man, and the dispensation of God. But the practical Inquirer—(I speak not of those who inquire for the gratification of curiosity, and still less of those who labor as students only to shine as disputants; but of one, who seeks the truth, because he feels the want of it),—the practical inquirer, I say, hath already placed his foot on the rock, if he have satisfied himself that whoever needs not a Redeemer is more than human. Remove from him the difficulties and objections that oppose or perplex his belief of a crucified Saviour; convince him of the reality of sin, which is impossible without a knowledge of its true nature and inevitable consequences; and then satisfy him as to the fact historically, and as to the truth spiritually, of a redemption therefrom by Christ; do this for him, and there is little fear that he will permit either logical quirks or metaphysical puzzles to contravene the plain dictate of his common sense, that the sinless One who redeemed mankind from sin, must have been more than man; and that He who brought light and immortality into the world, could not in his own nature have been an inheritor of death and darkness. It is morally impossible that a man with these convictions should suffer the objection of incomprehensibility, and this on a subject of faith, to overbalance the manifest absurdity and contradiction in the notion of a Mediator between God and the human race, at the same infinite distance from God as the race for whom he mediates.

The origin of Evil, meanwhile, is a question interesting only to the metaphysician, and in a system of moral and religious philosophy. The man of sober mind who seeks for truths that possess a moral and practical interest, is content to be certain, first, that evil must have had a beginning, since otherwise it must either be God, or a co-eternal and co-equal rival of God; both impious notions, and the latter foolish to boot:—secondly, that it could not originate in God; for if so, it would be at once evil and not evil, or God would be at once God, that is, infinite goodness, and not God—both alike impossible positions. Instead, therefore, of troubling himself with this barren controversy, he more profitably turns his inquiries to that evil which most concerns himself, and of which he may find the origin.

The entire scheme of necessary Faith may be reduced to two

heads; first, the object and occasion, and secondly, the fact and effect,—of our redemption by Christ: and to this view does the order of the following Comments correspond. I have begun with Original Sin, and proceeded in the following Aphorism to the doctrine of Redemption. The Comments on the remaining Aphorisms are all subsidiary to these, or written in the hope of making the minor tenets of general belief be believed in a spirit worthy of these. They are, in short, intended to supply a febrifuge against aguish scruples and horrors, the hectic of the soul; —and, in Milton's words, "for servile and thrall-like fear, to substitute that adoptive and cheerful boldness, which our new alliance with God requires of us as Christians." Not the origin of evil, not the chronology of sin, or the chronicles of the original sinner; but sin originant, underived from without, and no passive link in the adamantine chain of effects, each of which is in its turn an instrument of causation, but no one of them a cause; —not with sin inflicted, which would be a calamity;—not with sin (that is, an evil tendency) implanted, for which let the planter be responsible;—but I begin with original sin. And for this purpose I have selected the Aphorism from the ablest and most formidable antagonist of this doctrine, Bishop Jeremy Taylor, and from the most eloquent work of this most eloquent of divines.* Had I said, of men, Cicero would forgive me, and Demosthenes nod assent!†

* See the notes on J. Taylor, *Lit. Rem.* V. p. 194–218.—*Ed.*

† It does not appear that the Church of England demands the literal understanding of the document contained in the second (from verse 8) and third chapters of Genesis as a point of faith, or regards a different interpretation as affecting the orthodoxy of the interpreter:* divines of the most unimpeachable orthodoxy and the most averse to the allegorizing of Scripture history in general, having from the earliest ages of the Christian Church adopted or permitted it in this instance. And indeed no unprejudiced man can pretend to doubt, that if in any other work of Eastern origin he met with trees of life and of knowledge; or talking and conversable snakes:

Inque rei signum serpentem serpere jussum;

he would want no other proofs that it was an allegory he was reading, and intended to be understood as such. Nor, if we suppose him conversant with Oriental works of any thing like the same antiquity, could it surprise him to find events of true history in connection with, or historical person-

* See Bp. Horsley's Sermon xvi. 2 Peter i. 20, 21.—*Ed.*

APHORISM X.

ON ORIGINAL SIN.

Jeremy Taylor.

The question is not whether there be any such thing as original Sin: for it is certain, and confessed on all hands almost. For my part I can not but confess that to be, which I feel and groan under, and by which all the world is miserable.

ages among the actors and interlocutors of, the parable. In the temple-language of Egypt the serpent was the symbol of the understanding in its twofold function, namely, as the faculty of means to proximate or medial ends, analogous to the instinct of the more intelligent animals, ant, bee, beaver, and the like, and opposed to practical reason, as the determinant of the ultimate end; and again, as the discursive and logical faculty possessed individually by each individual—the *λόγος ἐν ἑκάστῳ*, in distinction from the *νοῦς*, that is, intuitive reason, the source of ideas and absolute truths, and the principle of the necessary and the universal in our affirmations and conclusions. Without or in contravention to the reason—(that is, the *spiritual* mind of St. Paul, and *the light that lighteth every man* of St. John)—this understanding (*φρόνημα σαρκὸς*, or carnal mind) becomes the sophistic principle, the wily tempter to evil by counterfeit good; the pandar and advocate of the passions and appetites: ever in league with, and always first applying to, the desire, as the inferior nature in man, the woman in our humanity; and through the desire prevailing on the will (the manhood, *virtus*) against the command of the universal reason, and against the light of reason in the will itself. This essential inherence of an intelligential principle (*φῶς νοερόν*) in the will (*ἀρχὴ θελητική*), or rather the Will itself thus considered, the Greeks expressed by an appropriate word, *βουλή*. This, but little differing from Origen's interpretation or hypothesis, is supported and confirmed by the very old tradition of the *homo androgynus*, that is, that the original man, the individual first created, was bisexual;—a chimæra, of which, and of many other mythological traditions, the most probable explanation is, that they were originally symbolical glyphs or sculptures, and afterwards translated into words, yet literally, that is, into the common names of the several figures and images composing the symbol; while the symbolic meaning was left to be deciphered as before, and sacred to the initiate. As to the abstruseness and subtlety of the conceptions, this is so far from being an objection to this oldest gloss on this venerable relic of Semitic, not impossibly ante-diluvian, philosophy, that to those who have carried their researches farthest back into Greek, Egyptian, Persian, and Indian antiquity, it will seem a strong confirmation. Or if I chose to address the skeptic in the language of the day, I might remind him that as alchemy went before chemistry, and astrology before astronomy, so in all countries of civilized men have metaphysics outrun common sense. Fortunately for us that they have so! For from all we know

Adam turned his back upon the sun, and dwelt in the dark and the shadow. He sinned, and fell into God's displeasure, and was made naked of all his supernatural endowments, was ashamed and sentenced to death, and deprived of the means of long life, and of the sacrament and instrument of immortality, I mean the

of the unmetaphysical tribes of New Holland and elsewhere, a common sense not preceded by metaphysics is no very enviable possession. O be not cheated, my youthful Reader, by this shallow prate! The creed of true common sense is composed of the results of scientific meditation, observation, and experiment, as far as they are generally intelligible. It differs therefore in different countries, and in every different age of the same country. The common sense of a people is the movable *index* of its average judgment and information. Without metaphysics science could have had no language, and common sense no materials.

But to return to my subject. It can not be denied, that the Mosaic narrative thus interpreted gives a just and faithful exposition of the birth and parentage and successive moments of phenomenal sin (*peccatum phænomenon; crimen primarium et commune*), that is, of sin as it reveals itself in time, and is an immediate object of consciousness. And in this sense most truly does the Apostle assert, that in Adam we all fell. The first human sinner is the adequate representative of all his successors. And with no less truth may it be said, that it is the same Adam that falls in every man, and from the same reluctance to abandon the too dear and undivorceable Eve: and the same Eve tempted by the same serpentine and perverted understanding, which, framed originally to be the interpreter of the reason and the ministering angel of the spirit, is henceforth sentenced and bound over to the service of the animal nature, its needs and its cravings, dependent on the senses for all its materials, with the world of sense for its appointed sphere: *Upon thy belly shalt thou go, and dust shalt thou eat all the days of thy life.* I have shown elsewhere, that as the instinct of the mere intelligence differs in degree not in kind, and circumstantially, not essentially, from the *vis vitæ*, or vital power in the assimilative and digestive functions of the stomach and other organs of nutrition, even so the Understanding in itself, and distinct from the Reason and Conscience, differs in degree only from the instinct in the animal. It is still but *a beast of the field*, though *more subtle than any beast of the field*, and therefore in its corruption and perversion *cursed above any*;—a pregnant word! of which if the Reader wants an exposition or paraphrase, he may find one more than two thousand years old among the fragments of the poet Menander. This is the *understanding* which in its *every thought* is to be brought *under obedience to faith*; which it can scarcely fail to be, if only it be first subjected to the reason, of which spiritual faith is even the blossoming and the fructifying process. For it is indifferent whether I say that Faith is the interpenetration of the Reason and the Will, or that it is at once the assurance and the commencement of the approaching union between the reason and

tree of life.* He then fell under the evils of a sickly body, and a passionate, ignorant, and uninstructed soul. His sin made him sickly, his sickness made him peevish: his sin left him ignorant, his ignorance made him foolish and unreasonable. His sin left him to his nature: and by his nature, whoever was to be born at all, was to be born a child, and to do before he could understand, and to be bred under laws to which he was always bound, but which could not always be exacted; and he was to choose when he could not reason, and had passions most strong

the intelligible realities, the living and substantial truths, that are even in this life its most proper objects.

I have thus put the Reader in possession of my own opinions respecting the narrative in *Gen.* ii. and iii. *Ἔστιν οὖν δὴ, ὡς ἔμοιγε δοκεῖ, ἵερος, μῦθος, ἀληθέστατον καὶ ἀρχαιότατον φιλοσόφημα, εὐσέβεσι μὲν σέβασμα, συνετοίς τε φωνᾶν· ἐς δὲ τὸ πᾶν ἑρμήνεως χατίζει.* Or I might ask with Augustine, why not both? Why not at once symbol and history? Or rather how should it be otherwise? Must not of necessity the first man be a symbol of mankind in the fullest force of the word symbol, rightly defined;—a sign included in the idea which it represents;—that is, an actual part chosen to represent the whole, as a lip with a chin prominent is a symbol of man; or a lower form or *species* of a higher in the same kind; thus magnetism is the symbol of vegetation, and of the vegetative and reproductive power in animals; the instinct of the ant-tribe or the bee is a symbol of the human understanding. And this definition of the word is of great practical importance, inasmuch as the symbolical is hereby distinguished *toto genere* from the allegoric and metaphorical. But, perhaps, parables, allegories, and allegorical or typical applications, are incompatible with inspired Scripture! The writings of St. Paul are sufficient proof of the contrary. Yet I readily acknowledge that allegorical applications are one thing, and allegorical interpretation another: and that where there is no ground for supposing such a sense to have entered into the intent and purpose of the sacred penman, they are not to be commended. So far indeed am I from entertaining any predilection for them, or any favorable opinion of the Rabbinical commentators and traditionists, from whom the fashion was derived, that in carrying it as far as our own Church has carried it, I follow her judgment, not my own. Indeed I know but one other part of the Scriptures not universally held to be parabolical, which, not without the sanction of great authorities, I am disposed to regard as an apologue or parable, namely, the book of Jonah; the reasons for believing the Jewish Nation collectively to be therein impersonated seeming to me unanswerable. And it is my deliberate and conscientious conviction, that the proofs of such interpretation having been the intention of the inspired writer or compiler of the book of Genesis lie on the face of the narrative itself.

* *Rom.* v. 14.—Who were they who *had not sinned after the similitude of Adam's transgression;* and over whom notwithstanding, *death reigned?*

when he had his understanding most weak; and the more need he had of a curb, the less strength he had to use it! And this being the case of all the world, what was every man's evil became all men's greater evil; and though alone it was very bad, yet when they came together it was made much worse. Like ships in a storm, every one alone hath enough to do to outride it; but when they meet, besides the evils of the storm, they find the intolerable calamity of their mutual concussion; and every ship that is ready to be oppressed with the tempest, is a worse tempest to every vessel against which it is violently dashed. So it is in mankind. Every man hath evil enough of his own, and it is hard for a man to live *up to the rule of his own reason and conscience.* But when he hath parents and children, friends and enemies, buyers and sellers, lawyers and clients, a family and a neighborhood—then it is that every man dashes against another, and one relation requires what another denies; and when one speaks another will contradict him; and that which is well spoken is sometimes innocently mistaken; and that upon a good cause produces an evil effect; and by these, and ten thousand other concurrent causes, man is made more than most miserable *

COMMENT.

The first question we should put to ourselves, when we have to read a passage that perplexes us in a work of authority, is: What does the writer mean by all this? And the second question should be, What does he intend by all this? In the passage before us, Taylor's meaning is not quite clear. A sin is an evil which has its ground or origin in the agent, and not in the compulsion of circumstances. Circumstances are compulsory from the absence of a power to resist or control them: and if this absence likewise be the effect of circumstance (that is, if it have been neither directly nor indirectly caused by the agent himself), the evil derives from the circumstances; and therefore (in the Apostle's sense of the word, sin, when he speaks of the *exceeding sinfulness* of sin) such evil is not sin; and the person who suffers it, or who is the compelled instrument of its infliction on others, may feel regret, but can not feel remorse. So likewise of the word origin, original, or originant. The Reader can not too early

* *Deus Justificatus*, with some slight omissions and alterations.—*Ed.*

be warned that it is not applicable, and, without abuse of language, can never be applied, to a mere link in a chain of effects, where each, indeed, stands in the relation of a cause to those that follow, but is at the same time the effect of all that precede. For in these cases a cause amounts to little more than an antecedent. At the utmost it means only a conductor of the causative influence; and the old axiom, *causa causæ causa causati*, applies with a never-ending regress to each several link, up the whole chain of nature. But this is Nature: and no natural thing or act can be called originant,* or be truly said to have an origin† in any other. The moment we assume an origin in na-

* * * * wherein they are not guilty,
Since Nature can not choose his origin.
Hamlet, Act I. sc. iv.—*Am. Ed.*

† This sense of the word is implied even in its metaphorical or figurative use. Thus we may say of a river that it originates in such or such a fountain; but the water of a canal is derived from such or such a river. The power which we call Nature, may be thus defined: a power subject to the law of continuity (*lex continui; nam in natura non datur saltus*) which law the human understanding, by a necessity arising out of its own constitution, can conceive only under the form of cause and effect. That this form or law of cause and effect is, relatively to the world without, or to things as they subsist independently of our perceptions, only a form or mode of thinking; that it is a law inherent in the understanding itself just as the symmetry of the miscellaneous objects seen by the kaleidoscope inheres in, or results from, the mechanism of the kaleidoscope itself—this becomes evident as soon as we attempt to apply the preconception directly to any operation of nature. For in this case we are forced to represent the cause as being at the same instant the effect, and *vice versa* the effect as being the cause—a relation which we seek to express by the terms action and re-action; but for which the term reciprocal action, or the law of reciprocity (*Wechselwirkung*), would be both more accurate and more expressive.

These are truths which can scarcely be too frequently impressed on the mind that is in earnest in the wish to reflect aright. Nature is a line in constant and continuous evolution. Its beginning is lost in the supernatural: and for our understanding therefore it must appear as a continuous line without beginning or end. But where there is no discontinuity there can be no origination, and every appearance of origination in nature is but a shadow of our own casting. It is a reflection from our own will or spirit. Herein, indeed, the will consists. This is the essential character by which Will is opposed to Nature, as spirit, and raised above nature as self-determining spirit—this namely, that it is a power of originating an act or state.

A young friend, or as he was pleased to describe himself, a pupil of mine,

ture, a true beginning, an actual first—that moment we rise above nature, and are compelled to assume a supernatural power. (*Gen.* i. 1.)

It will be an equal convenience to myself and to my Reader, to let it be agreed between us, that we will generalize the word

who is beginning to learn to think, asked me to explain by an instance what is meant by "originating an act or state." My answer was—This morning I awoke with a dull pain, which I knew from experience the getting up would remove: and yet by adding to the drowsiness and by weakening or depressing the volition (*voluntas sensorialis seu mechanica*), the very pain seemed to hold me back, to fix me, as it were, to the bed. After a peevish ineffectual quarrel with this painful disinclination, I said to myself: Let me count twenty, and the moment I come to nineteen I will leap out of bed So said, and so done. Now should you ever find yourself in the same or in a similar state, and should attend to the goings-on within you, you will learn what I mean by originating an act. At the same time you will see that it belongs exclusively to the will (*arbitrium*); that there is nothing analogous to it in outward experiences; and that I had, therefore, no way of explaining it but by referring you to an act of your own, and to the peculiar self-consciousness preceding and accompanying it. As we know what life is by being, so we know what will is by acting. That in willing, replied my friend, we appear to ourselves to constitute an actual beginning, and that this seems unique, and without any example in our sensible experience, or in the *phænomena* of nature, is an undeniable fact. But may it not be an illusion arising from our ignorance of the antecedent causes? You may suppose this, I rejoined:—that the soul of every man should impose a lie on itself; and that this lie, and the acting on the faith of its being the most important of all truths, and the most real of all realities, should form the main contra-distinctive character of humanity, and the only basis of that distinction between things and persons on which our whole moral and criminal law is grounded;—you may suppose this;—I can not, as I could in the case of an arithmetical or geometrical proposition, render it impossible for you to suppose it. Whether you can reconcile such a supposition with the belief of an all-wise Creator, is another question. But, taken singly, it is doubtless in your power to suppose this. Were it not, the belief of the contrary would be no subject of a command, no part of a moral or religious duty. You would not, however, suppose it without a reason. But all the pretexts that ever have been or ever can be offered for this supposition, are built on certain notions of the understanding that have been generalized from conceptions; which conceptions, again, are themselves generalized or abstracted from objects of sense. Neither the one nor the other, therefore, have any force except in application to objects of sense, and within the sphere of sensible experience. What but absurdity can follow, if you decide on spirit by the laws of matter;—if you judge that, which if it be at all must be supersensual, by that faculty of your mind, the very definition of which is "the faculty judging according to sense?"

circumstance, so as to understand by it, as often as it occurs in this Comment, all and every thing not connected with the Will, past or present, of a free agent. Even though it were the blood in the chambers of his heart, or his own inmost sensations, we will regard them as circumstantial, extrinsic, or from without.

In this sense of the word, original, and in the sense before given of sin, it is evident that the phrase, Original Sin, is a pleonasm, the epithet not adding to the thought, but only enforcing it. For if it be sin, it must be original; and a state or act, that has not its origin in the will, may be calamity, deformity, disease, or mischief; but a sin it can not be. It is not enough that the act appears voluntary, or that it is intentional; or that it has the most hateful passions or debasing appetite for its proximate cause

These then are unworthy the name of reasons: they are only pretexts. But without reason to contradict your own consciousness in defiance of your own conscience, is contrary to reason. Such and such writers, you say, have made a great sensation. If so, I am sorry for it; but the fact I take to be this. From a variety of causes the more austere sciences have fallen into discredit, and impostors have taken advantage of the general ignorance to give a sort of mysterious and terrific importance to a parcel of trashy sophistry, the authors of which would not have employed themselves more irrationally in submitting the works of Raffaelle or Titian to canons of criticism deduced from the sense of smell. Nay, less so. For here the objects and the organs are disparate: while in the other case they are absolutely diverse. I conclude this note by reminding the Reader, that my first object is to make myself understood. When he is in full possession of my meaning, then let him consider whether it deserves to be received as the truth. Had it been my immediate purpose to make him believe me as well as understand me, I should have thought it necessary to warn him that a finite will does indeed originate an act, and may originate a state of being; but yet only in and for the agent himself. A finite will constitutes a true beginning; but with regard to the series of motions and changes by which the free act is manifested and made effectual, the finite will gives a beginning only by coincidence with that Absolute Will, which is at the same time Infinite Power. Such is the language of religion, and of philosophy too in the last instance. But I express the same truth in ordinary language when I say, that a finite will or the will of a finite free agent, acts outwardly by confluence with the laws of nature.

(The student will find the fullest development that has yet been made of this most fundamental and most important distinction between Nature and Spirit, or Will, in Kant's *Kritik der practischen Vernunft*, and in Jacobi's *Von göttlichen Dingen*, pp. 388–428, vol. iii. Leipsic, 1816. See also Fichte's *Bestimmung des Menschen*, p. 256, et seq. for many forcible statements respecting the Will as *originant* in its essence.—*Am. Ed.*)

and accompaniment. All these may be found in a madhouse, where neither law nor humanity permits us to condemn the actor of sin. The reason of law declares the maniac not a free-agent; and the verdict follows of course—Not guilty. Now mania, as distinguished from idiocy, frenzy, delirium, hypochondria, and derangement (the last term used specifically to express a suspension or disordered state of the understanding or adaptive power), is the occultation or eclipse of reason, as the power of ultimate ends. The maniac, it is well known, is often found clever and inventive in the selection and adaptation of means to his ends; but his ends are madness. He has lost his reason. For though reason in finite beings, is not the will—or how could the will be opposed to the reason?—yet it is the condition, the *sine qua non* of a free will.

We will now return to the extract from Taylor on a theme of deep interest in itself, and trebly important from its bearings. For without just and distinct views respecting the Article of Original Sin, it is impossible to understand aright any one of the peculiar doctrines of Christianity. Now my first complaint is, that the eloquent Bishop, while he admits the fact as established beyond controversy by universal experience, yet leaves us wholly in the dark as to the main point, supplies us with no answer to the principal question—why he names it Original Sin? It can not be said, We know what the Bishop means, and what matters the name?—for the nature of the fact, and in what light it should be regarded by us, depends on the nature of our answer to the question, whether Original Sin is or is not the right and proper designation. I can imagine the same *quantum* of sufferings, and yet if I had reason to regard them as symptoms of a commencing change, as pains of growth, the temporary deformity and misproportions of immaturity, or (as in the final sloughing of the caterpillar) the throes and struggles of the waxing or evolving Psyche, I should think it no Stoical flight to doubt, how far I was authorized to declare the circumstance an evil at all. Most assuredly I would not express or describe the fact as an evil having an origin in the sufferers themselves, or as sin.

Let us, however, waive this objection. Let it be supposed that the Bishop uses the word in a different and more comprehensive sense, and that by sin he understands evil of all kind connected with or resulting from actions—though I do not see how we can represent the properties even of inanimate bodies (of poisonous substances for instance) except as acts resulting from the constitution of such bodies. Or if this sense, though not unknown to the mystic divines, should be too comprehensive and remote, I will suppose the Bishop to comprise under the term Sin, the evil accompanying or consequent on human actions and purposes:—though here, too, I have a right to be informed, for what reason and on what grounds sin is thus limited to human agency? And truly, I should be at no loss to assign the reason. But then this reason would instantly bring me back to my first definition; and any other reason, than that the human agent is endowed with reason, and with a will which can place itself either in subjection or in opposition to his reason—in other words, that man is alone of all known animals a responsible creature—I neither know nor can imagine.

Thus, then, the sense which Taylor—and with him the antagonists generally of this Article as propounded by the first Reformers—attaches to the words, Original Sin, needs only be carried on into its next consequence, and it will be found to imply the sense which I have given—namely, that sin is evil having an origin. But inasmuch as it is evil, in God it can not originate: and yet in some Spirit (that is, in some supernatural power) it must. For in nature there is no origin. Sin therefore is spiritual evil: but the spiritual in man is the will. Now when we do not refer to any particular sins, but to that state and constitution of the will, which is the ground, condition, and common cause of all sins; and when we would further express the truth, that this corrupt nature of the will must in some sense or other be considered as its own act, that the corruption must have been self-originated;—in this case and for this purpose we may, with no less propriety than force, entitle this dire spiritual evil and source of all evil, which is absolutely such, Original Sin. I have said, the corrupt nature of the will. I might add, that the admission of a nature into a spiritual essence by its own act is a corruption.

Such, I repeat, would be the inevitable conclusion, if Taylor's sense of the term were carried on into its immediate consequences. But the whole of his most eloquent Treatise makes it certain that Taylor did not carry it on: and consequently Original Sin, according to his conception, is a calamity, which being common to all men must be supposed to result from their common nature ;—in other words, the universal calamity of human nature.

Can we wonder, then, that a mind, a heart, like Taylor's, should reject, that he should strain his faculties to explain away the belief that this calamity, so dire in itself, should appear to the All-merciful God a rightful cause and motive for inflicting on the wretched sufferers a calamity infinitely more tremendous ;—nay, that it should be incompatible with Divine Justice not to punish it by everlasting torment? Or need we be surprised if he found nothing that could reconcile his mind to such a belief, in the circumstance that the acts now consequent on this calamity, and either directly or indirectly effects of the same, were, five or six thousand years ago in the instance of a certain individual and his accomplice, anterior to the calamity, and the cause or occasion of the same ;—that what in all other men is disease, in these two persons was guilt ;—that what in us is hereditary, and consequently nature, in them was original, and consequently sin? Lastly, might it not be presumed, that so enlightened, and at the same time so affectionate, a divine would even fervently disclaim and reject the pretended justifications of God grounded on flimsy analogies drawn from the imperfections of human ordinances and human justice-courts—some of very doubtful character even as human institutes, and all of them just only as far as they are necessary, and rendered necessary chiefly by the weakness and wickedness, the limited powers and corrupt passions, of mankind? The more confidently might this be presumed of so acute and practised a logician, as Taylor, in addition to his other extraordinary gifts, is known to have been, when it is demonstrable that the most current of these justifications rests on a palpable equivocation: namely, the gross misuse of the word Right.* An instance will explain my meaning. In as far as,

* It may conduce to the readier comprehension of this point if I say, that the equivoque consists in confounding the almost technical sense of the noun substantive, right (a sense most often determined by the genitive case following, as the right of property, the right of husbands to chastise their wives, and so forth) with the popular sense of the adjective, right: though this likewise has, if not a double sense, yet a double application ;—the first, when it is used to express the fitness of a mean to a relative end; for example, "the right way to obtain the right distance at which a picture should be examined," and the like; and the other, when it expresses a perfect conformity and commensurateness with the immutable idea of equity, or per-

from the known frequency of dishonest or mischievous persons, it may have been found necessary, in so far is the law justifiable in giving landowners the right of proceeding against a neighbor or fellow-citizen for even a slight trespass on that which the law has made their property: nay, of proceeding in sundry instances criminally and even capitally. But surely, either there is no religion in the world, and nothing obligatory in the precepts of the Gospel, or there are occasions in which it would be very wrong in the proprietor to exercise the right, which yet it may be highly expedient that he should possess. On this ground it is, that religion is the sustaining opposite of the law.

That Taylor, therefore, should have striven fervently against the Article so interpreted and so vindicated, is (for me at least) a subject neither of surprise nor of complaint. It is the doctrine which he substitutes; it is the weakness and inconsistency betrayed in the defence of this substitute; it is the unfairness with which he blackens the established Article—for to give it, as it had been caricatured by a few Ultra-Calvinists during the fever

fect rectitude. Hence the close connection between the words righteousness and godliness, that is, godlikeness.

I should be tempted to subjoin a few words on a predominating doctrine closely connected with the present argument—the Paleyan principle of general consequences; but the inadequacy of this principle as a criterion of right and wrong, and above all its utter unfitness as a moral guide, have been elsewhere so fully stated (*Friend*, Essay xv, II, p. 285), that even in again referring to the subject I must shelter myself under Seneca's rule, that what we can not too frequently think of, we can not too often be made to recollect. It is, however, of immediate importance to the point in discussion, that the reader should be made to see how altogether incompatible the principle of judging by general consequences is with the idea of an Eternal, Omnipresent, and Omniscient Being;—that he should be made aware of the absurdity of attributing any form of generalization to the All-perfect Mind. To generalize is a faculty and function of the human understanding, and from the imperfection and limitation of the understanding are the use and the necessity of generalizing derived. Generalization is a substitute for intuition, for the power of intuitive, that is, immediate knowledge. As a substitute, it is a gift of inestimable value to a finite intelligence, such as man in his present state is endowed with and capable of exercising; but yet a substitute only, and an imperfect one to boot. To attribute it to God is the grossest anthropomorphism: and grosser instances of anthropomorphism than are to be found in the controversial writings on Original Sin and Vicarious Satisfaction, the records of superstition do not supply.

of the (so-called) Quinquarticular controversy, was in effect to blacken it—and then imposes another scheme, to which the same objections apply with even increased force, a scheme which seems to differ from the former only by adding fraud and mockery to injustice;—these are the things that excite my wonder; it is of these that I complain. For what does the Bishop's scheme amount to? God, he tells us, required of Adam a perfect obedience, and made it possible by endowing him "with perfect rectitude and supernatural heights of grace" proportionate to the obedience which he required. As a consequence of his disobedience, Adam lost this rectitude, this perfect sanity and proportionateness of his intellectual, moral and corporeal state, powers and impulses; and as the penalty of his crime, he was deprived of all supernatural aids and graces. The death, with whatever is comprised in the Scriptural sense of the word, death, began from that moment to work in him, and this consequence he conveyed to his offspring, and through them to all his posterity, that is, to all mankind. They were born diseased in mind, body and will. For what less than disease can we call a necessity of error and a predisposition to sin and sickness? Taylor, indeed, asserts, that though perfect obedience became incomparably more difficult, it was not, however, absolutely impossible. Yet he himself admits that the contrary was universal; that of the countless millions of Adam's posterity, not a single individual ever realized, or approached to the realization of, this possibility; and (if my memory* does not deceive me) Taylor himself has elsewhere exposed—and if he has not, yet common sense will do it for him—the sophistry in asserting of a whole what may be true of the whole, but is in fact true

* I have, since this page was written, met with several passages in the Treatise on Repentance, the Holy Living and Dying, and the Worthy Communicant, in which the Bishop asserts without scruple the impossibility of total obedience; and on the same grounds as I have given.

[See the Doctrine and Practice of Repentance, c. I. s. 2, "—who—conclude that is possible to keep the commandments, though as yet no man ever did, but he that did it for us all." xv. "But in the moral sense, that is, when we consider what man is, and what are his strengths, and how many his enemies, and how soon he falls, and that he forgets when he should remember, and his faculties are asleep when they should be awake, and he is hindered by intervening accidents, and weakened and determined by superinduced qualities, habits and necessities,—the keeping of the commandments is morally impossible." xxxiv.—*Ed.*]

only of each of its component parts. Any one may snap a horse-hair: therefore, any one may perform the same feat with the horse's tail. On a level floor (on the hardened sand for instance, of a sea-beach) I chalk two parallel straight lines, with a width of eight inches. It is possible for a man, with a bandage over his eyes, to keep within the path for two or three paces: therefore, it is possible for him to walk blindfold for two or three leagues without a single deviation! And this possibility would suffice to acquit me of injustice, though I had placed man-traps within an inch of one line, and knew that there were pit-falls and deep wells beside the other!

This assertion, therefore, without adverting to its discordance with, if not direct contradiction to, the tenth and thirteenth Articles of our Church, I shall not, I trust, be thought to rate below its true value, if I treat it as an infinitesimal possibility that may be safely dropped in the calculation: and so proceed with the argument. The consequence then of Adam's crime was, by a natural necessity, inherited by persons who could not (the Bishop affirms) in any sense have been accomplices in the crime or partakers in the guilt: and yet consistently with the divine holiness, it was not possible that the same perfect obedience should not be required of them. Now what would the idea of equity, what would the law inscribed by the Creator on the heart of man, seem to dictate in this case? Surely, that the supplementary aids, the supernatural graces correspondent to a law above nature, should be increased in proportion to the diminished strength of the agents, and the increased resistance to be overcome by them. But no! not only the consequence of Adam's act, but the penalty due to his crime, was perpetuated. His descendants were despoiled or left destitute of these aids and graces, while the obligation to perfect obedience was continued; an obligation too, the non-fulfilment of which brought with it death and the unutterable woe that cleaves to an immortal soul forever alienated from its Creator.

Observe that all these results of Adam's fall enter into Bishop Taylor's scheme of Original Sin equally as into that of the first Reformers. In this respect the Bishop's doctrine is the same with that laid down in the Articles and Homilies of the English Church. The only difference that has hitherto appeared, consists in the aforesaid mathematical possibility of fulfilling the whole law, which in the Bishop's scheme is affirmed to remain still in human nature,* or (as it is elsewhere expressed) in the nature of the human will.† But though it were possible to grant this existence of a power in all men, which in no man was ever exemplified, and where the non-actualization of such power is, *à priori*, so certain, that the belief or imagination of the contrary in any individual is expressly given us by the Holy Spirit as a test, whereby it may be known that *the truth is not in him*, as an infallible sign of imposture or self-delusion!—though it were possible to grant this, which, consistently with Scripture and the principles of reasoning which we apply in all other cases, it is not possible to grant; and though it were possible likewise to over-

* "There is a natural possibility and a moral: there are abilities in every man to do any thing that is there commanded, and he that can do well today, may do so to-morrow; in the nature of things this is true: and since every sin is a breach of law, which a man might and ought to have kept, it is naturally certain, that whenever any man did break the commandment, he might have done otherwise. In man, therefore, speaking naturally and of the physical possibilities of things, there is by those assistances which are given in the Gospel, ability to keep the commandments evangelical. But in the moral sense," &c. *ubi supra.—Ed.*

† Availing himself of the equivocal sense, and (I most readily admit) the injudicious use of the word "free" in the—even on this account—faulty phrase, "free only to sin," Taylor treats the notion of a power in the will of determining itself to evil without an equal power of determining itself to good, as a "foolery." I would this had been the only instance in his *Deus Justificatus* of that inconsiderate contempt so frequent in the polemic treatises of minor divines, who will have ideas of reason, spiritual truths that can only be spiritually discerned, translated for them into adequate conceptions of the understanding. The great articles of Corruption and Redemption are propounded to us as spiritual mysteries; and every interpretation that pretends to explain them into comprehensible notions, does by its very success furnish presumptive proof of its failure. The acuteness and logical dexterity, with which Taylor has brought out the falsehood, or semblance of falsehood, in the Calvinistic scheme, are truly admirable. Had he next concentred his thoughts in tranquil meditation, and asked himself: what then is the truth?—if a Will be at all, what must a Will be?—he might, I think, have seen that a nature in a will implies already a corruption of that will: that a nature is as inconsistent with freedom as free choice with an incapacity of choosing aught but evil. And lastly, a free power in a nature to fulfil a law above nature!—I, who love and honor this good and great man with all the reverence that can dwell "on this side idolatry," dare not retort on this assertion the charge of foolery; but I find it a paradox as startling to my reason as any of the hard sayings of the Dort divines were to his understanding.

look the glaring sophistry of concluding in relation to a series of indeterminate length, that whoever can do any one, can therefore do all; a conclusion, the futility of which must force itself on the common sense of every man who understands the proposition; still the question will arise—Why, and on what principle of equity, were the unoffending sentenced to be born with so fearful a disproportion of their powers to their duties? Why were they subjected to a law, the fulfilment of which was all but impossible, yet the penalty on the failure tremendous? Admit that for those who had never enjoyed a happier lot, it was no punishment to be made to inhabit a ground which the Creator had cursed, and to have been born with a body prone to sickness, and a soul surrounded with temptation, and having the worst temptation within itself in its own temptability;—to have the duties of a Spirit with the wants and appetites of an Animal! Yet on such imperfect creatures, with means so scanty and impediments so numerous, to impose the same task-work that had been required of a creature with a pure and entire nature, and provided with supernatural aids—if this be not to inflict a penalty; yet to be placed under a law, the difficulty of obeying which is infinite, and to have momently to struggle with this difficulty, and to live momently in hazard of these consequences—if this be no punishment;—words have no correspondence with thoughts, and thoughts are but shadows of each other, shadows that own no substance for their antitype.

Of such an outrage on common sense Taylor was incapable. He himself calls it a penalty; he admits that in effect it is a punishment: nor does he seek to suppress the question that so naturally arises out of this admission;—on what principle of equity were the innocent offspring of Adam punished at all? He meets it, and puts in an answer. He states the problem, and gives his solution—namely, that "God on Adam's account was so exasperated with mankind, that being angry he would still continue the punishment!"—"The case" (says the Bishop) "is this: Jonathan and Michal were Saul's children. It came to pass that seven of Saul's issue were to be hanged: all equally innocent, equally culpable." [Before I quote further, I feel myself called on to remind the reader, that these last two words were added by Taylor, without the least grounds in Scripture, according to which (2 *Sam.* xxi.) no crime was laid to their charge, no blame imputed to them. Without any pretence of culpable conduct on their part, they were arraigned as children of Saul, and sacrificed to a point of state-expedience. In recommencing the quotation, therefore, the reader ought to let the sentence conclude with the words—] "all equally innocent." David took the five sons of Michal, for she had left him unhandsomely. Jonathan was his friend: and therefore he spared his son, Mephibosheth. Now here it was indifferent as to the guilt of the persons (*bear in mind, Reader, that no guilt was attached to any of them!*) whether David should take the sons of Michal, or Jonathan's; but it is likely that as upon the kindness that David had to Jonathan, he spared his son: so upon the just provocation of Michal, he made that evil fall upon them, which, it may be, they should not have suffered, if their mother had been kind. Adam was to God, as Michal to David."*

This answer, this solution, proceeding too from a divine so preeminently gifted, and occurring (with other passages not less startling) in a vehement refutation of the received doctrine, on the express ground of its opposition to the clearest conceptions and best feelings of mankind—this it is that surprises me. It is of this that I complain. The Almighty Father exasperated with those, whom the Bishop has himself in the same Treatise described as "innocent and most unfortunate"—the two things best fitted to conciliate love and pity! Or though they did not remain innocent, yet those whose abandonment to a mere nature, while they were left amenable to a law above nature, he affirms to be the irresistible cause, that they one and all did sin! And this decree illustrated and justified by its analogy to one of the worst actions of an imperfect mortal! From such of my Readers as will give a thoughtful perusal to these works of Taylor, I dare anticipate a concurrence with the judgment which I here transcribe from the blank space at the end of the *Deus Justificatus* in my own copy; and which, though twenty years have elapsed since it was written, I have never seen reason to recant or modify. "This most eloquent Treatise may be compared to a statue of Janus, with the one face, which we must suppose fronting the Calvinistic tenet, entire and fresh, as from the master's hand; beaming with life and force, witty scorn on the lip, and a brow at once bright and weighty with satisfying reason:—the other,

* Vol. ix. p. 5, 6. Heber's edit.—*Ed.*

looking toward the "something to be put in its place," maimed, featureless, and weather-bitten into an almost visionary confusion and indistinctness."*

With these expositions I hasten to contrast the Scriptural article respecting Original Sin, or the corrupt and sinful nature of the human Will, and the belief which alone is required of us as Christians. And here the first thing to be considered, and which will at once remove a world of error, is; that this is no tenet first introduced or imposed by Christianity, and which, should a man see reason to disclaim the authority of the Gospel, would no longer have any claim on his attention. It is no perplexity that a man may get rid of by ceasing to be a Christian, and which has no existence for a philosophic Deist. It is a fact affirmed, indeed, in the Christian Scriptures alone with the force and frequency proportioned to its consummate importance; but a fact acknowledged in every religion that retains the least glimmering of the patriarchal faith in a God infinite, yet personal:—a fact assumed or implied as the basis of every religion, of which any relics remain of earlier date than the last and total apostasy of the Pagan world, when the faith in the great I Am, the Creator, was extinguished in the sensual Polytheism, which is inevitably the final result of Pantheism, or the worship of Nature; and the only form under which the Pantheistic scheme—that, according to which the World is God, and the material universe itself the one only absolute Being—can exist for a people, or become the popular creed. Thus in the most ancient books of the Brahmins, the deep sense of this fact, and the doctrines grounded on obscure traditions of the promised remedy, are seen struggling, and now gleaming, now flashing, through the mist of Pantheism, and producing the incongruities and gross contradictions of the Brahmin Mythology; while in the rival sect—in that most strange *phænomenon*, the religious Atheism of the Buddhists, with whom God is only universal matter considered abstractedly from all particular forms—the fact is placed among the delusions natural to man, which, together with other superstitions grounded on a supposed essential difference between right and wrong, the sage is to decompose and precipitate from the *menstruum* of his more refined apprehensions! Thus in denying the fact, they virtually acknowledge it.

* See Lit. Remains, V. pp. 213, 214.

From the remote East, turn to the mythology of the Lesser Asia, to the descendants of Javan, who dwelt in the tents of Shem, and possessed the isles. Here, again, and in the usual form of an historic solution, we find the same fact, and as characteristic of the human race, stated in that earliest and most venerable *mythus*, or symbolic parable of Prometheus—that truly wonderful fable, in which the characters of the rebellious Spirit and of the Divine Friend of mankind (Θεὸς φιλάνθρωπος) are united in the same person ;* thus in the most striking manner noting the forced amalgamation of the Patriarchal tradition with the incongruous scheme of Pantheism. This and the connected tale of Io, which is but the sequel of the Prometheus, stand alone in the Greek Mythology, in which elsewhere both gods and men are mere powers and products of nature. And most noticeable it is, that soon after the promulgation and spread of the Gospel had awakened the moral sense, and had opened the eyes even of its wiser enemies to the necessity of providing some solution of this great problem of the moral world, the beautiful parable of Cupid and Psyche was brought forward as a rival Fall of Man : and the fact of a moral corruption connatural with the human race was again recognized. In the assertion of Original Sin the Greek Mythology rose and set.

But not only was the fact acknowledged of a law in the nature of man resisting the law of God (and whatever is placed in active and direct oppugnancy to the good is, *ipso facto*, positive evil) ; it was likewise an acknowledged mystery, and one which by the nature of the subject must ever remain such—a problem, of which any other solution than the statement of the fact itself was demonstrably impossible. That it is so, the least reflection will suffice to convince every man, who has previously satisfied himself that he is a responsible being. It follows necessarily from the postulate of a responsible will. Refuse to grant this, and I have not a word to say. Concede this, and you concede all. For this is the essential attribute of a will, and contained in the very idea, that whatever determines the will, acquires this power from a previous determination of the will itself. The will is ultimately self-determined, or it is no longer a will under the law of perfect freedom, but a nature under the mechanism of cause and effect. And if by an act, to which it had determined

* See Lit. Remains, IV. pp. 344–365.—*Ed.*

itself, it has subjected itself to the determination of nature (in the language of St. Paul, to the law of the flesh), it receives a nature into itself, and so far it becomes a nature: and this is a corruption of the will and a corrupt nature. It is also a fall of man, inasmuch as his will is the condition of his personality; the ground and condition of the attribute which constitutes him man. And the ground-work of personal being is a capacity of acknowledging the moral law (the law of the Spirit, the law of freedom, the Divine Will) as that which should, of itself, suffice to determine the will to a free obedience of the law, the law working therein by its own exceeding lawfulness.* This, and this alone, is positive good; good in itself, and independent of all relations. Whatever resists, and, as a positive force, opposes this in the will, is therefore evil. But an evil in the will, is an evil will; and as all moral evil (that is, all evil that is evil without reference to its contingent physical consequences) is of the will, this evil will must have its source in the will. And thus we might go back from act to act, from evil to evil, *ad infinitum*, without advancing a step.

We call an individual a bad man, not because an action of his is contrary to the law, but because it has led us to conclude from it some principle opposed to the law, some private maxim or by-law in his will contrary to the universal law of right reason in the conscience, as the ground of the action. But this evil principle again must be grounded in some other principle which has been made determinant of his will by the will's own self-determination. For if not, it must have its ground in some necessity of nature, in some instinct or propensity imposed, not acquired, another's work not his own. Consequently neither act nor principle could be imputed; and relatively to the agent, not original, not sin.

Now let the grounds on which the fact of an evil inherent in the will is affirmable in the instance of any one man, be supposed equally applicable in every instance, and concerning all men: so that the fact is asserted of the individual, not because he has committed this or that crime, or because he has shown himself to be this or that man, but simply because he is a man. Let the evil be supposed such as to imply the impossibility of an individual's referring to any particular time at which it might be con-

* If the law worked on the will, it would be the working of an intrinsic and alien force, and, as St. Paul profoundly argues, would prove the will sinful.

ceived to have commenced, or to any period of his existence at which it was not existing. Let it be supposed, in short, that the subject stands in no relation whatever to time, can neither be called in time nor out of time; but that all relations of time are as alien and heterogeneous in this question, as the relations and attributes of space (north or south, round or square, thick or thin) are to our affections and moral feelings. Let the Reader suppose this, and he will have before him the precise import of the Scriptural doctrine of Original Sin; or rather of the fact acknowledged in all ages, and recognized, but not originating, in the Christian Scriptures.

In addition to this it will be well to remind the inquirer, that the steadfast conviction of the existence, personality, and moral attributes of God, is presupposed in the acceptance of the Gospel, or required as its indispensable preliminary. It is taken for granted as a point which the hearer had already decided for himself, a point finally settled and put at rest: not by the removal of all difficulties, or by any such increase of insight as enabled him to meet every objection of the Epicurean or the Skeptic, with a full and precise answer; but because he had convinced himself that it was folly as well as presumption in so imperfect a creature to expect it; and because these difficulties and doubts disappeared at the beam, when tried against the weight and convictive power of the reasons in the other scale. It is, therefore, most unfair to attack Christianity, or any article which the Church has declared a Christian doctrine, by arguments, which, if valid, are valid against all religion. Is there a disputant who scorns a mere postulate, as the basis of any argument in support of the faith; who is too high-minded to beg his ground, and will take it by a strong hand? Let him fight it out with the Atheists, or the Manicheans; but not stoop to pick up their arrows, and then run away to discharge them at Christianity or the Church!

The only true way is to state the doctrine, believed as well by Saul of Tarsus, *yet breathing out threatenings and slaughter against* the Church of Christ, as by Paul the Apostle, *fully preaching the Gospel of Christ.* A moral evil is an evil that has its origin in a will. An evil common to all must have a ground common to all. But the actual existence of moral evil we are bound in conscience to admit; and that there is an evil common to all is a fact; and this evil must therefore have a common ground. Now this evil ground can not originate in the Divine Will: it must therefore be referred to the will of man. And this evil ground we call original sin. It is a mystery, that is, a fact, which we see, but can not explain; and the doctrine a truth which we apprehend, but can neither comprehend nor communicate. And such by the quality of the subject (namely, a responsible will) it must be, if it be truth at all.

A sick man, whose complaint was as obscure as his sufferings were severe and notorious, was thus addressed by a humane stranger: "My poor Friend! I find you dangerously ill, and on this account only, and having certain information of your being so, and that you have not wherewithal to pay for a physician, I have come to you. Respecting your disease, indeed, I can tell you nothing that you are capable of understanding, more than you know already, or can only be taught by reflection on your own experience. But I have rendered the disease no longer irremediable. I have brought the remedy with me: and I now offer you the means of immediate relief, with the assurance of gradual convalescence, and a final perfect cure; nothing more being required on your part, but your best endeavors to follow the prescriptions I shall leave with you. It is, indeed, too probable, from the nature of your disease, that you will occasionally neglect or transgress them. But even this has been calculated on in the plan of your cure, and the remedies provided, if only you are sincere and in right earnest with yourself, and have your heart in the work. Ask me not how such a disease can be conceived possible. Enough for the present that you know it to be real: and I come to cure the disease, not to explain it."

Now, what if the patient or some of his neighbors should charge this good Samaritan with having given rise to the mischievous notion of an inexplicable disease, involving the honor of the king of the country,—should inveigh against him as the author and first introducer of the notion, though of the numerous medical works composed ages before his arrival, and by physicians of the most venerable authority, it was scarcely possible to open a single volume without finding some description of the disease, or some lamentation of its malignant and epidemic character;—and, lastly, what if certain pretended friends of this good Samaritan, in their zeal to vindicate him against this absurd charge, should assert that he was a perfect stranger to this disease, and boldly deny that he had ever said or done any thing connected with it, or that implied its existence?

In this apologue or imaginary case, Reader! you have the true bearings of Christianity on the fact and doctrine of Original Sin. The doctrine (that is, the confession of a known fact) Christianity has only in common with every religion, and with every philosophy, in which the reality of a responsible will, and the essential difference between good and evil, have been recognized. Peculiar to the Christian religion are the remedy and (for all purposes but those of a merely speculative curiosity) the solution. By the annunciation of the remedy it affords all the solution which our moral interests require; and even in that which remains, and must remain, unfathomable, the Christian finds a new motive to walk humbly with the Lord his God.

Should a professed believer ask you, whether that which is the ground of responsible action in your will could in any way be responsibly present in the will of Adam,—answer him in these words: "You, Sir! can no more demonstrate the negative, than I can conceive the affirmative. The corruption of my will may very warrantably be spoken of as a consequence of Adam's fall, even as my birth of Adam's existence; as a consequence, a link in the historic chain of instances, whereof Adam is the first. But that it is on account of Adam; or that this evil principle was, *à priori*, inserted or infused into my will by the will of another—which is indeed a contradiction in terms, my will in such case being no will—this is nowhere asserted in Scripture explicitly or by implication." It belongs to the very essence of the doctrine, that in respect of original sin every man is the adequate representative of all men. What wonder, then, that where no inward ground of preference existed, the choice should be determined by outward relations, and that the first in time should be taken as the diagram! Even in the book of Genesis the word Adam is distinguished from a proper name by an article before it. It is *the* Adam, so as to express the *genus*, not the individual—or rather, perhaps, I should say, as well as the individual. But that the word with its equivalent, the *old man*, is used symbolically and universally by St. Paul (1 *Cor.* xv. 22, 45. *Eph.* iv. 22. *Col.* iii. 9. *Rom.* vi. 6), is too evident to need any proof.

I conclude with this remark. The doctrine of Original Sin concerns all men. But it concerns Christians in particular no otherwise than by its connection with the doctrine of Redemption; and with the divinity and divine humanity of the Redeemer, as a corollary or necessary inference from both mysteries. Beware of arguments against Christianity, which can not stop there, and consequently ought not to have commenced there. Something I might have added to the clearness of the preceding views, if the limits of the Work had permitted me to clear away the several delusive and fanciful assertions respecting the state* of our first parents, their wisdom, science, and angelic faculties, assertions without the slightest ground in Scripture:—or, if consistently with the wants and preparatory studies of those, for whose use this Volume was especially intended, I could have entered into the momentous subject of a spiritual fall or apostasy antecedent to the formation of man—a belief the Scriptural grounds of which are few and of diverse interpretation, but which has been almost universal in the Christian Church. Enough however has been given, I trust, for the Reader to see and (as far as the subject is capable of being understood) to understand this long controverted article, in the sense in which alone it is binding on his faith. Supposing him therefore to know the meaning of Original Sin, and to have decided for himself on the fact of its actual existence, as the antecedent ground and occasion of Christianity, we may now proceed to Christianity itself, as the edifice raised on this ground, that is, to the great constituent article of the faith in Christ, as the remedy of the disease—the doctrine of Redemption.

But before I proceed to this great doctrine, let me briefly remind the young and friendly pupil, to whom I would still be supposed to address myself, that in the following Aphorisms the word science is used in its strict and narrowest sense. By a science I here mean any chain of truths which are either absolutely certain, or necessarily true for the human mind, from the laws and constitution of the mind itself. In neither case is our conviction derived, or capable of receiving any addition, from outward experience, or empirical *data*—that is, matters of fact given to us through the *medium* of the senses—though these

* For a specimen of these Rabbinical dotages, I refer, not to the writings of mystics and enthusiasts, but to the shrewd and witty Dr. South, one of whose most elaborate sermons stands prominent among the many splendid extravaganzas on this subject. (See *Sermons*, II. *Gen.* i. 27.—*Ed.*)

data may have been the occasion, or may even be an indispensable condition, of our reflecting on the former, and thereby becoming conscious of the same. On the other hand, a connected series of conclusions grounded on empirical *data*, in contra-distinction from science, I beg leave (no better term occurring) in this place and for this purpose to denominate a scheme.

APHORISM XI.

In whatever age and country it is the prevailing mind and character of the nation to regard the present life as subordinate to a life to come, and to mark the present state, the world of their senses, by signs, instruments, and mementos of its connection with a future state and a spiritual world ;—where the mysteries of faith are brought within the hold of the people at large, not by being explained away in the vain hope of accommodating them to the average of their understanding, but by being made the objects of love by their combination with events and epochs of history, with national traditions, with the monuments and dedications of ancestral faith and zeal, with memorial and symbolical observances, with the realizing influences of social devotion, and, above all, by early and habitual association with acts of the will,—there Religion is. There, however obscured by the hay and straw of human will-work, the foundation is safe. In that country and under the predominance of such maxims, the National Church is no mere State-institute. It is the state itself in its intensest federal union ; yet at the same moment the guardian and representative of all personal individuality. For the Church is the shrine of morality : and in morality alone the citizen asserts and reclaims his personal independence, his integrity. Our outward acts are efficient, and most often possible, only by coalition. As an efficient power, the agent is but a fraction of unity ; he becomes an *integer* only in the recognition and performance of the moral law. Nevertheless it is most true (and a truth which can not with safety be overlooked) that morality, as morality, has no existence for a people. It is either absorbed and lost in the quicksands of prudential *calculus*, or it is taken up and transfigured into the duties and mysteries of religion. And no wonder : since morality (including the personal being, the I am, as its subject) is itself a mystery, and the ground and *suppositum* of all other mysteries, relatively to man.

APHORISM XII.

PALEY NOT A MORALIST.

Schemes of conduct, grounded on calculations of self-interest, or on the average consequences of actions, supposed to be general, form a branch of Political Economy, to which let all due honor be given. Their utility is not here questioned. But however estimable within their own sphere such schemes, or any one of them in particular, may be, they do not belong to moral science, to which, both in kind and purpose, they are in all cases foreign, and, when substituted for it, hostile. Ethics, or the science of Morality, does indeed in no wise exclude the consideration of action; but it contemplates the same in its originating spiritual source, without reference to space, or time, or sensible existence. Whatever springs out of *the perfect law of freedom*, which exists only by its unity with the will of God, its inherance in the Word of God, and its communion with the Spirit of God—that (according to the principles of moral science) is good—it is light and righteousness and very truth. Whatever seeks to separate itself from the divine principle, and proceeds from a false centre in the agent's particular will, is evil—a work of darkness and contradiction. It is sin and essential falsehood. Not the outward deed, constructive, destructive, or neutral,—not the deed as a possible object of the senses,—is the object of ethical science. For this is no compost, *collectorium* or inventory of single duties; nor does it seek in the multitudinous sea, in the predetermined wave, and tides and currents of nature, that freedom which is exclusively an attribute of Spirit. Like all other pure sciences, whatever it enunciates, and whatever it concludes, it enunciates and concludes absolutely. Strictness is its essential character; and its first proposition is, *Whosoever shall keep the whole law, and yet offend in one point, he is guilty of all.* For as the will or spirit, the source and substance of moral good, is one and all in every part; so must it be the totality, the whole articulated series of single acts, taken as unity, that can alone, in the severity of science, be recognized as the proper counterpart and adequate representative of a good will. Is it in this or that limb, or not rather in the whole body, the entire *organismus*, that the law of Life reflects itself? Much less, then, can the law of the Spirit work in fragments.

APHORISM XIII.

Wherever there exists a permanent* learned class, having authority, and possessing the respect and confidence of the country; and wherever the science of ethics is acknowledged and taught in this class, as a regular part of a learned education, to its future members generally, but as the special study and indispensable ground-work of such as are intended for holy orders;—there the article of Original Sin will be an axiom of faith in all classes. Among the learned an undisputed truth, and with the people a fact, which no man imagines it possible to deny: and the doctrine, thus interwoven in the faith of all, and coeval with the consciousness of each, will, for each and all, possess a reality, subjective indeed, yet virtually equivalent to that which we intuitively give to the objects of our senses.

With the learned this will be the case, because the article is the first—I had almost said spontaneous—product of the application of modern science to history, of which it is the interpreter. A mystery in its own right, and by the necessity and essential character of its subject—(for the will, like the life, in every act and product pre-supposes to itself a past always present, a present that evermore resolves itself into a past)—the doctrine of Original Sin gives to all the other mysteries of religion a common basis, a connection of dependency, an intelligibility of relation, and a total harmony, which supersede extrinsic proof. There is here that same proof from unity of purpose, that same evidence of symmetry, which in the contemplation of a human skeleton flashed conviction on the mind of Galen, and kindled meditation into a hymn of praise.

* A learned order must be supposed to consist of three classes. First, those who are employed in adding to the existing sum of power and knowledge. Second, and most numerous class, those whose office it is to diffuse through the community at large the practical results of science, and that kind and degree of knowledge and cultivation, which for all is requisite or clearly useful. Third, the formers and instructors of the second—in schools, halls and universities, or through the *medium* of the press. The second class includes not only the Parochial Clergy, and all others duly ordained to the ministerial office; but likewise all the members of the legal and medical professions, who have received a learned education under accredited and responsible teachers.—(*See the Church and State*, VI. p. 51.—*Ed.*

Meanwhile the people, not goaded into doubt by the lessons and examples of their teachers and superiors; not drawn away from the fixed stars of heaven—the form and magnitude of which are the same for the naked eye of the shepherd as for the telescope of the sage—from the immediate truths, I mean of Reason and Conscience, to an exercise to which they have not been trained,—of a faculty which has been imperfectly developed,—on a subject not within the sphere of the faculty, nor in any way amenable to its judgment;—the people will need no arguments to receive a doctrine confirmed by their own experience from within and from without, and intimately blended with the most venerable traditions common to all races, and the traces of which linger in the latest twilight of civilization.

Among the revulsions consequent on the brute bewilderments of a Godless revolution, a great and active zeal for the interests of religion may be one. I dare not trust it, till I have seen what it is that gives religion this interest, till I am satisfied that it is not the interests of this world; necessary and laudable interests, perhaps, but which may, I dare believe, be secured as effectually and more suitably by the prudence of this world, and by this world's powers and motives. At all events, I find nothing in the fashion of the day to deter me from adding, that the reverse of the preceding—that where Religion is valued and patronized as a supplement of Law, or an aid extraordinary of Police; where moral science is exploded as the mystic jargon of dark ages; where a lax system of consequences, by which every iniquity on earth may be (and how many have been!) denounced and defended with equal plausibility, is publicly and authoritatively taught as Moral Philosophy; where the mysteries of religion, and truths supersensual, are either cut and squared for the comprehension of the Understanding, the faculty judging according to sense, or desperately torn asunder from the Reason, nay fanatically opposed to it; lastly, where private* interpretation is

* The Author of the Statesman's Manual must be the most inconsistent of men, if he can be justly suspected of a leaning to the Romish Church; or if it be necessary for him to repeat his fervent Amen to the wish and prayer of our late good old king, that "every adult in the British Empire should be able to read his Bible, and have a Bible to read!" Nevertheless, it may not be superfluous to declare, that in thus protesting against the license of private interpretation, I do not mean to condemn the exercise or deny the right of individual judgment. I condemn only the pretended right

every thing, and the Church nothing—there the mystery of Original Sin will be either rejected, or evaded, or perverted into the monstrous fiction of hereditary sin,—guilt inherited; in the mystery of Redemption metaphors will be obtruded for the reality; and in the mysterious appurtenants and symbols of Redemption (regeneration, grace, the Eucharist, and spiritual communion) the realities will be evaporated into metaphors.

APHORISM XIV.

Leighton.

As in great maps or pictures you will see the border decorated with meadows, fountains, flowers, and the like, represented in it, but in the middle you have the main design: so amongst the works of God is it with the fore-ordained redemption of man. All his other works in the world, all the beauty of the creatures, the succession of ages, and the things that come to pass in them, are but as the border to this as the mainpiece. But as a foolish unskilful beholder, not discerning the excellency of the principal piece in such maps or pictures, gazes only on the fair border, and goes no farther—thus do the greatest part of us as to this great work of God, the redemption of our personal being, and the re-union of the human with the divine, by and through the divine humanity of the Incarnate Word.

APHORISM XV.

Luther.

It is a hard matter, yea, an impossible thing, for thy human strength, whosoever thou art (without God's assistance), at such

of every individual, competent and incompetent, to interpret Scripture in a sense of his own, in opposition to the judgment of the Church, without knowledge of the originals or of the languages, the history, customs, opinions and controversies of the age and country in which they were written; and where the interpreter judges in ignorance or in contempt of uninterrupted tradition, the unanimous consent of Fathers and Councils, and the universal faith of the Church in all ages. It is not the attempt to form a judgment, which is here called in question; but the grounds, or rather the no-grounds on which the judgment is formed and relied on.

My fixed principle is: that a Christianity without a Church exercising spiritual authority is vanity and delusion. And my belief is, that when Popery is rushing in on us like an inundation, the nation will find it to be so. I say Popery: for this too I hold for a delusion that Romanism or Roman Catholicism is separable from Popery. Almost as readily could I suppose a circle without a centre.

a time when Moses setteth on thee with the Law (see Aphorism XII.),—when the holy Law written in thy heart accuseth and condemneth thee, forcing thee to a comparison of thy heart therewith, and convicting thee of the incompatibleness of thy will and nature with Heaven and holiness and an immediate God—that then thou shouldst be able to be of such a mind as if no law nor sin had ever been! I say it is in a manner impossible that a human creature, when he feeleth himself assaulted with trials and temptations, and the conscience hath to do with God, and the tempted man knoweth that the root of temptation is within him, should obtain such mastery over his thoughts as then to think no otherwise than that from everlasting nothing hath been but only and alone Christ, altogether grace and deliverance!

COMMENT.

In irrational agents, namely, the brute animals, the will is hidden or absorbed in the law. The law is their nature. In the original purity of a rational agent the uncorrupted will is identical with the law. Nay, inasmuch as a will perfectly identical with the law is one with the Divine Will, we may say, that in the unfallen rational agent, the will constitutes the law.* But it is evident that the holy and spiritual power and light, which by a *prolepsis* or anticipation we have named law, is a grace, an inward perfection, and without the commanding, binding, and menacing character which belongs to a law, acting as a master or sovereign distinct from, and existing, as it were, externally for, the agent who is bound to obey it. Now this is St. Paul's sense of the word, and on this he grounds his whole reasoning. And hence too arises the obscurity and apparent paradoxy of several texts. That the law is a law for you; that it acts on the will

* In fewer words thus: For the brute animals, their nature is their law;—for what other third law can be imagined, in addition to the law of nature, and the law of reason? Therefore: in irrational agents the law constitutes the will. In moral and rational agents the will constitutes, or ought to constitute, the law: I speak of moral agents, unfallen. For the personal will comprehends the idea as a reason, and it gives causative force to the idea, as a practical reason. But idea with the power of realizing the same is a law; or say:—the spirit comprehends the moral idea, by virtue of its rationality, and it gives to the idea causative power, as a will. In every sense, therefore, it constitutes the law, supplying both the elements of which it consists, namely, the idea, and the realizing power.

not in it; that it exercises an agency from without, by fear and coercion; proves the corruption of your will, and presupposes it. Sin in this sense came by the law: for it has its essence, as sin, in that counter-position of the holy principle to the will, which occasions this principle to be a law. Exactly (as in all other points) consonant with the Pauline doctrine is the assertion of John, when—speaking of the re-adoption of the redeemed to be sons of God, and the consequent resumption (I had almost said re-absorption) of the law into the will (νόμον τέλειον τὸν τῆς ἐλευθερίας, *James* i. 25)—he says, *For the law was given by Moses, but grace and truth came by Jesus Christ.** That by the law St. Paul meant only the ceremonial law, is a notion that could originate only in utter inattention to the whole strain and bent of the Apostle's argument.

APHORISM XVI.

Leighton and Coleridge.

Christ's death was both voluntary and violent. There was external violence: and that was the accompaniment, or at most the occasion, of his death. But there was internal willingness, the spiritual will, the will of the Spirit, and this was the proper cause. By this Spirit he was restored from death: neither indeed *was it possible for him to be holden of it. Being put to death in the flesh, but quickened by the Spirit,* says St. Peter. But he is likewise declared elsewhere to have died by that same Spirit, which here, in opposition to the violence, is said to quicken him. Thus *Heb.* ix. 14, *Through the eternal Spirit he offered himself.* And even from Peter's words, and without the epithet eternal, to aid the interpretation, it is evident that *the Spirit,* here opposed to the flesh by body or animal life, is of a higher nature and power than the individual soul, which can not of itself return to reinhabit or quicken the body.

If these points were niceties, and an over-refining in doctrine, is it to be believed that the Apostles, John, Peter, and Paul, with the author of the Epistle to the Hebrews, would have laid so great a stress on them? But the true life of Christians is to eye Christ in every step of his life—not only as their rule but as their strength: looking to him as their pattern both in doing and in suffering, and drawing power from him for going through both:

* *John* i. 17.—*Ed.*

being without him able for nothing. Take comfort, then, thou that believest! *It is he that lifts up the soul from the gates of death;* and he hath said, *I will raise thee up at the last day.* Thou that believest *in* him, believe him and take comfort. Yea, when thou art most sunk in thy sad apprehensions, and he far off to thy thinking, then is he nearest to raise and comfort thee: as sometimes it grows darkest immediately before day.

APHORISM XVII.

Leighton and Coleridge.

Would any of you be cured of that common disease, the fear of death? Yet this is not the right name of the disease, as a mere reference to our armies and navies is sufficient to prove: nor can the fear of death, either as loss of life or pain of dying, be justly held a common disease. But would you be cured of the fear and fearful questionings connected with the approach of death? Look this way, and you shall find more than you seek. Christ, the Word that was from the beginning, and was made flesh and dwelt among men, died. And he, who dying conquered death in his own person, conquered sin and death, which is the wages of sin, for thee. And of this thou mayest be assured, if only thou believe in him and love him. I need not add, keep his commandments: since where faith and love are, obedience in its threefold character, as effect, reward, and criterion, follows by that moral necessity which is the highest form of freedom. The grave is thy bed of rest, and no longer the cold bed: for thy Saviour has warmed it, and made it fragrant.

If then it be health and comfort to the faithful that Christ descended into the grave, with especial confidence may we meditate on his return from thence, *quickened by the Spirit:* this being to those who are in him the certain pledge, yea, the effectual cause of that blessed resurrection for which they themselves hope. There is that union betwixt them and their Redeemer, that they shall rise by the communication and virtue of his rising: not simply by his power—for so the wicked likewise to their grief shall be raised: but *they by his life as their life.*

COMMENT ON THE THREE PRECEDING APHORISMS.

To the Reader, who has consented to submit his mind to my temporary guidance, and who permits me to regard him as my pupil or junior fellow-student, I continue to address myself. Should he exist only in my imagination, let the bread float on the waters! If it be the Bread of Life, it will not have been utterly cast away.

Let us pause a moment, and review the road we have passed over since the transit from Religious Morality to Spiritual Religion. My first attempt was to satisfy you, that there is a spiritual principle in man, and to expose the sophistry of the arguments in support of the contrary. Our next step was to clear the road of all counterfeits, by showing what is not the Spirit, what is not spiritual religion. And this was followed by an attempt to establish a difference in kind between religious truths and the deductions of speculative science; yet so as to prove, that the former are not only equally rational with the latter, but that they alone appeal to reason in the fulness and living reality of their power. This and the state of mind requisite for the formation of right convictions respecting spiritual truths, afterwards employed our attention. Having then enumerated the Articles of the Christian Faith peculiar to Christianity, I entered on the great object of the present Work: namely, the removal of all valid objections to these articles on grounds of right reason or conscience. But to render this practicable, it was necessary, first, to present each article in its true Scriptural purity, by exposure of the caricatures of misinterpreters; and this, again, could not be satisfactorily done till we were agreed respecting the faculty entitled to sit in judgment on such questions. I early foresaw that my best chance (I will not say, of giving an insight into the surpassing worth and transcendent reasonableness of the Christian scheme; but) of rendering the very question intelligible, depended on my success in determining the true nature and limits of the human Understanding, and in evincing its diversity from Reason. In pursuing this momentous subject, I was tempted in two or three instances into disquisitions, which if not beyond the comprehension, were yet unsuited to the taste, of the persons for whom the Work was principally intended. These, however, I have separated from the running text, and compressed into notes. The Reader will at worst, I hope, pass them by as a leaf or two of waste paper, willingly given by him to those for whom it may not be paper wasted. Nevertheless, I can not conceal that the subject itself supposes, on the part of the Reader, a steadiness in self-questioning, a pleasure in referring to his own inward experience for the facts asserted by the Author, which can only be expected from a person who has fairly set his heart on arriving at clear and fixed conclusions in matters of faith. But where this interest is felt, nothing more than a common capacity, with the ordinary advantages of education, is required for the complete comprehension both of the argument and the result. Let but one thoughtful hour be devoted to the pages 183–190. In all that follows, the Reader will find no difficulty in understanding my meaning, whatever he may have in adopting it.

The two great moments of the Christian Religion are, Original Sin and Redemption; that the ground, this the superstructure of our faith. The former I have exhibited, first, according to the scheme of the Westminster Divines and the Synod of Dort; then, according to the* scheme of a contemporary Arminian divine;

* To escape the consequences of this scheme, some Arminian divines have asserted that the penalty inflicted on Adam, and continued in his posterity, was simply the loss of immortality—death as the utter extinction of personal being: immortality being regarded by them (and not, I think, without good reason) as a supernatural attribute, and its loss therefore involved in the forfeiture of supernatural graces. This theory has its golden side: and, as a private opinion, is said to have the countenance of more than one dignitary of our Church, whose general orthodoxy is beyond impeachment. For here the penalty resolves itself into the consequence, and this the natural and naturally inevitable consequence of Adam's crime. For Adam, indeed, it was a positive punishment: a punishment of his guilt, the justice of which who could have dared arraign? While for the offspring of Adam it was simply a not super-adding to their nature the privilege by which the original man was contra-distinguished from the brute creation—a mere negation of which they had no more right to complain than any other species of animals. God in this view appears only in his attribute of mercy, as averting by supernatural interposition a consequence naturally inevitable. This is the golden side of the theory. But if we approach to it from the opposite direction, it first excites a just scruple, from the countenance it seems to give to the doctrine of Materialism. The supporters of this scheme do not, I presume, contend that Adam's offspring would not have been born men, but have formed a new species of beasts! And if not, the notion of a rational and self-conscious soul, perishing utterly with the dissolution of the organized body, seems to require, nay, almost involves, the opinion that the soul is a quality or accident of the body,—a mere harmony resulting from organization.

But let this pass unquestioned. Whatever else the descendants of Adam might have been without the intercession of Christ, yet (this intercession

and lastly, in contrast with both schemes, I have placed what I firmly believe to be the Scriptural sense of this article, and vindicated its entire conformity with reason and experience. I now proceed to the other momentous article—from the necessitating occasion of the Christian dispensation to Christianity itself. For Christianity and Redemption are equivalent terms. And here my comment will be comprised in a few sentences: for I confine my views to the one object of clearing this awful mystery from those too current misrepresentations of its nature and import, that have laid it open to scruples and objections, not to such as shoot

having been effectually made) they are now endowed with souls that are not extinguished together with the material body.—Now unless these divines teach likewise the Romish figment of Purgatory, and to an extent in which the Church of Rome herself would denounce the doctrine as an impious heresy: unless they hold, that a punishment temporary and remedial is the worst evil that the impenitent have to apprehend in a future state; and that the spiritual death declared and foretold by Christ, *the death eternal where the worm never dies*, is neither death nor eternal, but a certain *quantum* of suffering in a state of faith, hope, and progressive amendment—unless they go these lengths (and the divines here intended are orthodox Churchmen, men who would not knowingly advance even a step on the road towards them)—then I fear that any advantage their theory might possess over the Calvinistic scheme in the article of Original Sin, would be dearly purchased by increased difficulties, and an ultra-Calvinistic narrowness in the article of Redemption. I at least find it impossible, with my present human feelings, not to imagine that even in heaven it would be a fearful thing to know, that in order to my elevation to a lot infinitely more desirable than by nature it would have been, the lot of so vast a multitude had been rendered infinitely more calamitous; and that my felicity had been purchased by the everlasting misery of my fellow-men, who, if no redemption had been provided, after inheriting the pains and pleasures of earthly existence during the numbered hours, and the few and evil—evil yet few—days of the years of their mortal life, would have fallen asleep to wake no more,—would have sunk into the dreamless sleep of the grave, and have been as the murmur and the plaint, and the exulting swell and the sharp scream, which the unequal gust of yesterday snatched from the strings of a wind-harp.

In another place I have ventured to question the spirit and tendency of Taylor's Work on Repentance.* But I ought to have added, that to discover and keep the true medium in expounding and applying the efficacy of Christ's Cross and Passion, is beyond comparison the most difficult and delicate point of practical divinity—and that which especially needs a guidance from above.

* See also Literary Remains, V. pp. 194–212.—*Ed.*

forth from an unbelieving heart—(against these a sick bed will be a more effectual antidote than all the argument in the world)—but to such scruples as have their birth-place in the reason and moral sense. Not that it is a mystery—not that *it passeth all understanding;* if the doctrine be more than a hyperbolical phrase, it must do so;—but that it is at variance with the law revealed in the conscience; that it contradicts our moral instincts and intuitions—this is the difficulty which alone is worthy of an answer. And what better way is there of correcting the misconceptions than by laying open the source and occasion of them? What surer way of removing the scruples and prejudices, to which these misconceptions have given rise, than by propounding the mystery itself—namely, the Redemptive Act, as the transcendent cause of salvation—in the express and definite words in which it was enunciated by the Redeemer Himself?

But here, in addition to the three Aphorisms preceding, I interpose a view of Redemption as appropriated by faith, coincident with Leighton's, though for the greater part expressed in my own words. This I propose as the right view. Then follow a few sentences transcribed from Field (an excellent divine of the reign of James I., of whose work on the Church,* it would be difficult to speak too highly), containing the questions to be solved, and which are numbered as an Aphorism, rather to preserve the uniformity of appearance, than as being strictly such. Then follows the Comment: as part and commencement of which the Reader will consider the two paragraphs of pp. 172–3, written for this purpose, and in the foresight of the present inquiry: and I entreat him therefore to begin the Comment by re-perusing these.

APHORISM XVIII.

Steadfast by faith. This is absolutely necessary for resistance to the evil principle. There is no standing out without some firm ground to stand on: and this faith alone supplies. By faith in the love of Christ the power of God becomes ours. When the soul is beleaguered by enemies, weakness on the walls, treachery at the gates, and corruption in the citadel, then by faith she says—Lamb of God slain from the foundation of the world! Thou art my strength! I look to thee for deliverance! And thus she

* See Literary Remains, V. pp. 52–73.—*Ed.*

overcomes. The pollution (*miasma*) of sin is precipitated by his blood, the power of sin is conquered by his Spirit. The Apostle says not—steadfast by your own resolutions and purposes; but—*steadfast by faith.* Nor yet steadfast in your will, but steadfast in the faith. We are not to be looking to, or brooding over ourselves, either for accusation or for confidence, or (by a deep yet too frequent self-delusion) to obtain the latter by making a merit to ourselves of the former. But we are to look to Christ and *him crucified.* The law *that is very nigh to thee, even in thy heart:* the law that condemneth and hath no promise; that stoppeth the guilty past in its swift flight, and maketh it disown its name; the law will accuse thee enough. Linger not in the justice-court listening to thy indictment. Loiter not in waiting to hear the sentence. No, anticipate the verdict. Appeal to Cæsar. Haste to the king for a pardon. Struggle thitherward, though in fetters; and cry aloud, and collect the whole remaining strength of thy will in the outcry—*I believe; Lord, help my unbelief!* Disclaim all right of property in thy fetters. Say that they belong to the old man, and that thou dost but carry them to the grave, to be buried with their owner! Fix thy thought on what Christ did, what Christ suffered, what Christ is—as if thou wouldst fill the hollowness of thy soul with Christ. If he emptied himself of glory to become sin for thy salvation, must not thou be emptied of thy sinful self to become righteousness in and through his agony and the effective merits of his Cross?* By what other

* *God manifested in the flesh* is eternity in the form of time. But eternity in relation to time is as the absolute to the conditional, or the real to the apparent, and Redemption must partake of both;—always perfected, for it is a *Fiat* of the Eternal;—continuous, for it is a process in relation to man; the former the alone objectively, and therefore universally, true. That Redemption is an *opus perfectum*, a finished work, the claim to which is conferred in Baptism: that a Christian can not speak or think as if his redemption by the blood, and his justification by the righteousness of Christ alone, were future or contingent events, but must both say and think, I have been redeemed, I am justified; lastly, that for as many as are received into his Church by Baptism, Christ has condemned sin in the flesh, has made it dead in law, that is, no longer imputable as guilt, has destroyed the objective reality of sin:—these are truths, which all the Reformed Churches, Swedish, Danish, Evangelical (or Lutheran), the Reformed (the Calvinistic in mid-Germany, Holland, France, and Geneva, so called), lastly, the Church of England, and the Church of Scotland—nay, the best and most learned divines of the Roman Catholic Church have united in upholding as most

means, in what other form, is it possible for thee to stand in the presence of the Holy One? With what mind wouldst thou come before God, if not with the mind of Him, in whom alone God loveth the world? With good advice, perhaps, and a little assistance, thou wouldst rather cleanse and patch up a mind of

certain and necessary articles of faith, and the effectual preaching of which Luther declares to be the appropriate criterion *stantis vel cadentis Ecclesiæ*. The Church is standing or falling, according as this doctrine is supported, or overlooked, or countervened. Nor has the contrary doctrine, according to which the baptized are yet each individually to be called, converted, and chosen, with all the corollaries from this assumption, the watching for signs and sensible assurances, the frames, and the states, and the feelings, and the sudden conversions, the contagious fever-boils of the (most unfitly, so called) Evangelicals, and Arminian Methodists of the day, been in any age taught or countenanced by any known and accredited Christian Church, or by any body and succession of learned divines. On the other hand, it has rarely happened that the Church has not been troubled by Pharisaic and fanatical individuals, who have sought, by working on the fears and feelings of the weak and unsteady, that celebrity which they could not obtain by learning and orthodoxy; and alas! so subtle is the poison, and so malignant in its operation, that it is almost hopeless to attempt the cure of any person, once infected, more particularly when, as most often happens, the patient is a woman. Nor does Luther, in his numerous and admirable discourses on this point, conceal or palliate the difficulties which the carnal mind, that works under many and different disguises, throws in the way to prevent the laying firm hold of the truth. One most mischievous and very popular misbelief must be cleared away in the first instance—the presumption, I mean, that whatever is not quite simple, and what any plain body can understand at the first hearing, can not be of necessary belief, or among the fundamental articles or essentials of Christian faith. A docile childlike mind, a deference to the authority of the Churches, a presumption of the truth of doctrines that have been received and taught as true by the whole Church in all times; reliance on the positive declarations of the Apostle—in short, all the convictions of the truth of a doctrine that are previous to a perfect insight into its truth, because these convictions, with the affections and dispositions accompanying them, are the very means and conditions of attaining to that insight—and study of, and quiet meditation on, them with a gradual growth of spiritual knowledge and earnest prayer for its increase; all these, to each and all of which the young Christian is so repeatedly and fervently exhorted by St. Paul, are to be superseded, because, forsooth, truths needful for all men must be quite simple and easy, and adapted to the capacity of all, even of the plainest and dullest understanding! What can not be poured all at once on a man, can only be supererogatory drops from the emptied shower-bath of religious instruction! But surely, the more rational inference would be, that the faith, which is to save the whole man, must have its roots and justifying grounds in the very depths of our being. And

thy own, and offer it as thy admission-right, thy qualification to Him who *charged his angels with folly!* Oh! take counsel of thy reason. It will show thee how impossible it is that even a world should merit the love of eternal wisdom and all-sufficing beatitude, otherwise than as it is contained in that all-perfect Idea, in which the Supreme Spirit contemplateth himself and the plenitude of his infinity—the Only-Begotten before all ages, *the beloved Son, in whom the Father* is indeed *well pleased!*

And as the mind, so the body with which it is to be clothed; as the indweller, so the house in which it is to be the abiding-place.* There is but one wedding-garment, in which we can

he who can read the writings of the Apostles, John and Paul, without finding in almost every page a confirmation of this, must have looked at them, as at the sun in an eclipse, through blackened glasses.

* St. Paul blends both forms of expression, and asserts the same doctrine, when speaking of the *celestial body* provided for *the new man* in the spiritual flesh and blood, that is, the informing power and vivific life of the incarnate Word: for the blood is the life, and the flesh the power)—when speaking, I say, of this *celestial body* as a *house not made with hands, eternal in the heavens*, yet brought down to us, made appropriable by faith, and ours—he adds, *for in this earthly house* (that is, this mortal life, as the inward principle or energy of our tabernacle, or outward and sensible body) *we groan, earnestly desiring to be clothed upon with our house which is from heaven: not that we would be unclothed, but clothed upon, that mortality might be swallowed up of life.* 2 Cor. v. 1–4.

The last four words of the first verse (*eternal in the heavens*) compared with the conclusion of v. 2 (*which is from heaven*), present a coincidence with *John* iii. 13, "*And no man hath ascended up to heaven, but he that came down from heaven, even the Son of Man, which is in heaven.*" Would not the coincidence be more apparent, if the words of John had been rendered word for word, even to a disregard of the English idiom, and with what would be servile and superstitious fidelity in the translation of a common classic? I can see no reason why the *οὐδεὶς*, so frequent in St. John, should not be rendered literally, no one; and there may be a reason why it should. I have some doubt likewise respecting the omission of the definite articles *τὸν, τοῦ, τῷ*—and a greater as to the *ὁν ὢν*, both in this place and in *John* i. 18, being adequately rendered by our *which is.* What sense some of the Greek Fathers attached to, or inferred from, St. Paul's *in the heavens*, the theological student (and to theologians is this note principally addressed) may find in Waterland's letters to a Country Clergyman—a divine, whose judgment and strong sound sense are as unquestionable as his learning and orthodoxy. A Clergyman, in full orders, who has never read the works of Bull and Waterland, has a duty yet to perform.

Let it not be objected, that, forgetful of my own professed aversion to allegorical interpretations, I have, in this note, fallen into the fond humor

sit down at the marriage feast of Heaven: and that is the bridegroom's own gift, when he gave himself for us, that we might live in him and he in us. There is but one robe of righteousness, even the spiritual body, formed by the assimilative power of faith, for whoever eateth the flesh of the Son of Man, and drinketh his blood. Did Christ come from Heaven, did the Son of God leave the glory *which he had with his Father before the world began*, only to show us a way to life, to teach truths, to tell us of a resurrection? Or saith he not, *I am the way—I am the truth—I am the resurrection and the life?*

APHORISM XIX.

Field.

The Romanists teach that sins committed after Baptism (that is, for the immense majority of Christians having Christian pa-

of the mystic divines, and allegorizers of Holy Writ. There is, believe me, a wide difference between symbolical and allegorical. If I say that the flesh and blood (*corpus noumenon*) of the Incarnate Word are power and life, I say likewise that this mysterious power and life are verily and actually the flesh and blood of Christ. They are the allegorizers who turn the sixth chapter of the Gospel according to St. John, *the hard saying—who can hear it?*—after which time many of Christ's disciples, who had been eye-witnesses of his mighty miracles, who had heard the sublime morality of his Sermon on the Mount, had glorified God for the wisdom which they had heard, and had been prepared to acknowledge, *This is indeed the Christ,*—went back and walked no more with him!—the hard sayings, which even the Twelve were not yet competent to understand farther than that they were to be spiritually understood; and which the chief of the Apostles was content to receive with an implicit and anticipative faith!—they, I repeat, are the allegorizers who moralize these hard sayings, these high words of mystery, into a hyperbolical metaphor *per catachresin*, which only means a belief of the doctrine which Paul believed, an obedience to the law respecting which Paul *was blameless*, before the voice called him on the road to Damascus! What every parent, every humane preceptor, would do when a child had misunderstood a metaphor or apologue in a literal sense, we all know. But the meek and merciful Jesus suffered many of his disciples to fall off from eternal life, when, to retain them, he had only to say,—O ye simple ones! why are ye offended? My words, indeed, sound strange; but I mean no more than what you have often and often heard from me before, with delight and entire acquiescence!—*Credat Judæus! Non ego.* It is sufficient for me to know that I have used the language of Paul and John, as it was understood and interpreted by Justin Martyr, Tertullian, Irenæus, and (if he does not err) by the whole Christian Church then existing. [See Table Talk. VI. 316, 317.—*Ed.*]

rents, all their sins from the cradle to the grave) are not so remitted for Christ's sake, but that we must suffer that extremity of punishment which they deserve: and therefore either we must afflict ourselves in such sort and degree of extremity as may answer the demerit of our sins, or be punished by God, here, or in the world to come, in such degree and sort that his justice may be satisfied. [As the encysted venom, or poison-bag, beneath the adder's fang, so does this doctrine lie beneath the tremendous power of the Romish Hierarchy. The demoralizing influence of this dogma, and that it curdled the very life-blood in the veins of Christendom, it was given to Luther, beyond all men since Paul, to see, feel, and promulgate. And yet in his large Treatise on Repentance, how near to the spirit of this doctrine—even to the very walls and gates of Babylon—was Jeremy Taylor driven, in recoiling from the fanatical extremes of the opposite error!] But they that are orthodox, teach that it is injustice to require the paying of one debt twice. * * * It is no less absurd to say, as the Papists do, that our satisfaction is required as a condition, without which Christ's satisfaction is not applicable unto us, than to say, Peter hath paid the debt of John, and he to whom it was due accepteth of the payment on the condition that John pay it himself also. * * * The satisfaction of Christ is communicated and applied unto us without suffering the punishment that sin deserveth [and essentially involveth], upon the condition of our faith and repentance. [To which I would add: Without faith there is no power of repentance: without a commencing repentance no power to faith: and that it is in the power of the will either to repent or to have faith in the Gospel sense of the words, is itself a consequence of the redemption of mankind, a free gift of the Redeemer: the guilt of its rejection, the refusing to avail ourselves of the power, being all that we can consider as exclusively attributable to our own act.]

COMMENT. (CONTAINING AN APPLICATION OF THE PRINCIPLES LAID DOWN IN PP. 235–6.)

Forgiveness of sin, the abolition of guilt, through the redemptive power of Christ's love, and of his perfect obedience during his voluntary assumption of humanity, is expressed, on account of the resemblance of the consequences in both cases, by the payment of a debt for another, which debt the payer had not himself incurred. Now the impropriation of this metaphor—(that is, the taking it literally)—by transferring the sameness from the consequents to the antecedents, or inferring the identity of the causes from a resemblance in the effects—this is the point on which I am at issue: and the view or scheme of Redemption grounded on this confusion I believe to be altogether un-Scriptural.

Indeed, I know not in what other instance I could better exemplify the species of sophistry noticed in p. 245, as the Aristotelean μετάβασις εἰς ἄλλο γένος, or clandestine passing over into a diverse kind. The purpose of a metaphor is to illustrate a something less known by a partial identification of it with some other thing better understood, or at least more familiar. Now the article of Redemption may be considered in a two-fold relation—in relation to the antecedent, that is, the Redeemer's act, as the efficient cause and condition of redemption; and in relation to the consequent, that is, the effects in and for the Redeemed. Now it is the latter relation, in which the subject is treated of, set forth, expanded, and enforced by St. Paul. The mysterious act, the operative cause, is transcendent. *Factum est:* and beyond the information contained in the enunciation of the fact, it can be characterized only by the consequences. It is the consequences of the act of Redemption, which the zealous Apostle would bring home to the minds and affections both of Jews and Gentiles. Now the Apostle's opponents and gainsayers were principally of the former class. They were Jews: not only Jews unconverted, but such as had partially received the Gospel, and who, sheltering their national prejudices under the pretended authority of Christ's original Apostles and the Church in Jerusalem, set themselves up against Paul as followers of Cephas. Add too, that Paul himself was *a Hebrew of the Hebrews;* intimately versed *in the Jews' religion above many his equals in his own nation, and above measure zealous of the traditions of his fathers.* It might, therefore, have been anticipated that his reasoning would receive its outward forms and language, that it would take its predominant colors, from his own past, and his opponents' present, habits of thinking; and that his figures, images, analogies and references would be taken preferably from objects, opinions, events, and ritual observances ever uppermost in the imaginations of his own countrymen. And such we find them; —yet so judiciously selected, that the prominent forms, the figures of most frequent recurrence, are drawn from points of belief and practice, forms, laws, rites and customs, which then prevailed through the whole Roman world, and were common to Jew and Gentile.

Now it would be difficult if not impossible to select points better suited to this purpose, as being equally familiar to all, and yet having a special interest for the Jewish converts, than those are from which the learned Apostle has drawn the four principal metaphors, by which he illustrates the blessed consequences of Christ's redemption of mankind. These are: 1. Sin offerings, sacrificial expiation. 2. Reconciliation, atonement, καταλλαγή.*

.* This word occurs but once in the New Testament, *Rom.* v. 11, the marginal rendering being *reconciliation.* The personal noun, καταλλακτής, is still in use with the modern Greeks for a money-changer, or one who takes the debased currency, so general in countries under a despotic or other dishonest government, in exchange for sterling coin or bullion; the purchaser paying the καταλλαγή, that is, the difference. In the elder Greek writers, the verb means to exchange for an opposite, as, καταλλάσσετο τὴν ἔχθρην τοῖς στασιώταις—He exchanged within himself enmity for friendship (that is, he reconciled himself), with his party;—or, as we say, made it up with them, an idiom which (with whatever loss of dignity) gives the exact force of the word. He made up the difference. The Hebrew word, of very frequent occurrence in the Pentateuch, which we render by the substantive atonement, has its radical or visual image in *copher*, pitch. *Gen.* vi. 14, *Thou shalt pitch it within and without with pitch;*—hence to unite, to fill up a breach or leak, the word expressing both the act, namely the bringing together what had been previously separated, and the means, or material, by which the re-union is effected, as in our English verbs, to caulk, to solder, to *poy* or pay (from *poix*, pitch), and the French *suiver.* Thence, metaphorically, expiation, the *piacula* having the same root, and being grounded on another property or use of gums and resins, the supposed cleansing powers of their fumigation; *Numb.* viii. 21: *made atonement for the Levites to cleanse them.*—Lastly (or if we are to believe the Hebrew Lexicons, properly and most frequently) it means ransom. But if by proper, the interpreters mean primary and radical, the assertion does not need a confutation: all radicals belonging to one or other of three classes:—1. Interjections, or sounds expressing sensations or passions. 2. Imitations of sounds, as splash, roar, whiz, &c. 3. and principally, visual images, objects of sight. But as to frequency, in all the numerous (fifty I believe) instances of the word in the Old Testament, I have not found one in which it can, or at least need, be rendered by ransom: though beyond all doubt ransom is used in the Epistle to Timothy as an equivalent term.

3. Ransom from slavery, redemption, the buying back again, or being bought back. 4. Satisfaction of a creditor's claims by a payment of the debt. To one or other of these four heads all the numerous forms and exponents of Christ's mediation in St. Paul's writings may be referred. And the very number and variety of the words or *periphrases* used by him to express one and the same thing, furnish the strongest presumptive proof that all alike were used metaphorically. [In the following notation, let the small letters represent the effects or consequences, and the capitals the efficient causes or antecedents. Whether by causes we mean acts or agents, is indifferent. Now let X signify a transcendent, that is, a cause beyond our comprehension, and not within the sphere of sensible experience ; and on the other hand, let A, B, C, and D represent each one known and familiar cause, in reference to some single and characteristic effect : namely, A in reference to k, B to l, C to m, and D to n. Then I say X + k l m n is in different places expressed by A + k ; B + l ; C + m ; D + n. And these I should call metaphorical exponents of X.]

Now John, the beloved disciple, who leaned on the Lord's bosom, the Evangelist κατὰ πνεῦμα, that is according to the spirit, the inner and substantial truth of the Christian Creed—John, recording the Redeemer's own words, enunciates the fact itself, to the full extent in which it is enunciable for the human mind, simply and without any metaphor, by identifying it in kind with a fact of hourly occurrence—expressing it, I say, by a familiar fact the same in kind with that intended, though of a far lower dignity ;—by a fact of every man's experience, known to all, yet not better understood than the fact described by it. In the redeemed it is a re-generation, a birth, a spiritual seed impregnated and evolved, the germinal principle of a higher and enduring life, of a spiritual life—that is, a life the actuality of which is not dependent on the material body, or limited by the circumstances and processes indispensable to its organization and subsistence. Briefly, it is the differential of immortality, of which the assimilative power of faith and love is the integrant, and the life in Christ the integration.

But even this would be an imperfect statement, if we omitted the awful truth, that besides that dissolution of our earthly tabernacle which we call death, there is another death, not the mere negation of life, but its positive opposite. And as there is a mystery of life, and an assimilation to the principle of life, even to him who is the Life; so is there a mystery of death, and an assimilation to the principle of evil; a fructifying of the corrupt seed, of which death is the germination. Thus the regeneration to spiritual life is at the same time a redemption from the spiritual death.

Respecting the Redemptive Act itself, and the Divine Agent, we know from revelation that he *was made a quickening* (ζωοποιοῦν, life-making) *Spirit*: and that in order to this it was necessary that God should be *manifested in the flesh;* that the Eternal Word, through whom and by whom the world (κόσμος, the order, beauty, and sustaining law of visible natures) was and is, should be made flesh, assume our humanity personally, fulfil all righteousness, and so suffer and so die for us, as in dying to conquer death for as many as should receive him. More than this, the mode, the possibility, we are not competent to know. It is, as hath been already observed concerning the primal act of apostasy, a mystery by the necessity of the subject—a mystery which at all events it will be time enough for us to seek and expect to understand, when we understand the mystery of our natural life, and its conjunction with mind and will and personal identity. Even the truths that are given to us to know, we can know only through faith in the spirit. They are spiritual things, which must be spiritually discerned. Such, however, being the means and the effects of our redemption, well might the fervent Apostle associate it with whatever was eminently dear and precious to erring and afflicted mortals, and (where no expression could be commensurate, no single title be other than imperfect) seek from similitude of effect to describe the superlative boon, by successively transferring to it, as by a superior claim, the name of each several act and ordinance, habitually connected in the minds of all his hearers with feelings of joy, confidence, and gratitude.

Do you rejoice when the atonement made by the priest has removed the civil stain from your name, restored you to your privileges as a son of Abraham, and replaced you in the respect of your brethren?—Here is an atonement which takes away a deeper and worse stain, an eating canker-spot in the very heart of your personal being. This, to as many as receive it, gives the privilege to become sons of God (*John* i. 12); this will admit you to the society of angels, and insure to you the rights of brotherhood with spirits made perfect (*Heb.* xii. 22). Here is a sacrifice, a sin-offering for the whole world: and a High Priest, who is indeed a Mediator; who, not in type or shadow, but in very truth, and in his own right, stands in the place of Man to God, and of God to Man; and who receives as a Judge what he offered as an advocate.

Would you be grateful to one who had ransomed you from slavery under a bitter foe, or who brought you out of captivity? Here is redemption from a far direr slavery, the slavery of sin unto death; and he who gave himself for the ransom, has taken captivity captive.

Had you by your own fault alienated yourself from your best, your only sure friend;—had you, like a prodigal, cast yourself out of your Father's house;—would you not love the good Samaritan, who should reconcile you to your friend? Would you not prize above all price the intercession, which had brought you back from husks, and the tending of swine, and restored you to your father's arms, and seated you at your father's table?

Had you involved yourselves in a heavy debt for certain gewgaws, for high-seasoned meats, and intoxicating drinks, and glistering apparel, and in default of payment had made yourself over as a bondsman to a hard creditor, who, it was foreknown, would enforce the bond of judgment to the last tittle;—with what emotions would you not receive the glad tidings that a stranger, or a friend whom in the days of your wantonness you had neglected and reviled, had paid the debt for you, had made satisfaction to your creditor? But you have incurred a debt of death to the evil nature; you have sold yourself over to sin; and, relatively to you, and to all your means and resources, the seal on the bond is the seal of necessity. Its stamp is the nature of evil. But the stranger has appeared, the forgiving friend has come, even the Son of God from heaven: and to as many as have faith in his name, I say—the debt is paid for you;—the satisfaction has been made.

Now, to simplify the argument, and at the same time to bring the question to the test, we will confine our attention to the figure last mentioned, namely, the satisfaction of a debt. Passing by our modern *Alogi*, who find nothing but metaphors in either Apostle, let us suppose for a moment, with certain divines, that our Lord's words, recorded by John, and which in all places repeat and assert the same analogy, are to be regarded as metaphorical; and that it is the varied expressions of St. Paul that are to be literally interpreted: for example, that sin is, or involves, an infinite debt (in the proper and law-court sense of the word, debt)—a debt owing by us to the vindictive justice of God the Father, which can only be liquidated by the everlasting misery of Adam and all his posterity, or by a sum of suffering equal to this. Likewise, that God the Father, by his absolute decree, or (as some divines teach) through the necessity of his unchangeable justice, had determined to exact the full sum: which must, therefore, be paid either by ourselves or by some other in our name and behalf. But besides the debt which all mankind contracted in and through Adam, as a *homo publicus*, even as a nation is bound by the acts of its head or its plenipotentiary, every man (say these divines) is an insolvent debtor on his own score. In this fearful predicament the Son of God took compassion on mankind, and resolved to pay the debt for us, and to satisfy the divine justice by a perfect equivalent. Accordingly, by a strange yet strict consequence, it has been holden, by more than one of these divines, that the agonies suffered by Christ were equal in amount to the sum total of the torments of all mankind here and hereafter, or to the infinite debt, which in an endless succession of instalments we should have been paying to the divine justice, had it not been paid in full by the Son of God incarnate!

It is easy to say—"O but I do not hold this, or we do not make this an article of our belief!" The true question is: "Do you take any part of it; and can you reject the rest without being inconsequent?" Are debt, satisfaction, payment in full, creditor's rights, and the like, *nomina propria*, by which the very nature of Redemption and its occasion are expressed;—or are they, with several others, figures of speech for the purpose of illustrating the nature and extent of the consequences and effects of the Redemptive Act, and to excite in the receivers a due sense of the magnitude and manifold operation of the boon, and of the love and gratitude due to the Redeemer? If still you reply, the former: then, as your whole theory is grounded on a notion of justice, I ask you—Is this justice a moral attribute? But morality commences with, and begins in, the sacred distinction between thing and person. On this distinction all law, human and divine, is grounded: consequently, the law of justice. If you attach any meaning to the term justice, as applied to God, it must be the same to which you refer when you affirm or deny it of any other personal agent—save only, that in its attribution to God, you speak of it as unmixed and perfect. For if not, what do you mean? And why do you call it by the same name? I may, therefore, with all right and reason, put the case as between man and man. For should it be found irreconcilable with the justice which the light of reason, made law in the conscience, dictates to man, how much more must it be incongruous with the all-perfect justice of God! Whatever case I should imagine would be felt by the reader as below the dignity of the subject, and in some measure jarring with his feelings; and in other respects the more familiar the case, the better suited to the present purpose.

A sum of £1000 is due from James to Peter, for which James has given a bond. He is insolvent, and the bond is on the point of being put in suit against him, to James's utter ruin. At this moment Matthew steps in, pays Peter the thousand pounds, and discharges the bond. In this case, no man would hesitate to admit, that a complete satisfaction had been made to Peter. Matthew's £1000 is a perfect equivalent for the sum which James was bound to have paid, and which Peter had lent. It is the same thing, and this is altogether a question of things. Now instead of James's being indebted to Peter in a sum of money which (he having become insolvent) Matthew pays for him, let me put the case, that James had been guilty of the basest and most hard-hearted ingratitude to a most worthy and affectionate mother, who had not only performed all the duties and tender offices of a mother, but whose whole heart was bound up in this her only child—who had foregone all the pleasures and amusements of life in watching over his sickly childhood, had sacrificed her health and the far greater part of her resources to rescue him from the consequences of his follies and excesses during his youth and early manhood; and to procure for him the means of his present rank and affluence—all which he had repaid by neglect, desertion, and open profligacy. Here the mother stands in the relation of the creditor: and here too, I will suppose the same generous friend to interfere, and to perform with the greatest tenderness and constancy all those duties of a grateful and affectionate son, which James ought to have performed. Will this satisfy the mother's claims on James, or entitle him to her esteem, approbation, and blessing? Or what if Matthew the vicarious son, should at length address her in words to this purpose: "Now, I trust you are appeased, and will be henceforward reconciled to James. I have satisfied all your claims on him. I have paid his debt in full: and you are too just to require the same debt to be paid twice over. You will therefore regard him with the same complacency, and receive him into your presence with the same love, as if there had been no difference between him and you. For I have made it up." What other reply could the swelling heart of the mother dictate than this: "O misery! and is it possible that you are in league with my unnatural child to insult me? Must not the very necessity of your abandonment of your propher sphere form an additional evidence of his guilt? Must not the sense of your goodness teach me more fully to comprehend, more vividly to feel, the evil in him? Must not the contrast of your merits magnify his demerits in his mother's eye, and at once recall and embitter the conviction of the canker-worm in his soul?"

If indeed by the force of Matthew's example, by persuasion, or by additional and more mysterious influences, or by an inward co-agency, compatible with the existence of a personal will, James should be led to repent; if through admiration and love of this great goodness gradually assimilating his mind to the mind of his benefactor, he should in his own person become a grateful and dutiful child—then doubtless the mother would be wholly satisfied? But then the case is no longer a question of things, or a matter of debt payable by another. Nevertheless, the effect,—and the Reader will remember that it is the effects and consequences of Christ's mediation, on which St. Paul is dilating—the effect to James is similar in both cases, that is in the case of James, the debtor, and of James, the undutiful son. In both cases, James is liberated from a grievous burthen: and in both cases, he has to attribute his liberation to the act and free grace of another. The only difference is, that in the former case (namely, the payment of the debt) the beneficial act is, singly and without requiring any reaction or co-agency on the part of James, the efficient cause of his liberation; while in the latter case (namely, that of Redemption) the beneficial act is the first, the indispensable condition, and then, the co-efficient.

The professional student of theology will, perhaps, understand the different positions asserted in the preceding argument more readily if they are presented synoptically, that is, brought at once within his view, in the form of answers to four questions, comprising the constituent parts of the Scriptural doctrine of Redemption. And I trust that my lay readers of both sexes will not allow themselves to be scared from the perusal of the following short catechism, by half a dozen Latin words, or rather words with Latin endings, that translate themselves into English, when I dare assure them, that they will encounter no other obstacle to their full and easy comprehension of the contents.

SYNOPSIS OF THE CONSTITUENT POINTS IN THE DOCTRINE OF REDEMPTION, IN FOUR QUESTIONS, WITH CORRESPONDENT ANSWERS.

QUESTIONS.

Who (or What) is the
1. *Agens causator?*
2. *Actus causativus?*
3. *Effectum causatum?*
4. *Consequentia ab effecto?*

ANSWERS.

I. The Agent and personal Cause of the Redemption of mankind is—the co-external Word and only begotten Son of the Living God, incarnate, tempted, agonizing (*agonistes* ἀγωνιζόμενος), crucified, submitting to death, resurgent, communicant of his Spirit, ascendent, and obtaining for his Church the descent and communion of the Holy Spirit, the Comforter.

II. The Causative Act is—a spiritual and transcendent mystery, *that passeth all understanding*.

III. The Effect Caused is—the being born anew; as before in the flesh to the world, so now born in the spirit to Christ.

IV. The Consequences from the Effect are—sanctification from sin, and liberation from the inherent and penal consequences of sin in the world to come, with all the means and processes of sanctification by the Word and the Spirit: these consequents being the same for the sinner relatively to God and his own soul, as the satisfaction of a debt for a debtor relatively to his creditor;

as the sacrificial atonement made by the priest for the transgressor of the Mosaic Law; as the reconciliation to an alienated parent for a son who had estranged himself from his father's house and presence; and as a redemptive ransom for a slave or captive.

Now I complain, that this metaphorical naming of the transcendent causative act through the *medium* of its proper effects from actions and causes of familiar occurrence connected with the former by similarity of result, has been mistaken for an intended designation of the essential character of the causative act itself; and that thus divines have interpreted *de omni* what was spoken *de singulo*, and magnified a partial equation into a total identity.

I will merely hint to my more learned readers, and to the professional students of theology, that the origin of this error is to be sought for in the discussions of the Greek Fathers, and (at a later period) of the Schoolmen, on the obscure and abysmal subject of the divine A-seity, and the distinction between the θέλημα and the βουλή, that is, the Absolute Will, as the universal ground of all being, and the election and purpose of God in the Personal Idea, as the Father. And this view would have allowed me to express what I believe to be the true import and Scriptural idea of Redemption in terms much more nearly resembling those used ordinarily by the Calvinistic divines, and with a conciliative show of coincidence. But this motive was outweighed by the reflection, that I could not rationally have expected to be understood by those to whom I most wish to be intelligible: *et si non vis intelligi, cur vis legi?*

Not to countervene the purpose of a *Synopsis*, I have detached the confirmative or explanatory remarks from the answers to questions II. and III., and place them below as *scholia*. A single glance of the eye will enable the reader to re-connect each with the sentence it is supposed to follow.

SCHOLIUM TO ANS. II.

Nevertheless, the fact or actual truth having been assured to us by revelation, it is not impossible, by steadfast meditation on the idea and supernatural character of a personal Will, for a mind spiritually disciplined to satisfy itself, that the redemptive Act supposes (and that our redemption is even negatively conceivable only on the supposition of) an Agent who can at once act on the Will as an exciting cause, *quasi ab extra ;* and in the Will, as the condition of its potential, and the ground of its actual, being.

SCHOLIUM TO ANS. III.

Where two subjects, that stand to each other in the relation of antithesis or contradistinction, are connected by a middle term common to both, the sense of this middle term is indifferently determinable by either ; the preferability of the one or the other in any given case being decided by the circumstance of our more frequent experience of, or greater familiarity with, the term in this connection. Thus, if I put hydrogen and oxygen gas, as opposite poles, the term gas is common to both ; and it is a matter of indifference by which of the two bodies I ascertain the sense of the term. But if, for the conjoint purposes of connection and contrast, I oppose transparent crystallized alumen to opaque derb or uncrystallized alumen ;—it may easily happen to be far more convenient for me to show the sense of the middle term, that is alumen, by a piece of pipe-clay than by a sapphire or ruby ; especially if I should be describing the beauty and preciousness of the latter to a peasant woman, or in a district where a ruby was a rarity which the fewest only had an opportunity of seeing. This is a plain rule of common logic directed in its application by common sense.

Now let us apply this to the case in hand. The two opposites here are Flesh and Spirit : this in relation to Christ, that in relation to the world ; and these two opposites are connected by the middle term, Birth, which is of course common to both. But for the same reason, as in the instance last-mentioned, the interpretation of the common term is to be ascertained from its known sense, in the more familiar connection—birth, namely, in relation to our natural life and to the organized body, by which we belong to the present world. Whatever the word signifies in this connection, the same essentially in kind, though not in dignity and value, must be its signification in the other. How else could it be (what yet in this text it undeniably is), the *punctum indifferens*, or *nota communis* of the *thesis*, Flesh or the World and the *antithesis* Spirit or Christ? We might therefore, upon the supposition of a writer having been speaking of river-water in distinction from rain-water, as rationally pretend that in the latter phrase, the term, water, was to be understood metaphorically, as that the word, Birth, is a metaphor, and means only so and so in the Gospel according to St. John.

There is, I am aware, a numerous and powerful party in our Church, so numerous and powerful as not seldom to be entitled *the* Church, who hold and publicly teach, that "Regeneration is only Baptism." Nay, the writer of the article on the lives of Scott and Newton, in our ablest and most respectable Review, is but one among many who do not hesitate to brand the contrary opinion as heterodoxy, and schismatical superstition.* I trust that I think as seriously as most men of the evil of schism; but with every disposition to pay the utmost deference to an acknowledged majority, including, it is said, a very large proportion of the present dignitaries of our Church, I can not but think it a sufficient reply, that if Regeneration means Baptism, Baptism must mean Regeneration; and this too, as Christ himself has declared, a regeneration in the Spirit. Now I would ask these divines this simple question: Do they believingly suppose a spiritual regenerative power and agency inhering in or accompanying the sprinkling of a few drops of water on an infant's face? They can not evade the question by saying that Baptism is a type or sign. For this would be to supplant their own assertion, that Regeneration means Baptism, by the contradictory admission, that Regeneration is the *significatum*, of which Baptism is the significant. Unless, indeed, they would incur the absurdity of saying, that Regeneration is a type of Regeneration, and Baptism a type of itself—or that Baptism only means Baptism! And this indeed is the plain consequence to which they might be driven, should they answer the above question in the negative.

But if their answer be, "Yes! we do suppose and believe this efficiency in the Baptismal act"—I have not another word to say. Only, perhaps, I might be permitted to express a hope that, for consistency's sake, they would speak less slightingly of the insufflation, and extreme unction, used in the Romish Church; notwithstanding the not easily to be answered arguments of our Christian Mercury, the all-eloquent Jeremy Taylor, respecting the latter,—"which, since it is used when the man is above half dead, when he can exercise no act of understanding, it must needs be nothing.

* See Quart. Review, vol. xxxi. p. 26.—*Ed.*

For no rational man can think, that any ceremony can make a spiritual change without a spiritual act of him that is to be changed; nor that it can work by way of nature, or by charm, but morally and after the manner of reasonable creatures."*

It is too obvious to require suggestion, that these words here quoted apply with yet greater force and propriety to the point in question; as the babe is an unconscious subject, which the dying man need not be supposed to be. My avowed convictions respecting Regeneration with the spiritual Baptism, as its condition and initiative (*Luke* iii. 16; *Mark* i. 7; *Matt.* iii. 11), and of which the sacramental rite, the Baptism of John, was appointed by Christ to remain as the sign and figure; and still more, perhaps, my belief respecting the mystery of the Eucharist,—concerning which I hold the same opinions as Bucer,† Peter Martyr, and presumably, Cranmer himself—these convictions and this belief will, I doubt not, be deemed by the orthodox *de more Grotii*, who improve the letter of Arminius with the spirit of Socinus, sufficient *data* to bring me in guilty of irrational and superstitious mysticism. But I abide by a maxim which I learned at an early period of my theological studies, from Benedict Spinoza. Where the alternative lies between the absurd and the incomprehensible, no wise man can be at a loss which of the two to prefer. To be called irrational, is a trifle: to be so, and in matters of religion, is far otherwise: and whether the irrationality consists in men's believing (that is, in having persuaded themselves that they believe) against reason, or without reason, I have been early instructed to consider it as a sad and serious evil, pregnant with mischiefs, political and moral. And by none of my numerous instructors so impressively as by that great and shining light of our Church in the æra of her intellectual splendor, Bishop Jeremy Taylor: from one of whose works,‡ and that of especial authority for the safety as well as for the importance of the principle, inasmuch as it was written expressly *ad populum*, I will now, both for its own intrinsic worth, and to relieve the attention, wearied, perhaps, by the length and argumentative character of the preceding discussion, interpose the following Aphorism.

* Dedicat. to Holy Dying.—*Ed.*

† Strype—Cranmer, Append.—*Ed.*

‡ Worthy Communicant, c. iii. s. 5.—*Ed.*

APHORISM XX.

Taylor.

Whatever is against right reason, that no faith can oblige us to believe. For though reason is not the positive and affirmative measure of our faith, and our faith ought to be larger than (speculative) reason, and take something into her heart, that reason can never take into her eye; yet in all our creed there can be nothing against reason. If reason justly contradicts an article, it is not of the household of faith. In this there is no difficulty, but that in practice we take care that we do not call that reason, which is not so.* For although reason is a right judge,† yet it ought not to pass sentence in an inquiry of faith, until all the information be brought in; all that is within, and all that is without, all that is above, and all that is below; all that concerns it in experience, and all that concerns it in act; whatsoever is of pertinent observation, and whatsoever is revealed. For else reason may argue very well, and yet conclude falsely. It may conclude well in logic, and yet infer a false proposition in theology.‡ But when our judge is fully and truly informed in all that whence she is to make her judgment, we may safely follow her whithersoever she invites us.

APHORISM XXI.

Taylor.

He that speaks against his own reason, speaks against his own conscience: and therefore it is certain, no man serves God with a good conscience, who serves him against his reason.

APHORISM XXII.

Taylor.

By the eye of reason through the telescope of faith, that is, revelation, we may see what without this telescope we could never have known to exist. But as one that shuts the eye hard,

* See *ante*, p. 241.—*Ed.*

† Which it could not be in respect of spiritual truths and objects supersensuous, if it were the same with, and merely another name for the faculty judging according to sense—that is, the understanding, or (as Taylor most often calls it in distinction from reason) discourse (*discursus seu facultas discursiva vel discursoria*). The reason, so instructed and so actuated as Taylor requires in the sentences immediately following, is what I have called the Spirit. [See *ante*, pp. 252, 253.—*Ed.*

‡ See *ante*, p. 236.—*Ed.*

and with violence curls the eye-lid, forces a fantastic fire from the crystalline humor, and espies a light that never shines, and sees thousands of little fires that never burn ; so is he that blinds the eye of reason, and pretends to see by an eye of faith. He makes little images of notions, and some atoms dance before him ; but he is not guided by the light, nor instructed by the proposition, but sees like a man in his sleep. In no case can true reason and a right faith oppose each other.

NOTE PREFATORY TO APHORISM XXIII.

Less on my own account, than in the hope of forearming my youthful friends, I add one other transcript from Bishop Taylor, as from a writer to whose name no taint or suspicion of Calvinistic or schismatical tenets can attach, and for the purpose of softening the offence which, I can not but foresee, will be taken at the positions asserted in the first paragraph of Aphorism VII. p. 229, and the documental proofs of the same in pp. 231, 232 ; and this by a formidable party composed of men ostensibly of the most dissimilar creeds, regular Church-divines, voted orthodox by a great majority of suffrages, and the so-called free-thinking Christians, and Unitarian divines. It is the former class alone that I wish to conciliate : so far at least as it may be done by removing the aggravation of novelty from the offensive article. And surely the simple re-assertion of one of "the two great things," which Bishop Taylor could assert as a fact,—which, he took for granted, that no Christian would think of controverting, —should at least be controverted without bitterness by his successors in the Church. That which was perfectly safe and orthodox in 1657, in the judgment of a devoted Royalist and Episcopalian, ought to be at most but a venial heterodoxy in 1825. For the rest, I am prepared to hear in answer—what has already been so often and with such theatrical effect dropped as an extinguisher on my arguments—the famous concluding period of the fourth book of Paley's Moral and Political Philosophy, declared by Dr. Parr to be the finest prose passage in English literature. Be it so. I bow to so great an authority. But if the learned doctor would impose it on me as the truest as well as the finest, or expect me to admire the logic equally with the rhetoric —*ἀφίσταμαι*—I start off. As I have been un-English enough to find Pope's tomb-epigram on Sir Isaac Newton nothing better than a gross and wrongful falsehood, conveyed in an enormous and irreverent hyperbole ; so with regard to this passage in question, free as it is from all faults of taste, I have yet the hardihood to confess, that in the sense in which the words "discover" and "prove" are here used and intended, I am not convinced of the truth of the principle (that he alone discovers who proves), and I question the correctness of the particular case, brought as instance and confirmation. I doubt the validity of the assertion as a general rule ; and I deny it, as applied to matters of faith, to the verities of religion, in the belief of which there must always be somewhat of moral election, "an act of the will in it as well as of the understanding, as much love in it as discursive power. True Christian faith must have in it something of in-evidence, something that must be made up by duty and by obedience."*— But most readily do I admit, and most fervently do I contend that the miracles worked by Christ, both as miracles and as fulfilments of prophecy, both as signs and as wonders, made plain discovery, and gave unquestionable proof, of his divine character and authority; that they were to the whole Jewish nation true and appropriate evidences, that He was indeed come who had promised and declared to their forefathers, *Behold your God will come with vengeance, even God with a recompense. He will come and save you.*† I receive them as proofs, therefore, of the truth of every word which he taught who was himself The Word; and as sure evidences of the final victory over death and of the life to come, in that they were manifestations of Him, who said : *I am the resurrection and the life!*

The obvious inference from the passage in question, if not its express import, is : *Miracula experimenta crucis esse, quibus solis probandum erat, homines non, pecudum instar, omnino perituros esse.* Now this doctrine I hold to be altogether alien from the spirit, and without authority in the letter, of Scripture. I can recall nothing in the history of human belief that should induce me, I find nothing in my own moral being that enables me, to understand it. I can, however, perfectly well understand, the readiness of those divines in *hoc Paleii dictum ore pleno jurare, qui nihil aliud in toto Evangelio invenire posse profitentur.*

* J. Taylor's Worthy Communicant.—*Ed.*

† *Isaiah* xxxiv. compared with *Matt.* x. 34, and *Luke* xii. 49.—*Ed.*

The most unqualified admiration of this superlative passage I find perfectly in character for those, who while Socinianism and Ultra-Socinianism, are spreading like the roots of an elm, on and just below the surface, through the whole land, and here and there at least have even dipped under the garden-fence of the Church, and blunted the edge of the laborer's spade in the gayest parterres of our Baalhamon,—who,—while heresies, to which the framers and compilers of our Liturgy, Homilies, and Articles would have refused the very name of Christianity, meet their eyes on the list of religious denominations for every city and large town throughout the kingdom—can yet congratulate themselves with Dr. Paley, in his book on the Evidences,* that the rent has not reached the foundation ;—that is, that the corruption of man's will ; that the responsibility of man in any sense in which it is not equally predicable of dogs and horses ; that the divinity of our Lord, and even his pre-existence ; that sin, and redemption through the merits of Christ ; and grace ; and the especial aids of the Spirit ; and the efficacy of prayer ; and the subsistency of the Holy Ghost ; may all be extruded without breach or rent in the essentials of Christian Faith ;—that a man may deny and renounce them all, and remain a fundamental Christian, notwithstanding! But there are many who can not keep up with Latitudinarians of such a stride ; and I trust that the majority of serious believers are in this predicament. Now for all these it would seem more in character to be of Bishop Taylor's opinion, that the belief in question is presupposed in a convert to the truth in Christ—but at all events not to circulate in the great whispering-gallery of the religious Public suspicions and hard thoughts of those who, like myself, are of this opinion ; who do not dare decry the religious instincts of humanity as a baseless dream ; who hold, that to excavate the ground under the faith of all mankind, is a very questionable method of building up our faith as Christians ; who fear, that instead of adding to, they should detract from the honor of the Incarnate Word by disparaging the light of the Word, that was in the beginning, and which lighteth every man ; and who, under these convictions, can tranquilly leave it to be disputed, in some new Dialogues in the shades, between the fathers of the Unitarian Church on the one side, and Maimonides, Moses Mendelssohn, and Lessing on the other, whether the fa-

* *Conclusion*, Part III. ch. 8.—*Ed.*

mous passage in Paley does or does not contain the three dialectic flaws, *petitio principii*, *argumentum in circulo*, and *argumentum contra rem a premisso rem ipsam includente.*

Yes! fervently do I contend, that to satisfy the understanding that there is a future state, was not the specific object of the Christian Dispensation; and that neither the belief of a future state, nor the rationality of this belief, is the exclusive attribute of the Christian religion. An essential, a fundamental, article of all religion it is, and therefore of the Christian; but otherwise than as in connection with the salvation of mankind from the terrors of that state, among the essential articles peculiar to the Gospel Creed (those, for instance, by which it is *contra*-distinguished from the creed of a religious Jew), I do not place it. And before sentence is passed against me, as heterodox, on this ground, let not my judges forget who it was that assured us, that if a man did not believe in a state of retribution after death, previously and on other grounds, *neither would he believe, though a man should be raised from the dead.*

Again, I am questioned as to my proofs of a future state by men who are so far, and only so far, professed believers, that they admit a God, and the existence of a law from God. I give them: and the questioners turn from me with a scoff or incredulous smile. Now should others of a less scanty creed infer the weakness of the reasons assigned by me from their failure in convincing these men; may I not remind them, who it was, to whom a similar question was proposed by men of the same class? But at all events it will be enough for my own support to remember it; and to know that HE held such questioners, who could not find a sufficing proof of this great all-concerning verity in the words, *The God of Abraham, the God of Isaac, and the God of Jacob* unworthy of any other answer—men not to be satisfied by any proof—by any such proofs, at least, as are compatible with the ends and purposes of all religious conviction;—by any proofs that would not destroy the faith they were intended to confirm, and reverse the whole character and quality of its effects and influences. But if, notwithstanding all here offered in defence of my opinion, I must still be adjudged heterodox and in error,—what can I say but that *malo cum Platone errare*, and take refuge behind the ample shield of Bishop Jeremy Taylor?

APHORISM XXIII.

Taylor.

In order to his own glory, and for the manifestation of his goodness, and that the accidents of this world might not overmuch trouble those good men who suffered evil things, God was pleased to do two great things. The one was: that he sent his Son into the world to take upon him our nature, that every man might submit to a necessity, from which God's own Son was not exempt, when it behooved even Christ to suffer, and so to enter into glory. The other great thing was: that God did not only by revelation and the sermons of the Prophets to his Church, but even to all mankind competently teach, and effectively persuade, that the soul of man does not die; that though things were ill here, yet to the good who usually feel most of the evils of this life, they should end in honor and advantages. And therefore Cicero had reason on his side to conclude, that there is a time and place after this life, wherein the wicked shall be punished, and the virtuous rewarded; when he considered that Orpheus and Socrates, and many others, just men and benefactors of mankind, were either slain or oppressed to death by evil men. *And all these received not the promise.* But when virtue made men poor, and free speaking of brave truths made the wise to lose their liberty: when an excellent life hastened an opprobrious death, and the obeying reason and our conscience lost us our lives, or at least all the means and conditions of enjoying them: it was but time to look about for another state of things where justice should rule, and virtue find her own portion. And therefore men cast out every line, and turned every stone, and tried every argument: and sometimes proved it well, and when they did not, yet they believed strongly; and they were sure of the thing, when they were not sure of the argument.*

COMMENT.

A fact may be truly stated, and yet the cause or reason assigned for it mistaken, or inadequate, or *pars pro toto*,—one only or few of many that might or should have been adduced. The preceding Aphorism is an instance in point. The *phænomenon* here brought forward by the Bishop, as the ground and occasion

* Sermon at the Funeral of Sir George Dalston.—*Ed.*

of men's belief of a future state—namely, the frequent, not to say ordinary, disproportion between moral worth and worldly prosperity—must, indeed, at all times and in all countries of the civilized world have led the observant and reflecting few, the men of meditative habits and strong feelings of natural equity, to a nicer consideration of the current belief, whether instinctive or traditional. By forcing the soul in upon herself, this enigma of Saint and Sage from Job, David and Solomon, to Claudian and Boetius,—this perplexing disparity of success and desert,—has, I doubt not, with such men been the occasion of a steadier and more distinct consciousness of a something in man different in kind, and which not merely distinguishes but contradistinguishes him from brute animals—at the same time that it has brought into closer view an enigma of yet harder solution—the fact, I mean, of a contradiction in the human being, of which no traces are observable elsewhere in animated or inanimate nature:—a struggle of jarring impulses; a mysterious diversity between the injunctions of the mind and the elections of the will; and (last not least) the utter incommensurateness and the unsatisfying qualities of the things around us, that yet are the only objects which our senses discover, or our appetites require us to pursue: —hence for the finer and more contemplative spirits the ever-strengthening suspicion, that the two *phenomena* must in some way or other stand in close connection with each other, and that the riddle of fortune and circumstance is but a form or effluence of the riddle of man:—and hence again, the persuasion, that the solution of both problems is to be sought for—hence the presentiment, that this solution will be found—in the contra-distinctive constituent of humanity, in the something of human nature which is exclusively human:—and—as the objects discoverable by the senses, as all the bodies and substances that we can touch, measure, and weigh, are either mere totals, the unity of which results from the parts, and is of course only apparent; or substances, the unity of action of which is owing to the nature or arrangement of the partible bodies which they actuate or set in motion (steam for instance, in a steam-engine;)—as on the one hand the condition and known or conceivable properties of all the objects which perish and utterly cease to be, together with all the properties which we ourselves have in common with these perishable things, differ in kind from the acts and properties peculiar to our humanity, so that the former can not even be conceived, can not without a contradiction in terms, be predicated, of the proper and immediate subject of the latter—(for who would not smile at an ounce of truth, or a square foot of honor?)—and as, on the other hand, whatever things in visible nature have the character of permanence, and endure amid continual flux unchanged like a rainbow in a fast-flying shower (for example, beauty, order, harmony, finality, law), are all akin to the *peculia* of humanity, are all *congenera* of mind and will, without which indeed they would not only exist in vain, as pictures for moles, but actually not exist at all;—hence, finally, the conclusion that the soul of man, as the subject of mind and will, must likewise possess a principle of permanence, and be destined to endure. And were these grounds lighter than they are, yet as a small weight will make a scale descend, where there is nothing in the opposite scale, or painted weights, which have only an illusive relief or prominence; so in the scale of immortality slight reasons are in effect weighty, and sufficient to determine the judgment, there being no counterweight, no reasons against them, and no facts in proof of the contrary, that would not prove equally well the cessation of the eye on the removal or diffraction of the eye-glass, and the dissolution or incapacity of the musician on the fracture of his instrument or its strings.

But though I agree with Taylor so far, as not to doubt that the misallotment of worldly goods and fortunes was one principal occasion, exciting well-disposed and spiritually awakened natures by reflections and reasonings, such as I have here supposed, to mature the presentiment of immortality into full consciousness, into a principle of action and a well-spring of strength and consolation; I can not concede to this circumstance any thing like the importance and extent of efficacy which he in this passage attributes to it. I am persuaded, that as the belief of all mankind, of all* tribes, and nations, and languages, in all ages, and in all

* I say *all:* for the accounts of one or two travelling French philosophers, professed atheists and partisans of infidelity, respecting one or two African hordes, Caffres, and poor outlawed Boschmen, hunted out of their humanity, ought not to be regarded as exceptions. And as to Hearne's assertion respecting the non-existence and rejection of the belief among the Copper-Indians, it is not only hazarded on very weak and insufficient grounds, but he himself, in another part of his work, unconsciously supplies

states of social union, it must be referred to far deeper grounds, common to man as man; and that its fibres are to be traced to the tap-root of humanity. I have long entertained, and do not hesitate to avow, the conviction that the argument from universality of belief urged by Barrow and others in proof of the first article of the Creed, is neither in point of fact—for two very different objects may be intended, and two or more diverse and even contradictory conceptions may be expressed, by the same name—nor in legitimacy of conclusion as strong and unexceptionable, as the argument from the same ground for the continuance of our personal being after death. The bull-calf butts with smooth and unarmed brow. Throughout animated nature, of each characteristic organ and faculty there exists a pre-assurance, an instinctive and practical anticipation; and no pre-assurance common to a whole species does in any instance prove delusive.* All other prophecies of nature have their exact fulfilment—in every other *ingrafted word* of promise, Nature is found true to her word; and is it in her noblest creature that she tells her first lie?—(The Reader will, of course, understand, that I am here speaking in the assumed character of a mere naturalist, to whom no light of revelation had been vouchsafed; one, who

> ———————— with gentle heart
> Had worship'd Nature in the hill and valley,
> Not knowing what he loved, but loved it all.)

Whether, however, the introductory part of the Bishop's argument is to be received with more or less qualification, the fact itself, as stated in the concluding sentence of the Aphorism, remains unaffected, and is beyond exception true.

data, from whence the contrary may safely be concluded. Hearne, perhaps, put down his friend Motannabbi's Fort-philosophy for the opinion of his tribe; and from his high appreciation of the moral character of this murderous gymnosophist, it might, I fear, be inferred, that Hearne himself was not the very person one would, of all others, have chosen for the purpose of instituting the inquiry.

* See Baron Field's Letters from New South Wales. The poor natives, the lowest in the scale of humanity, evince no symptom of any religion, or the belief of any superior power as the maker of the world; but yet have no doubt that the spirits of their ancestors survive in the form of porpoises, and mindful of their descendants, with imperishable affection, drive the whales ashore for them to feast on.

If other argument and yet higher authority were required, I might refer to St. Paul's Epistle to the Romans, and to the Epistle to the Hebrews, which whether written by Paul, or, as Luther conjectured, by Apollos, is out of all doubt the work of an Apostolic man filled with the Holy Spirit, and composed while the Temple and the glories of the Temple worship were yet in existence. Several of the Jewish and still Judaizing converts had begun to vacillate in their faith, and to *stumble at the stumbling-stone* of the contrast between the pomp and splendor of the old Law, and the simplicity and humility of the Christian Church. To break this sensual charm, to unfascinate these bedazzled brethren, the writer to the Hebrews institutes a comparison between the two religions, and demonstrates the superior spiritual grandeur, the greater intrinsic worth and dignity of the religion of Christ. On the other hand, at Rome where the Jews formed a numerous, powerful, and privileged class (many of them, too, by their proselyting zeal and frequent disputations with the priests and philosophers trained and exercised polemics), the recently-founded Christian Church was, it appears, in greater danger from the reasonings of the Jewish doctors and even of its own Judaizing members, respecting the use of the new revelation. Thus the object of the Epistle to the Hebrews was to prove the superiority of the Christian religion; the object of the Epistle to the Romans to prove its necessity. Now there was one argument extremely well calculated to stagger a faith newly transplanted and still loose at its roots, and which if allowed, seemed to preclude the possibility of the Christian religion, as an especial and immediate revelation from God—on the high grounds, at least, on which the Apostle of the Gentiles placed it, and with the exclusive rights and superseding character, which he claimed for it. "You admit" (said they) "the divine origin and authority of the Law given to Moses, proclaimed with thunders and lightnings and the voice of the Most High heard by all the people from Mount Sinai, and introduced, enforced, and perpetuated by a series of the most stupendous miracles. Our religion, then, was given by God: and can God give a perishable imperfect religion? If not perishable, how can it have a successor? If perfect, how can it need to be superseded? The entire argument is indeed comprised in the latter attribute of our law. We know, from an authority which you yourselves acknowledge for divine, that our religion is perfect. *He is the rock, and his work is perfect.* (*Deut.* xxxii. 4.) If then the religion revealed by God himself to our forefathers is perfect, what need have we of another ?"—This objection, both from its importance and from its extreme plausibility, for the persons at least to whom it was addressed, required an answer in both Epistles. And accordingly the answer is included in the one (that to the Hebrews) and it is the especial purpose and main subject of the other. And how does the Apostle answer it ? Suppose—and the thing is not impossible*—a man of sense, who had studied the evidences of Priestley and Paley with Warburton's Divine Legation, but who should be a perfect stranger to the writings of St. Paul, and that I put this question to him :—"What do you think, will St. Paul's answer be ?" "Nothing," he would reply, "can be more obvious. It is in vain, the Apostle will urge, that you bring your notions of probability and inferences from the arbitrary interpretation of a word in an absolute rather than a relative sense, to invalidate a known fact. It is a fact, that your religion is (in your sense of the word) not perfect : for it is deficient in one of the two essential constituents of all true religion, the belief of a future state on solid and sufficient grounds. Had the doctrine indeed been revealed, the stupendous miracles, which you most truly affirm to have accompanied and attested the first promulgation of your religion, would have supplied the requisite proof. But the doctrine was not revealed ; and your belief of a future state rests upon no solid grounds. You believe it (as far as you believe it, and as many of you as profess this belief) without revelation, and without the only proper and sufficient evidence of

* The case here supposed actually occurred in my own experience in the person of a Spanish refugee, of English parents, but from his tenth year resident in Spain, and bred in a family of wealthy, but ignorant and bigoted, Roman Catholics. In mature manhood he returned to England, disgusted with the conduct of the priests and monks, which had indeed for some years produced on his mind its so common effect among the better-informed natives of the south of Europe—a tendency to Deism. The results, however, of the infidel system in France, with his opportunities of observing the effects of irreligion on the French officers in Spain, on the one hand ; and the undeniable moral and intellectual superiority of Protestant Britain on the other, had not been lost on him : and here he began to think for himself and resolved to study the subject. He had gone through Bishop Warburton's Divine Legation, and Paley's Evidences ; but had never read the Gospels consecutively. and the Epistles not at all.

its truth. Your religion, therefore, though of divine origin, is (if taken in disjunction from the new revelation, which I am commissioned to proclaim) but a *religio dimidiata*; and the main purpose, the proper character, and the paramount object of Christ's mission and miracles, is to supply the missing half by a clear discovery of a future state; and (since " he alone discovers who proves") by proving the truth of the doctrine now for the first time declared with the requisite authority, by the requisite, appropriate, and alone satisfactory evidences."

But is this the Apostle's answer to the Jewish oppugners, and the Judaizing false brethren of the Church of Christ? It is not the answer, it does not resemble the answer, returned by the Apostle. It is neither parallel nor corradial with the line of argument in either of the two Epistles, or with any one line; but it is a chord that traverses them all, and only touches where it cuts across. In the Epistle to the Hebrews, the directly contrary position is repeatedly asserted: and in the Epistle to the Romans, it is everywhere supposed. The death to which the Law sentenced all sinners (and which even the Gentiles without the revealed law had announced to them by their consciences, *the judgment of God having been made known even to them*) must be the same death, from which they were saved by the faith of the Son of God; or the Apostle's reasoning would be senseless, his *antithesis* a mere equivoque, a play on a word, *quod idem sonat, aliud vult.* Christ *redeemed mankind from the curse of the law;* and we all know, that it was not from temporal death, or the penalties and afflictions of the present life, that believers had been redeemed. The Law of which the inspired sage of Tarsus is speaking, from which no man can plead excuse; the Law, miraculously delivered in thunders from Mount Sinai, which was inscribed on tables of stone for the Jews, and written in the hearts of all men (*Rom.* ii. 15) the law *holy and spiritual!* What was the great point, of which this law, in its own name offered no solution; the mystery which it left behind the veil, or in the cloudy tabernacle of types and figurative sacrifices? Whether there was a judgment to come, and souls to suffer the dread sentence? Or was it not far rather —what are the means of escape; where may grace be found and redemption? St. Paul says, the latter. The law brings condemnation: but the conscience-sentenced transgressor's question, "What shall I do to be saved? Who will intercede for me?" it dismisses as beyond its jurisdiction and takes no cognizance thereof, save in prophetic murmurs or mute out-shadowings of mystic ordinances and sacrificial types. Not therefore, that there is a life to come, and a future state; but what each individual soul may hope for itself therein: and on what grounds: and that this state has been rendered an object of aspiration and fervent desire, and a source of thanksgiving and exceeding great joy; and by whom, and through whom, and for whom, and by what means, and under what conditions—these are the peculiar and distinguishing fundamentals of the Christian Faith. These are the revealed lights and obtained privileges of the Christian Dispensation. Not alone the knowledge of the boon, but the precious inestimable boon itself, is the *grace and truth that came by Jesus Christ.* I believe Moses, I believe Paul; but I believe in Christ.

APHORISM XXIV.

ON BAPTISM.

Leighton.

In those days came John the Baptist, preaching.—It will suffice for our present purpose, if by these* words we direct the attention to the origin, or at least first Scriptural record, of Baptism, and to the combinement of preaching therewith; their aspect each to the other, and their concurrence to one excellent end; the word unfolding the sacrament, and the sacrament sealing the word; the word as a light, informing and clearing the sense of the seal; and this again as a seal, confirming and ratifying the truth of the word; as you see some significant seals, or engraven signets, have a word about them expressing their sense.

But truly the word is a light, and the sacraments have in them of the same light illuminating them. This sacrament of Bap-

* By certain Biblical philologists of the Teutonic school (men distinguished by learning, but still more characteristically by hardihood in conjecture, and who suppose the Gospels to have undergone several successive revisions and enlargements by, or under the authority of, the sacred historians) these words are contended to have been, in the first delivery, the common commencement of all the Gospels *κατὰ σάρκα* (that is, according to the flesh), in distinction from St. John's or the Gospel *κατὰ πνεῦμα* (that is, according to the Spirit).

tism, the ancients do particularly express by light. Yet are they both nothing but darkness to us, till the same light shine in our hearts; for till then we are nothing but darkness ourselves, and therefore the most luminous things are so to us. Noonday is as midnight to a blind man. And we see these ordinances, the word and the sacrament, without profit or comfort for the most part, because we have not that divine light within us. And we have it not, because we ask it not.

COMMENT, OR AN AID TO REFLECTION IN THE FORMING OF A SOUND JUDGMENT RESPECTING THE PURPORT AND PURPOSE OF THE BAPTISMAL RITE, AND A JUST APPRECIATION OF ITS VALUE AND IMPORTANCE.

A born and bred Baptist, and paternally descended from the old orthodox Non-conformists, and both in his own and his father's right a very dear friend of mine, had married a member of the National Church. In consequence of an anxious wish expressed by his lady for the baptism of their first child, he solicited me to put him in possession of my views respecting this controversy; though principally as to the degree of importance which I attached to it. For as to the point itself, his natural prepossession in favor of the persuasion in which he was born had been confirmed by a conscientious examination of the arguments on both sides. As the comment on the preceding Aphorism, or rather as an expansion of its subject-matter, I will give the substance of the conversation: and amply shall I have been remunerated, should it be read with the interest and satisfaction with which it was heard. More particularly, should any of my Readers find themselves under the same or similar circumstances.

Our discussion is rendered shorter and more easy by our perfect agreement in certain preliminary points. We both disclaim alike every attempt to explain any thing into Scripture, and every attempt to explain any thing out of Scripture. Or if we regard either with a livelier aversion it is the latter, as being the more fashionable and prevalent. I mean the practice of both high and low Grotian divines to explain away positive assertions of Scripture on the pretext, that the literal sense is not agreeable to reason, that is, their particular reason. And inasmuch as (in the only right sense of the word) there is no such thing as a particular reason, they must, and in fact they do, mean that the literal sense is not accordant to their understanding, that is, to the notions which their understandings have been taught and accustomed to form in their school of philosophy. Thus a Platonist who should become a Christian would at once, even in texts susceptible of a different interpretation, recognize, because he would expect to find, several doctrines which the disciple of the Epicurean or mechanic school will not receive on the most positive declarations of the divine word. And as we agree in the opinion that the *Minimi-fidian* party err grievously in the latter point, so I must concede to you, that too many Pædo-baptists (assertors of Infant Baptism) have erred, though less grossly, in the former. I have, I confess, no eye for these smoke-like wreaths of inference, this ever-widening spiral *ergo* from the narrow aperture of perhaps a single text; or rather an interpretation forced into it by construing an idiomatic phrase in an artless narrative with the same absoluteness as if it had formed part of a mathematical problem. I start back from these inverted pyramids, where the apex is the base. If I should inform any one that I had called at a friend's house, but had found nobody at home, the family having all gone to the play; and if he on the strength of this information should take occasion to asperse my friend's wife for unmotherly conduct in taking an infant six months old to a crowded theatre; would you allow him to press on the words "nobody" and "all the family," in justification of the slander? Would you not tell him, that the words were to be interpreted by the nature of the subject, the purpose of the speaker, and their ordinary acceptation; and that he must or might have known, that infants of that age would not be admitted into the theatre? Exactly so, with regard to the words, *he and all his household.* Had Baptism of infants at that early period of the Gospel been a known practice, or had this been previously demonstrated,—then indeed the argument, that in all probability there were infants or young children in so large a family, would be no otherwise objectionable than as being superfluous, and a sort of anticlimax in logic. But if the words are cited as the proof, it would be a clear *petitio principii*, though there had been nothing else against it. But when we turn back to the Scriptures preceding the narrative, and find repentance and belief demanded as the terms and indispensable conditions of Baptism—then the case above imagined applies in its full force. Equally vain is the pretended analogy from Circumcision, which was no Sacrament at all; but the means and mark of national distinction. In the first instance it was, doubtless, a privilege or mark of superior rank conferred on the descendants of Abraham. In the Patriarchal times this rite was confined (the first governments being theocracies) to the priesthood, who were set apart to that office from their birth. At a later period this token of the premier class was extended to kings. And thus, when it was re-ordained by Moses for the whole Jewish nation, it was at the time said—Ye are all priests and kings; ye are a consecrated people. In addition to this, or rather in aid of this, Circumcision was intended to distinguish the Jews by some indelible sign; and it was no less necessary that Jewish children should be recognizable as Jews than Jewish adults—not to mention the greater safety of the rite in infancy. Nor was it ever pretended that any grace was conferred with it, or that the rite was significant of any inward or spiritual operation. In short, an unprejudiced and competent reader need only peruse the first thirty-three paragraphs of the eighteenth section of Taylor's Liberty of Prophesying; and then compare with these the remainder of the section added by him after the Restoration: those, namely, in which he attempts to overthrow his own arguments. I had almost said, affects: for such is the feebleness, and so palpable the sophistry, of his answers, that I find it difficult to imagine that Taylor himself could have been satisfied with them. The only plausible arguments apply with equal force to Baptist and Pædo-baptist; and would prove, if they proved any thing, that both were wrong, and the Quakers only in the right.

Now, in the first place, it is obvious, that nothing conclusive can be drawn from the silence of the New Testament respecting a practice, which, if we suppose it already in use, must yet, from the character of the first converts, have been of comparatively rare occurrence; and which, from the predominant and more concerning objects and functions of the Apostolic writers (1 *Cor.* i. 17), was not likely to have been mentioned otherwise than incidentally, and very probably therefore might not have occurred to them to mention at all. But, secondly, admitting that the practice was introduced at a later period than that in which the Acts of the Apostles and the Epistles were composed: I should yet be fully satisfied, that the Church exercised herein a sound*

* That every the least permissible form and ordinance, which at different

discretion. On either supposition, therefore, it is never without regret that I see a divine of our Church attempting to erect forts on a position so evidently commanded by the stronghold of his antagonists. I dread the use which the Socinians may make of their example, and the Papists of their failure. Let me not, however, deceive you. (The Reader understands, that I suppose myself conversing with a Baptist.) I am of opinion, that the divines on your side are chargeable with a far more grievous mistake, that of giving a carnal and Judaizing interpretation to the various Gospel texts in which the terms, *baptism* and *baptize*, occur, contrary to the express and earnest admonitions of the Apostle Paul. And this I say without in the least retracting my former concession, that the texts appealed to, as commanding or authorizing Infant Baptism, are all without exception made to bear a sense neither contained nor deducible; and likewise that (historically considered) there exists no sufficient positive evidence that the Baptism of infants was instituted by the Apostles in the practice of the Apostolic age.*

times it might be expedient for the Church to enact, are pre-enacted in the New Testament; and that whatever is not to be found there, ought to be allowed nowhere—this has been asserted. But that it has been proved, or even rendered plausible; or that the tenet is not to be placed among the revulsionary results of the Scripture-slighting will-worship of the Romish Church; it will be more sincere to say I disbelieve, than that I doubt. It was chiefly, if not exclusively, in reference to the extravagances built on this tenet, that the great Selden ventured to declare that the words, *Scrutamini Scripturas*, had set the world in an uproar.

Extremes appear to generate each other; but if we look steadily, there will most often be found some common error, that produces both as its positive and negative poles. Thus superstitions go by pairs, like the two Hungarian sisters, always quarrelling and inveterately averse, but yet joined at the trunk.

* More than this I do not consider as necessary for the argument. And as to Robinson's assertion in his History of Baptism, that Infant Baptism did not commence till the time of Cyprian, who, condemning it as a general practice, allowed it in particular cases by a dispensation of charity: and that it did not actually become the ordinary rule of the Church, till Augustine, in the fever of his Anti-Pelagian dispute had introduced the Calvinistic interpretation of Original Sin, and the dire state of infants dying unbaptized—I am so far from acceding to them, that I reject the whole statement as rash, and not only unwarranted by the authorities he cites, but unanswerably confuted by Baxter, Wall, and many other learned Pædo-baptists before and since the publication of his work. I confine myself to the

Lastly, we both coincide in the full conviction, that it is neither the outward ceremony of Baptism, under any form or circumstances, nor any other ceremony, but such a faith in Christ as tends to produce a conformity to his holy doctrines and example in heart and life, and which faith is itself a declared mean and condition of our partaking of his spiritual body, and of being *clothed upon* with his righteousness,—that properly makes us Christians, and can alone be enjoined as an article of faith necessary to salvation, so that the denial thereof may be denounced as a damnable heresy. In the strictest sense of essential, this alone is the essential in Christianity, that the same spirit should be growing in us which was in the fulness of all perfection in Christ Jesus Whatever else is named essential, is such because, and only as far as, it is instrumental to this, or evidently implied herein. If the Baptists hold the visible right to be indispensable to salvation, with what terror must they not regard every disease that befalls their children between youth and infancy! But if they are saved by the faith of the parent, then the outward rite is not essential to salvation, otherwise than as the omission should arise from a spirit of disobedience: and in this case it is the cause not the effect, the wilful and unbaptized heart, not the unbaptizing hand, that perils it. And surely it looks very like an inconsistency to admit the vicarious faith of the parents, and the therein implied promise, that the child shall be Christianly bred up, and as much as in them lies prepared for the communion of saints—to admit this, as safe and sufficient in their own instance, and yet to denounce the same belief and practice as hazardous and unavailing in the Church—the same, I say, essentially, and only differing from their own by the presence of two or three Christian friends as additional securities, and by the promise being expressed!

But you, my filial friend! have studied Christ under a better teacher—the spirit of adoption, even the spirit that was in Paul, and which still speaks to us out of his writings. You remember and admire the saying of an old divine, that a ceremony duly instituted is a chain of gold around the neck of faith; but if in the wish to make it co-essential and consubstantial, you draw it closer and closer, it may strangle the faith it was meant to deck

assertion—not that Infant Baptism was not—but that there exist no sufficient proofs that it was—the practice of the Apostolic age.

and designate. You are not so unretentive a scholar as to have forgotten the *pateris et auro* of your Virgil: or if you were, you are not so inconsistent a reasoner as to translate the Hebraism, spirit and fire, in one place by spiritual fire, and yet refuse to translate water and spirit by spiritual water in another place; or if, as I myself think, the different position marks a different sense, yet that the former must be *ejusdem generis* with the latter—the water of repentance, reformation in conduct; and the spirit that which purifies the inmost principle of action, as fire purges the metal substantially, and not cleansing the surface only.

But in this instance, it will be said, the ceremony, the outward and visible sign, is a Scripture ordinance. I will not reply that the Romish priest says the same of the anointing of the sick with oil and the imposition of hands. No, my answer is: that this is a very sufficient reason for the continued observance of a ceremonial rite so derived and sanctioned, even though its own beauty, simplicity, and natural significancy had pleaded less strongly in its behalf. But it is no reason why the Church should forget that the perpetuation of a thing does not alter the nature of the thing, and that a ceremony to be perpetuated is to be perpetuated as a ceremony. It is no reason why, knowing and experiencing even in the majority of her own members the proneness of the human mind to superstition,* the Church might not rightfully and piously adopt the measures best calculated to check this tendency, and to correct the abuse to which it had led in any particular rite. But of superstitious notions respecting the Baptismal ceremony, and of abuse resulting, the instances were flagrant and notorious. Such, for instance, was the frequent deferring of the Baptismal rite to a late period of life, and even to the deathbed, in the belief that the mystic water would cleanse the baptized person from all sin, and (if he died immediately after the performance of the ceremony), send him pure and spotless into the other world.

Nor is this all. The preventive remedy applied by the Church is legitimated as well as additionally recommended by the following consideration. Where a ceremony answered and was in-

* Let me be permitted to repeat and apply the note in a former page. Superstition may be defined as *superstantium* (*cujusmodi sunt ceremoniæ et signa externa quæ, nisi in significando, nihili sunt et pœne nihil*) *substantiatio.*

tended to answer several purposes, which purposes at its first institution were blended in respect of the time, but which afterwards by change of circumstances (as when, for instance, a large and ever-increasing proportion of the members of the Church, or those who at least bore the Christian name, were of Christian parents) were necessarily dis-united—then either the Church has no power or authority delegated to her (which is shifting the ground of controversy), or she must be authorized to choose and determine, to which of the several purposes the ceremony should be attached. Now one of the purposes of Baptism was—the making it publicly manifest, first, what individuals were to be regarded by the World (*Phil.* ii. 15) as belonging to the visible communion of Christians: inasmuch as by their demeanor and apparent condition, the general estimation of *the city set on a hill and not to be hid* (*Matth.* v. 14) could not but be affected—the city that even *in the midst of a crooked and perverse nation* was bound not only to give no cause, but by all innocent means, to prevent every occasion, of *rebuke*. Secondly, to mark out, for the Church itself, those that were entitled to that especial dearness, that watchful and disciplinary love and loving-kindness, which over and above the affections and duties of philanthropy and universal charity, Christ himself had enjoined, and with an emphasis and in a form significant of its great and especial importance,—*A new commandment I give unto you, that ye love one another.* By a charity wide as sunshine, and comprehending the whole human race, the body of Christians was to be placed in contrast with the proverbial misanthropy and bigotry of the Jewish Church and people: while yet they were to be distinguished and known to all men, by the peculiar love and affection displayed by them towards the members of their own community; thus exhibiting the intensity of sectarian attachment, yet by the no less notorious and exemplary practice of the duties of universal benevolence, secured from the charge so commonly brought against it, of being narrow and exclusive. "How kind these Christians are to the poor and afflicted, without distinction of religion or country; but how they love each other!"

Now combine with this the consideration before urged—the duty, I mean, and necessity of checking the superstitious abuse of the Baptismal rite: and I then ask, with confidence, in what way could the Church have exercised a sound discretion more wisely, piously, or effectively, than by fixing, from among the several ends and purposes of baptism, the outward ceremony to the purposes here mentioned? How could the great body of Christians be more plainly instructed as to the true nature of all outward ordinances? What can be conceived better calculated to prevent the ceremony from being regarded as other and more than a ceremony, if not the administration of the same on an object (yea, a dear and precious object) of spiritual duties, though the conscious subject of spiritual operations and graces only by anticipation and in hope;—a subject unconscious as a flower of the dew falling on it, or the early rain, and thus emblematic of the myriads who (as in our Indian empire, and henceforward, I trust, in Africa) are temporally and even morally benefited by the outward existence of Christianity, though as yet ignorant of its saving truth? And yet, on the other hand, what more reverential than the application of this the common initiatory rite of the East sanctioned and appropriated by Christ—its application, I say, to the very subjects, whom he himself commanded to be brought to him—the children in arms, respecting whom *Jesus was much displeased with his disciples, who had rebuked those that brought them?* What more expressive of the true character of that originant yet generic stain, from which the Son of God, by his mysterious Incarnation and Agony and Death and Resurrection, and by the Baptism of the Spirit, came to cleanse the children of Adam, than the exhibition of the outward element to infants, free from and incapable of crime, in whom the evil principle was present only as potential being, and whose outward semblance represented the kingdom of Heaven? And can it—to a man, who would hold himself deserving of *anathema maranatha* (1 *Cor*. xvi. 22) if he did not *love the Lord Jesus*—can it be nothing to such a man, that the introduction and commendation of a new inmate, a new spiritual ward, to the assembled brethren in Christ (—and this, as I have shown above, was one purpose of the Baptismal ceremony—) does in the Baptism of an infant recall our Lord's own presentation in the Temple on the eighth day after his birth? Add to all these considerations the known fact of the frequent exposure and the general light regard of infants, at the time when Infant Baptism is by the Baptists supposed to have been first ruled by the Catholic Church, not overlooking the humane and charitable motives, that influenced

Cyprian's decision in its favor. And then make present to your imagination, and meditatively contemplate the still continuing tendency, the profitable, the beautiful effects of this ordinance now and for so many centuries back, on the great mass of the population throughout Christendom—the softening, elevating exercise of faith, and the conquest over the senses, while in the form of a helpless crying babe the presence, and the unutterable worth and value, of an immortal being made capable of everlasting bliss are solemnly proclaimed and carried home to the mind and heart of the hearers and beholders! Nor will you forget the probable influence on the future education of the child, the opportunity of instructing and impressing the friends, relatives, and parents in their best and most docile mood. These are, indeed, the *mollia tempora fandi.*

It is true, that by an unforeseen accident, and through the propensity of all zealots to caricature partial truth into total falsehood—it is too true, that a tree the very contrary in quality of that shown to Moses (*Exod.* xv. 25) was afterwards *cast into the sweet waters from this fountain*, and made them like *the waters of Marah*, too bitter to be drunk. I allude to the Pelagian controversy, the perversion of the article of Original Sin by Augustine, and the frightful conclusions which this *durus pater infantum* drew from the article thus perverted. It is not, however, to the predecessors of this African, whoever they were that authorized Pædo-Baptism, and at whatever period it first became general—it is not to the Church at the time being, that these consequences are justly imputable. She had done her best to preclude every superstition, by allowing, in urgent cases, any and every adult, man and woman, to administer the ceremonial part, the outward rite of Baptism: but reserving to the highest functionary of the Church (even to the exclusion of the co-presbyters) the more proper and spiritual purpose, namely, the declaration of repentance and belief, the free choice of Christ as his Lord, and the open profession of the Christian title by an individual in his own name and by his own deliberate act. This office of religion, the essentially moral and spiritual nature of which could not be mistaken, this most solemn office the Bishop alone was to perform.

Thus—as soon as the purposes of the ceremonial rite were by change of circumstances divided, that is, took place at different periods of the believer's life—to the outward purposes, where the effect was to be produced on the consciousness of others, the Church continued to affix the outward rite; while to the substantial and spiritual purpose, where the effect was to be produced on the individual's own mind, she gave its beseeming dignity by an ordinance not figurative, but standing in the direct cause and relation of means to the end.

In fine, there are two great purposes to be answered, each having its own subordinate purposes and desirable consequences. The Church answers both, the Baptists one only. If, nevertheless, you would still prefer the union of the Baptismal rite with the Confirmation, and that the presentation of infants to the assembled Church had formed a separate institution, avowedly prospective—I answer: first, that such for a long time and to a late period was my own judgment. But even then it seemed to me a point, as to which an indifference would be less inconsistent in a lover of truth, than a zeal to separation in a professed lover of peace. And secondly, I would revert to the history of the Reformation, and the calamitous accident of the Peasants' War: when the poor ignorant multitude, driven frantic by the intolerable oppressions of their feudal lords, rehearsed all the outrages that were acted in our own times by the Parisian populace headed by Danton, Marat, and Robespierre; and on the same outrageous principles, and in assertion of the same rights of brutes to the subversion of all the duties of men. In our times, most fortunately for the interest of religion and morality, or of their prudential substitutes at least, the name of Jacobin was everywhere associated with that of Atheist and Infidel. Or rather, Jacobinism and Infidelity were the two heads of the revolutionary Geryon—connatural misgrowths of the same monster-trunk. In the German convulsion, on the contrary, by a mere but most unfortunate accident, the same code of Caliban jurisprudence, the same sensual and murderous excesses, were connected with the name of Anabaptist. The abolition of magistracy, community of goods, the right of plunder, polygamy, and whatever else was fanatical, were comprised in the word Anabaptism. It is not to be imagined that the Fathers of the Reformation could, without a miraculous influence, have taken up the question of Infant Baptism with the requisite calmness and freedom of spirit. It is not to be wished that they should have entered on the discussion. Nay, I will go farther. Unless the abolition of Infant Baptism can be shown to be involved in some fundamental article of faith, unless the practice could be proved fatal or imminently perilous to salvation, the Reformers would not have been justified in exposing the yet tender and struggling cause of Protestantism to such certain and violent prejudices as this innovation would have excited. Nothing less than the whole substance and efficacy of the Gospel Faith was the prize, which they had wrestled for and won; but won from enemies still in the field, and on the watch to retake, at all costs, the sacred treasure, and consign it once again to darkness and oblivion. If there be *a time for all things*, this was not the time for an innovation that would and must have been followed by the triumph of the enemies of Scriptural Christianity, and the alienation of the governments that had espoused and protected it.

Remember I say this on the supposition of the question's not being what you do not pretend it to be, an essential of the Faith by which we are saved. But should it likewise be conceded that it is a disputable point—and that in point of fact it is and has been disputed by divines whom no pious Christian of any denomination will deny to have been faithful and eminent servants of Christ; should it, I say, be likewise conceded that the question of Infant Baptism is a point, on which two Christians, who perhaps differ on this point only, may differ without giving just ground for impeaching the piety or competence of either; in this case I am obliged to infer that the person who at any time can regard this difference as singly warranting a separation from a religious community, must think of schism under another point of view than that in which I have been taught to contemplate it by St. Paul in his Epistles to the Corinthians.

Let me add a few words on a diversity of doctrine closely connected with this;—the opinions of Doctors Mant and D'Oyly as opposed to those of the (so called) Evangelical clergy. "The Church of England (says Wall*) does not require assent and con-

* Conference between Two Men that had Doubts about Infant Baptism. By W. Wall, Author of the History of Infant Baptism, and Vicar of Shoreham in Kent. A very sensible little tract, and written in an excellent spirit; but it failed, I confess, in satisfying my mind as to the existence of any decisive proofs or documents of Infant Baptism having been an Apostolic usage, or specially intended in any part of the New Testament; though

sent" to either opinion "in order to lay communion." But I will suppose the person a minister: but minister of a Church which has expressly disclaimed all pretence to infallibility; a Church which in the construction of its Liturgy and Articles is known to have worded certain passages for the purpose of rendering them subscribable by both A and Z—that is, the opposite parties as to

deducible generally from many passages, and in perfect accordance with the spirit of the whole.

A mighty wrestler in the cause of spiritual religion and Gospel morality, in whom more than in any other contemporary I seem to see the spirit of Luther revived, expressed to me his doubts whether we have a right to deny that an infant is capable of a spiritual influence. To such a man I could not feel justified in returning an answer *ex tempore*, or without having first submitted my convictions to a fresh revisal. I owe him, however, a deliberate answer; and take this opportunity of discharging the debt.

The objection supposes and assumes the very point which is denied, or at least disputed—namely, that Infant Baptism is specially enjoined in the Scriptures. If an express passage to this purport had existed in the New Testament—the other passages, which evidently imply a spiritual operation under the condition of a preceding spiritual act on the part of the person baptized, remaining as now—then indeed, as the only way of removing the apparent contradiction, it might be allowable to call on the Anti-pædobaptist to prove the negative—namely, that an infant a week old is not a subject capable or susceptible of spiritual agency. And, *vice versa*, should it be made known to us, that infants are not without reflection and self-consciousness—then, doubtless, we should be entitled to infer that they were capable of a spiritual operation, and consequently of that which is signified in the Baptismal rite administered to adults. But what does this prove for those who not only can not show, but who do not themselves profess to believe the self-consciousness of a new-born babe, but who rest the defence of Infant Baptism on the assertion, that God was pleased to affix the performance of this rite to his offer of salvation as the indispensable, though arbitrary, condition of the infant's salvability?—As kings, in former ages, when they conferred lands in perpetuity, would sometimes, as the condition of the tenure, exact from the beneficiary a hawk, or some trifling ceremony, as the putting on or off of their sandals, or whatever royal caprice or the whim of the moment, might suggest. But you, honored Irving, are as little disposed as I am, to favor such doctrine!

Friend pure of heart and fervent! we have learnt
A different lore. We may not thus profane
The idea and name of Him whose absolute will
Is reason, truth supreme, essential order.*

---

* See Church and State, VI. pp. 114, 115, note.—*Ed.*

the points in controversy. I suppose this person's convictions those of Z, and that out of five passages there are three, the more natural and obvious sense of which is in his favor; and two of which, though not absolutely precluding a different sense, yet the more probable interpretation is in favor of A, that is, of those who do not consider the Baptism of an infant as prospective, but hold it to be an *opus operans et in præsenti*. Then I say, that if such a person regards these two sentences or single passages as obliging or warranting him to abandon the flock intrusted to his charge, and either to join such as are the avowed enemies of the Church on the double ground of its particular constitution and of its being an establishment, or to set up a separate church for himself—I can not avoid the conclusion, that either his conscience is morbidly sensitive in one speck to the exhaustion of the sensibility in a far larger portion; or that he must have discovered some mode beyond the reach of my conjectural powers, of interpreting the Scriptures enumerated in the following excerpt from the popular Tract before cited, in which the writer expresses an opinion to which I assent with my whole heart, namely:

"That all Christians in the world that hold the same fundamentals ought to make one Church, though differing in lesser opinions; and that the sin, the mischief, and danger to the souls of men, that divide into those many sects and parties among us, does (for the most of them) consist not so much in the opinions themselves, as in their dividing and separating for them. And in support of this tenet, I will refer you to some plain places of Scripture, which if you please now to peruse, I will be silent the while. See what our Saviour himself says, *John* x. 16. *John* xvi. 11. And what the primitive Christians practised, *Acts* ii. 46, and iv. 32. And what St. Paul says, 1 *Cor*. i. 10, 11, 12, and 2, 3, 4, also, the whole 12th chapter: *Eph*. ii. 17, &c. to the end. Where the Jewish and Gentile Christians are showed to be *one body, one household, one temple fitly framed together:* and these were of different opinions in several matters. Likewise chap. iii. 6, iv. 1–13, *Phil*. ii. 1, 2, where he uses the most solemn adjurations to this purpose. But I would more especially recommend to you the reading of *Gal*. v. 20, 21. *Phil*. iii. 15, 16, the 14th chapter to the *Romans*, and part of the 15th, to verse 7, and also *Rom*. xv. 17.

"Are not these passages plain, full, and earnest? Do you

find any of the uncontroverted points to be determined by Scripture in words nigh so plain or pathetic ?"

If I had addressed the ministers recently seceded, I would have first proved from Scripture and reason the justness of their doctrines concerning Baptism and conversion. 2. I would have shown, that even in respect of the Prayer-book and Homilies of the Church of England, taken as a whole, their opponents were comparatively as ill off as themselves, if not worse. 3. That the few mistakes or inconvenient phrases of the Baptismal Service did not impose on the conscience the necessity of resigning the pastoral office. 4. That even if they did, this would by no means justify schism from lay-membership : or else there could be no schism except from an immaculate and infallible Church. Now, as our Articles have declared that no Church is or ever was such, it would follow that there is no such sin as that of schism, that is, that St. Paul wrote falsely or idly. 5. That the escape through the channel of dissent is from the frying-pan to the fire—or, to use a less worn and vulgar simile, the escape of a leech from a glass-jar of water into the naked and open air. But never, never, would I in one breath allow my Church to be fallible, and in the next contend for her absolute freedom from all error—never confine inspiration and perfect truth to the Scriptures, and then scold for the perfect truth of each and every word in the Prayer-book. Enough for me, if in my heart of hearts, free from all fear of man and all lust of preferment, I believe (as I do) the Church of England to be the most Apostolic Church ; that its doctrines and ceremonies contain nothing dangerous to righteousness or salvation ; and that the imperfections in its Liturgy are spots indeed, but spots on the sun, which impede neither its light nor its heat, so as to prevent the good seed from growing in a good soil, and producing fruits of redemption.

[* "8 May, 1828. I see the necessity of greatly expanding and clearing up the chapter on Baptism in the Aids to Reflection, and of proving the substantial accordance of my scheme with that of our Church.

* The paragraphs which the Editor has, after some consideration, thought it advisable to print within brackets in the text of this edition of the Aids to Reflection, are taken from one of the deeply interesting Note Books, kept by Mr. Coleridge with great care during the later years of his life. The material contents of these Books are in process of publication.—*Ed.*

"I still say that an assertion of an act of the Spirit in time—that at the moment of the uttering of the words, *I baptize thee in the name, &c.*, it may be declared, 'Now the Spirit begins to act'—is false in philosophy, and contrary to Scripture; and that our Church Service needs no such hypothesis. Further, I still say that the communication of the Spirit as of a power in principle not yet possessed to an unconscious agent by human ministry, is without precedent or warrant in Scripture;—that the nature of the Spirit communicated by the Apostles by imposition of hands, is a very difficult question; and that the reasons for supposing it to be certain miraculous gifts of the Spirit, peculiar to the first age of Christianity, and during the formation of the Church, are neither few nor insignificant.

"Further, I say that in itself it might be indifferent, whether, the outward Rite of Baptism formed the initiation into the Baptismal period, εἰς τὸ φωτίζειν, or the finale and coronation:—that from the necessity of the circumstances, that is, the non-existence of the Church as the sponsor and security for the undertaking of the enlightening process, and the adult age of the persons to be baptized, the latter was, and could not but be, the practice of the Apostolic age;—but that in after-times both the commencement and the close were ritually solemnized;—in the first, the Church conferring all the privileges of Christianity;—in the second, the donee acknowledging the gift, and declaring his consent to the conditions, and the Church confirming the gift, and receiving the individual as, ἤδη πεφωτισμένον, and no longer, ἐν τῷ φωτίζεσθαι, as one being enlightened. Now it is notorious that during the first two centuries, the catechumens generally were not baptized, and that their baptism was immediately followed by admission to the Eucharist. And such was the force of custom, that when the baptism of infants became the rule of the Church, the Eucharist was administered to them;—a practice which greatly obscured, if it did not destroy, the beautiful harmony and distinct significancy of the two Rites as symbolic,—the one of the Light of the Word, the other of the Life; and therefore with great reason was the practice discontinued.

"Observe, I do not deny—God forbid! the possibility or the reality of the influence of the Spirit on the soul of the infant. His first smile bespeaks a reason—the Light from the Life of the Word—as already existent; and where the Word is, there will the Spirit act. Still less do I think lightly of the graces which the child receives, as a living part of the Church, and whatever flows from the Communion of Saints, and the περιχώρησις of the Spirit. Our Church most wisely and scripturally precludes all the mischievous fanaticism of moments of conversion. Except the time when the Church receives the subject into her own body, and co-organizes the person therewith, no time can be specified for the Spirit's descent and incoming. For the operations of the Spirit are as little referable to Time as to Space; but in reference to our principles of conduct toward, and judgment concerning, our neighbors, the Church declares, that before the time of the Baptism, there is no authority for asserting,—and that since the time there is no authority for denying,—that gift and regenerate presence of the Holy Spirit, promised by an especial covenant to the members of Christ's mystical body; and consequently, no just pretence for expecting or requiring another new initiation or birth into the state of Grace."]

CONCLUSION.

I AM not so ignorant of the temper and tendency of the age in which I live, as either to be unprepared for the sort of remarks which the literal interpretation of the Evangelist will call forth, or to attempt an answer to them. Visionary ravings, obsolete whimsies, transcendental trash, and the like, I leave to pass at the price current among those who are willing to receive abusive phrases as substitutes for argument. Should any suborner of anonymous criticism have engaged some literary bravo or buffoon beforehand to vilify this Work, as in former instances, I would give a friendly hint to the operative critic, that he may compile an excellent article for the occasion, and with very little trouble, out of Warburton's Tract on Grace and the Spirit, and the Preface to the same. There is, however, one objection, which will so often be heard from men, whose talents and reputed moderation must give a weight to their words, that I owe it both to my own character and to the interests of my readers, not to leave it unnoticed. The charge will probably be worded in this way:—There is nothing new in all this. (As if novelty were any merit in questions of revealed religion!) It is mysticism, all taken out of William Law, after he had lost his senses in brooding over the visions of a delirious German cobbler, Jacob Böhme.

Of poor Jacob Böhme I have delivered my sentiments at large in another work. Those who have condescended to look into his writings must know that his characteristic errors are: first, the mistaking the accidents and peculiarities of his own overwrought mind for realities and modes of thinking common to all minds: and secondly, the confusion of Nature, that is, the active powers communicated to matter, with God the Creator. And if the same persons have done more than merely looked into the present Volume, they must have seen, that to eradicate, and, if possible, to preclude both the one and the other, stands prominent among its avowed objects.

Of William Law's Works I am acquainted with the Serious Call; and besides this I remember to have read a small Tract on Prayer, if I mistake not, as I easily may, it being at least six-and-twenty years since I saw it. He may in this or in other tracts have quoted the same passages from the fourth Gospel which I have done. But surely this affords no presumption that my conclusions are the same with his; still less, that they are drawn from the same premisses; and least of all, that they were adopted from his writings. Whether Law has used the phrase, assimilation by faith, I know not; but I know that I should expose myself to a just charge of an idle parade of my reading, if I recapitulated the tenth part of the authors, ancient and modern, Romish and Reformed, from Law to Clemens Alexandrinus and Irenæus, in whose works the same phrase occurs in the same sense. And after all, on such a subject, how worse than childish is the whole dispute!

Is the fourth Gospel authentic? And is the interpretation I have given true or false? These are the only questions which a wise man would put, or a Christian be anxious to answer. I not only believe it to be the true sense of the texts; but I assert that it is the only true, rational, and even tolerable sense. And this position alone I conceive myself interested in defending. I have studied with an open and fearless spirit the attempts of sundry learned critics of the Continent to invalidate the authenticity of this Gospel, before and since Eichorn's Vindication. The result has been a clearer assurance and (as far as this was possible) a yet deeper conviction of the genuineness of all the writings which the Church has attributed to this Apostle. That those, who have formed an opposite conclusion, should object to the use of expressions which they had ranked among the most obvious marks of spuriousness, follows as a matter of course. But that men, who with a clear and cloudless assent receive the sixth chapter of this Gospel as a faithful, nay, inspired record of an actual discourse, should take offence at the repetition of words which the Redeemer himself, in the perfect foreknowledge that they would confirm the disbelieving, alienate the unsteadfast, and transcend the present capacity even of his own elect, had chosen as the most appropriate; and which, after the most decisive proofs that they were misinterpreted by the greater number of his hearers, and not understood by any, he nevertheless repeated with stronger emphasis and without comment as the only appropriate symbols of the great truth he was declaring, and to realize which ἐγένετο σαρξ;*—that in their own discourses these men should hang back from all express reference to these words, as if they were afraid or ashamed of them, though the earliest recorded ceremonies and liturgical forms of the primitive Church are absolutely inexplicable, except in connection with this discourse, and with the mysterious and spiritual, not allegorical and merely ethical, import of the same; and though this import is solemnly and in the most unequivocal terms asserted and taught by their own Church, even in her Catechism, or compendium of doctrines necessary for all her members;—this I may perhaps understand; but this I am not able to vindicate or excuse.

There is, however, one opprobrious phrase which it may be profitable for my younger readers that I should explain, namely, Mysticism. And for this purpose I will quote a sentence or two from a dialogue which, had my prescribed limits permitted, I should have attached to the present work; but which with an Essay† on the Church, as instituted by Christ, and as an establishment of the State, and a series of Letters‡ on the right and the superstitious use and estimation of the Bible, will hereafter appear by themselves, should the reception given to the present Volume encourage or permit the publication.

* Of which our *he was made flesh*, is a very inadequate translation. The Church of England in this as in other doctrinal points has preserved the golden mean between the superstitious reverence of the Romanists, and the avowed contempt of the Sectarians, for the writings of the Fathers, and the authority and unimpeached traditions of the Church during the first three or four centuries. And how, consistently with this honorable characteristic of our Church, a minister of the same could, on the Sacramentary scheme now in fashion, return even a plausible answer to Arnauld's great work on Transubstantiation (not without reason the boast of the Romish Church), exceeds my powers of conjecture.

† See the Church and State, VI.—*Ed.*

‡ See Confessions of an Inquiring Spirit. 1840. V.—*Ed.*

MYSTICS AND MYSTICISM.

Antinous.—"What do you call Mysticism? And do you use the word in a good or in a bad sense?"

Nous.—"In the latter only; as far, at least, as we are now concerned with it. When a man refers to inward feelings and experiences, of which mankind at large are not conscious, as evidences of the truth of any opinion—such a man I call a Mystic: and the grounding of any theory or belief on accidents and anomalies of individual sensations or fancies, and the use of peculiar terms invented, or perverted from their ordinary significations, for the purpose of expressing these idiosyncracies and pretended facts of interior consciousness, I name Mysticism. Where the error consists simply in the Mystic's attaching to these anomalies of his individual temperament the character of reality, and in receiving them as permanent truths, having a subsistence in the Divine Mind, though revealed to himself alone; but entertains this persuasion without demanding or expecting the same faith in his neighbors—I should regard it as a species of enthusiasm, always indeed to be deprecated, but yet capable of co-existing with many excellent qualities both of head and heart. But when the Mystic, by ambition or still meaner passions, or (as sometimes is the case) by an uneasy and self-doubting state of mind which seeks confirmation in outward sympathy, is led to impose his faith, as a duty, on mankind generally: and when with such views he asserts that the same experiences would be vouchsafed, the same truths revealed, to every man, but for his secret wickedness and unholy will;—such a Mystic is a fanatic, and in certain states of the public mind, a dangerous member of society. And most so in those ages and countries in which fanatics of elder standing are allowed to persecute the fresh competitor. For under these predicaments, Mysticism, though originating in the singularities of an individual nature, and therefore essentially anomalous, is nevertheless highly contagious. It is apt to collect a swarm and cluster *circum fana*, around the new fane; and therefore merits the name of *fanaticism*, or as the Germans say, *Schwärmerey*, that is, swarm-making."

We will return to the harmless species, the enthusiastic Mystics;—a species that may again be subdivided into two ranks.

And it will not be other than germane to the subject, if I endeavor to describe them in a sort of allegory or parable. Let us imagine a poor pilgrim benighted in a wilderness or desert, and pursuing his way in the starless dark with a lantern in his hand. Chance or his happy genius leads him to an *oasis* or natural garden, such as in the creations of my youthful fancy I supposed Enos,* the child of Cain, to have found. And here, hungry and thirsty, the way-wearied man rests at a fountain ; and the taper of his lantern throws its light on an over-shadowing tree, a boss of snow-white blossoms, through which the green and growing fruits peeped, and the ripe golden fruitage glowed. Deep, vivid, and faithful are the impressions, which the lovely imagery comprised within the scanty circle of light makes and leaves on his memory. But scarcely has he eaten of the fruits and drunk of the fountain, ere scared by the roar and howl from the desert he hurries forward : and as he passes with hasty steps through grove and glade, shadows and imperfect beholdings and vivid fragments of things distinctly seen blend with the past and present shapings of his brain. Fancy modifies sight. His dreams transfer their forms to real objects ; and these lend a substance and an outness

* Will the Reader forgive me if I attempt at once to illustrate and relieve the subject by annexing the opening lines of a poem composed in the same year in which I wrote the Ancient Mariner and the first Book of Christabel ?

"Encinctur'd with a twine of leaves,
That leafy twine his only dress !
A lovely boy was plucking fruits
In a moonlight wilderness.
The moon was bright, the air was free,
And fruits and flowers together grew
On many a shrub and many a tree :
And all put on a gentle hue,
Hanging in the shadowy air
Like a picture rich and rare.
It was a climate where, they say,
The night is more beloved than day.
But who that beauteous boy beguiled
That beauteous boy, to linger here ?
Alone, by night, a little child,
In place so silent and so wild—
Has he no friend, no loving mother near ?"

WANDERINGS OF CAIN.
Poet. Works, VII. p. 292.—*Ed.*

to his dreams. Apparitions greet him; and when at a distance from this enchanted land, and on a different track, the dawn of day discloses to him a caravan, a troop of his fellow-men, his memory, which is itself half fancy, is interpolated afresh by every attempt to recall, connect, and piece out his recollections. His narration is received as a madman's tale. He shrinks from the rude laugh and contemptuous sneer, and retires into himself. Yet the craving for sympathy, strong in proportion to the intensity of his convictions, impels him to unbosom himself to abstract auditors; and the poor quietist becomes a penman, and, all too poorly stocked for the writer's trade, he borrows his phrases and figures from the only writings to which he has had access, the sacred books of his religion. And thus I shadow out the enthusiastic Mystic of the first sort; at the head of which stands the illuminated Teutonic theosopher and shoemaker, honest Jacob Böhme, born near Gorlitz, in Upper Lusatia, in the 17th of our Elizabeth's reign, and who died in the 22d of her successor's.

To delineate a Mystic of the second and higher order, we need only endow our pilgrim with equal gifts of nature, but these developed and displayed by all the aids and arts of education and favorable fortune. He is on his way to the Mecca of his ancestral and national faith, with a well-guarded and numerous procession of merchants and fellow-pilgrims, on the established track. At the close of day the caravan has halted: the full moon rises on the desert: and he strays forth alone, out of sight but to no unsafe distance; and chance leads him, too, to the same oasis or islet of verdure on the sea of sand. He wanders at leisure in its maze of beauty and sweetness, and thrids his way through the odorous and flowering thickets into open spots of greenery, and discovers statues and memorial characters, grottos, and refreshing caves. But the moonshine, the imaginative poesy of Nature, spreads its soft shadowy charm over all, conceals distances, and magnifies heights, and modifies relations; and fills up vacuities with its own whiteness, counterfeiting substance; and where the dense shadows lie, makes solidity imitate hollowness; and gives to all objects a tender visionary hue and softening. Interpret the moonlight and the shadows as the peculiar genius and sensibility of the individual's own spirit; and here you have the other sort; a Mystic, an enthusiast of a nobler breed—a Fenelon. But the residentiary, or the frequent visitor of the favored spot, who has scanned its beauties by steady daylight, and mastered its true proportions and lineaments,—he will discover that both pilgrims have indeed been there. He will know, that the delightful dream, which the latter tells, is a dream of truth; and that even in the bewildered tale of the former there is truth mingled with the dream.

But the source, the spring-head, of the charges which I anticipate, lies deep. Materialism, conscious and avowed Materialism, is in ill repute: and a confessed Materialist therefore a rare character. But if the faith be ascertained by the fruits: if the predominant, though most often unsuspected, persuasion is to be learnt from the influences, under which the thoughts and affections of the man move and take their direction; I must reverse the position. Only not all are Materialists. Except a few individuals, and those for the most part of a single sect: every one who calls himself a Christian, holds himself to have a soul as well as a body. He distinguishes mind from matter, the subject of his consciousness from the objects of the same. The former is his mind: and he says, it is immaterial. But though subject and substance are words of kindred roots, nay, little less than equivalent terms, yet nevertheless it is exclusively to sensible objects, to bodies, to modifications of matter, that he habitually attaches the attributes of reality, of substance. Real and tangible, substantial and material, are synonymes for him. He never indeed asks himself, what he means by mind? But if he did, and tasked himself to return an honest answer—as to what, at least, he had hitherto meant by it—he would find, that he had described it by negatives, as the opposite of bodies, for example, as a somewhat opposed to solidity, to visibility, and the like, as if you could abstract the capacity of a vessel, and conceive of it as a somewhat by itself, and then give to the emptiness the properties of containing, holding, being entered, and so forth. In short, though the proposition would perhaps be angrily denied in words, yet in fact he thinks of his mind, as a property, or accident of a something else, that he calls a soul or spirit: though the very same difficulties must recur, the moment he should attempt to establish the difference. For either this soul or spirit is nothing but a thinner body, a finer mass of matter: or the attribute of self-subsistency vanishes from the soul on the same grounds, on which it is refused to the mind.

I am persuaded, however, that the dogmatism of the Corpuscular School, though it still exerts an influence on man's notions and phrases, has received a mortal blow from the increasingly dynamic spirit of the physical sciences now highest in public estimation. And it may safely be predicted that the results will extend beyond the intention of those, who are gradually effecting this revolution. It is not Chemistry alone that will be indebted to the genius of Davy, Oersted, and their compeers: and not as the founder of physiology and philosophic anatomy alone, will mankind love and revere the name of John Hunter. These men have not only taught, they have compelled us to admit, that the immediate objects of our senses, or rather the grounds of the visibility and tangibility of all objects of sense, bear the same relation and similar proportion to the intelligible object—that is, to the object which we actually mean when we say, " It is such or such a thing," or "I have seen this or that,"—as the paper, ink, and differently combined straight and curved lines of an edition of Homer bear to what we understand by the words, Iliad and Odyssey. Nay, nothing would be more easy than so to construct the paper, ink, painted capitals, and the like, of a printed disquisition on the eye, or the muscles and cellular texture (that is, the flesh) of the human body, as to bring together every one of the sensible and ponderable stuffs or elements, that are sensuously perceived in the eye itself, or in the flesh itself. Carbon and nitrogen, oxygen and hydrogen, sulphur, phosphorus, and one or two metals and metallic bases, constitute the whole. It can not be these therefore, that we mean by an eye, by our body. But perhaps it may be a particular combination of these? Now here comes a question: In this term do you or do you not include the principle, the operating cause, of the combination? If not, then detach this eye from the body. Look steadily at it—as it might lie on the marble slab of a dissecting-room. Say it were the eye of a murderer, a Bellingham: or the eye of a murdered patriot, a Sidney!—Behold it, handle it, with its various accompaniments or constituent parts, of tendon, ligament, membrane, blood-vessel, gland, humors; its nerves of sense, of sensation, and of motion. Alas! all these names, like that of the organ itself, are so many anachronisms, figures of speech, to express that which has been: as when the guide points with his finger to a heap of stones, and tells the traveller, " That is Babylon, or Persepolis."—Is this cold jelly *the light of the body?* Is this the *micranthropos* in the marvellous microcosm? Is this what you mean when you well describe the eye as the telescope and the mirror of the soul, the seat and agent of an almost magical power?

Pursue the same inquisition with every other part of the body, whether integral or simply ingredient; and let a Berzelius or a Hatchett be your interpreter, and demonstrate to you what it is that in each actually meets your senses. And when you have heard the scanty catalogue, ask yourself if these are indeed the living flesh, the blood of life? Or not far rather—I speak of what, as a man of common sense, you really do, not what, as a philosopher, you ought to believe—is it not, I say, far rather the distinct and individualized agency that by the given combinations utters and bespeaks its presence? Justly and with strictest propriety of language may I say, speaks. It is to the coarseness of our senses, or rather to the defect and limitation of our percipient faculty, that the visible object appears the same even for a moment. The characters which I am now shaping on this paper, abide. Not only the forms remain the same, but the particles of the coloring stuff are fixed, and, for an indefinite period at least, remain the same. But the particles that constitute the size, the visibility of an organic structure, are in perpetual flux. They are to the combining and constitutive power as the pulses of air to the voice of a discourser; or of one who sings a roundelay. The same words may be repeated; but in each second of time the articulated air hath passed away, and each act of articulation appropriates and gives momentary form to a new and other portion. As the column of blue smoke from a cottage chimney in the breathless summer noon, or the steadfast-seeming cloud on the edge point of a hill in the driving air-current, which momently condensed and recomposed is the common phantom of a thousand successors;—such is the flesh, which our bodily eyes transmit to us; which our palates taste; which our hands touch.

But perhaps the material particles possess this combining power by inherent reciprocal attractions, repulsions, and elective affinities; and are themselves the joint artists of their own combinations? I will not reply, though well I might, that this would be to solve one problem by another, and merely to shift the mystery. It will be sufficient to remind the thoughtful querist, that even herein consists the essential difference, the contra-distinction, of an organ from a machine; that not only the characteristic shape is evolved from the invisible central power, but the material mass itself is acquired by assimilation. The germinal power of the plant transmutes the fixed air and the elementary base of water into grass or leaves; and on these the organific principle in the ox or the elephant exercises an alchemy still more stupendous. As the unseen agency weaves its magic eddies, the foliage becomes indifferently the bone and its marrow, the pulpy brain, or the solid ivory. That what you see is blood, is flesh, is itself the work, or shall I say, the translucence, of the invisible energy, which soon surrenders or abandons them to inferior powers (for there is no pause nor chasm in the activities of nature), which repeat a similar metamorphosis according to their kind;—these are not fancies, conjectures, or even hypotheses, but facts; to deny which is impossible, not to reflect on which is ignominious. And we need only reflect on them with a calm and silent spirit to learn the utter emptiness and unmeaningness of the vaunted Mechanico-corpuscular philosophy, with both its twins, Materialism on the one hand, and Idealism, rightlier named subjective Idolism, on the other: the one obtruding on us a world of spectres and apparitions; the other a mazy dream.*

Let the Mechanic or Corpuscular scheme, which in its absoluteness and strict consistency was first introduced by Des Cartes, be judged by the results. By its fruits shall it be known.

In order to submit the various *phænomena* of moving bodies to geometrical construction, we are under the necessity of abstracting from corporeal substance all its positive properties, and obliged to consider bodies as differing from equal portions of space†

* See the Author's *Theory of Life*, Appendix C.—*Am. Ed.*

† Such is the conception of body in Des Cartes' own system. Body is everywhere confounded with matter, and might in the Cartesian sense be defined space or extension, with the attribute of visibility. As Des Cartes at the same time zealously asserted the existence of intelligential beings, the reality and independent self-subsistence of the soul, Berkeleyanism or Spinosism was the immediate and necessary consequence. Assume a plurality of self-subsisting souls, and we have Berkeleyanism; assume one only (*unam et unicam substantiam*), and you have Spinosism, that is, the assertion of one infinite Self-subsistent, with the two attributes of thinking and appearing. *Cogitatio infinita sine centro, et omniformis apparitio.* How far the Newtonian *vis inertiæ* (interpreted any otherwise than as an arbitrary term=x y z, to represent the unknown but necessary supplement or inte-

only by figure and mobility. And as a fiction of science, it would be difficult to overvalue this invention. It possesses the same merits in relation to geometry that the atomic theory has in relation to algebraic calculus. But in contempt of common sense, and in direct opposition to the express declarations of the inspired historian (*Gen.* i.), and to the tone and spirit of the Scriptures throughout, Des Cartes propounded it as truth of fact, and instead of a world created and filled with productive forces by the almighty *Fiat*, left a lifeless machine whirled about by the dust of its own grinding: as if death could come from the living fountain of life; nothingness and phantom from the plenitude of reality, the absoluteness of creative will!

Holy! Holy! Holy! let me be deemed mad by all men, if such be thy ordinance: but, O! from such madness save and preserve me, my God!

When, however, after a short interval, the genius of Kepler, expanded and organized in the soul of Newton, and there (if I may hazard so bold an expression) refining itself into an almost celestial clearness, had expelled the Cartesian *vortices*;* then the

gration of the Cartesian notion of body) has patched up the flaw, I leave for more competent judges to decide. But should any one of my Readers feel an interest in the speculative principles of natural philosophy, and should be master of the German language, I warmly recommend for his perusal the earliest known publication of the great founder of the Critical Philosophy, (written in the twenty-second year of his age!) on the then eager controversy between the Leibnitzian and the French and English Mathematicians, respecting the living forces—*Gedanken von der wahren Schätzung der lebendigen Kräfte:* 1747—in which Kant demonstrates the right reasoning to be with the latter; but the truth of the fact, the evidence of experience, with the former; and gives the explanation, namely: body, or corporeal nature, is something else and more than geometrical extension, even with the addition of a *vis inertiæ*. And Leibnitz, with the Bernouillis, erred in the attempt to demonstrate geometrically a problem not susceptible of geometrical construction. This tract, with the succeeding *Himmels-System*, may with propriety be placed, after the *Principia* of Newton, among the striking instances of early genius; and as the first product of the dynamic philosophy in the physical sciences, from the time, at least, of Giordano Bruno, whom the idolaters burned for an Atheist, at Rome, in the year 1600.—[See The Friend, II. p. 110 note.—*Ed.*]

* For Newton's own doubtfully suggested ether or most subtle fluid, as the ground and immediate agent in the *phænomena* of universal gravitation, was either not adopted or soon abandoned by his disciples; not only as introducing, against his own canons of right reasoning, an *ens imaginarium*

necessity of an active power, of positive forces present in the material universe, forced itself on the conviction. For as a law without a lawgiver is a mere abstraction; so a law without an agent to realize it, a constitution without an abiding executive, is, in fact, not a law but an idea. In the profound emblem of the great tragic poet, it is the powerless Prometheus fixed on a barren rock. And what was the result? How was this necessity provided for? God himself—my hand trembles as I write! Rather, then let me employ the word, which the religious feeling, in its perplexity, suggested as the substitute—the Deity itself was declared to be the real agent, the actual gravitating power! The law and the lawgiver were identified. God (says Dr. Priestley) not only does, but is every thing. *Jupiter est quodcunque vides.* And thus a system, which commenced by excluding all life and immanent activity from the visible universe, and evacuating the natural world of all nature, ended by substituting the Deity, and reducing the Creator to a mere *anima mundi:* a scheme that has no advantage over Spinosism but its inconsistency, which does indeed make it suit a certain order of intellects, who, like the *pleuronectæ* (or flat fish) in ichthyology which have both eyes on the same side, never see but half of a subject at one time, and forgetting the one before they get to the other are sure not to detect any inconsistency between them.

And what has been the consequence? An increasing unwillingness to contemplate the Supreme Being in his personal attributes: and thence a distaste to all the peculiar doctrines of the Christian Faith, the Trinity, the Incarnation of the Son of God, and Redemption. The young and ardent, ever too apt to mistake the inward triumph in the detection of error for a positive love of truth, are among the first and most frequent victims to this epidemic *fastidium.* Alas! even the sincerest seekers after light are not safe from the contagion. Some have I known, con-

into physical science, a suffiction in the place of a legitimate supposition; but because the substance (if assumed to exist) must itself form part of the problem which it was meant to solve. Meantime Leibnitz's pre-established harmony, which originated in Spinosa, found no acceptance; and, lastly, the notion of a corpuscular substance, with properties put into it, like a pincushion hidden by the pins, could pass with the unthinking only for any thing more than a confession of ignorance, or technical terms expressing a *hiatus* of scientific insight.

stitutionally religious—I speak feelingly; for I speak of that which for a brief period was my own state—who under this unhealthful influence have been so estranged from the heavenly Father, the living God, as even to shrink from the personal pronouns as applied to the Deity. But many do I know, and yearly meet with, in whom a false and sickly taste co-operates with the prevailing fashion: many, who find the God of Abraham, Isaac, and Jacob, far too real, too substantial; who feel it more in harmony with their indefinite sensations

> To worship Nature in the hill and valley,
> Not knowing what they love:—

and (to use the language, but not the sense or purpose, of the great poet of our age) would fain substitute for the Jehovah of their Bible

> A sense sublime
> Of something far more deeply interfused,
> Whose dwelling is the light of setting suns,
> And the round ocean and the living air;
> A motion and a spirit, that impels
> All thinking things, all objects of all thought,
> And rolls through all things! WORDSWORTH.

And this from having been educated to understand the Divine Omnipresence in any sense rather than the only safe and legitimate one, the presence of all things to God!

Be it, however, that the number of such men is comparatively small; and be it (as in fact it often is) but a brief stage, a transitional state, in the process of intellectual growth. Yet among a numerous and increasing class of the higher and middle ranks, there is an inward withdrawing from the life and personal being of God, a turning of the thoughts exclusively to the so-called physical attributes, to the omnipresence in the counterfeit form of ubiquity, to the immensity, the infinity, the immutability;—the attributes of space with a notion of power as their *substratum*,—a Fate, in short, not a moral Creator and Governor. Let intelligence be imagined, and wherein does the conception of God differ essentially from that of gravitation (conceived as the cause of gravity) in the understanding of those, who represent the Deity not only as a necessary but as a necessitated being; those, for whom justice is but a scheme of general laws; and holiness, and the divine hatred of sin, yea, and sin itself, are words without meaning, or accommodations to a rude and barbarous race? Hence, I more than fear the prevailing taste for books of natural theology, physico-theology, demonstrations of God from Nature, evidences of Christianity, and the like. Evidences of Christianity! I am weary of the word. Make a man feel the want of it; rouse him, if you can, to the self-knowledge of his need of it; and you may safely trust it to its own evidence,—remembering only the express declaration of Christ himself: *No man cometh to me, unless the Father leadeth him.* Whatever more is desirable—I speak now with reference to Christians generally, and not to professed students of theology—may, in my judgment, be far more safely and profitably taught, without controversy or the supposition of infidel antagonists, in the form of Ecclesiastical history.

The last fruit of the Mechanico-corpuscular philosophy, say rather of the mode and direction of feeling and thinking produced by it on the educated class of society—or that result, which as more immediately connected with my present theme I have reserved for the last—is the habit of attaching all our conceptions and feelings, and of applying all the words and phrases expressing reality to the objects of the senses: more accurately speaking to the images and sensations by which their presence is made known to us. Now I do not hesitate to assert, that it was one of the great purposes of Christianity, and included in the process of our redemption, to rouse and emancipate the soul from this debasing slavery to the outward senses, to awaken the mind to the true *criteria* of reality, namely, permanence, power, will manifested in act, and truth operating as life. *My words,* said Christ, *are spirit:* and they (that is, the spiritual powers expressed by them) *are truth;* that is, very being. For this end our Lord, who came from heaven to *take captivity captive,* chose the words and names, that designate the familiar yet most important objects of sense, the nearest and most concerning things and incidents of corporeal nature; water, flesh, blood, birth, bread! But he used them in senses, that could not without absurdity be supposed to respect the mere *phænomena,* water, flesh, and the like; in senses that by no possibility could apply to the color, figure, specific mode of touch or taste produced on ourselves, and by which we are made aware of the presence of the things and understand them—*res, quæ sub apparitionibus istis statuendæ sunt.* And this awful recalling of the drowsed soul from the dreams and phantom world of sensuality to *actual* reality,—how has it been evaded! These words, that were spirit,—these mysteries, which even the Apostles must wait for the Paraclete in order to comprehend—these spiritual things which can only be spiritually discerned,—were mere metaphors, figures of speech, oriental hyperboles! "All this means only morality!" Ah! how far nearer to the truth would these men have been, had they said that morality means all this!

The effect, however, has been most injurious to the best interests of our Universities, to our incomparably constituted Church, and even to our national character. The few who have read my two Lay Sermons are no strangers to my opinions on this head; and in my treatise on the Church and Churches, I shall, if Providence vouchsafe, submit them to the Public, with their grounds and historic evidences in a more systematic form.

I have, I am aware, in this present Work furnished occasion for a charge of having expressed myself with slight and irreverence of celebrated names, especially of the late Dr. Paley. O, if I were fond and ambitious of literary honor, of public applause, how well content should I be to excite but one third of the admiration which, in my inmost being, I feel for the head and heart of Paley! And how gladly would I surrender all hope of contemporary praise, could I even approach to the incomparable grace, propriety, and persuasive facility of his writings! But on this very account I believe myself bound in conscience to throw the whole force of my intellect in the way of this triumphal car, on which the tutelary genius of modern idolatry is borne, even at the risk of being crushed under the wheels. I have at this moment before my eyes the eighteenth of his Posthumous Discourses: the amount of which is briefly this,—that all the words and passages in the New Testament which express and contain the peculiar doctrines of Christianity, the paramount objects of the Christian Revelation, all those which speak so strongly of the value, benefit, and efficacy of the death of Christ, assuredly mean something: but what they mean, nobody, it seems, can tell! But doubtless we shall discover it, and be convinced that there is a substantial sense belonging to these words in a future state! Is there an enigma or an absurdity in the Koran or the Vedas, which might not be defended on the same pretence? A similar impression, I confess, was left on my mind by Dr. Magee's statement or exposition (*ad normam Grotianam*) of the doctrine of Redemption; and deeply did it disappoint the high expectations, sadly did it chill the fervid sympathy, which his introductory chapter, his manly and masterly disquisition on the sacrificial rites of Paganism, had raised in my mind.

And yet I can not read the pages of Paley, here referred to aloud, without the liveliest sense, how plausible and popular they will sound to the great majority of readers. Thousands of sober, and in other way pious, Christians will echo the words, together with Magee's kindred interpretation of the death of Christ, and adopt the doctrine for their make-faith; and why? It is feeble. And whatever is feeble is always plausible: for it favors mental indolence. It is feeble: and feebleness, in the disguise of confessing and condescending strength, is always popular. It flatters the reader by removing the apprehended distance between him and the superior author; and it flatters him still more by enabling him to transfer to himself, and to appropriate, this superiority; and thus to make his very weakness the mark and evidence of his strength. Ay, quoth the rational Christian—or with a sighing, self-soothing sound between an Ay and an Ah!—I am content to think with the great Dr. Paley, and the learned Archbishop of Dublin—

Man of sense! Dr. Paley was a great man, and Dr. Magee is a learned and exemplary prelate; but You do not think at all!

With regard to the convictions avowed and enforced in my own Work, I will continue my address to the man of sense in the words of an old philosopher:—*Tu vero crassis auribus et obstinato corde respuis quæ forsitan vere perhibeantur. Minus hercule calles pravissimis opinionibus ea putari mendacia, quæ vel auditu nova, vel visu rudia, vel certe supra captum cogitationis (extemporaneæ tuæ) ardua videantur: quæ si paulo accuratius exploraris, non modo compertu evidentia, sed etiam factu facilia, senties.**

In compliance with the suggestion of a friend, the celebrated conclusion of the fourth book of Paley's Moral and Political Philosophy, referred to in p. 258, of this Volume, is here transprinted for the convenience of the Reader:—

* *Apul. Metam.* I.—*Ed.*

"Had Jesus Christ delivered no other declaration than the following—*The hour is coming, in the which all that are in the grave shall hear his voice, and shall come forth: they that have done good, unto the resurrection of life, and they that have done evil, unto the resurrection of damnation;*—he had pronounced a message of inestimable importance, and well worthy of that splendid apparatus of prophecy and miracles with which his mission was introduced and attested: a message in which the wisest of mankind would rejoice to find an answer to their doubts, and rest to their inquiries. It is idle to say, that a future state had been discovered already;—it had been discovered as the Copernican system was;—it was one guess among many. He alone discovers, who proves; and no man can prove this point, but the teacher who testifies by miracles that his doctrine comes from God."

Pædianus says of Virgil,—*Usque adeo expers invidiæ ut siquid erudite dictum inspiceret alterius, non minus gauderet ac si suum esset.* My own heart assures me that this is less than the truth: that Virgil would have read a beautiful passage in the work of another with a higher and purer delight than in a work of his own, because free from the apprehension of his judgment being warped by self-love, and without that repressive modesty akin to shame, which in a delicate mind holds in check a man's own secret thoughts and feelings, when they respect himself. The cordial admiration with which I peruse the preceding passage as a master-piece of composition would, could I convey it, serve as a measure of the vital importance I attach to the convictions which impelled me to animadvert on the same passage as doctrine.

APPENDIX A.

SUMMARY OF THE SCHEME OF THE ARGUMENT TO PROVE THE DIVERSITY IN KIND OF THE REASON AND THE UNDERSTANDING. SEE p. 188.

THE position to be proved is the difference in kind of the understanding from the reason.

The axiom, on which the proof rests, is: subjects, which require essentially different general definitions, differ in kind and not merely in degree. For difference in degree forms the ground of specific definitions, but not of generic or general.

Now reason is considered either in relation to the will and moral being, when it is termed the practical* reason = A: or relatively to the intellective and sciential faculties, when it is termed theoretic or speculative reason = *a*. In order therefore to be compared with the reason, the understanding must in like manner be distinguished into the understanding as a principle of action, in which relation I call it the adaptive power, or the faculty of selecting and adapting means and medial of proximate ends = B: and the understanding, as a mode and faculty of thought, when it is called reflection = *b*. Accordingly, I give the general definitions of these four: that is, I describe each severally by its essential characters: and I find, that the definition of A differs *toto genere* from that of B, and the definition of *a* from that of *b*.

Now subjects that require essentially different definitions do themselves differ in kind. But Understanding and Reason require essentially different definitions. Therefore Understanding and Reason differ in kind.

* The Practical Reason alone is Reason in the full and substantive sense. It is Reason in its own sphere of perfect freedom; as the source of ideas, which ideas, in their conversion to the responsible Will, become ultimate ends. On the other hand, Theoretic Reason, as the ground of the universal and absolute in all logical conclusion, is rather the light of Reason in the Understanding, and known to be such by its contrast with the contingency and particularity which characterize all the proper and indigenous growths of the Understanding.

APPENDIX B.

WHAT is Instinct ?* As I am not quite of Bonnet's opinion "that philosophers will in vain torment themselves to define instinct until they have spent some time in the head of the animal without actually being that animal," I shall endeavor to explain the use of the term. I shall not think it necessary to controvert the opinions which have been offered on this subject, whether the ancient doctrine of Descartes, who supposed that animals were mere machines; or the modern one of Lamark, who attributes instincts to habits impressed upon the organs of animals, by the constant efflux of the nervous fluid to these organs to which it has been determined in their efforts to perform certain actions, to which their necessities have given birth. And it will be here premature to offer any refutation of the opinions of those who contend for the identity of this faculty with reason, and maintain that all the actions of animals are the result of invention and experience;—an opinion maintained with considerable plausibility by Dr. Darwin.

"Perhaps the most ready and certain mode of coming to a conclusion in this intricate inquiry will be by the apparently circuitous route of determining first, what we do not mean by the word. Now we certainly do not mean, in the use of the term, any act of the vital power in the production or maintenance of an organ: nobody thinks of saying that the teeth grow by instinct, or that when the muscles are increased in vigor and size in consequence of exercise, it is from such a cause or principle. Neither do we attribute instinct to the direct functions of the organs in providing for the continuance and sustentation of the whole co-organized body. No one talks of the liver secreting bile, or of the heart acting for the propulsion of the blood, by instinct. Some, indeed, have maintained that breathing, even voiding the excrement and urine, are instinctive operations; but surely these, as well as the former, are automatic, or at least are the necessary result of the organization of the parts in and by which the actions are produced. These instances seem to be, if I may so say, below instinct. But again, we do not attribute instinct to any actions preceded by a will conscious of its whole purpose, calculating

* Green's Vital Dynamics, Appendix F, p. 88. See ante, p. 257.—*Ed.*

its effects, and predetermining its consequences, nor to any exercise of the intellectual powers, of which the whole scope, aim, and end are intellectual. In other terms, no man who values his words will talk of the instinct of a Howard, or of the instinctive operations of a Newton or Leibnitz, in those sublime efforts, which ennoble and cast a lustre, not less on the individuals than on the whole human race.

"To what kind or mode of action shall we then look for the legitimate application of the term? In answer to this query, we may, I think, without fear of the consequences, put the following cases as exemplifying and justifying the use of the term, Instinct, in an appropriate sense. First, when there appears an action, not included either in the mere functions of life, acting within the sphere of its own organismus; nor yet an action attributable to the intelligent will or reason: yet at the same time, not referable to any particular organ, we then declare the presence of an Instinct. We might illustrate this in the instance of a bull-calf butting before he has horus, in which the action can have no reference to its internal economy, to the presence of a particular organ, or to an intelligent will. Secondly, likewise if it be not indeed included in the first, we attribute Instinct where the organ is present, if only the act is equally anterior to all possible experience on the part of the individual agent, as for instance, when the beaver employs its tail for the construction of its dwelling; the tailor-bird its bill for the formation of its pensile habitation; the spider its spinning organ for fabricating its artfully woven nets, or the viper its poison fang for its defence. And lastly, generally, where there is an act of the whole body as one animal, not referable to a will conscious of its purpose, nor to its mechanism, nor to a habit derived from experience, nor previous frequent use. Here with most satisfaction, and without doubt of the propriety of the word, we declare an Instinct; as examples of which, we may adduce the migratory habits of birds, the social instincts of the bees, the construction of their habitations, composed of cells formed with geometrical precision, adapted in capacity to different orders of the society, and forming storehouses for containing a supply of provisions; not to mention similar instances in wasps, ants, termites; and the endless contrivances for protecting the future progeny.

"But if it be admitted that we have rightly stated the application of the term, what we may ask is contained in the examples adduced, or what inferences are we to make as to the nature of Instinct itself, as a source and principle of action? We shall, perhaps, best aid ourselves in the inquiry by an example, and let us take a very familiar one of a caterpillar taking its food. The caterpillar seeks at once the plant, which furnishes the appropriate aliment, and this even as soon as it creeps from the ovum; and the food being taken into the stomach, the nutritious part is separated from the innutritious, and is disposed of for the support of the animal. The question then is, what is contained in this instance of instinct? In the first place what does the vital power in the stomach do, if we generalize the account of the process, or express it in its most general terms? Manifestly it selects and applies appropriate means to an immediate end, prescribed by the constitution; first of the particular organ, and then of the whole body or organismus. This we have admitted is not instinct. But what does the caterpillar do? Does it not also select and apply appropriate means to an immediate end prescribed by its particular organization and constitution? But there is something more; it does this according to circumstances; and this we call Instinct. But may there not be still something more involved? What shall we say of Hüber's humble-bees? A dozen of these were put under a bell glass along with a comb of about ten silken cocoons, so unequal in height as not to be capable of standing steadily; to remedy this, two or three of the humble-bees got upon the comb, stretched themselves over its edge, and with their heads downwards, fixed their forefeet on the table on which the comb stood, and so with their hindfeet kept the comb from falling: when these were weary others took their places. In this constrained and painful posture, fresh bees relieving their comrades at intervals, and each working in its turn, did these affectionate little insects support the comb for nearly three days; at the end of which time they had prepared sufficient wax to build pillars with it. And what is still further curious, the first pillars having got displaced, the bees had again recourse to the same manœuvre. What then is involved in this case? Evidently the same selection and appropriation of means to an immediate end as before; but observe! according to varying circumstances.

"And here we are puzzled; for this becomes Understanding. At least no naturalist, however predetermined to contrast and oppose Instinct to Understanding, but ends at last in facts in which he himself can make out no difference. But are we hence to conclude that the instinct is the same, and identical with the human understanding? Certainly not; though the difference is not in the essential of the definition, but in an addition to, or modification of, that which is essentially the same in both. In such cases, namely, as that which we have last adduced, in which instinct assumes the semblance of understanding, the act indicative of instinct is not clearly prescribed by the constitution or laws of the animal's peculiar organization, but arises out of the constitution and previous circumstances of the animal, and those habits, wants, and that predetermined sphere of action and operation which belong to the race, and beyond the limits of which it does not pass. If this be the case, I may venture to assert that I have determined an appropriate sense for instinct: namely, that it is a power of selecting and applying appropriate means to an immediate end, according to circumstances and the changes of circumstances, these being variable and varying; but yet so as to be referable to the general habits, arising out of the constitution and previous circumstances of the animal considered not as an individual, but as a race.

"We may here, perhaps, most fitly explain the error of those who contend for the identity of Reason and Instinct, and believe that the actions of animals are the result of invention and experience. They have, no doubt, been deceived, in their investigation of Instinct, by an efficient cause simulating a final cause; and the defect in their reasoning has arisen in consequence of observing in the instinctive operations of animals the adaptation of means to a relative end, from the assumption of a deliberate purpose. To this freedom or choice in action and purpose, instinct, in any appropriate sense of the word, can not apply, and to justify and explain its introduction, we must have recourse to other and higher faculties than any manifested in the operations of instinct. It is evident, namely, in turning our attention to the distinguishing character of human actions, that there is, as in the inferior animals, a selection and appropriation of means to ends—but it is (not only according to circumstances, not only according to varying circumstances, but it is) according to varying purposes. But this is an attribute of the intelligent will, and no longer even mere understanding.

"And here let me observe that the difficulty and delicacy of this investigation are greatly increased by our not considering the understanding (even our own) in itself, and as it would be were it not accompanied with and modified by the co-operation of the will, the moral feeling, and that faculty, perhaps best distinguished by the name of Reason, of determining that which is universal and necessary, of fixing laws and principles whether speculative or practical, and of contemplating a final purpose or end. This intelligent will,—having a self-conscious purpose, under the guidance and light of the reason, by which its acts are made to bear as a whole upon some end in and for itself, and to which the understanding is subservient as an organ or the faculty of selecting and appropriating the means—seems best to account for that progressiveness of the human race, which so evidently marks an insurmountable distinction and impassable barrier between man and the inferior animals; but which would be inexplicable, were there no other difference than in the degree of their intellectual faculties.

"Man doubtless has his instincts, even in common with the inferior animals, and many of these are the germs of some of the best feelings of his nature. What, amongst many, might I present as a better illustration, or more beautiful instance, than the *storge* or maternal instinct? But man's instincts are elevated and ennobled by the moral ends and purposes of his being. He is not destined to be the slave of blind impulses, a vessel purposeless, unmeant. He is constituted by his moral and intelligent will, to be the first freed being, the master-work and the end of nature; but this freedom and high office can only co-exist with fealty and devotion to the service of truth and virtue. And though we may even be permitted to use the term instinct, in order to designate those high impulses which in the minority of man's rational being, shape his acts unconsciously to ultimate ends, and which in constituting the very character and impress of the humanity reveal the guidance of Providence; yet the convenience of the phrase, and the want of any other distinctive appellation for an influence *de supra*, working unconsciously in and on the whole human race, should not induce us to forget that the term instinct is only strictly applicable to the adaptive power, as the faculty, even in its highest proper form, of selecting and adapting appropriate means to proximate ends according to varying circumstances,—a faculty which, however, only differs from human understanding in consequence of the latter being enlightened by reason, and that the principles which actuate man as ultimate ends, and are designed for his conscious possession and guidance, are best and most properly named Ideas."

APPENDIX C.

The following tract published in England under the title of *Hints towards the Formation of a more Comprehensive Theory of Life, by S. T. Coleridge*, is inserted here, because it contains a fuller and more systematic development of the general views presented on pages 357–359 of the *Aids to Reflection.* This seems to be its most appropriate place in the collection, and the reader will find it both in matter and form, one of the most profound and elegant exhibitions that have yet been made of the Dynamic Theory of Life.—*Am. Ed.*

THEORY OF LIFE.

When we stand before the bust of John Hunter, or as we enter the magnificent museum furnished by his labors, and pass slowly, with meditative observation, through this august temple, which the genius of one great man has raised and dedicated to the wisdom and uniform working of the Creator, we perceive at every step the guidance, we had almost said, the inspiration, of those profound ideas concerning Life, which dawn upon us indeed, through his written works, but which he has here presented to us in a more perfect language than that of words—the language of God himself, as uttered by Nature.

That the true idea of Life existed in the mind of John Hunter I do not entertain the least doubt; but it may, perhaps, be doubted whether his incessant occupation, and his stupendous industry in the service, both of his contemporaries and of posterity, added to his comparatively slight acquaintance with the arts and aids of logical arrangement, permitted him fully to unfold and arrange it in distinct, clear, and communicable conceptions. Assuredly, however, I may, without incurring the charge of arrogance or detraction, venture to assert that, in his writings the light which occasionally flashes upon us seems at other times, and more frequently, to struggle through an unfriendly medium, and even sometimes to suffer a temporary occultation. At least, in order to dissipate the undeniable obscurities, and to reconcile the apparent contradictions found in his works,—to distinguish, in short, the numerous passages in which without, perhaps, losing sight internally of his own peculiar belief, he yet falls into the phraseology and mechanical solutions of his age,—we must distinguish such passages from those in which the form corresponds to the substance, and in which, therefore, the nature and essential laws of vital action are expressed, as far as his researches had unveiled them to his own mind, without disguise. To effect this, we must, as it were, climb up on his shoulders, and look at the same objects in a distincter form, because seen from the more commanding point of view furnished by himself. This has, indeed, been more than once attempted already, and, in one instance, with so evident a display of power and insight as announces in the assertor and vindicator of the Hunterian Theory a congenial intellect, and a disciple in whom Hunter himself would have exulted. Would that this attempt had been made on a larger scale, that the writer to whom I refer* had in consequence developed his opinions systematically, and carried them yet further back, even to their ultimate principle!

But this the scientific world has yet to expect; or it is more than probable that the present humble endeavor would have been superseded, or confined, at least, to the task of restating the opinion of my predecessor with such modifications as the differences that will always exist between men who have thought independently, and each for himself, have never failed to introduce, even on problems of far easier and more obvious solution.

Without further preface or apology, therefore, I shall state at once my objections to all the definitions that have hitherto been given of Life, as meaning too much or too little, with an exception, however, in favor of those which mean nothing at all; and even these last must, in certain cases, receive an honor they do not merit, and be confuted, or rather detected, on account of their too general acceptance, and the incalculable power of words over the minds of men in proportion to the remoteness of the subject from the cognizance of the senses.

It would be equally presumptuous and unreasonable should I, with a late writer on this subject, "exhort the reader to be particularly on his guard against loose and indefinite expressions;" but I perfectly agree with him that they are the bane of all science, and have been remarkably injurious in the different departments of physiology.

The attempts to explain the nature of Life, which have fallen within my knowledge, presuppose the arbitrary division of all that surrounds us into things with life, and things without life—a division grounded on a mere assumption. At the best, it can be regarded only as a hasty deduction from the first superficial notices of the objects that surround us, sufficient, perhaps, for the purpose of ordi-

* Mr. Abernethy.

nary discrimination, but far too indeterminate and diffluent to be taken unexamined by the philosophic inquirer. The positions of science must be tried in the jeweller's scales, not like the mixed commodities of the market, on the weigh-bridge of common opinion and vulgar usage. Such, however, has been the procedure in the present instance, and the result has been answerable to the coarseness of the process. By a comprisal of the *petitio principii* with the *argumentum in circulo*,—in plain English, by an easy logic, which begins with begging the question, and then moving in a circle, comes round to the point where it began,—each of the two divisions has been made to define the other by a mere reassertion of their assumed contrariety. The physiologist has luminously explained Y plus X by informing us that it is a somewhat that is the antithesis of Y minus X; and if we ask, what then is Y — X? the answer is, the antithesis of Y + X, a reciprocation of great service, that may remind us of the twin sisters in the fable of the Lamiæ, with but one eye between them both, which each borrowed from the other as either happened to want it; but with this additional disadvantage, that in the present case it is after all but an eye of glass. The definitions themselves will best illustrate our meaning. I will begin with that given by Bichat. "Life is the sum of all the functions by which death is resisted," in which I have in vain endeavored to discover any other meaning than that life consists in being able to live. This author, with a whimsical gravity, prefaces his definition with the remark, that the nature of life has hitherto been sought for in *abstract* considerations; as if it were possible that four more inveterate abstractions could be brought together in one sentence than are here assembled in the words, life, death, function, and resistance. Similar instances might be cited from Richerand and others. The word Life is translated into other more learned words; and this *paraphrase* of the *term* is substituted for the *definition* of the *thing*, and therefore (as is always the case in every *real* definition as contra-distinguished from a *verbal* definition), for at least a partial *solution* of the *fact*. Such as these form the *first* class.—The second class takes some one particular function of Life common to all living objects,—nutrition, for instance; or, to adopt the phrase most in vogue at present, assimilation, for the purposes of reproduction and growth. Now this, it is evident, can be an appropriate definition only of the very lowest species, as of a Fungus or a Mollusca; and just as comprehensive an idea of the mystery of Life, as a Mollusca might give, can this definition afford. But this is not the only objection. For, *first*, it is not pretended that we begin with seeking for an organ evidently appropriated to nutrition, and then infer that the substance in which such an organ is found *lives*. On the contrary, in a number of cases among the obscurer animals and vegetables we infer the organ from the pre-established fact of its life. *Secondly*, it identifies the process itself with a certain range of its forms, those, namely, by which it is manifested in animals and vegetables. For this, too, no less than the former, presupposes the arbitrary division of all things into not living and lifeless, on which, as I before observed, all these definitions are grounded. But it is sorry logic to take the proof of an affirmative in one thing as the proof of the negative in another. All animals that have lungs breathe, but it would be a childish oversight to deduce the converse, viz. all animals that breathe have lungs. The theory in which the French chemists organized the discoveries of Black, Cavendish, Priestley, Scheele, and other English and German philosophers, is still, indeed, the reigning theory, but rather, it should seem, from the absence of a rival sufficiently popular to fill the throne in its stead, than from the continuance of an implicit belief in its own stability. We no longer at least cherish that intensity of faith which, before Davy commenced his briliant career, had not only identified it with chemistry itself, but had substituted its nomenclature, even in common conversation, for the far more philosophic language which the human race had abstracted from the laboratory of Nature. I may venture to prophesy that no future Beddoes will make it the corival of the mathematical sciences in demonstrative evidence. I think it a matter of doubt whether, during the period of its supposed infallibility, physiology derived more benefit from the extension, or injury from the misdirection, of its views. Enough of the latter is fresh in recollection to make it but an equivocal compliment to a physiological position, that it must stand or fall with the corpuscular philosophy, as modified by the French theory of chemistry. Yet should it happen (and the event is not impossible, nor the supposition altogether absurd), that more and more decisive facts should present themselves in confirmation of the metamorphosis of elements, the position that life consists in assimilation would either cease to be distinctive, or fall back into the former class as an identical proposition, namely, that Life, meaning by the word that sort of growth which takes place by means of a peculiar organization, consists in that sort of growth which is peculiar to organized life. *Thirdly*, the definition involves a still more egregious flaw in the reasoning, namely, that of *cum hoc, ergo propter hoc* (or the assumption of causation from mere coexistence); and this, too, in its very worst form. For it is not *cum hoc solo, ergo propter hoc*, which would in many cases supply a presumptive proof by induction, but *cum hoc, et plurimis aliis, ergo propter hoc!* Shell, of some kind or other, is common to the whole order of testacea, but it would be absurd to define the *vis vitæ* of testaceous animals as existing in the shell, though we know it to be the constant accompaniment, and have every reason to believe the constant effect, of the specific life that acts in those animals. Were we (*argumenti causâ*) to imagine shell coextensive with the organized creation, this would produce no abatement in the falsity of the reasoning. Nor does the flaw stop here; for a physiological, that is, a real, definition, as distinguished from the verbal definitions of lexicography, must consist neither in any single property or function of the thing to be defined, nor yet in all collectively, which latter, indeed, would be a history, not a definition. It must consist, therefore, in the *law* of the thing, or in such an *idea* of it, as being admitted, all the properties and functions are admitted by implication. It must likewise be so far *causal*, that a full insight having been obtained of the law, we derive from it a progressive insight into the necessity and *generation* of the phenomena of which it is the law. Suppose a disease in question, which appeared always accompanied with certain symptoms in certain stages, and with some one or more symptoms in all stages—say deranged digestion, capricious alternation of vivacity and languor, headache, dilated pupil, diminished sensibility to light, &c.—Neither the men who selected the one constant symptom, nor he who enumerated all the symptoms, would give the scientific definition *talem scilicet, quali scientia fit vel datur*, but the man who at once named and defined the disease hydrocephalus, producing pressure on the brain. For it is the essence of a scientific definition to be causative, not by introduction of imaginary somewhats, natural or supernatural, under the name of causes, but by announcing the law of action in the particular case, in subordination to the common law of which all the phenomena are modifications or results.

Now in the definition on which, as the representative of a whole class, we are *now* animadverting, a single effect is given as constituting the cause. For nutrition by digestion is certainly necessary to life, only under certain circumstances, but that life is previously necessary to digestion is absolutely certain under all circumstances. Besides, what other phenomenon of Life would the conception of assimilation, *per se*, or as it exists in the lowest order of animals, involve or explain? How, for instance, does it include sensation, locomotion, or habit? or if the two former should be taken as distinct from life, *toto genere*, and supervenient to it, we then ask what conception is given of *vital* assimilation as contra-distinguished from that of the nucleus of a crystal?

Lastly, this definition confounds the Law of Life, or the primary and universal form of vital agency, with the conception, Animals. For the kind, it substitutes the representative of its degrees and modifications. But the first and most important office of science, physical, or physiological, is to contemplate the power in kind, abstracted from the degree. The ideas of caloric, whether as substance or property, and the conception of latent heat, the heat in ice, &c., that excite the wonder or the laughter of the vulgar, though susceptible of the most important practical applications, are the result of this abstraction; while the only purpose to which a definition like the preceding could become subservient, would be in supplying a nomenclature with the character of the most common species of a genus—its *genus generalissimum*, and even this would be useless in the present instance, inasmuch as it presupposes the knowledge of the things characterized.

The third class, and far superior to the two former, selects some property characteristic of all living bodies, not merely found in all *animals* alike, but existing equally in all parts of all living things, both animals and plants. Such, for instance, is the definition of Life, as consisting in anti-putrescence, or the power of resisting putrefaction. Like all the others, however, even this confines the idea of Life to those degrees or concentrations of it, which manifest themselves in organized beings, or rather in those the organization of which is apparent to us. Consequently, it substitutes an abstract term, or generalization of effects, for the idea, or superior form of causative agency. At best, it describes the *vis vitæ* by one only of its many influences. It is however, as we have said before, preferable to the former, because it is not, as they are, altogether unfruitful, inasmuch as it attests, less equivocally than any other sign, the presence or absence of that degree of the *vis vitæ* which is the necessary condition of organic or self-renewing power. It throws no light, however, on the law or principle of action; it does not increase our insight into the other phenomena; it presents to us no *inclusive* form, out of which the other forms may be developed, and finally, its defect as a definition may be detected by generalizing it into a higher formula, as a power which, during its continuance, resists or subordinates heterogeneous and adverse powers. Now this holds equally true of chemical relatively to the mechanical powers; and really affirms no more of Life than may be equally affirmed of every form of being, namely, that it tends to preserve itself, and resists, to a certain extent, whatever is incompatible with the laws that constitute its particular state for the time being. For it is not true only of the great divisions or classes into which we have found it expedient to distinguish, while we generalize, the powers acting in nature, as into intellectual, vital, chemical, mechanical; but it holds equally true of the degrees, or species of each of these genera relatively to each other: as in the decomposition of the alkalies by heat, or the galvanic spark. Like the combining power of Life, the copula here resists for awhile the attempts to dissolve it, and then yields, to reappear in new phenomena.

It is a wonderful property of the human mind, that when once a momentum has been given to it in a fresh direction, it pursues the new path with obstinate perseverance, in all conceivable bearings, to its utmost extremes. And by the startling consequences which arise out of these extremes, it is first awakened to its error, and either recalled to some former track, or receives some fresh impulse, which it follows with the same eagerness, and admits to the same monopoly. Thus in the 13th century the first science which roused the intellects of men from the torpor of barbarism, was, as in all countries ever has been, and ever must be the case, the science of *Metaphysics* and *Ontology*. We first seek what can be found at home, and what wonder if truths, that appeared to reveal the secret depths of our own souls, should take possession of the whole mind, and all truths appear trivial which could not either be evolved out of similar principles, by the same process, or at least brought under the same forms of thought, by perceived or imagined analogies? And so it was. For more than a century men continued to invoke the oracle of their own spirits, not only concerning its own forms and modes of being, but likewise concerning the laws of external nature. All attempts at philosophical explication were commenced by a mere effort of the understanding, as the power of abstraction; or by the imagination, transferring its own experiences to every object presented from without. By the former, a class of phenomena were in the first place abstracted, and fixed in some general term: of course this could designate only the impressions made by the outward objects, and so far, therefore, having been thus metamorphosed, they were effects of these objects; but then made to supply the place of their own causes, under the name of occult qualities. Thus the properties peculiar to gold, were abstracted from those it possessed in common with other bodies, and then generalized in the term *Aureity:* and the inquirer was instructed that the Essence of Gold, or the cause which constituted the peculiar modification of matter called gold, was the power of aureity. By the latter, *i. e.* by the imagination, thought and will were superadded to the occult quality, and every form of nature had its appropriate Spirit, to be controlled or conciliated by an appropriate ceremonial. This was entitled its SUBSTANTIAL FORM. Thus, physic became a sort of dull poetry, and the art of medicine (for physiology could scarcely be said to exist) was a system of magic, blended with traditional empiricism. Thus the forms of thought proceeded to act in their own emptiness, with no attempt to fill or substantiate them by the information of the senses, and all the branches of science formed so many sections of logic and metaphysics. And so it continued, even to the time that the Reformation sounded the second trumpet, and the authority of the schools sank with that of the hierarchy, under the intellectual courage and activity which this great revolution had inspired. Power, once awakened, cannot rest in one object. All the sciences partook of the new influences. The world of experimental philosophy was soon mapped out for posterity by the comprehensive and enterprising genius of Bacon, and the laws explained by which experiment could be dignified into experience.* But no sooner was the impulse given, than the same propensity was made manifest of looking at all things in the one point of view which chanced to be of predominant attraction. Our Gilbert, a man of genuine philosophical genius, had no sooner multiplied the facts of magnetism, and extended our knowledge concerning the property of magnetic bodies, but all things in heaven, and earth, and in the waters beneath the earth, were resolved into *magnetic* influences.

Shortly after a new light was struck by Harriott and Descartes, with their contemporaries, or immediate predecessors, and the restoration of ancient geometry, aided by the modern invention of algebra, placed the science of mechanism on the philosophic throne. How widely this domination spread, and how long it continued, if, indeed, even now it can be said to have abdicated its pretensions, the reader need not be reminded. The sublime discoveries of Newton, and, together with these, his not less fruitful than wonderful application, of the higher mathesis to the movements of the celestial bodies, and to the laws of light, gave almost a religious sanction to the corpuscular system and mechanical theory. It became synonymous with philosophy itself. It was the sole portal at which truth was permitted to enter. The human body was treated of as an hydraulic machine, the operations of medicine were solved, and alas! even directed by reference partly to gravitation and the laws of motion, and partly by chemistry, which itself, however, as far as its theory was concerned, was but a branch of mechanics working exclusively by imaginary wedges, angles, and spheres. Should the reader chance to put his hand on the 'Principles of Philosophy,' by La Forge, an immediate disciple of Descartes, he may see the phenomena of sleep solved in a copper-plate engraving, with all the figures into which the globules of the blood shaped themselves, and the results demonstrated by mathematical calculations. In short, from the time of Kepler† to that of Newton, and from Newton to Hartley, not only all things in external nature, but the subtlest mysteries of life and organization, and even of the intellect and moral being, were conjured within the magic circle of mathematical formulæ. And now a new light was struck by the discovery of electricity, and, in every sense of the word, both playful and serious, both for good and for evil, it may be affirmed to have electrified the whole frame of natural philosophy. Close on its heels followed the momentous discovery of the principal gases by Scheele and Priestley, the composition of water

* Experiment, as an organ of reason, not less distinguished from the blind or dreaming industry of the alchemists, than it was successfully opposed to the barren subtleties of the schoolmen.

† Whose own mind, however, was not comprehended in the vortex; where Kepler erred it was in the other extreme.

by Cavendish, and the doctrine of latent heat by Black. The scientific world was prepared for a new dynasty; accordingly, as soon as Lavoisier had reduced the infinite variety of chemical phenomena to the actions, reactions, and interchanges of a few elementary substances, or at least excited the expectation that this would speedily be effected, the hope shot up, almost instantly, into full faith, that it had been effected. Henceforward the new path, thus brilliantly opened, became the common road to all departments of knowledge: and, to this moment, it has been pursued with an eagerness and almost epidemic enthusiasm which, scarcely less than its political revolutions, characterize the spirit of the age. Many and inauspicious have been the invasions and inroads of this new conqueror into the rightful territories of other sciences; and strange alterations have been made in less harmless points than those of terminology, in homage to an art unsettled, in the very ferment of imperfect discoveries, and either without a theory, or with a theory maintained only by composition and compromise. Yet this very circumstance has favored its encroachments, by the gratifications which its novelty affords to our curiosity, and by the keener interest and higher excitement which an unsettled and revolutionary state is sure to inspire. He who supposes that science possesses an immunity from such influences knows little of human nature. How, otherwise, could men of strong minds and sound judgments have attempted to penetrate by the clue of chemical experiment, the secret recesses, the sacred adyta of organic life, without being aware that chemistry must needs be at its extreme limits, when it has approached the threshold of a higher power? Its own transgressions, however, and the failure of its enterprises will become the means of defining its absolute boundary, and we shall have to guard against the opposite error of rejecting its aid altogether as analogy, because we have repelled its ambitious claims to an identity with the vital powers.

Previously to the submitting my own ideas on the subject of life, and the powers into which it resolves itself, or rather in which it is manifested to *us*, I have hazarded this apparent digression from the anxiety to *preclude certain suspicions*, which the subject itself is so fitted to awaken, and while I anticipate the charges, to plead in answer to each a full and unequivocal—not guilty!

In the first place, therefore, I distinctly disclaim all intention of explaining life into an occult quality; and retort the charge on those who can satisfy themselves with defining it as the peculiar power by which death is resisted.

Secondly. Convinced—by revelation, by the consenting authority of all countries, and of all ages, by the imperative voice of my own conscience, and by that wide chasm between man and the noblest animals of the brute creation, which no perceivable or conceivable difference of organization is sufficient to overbridge—that I have a rational and responsible soul, I think far too reverentially of the same to degrade it into an hypothesis, and cannot be blind to the contradiction I must incur, if I assign that soul which I believe to constitute the peculiar nature of man as the cause of functions and properties, which man possesses in common with the oyster and the mushroom.*

Thirdly, while I disclaim the error of Stahl in deriving the phenomena of life from the unconscious actions of the rational soul, I repel with still greater earnestness the assertion and even the supposition that the functions are the offspring of the structure, and "Life† the result of organization," connected with it as effect with cause. Nay, the position seems to me little less strange, than as if a man should say, that building with all the included handicraft, of plastering, sawing, planing, &c. were the offspring of the house; and that the mason and carpenter were the result of a suite of chambers, with the passages and staircases that lead to them. To make A the offspring of B, when the very existence of B as B presupposes the existence of A, is preposterous in the *literal* sense of the word, and a consummate instance of the *hysteron proteron* in logic. But if I reject the organ as the *cause* of that, of which it is the organ, though I might admit it among the *conditions* of its actual functions; for the same reason I must reject *fluids* and *ethers* of all kinds, magnetical, electrical, and universal, to whatever quintessential thinness they may be treble distilled, and (as it were) super-substantiated. With these, I abjure likewise all *chemical* agencies, compositions, and decompositions, were it only that as stimulants they suppose a stimulability *sui generis*, which is but another paraphrase for life. Or if they are themselves at once both the excitant and the excitability, I miss the connecting link between this imaginary ether and the visible body, which then becomes no otherwise distinguished from inanimate matter, than by its juxtaposition in mere space, with an heterogeneous inmate, the cycle of whose actions revolves within itself. Besides which I should think that I was confounding metaphors and realities most absurdly, if I imagined that I had a greater insight into the meaning and possibility of a living alcohol, than of a living quicksilver. In short, visible SURFACE and *power* of any kind, much more the *power* of life, are ideas which the very forms of the human under-

* But still less would I avail myself of its acknowledged inappropriateness to the purposes of physiology, in order to cast a self-complacent sneer on the soul itself, and on all who believe in its existence. First, because in my opinion it would be impertinent; secondly, because it would be imprudent and injurious to the character of my profession; and, lastly, because it would argue an irreverence to the feelings of mankind, which I deem scarcely compatible with a good heart, and a degree of arrogance and presumption which I have never found, except in company with a corrupt taste and a shallow capacity.

† Vide Lawrence's Lecture.

standing make it impossible to identify. But whether the powers which manifest themselves to us under certain conditions in the forms of electricity, or chemical attraction, have any analogy to the power which manifests itself in growth and organization, is altogether a different question, and demands altogether a different chain of reasoning: if it be indeed a tree of knowledge, it will be known by its fruits, and these will depend not on the mere assertion, but on the inductions by which the position is supported, and by the additions which it makes to our insight into the nature of the facts it is meant to illustrate.

To *account* for Life is one thing: to explain Life another. In the first we are supposed to state something prior (if not in time, yet in the order of Nature) to the thing accounted for, as the ground or cause of that thing, or (which comprises the meaning and force of both words) as its *sufficient cause, quæ et facit, et subest.* And to this, in the question of Life, I know no possible answer, but GOD. To account for a thing is to see into the principle of its possibility, and from that principle to evolve its being. Thus the mathematician demonstrates the truths of geometry by constructing them. It is an admirable remark of Joh. Bapt. a Vico, in a Tract published at Naples, 1710,* "Geometrica ideò demonstramus, quia facimus; physica si demonstrare possimus, faceremus. Metaphysici veri claritas eadem ac lucis, quam non nisi per opaca cognoscimus; nam non lucem sed lucidas res videmus. Physica sunt opaca, nempe formata et finita, in quibus Metaphysici veri lumen videmus." The reasoner who assigns structure or organization as the antecedent of Life, who names the former a cause, and the *latter* its effect, *he* it is who pretends to account for life. Now Euclid would, with great right, demand of such a philosopher to *make* Life; in the same sense, I mean, in which Euclid makes an Icosaedron, or a figure of twenty sides, namely, in the understanding or by an intellectual construction. An argument which, of itself, is sufficient to prove the untenable nature of Materialism.

To explain a power, on the other hand, is (the power itself being assumed, though not comprehended, *ut qui datur, non intelligitur*) to unfold or spread it out: *ex implicito planum facere.* In the present instance, such an explanation would consist in the reduction of the idea of Life to its simplest and most comprehensive form or mode of action; that is, to some characteristic *instinct* or *tendency*, evident in all its manifestations, and involved in the idea itself. This assumed as existing in *kind*, it will be required to present an ascending series of corresponding phenomena as involved *in*, proceeding *from*, and so far therefore explained *by*, the supposition of its progressive inten-

* Joh. Bapt. a Vico, Neapol. Reg. eloq. Professor, de antiquissima Italorum sapientia ex lingua Latina originibus eruendâ: libri tres. Neap., 1710.

sity and of the gradual enlargement of its sphere, the necessity of which again must be contained in the idea of the tendency itself. In other words, the tendency having been given in *kind*, it is required to render the phenomena intelligible as its different degrees and modifications. Still more perfect will the explanation be, should the necessity of this progression and of these ascending gradations be contained in the assumed idea of life, as thus defined by the general form and common purport of all its various tendencies. This done, we have only to add the conditions common to all its phenomena, and those appropriate to each place and rank, in the scale of ascent, and then proceed to determine the primary and constitutive forms, *i. e.* the elementary powers in which this tendency realizes itself under different degrees and conditions.*

* The object I have proposed to myself, and wherein its distinction exists, may be thus illustrated. A complex machine is presented to the common view, the moving power of which is hidden. Of those who are studying and examining it, *one* man fixes his attention on some one application of that power, on certain effects produced by that particular application, and on a certain part of the structure evidently appropriated to tho production of these effects, neither the one or other of which he had discovered in a neighboring machine, which he at the same time asserts to be quite distinct from the former, and to be moved by a power altogether different, though many of the works and operations are, he admits, common to both machines. In this supposed peculiarity he places the essential character of the former machine, and defines it by the presence of that which is, or which he supposes to be, absent in the latter. Supposing that a stranger to both were about to visit the two machines, this peculiarity would be so far useful as that it might enable him to distinguish the one from the other, and thus to look in the proper place for whatever else he had heard remarkable concerning either; not that he or his informant would understand the machine any better or otherwise, than the common character of a whole class in the nomenclature of botany would enable a person to understand all, or any one of the plants contained in that class. But if, on the other hand, the machine in question were such as no man was a stranger to, if even the supposed peculiarity, either by its effects, or by the construction of that portion of the works which produced them, were equally well known to all men, in this case we can conceive no use at all of such a definition; for at the best it could only be admitted as a definition for the purposes of nomenclature, which never adds to knowledge, although it may often facilitate its communication. But in this instance it would be nomenclature misplaced, and without an object. Such appears to me to be the case with all those definitions which place the essence of Life in nutrition, contractility, &c. As the second instance, I will take the inventor and maker of the machine himself, who knows its moving power, or perhaps himself constitutes it, who is, as it were, the soul of the work, and in whose mind all its parts, with all their bearings and relations, had pre-existed long before the machine itself had been put together. In him therefore there would reside, what it would be presumption to attempt to acquire, or to pretend to communicate, the most perfect insight not only of the machine itself, and of all its various operations, but of its ultimate principle and its essential causes. The mysterious ground, the efficient causes of vitality, and whether different lives differ absolutely or only in degree, He alone can know who not only said, "Let the earth bring forth the living creature, the beast of the earth after his kind, and it was so;" but who said, "Let us make man in our image, who himself breathed into his nostrils the breath of Life, and *man* became a living soul."

The third case which I would apply to my own attempt would be that of the inquirer, who, presuming to know nothing of the power that moves the whole machine, takes those parts of it which are presented to his view, seeks to reduce its various movements to as few and simple laws of motion as possible, and out of their separate and conjoint action proceeds to explain and appropriate the structure and relative positions of the

What is Life? Were such a question proposed, we should be tempted to answer, what is *not* Life that really *is?* Our reason convinces us that the quantities of things, taken abstractedly as quantity, exist only in the relations they bear to the percipient; in plainer words, they exist only in our minds, *ut quorum esse est percipi.* For if the definite quantities have a ground, and therefore a reality, in the external world, and independent of the mind that perceives them, this ground is *ipso facto* a quality; the very etymon of this word showing that a quality, not taken in its own nature but in relation to another thing, is to be defined *causa sufficiens, entia, de quibus loquimur; esse talia, qualia sunt.* Either the quantities perceived exist only in the perception, or they have likewise a real existence. In the former case, the quality (the word is here used in an active sense) that determines them belongs to Life, *per ipsam hypothesin;* and in the other case, since by the agreement of all parties Life may exist in other forms than those of consciousness, or even of sensibility, the *onus probandi* falls on those who assert of any quality that it is *not* Life. For the analogy of all that we know is clearly in favor of the contrary supposition, and if a man would analyze the meaning of his own words, and carefully distinguish his perceptions and sensations from the external cause exciting them, and at the same time from the quantity or superficies under which that cause is acting, he would instantly find himself, if we mistake not, involuntarily identifying the ideas of Quality and Life. Life, it is admitted on all hands, does not necessarily imply consciousness or sensibility; and we, for our parts, can not see that the irritability which metals manifest to galvanism, can be more remote from that which may be supposed to exist in the tribe of lichens, or in the helvellæ, pezizee, &c., than the latter is from the phenomena of excitability in the human body, whatever name it may be called by, or in whatever way it may modify itself.* That the mere act of growth does not constitute the idea of Life, or the absence of that act exclude it, we have a proof in every egg before it is placed under the hen, and in every grain of corn before it is put into the soil. All that could be deduced by fair reasoning would amount to this only, that the life of metals, as the power which affects and determines their comparative cohesion, ductility, &c., was yet lower on the scale than the Life which produces the first attempts of

works. In obedience to the canon,—"Principia non esse multiplicanda præter summam necessitatem cui suffragamur non ideo quia causalem in mundo unitatem vel ratione vel experientiâ perspiciamus, sed illam ipsam indagamus impulsu intellectûs, qui tantundem sibi in explicotaine phænomenorum profecisse videtur quantum ab eodem principio ad plurima rationata descendere ipsi concessum est."

* The arborescent forms on a frosty morning, to be seen on the window and pavement, must have *some* relation to the more perfect forms developed in the vegetable world.

organization, in the almost shapeless tremella, or in such fungi as grow in the dark recesses of the mine.

If it were asked, to what purpose or with what view we should generalize the idea of Life thus broadly, I should not hesitate to reply that, were there no other use conceivable, there would be *some* advantage in merely destroying an arbitrary assumption in natural philosophy, and in reminding the physiologists that they could not hear the life of metals asserted with a more contemptuous surprise than they themselves incur from the vulgar, when they speak of the Life in mould or mucor. But this is not the case. This wider view not only precludes a groundless assumption, it likewise fills up the arbitrary chasm between physics and physiology, and justifies us in using the former as means of insight into the latter, which would be contrary to all sound rules of ratiocination if the powers working in the objects of the two sciences were absolutely and essentially diverse. For as to abstract the idea of *kind* from that of *degrees*, which are alone designated in the language of common use, is the first and indispensable step in philosophy, so are we the better enabled to form a notion of the *kind*, the lower the *degree* and the simpler the form is in which it appears to us. We study the complex in the simple; and only from the intuition of the lower can we safely proceed to the intellection of the higher degrees. The only danger lies in the leaping from low to high, with the neglect of the intervening gradations. But the same error would introduce discord into the gamut, *et ab abusu contra usum non valet consequentia.* That these degrees will themselves bring forth secondary kinds sufficiently distinct for all the purposes of science, and even for common sense, will be seen in the course of this inquisition: for this is one proof of the essential vitality of nature, that she does not ascend as links in a suspended chain, but as the steps in a ladder; or rather she at one and the same time *ascends* as by a climax, and expands as the concentric circles on the lake from the point to which the stone in its fall had given the first impulse. At all events, a contemptuous rejection of this mode of reasoning would come with an ill grace from a medical philosopher, who cannot combine any three phenomena of health or of disease without the assumption of powers, which he is compelled to deduce without being able to demonstrate; nay, even of material substances as the *vehicles* of these powers, which he can never expect to exhibit before the senses.

From the preceding it should appear, that the most comprehensive formula to which life is reducible, would be that of the internal copula of bodies, or (if we may venture to borrow a phrase from the Platonic school) the *power* which discloses itself from within as a principle of *unity* in the *many*. But that there is a physiognomy in words, which, without reference to their fitness or necessity, make unfavorable as well as favorable impressions, and that every unusual term in an abstruse research incurs the risk of being denominated jargon, I should at the same time have borrowed a scholastic *term*, and defined life *absolutely*, as the principle of unity in *multeity*, as far as the former, the unity to wit, is produced *ab intra;* but *eminently* (*sensu eminenti*), I define life as *the principle of individuation*, or the power which unites a given *all* into a *whole* that is presupposed by all its parts. The link that combines the two, and acts throughout both, will, of course, be defined by the *tendency* to *individuation.* Thus, from its utmost *latency*, in which life is one with the elementary powers of mechanism, that is, with the powers of mechanism considered as qualitative and actually synthetic, to its highest manifestation (in which, as the *vis vitæ vivida*, or life *as* life, it subordinates and modifies these powers, becoming contra-distinguished from mechanism,* *ab extra*, under the form of organization), there is an ascending series of intermediate classes, and of analogous gradations in each class. To a reflecting mind, indeed, the very fact that the powers peculiar to life in living animals *include* cohesion, elasticity, &c. (or, in the words of a late publication, "that living matter exhibits these physical properties,"†) would demonstrate that, in the truth of things, they are homogeneous, and that both the classes are but degrees and different dignities of one and the same tendency. For the latter are not subjected to the former as a lever, or walking-stick to the muscles; the more intense the life is, the less does *elasticity*, for instance, appear *as* elasticity. It sinks down into the nearest approach to its *physical* form by a series of degrees from the contraction and elongation of the irritable muscle to the physical hardness of the insensitive nail. The lower powers are *assimilated*, not merely *employed*, and assimilation presupposes the homogeneous nature of the thing assimilated; else it is a miracle, only not the same as that of a *creation*, because it would imply that additional and equal miracle of annihilation. In short, all the impossibilities which the acutest of the reformed Divines have detected in the hypothesis of transubstantiation would apply, *totidem verbis et syllabis*, to that of assimilation, if the objects and the agents were really heterogeneous. Unless, therefore, a thing can exhibit properties which do not belong to it, the very admission that living matter exhibits *physical* properties, includes the further admission, that those physical or dead properties are themseves vital

* Thus we may say that whatever is organized from without, is a product of mechanism; whatever is mechanized from within, is a production of organization.

† "The matter that surrounds us is divided into two great classes, living and dead; the latter is governed by physical laws, such as attraction, gravitation, chemical affinity; and it exhibits physical properties, such as cohesion, elasticity, divisibility, &c. Living matter also exhibits these properties, and is subject, in great measure, to physical laws. But living bodies are endowed moreover with a set of properties altogether different from these, and contrasting with them very remarkably." (Vide Lawrence's Lectures, p. 121.)

in essence, really *distinct* but in appearance only *different;* or in absolute contrast with each other.

In all cases that which, *abstractly* taken, is the definition of the *kind*, will, when applied *absolutely*, or in its fullest sense, be the definition of the highest *degree* of that kind. If life, in general, be defined *vis ab intra, cujus proprium est coadunare plura in rem unicam, quantùm est res unica;* the unity will be more intense in proportion as it constitutes each particular thing a whole of itself; and yet more, again, in proportion to the number and interdependence of the parts, which it unites as a whole. But a whole composed, *ab intra*, of different parts, so far interdependent that each is reciprocally means and end, is an individual, and the individuality is most intense where the greatest dependence of the parts on the whole is combined with the greatest dependence of the whole on its parts; the first (namely, the dependence of the parts on the whole) being absolute; the second (namely, the dependence of the whole on its parts) being proportional to the importance of the relation which the parts have to the whole, that is, as their action extends more or less beyond themselves. For this spirit of the whole is most expressed in that part which derives its importance as an End from its importance as a Mean, relatively to all the parts under the same copula.

Finally, of individuals, the living power will be most intense in that individual which, as a whole, has the greatest number of integral parts presupposed in it; when, moreover, these integral parts, together with a proportional increase of their interdependence, as *parts*, have themselves most the character of wholes in the sphere occupied by them. A mathematical point, line, or surface, is an *ens rationis*, for it expresses an intellectual act; but a physical atom is *ens fictitium*, which may be made subservient, as ciphers are in arithmetic, to the purposes of hypothetical construction, *per regulam falsi;* but transferred to *Nature*, it is in the strictest sense an *absurd* quantity; for extension, and consequently divisibility, or *multeity** (for space can not be divided), is the indispensable condition, under which alone any thing can *appear* to us, or even be *thought* of, as a *thing*. But if it should be replied, that the elementary particles are atoms not positively, but by such a hardness communicated to them as is relatively invincible, I should remind the asserter that *temeraria citatio supernaturalium est pulvinar intellectûs pigri*, and that he who requires me to believe a miracle of his own dreaming, must first work a mira-

* Much against my will I repeat this scholastic term, *multeity*, but I have sought in vain for an unequivocal word of a less repulsive character, that would convey the notion in a positive and not comparative sense in kind, as opposed to the *unum et simplex*, not in degree, as contracted with the *few*. We can conceive no reason that can be adduced in justification of the word *caloric*, as invented to distinguish the external cause of the sensation heat, which would not equally authorize the introduction of a technical term in this instance.

cle to convince me that he had dreamt by inspiration. Add too, the gross inconsistency of resorting to an immaterial influence in order to complete a system of materialism, by the exclusion of all modes of existence which the theorist cannot in imagination, at least, *finger* and *peep* at! Each of the preceding gradations, as above defined, might be represented as they exist, and are realized in Nature. But each would require a work for itself, co-extensive with the science of metals, and that of fossils (both as geologically applied); of crystallization; and of vegetable and animal physiology, in all its distinct branches. The nature of the present essay scarcely permits the space sufficient to illustrate our meaning. The proof of its probability (for to that only can we arrive by so partial an application of the hypothesis), is to be found in its powers of solving the particular class of phenomena, that form the subjects of the present inquisition, more satisfactorily and profitably than has been done, or even attempted before.

Exclusively, therefore, for the purposes of *illustration*, I would take as an instance of the first step, the metals, those, namely, that are capable of permanent reduction. For, by the established laws of nomenclature, the others (as sodium, potassium, calcium, silicium, &c.) would be entitled to a class of their own, under the name of *bases*. It is long since the chemists have despaired of decomposing this class of bodies. They still remain, one and all, as elements or simple bodies, though, on the principles of the corpuscularian philosophy, nothing can be more improbable than that they really are such; and no reason has or can be assigned on the grounds of that system, why, in no one instance, the contrary has not been proved. But this is at once explained, if we assume them as the simplest form of unity, namely, the unity of powers and properties. For these, it is evident, may be endlessly modified, but can never be decomposed. If I were asked by a philosopher who had previously extended the attribute of Life to the *Byssus speciosa*, and even to the crustaceous matter, or outward bones of a lobster, &c., whether the ingot of gold expressed *life*, I should answer without hesitation, as the *ingot* of gold assuredly not, for its form is accidental and *ab extra*. It may be added to or detracted from without in the least affecting the nature, state, or properties in the specific matter of which the ingot consists. But as *gold*, as that special union of absolute and of relative gravity, ductility, and hardness, which, wherever they are found, constitute *gold*, I should answer no less fearlessly, in the affirmative. But I should further add, that of the two counteracting tendencies of nature, namely, that of *detachment* from the universal life, which universality is represented to us by gravitation, and that of *attachment* or reduction into it, this and the other noble metals represented the units in which the latter tendency, namely, that of identity with the life of nature, subsisted in the greatest overbalance over the former. It is the form of unity with the least degree of tendency to individuation.

Rising in the ascent, I should take, as illustrative of the second step, the various forms of crystals as a union, not of powers only, but of parts, and as the simplest forms of composition in the next narrowest sphere of affinity. Here the form, or apparent *quantity*, is manifestly the result of the *quality*, and the chemist himself not seldom admits them as infallible characters of the substances united in the whole of a given crystal.

In the first step, we had Life, as the mere *unity* of powers; in the second we have the simplest forms of *totality* evolved. The third step is presented to us in those vast formations, the tracing of which generically would form the science of Geology, or its history in the strict sense of the word, even as their description and diagnostics constitute its preliminaries.

Their claim to this rank I cannot here even attempt to support. It will be sufficient to explain my reason for having assigned it to them, by the avowal, that I regard them in a twofold point of view: 1st, as the residue and product of vegetable and animal life; 2d, as manifesting the tendencies of the Life of Nature to vegetation or animalization. And this process I believe—in one instance by the peat morasses of the northern, and in the other instance by the coral banks of the southern hemisphere—to be still connected with the present order of vegetable and animal Life, which constitutes the fourth and last step in these wide and comprehensive divisions.

In the lowest forms of the vegetable and animal world we perceive totality dawning into *individuation*, while in man, as the highest of the class, the individuality is not only perfected in its corporeal sense, but begins a new series beyond the appropriate limits of physiology. The tendency to individuation, more or less obscure, more or less obvious, constitutes the common character of all classes, as far as they maintain for themselves a distinction from the universal life of the planet; while the degrees, both of intensity and extension, to which this tendency is realized, form the species, and their ranks in the great scale of ascent and expansion.

In the treatment of a subject so vast and complex, within the limits prescribed for an essay like the present, where it is impossible not to say either too much or too little (and too much because too little), an author is entitled to make large claims on the candor of his judges. Many things he must express inaccurately, not from ignorance or oversight, but because the more precise expression would have involved the necessity of a further explanation, and this another, even to the first elements of the science. This is an inconvenience which presses on the analytic method, on however large a scale it may be conducted, compared with the synthetic; and it must bear with a tenfold weight in the present instance, where we are not permitted to avail ourselves of its usual advantages as a counterbalance to its inherent defects. I shall have done all that I dared propose to myself, or that can be justly demanded of me by others, if I have succeeded in conveying a sufficiently clear, though indistinct and inadequate notion, so as of its many results to render intelligible that one which I am to apply to my particular subject, not as a truth already demonstrated, but as an hypothesis, which pretends to no higher merit than that of explaining the particular class of phenomena to which it is applied, and ask no other reward than a presumption in favor of the general system of which it affirms itself to be a dependent though integral part. By Life I everywhere mean the true Idea of Life, or that most general form under which Life manifests itself to us, which includes all its other forms. This I have stated to be the *tendency to individuation*, and the degrees or intensities of Life to consist in the progressive realization of this tendency. The power which is acknowledged to exist, wherever the realization is found, must subsist wherever the tendency is manifested. The power which comes forth and stirs abroad in the bird, must be latent in the egg. I have shown, moreover, that this tendency to individuate can not be conceived without the opposite tendency to connect, even as the centrifugal power supposes the centripetal, or as the two opposite poles constitute each other, and are the constituent acts of one and the same power in the magnet. We might say that the life of the magnet subsists in their union, but that it lives (acts or manifests itself) in their strife. Again, if the tendency be at once to individuate and to connect, to detach, but so as either to retain or to reproduce attachment, the individuation itself must be a tendency to the ultimate production of the highest and most comprehensive individuality. This must be the one great end of Nature, her ultimate production of the highest and most comprehensive individuality. This must be the one great end of Nature, her ultimate object, or by whatever other word we may designate that something which bears to a final cause the same relation that Nature herself bears to the Supreme Intelligence.

According to the plan I have prescribed for this inquisition, we are now to seek for the highest law, or most general form, under which this tendency acts, and then to pursue the same process with this, as we have already done with the tendency itself, namely, having stated the law in its highest abstraction, to present it in the different forms in which it appears and reappears in higher and higher dignities. I restate the question. The tendency having been ascertained, what is its most general law? I answer—*polarity*, or the essential dualism of Nature, arising out of its productive unity, and still tending to reaffirm it, either as equilibrium, indifference, or identity. In its *pro-*

ductive power, of which the product is the only measure, consists its incompatibility with mathematical calculus. For the full applicability of an abstract science ceases, the moment reality begins.* Life, then, we consider as the copula, or the unity of thesis and antithesis, position and counterposition,—Life itself being the positive of both; as, on the other hand, the two counterpoints are the necessary conditions of the *manifestations* of Life. These, by the same necessity, unite in a synthesis; which again, by the law of dualism, essential to all actual existence, expands, or *produces* itself, from the point into the *line*, in order again to converge, as the initiation of the same productive process in some intenser form of reality. Thus, in the identity of the two counter-powers, Life *sub*sists; in their strife it *con*sists: and in their reconciliation it at once dies and is born again into a new form, either falling back into the life of the whole, or starting anew in the process of individuation.

Whence shall we take our beginning? From Space, *istud litigium*

* For abstractions are the conditions and only subject of all abstract sciences. Thus the theorist (vide Dalton's Theory), who reduces the chemical process to the positions of atoms, would doubtless thereby render chemistry calculable, but that he commences by destroying the chemical process itself, and substitutes for it a *mote dance* of abstractions; for even the powers which he appears to leave real, those of attraction and repulsion, he immediately unrealizes by representing them as diverse and separable properties. We can abstract the quantities and the quantitative motion from masses, passing over or leaving for other sciences the question of what constitutes the masses, and thus apply not to the masses themselves, but to the abstractions therefrom,—the laws of geometry and universal arithmetic. And where the quantities are the infallible signs of real powers, and our chief concern with the masses is as SIGNS, sciences may be founded thereon of the highest use and dignity. Such, for instance, is the sublime science of astronomy, having for its objects the vast masses which "God placed in the firmament of the heaven to be for *signs* and for seasons, for days and years." For the whole doctrine of physics may be reduced to three great divisions: First, *quantitative motion*, which is proportioned to the quantity of matter exclusively. This is the science of weight or statics. Secondly, *relative motion*, as communicated to bodies externally by impact. This is the science of mechanics. Thirdly, *qualitative motion*, or that which is accordant to properties of matter, And this is chemistry. Now it is evident that the first two sciences presuppose that which forms the exclusive object of the third, namely, quality; for all quantity in nature is either itself derived, or at least derives its powers from some *quality*, as that of weight, specific cohesion, hardness, &c.; and therefore the attempt to reduce to the distances or impacts of atoms, under the assumptions of two powers, which are themselves declared to be no more than mere general terms for those quantities of motion and impact (the atom itself being a fiction formed by abstraction, and in truth a third occult quality for the purpose of explaining hardness and density), amounts to an attempt to destroy chemistry itself, and at the same time to exclude the sole reality and only positive contents of the very science into which that of chemistry is to be degraded. Now what qualities are to chemistry, *productiveness* is to the science of Life; and this being excluded, physiology or zoonomy would sink into chemistry, chemistry by the same process into mechanics, while mechanics themselves would lose the substantial principle, which, bending the lower extreme towards its apex, produces the organic circle of the sciences, and elevates them all into different arcs or stations of the one absolute science of Life.

This explanation, which in appearance only is a digression, was indispensably requisite to prevent the idea of polarity, which has been given as the universal law of Life, from being misunderstood as a mere refinement on those mechanical systems of physiology, which it has been my main object to explode.

philosophorum, which leaves the mind equally dissatisfied, whether we deny or assert its real existence. To make it wholly ideal, would be at the same time to idealize all phenomena, and to undermine the very conception of an external world. To make it real, would be to assert the existence of something, with the properties of nothing. It would far transcend the height to which a physiologist must confine his flights, should we attempt to reconcile this apparent contradiction. It is the duty and the privilege of the theologian to demonstrate, that *space* is the ideal organ by which the soul of man perceives the *omnipresence* of the Supreme Reality, as distinct from the works, which in him move, and live, and have their being; while the equal mystery of *Time* bears the same relation to his *Eternity*, or what is fully equivalent, his Unity.

Physiologically contemplated, Nature begins, proceeds, and ends in a contradiction; for the moment of absolute solution would be that in which Nature would cease to be Nature, *i. e.* a scheme of ever-varying relations; and physiology, in the ambitious attempt to solve phenomena into absolute realities, would itself become a mere web of verbal abstractions.

But it is in strict connection with our subject, that we should make the universal FORMS as well as the not less universal LAW of Life, clear and intelligible in the example of *Time* and *Space*, these being both the first specification of the principle, and ever after its indispensable symbols. First, a single act of self-inquiry will show the impossibility of distinctly conceiving the one without some involution of the other; either time expressed in space, in the form of the mathematical line, or space within time, as in the circle. But to form the first conception of a *real* thing, we state both as one in the idea, *duration*. The formula is: $\overbrace{A=B+B=A}=\overbrace{A=A}$, or the oneness of space and time, is the predicate of all *real* being.

But as little can we conceive the oneness, except as the mid-point producing itself on each side; that is, manifesting itself on two opposite poles. Thus, from identity we derive duality, and from both together we obtain polarity, synthesis, indifference, predominance. The line is Time + Space, under the predominance of Time: Surface is Space + Time, under the predominance of Space, while Line + Surface as the synthesis of units, is the circle in the first dignity; to the sphere in the second; and to the globe in the third. In short, neither can the antagonists appear but as two forces of one power, nor can the power be conceived by us but as the equatorial point of the two counteracting forces; of which the *hypomochlion* of the lever is as good an illustration as any thing can be that is thought of *mechanically* only, and exclusively of life. To make it adequate, we must substitute the idea of positive production for that of rest, or mere neutralization. To the fancy alone it is the null-point, or zero, but to the reason it is the *punctum saliens*, and the power itself in its eminence. Even in these, the most abstract and universal forms of all thought and perception—even in the ideas of time and space, we slip under them, as it were, a *substratum;* for we can not think of them but as far as they are co-inherent, and therefore as reciprocally the measures of each other. Nor, again, can we finish the process without having the idea of *motion* as its immediate product. Thus we say, that time has one dimension, and imagine it to ourselves as a line. But the line we have already proved to be the productive synthesis of time, with space under the predominance of time. If we exclude space by an abstract assumption, the time remains as a spaceless point, and represents the concentered power of unity and active negation, *i. e.* retraction, determination, and limit, *ab intra.* But if we assume the time as excluded, the line vanishes, and we leave space dimensionless, an indistinguishable ALL, and therefore the representative of absolute weakness and formlessness, but, for that very reason, of infinite capacity and formability.

We have been thus full and express on this subject, because these simple ideas of time, space, and motion; of length, breadth, and depth, are not only the simplest and universal, but the necessary symbols of all philosophic construction. They will be found the primary factors and elementary forms of every calculus and of every diagram in the algebra and geometry of a scientific physiology. Accordingly, we shall recognize the same forms under other names; but at each return more specific and intense; and the whole process repeated with ascending gradations of reality, *exempli gratiâ:* Time + space =motion; T*m* + space = line + breadth = depth; depth + motion = force; L*f* + B*f* =D*f*; LD*f* + BD*f* = attraction + repulsion = gravitation; and so on, even till they pass into outward phenomena, and form the intermediate link between productive powers and fixed products in light, heat, and electricity. If we pass to the construction of matter, we find it as the product, or *tertium aliud*, of antagonist powers of repulsion and attraction. Remove these powers, and the conception of matter vanishes into space—conceive repulsion only, and you have the same result. For infinite repulsion, uncounteracted and alone, is tantamount to infinite, dimensionless diffusion, and this again to infinite weakness; viz., to space. Conceive attraction alone, and as an infinite contraction, its product amounts to the absolute point, viz., to time. Conceive the synthesis of both, and you have matter as a fluxional antecedent, which, in the very act of formation, passes into body by its gravity, and yet in all bodies it still remains as their mass, which, being exclusively calculable under the law of gravitation, gives rise, as we before observed, to the science of statics, most improperly called celestial mechanics.

In strict consistence with the same philosophy which, instead of considering the powers of bodies to have been miraculously stuck into a prepared and pre-existing matter, as pins into a pin-cushion, conceives the powers as the productive factors, and the body or phenomenon as the fact, product, or fixture; we revert again to potentiated length in the power of magnetism; to surface in the power of electricity; and to the synthesis of both, or potentiated depth, in constructive, that is, chemical affinity. But while the two factors are as poles to each other, each factor has likewise its own poles, and thus in the simple cross—

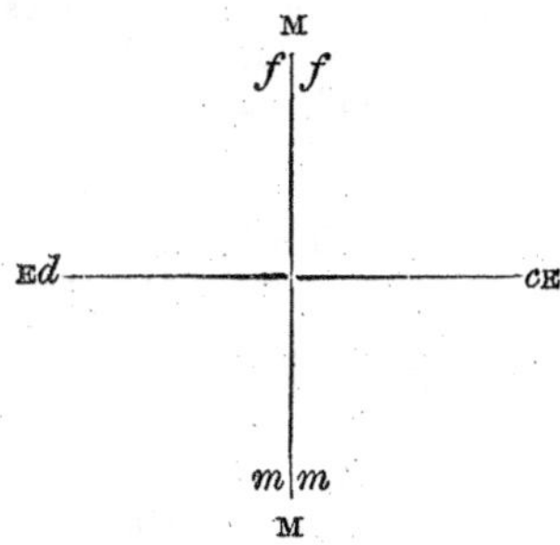

M M being the magnetic line, with *f f* its northern pole, or pole of attraction; and *m m* its south, or pole of repulsion, E E one of the lines that spring from each point of M M, with its east, or pole of contraction, and *d* its west, or pole of diffluence and expansion—we have presented to us the universal quadruplicity, or four elemental forms of power; in the endless proportions and modifications of which, the innumerable offspring of all-bearing Nature consist. Wisely docile to the suggestions of Nature herself, the ancients significantly expressed these forces under the names of earth, water, air, and fire; not meaning any tangible or visible substance so generalized, but the powers predominant, and, as it were, the living basis of each, which no chemical decomposition can ever present to the senses, were it only that their interpenetration and co-inherence first constitutes them sensible, and is the condition and meaning of a—*thing*. Already our more truly philosophical naturalists (Ritter, for instance) have begun to generalize the four great elements of chemical nomenclature, carbon, azote, oxygen, and hydrogen: the two former as the positive and negative pole of the magnetic axis, or as the power of fixity and mobility; and the two latter as the opposite poles, or plus and minus states of cosmical electricity, as the powers of contraction and dilatation, or of comburence and combustibility. These powers are to each other as longitude to latitude, and the poles of each relatively as north to south, and as east to west. For surely the reader will find no distrust in a system only because Nature, ever consistent with herself, presents us everywhere with harmonious and accordant symbols of her consistent doctrines. Nothing would be more easy than, by the ordinary principles of sound logic and common sense, to demonstrate the impossibility and expose the absurdity of the corpuscularian or mechanic system, or than to prove the untenable nature of any intermediate system. But we can not force any man into an insight or intuitive possession of the true philosophy, because we can not give him abstraction, intellectual intuition, or constructive imagination; because we can not organize for him an eye that can see, an ear that can listen to, or a heart that can feel, the harmonies of Nature, or recognize in her endless forms, the thousandfold realization of those simple and majestic laws, which yet in their absoluteness can be discovered only in the recesses of his own spirit,—not by that man, therefore, whose imaginative powers have been *ossified* by the continual reaction and assimilating influences of mere *objects* on his mind, and who is a prisoner to his own eye and its reflex, the passive fancy!—not by him in whom an unbroken familiarity with the organic world, as if it were mechanical, with the sensitive, but as if it were insensate, has engendered the coarse and hard spirit of a sorcerer. The former is unable, the latter unwilling, to master the absolute prerequisites. There is neither hope nor occasion for him "to cudgel his brains about it, he has no feeling of the business." If he do not see the necessity from without, if he have not learned the possibility from within, of interpenetration, of total intussusception, of the existence of all in each as the condition of Nature's unity and substantiality, and of the latency under the predominance of some one power, wherein subsists her life and its endless variety, as he must be, by habitual slavery to the eye, or its reflex, the passive fancy, under the influences of the corpuscularian philosophy, he has so paralyzed his imaginative powers as to be unable—or by that hardness and heart-hardening spirit of contempt, which is sure to result from a perpetual commune with the lifeless, he has so far debased his inward being—as to be unwilling to comprehend the pre-requisite, he must be content, while standing thus at the threshold of philosophy, to receive the results, though he can not be admitted to the deliberation—in other words, to act upon *rules* which he is incapable of understanding as LAWS, and to reap the harvest with the sharpened iron for which others have delved for him in the mine.

It is not improbable that there may exist, and even be discovered, higher forms and more akin to Life than those of magnetism, electricity, and constructive (or chemical) affinity appear to be, even in their finest known influences. It is not improbable that we may hereafter find ourselves justified in revoking certain of the latter, and unappropriating them to a yet unnamed triplicity; or that, being thus assisted, we may obtain a qualitative instead of a quantitative insight into vegetable animation, as distinct from animal, and that of the insect world from both. But in the present state of science, the magnetic, electric, and chemical powers are the last and highest of inorganic nature. These, therefore, we assume as presenting themselves again to us, in their next metamorphosis, as reproduction (*i. e.* growth and identity of the whole, amid the change or flux of all the parts), irritability and sensibility; reproduction corresponding to magnetism, irritability to electricity, and sensibility to constructive chemical affinity.

But before we proceed further, it behooves us to answer the objections contained in the following passage, or withdraw ourselves in time from the bitter contempt in which it would involve us. Acting under such a necessity, we need not apologize for the length of the quotation.

1. "If," says Mr. Lawrence, "the properties of living matter are to be explained in this way, why should not we adopt the same plan with physical properties, and account for gravitation, or chemical affinity, by the supposition of appropriate subtle fluids? Why does the irritability of a muscle need such an explanation, if explanation it can be called, more than the elective attraction of a salt?"

2. "To make the matter more intelligible, this vital principle is compared to magnetism, to electricity, and to galvanism; or it is roundly stated to be oxygen. 'Tis like a camel, or like a whale, or like what you please."

3. "You have only to grant that the phenomena of the sciences just alluded to depend on extremely fine and invisible fluids, superadded to the matters in which they are exhibited, and to allow further that Life, and magnetic, galvanic, and electric phenomena correspond perfectly; the existence of a subtile matter of Life will then be a very probable inference."

4. "On this illustration you will naturally remark, that the existence of the magnetic, electric, and galvanic fluids, which is offered as a proof of the existence of a vital fluid, is as much a matter of doubt as that of the vital fluid itself."

5. "It is singular, also, that the vital principle should be like both magnetism and electricity, when these two are not like each other."

6. "It would have been interesting to have had this illustration prosecuted a little further. We should have been pleased to learn whether the human body is more like a loadstone, a voltaic pile, or an electrical machine; whether the organs are to be regarded as Leyden jars, magnetic needles, or batteries."

7. "The truth is, there is no resemblance, no analogy, between Electricity and Life; the two orders of phenomena are completely

distinct; they are incommensurable. Electricity illustrates life no more than life illustrates electricity."*

To avoid unnecessary description, I shall refer to the passages by the numbers affixed to them, for that purpose, in the margin.

In reply to No. 1, I ask whether, in the nature of the mind, illustration and explanation must not of necessity proceed from the lower to the higher? or whether a boy is to be taught his addition, subtraction, multiplication, and division, by the highest branches of algebraic analysis? Is there any better way of systematic teaching, than that of illustrating each new step, or having each new step illustrated to him by its identity in kind with the step the next below it? though it be the only mode in which this objection can be answered, yet it seems affronting to remind the objector, of rules so simple as that the complex must even be illustrated by the more simple, or the less scrutible by that which is more subject to our examination.

In reply to No. 2, I first refer to the author's eulogy on Mr. Hunter, p. 163, in which he is justly extolled for having "surveyed the whole *system* of organized beings, from plants to man:" of course, therefore, *as a system*; and therefore under some *one common law*. Now in the very same sense, and no other, than that in which the writer himself by implication compares himself as a man to the *dermestes typographicus*, or the *fucus scorpioides*, do I compare the principle of Life to magnetism, electricity, and constructive affinity,—or rather to that power to which the two former are the thesis and antithesis, the latter the synthesis. But if to compare involve the sense of its etymon, and involve the sense of parity, I utterly deny that I do at all compare them; and, in truth, in no conceivable sense of the word is it applicable, any more than a geometrician can be affirmed to compare a polygon to a point, because he generates the line out of the point. The writer attributes to a philosophy essentially vital the barrenness of the mechanic system, with which alone his imagination

* I apprehend that by men of a certain school it would be deemed no demerit, even though they should never have condescended to look into any system of Aristotelian logic. It is enough for these gentlemen that they are experimentalists! Let it not, however, be supposed that they make more experiments than their neighbors, who consider induction as a means and not an end; or have stronger motives for making them, unless it can be believed that Tycho Brühe must have been urged to repeat his sweeps of the heavens with greater accuracy and industry than Herschel, for no better reason than that the former flourished before the theory of gravitation was perfected. No, but they have the honor of being mere experimentalists! If, however, we may not refer to logic, we may to common sense and common experience. It is not improbable, however, that they have both read and studied a book of hypothetical psychology on the assumptions of the crudest materialism, stolen too without acknowledgment from our David Hartley's Essay on Man, which is well known under the whimsical name of Condillac's Logic. But, as Mr. Brand has lately observed, "The French are a queer people," and we should not be at all surprised to hear of a book of fresh importation from Paris, on determinate proportions in chemistry, announced by the author in his title-page as a new and improved system either of arithmetic or geometry.

has been familiarized, and which, as hath been justly observed by a contemporary writer, is contra-distinguished from the former principally in this respect; that demanding for every mode and act of existence real or possible visibility, it knows only of distance and nearness, composition (or rather compaction) and decomposition, in short, the relations of unproductive particles to each other; so that in every instance the result is the exact sum of the component qualities, as in arithmetical addition. This is the philosophy of Death, and only of a dead nature can it hold good. In Life, and in the view of a vital philosophy, the two component counter-powers actually interpenetrate each other, and generate a higher third, including both the former, "ita tamen ut sit alia et major."

As a complete answer to No. 3, I refer the reader to many passages in the preceding and following pages, in which, on far higher and more demonstrative grounds than the mechanic system can furnish, I have exposed the unmeaningness and absurdity of these finer fluids, as applied even to electricity itself; unless, indeed, they are assumed as its product. But in addition I beg leave to remind the author, that it is incomparably more agreeable to all experience to originate the formative process in the *fluid*, whether fine or gross, than in corporeal *atoms*, in which we are not only deserted by all experience, but contradicted by the primary conception of body itself.

Equally inapplicable is No. 4: and of No. 5 I can only repeat, first, that I do not make Life *like* magnetism, or *like* electricity; that the difference between magnetism and electricity, and the powers illustrated by them, is an essential part of my system, but that the animal Life of man is the identity of all three. To whatever other system this objection may apply, it is utterly irrelevant to that which I have here propounded: though from the narrow limits prescribed to me, it has been propounded with an inadequacy painful to my own feelings.

The ridicule in No. 6 might be easily retorted; but as it could prove nothing, I will leave it where I found it, in a page where nothing is proved.

A similar remark might be sufficient for the bold and blank assertion (No. 7) with which the extract concludes; but that I feel some curiosity to discover what meaning the author attaches to the term analogy. Analogy implies a difference in sort, and not merely in degree; and it is the sameness of the end, with the difference of the means, which constitutes analogy. No one would say the lungs of a man were analogous to the lungs of a monkey, but any one might say that the gills of fish and the spiracula of insects are analogous to lungs. Now if there be any philosophers who have asserted that electricity as electricity is the *same* as Life, for that reason they can not be *analogous* to each other; and as no man in his senses, philosopher or not, is capable of imagining that the lightning which destroys a sheep, was a means to the same end with the principle of its organization; for this reason, too, the two powers can not be represented as analogous. Indeed I know of no system in which the word, as thus applied, would admit of an endurable meaning, but that which teaches us, that a mass of marrow in the skull is analogous to the rational soul, which Plato and Bacon, equally with the "poor Indian," believe themselves to have received from the Supreme Reason.

It would be blindness not to see, or affectation to pretend not to see, the work at which these sarcasms were levelled. The author of that work is abundantly able to defend his own opinions; yet I should be ambitious to address *him* at the close of the contest in the lines of the great Roman poet:

> "Et nos tela, Pater, ferrumque haud debile dextrâ
> Spargimus, et nostro sequitur, de vulnere sanguis."

In Mr. Abernethy's Lecture on the Theory of Life, it is impossible not to see a presentiment of a great truth. He has, if I may so express myself, caught it in the breeze: and we seem to hear the first glad opening and shout with which he springs forward to the pursuit. But it is equally evident that the prey has not been followed through its doublings and windings, or driven out from its brakes and covers into full and open view. Many of the least tenable phrases may be fairly interpreted as illustrations, rather than precise exponents of the author's meaning; at least, while they remain as a mere suggestion or annunciation of his ideas, and till he has expanded them over a larger sphere, it would be unjust to infer the contrary. But it is not with men, however strongly their professional merits may entitle them to reverence, that my concern is at present. If the opinions here supported are the same with those of Mr. Abernethy, I rejoice in his authority. If they are different, I shall wait with an anxious interest for an exposition of that difference.

Having reasserted that I no more confound magnetism with electricity, or the chemical process, than the mathematician confounds length with breadth, or either with depth; I think it sufficient to add that there are two views of the subject, the former of which I do not believe attributable to any philosopher, while both are alike disclaimed by me as forming any part of my views. The first is that which is supposed to consider electricity identical with life, as it subsists in organized bodies. The other considers electricity as everywhere present, and penetrating all bodies under the image of a subtile fluid or substance, which, in Mr. Abernethy's inquiry, I regard as little more than a mere diagram on his slate, for the purpose of fixing the attention on the intellectual conception, or as a possible *product* (in which case electricity must be a composite power), or at worst, as words *quæ humana incuria fudit.* This which, in inanimate Nature, is manifested now as magnetism, now as electricity, and now as chemical agency, is supposed, on entering an organized body, to constitute its vital *principle*, something in the same manner as the steam becomes the *mechanic* power of the steam-engine, in *consequence* of its compression by the steam-engine; or as the breeze that murmurs indistinguishably in the forest becomes the element, the substratum, of melody in the Æolian harp, and of consummate harmony in the organ. Now this hypothesis is as directly opposed to my view as supervention is to evolution, inasmuch as I hold the organized body itself, in all its marvellous contexture, to be the PRODUCT and representant of the power which is here supposed to have supervened to it. So far from admitting a *transfer*, I do not admit it even in electricity itself, or in the phenomena universally called electrical; among other points I ground my explanation of remote sympathy on the directly contrary supposition.

But my opinions will be best explained by a rapid exemplification in the processes of Nature, from the first rudiments of individualized life in the lowest classes of its two great poles, the vegetable and animal creation, to its crown and consummation in the human body; thus illustrating at once the unceasing *polarity of life, as the form of its process, and its tendency to progressive individuation as the law of its direction.*

Among the conceptions, of the mere ideal character of which the philosopher is well aware, and which yet become necessary from the necessity of assuming a beginning; the original fluidity of the planet is the chief. Under some form or other it is expressed or implied in every system of cosmogony and even of geology, from Moses to Thales, and from Thales to Werner. This assumption originates in the same law of mind that gave rise to the *prima materia* of the Peripatetic school. In order to *comprehend* and *explain* the *forms* of things, we must imagine a state *antecedent* to form. A chaos of heterogeneous substances, such as our Milton has described, is not only an *impossible* state (for this may be equally true of every other attempt), but it is *palpably* impossible. It presupposes, moreover, the thing it is intended to solve; and makes *that* an *effect* which had been called in as the explanatory *cause*. The requisite and only serviceable fiction, therefore, is the representation of CHAOS as one vast homogeneous drop! In this sense it may be even justified, as an appropriate symbol of the great fundamental truth that all things spring from, and subsist in, the endless strife between indifference and difference. The whole history of Nature is comprised in the specification of the transitional states from the one to the other. The symbol only is fictitious: the thing signified is not only grounded in truth—it is the law and actuating principle of all other truths, whether physical or intellectual.

Now, by magnetism in its widest sense, I mean the first and simplest *differential* act of Nature, as the power which works in *length*, and produces the first distinction between the indistinguishable by the generation of a *line*. Relatively, therefore, to fluidity, that is, to matter, the parts of which can not be distinguished from each other by figure, magnetism is the power of fixity; but, relatively to itself, magnetism, like every other power in Nature, is designated by its opposite poles, and must be represented as the magnetic axis, the northern pole of which signifies rest, attraction, fixity, coherence, or hardness; the element of EARTH in the nomenclature of *observation* and the CARBONIC principle in that of *experiment;* while the southern pole, as its antithesis, represents mobility, repulsion, incoherence, and fusibility; the element of air in the nomenclature of observation (that is, of Nature as it appears to us when unquestioned by art), and azote or nitrogen in the nomenclature of experiment (that is, of Nature in the state so beautifully allegorized in the Homeric fable of Proteus bound down, and forced to answer by Ulysses, after having been pursued through all his metamorphoses into his ultimate form*). That nothing real does or can exist corresponding to either pole *exclusively*, is involved in the very definition of a THING as the synthesis of opposing energies. That a thing *is*, is owing to the co-inherence therein of any two powers; but that it is *that* particular thing arises from the proportions in which these powers are co-present, either as predominance or as reciprocal neutralization; but under the modification of twofold power to which magnetism itself is, as the thesis to its antithesis.

The correspondent, in the world of the senses, to the magnetic axis, exists in the series of metals. The metalleity, as the universal base of the planet, is a necessary deduction from the principles of the system. From the infusible, though evaporable, diamond to nitrogen itself, the metallic nature of which has been long suspected by chemists, though still under the mistaken notion of an oxyde, we trace a series of metals from the maximum of coherence to positive fluidity, in all ordinary temperatures, we mean. Though, in point of fact, cold itself is but a superinduction of the one pole, or, what amounts to the same thing, the subtraction of the other, under the modifications afore described; and therefore are the metals indecomposible, because they are themselves the decompositions of the metallic axis, in all its degrees of longitude and latitude. Thus the substance of the planet from which it *is*, is metallic; while that which is ever *becoming*, is in like manner produced through the perpetual modification of the first by the opposite forces of the second; that is, by the principle of contraction and difference at the eastern extreme—the element of fire, or

* Such is the interpretation given by Lord Bacon. To which of the two gigantic intellects, the poet's or philosophic commentator's, the allegory belongs, I shall not presume to decide. Its extraordinary beauty and appropriateness remains the same in either case.

the oxygen of the chemists; and by the elementary power of dilatation, or universality at its western extreme—the ὕδωρ ἐν ὕδατι of the ancients, and the hydrogen of the laboratory.

It has been before noticed that the progress of Nature is more truly represented by the ladder, than by the suspended chain, and that she expands as by concentric circles. This is, indeed, involved in the very conception of individuation, whether it be applied to the different species or to the individuals. In what manner the evident interspace is reconciled with the equally evident continuity of the life of Nature, is a problem that can be solved by those minds alone, which have intuitively learnt that the whole *actual* life of Nature originates in the existence, and consists in the perpetual reconciliation, and as perpetual resurgency of the primary contradiction, of which universal polarity is the result and the exponent. From the first moment of the differential impulse—(the primæval chemical epoch of the Wernerian school)—when Nature, by the tranquil deposition of crystals, prepared, as it were, the fulcrum of her after-efforts, from this, her first, and in part *irrevocable*, self-contraction, we find, in each ensuing production, more and more tendency to independent existence in the increasing multitude of strata, and in the relics of the lowest orders, first of vegetable and then of animal life. In the schistous formations, which we must here assume as in great measure the residue of vegetable creations, that have sunk back into the universal life, and in the later predominant calcareous masses, which are the *caput mortuum* of animalized existence, we ascend from the laws of attraction and repulsion, as united in gravity, to magnetism, electricity, and constructive power, till we arrive at the point representative of a new and far higher intensity. For from this point flow, as in opposite directions, the two streams of vegetation and animalization, the former characterized by the predominance of magnetism in its highest power, as reproduction, the other by electricity intensified—as irritability, in like manner. The vegetable and animal world are the thesis and antithesis, or the opposite poles of organic life. We are not, therefore, to seek in either for analogies to the other, but for counterpoints. On the same account, the nearer the common source, the greater the likeness; the farther the remove, the greater the opposition. At the extreme limits of inorganic Nature, we may detect a dim and obscure prophecy of her ensuing process in the twigs and rude semblances that occur in crystallization of some of the copper ores, and in the well-known *arbor Dianæ*, and *arbor Veneris*. These latter Ritter has already ably explained by considering the oblique branches and their acute angles as the result of magnetic repulsion, from the presentation of the same poles, &c. In the CORALS and CONCHYLIA, the whole act and purpose of their existence seems to be that of connecting the animal with the inorganic world by the perpetual formation of calcareous earth. For the corals are nothing but polypi, which are characterized by still passing away and dissolving into the earth, which they had previously excreted, as if they were the first feeble effort of detachment. The power seems to step forward from out the inorganic world only to fall back again upon it, still, however, under a new form, and under the predominance of the more active pole of magnetism. The product must have the same connection, therefore, with azote, which the first rudiments of vegetation have with carbon: the one and the other exist not for their own sakes, but in order to produce the conditions best fitted for the production of higher forms. In the polypi, corallines, &c., individuality is in its first dawn; there is the same shape in them all, and a multitude of animals form, as it were, a common animal. And as the individuals run into each other, so do the different genera. They likewise pass into each other so indistinguishably, that the whole order forms a very network.

As the corals approach the conchylia, this interramification decreases. The tubipora forms the transition to the serpula; for the characteristic of all zoophytes, namely, the star shape of their openings, here disappears, and the tubiporæ are distinguished from the rest of the corals by this very circumstance, that the hollow calcareous pipes are placed side by side, without interbranching. In the serpula they have already become separate. How feeble this attempt is to individuate, is most clearly shown in their mode of generation. Notwithstanding the report of Professor Pallas, it still remains doubtful whether there exists any actual copulation among the polypi. The mere existence of a polypus suffices for its endless multiplication. They may be indefinitely propagated by cuttings, so languid is the power of individuation, so boundless that of reproduction. But the delicate jelly dissolves, as lightly as it was formed, into its own product, and it is probable that the Polynesia, as a future continent, will be the gigantic monument, not so much of their life, as of the life of Nature in them. Here we may observe the first instance of that general law, according to which Nature still assimilates her extreme points. In these, her first and feeblest attempts to animalize organization, it is latent, because undeveloped, and merely potential; while, in the human brain, the last and most consummate of her combined energies, it is again lost or disguised in the subtlety* and multiplicity of its evolution.

In the class immediately above (Mollusca) we find the individuals separate, a more determinate form, and in the higher species, the rudiment of nerves, as the first scarce distinguishable impress and exponent of sensibility; still, however, the vegetative reproduction is the predominant form; and even the nerves "which float in the same

* The Anatomical Demonstrations of the Brain, by Dr. Spurzheim, which I have seen, presented to me the most satisfactory proof of this.

cavity with the other viscera," are probably subservient to it, and extend their power in the increased intensity of the reproductive force. Still prevails the transitional state from the fluid to the solid; and the jelly, that rudiment in which all animals, even the noblest, have their commencement; constitutes the whole sphere of these rudimental animals.

In the snail and muscle, the residuum of the coral reappears, but refined and ennobled into a part of the animal. The whole class is characterized by the separation of the fluid from the solid. On the one side, a gelatinous semi-fluid; on the other side, an entirely inorganic, though often a most exquisitely mechanized, calcareous excretion! Animalization in general is, we know, contra-distinguished from vegetables in general by the predominance of azote in the chemical composition, and of irritability in the organic process. But in this and the foregoing classes, as being still near the common equator, or the punctum indifferentiæ, the carbonic principle still asserts its claims, and the force of reproduction struggles with that of irritability. In the unreconciled strife of these two forces consists the character of the *Vermes*, which appear to be the preparatory step for the next class. Hence the difficulties which have embarrassed the naturalists, who adopt the Linnæan classification, in their endeavors to discover determinate characters of distinction between the vermes and the insecta.

But no sooner have we passed the borders, than endless variety of form and the bold display of instincts announce, that Nature has succeeded. She has created the intermediate link between the vegetable world, as the product of the reproductive or magnetic power, and the animal as the exponent of sensibility. Those that live and are nourished, on the bodies of other animals, are comparatively few, with little diversity of shape, and almost all of the same natural family. These we may pass by as exceptions. But the insect world, taken at large, appears as an intenser life, that has struggled itself loose and become emancipated from vegetation, *Floræ liberti, et libertini!* If for the sake of a moment's relaxation we might indulge a Darwinian flight, though at the risk of provoking a smile, (not, I hope, a frown,) from sober judgment, we might imagine the life of insects an apotheosis of the petals, stamina, and nectaries, round which they flutter, or of the stems and pedicles, to which they adhere. Beyond and above this step, Nature seems to act with a sort of free agency, and to have formed the classes from choice and bounty. Had she proceeded no further, yet the whole vegetable, together with the whole insect creation, would have formed within themselves an entire and independent system of Life. All plants have insects, most commonly each genus of vegetables its appropriate genera of insects; and so reciprocally interdependent and necessary to each other are they, that we can almost as little think of vegetation without insects, as of insects without vegetation. Though probably the mere likeness of *shape*, in the *papilio*, and the papilionaceous plants, suggested the idea of the former, as the latter in a state of detachment, to our late poetical and theoretical brother; yet a something, that approaches to a graver plausibility, is given to this fancy of a flying blossom; when we reflect how many plants depend upon insects for their fructification. Be it remembered, too, that with few and very obscure exceptions, the irritable power and an analogon of voluntary motion first dawn on us in the vegetable world, in the stamina, and anthers, at the period of impregnation. Then, as if Nature had been encouraged by the success of the first experiment, both the one and the other appear as predominance and general character. THE INSECT WORLD IS THE EXPONENT OF IRRITABILITY, AS THE VEGETABLE IS OF REPRODUCTION.

With the ascent in power, the intensity of individuation keeps even pace; and from this we may explain all the characteristic distinctions between this class and that of the vermes. The almost homogeneous jelly of the animalcula infusoria became, by a vital oxydation, granular in the polypi. This granulation formed itself into distinct organs in the molluscæ; while for the snails, which are the next step, the animalized lime, that seemed the sole final cause of the life of the polypi, assumes all the characters of an ulterior purpose. Refined into a horn-like substance, it becomes to the snails the substitute of an organ, and their outward skeleton. Yet how much more manifold and definite, the organization of an insect, than that of the preceding class, the patient researches of Swammerdam and Lyonnet have evinced, to the delight and admiration of every reflecting mind.

In the insect, for the first time, we find the distinct commencement of a separation between the exponents of sensibility and those of irritability; *i. e.* between the *nervous* and the *muscular* system. The latter, however, asserts its pre-eminence throughout. The prodigal provision of organs for the purposes of respiration, and the marvellous powers which numerous tribes of insects possess, of accommodating the most corrupted airs, for a longer or shorter period, to the support of their excitability, would of itself lead us to presume, that here the *vis irritabilis* is the reigning dynasty. There is here no confluence of nerves into one reservoir, as evidence of the independent existence of sensibility *as* sensibility;—and therefore no counterpoise of a vascular system, as a distinct exponent of the irritable pole. The whole muscularity of these animals is the organ of irritability; and the nerves themselves are probably feeders of the motory power. The petty rills of sensibility flow into the full expanse of irritability, and there lose themselves. The nerves appertaining to the senses, on the other hand, are indistinct, and comparatively unimportant. The multitude of immovable eyes appear not so much conductors of light, as its ultimate recipient. We are almost tempted to believe that they constitute, rather than subserve, their sensorium.

These eye-facets form the sense of light, rather than organs of seeing. Their almost paradoxical number at least, and the singularity of their forms, render it probable that they impel the animal by some modification of its irritability, herein likewise containing a striking analogy to the known influence of light on plants, than as excitements of sensibility. The sense that is nearest akin to irritability, and which alone resides in the muscular system, is that of touch, or feeling. This, therefore, is the first sense that emerges. Being confined to absolute contact, it occupies the lowest rank; but for that very reason it is the ground of all the other senses, which act, according to the ratio of their ascent, at still increasing distances, and become more and more ideal, from the tentacles of the polypus, to the human eye; which latter might be defined the outward organ of the identity, or at least of the indifference, of the real and ideal. But as the calcareous residuum of the lowest class approaches to the nature of horn in the snail, so the cumbrous shell of the snail has been transformed into polished and movable plates of defensive armor in the insect. Thus, too, the same power of progressive individuation articulates the tentacula of the polypus and holothuria into antennæ; thereby manifesting the full emersion and eminency of irritability as a power which acts in, and gives its own character to, that of reproduction. The least observant must have noticed the lightning-like rapidity with which the insect tribes devour and eliminate their food, as by an instinctive necessity, and in the least degree for the purposes of the animal's own growth or enlargement. The same predominance of irritability, and at the same time a new start in individuation, is shown in the reproductive power as generation. There is now a regular projection, *ab intra ad extra*, for which neither sprouts nor cuttings can any longer be the substitutes. We have not space for further detail; but there is one point too strikingly illustrative and even confirmative of the proposed system, to be omitted altogether. We mean the curious fact, that the same characteristic tendency, *ad extra*, which in the males and females of certain insect tribes is realized in the functions of generation, conception, and parturiency, manifests and expands itself in the *sexless* individuals (which are always in this case the great majority of the species), as instincts of art, and in the construction of works completely detached and inorganic; while the geometric regularity of these works, which bears an analogy to crystallization, is demonstrably no more than the necessary result of uniform action in a compressed multitude.

Again, as the insect world, averaging the whole, comes nearest to plants (whose very essence is reproduction), in the multitude of their germs; so does it resemble plants in the sufficiency of a single impregnation for the evolution of myriads of detached lives. Even so, the metamorphoses of insects, from the egg to the maggot and caterpillar, and from these, through the nympha and aurelia into the perfect insect, are but a more individuated and intenser form of a similar transformation of the plant from the seed-leaflets, or cotyledons, through the stalk, the leaves, and the calyx, into the perfect flower, the various colors of which seem made for the reflection of light, as the antecedent grade to the burnished scales, and scale-like eyes of the insect. Nevertheless, with all this seeming prodigality of organic power, the whole tendency is *ad extra*, and the life of insects, as electricity in the quadrate, acts chiefly on the superficies of their bodies, to which we may add the negative proof arising from the absence of sensibility. It is well known, that the two halves of a divided insect have continued to perform, or attempt, each their separate functions, the trunkless head feeding with its accustomed voracity, while the headless trunk has exhibited its appropriate excitability to the sexual influence.

The intropulsive force, that sends the ossification inward as to the centre, is reserved for a yet higher step, and this we find embodied in the class of *fishes*. Even here, however, the process still seems imperfect, and (as it were) initiatory. The skeleton has left the surface, indeed, but the bones approach to the nature of gristle. To feel the truth of this, we need only compare the most perfect bone of a fish with the thigh-bones of the mammalia, and the distinctness with which the latter manifest the co-presence of the *magnetic* power in its solid parietes, of the *electrical* in its branching arteries, and of the third greatest power, viz., the *qualitative* and interior, in its marrow. The senses of fish are more distinct than those of insects. Thus, the intensity of its sense of smell has been placed beyond doubt, and rises in the extent of its sphere far beyond the irritable sense, or the feeling, in insects. I say the *feeling*, not the touch; for the touch seems, as it were, a supervention to the feeling, a perfection *given* to it by the reaction of the higher powers. As the feeling of the insect, in subtlety and virtual distance, rises above the solitary sense of taste* in the mollusca, so does the smell of the fish rise above the feeling of the insect. In the fish, likewise, the eyes are single and movable, while it is remarkable that the only insect that possesses this latter privilege, is an inhabitant of the waters. Finally, here first, unequivocally, and on a *large* scale (for I pretend not to control the freedom, in which the necessity of Nature is rooted, by the precise limits of a system),—here first, Nature exhibits, in the power of sensibility, the consummation of those vital forms (the *nisus formativi*)

* The remark on the feeling of the antennæ, compared with the touch of man, or even of the half-reasoning elephant, is yet more applicable to the taste, which in the segelatinous animals might, perhaps not inappropriately, be entitled the gastric sense.

the adequate and the sole measure of which is to be sought for in their several organic products. But as if a weakness of exhaustion had attended this advance in the same moment it was made, Nature seems necessitated to fall back, and re-exert herself on the lower ground which she had before occupied, that of the vital magnetism, or the power of reproduction. The intensity of this latter power in the fishes, is shown both in their voracity and in the number of their eggs, which we are obliged to calculate by *weight*, not by *tale*. There is an equal intensity both of the *immanent* and the *projective* reproduction, in which, if we take in the comparative number of individuals in each species, and likewise the different intervals between the acts, the fish (it is probable) would be found to stand in a similar relation to the insect, as the insect, in the latter point, stands to the system of vegetation. Meantime, the fish sinks a step below the insect, in the mode and circumstances of impregnation. To this we will venture to add, the predominance of *length*, as the *form* of growth in so large a proportion of the known orders of fishes, and not less of their rectilineal path of motion. In all other respects, the correspondence combined with the progress in individuation, is striking in the whole detail. Thus the eye, in addition to its movability, has besides acquired a saline moisture in its higher development, as accordant with the life of its element. Add to these the glittering covering in both, the splendor of the scales in the one answering to the brilliant plates in the other,—the luminous reservoirs of the fire-flies, —the phosphorescence and electricity of many fishes,—the same analoga of moral qualities, in their rapacity, boldness, modes of seizing their prey by surprise,—their gills, as presenting the intermediate state between the spiracula of the grade next below, and the lungs of the step next above, both extremes of which seem combined in the structure of birds and of their quill-feathers; but above all, the convexity of the crystalline lens, so much greater than in birds, quadrupeds, and man, and seeming to collect, in one powerful organ, the hundredfold microscopic facettes of the insect's *light* organs; and it will not be easy to resist the conviction, that the same power is at work in both, and reappears under higher auspices. The intention of Nature is repeated; but, as was to have been expected, with two main differences. First, that in the lower grade the reproductions themselves seem merged in those of irritability, from the very circumstance that the latter constitutes no pole, either to the former, or to sensibility. The force of irritability acts, therefore, in the insect world, in full predominance; while the emergence of sensibility in the fish calls forth the opposite pole of reproduction, as a *distinct* power, and causes therefore the irritability to flow, in part, into the power of reproduction. The second result of this ascent is the direction of the organizing power, *ad intra*, with the consequent greater simplicity of the exterior form, and the substitution of condensed and flexible force, with comparative unity of implements, for that variety of tools, almost as numerous as the several objects to which they are to be applied, which arises from, and characterizes the superficial life of the insect creation. This grade of ascension, however, like the former, is accompanied by an apparent retrograde movement. For from this very accession of vital intensity we must account for the absence in the fishes of all the formative, or rather (if our language will permit it) *fabricative* instincts. How could it be otherwise? These instincts are the surplus and projection of the organizing power in the direction *ad extra*, and could not, therefore, have been expected in the class of animals that represent the first intuitive effort of organization, and are themselves the product of its first movement in the direction *ad intra*. But Nature never loses what she has once learnt, though in the acquirement of each new power she intermits, or performs less energetically, the act immediately preceding. She often drops a faculty, but never fails to pick it up again. She may seem forgetful and absent, but it is only to recollect herself with *additional*, as well as *recruited* vigor, in some after and higher state; as if the sleep of powers, as well as of bodies, were the season and condition of their growth. Accordingly, we find these instincts again, and with them a wonderful synthesis of fish and insect, as a higher third, in the feathered inhabitants of the air. Nay, she seems to have gone yet further back, and having given B + C = D in the birds, so to have sported with one solitary instance of B + D = A in that curious animal the dragon, the anatomy of which has been recently given to the public by Tiedemann; from whose work it appears, that this creature presents itself to us with the wings of the insect, and with the nervous system, the brain, and the cranium of the bird, in their several rudiments.

The synthesis of fish and insect in the birds, might be illustrated equally in detail with the former; but it will be sufficient for our purpose, that as in both the former cases, the insect and the fish, so here in that of the birds, the powers are under the predominance of irritability; the sensibility being dormant in the first, awakening in the second, and awake, but still subordinate, in the third. Of this my limits confine me to a single presumptive proof, viz., the superiority in strength and courage of the female in the birds of prey. For herein, indeed, does the difference of the sexes universally consist, wherever both the forces are developed, that the female is characterized by quicker irritability, and the male by deeper sensibility. How large a stride has been now made by Nature in the progress of individuation, what ornithologist does not know? From a multitude of instances we select the most impressive, the power of sound, with the first rudiments of modulation! That all languages designate the melody of birds as singing (though according to Blumenbach man only sings, while birds do but whistle), demonstrates that it has been felt as, what indeed it is, a tentative and prophetic prelude of something yet to come. With this conjoin the power and the tendency to acquire articulation, and to imitate speech; conjoin the building instinct and the migratory, the monogamy of several species, and the pairing of almost all; and we shall have collected new instances of the usage (I dare not say law) according to which Nature lets fall, in order to resume, and steps backward the furthest, when she means to leap forwards with the greatest concentration of energy.

For lo! in the next step of ascent the power of sensibility has assumed her due place and rank: her minority is at an end, and the complete and universal presence of a nervous system unites absolutely, by instanteity of time what, with the due allowances for the transitional process, had before been either lost in sameness, or perplexed by multiplicity, or compacted by a finer mechanism. But with this, all the analogies with which Nature had delighted us in the preceding step seem lost, and, with the single exception of that more than valuable, that estimable philanthropist, the dog, and, perhaps, of the horse and elephant, the analogies to ourselves, which we can discover in the quadrupeds or quadrumani, are of our vices, our follies, and our imperfections. The facts in confirmation of both the propositions are so numerous and so obvious, the advance of Nature, under the predominance of the third synthetic power, both in the intensity of life and in the intenseness and extension of individuality, is so undeniable, that we may leap forward at once to the highest realization and reconciliation of both her tendencies, that of the most perfect detachment with the greatest possible union, to that last work, in which Nature did not assist as handmaid under the eye of her sovereign Master, who made Man in his own image, by superadding self-consciousness with self-government, and breathed into him a living soul.

The class of *Vermes* deposit a calcareous stuff, as if it had torn loose from the earth a piece of the gross mass which it must still drag about with it. In the insect class this residuum has refined itself. In the fishes and amphibia it is driven back or inward, the organic power begins to be intuitive, and sensibility appears. In the birds the bones have become hollow; while, with apparent proportional recess, but, in truth, by the excitement of the opposite pole, their exterior presents an actual vegetation. The bones of the mammalia are filled up, and their coverings have become more simple. Man possesses the most perfect osseous structure, the least and most insignificant covering. The whole force of organic power has attained an inward and centripetal direction. He has the whole world in counterpoint to him, but he contains an entire world within himself. Now, for the first time at the apex of the living pyramid, it is Man and Nature, but

Man himself is a syllepsis, a compendium of Nature—the Microcosm! Naked and helpless cometh man into the world. Such has been the complaint from eldest time; but we complain of our chief privilege, our ornament, and the connate mark of our sovereignty. *Porphyrigeniti sumus!* In Man the centripetal and individualizing tendency of all Nature is itself concentred and individualized—he is a revelation of Nature! Henceforward, he is referred to himself, delivered up to his own charge; and he who stands the most on himself, and stands the firmest, is the truest, because the most individual, Man. In social and political life this acme is inter-dependence; in moral life it is independence; in intellectual life it is genius. Nor does the form of polarity, which has accompanied the law of individuation up its whole ascent, desert it here. As the height, so the depth. The intensities must be at once opposite and equal. As the liberty, so must be the reverence for law. As the independence, so must be the service and the submission to the Supreme Will! As the ideal genius and the originality, in the same proportion must be the resignation to the real world, the sympathy and the inter-communion with Nature. In the conciliating mid-point, or equator, does the Man live, and only by its equal presence in both its poles can that life be manifested!

If it had been possible, within the prescribed limits of this essay, to have deduced the philosophy of Life synthetically, the evidence would have been carried over from section to section, and the *quod erat demonstrandum* at the conclusion of one section would reappear as the principle of the succeeding—the goal of the one would be the starting-post of the other. Positions arranged in my own mind, as intermediate and organic links of administration, must be presented to the reader in the first instance, at least, as a mere hypothesis. Instead of demanding his assent as a right, I must solicit a suspension of his judgment as a courtesy; and, after all, however firmly the hypothesis may support the phenomena piled upon it, we can deduce no more than a practical rule, grounded on a strong presumption. The license of arithmetic, however, furnishes instances that a rule may be usefully applied in practice, and for the particular purpose may be sufficiently authenticated by the result, before it has itself been duly demonstrated. It is enough, if only it hath been rendered fully intelligible.

In a system where every position proceeds from a scientific preconstruction, a power acting exclusively in length, would be magnetism by virtue of our own definition of the term. In like manner, a surface power would be electricity, as far as that system was concerned, whether it accorded or not with the facts ordinarily so called. But it is incumbent on us, who must treat the subject *analytically*, to show by experiment that magnetism does in fact act longitudinally, and electricity superficially; and that, consequently, the former is distinguished from, and yet contained in, the latter, as a straight line is distinguished from, yet contained in, a superficies.

First, that magnetism, in its conductors, seeks and follows length only, and by the length is itself conducted, has been proved by Brugmans, in his philosophical Essay on the Matter of Magnetism, where he relates that a magnet capable of supporting a body four times heavier than itself, and which acted as a magnetic needle at the distance of twenty inches, was so weakened by the interposition of three cast-iron plates of considerable thickness, as scarcely to move the magnetic needle from its place at a distance of only three inches. A similar experiment had been made by Descartes. I concluded, therefore, said Brugmans, that if the iron plates were interposed between the magnet and the needle lengthways, instead of breadthways or right across, the action of the magnet on the magnetic needle would, in consequence of this great increase of resistance, become still weaker, or perhaps evanescent. But not less to my surprise than my admiration, I found that the power of the magnet was so far from being *diminished* by this change in the relative position of the iron-plates; that, on the contrary, it now extended to a far greater distance than when no iron at all was interposed. Some time after the same philosopher, out of several iron bars, the sides of which were an inch broad each, composed a single bar of the length of more than ten feet, and observed the magnetism make its way through the whole mass. But, in order to try whether the action could be propagated to any length indefinitely, after several experiments with bars of intermediate lengths, in all of which he had succeeded, he tried a four-cornered iron rod, more than twenty feet long, and it was at this length that the magnetic power first began to be diminished. So far Brugmans.

But the shortest way for any one to convince himself of this relation of the magnetic power would be, in one and the same experiment, to interpose the same piece of iron between the magnet and the compass needle first *breadthways;* and in this case it will be found that the needle, which had been previously deflected by the magnet from its natural position at one of its poles, will instantly resume the same, either wholly or very nearly so—then to interpose the same piece of iron *lengthways;* in which case the position of the compass needle will be scarcely or not at all affected.

The assertion of Bernoulli and others, that the absolute force of the artificial magnet increases in the ratio of its superficies, stands corrected in the far more accurate experiments of Coulomb (published in his Treatise on Magnetism), which proves that the increase takes place (in a far greater degree) in the ratio of its length. The same naturalist even found means to determine that the directing powers of the needle, which he had measured by help of his *balance de tortion*, stand to the length of the needle in such a ratio as that, provided only the length of the needle is from forty to fifty times its diameter, the momenta of these directing powers will increase in the very same direct proportion as the length is increased. Nor is this all that may be deduced from the experiment last mentioned. If only the magnet be strong enough, it will show likewise that magnetism *seeks* the length. The proof is contained in the remarkable fact, that the iron interposed between the magnet and the magnetic needle *breadthways* constantly acquires its two opposite poles at both ends *lengthways*. Though the preceding experiments are abundantly sufficient to prove the position, yet the following deserves mention for the beautiful clearness of its evidence. If the magnetic power is determined exclusively by length, it is to be expected that it will manifest no force, where the piece of iron is of such a shape that no one dimension predominates. Bring a *cube* of iron near the magnetic needle and it will not exert the slightest degree of power beyond what belongs to it as mere iron. By the perfect equality of the dimension, the magnetism of the earth appears, as it were, perplexed and doubtful. Now, then, attach a second cube of iron to the first, and the instantaneous act of the iron on the magnetic needle will make it manifest that with the length thus given, the magnetic influence is given at the same moment.

That electricity, on the other hand, does not act in length merely, is clear, from the fact that every electric body is electric over its whole surface. But that electricity acts both in length and breadth, and *only* in length and breadth, and not in depth; in short, that the (so-called) electrical fluid in an electrified body spreads over the whole surface of that body without penetrating it, or tending *ad intra*, may be proved by direct experiment. Take a cylinder of wood, and bore an indefinite number of holes in it, each of them four lines in depth and four in diameter. Electrify this cylinder, and present to its superficies a small square of gold-leaf, held to it by an insulating needle of gum lac, and bring this square to an electrometer of great sensibility. The electrometer will instantly show an electricity in the gold-leaf, similar to that of the cylinder which had been brought into contact with it. The square of gold-leaf having thus been discharged of its electricity, put it carefully into one of the holes of the cylinder, *so*, namely, that it shall touch only the bottom of the hole, and present it again to the electrometer. It will be then found that the electrometer will exhibit no signs of electricity whatsoever. From this it follows, that the electricity which had been communicated to the cylinder had confined itself to the *surface*. If the time and the limit prescribed would admit, we could multiply experiments, all tending to prove the same law; but we must be content with the barely sufficient. But that the *chemical process* acts in *depth*, and first, therefore, *realizes* and integrates the fluxional power of magnetism and electricity, is involved in the *term* composition; and this will become still more convincing when we have learnt to regard *decomposition* as a mere co-relative, *i. e.* as decomposition relatively to the body decomposed, but composition *actually* and in respect of the substances, *into* which it was decomposed. The alteration in the specific gravity of metals in their chemical amalgams, interesting as the fact is in all points, is *decisive* in the present; for gravity is the sole *inward* of inorganic bodies—it *constitutes* their depth.

I can now, for the first time, give to my opinions that degree of intelligibility, which is requisite for their introduction as hypotheses; the experiments above related, understood as in the common mode of thinking, prove that the magnetic influence flows in length, the electric fluid by suffusion, and that chemical agency (whatever the main agent may be) is qualitative and *in intimis*. Now my hypothesis demands the converse of all this. I affirm that a power, acting exclusively in length, is (wherever it be found) *magnetism;* that a power which acts *both* in length and in breadth, and *only* in length and breadth, is (wherever it be found) *electricity;* and finally, that a power which, together with length and breadth, includes depth likewise, is (wherever it be found) *constructive agency*. That is but *one* phenomenon of magnetism, to which we have appropriated and confined the term magnetism; because of all the natural bodies at present known, iron, and one or two of its nearest relatives in the family of hard yet coherent metals, are the only ones, in which all the conditions are collected, under which alone the magnetic agency can appear in and during the act itself. When, therefore, I affirm the power of reproduction in organized bodies to be magnetism, I must be understood to mean that this power, as it exists in the magnet, and which we there (to use a strong phrase) catch in the very act, is to the same kind of power, working as reproductive, what the root is to the cube of that root. We no more confound the force in the compass needle with that of reproduction, than a man can be said to confound his liver with a lichen, because he affirms that both of them grow.

The same precautions are to be repeated in the identification of electricity with irritability; and the power of depth, for which we have yet no appropriated term, with sensibility. How great the distance is in all, and that the lowest degrees are adopted as the exponent terms, not for their own sakes, but merely because they may be used with less hazard of diverting the attention from the *kind* by peculiar properties arising out of the degree, is evident from the third instance, unless the theorist can be supposed insane enough to apply sensation in good earnest to the effervescence of an acid or an alkali, or to sympathize with the distresses of a vat of new beer when it is working. In whatever way the subject could be treated, it must have remained unintelligible to men who, if they think of space at all, abstract their notion of it from the contents of an exhausted receiver. With this, and with an ether, such men may work wonders; as what, indeed, can not be done with a plenum and a vacuum, when a theorist has privileged himself to assume the one, or the other, *ad libitum?*—in all innocence of heart, and undisturbed by the reflection that the two things can not both be true. That both time and space are mere abstractions I am well aware; but I know with equal certainty that what is *expressed* by them as the *identity* of both is the highest reality, and the root of all power, the power to suffer, as well as the power to act. However mere an *ens logicum* space may be, the *dimensions* of space are real, and the works of Galileo, in more than one elegant passage, prove with what awe and amazement they fill the mind that worthily contemplates them. Dismissing, therefore, all facts of degrees, as introduced merely for the purposes of illustration, I would make as little reference as possible to the magnet, the charged phial, or the processes of the laboratory, and designate the three powers in the process of our animal life, each by two co-relative terms, the one expressing the *form*, and the other the *object* and *product* of the power. My hypothesis will, therefore, be thus expressed, that the constituent forces of life in the human living body are—first, the power of length, or REPRODUCTION; second, the power of surface (that is, length and breadth), or IRRITABILITY; third, the power of depth, or SENSIBILITY. With this observation I may conclude these remarks, only reminding the reader that Life itself is neither of these separately, but the copula of all three—that Life, *as* Life, supposes a positive or universal principle in Nature, with a negative principle in every particular animal, the latter, or limitative power, constantly acting to individualize, and, as it were, *figure* the former. *Thus*, then, Life itself is not a *thing*—a self-subsistent *hypostasis*—but an *act* and *process;* which, pitiable as the prejudice will appear to the *forts esprits*, is a great deal more than either my reason would authorize or my conscience allow me to assert—concerning the Soul, as the principle both of Reason and Conscience.

THE STATESMAN'S MANUAL

THE

STATESMAN'S MANUAL;

OR, THE BIBLE THE BEST GUIDE TO POLITICAL SKILL AND FORESIGHT: A LAY SERMON, ADDRESSED TO THE HIGHER CLASSES OF SOCIETY,

WITH AN APPENDIX,

CONTAINING COMMENTS AND ESSAYS CONNECTED WITH THE STUDY OF THE INSPIRED WRITINGS.

BY SAMUEL TAYLOR COLERIDGE.

WITH THE AUTHOR'S LAST CORRECTIONS AND NOTES,

BY

HENRY NELSON COLERIDGE, ESQ., M.A.

NEW YORK:
HARPER & BROTHERS,
1853.

Ad isthæc quæso vos, qualiacunque primo videantur aspectu, attendite, ut qui vobis forsan insanire videar, saltem quibus insaniam rationibus cognoscatis.—GIORDANO BRUNO.

A LAY SERMON, &c.

For he established a testimony in Jacob and appointed a law in Israel; which he commanded our fathers, that they should make them known to their children: that the generation to come might know them, even the children which should be born; who should arise and declare them to their children: that they might set their hope in God, and not forget the works of God.—Psalm lxxviii. 5, 6, 7.

If our whole knowledge and information concerning the Bible had been confined to the one fact of its immediate derivation from God, we should still presume that it contained rules and assistances for all conditions of men under all circumstances; and therefore for communities no less than for individuals. The contents of every work must correspond to the character and designs of the work-master; and the inference in the present case is too obvious to be overlooked, too plain to be resisted. It requires, indeed, all the might of superstition to conceal from a man of common understanding the further truth, that the interment of such a treasure in a dead language must needs be contrary to the intentions of the gracious Donor. Apostasy itself dared not question the premisses: and that the practical consequence did not follow, is conceivable only under a complete system of delusion, which from the cradle to the death-bed ceases not to over-awe the will by obscure fears, while it pre-occupies the senses by vivid imagery and ritual pantomime. But to such a scheme all forms of sophistry are native. The very excellence of the Giver has been made a reason for withholding the gift; nay the transcendent value of the gift itself assigned as the motive of its detention. We may be shocked at the presumption, but need not be surprised at the fact, that a jealous priesthood should have ventured to represent the applicability of the Bible to all the wants and occasions of men as a wax-like pliancy to all their fancies and prepossessions. Faithful guardians of Holy Writ, they are constrained to make it useless in order to guard it from profanation; and those, whom they have most defrauded, are the readiest to justify the fraud. For imposture, organized into a comprehensive and self-consistent whole, forms a world of its own, in which inversion becomes the order of nature.

Let it not be forgotten, however (and I recommend the fact to the especial attention of those among ourselves, who are disposed to rest contented with an implicit faith and passive acquiescence) that the Church of Rome never ceased to avow the profoundest reverence for the Scriptures themselves, and what it forbids its vassals to ascertain, it not only permits, but commands them to take for granted.

Whether, and to what extent, this suspension of the rational functions, this spiritual slumber, will be imputed as a sin to the souls who are still under chains of Papal darkness, we are neither enabled or authorized to determine. It is enough for us to know that the land, in which we abide, has like another Goshen *been severed from the plague*, and that we have light in our dwellings. The road of salvation for us is a high road, and the wayfarers, though *simple, need not err therein*. The Gospel lies open in the market-place and on every window-seat, so that (virtually at least) *the deaf may hear the words of the book*. It is preached at every turning, so that the *blind may see* them. (Isa. xxix. 18.) The circumstances then being so different, if the result should prove similar, we may be quite certain that we shall not be holden guiltless. The ignorance which may be the excuse of others will be our crime. Our birth and denizenship in an enlightened and Protestant land will, with all our rights and franchises to boot, be brought in judgment against us, and stand first in the fearful list of blessings abused. The glories of our country will form the blazonry of our own impeachment, and the very name of Englishmen, of which we are almost all of us too proud, and for which scarcely any of us are enough thankful, will be annexed to that of Christians only to light up our shame and to aggravate our condemnation.

I repeat, therefore, that the habitual unreflectingness, which in certain countries may be susceptible of more or less palliation in most instances, can in this country be deemed blameless in none. The humblest and least educated of our countrymen must have wilfully neglected the inestimable privileges secured to all alike, if he has not himself found, if he has not from his own personal experience discovered, the sufficiency of the Scriptures* in all knowledge requisite for a right performance of his duty as a man and a Christian. Of the laboring classes, who in all countries form the great majority of the inhabitants, more than this is not demanded, more than this is not perhaps generally desirable. They are *not sought for in public counsel,* nor need they be found where politic sentences are spoken. It is enough if every one is wise in the working of his own craft: so best *will they maintain the state of the world.*

But you, my friends, to whom the following pages are more particularly addressed, as to men moving in the higher class of society,—you will, I hope, have availed yourselves of the ampler means intrusted to you by God's providence, for a more extensive study and a wider use of his revealed will and word. From you we have a right to expect a sober and meditative accommodation to your own times and country of those important truths declared in the inspired writings *for a thousand generations,* and of the awful examples, belonging to all ages, by which those truths are at once illustrated and confirmed. Would you feel conscious that you had shown yourselves unequal to your station in society,—would you stand degraded in your own eyes,—if you betrayed an utter want of information respecting the acts of human sovereigns and legislators? And should you not much rather be both ashamed and afraid to know yourselves inconversant with the acts and constitutions of God, whose law executeth itself, and whose Word is the foundation, the power, and the life of the universe? Do you hold it a requisite of your rank to show yourselves inquisitive concerning the expectations and plans of statesmen and state-councillors? Do you excuse it as natural curiosity, that you lend a listening ear to the guesses of state-gazers, to the dark hints and open revilings of our self-inspired state-fortune-tellers, the wizards, that peep and mutter and forecast, alarmists by trade, and malcontents for their bread? And should you not feel a deeper interest in predictions which are permanent prophecies, because they are at the same time eternal truths? Predictions which in containing the grounds of fulfilment involve the principles of foresight, and teach the science of the future in its perpetual elements?

* See App. (A.)—*Ed.*

But I will struggle to believe that of those whom I now suppose myself addressing there are few who have not so employed their greater leisure and superior advantages as to render these remarks, if not wholly superfluous, yet personally inapplicable. In common with your worldly inferiors, you will indeed have directed your main attention to the promises and the information conveyed in the records of the Evangelists and Apostles;—promises, that need only a lively trust in them, on our own part, to be the means as well as the pledges of our eternal welfare—information that opens out to our knowledge a kingdom that is not of this world, thrones that can not be shaken, and sceptres that can neither be broken nor transferred. Yet not the less on this account will you have looked back with a proportionate interest on the temporal destinies of men and nations, stored up for our instruction in the archives of the Old Testament: not the less will you delight to retrace the paths by which Providence has led the kingdoms of this world through the valley of mortal life;—paths engraved with the footmarks of captains sent forth from the God of armies;—nations in whose guidance or chastisement the arm of Omnipotence itself was made bare.

Recent occurrences have given additional strength and fresh force to our sage poet's eulogy on the Jewish Prophets;—

> As men divinely taught and better teaching
> The solid rules of civil government
> In their majestic unaffected style,
> Than all the oratory of Greece and Rome.
> In them is plainest taught and easiest learnt
> What makes a nation happy and keeps it so,
> What ruins kingdoms and lays cities flat. PAR. REG. iv. 354.

If there be any antidote to that restless craving for the wonders of the day, which in conjunction with the appetite for publicity is spreading like an efflorescence on the surface of our national character; if there exist means for deriving resignation from general discontent, means of building up with the very materials of political gloom that steadfast frame of hope which affords the only certain shelter from the throng of self-realizing alarms, at the same time that it is the natural home and workshop of all the active virtues; that antidote and these means must be sought for in the collation of the present with the past, in the habit of thoughtfully assimilating the events of our own age to those of the time before us. If this be a moral advantage derivable from history in general, rendering its study therefore a moral duty for such as possess the opportunities of books, leisure and education, it would be inconsistent even with the name of believers not to recur with pre-eminent interest to events and revolutions, the records of which are as much distinguished from all other history by their especial claims to divine authority, as the facts themselves were from all other facts by especial manifestation of divine interference. *Whatsoever things*, saith Saint Paul (Rom. xv. 4), *were written aforetime, were written for our learning; that we through patience and comfort of the Scriptures might have hope.*

In the infancy of the world signs and wonders were requisite in order to startle and break down that superstition,—idolatrous in itself and the source of all other idolatry,—which tempts the natural man to seek the true cause and origin of public calamities in outward circumstances, persons, and incidents: in agents therefore that were themselves but surges of the same tide, passive conductors of the one invisible influence, under which the total host of billows, in the whole line of successive impulse, swell and roll shoreward; there finally, each in its turn, to strike, roar, and be dissipated.

But with each miracle worked there was a truth revealed, which thenceforward was to act as its substitute. And if we think the Bible less applicable to us on account of the miracles, we degrade ourselves into mere slaves of sense and fancy, which are indeed the appointed medium between earth and heaven, but for that very cause stand in a desirable relation to spiritual truth then only, when, as a mere and passive medium, they yield a free passage to its light. It was only to overthrow the usurpation exercised in and through the senses, that the senses were miraculously appealed to; for reason and religion are their own evidence.* The natural sun is in this respect a symbol of the spiritual. Ere he is fully arisen, and while his glories are still under veil, he calls up the breeze to chase away the usurping vapors of the night-season, and thus converts the air itself into the minister of its own purification: not surely in proof or elucidation of the light from heaven, but to prevent its interception.

Wherever, therefore, similar circumstances co-exist with the

* See App. (B.)—*Ed.*

same moral causes, the principles revealed, and the examples recorded, in the inspired writings render miracles superfluous: and if we neglect to apply truths in expectation of wonders, or under pretext of the cessation of the latter, we tempt God, and merit the same reply which our Lord gave to the Pharisees on a like occasion. *A wicked and an adulterous generation seeketh after a sign, and there shall no sign be given to it, but the sign of the prophet Jonas* (Matt. xvi. 4)*:* that is, a threatening call to repentance.* Equally applicable and prophetic will the following verses be. *The queen of the South shall rise up in the judgment with the men of this generation and condemn them: for she came from the utmost parts of the earth to hear the wisdom of Solomon; and, behold, a greater than Solomon is here. —The men of Nineveh shall rise in judgment with this generation and shall condemn it; for they repented at the preaching of Jonas; and, behold, a greater than Jonas is here* (Luke xi. 31, 32). For have we not divine assurance that Christ is with his Church even to the end of the world? And what could the queen of the South, or the men of Nineveh have beholden, that could enter into competition with the events of our own times, in importance, in splendor, or even in strangeness and significancy?

The true origin of human events is so little susceptible of that kind of evidence which can compel our belief; so many are the disturbing forces which in every cycle of changes modify the motion given by the first projection; and every age has, or imagines it has, its own circumstances which render past experience no longer applicable to the present case; that there will never be wanting answers, and explanations, and specious flatteries of hope to persuade a people and its government that the history of the past is inapplicable to their case. And no wonder, if we read history for the facts instead of reading it for the sake of the general principles, which are to the facts as the root and sap of a tree to its leaves: and no wonder, if history so read should find a dangerous rival in novels, nay, if the latter should be preferred to the former on the score even of probability. I well remember, that when the examples of former Jacobins, as Julius Cæsar, Cromwell, and the like, were adduced in France and England at the commencement of the French Consulate, it was ridiculed as pedantry and pedant's ignorance to fear a repetition of usurpa-

* See App. (C.)—*Ed.*

tion and military despotism at the close of the enlightened eighteenth century! Even so, in the very dawn of the late tempestuous day, when the revolutions of Corcyra, the proscriptions of the Reformers, Marius, Cæsar, and the like, and the direful effects of the levelling tenets in the Peasants' War in Germany, were urged on the Convention, and its vindicators; I well remember that the *Magi* of the day, the true citizens of the world, the *plusquam-perfecti* of patriotism, gave us set proofs that similar results were impossible, and that it was an insult to so philosophical an age, to so enlightened a nation, to dare direct the public eye towards them as to lights of warning! Alas! like lights in the stern of a vessel they illumined the path only that had been past over!

The politic Florentine* has observed, that there are brains of three races. The one understands of itself; the other understands as much as is shown it by others; the third neither understands of itself, nor what is shown it by others. In our times there are more perhaps who belong to the third class from vanity and acquired frivolity of mind, than from natural incapacity. It is no uncommon weakness with those who are honored with the acquaintance of the great, to attribute national events to particular persons, particular measures, to the errors of one man, to the intrigues of another, to any possible spark of a particular occasion, rather than to the true proximate cause (and which alone deserves the name of a cause), the predominant state of public opinion. And still less are they inclined to refer the latter to the ascendency of speculative principles, and the scheme or mode of thinking in vogue. I have known men, who with significant nods and the pitying contempt of smiles have denied all influence to the corruptions of moral and political philosophy, and with much solemnity have proceeded to solve the riddle of the French Revolution by Anecdotes! Yet it would not be difficult, by an unbroken chain of historic facts, to demonstrate that the most important changes in the commercial relations of the world had their origin in the closets or lonely walks of uninterested theorists;—that the mighty epochs of commerce, that have changed the face of empires; nay, the most impor-

* *Sono di tre generazioni cervelli: l'uno intende per se; l'altro intende quanto da altri gli è mostro; e il terzo non intende nè per se stesso nè per dimostrazione di altri.* Il Principe, c. xxii.

tant of those discoveries and improvements in the mechanic arts, which have numerically increased our population beyond what the wisest statesmen of Elizabeth's reign deemed possible, and again doubled this population virtually; the most important, I say, of those inventions that in their results

——— best uphold
War by her two main nerves, iron and gold—

had their origin not in the cabinets of statesmen, or in the practical insight of men of business, but in the visions of recluse genius. To the immense majority of men, even in civilized countries, speculative philosophy has ever been, and must ever remain, a *terra incognita*. Yet it is not the less true, that all the epoch-forming revolutions of the Christian world, the revolutions of religion and with them the civil, social, and domestic habits of the nations concerned, have coincided with the rise and fall of metaphysical systems.* So few are the minds that really govern the machine of society, and so incomparably more numerous and more important are the indirect consequences of things, than their foreseen and direct effects.

It is with nations as with individuals. In tranquil moods and peaceable times we are quite practical. Facts only and cool common sense are then in fashion. But let the winds of passion swell, and straightway men begin to generalize; to connect by remotest analogies; to express the most universal positions of reason in the most glowing figures of fancy; in short, to feel particular truths and mere facts, as poor, cold, narrow, and incommensurate with their feelings.

With his wonted fidelity to nature, our own great poet has placed the greater number of his profoundest maxims and general truths, both political and moral, not in the mouths of men at ease, but of men under the influence of passion, when the mighty thoughts overmaster and become the tyrants of the mind that has brought them forth. In his Lear, Othello, Macbeth, Hamlet, principles of deepest insight and widest interest fly off like sparks from the glowing iron under the loud forge-hammer.†

* This thought might also be applied to, and exemplified by, the successive epochs in the history of the Fine Arts from the tenth century. 1827.

† It seems a paradox only to the unthinking, and it is a fact that none, but the unread in history, will deny, that in periods of popular tumult and

A calm and detailed examination of the facts justifies me to my own mind in hazarding the bold assertion, that the fearful blunders of the late dread Revolution, and all the calamitous mistakes of its opponents from its commencement even to the æra of loftier principles and wiser measures (an æra, that began with, and ought to be named from, the war of the Spanish and Portuguese insurgents) every failure with all its gloomy results may be unanswerably deduced from the neglect of some maxim or other that had been established by clear reasoning and plain facts in the writings of Thucydides, Tacitus, Machiavel, Bacon, or Harrington. These are red-letter names even in the almanacs of worldly wisdom : and yet I dare challenge all the critical benches of infidelity to point out any one important truth, any one efficient practical direction or warning, which did not pre-exist (and for the most part in a sounder, more intelligible, and more comprehensive form) in the Bible.

In addition to this, the Hebrew legislator, and the other inspired poets, prophets, historians and moralists of the Jewish Church have two peculiar advantages in their favor. First, their particular rules and prescripts flow directly and visibly from universal principles, as from a fountain : they flow from principles and ideas that are not so properly said to be confirmed by reasons as

innovation the more abstract a notion is, the more readily has it been found to combine, the closer has appeared its affinity, with the feelings of a people and with all their immediate impulses to action. At the commencement of the French Revolution, in the remotest villages every tongue was employed in echoing and enforcing the almost geometrical abstractions of the physiocratic politicians and economists. The public roads were crowded with armed enthusiasts disputing on the inalienable sovereignty of the people, the imprescriptible laws of the pure reason, and the universal constitution, which, as rising out of the nature and rights of man as man, all nations alike were under the obligation of adopting. Turn over the fugitive writings, that are still extant, of the age of Luther ; peruse the pamphlets and loose sheets that came out in flights during the reign of Charles I. and the Republic; and you will find in these one continued comment on the aphorism of Lord Bacon (a man assuredly sufficiently acquainted with the extent of secret and personal influence), that the knowledge of the speculative principles of men in general between the age of twenty and thirty, is the one great source of political prophecy. And Sir Philip Sidney regarded the adoption of one set of principles in the Netherlands, as a proof of the divine agency, and the fountain of all the events and successes of that Revolution.

to be reason itself. Principles in act and procession, disjoined from which, and from the emotions that inevitably accompany the actual intuition of their truth, the widest maxims of prudence are like arms without hearts, muscles without nerves. Secondly, from the very nature of those principles, as taught in the Bible, they are understood in exact proportion as they are believed and felt. The regulator is never separated from the main-spring. For the words of the Apostle are literally and philosophically true: *We* (that is the human race) *live by faith*. Whatever we do or know that in kind is different from the brute creation, has its origin in a determination of the reason to have faith and trust in itself. This, its first act of faith, is scarcely less than identical with its own being. *Implicite*, it is the *copula*—it contains the possibility—of every position, to which there exists any correspondence in reality.* It is itself, therefore, the realizing principle, the spiritual *substratum* of the whole complex body of truths. This primal act of faith is enunciated in the word, God: a faith not derived from, but itself the ground and source of, experience, and without which the fleeting chaos of facts would no more form experience, than the dust of the grave can of itself make a living man. The imperative and oracular form of the inspired Scripture is the form of reason itself in all things purely rational and moral.

If Scripture be the word of Divine Wisdom, we might anticipate that it would in all things be distinguished from other books, as the Supreme Reason, whose knowledge is creative, and antecedent to the things known, as distinguished from the understanding, or creaturely mind of the individual, the acts of which are posterior to the things which it records and arranges. Man alone was created in the image of God: a position groundless and inexplicable, if the reason in man do not differ from the understanding. For this the inferior animals (many at least) possess in degree: and assuredly the divine image or idea is not a thing of degrees.

* I mean that, but for the confidence which we place in the assertions of our reason and conscience, we could have no certainty of the reality and actual outness of the material world. It might be affirmed that in what we call "sleep" every one has a dream of his own; and that in what we call "awake," whole communities dream nearly alike. It is!—is a sense of reason: the senses can only say—It seems! 1827.

Hence it follows that what is expressed in the Scriptures is implied in all absolute science. The latter whispers what the former utter as with the voice of a trumpet. *As sure as God liveth*, is the pledge and assurance of every positive truth, that is asserted by the reason. The human understanding musing on many things snatches at truth, but is frustrated and disheartened by the fluctuating nature of its objects;* its conclusions therefore are timid and uncertain, and it hath no way of giving permanence to things but by reducing them to abstractions. *Hardly do we guess aright at things that are upon earth, and with labor do we find the things that are before us; but all certain knowledge is in the power of God, and a presence from above.* So only have the ways of men been reformed, and every doctrine that contains a saving truth, and all acts pleasing to God (in other words, all actions consonant with human nature, in its original intention) are through wisdom; that is, the rational spirit of man.

This then is the prerogative of the Bible; this is the privilege of its believing students. With them the principle of knowledge is likewise a spring and principle of action. And as it is the only certain knowledge, so are the actions that flow from it the only ones on which a secure reliance can be placed. The understanding may suggest motives, may avail itself of motives, and make judicious conjectures respecting the probable consequences of actions. But the knowledge taught in the Scriptures produces the motives, involves the consequences; and its highest *formula* is still: *As sure as God liveth*, so will it be unto thee! Strange as this position will appear to such as forget that motives can be causes only in a secondary and improper sense, inasmuch as the man makes the motive, not the motives the man; yet all history bears evidence to its truth. The sense of expediency, the cautious balancing of comparative advantages, the constant wakefulness to the *Cui bono?*—in connection with the *Quid mihi?*—all these are in their places in the routine of conduct, by which

* *Ποταμῷ γὰρ οὐκ ἔστιν ἐμβῆναι δὶς τῷ αὐτῷ καθ'* Ἡράκλειτον, *οὔτε θνητῆς οὐσίας δὶς ἅψασθαι κατὰ ἕξιν· ἀλλὰ ὀξύτητι καὶ τάχει μεταβολῆς σκίδνησι καὶ πάλιν συνάγει, μᾶλλον δὲ οὐδὲ πάλιν οὐδὲ ὕστερον ἀλλ' ἅμα συνίσταται καὶ ἀπολείπει, καὶ πρόσεισι καὶ ἄπεισι· ὅθεν οὐδ' εἰς τὸ εἶναι περαίνει τὸ γιγνόμενον αὐτῆς τῷ μηδέποτε λήγειν, μηδ' ἱστᾶσθαι τὴν γένεσιν, κ. τ. λ.*

PLUTARCH'S *De EI. apud Delphos* c. xviii.

the individual provides for himself the real or supposed wants of to-day and to-morrow: and in quiet times and prosperous circumstances a nation presents an aggregate of such individuals, a busy ant-hill in calm and sunshine. By the happy organization of a well-governed society the contradictory interests of ten millions of such individuals may neutralize each other, and be reconciled in the unity of the national interest. But whence did this happy organization first come? Was it a tree transplanted from Paradise, with all its branches in full fruitage? Or was it sowed in sunshine? Was it in vernal breezes and gentle rains that it fixed its roots, and grew and strengthened? Let history answer these questions. With blood was it planted; it was rocked in tempests; the goat, the ass, and the stag gnawed it; the wild boar has whetted his tusks on its bark. The deep scars are still extant on its trunk, and the path of the lightning may be traced among its higher branches. And even after its full growth, in the season of its strength, *when its height reached to the heaven, and the sight thereof to all the earth*, the whirlwind has more than once forced its stately top to touch the ground: it has been bent like a bow, and sprang back like a shaft. Mightier powers were at work than expediency ever yet called up; yea, mightier than the mere understanding can comprehend. One confirmation of the latter assertion you may find in the history of our country, written by the same Scotch philosopher who devoted his life to the undermining of the Christian religion; and expended his last breath in a blasphemous regret that he had not survived it;—by the same heartless sophist who, in this island, was the main pioneer of that atheistic philosophy, which in France transvenomed the natural thirst of truth into the *hydrophobia* of a wild and homeless skepticism; the Elias of that Spirit of Antichrist, which

——— still promising
Freedom, itself too sensual to be free,
Poisons life's amities and cheats the soul
Of faith, and quiet hope and all that lifts
And all that soothes the spirit!*

This inadequacy of the mere understanding to the apprehension of moral greatness we may trace in this historian's cool systematic attempt to steal away every feeling of reverence for every

* Poet. Works, VII. pp. 110, 111.—*Ed.*

great name by a scheme of motives, in which as often as possible the efforts and enterprises of heroic spirits are attributed to this or that paltry view of the most despicable selfishness. But in the majority of instances this would have been too palpably false and slanderous: and therefore the founders and martyrs of our Church and Constitution, of our civil and religious liberty, are represented as fanatics and bewildered enthusiasts. But histories incomparably more authentic than Mr. Hume's (nay, spite of himself even his own history) confirm by irrefragable evidence the aphorism of ancient wisdom, that nothing great was ever achieved without enthusiasm. For what is enthusiasm but the oblivion and swallowing up of self in an object dearer than self, or in an idea more vivid? How this is produced in the enthusiasm of wickedness, I have explained in the second Comment annexed to this Discourse. But in the genuine enthusiasm of morals, religion, and patriotism, this enlargement and elevation of the soul above its mere self attest the presence, and accompany the intuition, of ultimate principles alone. These alone can interest the undegraded human spirit deeply and enduringly, because these alone belong to its essence, and will remain with it permanently.

Notions, the depthless abstractions of fleeting *phænomena*, the shadows of sailing vapors, the colorless repetitions of rainbows, have effected their utmost when they have added to the distinctness of our knowledge. For this very cause they are of themselves adverse to lofty emotion, and it requires the influence of a light and warmth, not their own, to make them crystallize into a semblance of growth. But every principle is actualized by an idea; and every idea is living, productive, partaketh of infinity, and (as Bacon has sublimely observed) containeth an endless power of semination. Hence it is, that science, which consists wholly in ideas and principles, is power. *Scientia et potentia* (saith the same philosopher) *in idem coincidunt.* Hence too it is, that notions, linked arguments, reference to particular facts and calculations of prudence, influence only the comparatively few, the men of leisurely minds who have been trained up to them: and even these few they influence but faintly. But for the reverse, I appeal to the general character of the doctrines which have collected the most numerous sects, and acted upon the moral being of the converts with a force that might well seem supernatural. The great principles of our religion, the sublime ideas spoken out everywhere in the Old and New Testament, resemble the fixed stars, which appear of the same size to the naked as to the armed eye; the magnitude of which the telescope may rather seem to diminish than to increase. At the annunciation of principles, of ideas, the soul of man awakes and starts up, as an exile in a far distant land at the unexpected sounds of his native language, when after long years of absence, and almost of oblivion, he is suddenly addressed in his own mother-tongue. He weeps for joy, and embraces the speaker as his brother. How else can we explain the fact so honorable to Great Britain, that the poorest* amongst us will contend with as much enthusiasm as the richest for the rights of property? These rights are the spheres and necessary conditions of free agency. But free agency contains the idea of the free will; and in this he intuitively knows the sublimity, and the infinite hopes, fears, and capabilities of his own nature. On what other ground but the cognateness of ideas and principles to man as man does the nameless soldier rush to the combat in defence of the liberties or the honor of his country?—Even men wofully neglectful of the principles of religion will shed their blood for its truth.

Alas!—the main hindrance to the use of the Scriptures, as your manual, lies in the notion that you are already acquainted with its contents. Something new must be presented to you, wholly new and wholly out of yourselves; for whatever is within us must be as old as the first dawn of human reason. Truths of all others the most awful and mysterious and at the same time of universal interest are considered so true as to lose all the powers of truth, and lie bed-ridden in the dormitory of the soul, side by side with the most despised and exploded errors. But it should not be so with you! The pride of education, the sense of consistency should preclude the objection: for would you not be ashamed to apply it to the works of Tacitus, or of Shakspeare? Above all, the rank which you hold, the influence you possess, the powers you may be called to wield, give a special unfitness to this frivolous craving for novelty. To find no contradiction in

* The reader will remember the anecdote told with so much humor in Goldsmith's Essay. But this is not the first instance where the mind in its hour of meditation finds matter of admiration and elevating thought in circumstances that in a different mood had excited his mirth.

the union of old and new, to contemplate the Ancient of days, his words and his works, with a feeling as fresh as if they were now first springing forth at his *fiat*—this characterizes the minds that feel the riddle of the world and may help to unravel it. This, most of all things, will raise you above the mass of mankind, and therefore will best entitle and qualify you to guide and control them. You say, you are already familiar with the Scriptures. With the words, perhaps, but in any other sense you might as wisely boast of your familiar acquaintance with the rays of the sun, and under that pretence turn away your eyes from the light of heaven.

Or would you wish for authorities, for great examples? You may find them in the writings of Thuanus, of Clarendon, of More, of Raleigh; and in the life and letters of the heroic Gustavus Adolphus. But these, though eminent statesmen, were Christians, and might lie under the thraldom of habit and prejudice. I will refer you then to authorities of two great men, both pagans; but removed from each other by many centuries, and not more distant in their ages than in their characters and situations. The first shall be that of Heraclitus, the sad and recluse philosopher. *Πολυμαθίη νόον οὐ διδάσκει· Σίβυλλα δὲ μαινομένῳ στόματι ἀγελαστὰ καὶ ἀκαλλώπιστα καὶ ἀμύριστα φθεγγομένη χιλίων ἐτῶν ἐξικνεῖται τῇ φωνῇ διὰ τὸν θεόν.** Shall we hesitate to apply to the prophets of God, what could be affirmed of the Sibyls by a philosopher whom Socrates, the prince of philosophers, venerated for the profundity of his wisdom?

For the other, I will refer you to the darling of the polished court of Augustus, to the man whose works have been in all ages deemed the models of good sense, and are still the pocket companions of those who pride themselves on uniting the scholar

* Multiscience (or a variety and quantity of acquired knowledge) does not teach intelligence. But the Sibyl with wild enthusiastic mouth shrilling forth unmirthful, inornate, and unperfumed truths, reaches to a thousand years, with her voice through the power of God.

———Not hers
To win the sense by words of rhetoric,
Lip-blossoms breathing perishable sweets;
But by the power of the informing Word
Roll sounding onward through a thousand years
Her deep prophetic bodements.

Lit. Rem. V. p. 268.—*Ed.*

with the gentleman. This accomplished man of the world has given an account of the subjects of conversation between the illustrious statesmen who governed, and the brightest luminaries who then adorned, the empire of the civilized world:

> *Sermo oritur non de villis domibusve alienis*
> *Nec, male nec ne Lepos saltet. Sed quod magis ad nos*
> *Pertinet, et nescire malum est, agitamus: utrumne*
> *Divitiis homines, an sint virtute beati;*
> *Et quod sit natura boni, summumque quid ejus.**

Berkeley indeed asserts, and is supported in his assertion by the great statesmen, Lord Bacon and Sir Walter Raleigh, that without an habitual interest in these subjects a man may be a dexterous intriguer, but never can be a statesman.

But do you require some one or more particular passage from the Bible, that may at once illustrate and exemplify its applicability to the changes and fortunes of empires? Of the numerous chapters that relate to the Jewish tribes, their enemies and allies, before and after their division into two kingdoms, it would be more difficult to state a single one from which some guiding light might not be struck. And in nothing is Scriptural history more strongly contrasted with the histories of highest note in the present age, than in its freedom from the hollowness of abstractions. While the latter present a shadow-fight of things and quantities, the former gives us the history of men, and balances the important influence of individual minds with the previous state of the national morals and manners, in which, as constituting a specific susceptibility, it presents to us the true cause both of the influence itself, and of the weal or woe that were its consequents. How should it be otherwise? The histories and political economy of the present and preceding century partake in the general contagion of its mechanic philosophy, and are the product of an unenlivened generalizing understanding. In the Scriptures they are the living educts of the imagination; of that reconciling and mediatory power, which incorporating the reason in images of the sense, and organizing (as it were) the flux of the senses by the permanence and self-circling energies of the reason, gives birth to a system of symbols, harmonious in themselves, and consubstantial with the truths of which they are the conductors. These

* Hor. Serm. ii. t. 6, 71, &c.

are the *wheels* which Ezekiel beheld, when the hand of the Lord was upon him, and he saw visions of God as he sate among the captives by the river of Chebar. *Whithersoever the Spirit was to go, the* wheels *went, and thither was their spirit to go:—for the spirit of the living creature was in the* wheels *also.** The truths and the symbols that represent them move in conjunction and form the living chariot that bears up (for us) the throne of the Divine Humanity. Hence, by a derivative, indeed, but not a divided, influence, and though in a secondary yet in more than a metaphorical sense, the Sacred Book is worthily entitled *the Word of God.* Hence too, its contents present to us the stream of time continuous as life and a symbol of eternity, inasmuch as the past and the future are virtually contained in the present. According therefore to our relative position on the banks of this stream the Sacred History becomes prophetic, the Sacred Prophecies historical, while the power and substance of both inhere in its laws, its promises, and its comminations. In the Scriptures therefore both facts and persons must of necessity have a twofold significance, a past and a future, a temporary and a perpetual, a particular and a universal application. They must be at once portraits and ideals.

Eheu! paupertina philosophia in paupertinam religionem ducit:—A hunger-bitten and idea-less philosophy naturally produces a starveling and comfortless religion. It is among the miseries of the present age that it recognizes no *medium* between literal and metaphorical. Faith is either to be buried in the dead letter, or its name and honors usurped by a counterfeit product of the mechanical understanding, which in the blindness of self-complacency confounds symbols with allegories. Now an allegory is but a translation of abstract notions into a picture-language, which is itself nothing but an abstraction from objects of the senses; the principal being more worthless even than its phantom proxy, both alike unsubstantial, and the former shapeless to boot. On the other hand a symbol (*ὁ ἔστιν ἀεὶ ταυτηγόρικον*) is characterized by a translucence of the special in the individual, or of the general in the special, or of the universal in the general; above all by the translucence of the eternal through and in the temporal. It always partakes of the reality which it renders intelligible; and while it enunciates the whole, abides itself as a

* Ezek. i. 20.

living part in that unity of which it is the representative. The other are but empty echoes which the fancy arbitrarily associates with apparitions of matter, less beautiful but not less shadowy than the sloping orchard or hill-side pasture-field seen in the transparent lake below. Alas, for the flocks that are to be led forth to such pastures! *It shall even be as when a hungry man dreameth, and behold, he eateth; but he awaketh and his soul is empty: or as when a thirsty man dreameth, and behold he drinketh; but he awaketh and behold, he is faint!** O! that we would seek for the bread which was given from heaven, that we should eat thereof and be strengthened! O that we would draw at the well at which the flocks of our forefathers had living water drawn for them, even that water which, instead of mocking the thirst of him to whom it is given, becomes a well within himself *springing up to life everlasting!*

When we reflect how large a part of our present knowledge and civilization is owing, directly or indirectly, to the Bible; when we are compelled to admit, as a fact of history, that the Bible has been the main lever by which the moral and intellectual character of Europe has been raised to its present comparative height; we should be struck, methinks, by the marked and prominent difference of this book from the works which it is now the fashion to quote as guides and authorities in morals, politics, and history. I will point out a few of the excellences by which the one is distinguished, and shall leave it to your own judgment and recollection to perceive and apply the contrast to the productions of highest name in these latter days. In the Bible every agent appears and acts as a self-subsisting individual; each has a life of its own, and yet all are one life. The elements of necessity and free-will are reconciled in the higher power of an omnipresent Providence, that predestinates the whole in the moral freedom of the integral parts. Of this the Bible never suffers us to lose sight. The root is never detached from the ground. It is God everywhere: and all creatures conform to his decrees, the righteous by performance of the law, the disobedient by the sufferance of the penalty.

Suffer me to inform or remind you, that there is a threefold necessity. There is a logical, and there is a mathematical necessity; but the latter is always hypothetical, and both subsist

* Is. xxix. 8.—*Ed.*

formally only, not in any real object. Only by the intuition and immediate spiritual consciousness of the idea of God, as the One and Absolute, at once the ground and the cause, who alone containeth in himself the ground of his own nature, and therein of all natures, do we arrive at the third, which alone is a real objective, necessity. Here the immediate consciousness decides: the idea is its own evidence, and is insusceptible of all other. It is necessarily groundless and indemonstrable; because it is itself the ground of all possible demonstration. The reason hath faith in itself in its own revelations. Ο λόγος ἔφη. *Ipse dixit.* So it is: for it is so. All the necessity of causal relations (which the mere understanding reduces, and must reduce to co-existence and regular succession* in the objects of which they are predicated, and to habit and association in the mind predicating) depends on, or rather inheres in, the idea of the omnipresent and absolute: for this it is, in which the possible is one and the same with the real and the necessary. Herein the Bible differs from all the books of Greek philosophy, and in a two-fold manner. It doth not affirm a divine nature only, but a God: and not a God only, but the living God. Hence in the Scriptures alone is the *jus divinum*, or direct relation of the state and its magistracy to the Supreme Being, taught as a vital and indispensable part of all moral and of all political wisdom, even as the Jewish alone was a true theocracy.

Were it my object to touch on the present state of public affairs in this kingdom, or on the prospective measures in agitation respecting our sister island, I would direct your most serious meditations to the latter period of the reign of Solomon, and to the revolutions in the reign of Rehoboam, his successor. But I should tread on glowing embers. I will turn to a subject on which all men of reflection are at length in agreement—the causes of the Revolution and fearful chastisement of France. We have learned to trace them back to the rising importance of the commercial and manufacturing class, and its incompatibility with the old feudal privileges and prescriptions; to the spirit of sensuality and ostentation, which from the court had spread through all the towns and cities of the kingdom; to the predominance of a presumptuous and irreligious philosophy; to the extreme over-

* See Hume's Essays. The sophist evades, as Cicero long ago remarked, the better half of the predicament, which is not *præire* but *efficienter præire.*

rating of the knowledge and power given by the improvements of the arts and sciences, especially those of astronomy, mechanics, and a wonder-working chemistry; to an assumption of prophetic power, and the general conceit that states and governments might be and ought to be constructed as machines, every movement of which might be foreseen and taken into previous calculation; to the consequent multitude of plans and constitutions, of planners and constitution-makers, and the remorseless arrogance with which the authors and proselytes of every new proposal were ready to realize it, be the cost what it might in the established rights, or even in the lives, of men; in short, to restlessness, presumption, sensual indulgence, and the idolatrous reliance on false philosophy in the whole domestic, social, and political life of the stirring and effective part of the community: these all acting, at once and together, on a mass of materials supplied by the unfeeling extravagance and oppressions of the government, which *showed no mercy, and very heavily laid its yoke.*

Turn then to the chapter from which the last words were cited, and read the following seven verses; and I am deceived if you will not be compelled to admit that the Prophet revealed the true philosophy of the French revolution more than two thousand years before it became a sad irrevocable truth of history. *And thou saidst, I shall be a lady forever: so that thou didst not lay these things to thy heart, neither didst remember the latter end of it. Therefore, hear now this, thou that art given to pleasures, that dwellest carelessly, that sayest in thine heart, I am, and none else beside me! I shall not sit as a widow, neither shall I know the loss of children. But these two things shall come to thee in a moment, in one day; the loss of children, and widowhood; they shall come upon thee in their perfection, for the multitude of thy sorceries, and for the great abundance of thine enchantments. For thou hast trusted in thy wickedness; thou hast said, None seeth me. Thy wisdom and thy knowledge, it hath perverted thee; and thou hast said in thine heart, I am, and none else beside me. Therefore shall evil come upon thee, thou shalt not know* from whence it riseth: and*

* The reader will scarcely fail to find in this verse a remembrancer of the sudden setting-in of the frost, a fortnight before the usual time (in a country too where the commencement of the two seasons is in general scarcely less regular than that of the wet and dry seasons between the trop-

mischief shall fall upon thee, thou shalt not be able to put it off; and desolation shall come upon thee suddenly, which thou shalt not know. Stand now with thine enchantments, and with the multitude of thy sorceries, wherein thou hast labored from thy youth; if so be thou shalt be able to profit, if so be thou mayest prevail. Thou art wearied in the multitude of thy counsels. Let now the astrologers, the stargazers, the monthly prognosticators stand up, and save thee from these things that shall come upon thee. (Is. xlvii. 7, &c.)

There is a grace that would enable us to take up vipers, and the evil thing shall not hurt us: a spiritual alchemy which can transmute poisons into a *panacea*. We are counselled by our Lord himself to make unto ourselves friends of the Mammon of unrighteousness: and in this age of sharp contrasts and grotesque combinations it would be a wise method of sympathizing with the tone and spirit of the times, if we elevated even our daily newspapers and political journals into comments on the Bible.

When I named this Essay a Sermon, I sought to prepare the inquirers after it for the absence of all the usual softenings suggested by worldly prudence, of all compromise between truth and courtesy. But not even as a sermon would I have addressed the present discourse to a promiscuous audience; and for this reason I likewise announced it in the title-page, as exclusively *ad clerum*; that is (in the old and wide sense of the word), to men of clerkly acquirements of whatever profession. I would that the greater part of our publications could be thus directed, each to its appropriate class of readers. But this can not be. For among other odd burs and kecksies, the misgrowth of our luxuriant activity, we have now a Reading Public*—as strange

ics), which caused, and the desolation which accompanied, the flight from Moscow. The Russians baffled the physical forces of the imperial Jacobin, because they were inaccessible to his imaginary forces. The faith in St. Nicholas kept off at safe distance the more pernicious superstition of the destinies of Napoleon the Great. The English in the Peninsula overcame the real, because they set at defiance, and had heard only to despise, the imaginary powers of the irresistible Emperor. Thank Heaven! the heart of the country was sound at the core.

* Some participle passive in the diminutive form, *Eruditulorum Natio* for instance, might seem at first sight a fuller and more exact designation; but the superior force and humor of the former become evident whenever

a phrase, methinks, as ever forced a splenetic smile on the staid countenance of meditation; and yet no fiction. For our readers have, in good truth, multiplied exceedingly, and have waxed proud. It would require the intrepid accuracy of a Colquhoun to venture at the precise number of that vast company only, whose heads and hearts are dieted at the two public ordinaries of literature, the circulating libraries and the periodical press. But what is the result? Does the inward man thrive on this regimen? Alas! if the average health of the consumers may be judged of by the articles of largest consumption; if the secretions may be conjectured from the ingredients of the dishes that are found best suited to their palates; from all that I have seen, either of the banquet or the guests, I shall utter my *profaccia* with a desponding sigh. From a popular philosophy and a philosophic populace, Good Sense deliver us!

At present, however, I am to imagine for myself a very differ-

the phrase occurs as a step or stair in a *climax* of irony. By way of example take the following sentences, transcribed from a work demonstrating that the New Testament was intended exclusively for the primitive converts from Judaism, was accommodated to their prejudices, and is of no authority, as a rule of faith, for Christians in general. "The Reading Public in this enlightened age and thinking nation, by its favorable reception of liberal ideas, has long demonstrated the benign influence of that profound philosophy which has already emancipated us from so many absurd prejudices held in superstitious awe by our deluded forefathers. But the dark age yielded at length to the dawning light of reason and common sense at the glorious, though imperfect, Revolution. The people can be no longer duped or scared out of their imprescriptible and inalienable right to judge and decide for themselves on all important questions of government and religion. The scholastic jargon of jarring articles and metaphysical creeds may continue for a time to deform our Church-establishment; and like the grotesque figures in the niches of our old Gothic cathedrals, may serve to remind the nation of its former barbarism; but the universal suffrage of a free and enlightened Public," &c. &c.

Among the revolutions worthy of notice, the change in the nature of the introductory sentences and prefatory matter in serious books is not the least striking. The same gross flattery which disgusts us in the dedications to individuals in the elder writers, is now transferred to the nation at large, or the Reading Public: while the Jeremiads of our old moralists, and their angry denunciations concerning the ignorance, immorality, and irreligion of the People, appear (*mutatis mutandis*, and with an appeal to the worst passions, envy, discontent, scorn, vindictiveness) in the shape of bitter libels on ministers, parliament, the clergy: in short, on the State and Church, and all persons employed in them.

ent audience. I appeal exclusively to men, from whose station and opportunities I may dare to anticipate a respectable portion of that sound book-learnedness, into which our old public schools still continue to initiate their pupils. I appeal to men in whom I may hope to find, if not philosophy, yet occasional impulses at least to philosophic thought. And here, as far as my own experience extends, I can announce one favorable symptom. The notion of our measureless superiority in good sense to our ancestors, so general at the commencement of the French Revolution, and for some years before it, is out of fashion. We hear, at least, less of the jargon of this enlightened age. After fatiguing itself, as performer or spectator in the giddy figure-dance of political changes, Europe has seen the shallow foundations of its self-complacent faith give way; and among men of influence and property, we have now more reason to apprehend the stupor of despondence, than the extravagances of hope, unsustained by experience or of self-confidence not bottomed on principle.

In this rank of life the danger lies, not in any tendency to innovation, but in the choice of the means for preventing it. And here my apprehensions point to two opposite errors; each of which deserves a separate notice. The first consists in a disposition to think, that as the peace of nations has been disturbed by the diffusion of a false light, it may be re-established by excluding the people from all knowledge and all prospect of amelioration. O! never, never! Reflection and stirrings of mind, with all their restlessness, and all the errors that result from their imperfection, from the Too much, because Too little, are come into the world. The powers that awaken and foster the spirit of curiosity are to be found in every village: books are in every hovel. The infant's cries are hushed with picture-books: and the cottager's child sheds his first bitter tears over pages, which render it impossible for the man to be treated or governed as a child. Here as in so many other cases, the inconveniences that have arisen from a thing's having become too general are best removed by making it universal.

The other and contrary mistake proceeds from the assumption, that a national education will have been realized whenever the people at large have been taught to read and write. Now among the many means to the desired end, this is doubtless one, and not the least important. But neither is it the most so.

Much less can it be considered to constitute education, which consists in educing the faculties and forming the habits; the means varying according to the sphere in which the individuals to be educated are likely to act and become useful. I do not hesitate to declare, that whether I consider the nature of the discipline adopted,* or the plan of poisoning the children of the poor with a sort of potential infidelity under the "liberal idea" of teaching those points only of religious faith, in which all denominations agree, I can not but denounce the so-called Lancasterian schools as pernicious beyond all power of compensation by the new acquirement of reading and writing. But take even Dr. Bell's original and unsophisticated plan, which I myself regard as an especial gift of Providence to the human race; and suppose this incomparable machine, this vast moral steam-engine, to have been adopted and in free motion throughout the Empire; it would yet appear to me a most dangerous delusion to rely on it as if this of itself formed an efficient national education. We can not, I repeat, honor the scheme too highly as a prominent and necessary part of the great process; but it will neither supersede nor can it be substituted for sundry other measures, that are at least equally important. And these are such measures, too, as unfortunately involve the necessity of sacrifices on the side of the rich and powerful more costly and far more difficult than the yearly subscription of a few pounds;—such measures as demand more self-denial than the expenditure of time in a committee or of eloquence in a public meeting.

Nay, let Dr. Bell's philanthropic end have been realized, and the proposed *modicum* of learning have become universal; yet convinced of its insufficiency to stem the strong currents set in from an opposite point, I dare not assure myself that it may not be driven backward by them and become confluent with the evils which it was intended to preclude.†

* See Mr. Southey's Tract on the New or Madras system of education: especially toward the conclusion, where with exquisite humor as well as with his usual poignancy of wit he has detailed Joseph Lancaster's disciplinarian inventions. But even in the schools, that used to be called Lancasterian, these are, I believe, discontinued. The true perfection of discipline in a school is—the *maximum* of watchfulness with the *minimum* of punishment.

† See the Report of the House of Commons' Committee on the increase

What other measures I had in contemplation, it has been my endeavor to explain elsewhere. But I am greatly deceived, if one preliminary to an efficient education of the laboring classes be not the recurrence to a more manly discipline of the intellect on the part of the learned themselves, in short a thorough re-casting of the moulds, in which the minds of our gentry, the characters of our future land-owners, magistrates and senators are to receive their shape and fashion. O what treasures of practical wisdom would be once more brought into open day by the solution of this problem! Suffice it for the present to hint the master-thought. The first man, on whom the light of an idea dawned, did in that same moment receive the spirit and credentials of a lawgiver: and as long as man shall exist, so long will the possession of that antecedent knowledge (the maker and master of all profitable experience) which exists only in the power of an idea, be the one lawful qualification of all dominion in the world of the senses. Without this, experience itself is but a Cyclops walking backwards under the fascination of the past; and we are indebted to a lucky coincidence of outward circumstances and contingencies, least of all things to be calculated on in times like the present, if this one-eyed experience does not seduce its worshipper into practical anachronisms.

But alas! the halls of old philosophy have been so long deserted, that we circle them at shy distance as the haunt of phantoms and chimæras.* The sacred grove of Academus is holden in like regard with the unfoodful trees in the shadowy world of Maro that had a dream attached to every leaf. The very terms of ancient wisdom are worn out, or (far worse!) stamped on baser metal: and whoever should have the hardihood to reproclaim its solemn truths must commence with a glossary.

In reviewing the foregoing pages, I am apprehensive that they may be thought to resemble the overflow of an earnest mind rather than an orderly premeditated composition. Yet this imperfection of form will not be altogether uncompensated, if it should be the means of presenting with greater liveliness the feelings and impressions under which they were written. Still less shall I regret this defect if it should induce some future

of crime;—within the last twenty years quintupled over all England, and in several counties decupled. 28th September, 1828.

* See App. (E.)—*Ed.*

traveller engaged in the like journey to take the same station and to look through the same *medium* at the one main object which amid all my discursions I have still kept in view. The more, however, doth it behoove me not to conclude this address without attempting to recapitulate in as few and as plain words as possible the sum and substance of its contents.

There is a state of mind indispensable for all perusal of the Scriptures to edification, which must be learned by experience, and can be described only by negatives. It is the direct opposite of that which, if a moral passage of Scripture were cited, would prompt a man to reply, "Who does not know this?" But if the quotation should have been made in support of some article of faith, this same habit of mind will betray itself in different individuals, by apparent contraries, which yet are but the two poles, or *plus* and *minus* states, of the same influence. The latter, or the negative, pole may be suspected, as often as you hear a comment on some high and doctrinal text introduced with the words, "It only means so and so!" For instance, I object to a professed free-thinking Christian the following solemn enunciation of *the riches of the glory of the mystery hid from ages and from generations* by the philosophic Apostle of the Gentiles:—*Who* (namely, the Father) *hath delivered us from the power of darkness and hath translated us into the kingdom of his dear Son: In whom we have redemption through his blood, even the forgiveness of sins: Who is the image of the invisible God, the first-born* of every creature: For by him were all things created, that are in heaven, and that are in earth, visible and invisible, whether they be thrones, or dominions, or principalities, or powers: all things were created by him, and for him: And he is before all things, and by him all things consist. And he is the head of the body, the Church: who is the beginning, the first-born from the dead; that in all things he might have the pre-eminence. For it pleased the Father that in him should all fulness dwell: And, having made peace through the blood of his cross, by him to reconcile all things unto himself; by him, I say, whether they be things in earth, or things in heaven.* Col. i. 13, &c. What is the reply?—Why, that by these words (very

* A mistaken translation. The words should be: *Begotten before any kind of creation;* and even this does not convey the full sense of the superlative, πρωτότοκος. (See Table Talk, VI. 478, (note.)—*Ed.*)

bold and figurative words it must be confessed, yet still) St. Paul only meant that the universal and eternal truths of morality and a future state had been reproclaimed by an inspired teacher and confirmed by miracles!* The words only mean, Sir, that a state of retribution after this life had been proved by the fact of Christ's resurrection—that is all!

Of the positive pole, on the other hand, language to the following purport is the usual exponent. "It is a mystery: and we are bound to believe the words without presuming to inquire into the meaning of them." That is, we believe in St. Paul's veracity; and that is enough. Yet St. Paul repeatedly presses on his hearers that thoughtful perusal of the Sacred Writings, and those habits of earnest though humble inquiry which, if the heart only have been previously regenerated, would lead them *to a full assurance* of understanding εἰς ἐπίγνωσιν, (*to an entire assent of the mind; to a spiritual intuition, or positive inward knowledge by experience*) of the *mystery of God, and of the Father, and of Christ*, in which (*nempe*, μυστηρίῳ) *are hid all the treasures of wisdom and knowledge.* Col. ii. 2, 3.

To expose the inconsistency of both these extremes, and by inference to recommend that state of mind, which looks forward to *the fellowship of the mystery of the faith as a spirit of wisdom and revelation in the* knowledge *of God, the eyes of the* understanding *being enlightened* (Eph. i. 17–18)—this formed my general purpose. Long has it been at my heart! I consider it as the contra-distinguishing principle of Christianity that in it alone πᾶς πλοῦτος τῆς πληροφορίας τῆς συνέσεως (the understanding in its utmost power and opulence) culminates in faith, as in its crown of glory, at once its light and its remuneration. On this most important point I attempted long ago to preclude, if possible, all misconception and misinterpretation of my opinions. Alas! in this time of distress and embarrassment the sentiments have a more especial interest, a more immediate application, than

* But I shall scarcely obtain an answer to certain difficulties involved in this free and liberal interpretation: for example, that with the exception of a handful of rich men considered as little better than infidels, the Jews were as fully persuaded of these truths as Christians in general are at the present day. Moreover that this inspired teacher had himself declared that if the Jews did not believe on the evidence of Moses and the Prophets, neither would they though a man should rise from the dead.

when they were first written. If (I observed)* it be a truth attested alike by common feeling and common sense, that the greater part of human misery depends directly on human vices, and the remainder indirectly, by what means can we act on men, so as to remove or preclude their vices and purify their principles of moral election? The question is not by what means each man is to alter his own character;—in order to this, all the means prescribed, and all the aidances given by religion may be necessary for him. Vain of themselves may be—

> The sayings of the wise
> In ancient and in modern books enroll'd
>
> . . . .
>
> Unless he feel within
> Some source of consolation from above,
> Secret refreshings, that repair his strength,
> And fainting spirits uphold. SAMSON AGONISTES.

This is not the question. Virtue would not be virtue could it be given by one fellow-creature to another. To make use of all the means and appliances in our power to the actual attainment of rectitude, is the abstract of the duty which we owe to ourselves: to supply those means as far as we can, comprises our duty to others. The question then is, what are these means? Can they be any other than the communication of knowledge and the removal of those evils and impediments which prevent its reception? It may not be in our power to combine both, but it is in the power of every man to contribute to the former, who is sufficiently informed to feel that it is his duty. If it be said, that we should endeavor not so much to remove ignorance, as to make the ignorant religious: religion herself through her sacred oracles answers for me, that all effective faith pre-supposes knowledge and individual conviction. If the mere acquiescence in truth, uncomprehended and unfathomed, were sufficient, few indeed would be the vicious and the miserable, in this country at least where speculative infidelity is, Heaven be praised! confined to a small number. Like bodily deformity, there is one instance here and another there; but three in one place are already an undue proportion. It is highly worthy of observation that the inspired Writings received by Christians are distinguishable from all other books pretending to inspiration, from the scriptures of the Bra-

* The Friend, II. p. 99.—*Ed.*

mins, and even from the Koran, in their strong and frequent recommendations of truth. I do not here mean veracity, which can not but be enforced in every code which appeals to the religious principle of man; but knowledge. This is not only extolled as the crown and honor of a man, but to seek after it is again and again commanded us as one of our most sacred duties. Yea, the very perfection and final bliss of the glorified spirit is represented by the Apostle as a plain aspect or intuitive beholding of truth in its eternal and immutable source. Not that knowledge can of itself do all. The light of religion is not that of the moon, light without heat; but neither is its warmth that of the stove, warmth without light. Religion is the sun whose warmth indeed swells, and stirs, and actuates the life of nature, but who at the same time beholds all the growth of life with a master-eye, makes all objects glorious on which he looks, and by that glory visible to others.

For this cause I bow my knees unto the Father of our Lord Jesus Christ, that he would grant you according to the riches of his glory, to be strengthened with might by his Spirit in the inner man; that Christ may dwell in your hearts by faith; that ye being rooted and grounded in love, may be able to comprehend with all saints what is the breadth, and length, and depth, and height; and to know the love of Christ which passeth all knowledge, that ye might be filled with the fulness of God. (Eph. iii. 14–19.) For to know God is (by a vital and spiritual act in which to know and to possess are one and indivisible)—to know God, I say, is—to acknowledge him as the infinite clearness in the incomprehensible fulness, and fulness incomprehensible with infinite clearness.

This, then, comprises my first purpose, which is in a two-fold sense general: for in the substance, if not in the form, it belongs to all my countrymen and fellow-Christians without distinction of class, while for its object it embraces the whole of the inspired Scriptures from the recorded first day of heaven and earth, ere the light was yet gathered into celestial lamps or reflected from their revolving mirrors, to the predicted Sabbath of the new creation, when heaven and earth shall have become one city with neither *sun nor moon to shine in it;* for the glory of God shall lighten it and the Lamb be the light thereof. My second purpose is after the same manner in a two-fold sense specific: for as this Sermon is nominally addressed to, so was it for the greater part exclusively intended for, the perusal of the learned: and its object likewise is to urge men so qualified to apply their powers and attainments to an especial study of the Old Testament as teaching the elements of political science.

It is asked, in what sense I use these words? I answer: in the same sense as the terms are employed when we refer to Euclid for the elements of the science of geometry, only with one difference arising from the diversity of the subject. With one difference only; but that one how momentous! All other sciences are confined to abstractions, unless when the term science is used in an improper and flattering sense.—Thus we may speak without boast of natural history; but we have not yet attained to a science of nature. The Bible alone contains a science of realities: and therefore each of its elements is at the same time a living germ, in which the present involves the future, and in the finite the infinite exists potentially. That hidden mystery in every the minutest form of existence, which contemplated under the relations of time presents itself to the understanding retrospectively, as an infinite ascent of causes, and prospectively as an interminable progression of effects;—that which contemplated in space is beholden intuitively as a law of action and re-action, continuous and extending beyond all bound;—this same mystery freed from the *phænomena* of time and space, and seen in the depth of real being, reveals itself to the pure reason as the actual immanence or in-being* of all in each. Are we struck with admiration at beholding the cope of heaven imaged in a dew-drop? The least of the *animalculæ* to which that drop would be an ocean, contains in itself an infinite problem of which God omnipresent is the only solution. The slave of custom is roused by the rare and the accidental alone; but the axioms of the unthinking are to the philosopher the deepest problems as being the nearest to the mysterious root, and partaking at once of its darkness and its pregnancy.

O what a mine of undiscovered treasures, what a new world of power and truth would the Bible promise to our future meditation, if in some gracious moment one solitary text of all its inspired contents should but dawn upon us in the pure untroubled

* In-being is the word chosen by Bishop Sherlock to express this sense. See his Tract on the Athanasian Creed. 1827.

brightness of an idea, that most glorious birth of the God-like within us, which even as the light, its material symbol, reflects itself from a thousand surfaces, and flies homeward to its Parent Mind enriched with a thousand forms, itself above form and still remaining in its own simplicity and identity! O for a flash of that same light, in which the first position of geometric science that ever loosed itself from the generalizations of a groping and insecure experience, for the first time revealed itself to a human intellect in all its evidence and all its fruitfulness, transparence without *vacuum*, and plenitude without opacity! O that a single gleam of our own inward experience would make comprehensible to us the rapturous Eureka, and the grateful hecatomb, of the philosopher of Samos;—or that vision which from the contemplation of an arithmetical harmony rose to the eye of Kepler, presenting the planetary world, and all its orbits in the divine order of their ranks and distances;—or which, in the falling of an apple, revealed to the ethereal intuition of our own Newton the constructive principle of the material universe. The promises which I have ventured to hold forth concerning the hidden treasures of the Law and the Prophets will neither be condemned as paradox or as exaggeration by the mind that has learned to understand the possibility, that the reduction of the sands of the sea to number should be found a less stupendous problem by Archimedes than the simple conception of the Parmenidean ONE. What however is achievable by the human understanding without this light, may be comprised in the epithet, κενόσπουδοι: and a melancholy comment on that phrase would the history of human cabinets and legislators for the last thirty years furnish! The excellent Barrow, the last of the disciples of Plato and Archimedes among our modern mathematicians, shall give the description and state the value: and in his words I shall conclude.

"*Aliud agere*, to be impertinently busy, doing that which conduceth to no good purpose, is in some respect worse than to do nothing. Of such industry we may understand that of the Preacher, *The labor of the foolish wearieth every one of them.*"

APPENDIX.

APPENDIX,

CONTAINING COMMENTS AND ESSAYS.

(A.)

In this use of the word 'sufficiency,' I pre-suppose on the part of the reader or hearer an humble and docile state of mind, and above all the practice of prayer, as the necessary condition of such a state, and the best if not the only means of becoming sincere to our own hearts. Christianity is especially differenced from all other religions by being grounded on facts which all men alike have the same means of ascertaining with equal facility, and which no man can ascertain for another. Each person must be herein querist and respondent to himself; Am I sick, and therefore need a physician?—Am I in spiritual slavery, and therefore need a ransomer?—Have I given a pledge, which must be redeemed, and which I can not redeem by my own resources?—Am I at one with God, and is my will concentric with that holy power, which is at once the constitutive will and the supreme reason of the universe?—If not, must I not be mad if I do not seek, and miserable if I do not discover and embrace, the means of atonement?* To collect, to weigh, and to appreciate historical proofs and presumptions is not equally within the means and opportunities of every man. The testimony of books of history is one of the strong and stately pillars of the Church of Christ; but it is not the foundation, nor can it without loss of essential faith be mistaken or substituted for the foundation. There is a sect, which in its scornful pride of antipathy to mysteries (that is, to all those doctrines of the pure and intuitive reason, which transcend the understanding, and can never be contemplated by it, but through a false and falsifying perspective) affects to condemn all inward and preliminary experience as enthusiastic delusion or fanatical contagion. Historic evidence, on the other hand, these men treat, as the Jews of old treated the brazen

* This is a mistaken etymology, and consequently a dull, though unintentional, pun. Our *atone* is, doubtless, of the same stock with the Teutonic *aussöhnen*, *versöhnen*, the Anglo-Saxon taking the *t* for the *s*.

serpent, which was the relic and evidence of the miracles worked by Moses in the wilderness. They turned it into an idol: and therefore Hezekiah (*who clave to the Lord, and did right in the sight of the Lord, so that after him was none like him, among all the kings of Judah, nor any that were before him*) not only *removed the high places, and brake the images, and cut down the groves;* but likewise *brake in pieces the brazen serpent that Moses had made: for the children of Israel did burn incense to it.* (2 Kings xviii.)

To preclude an error so pernicious, I request that to the wilful neglect of those outward ministrations of the word which all Englishmen have the privilege of attending, the reader will add the setting at naught likewise of those inward means of grace, without which the language of the Scriptures, in the most faithful translation and in the purest and plainest English, must nevertheless continue to be a dead language,—a sun-dial by moonlight.

(B.)

Reason and Religion differ only as a two-fold application of the same power. But if we are obliged to distinguish, we must ideally separate. In this sense I affirm that reason is the knowledge of the laws of the whole considered as one; and as such it is contra-distinguished from the understanding, which concerns itself exclusively with the quantities, qualities, and relations of particulars in time and space. The understanding, therefore, is the science of *phænomena*, and of their subsumption under distinct kinds and sorts (*genera* and *species*). Its functions supply the rules and constitute the possibility of experience; but remain mere logical forms except as far as materials are given by the sense or sensations. The reason, on the other hand, is the science of the universal, having the ideas of oneness and allness as its two elements or primary factors. In the language of the old Schools,

$$\text{Unity} + \text{Omneity} = \text{Totality}.$$

The reason first manifests itself in man by the tendency to the com prehension of all as one. We can neither rest in an infinite that is not at the same time a whole, nor in a whole that is not infinite. Hence the natural man is always in a state either of resistance or of captivity to the understanding and the fancy, which can not represent totality without limit: and he either loses the one in the striving after the infinite, that is, atheism with or without polytheism, or he loses the infinite in the striving after the one, and then sinks into anthropomorphic monotheism.

The rational intellect, therefore, taken abstractedly and unbalanced, did, in itself (*ye shall be as Gods*, Gen. iii. 5), and in its consequences (the lusts of the flesh, the eye, and the understanding, as in v. 5), form the original temptation, through which men fell: and in all ages has continued to originate the same, even from Adam, in whom we all fell, to the atheists who deified the human reason in the person of a harlot during the earlier period of the French Revolution.

To this tendency, therefore, religion, as the consideration of the particular and individual (in which respect it takes up and identifies with itself the excellence of the understanding), but of the individual, as it exists and has its being in the universal (in which respect it is one with the pure reason)—to this tendency, I say, religion assigns the due limits, and is the echo of the *voice of the Lord God walking in the garden.* Hence in all the ages and countries of civilization religion has been the parent and fosterer of the fine arts, as of poetry, music, painting, and the like, the common essence of which consists in a similar union of the universal and the individual. In this union, moreover, is contained the true sense of the ideal. Under the old Law the altar, the curtains, the priestly vestments, and whatever else was to represent the beauty of holiness, had an ideal character: and the Temple itself was a master-piece of ideal beauty.

There exists in the human being, at least in man fully developed, no mean symbol of tri-unity in reason, religion, and the will. For each of the three, though a distinct agency, implies and demands the other two, and loses its own nature at the moment that from distinction it passes into division or separation. The perfect frame of a man is the perfect frame of a state: and in the light of this idea we must read Plato's Republic.*

The comprehension, impartiality, and far-sightedness of reason (the legislative of our nature) taken singly and exclusively, becomes mere visionariness in intellect, and indolence or hard-heartedness in morals. It is the science of cosmopolitism without country, of philanthropy without neighborliness or consanguinity, in short, of all the impostures of that philosophy of the French Revolution, which would sacrifice each to the shadowy idol of all. For Jacobinism is *monstrum hybridum*, made up in part of despotism, or the lust of rule grounded in selfness; and in part of abstract reason misapplied to objects that belong entirely to experience and the understanding. Its instinct and mode of action are in strict correspondence with its origin. In all places, Jacobinism betrays its mixed parentage and nature by applying to the brute passions and physical force of the multitude (that is, to man as a mere animal) in order to build up government and the frame of society on natural rights instead of social privileges, on the universals of abstract reason instead of positive institutions, the lights of specific experience, and the modifications of existing circumstances.

* If I judge rightly, this celebrated work is to 'The History of the Town of Man-soul,' what Plato was to John Bunyan.

Right in its most proper sense is the creature of law and statute, and only in the technical language of the courts has it any substantial and independent sense. In morals, right is a word without meaning except as the correlative of duty.

From all this it follows, that reason as the science of all as a whole must be interpenetrated by a power, that represents the concentration of all in each—a power that acts by a contraction of universal truths into individual duties, such contraction being the only form in which those truths can attain life and reality. Now this is religion, which is the executive of our nature, and on this account the name of highest dignity, and the symbol of sovereignty. To the same purport I have elsewhere defined religion as philosophy evolved from idea into act and fact by the superinduction of the extrinsic conditions of reality.

Yet even religion itself, if ever in its too exclusive devotion to the specific and individual it neglects to interpose the contemplation of the universal, changes its being into superstition, and becoming more and more earthly and servile, as more and more estranged from the one in all, goes wandering at length with its pack of amulets, bead-rolls, periapts, fetisches, and the like pedlery, on pilgrimages to Loretto, Mecca, or the temple of Juggernaut, arm in arm with sensuality on one side and self-torture on the other, followed by a motley group of friars, pardoners, faquirs, gamesters, flagellants, mountebanks, and harlots.

But neither can reason or religion exist or co-exist as reason and religion, except as far as they are actuated by the will (the Platonic θυμὸς), which is the sustaining, coercive and ministerial power, the functions of which in the individual correspond to the officers of war and police in the ideal Republic of Plato. In its state of immanence or indwelling in reason and religion, the will appears indifferently as wisdom or as love: two names of the same power, the former more intelligential, the latter more spiritual, the former more frequent in the Old, the latter in the New, Testament. But in its utmost abstraction and consequent state of reprobation, the will becomes Satanic pride and rebellious self-idolatry in the relations of the spirit to itself, and remorseless despotism relatively to others; the more hopeless as the more obdurate by its subjugation of sensual impulses, by its superiority to toil and pain and pleasure; in short, by the fearful resolve to find in itself alone the one absolute motive of action, under which all other motives from within and from without must be either subordinated or crushed.

This is the character which Milton has so philosophically as well as sublimely embodied in the Satan of his Paradise Lost. Alas! too often has it been embodied in real life. Too often has it given a dark and savage grandeur to the historic page. And wherever it has appeared, under whatever circumstances of time and country, the same ingredients have gone to its composition; and it has been identified by the same attributes. Hope in which there is no cheerfulness; steadfastness within and immovable resolve, with outward restlessness and whirling activity; violence with guile; temerity with cunning; and, as the result of all, interminableness of object with perfect indifference of means; these are the qualities that have constituted the commanding genius; these are the marks, that have characterized the masters of mischief, the liberticides, and mighty hunters of mankind, from Nimrod to Bonaparte. And from inattention to the possibility of such a character as well as from ignorance of its elements, even men of honest intentions too frequently become fascinated. Nay, whole nations have been so far duped by this want of insight and reflection as to regard with palliative admiration, instead of wonder and abhorrence, the Molochs of human nature, who are indebted for the larger portion of their meteoric success to their total want of principle, and who surpass the generality of their fellow-creatures in one act of courage only, that of daring to say with their whole heart, "Evil, be thou my good!"—All system so far is power; and a systematic criminal, self-consistent and entire in wickedness, who entrenches villany within villany, and barricadoes crime by crime, has removed a world of obstacles by the mere decision, that he will have no obstacles, but those of force and brute matter.

I have only to add a few sentences, in completion of this comment, on the conscience* and on the understanding. The conscience is neither reason, religion, or will, but an experience *sui generis* of the coincidence of the human will with reason and religion. It might, perhaps, be called a spiritual sensation; but that there lurks a contradiction in the terms, and that it is often deceptive to give a common or generic name to that, which being unique, can have no fair analogy. In strictness, therefore, the conscience is neither a sensation nor a sense; but a testifying state, best described in the words of Scripture, as *the peace of God that passeth all understanding.*

Of the latter faculty, namely, of the understanding, considered in and of itself the Peripatetic aphorism, *nihil in intellectu quod non prius in sensu*, is strictly true as well as the legal maxim, *de rebus non apparentibus et non existentibus eadem est ratio.* The eye is not more inappropriate to sound, than the mere understanding to the modes and laws of spiritual existence. In this sense I have used the term; and in this sense I assert that the understanding or experiential faculty, unirradiated by the reason and the spirit, has no appropriate

* I have this morning read with high delight an admirable representation of what men in general think, and what ought to be thought, concerning the conscience in the translation of Swedenborg's Universal Theology of the New Church. II. pp. 361–370.
6 January, 1821.

object but the material world in relation to our worldly interests. The far-sighted prudence of man, and the more narrow but at the same time far less fallible cunning of the fox, are both no other than a nobler substitute for salt, in order that the hog may not putrefy before its destined hour.

It must not, however, be overlooked that this insulation of the understanding is our own act and deed. The man of healthful and undivided intellect uses his understanding* in this state of abstraction only as a tool or organ; even as the arithmetician uses numbers, that is, as the means not the end of knowledge. Our Shakspeare in agreement both with truth and the philosophy of his age names it "discourse of reason," as an instrumental faculty belonging to reason: and Milton opposes the discursive to the intuitive, as the lower to the higher,

Differing but in degree, in kind the same.

Of the discursive understanding, which forms for itself general notions and terms of classification for the purpose of comparing and arranging *phænomena*, the characteristic is clearness without depth. It contemplates the unity of things in their limits only, and is consequently a knowledge of superficies without substance. So much so indeed that it entangles itself in contradictions in the very effort of

* Perhaps the safer use of the term, understanding, for general purposes, is, to take it as the mind, or rather as the man himself considered as a concipient as well as percipient being, and reason as a power supervening. The want of a clear notion respecting the nature of reason may be traced to the difficulty of combining the notion of an organ of sense, or a new sense, with the notion of the appropriate and peculiar objects of that sense, so that the idea evolved from this *synthesis* shall be the identity of both. By reason we know that God is: but God is himself the Supreme Reason. And this is the proper difference between all spiritual faculties and the bodily senses;—the organs of spiritual apprehension having objects consubstantial with themselves (ὁμοούσια), or being themselves their own objects, that is, self-contemplative.

Reason may or rather must be used in two different yet correlative senses, which are nevertheless in some measure reunited by a third. In its highest sense, and which is the ground and source of the rest, reason is being, the Supreme Being contemplated objectively, and in abstraction from the personality. The Word or Logos is life, and communicates life; is light and communicates light. Now this light contemplated *in abstracto* is reason. Again as constituents of reason we necessarily contemplate unity and distinctity. Now the latter as the polar opposite to the former implies plurality: therefore I use the plural, distinctities, and say, that the distinctities considered apart from the unity are the ideas, and reason is the ground and source of ideas. This is the first and absolute sense.

The second sense comes when we speak of ourselves as possessing reason; and this we can no otherwise define than as the capability with which God had endowed man of beholding, or being conscious of, the divine light. But this very capability is itself that light, not as the divine light, but as the life or indwelling of the living Word, which is our light; that is, a life whereby we are capable of the light, and by which the light is present to us, as a being which we may call ours, but which I can not call mine: for it is the life that we individualize, while the light, as its correlative opposite, remains universal.

Most pregnant is the doctrine of opposite correlatives as applied to Deity, but only as manifested in man, not to the Godhead absolutely. 1827.

comprehending the idea of substance. The completing power which unites clearness with depth, the plenitude of the sense with the comprehensibility of the understanding, is the imagination, impregnated with which the understanding itself becomes intuitive, and a living power. The reason (not the abstract reason, not the reason as the mere organ of science, or as the faculty of scientific principles and schemes *à priori;* but reason), as the integral spirit of the regenerated man, reason substantiated and vital, *one only*, yet *manifold, overseeing all, and going through all* understanding; *the breath of the power of God, and a pure influence from the glory of the Almighty;* which *remaining in itself* regenerateth all other powers, *and in all ages entering into holy souls maketh them friends of God and prophets;* (Wisdom of Solomon, c. vii.) this reason without being either the sense, the understanding, or the imagination, contains all three within itself, even as the mind contains its thoughts, and is present in and through them all; or as the expression pervades the different features of an intelligent countenance. Each individual must bear witness of it to his own mind, even as he describes life and light: and with the silence of light it describes itself, and dwells in us only as far as we dwell in it. It can not in strict language be called a faculty, much less a personal property, of any human mind. He, with whom it is present, can as little appropriate it, whether totally or by partition, as he can claim ownership in the breathing air or make an inclosure in the cope of heaven.

The object of the preceding discourse was to recommend the Bible, as the end and centre of our reading and meditation. I can truly affirm of myself, that my studies have been profitable and availing to me only so far as I have endeavored to use all my other knowledge as a glass enabling me to receive more light in a wider field of vision from the word of God. If you have accompanied me thus far, thoughtful reader, let it not weary you if I digress for a few moments to another book, likewise a revelation of God—the great book of his servant Nature. That in its obvious sense and literal interpretation it declares the being and attributes of the Almighty Father, none but the fool in heart has ever dared gainsay. But it has been the music of gentle and pious minds in all ages, it is the poetry of all human nature, to read it likewise in a figurative sense, and to find therein correspondences and symbols of the spiritual world.

I have at this moment before me, in the flowery meadow, on which my eye is now reposing, one of its most soothing chapters, in which there is no lamenting word, no one character of guilt or anguish. For never can I look and meditate on the vegetable creation without a feeling similar to that with which we gaze at a beautiful infant that has fed itself asleep at its mother's bosom, and smiles in its strange dream of obscure yet happy sensations. The same tender and genial pleasure takes possession of me, and this pleasure is checked and drawn inward by the like aching melancholy, by the same whispered remonstrance, and made restless by a similar impulse of aspiration. It seems as if the soul said to herself: From this state hast thou fallen! Such shouldst thou still become, thyself all permeable to a holier power! thyself at once hidden and glorified by its own transparency, as the accidental and dividuous in this quiet and harmonious object is subjected to the life and light of nature; to that life and light of nature, I say, which shines in every plant and flower, even as the transmitted power, love and wisdom of God over all fills, and shines through, nature! But what the plant is by an act not its own and unconsciously—that must thou make thyself to become—must by prayer and by a watchful and unresisting spirit, join at least with the preventive and assisting grace to make thyself, in that light of conscience which inflameth not, and with that knowledge which puffeth not up!

But further, and with particular reference to that undivided reason, neither merely speculative or merely practical, but both in one, which I have in this annotation endeavored to contra-distinguish from the understanding, I seem to myself to behold in the quiet objects, on which I am gazing, more than an arbitrary illustration, more than a mere *simile*, the work of my own fancy. I feel an awe, as if there were before my eyes the same power as that of the reason—the same power in a lower dignity, and therefore a symbol established in the truth of things. I feel it alike, whether I contemplate a single tree or flower, or meditate on vegetation throughout the world, as one of the great organs of the life of nature. Lo!*—with the rising sun it commences its outward life and enters into open communion with all the elements, at once assimilating them to itself and to each other. At the same moment it strikes its roots and unfolds its leaves, absorbs and respires, steams forth its cooling vapor and finer fragrance, and breathes a repairing spirit, at once the food and tone of the atmosphere, into the atmosphere that feeds it. Lo!—at the touch of light how it returns an air akin to light, and yet with the same pulse effectuates its own secret growth, still contracting to fix what expanding it had refined. Lo!—how upholding the ceaseless plastic motion of the parts in the profoundest rest of the whole it becomes the visible *organismus* of the entire silent or elementary life of nature and, therefore, in incorporating the one extreme becomes the symbol of the

* The remainder of this paragraph might properly form the conclusion of a disquisition on the spirit, as suggested by meditative observation of natural objects, and of our own thoughts and impulses without reference to any theological dogma, or any religious obligation to receive it as a revealed truth, but traced to the law of the dependence of the particular on the universal, the first being the organ of the second, as the lungs in relation to the atmosphere, the eye to light, crystal to fluid, figure to space, and the like.—1822.

other; the natural symbol of that higher life of reason, in which the whole series (known to us in our present state of being) is perfected, in which, therefore, all the subordinate gradations recur, and are re-ordained *in more abundant honor*. We had seen each in its own cast, and we now recognize them all as co-existing in the unity of a higher form, the crown and completion of the earthly, and the mediator of a new and heavenly series.* Thus finally, the vegetable creation, in the simplicity and uniformity of its internal structure symbolizing the unity of nature, while it represents the omniformity of her delegated functions in its external variety and manifoldness, becomes the record and chronicle of her ministerial acts, and enchases the vast unfolded volume of the earth with the hieroglyphics of her history.

O!—if as the plant to the orient beam, we would but open out our minds to that holier light, which '*being compared with light is found before it, more beautiful than the sun, and above all the order of stars*,' (Wisdom of Solomon, vii. 29)—ungenial, alien, and adverse to our very nature would appear the boastful wisdom which, beginning in France, gradually tampered with the taste and literature of all the most civilized nations of Christendom, seducing the understanding from its natural allegiance, and therewith from all its own lawful claims, titles, and privileges. It was placed as a ward of honor in the courts of faith and reason; but it chose to dwell alone, and became a harlot by the way-side. The commercial spirit, and the ascendency of the experimental philosophy which took place at the close of the seventeenth century, though both good and beneficial in their own kinds, combined to foster its corruption. Flattered and dazzled by

* It may be shown that the *plus* or universal, which man as the *minus* or individual finds his correlative pole, can only be God. I. This may be proved, exhaustively, that all lower universals are already attached to lower particulars. II. It may be proved by the necessity of harmonic correspondence. The principle of personal individuality being the transcendent—(that is, the highest *species* of *genus* X, in which X rises, *moritur, at dum moritur resurgit*, into the higher *genus* Y)—the personal principle, I say, being the transcendent of all particulars, requires for its correspondent opposite the transcendent of all universals: and this is God. The doctrine of the spirit thus generally conceived, and without being matured into any more distinct conceptions by revealed Scripture, is the ground of theopathy, religious feeling, or devoutness; while the reason,—as contra-distinguished from the understanding by logical processes, without reference to revelation or to reason *sensu eminenti*, as the self-subsistent Reason or *Logos*, and merely considered as the endowment of the human will and mind, having two definitions accordingly as it is exercised practically or intellectually,—is the ground of theology, or religious belief. Both are good in themselves as far as they go, and productive—the former—of a sensibility to the beautiful in art and nature, of imaginativeness and moral enthusiasm;—the latter—of insight, comprehension, and a philosophic mind. They are good in themselves, and the preconditions of the better; and therefore these disquisitions would form an appropriate conclusion to The Aids to Reflection. For as many as are wanting either in leisure or inclination, or belief of their own competency to go further—from the miscellaneous to the systematic—that volume is a whole, and for them the whole work. While for others these disquisitions form the drawbridge, the connecting link, between the disciplinary and preparatory rules and exercises of reflection, and the system of faith and philosophy of S. T. C.—1827.

the real or supposed discoveries which it had made, the more the understanding was enriched, the more did it become debased; till science itself put on a selfish and sensual character, and immediate utility, in exclusive reference to the gratification of the wants and appetites of the animal, the vanities and caprices of the social, and the ambition of the political, man was imposed as the test of all intellectual powers and pursuits. Worth was degraded into a lazy synonyme of value; and value was exclusively attached to the interest of the senses. But though the growing alienation and self-sufficiency of the understanding was perceptible at an earlier period, yet it seems to have been about the middle of the last century, under the influence of Voltaire, D'Alembert, Diderot, say generally of the so-called Encyclopedists, and alas!—of their crowned proselytes and disciples, Frederick, Joseph, and Catherine,—that the human understanding, and this too in its narrowest form, was tempted to throw off all show of reverence to the spiritual and even to the moral powers and impulses of the soul; and usurping the name of reason openly joined the banners of Antichrist, at once the pander and the prostitute of sensuality, and whether in the cabinet, laboratory, the dissecting room, or the brothel, alike busy in the schemes of vice and irreligion. Well and truly might it, thus personified in our fancy, have been addressed in the words of the evangelical Prophet, which I have once before quoted. *Thou hast said, None seeth me. Thy wisdom and thy knowledge, it hath perverted thee—and thou hast said in thy heart, I am, and there is none beside me.* (Isaiah xlvii. 10.)

Prurient, bustling, and revolutionary, this French wisdom has never more than grazed the surfaces of knowledge. As political economy, in its zeal for the increase of food it habitually overlooked the qualities and even the sensations of those that were to feed on it. As ethical philosophy, it recognized no duties which it could not reduce into debtor and creditor accounts on the ledgers of self-love, where no coin was sterling which could not be rendered into agreeable sensations. And even in its height of self-complacency as chemical art, greatly am I deceived if it has not from the very beginning mistaken the products of destruction, *cadavera rerum*, for the elements of composition: and most assuredly it has dearly purchased a few brilliant inventions at the loss of all communion with life and the spirit of nature. As the process, such the result;—a heartless frivolity alternating with a sentimentality as heartless; an ignorant contempt of antiquity; a neglect of moral self-discipline; a deadening of the religious sense, even in the less reflecting forms of natural piety; a scornful reprobation of all consolations and secret refreshings from above,—and as the *caput mortuum* of human nature evaporated, a French nature of rapacity, levity, ferocity, and presumption.

Man of understanding, canst thou command the stone to lie, canst thou bid the flower bloom, where thou hast placed it in thy classification?—Canst thou persuade the living or the inanimate to stand separate even as thou hast separated them?—And do not far rather all things spread out before thee in glad confusion and heedless intermixture, even as a lightsome chaos on which the Spirit of God is moving?—Do not all press and swell under one attraction, and live together in promiscuous harmony, each joyous in its own kind, and in the immediate neighborhood of myriad others that in the system of thy understanding are distant as the poles?—If to mint and to remember names delight thee, still arrange and classify and pore and pull to pieces, and peep into death to look for life, as monkeys put their hands behind a looking-glass! Yet consider in the first sabbath which thou imposest on the busy discursion of thought, that all this is at best little more than a technical memory: that like can only be known by like: that as truth is the correlative of being, so is the act of being the great organ of truth: that in natural no less than in moral science, *quantum sumus, scimus.*

That which we find in ourselves is (*gradu mutato*) the substance and the life of all our knowledge. Without this latent presence of the 'I am,' all modes of existence in the external world would flit before us as colored shadows, with no greater depth, root, or fixure, than the image of a rock hath in a gliding stream or the rainbow on a fast-sailing rain-storm. The human mind is the compass, in which the laws and actuations of all outward essences are revealed as the dips and declinations. (The application of geometry to the forces and movements of the material world is both proof and instance.) The fact, therefore, that the mind of man in its own primary and constituent forms represents the laws of nature, is a mystery which of itself should suffice to make us religious: for it is a problem of which God is the only solution, God, the one before all, and of all, and through all!—True natural philosophy is comprised in the study of the science and language of symbols. The power delegated to nature is all in every part: and by a symbol I mean, not a metaphor or allegory or any other figure of speech or form of fancy, but an actual and essential part of that, the whole of which it represents. Thus our Lord speaks symbolically when he says that *the eye is the light of the body.* The genuine naturalist is dramatic poet in his own line: and such as our myriad-minded Shakspeare is, compared with the Racines and Metastasios, such and by a similar process of self-transformation would the man be, compared with the doctors of the mechanic school, who should construct his physiology on the heaven-descended, Know Thyself.

Even *the visions of the night* speak to us of powers within us that are not dreamt of in their day-dream of philosophy. The dreams, which we most often remember, are produced by the nascent sensations and inward *motiunculæ* (the fluxions) of the waking state. Hence, too, they are more capable of being remembered, because passing more gradually into our waking thoughts they are more likely to associate with our first perceptions after sleep. Accordingly, when the nervous system is approaching to the waking state, a sort of under-consciousness blends with our dreams, that in all we imagine as seen or heard our own self is the ventriloquist, and moves the slides in the magic-lantern. We dream about things.

But there are few persons of tender feelings and reflecting habits, who have not, more or less often in the course of their lives, experienced dreams of a very different kind, and during the profoundest sleep that is compatible with after-recollection,—states, of which it would scarcely be too bold to say that we dream the things themselves: so exact, minute, and vivid beyond all power of ordinary memory is the portraiture, so marvellously perfect is our brief *metempsychosis* into the very being, as it were, of the person who seems to address us. The dullest wight is at times a Shakspeare in his dreams. Not only may we expect that men of strong religious feelings, but little religious knowledge, will occasionally be tempted to regard such occurrences as supernatural visitations; but it ought not to surprise us, if such dreams should sometimes be confirmed by the event, as though they had actually possessed a character of divination. For who shall decide, how far a perfect reminiscence of past experiences (of many perhaps that had escaped our reflex consciousness at the time)—who shall determine, to what extent this reproductive imagination, unsophisticated by the will, and undistracted by intrusions from the senses, may or may not be concentered and sublimed into foresight and presentiment?—There would be nothing herein either to foster superstition on the one hand, or to justify contemptuous disbelief on the other. Incredulity is but credulity seen from behind, bowing and nodding assent to the habitual and the fashionable.

To the touch (or feeling) belongs the proximate; to the eye the distant. Now little as I might be disposed to believe, I should be still less inclined to ridicule, the conjecture that in the recesses of our nature, and undeveloped, there might exist an inner sense (and therefore appertaining wholly to time)—a sense hitherto without a name, which as a higher third combined and potentially included both the former. Thus gravitation combines and includes the powers of attraction and repulsion, which are the constituents of matter, as distinguished from body. And thus, not as a compound, but as a higher third, it realizes matter (of itself *ens fluxionale et præfluum*) and constitutes it body. Now suppose that this nameless inner sense stood to the relations of time as the power of gravitation to those of space? *A priori*, a presence to the future is not more mysterious or transcendent than a presence to the distant, than a power equally immediate to the most remote objects, as it is to the central mass of its own body, toward which it seems, as it were, enchanting them: for instance, the gravity in the sun and moon to the spring-tides of our ocean. The true reply to such an *hypothesis* would be, that as there is nothing to be said against its possibility, there is, likewise, nothing to be urged for its reality; and that the facts may be rationally explained without it.

It has been asked why knowing myself to be the object of personal slander (slander as unprovoked as it is groundless, unless acts of kindness are provocation) I furnish this material for it by pleading in palliation of so chimerical a fancy. With that half-playful sadness, which at once sighs and smiles, I answered: why not for that very reason? —namely, in order that my calumniator might have, if not a material, yet some basis for the poison-gas of his invention to combine with? —But no,—pure falsehood is often for the time the most effective; for how can a man confute what he can only contradict?—Our opinions and principles can not prove an *alibi.* Think only what your feelings would be if you heard a wretch deliberately perjure himself in support of an infamous accusation, so remote from all fact, so smooth and homogeneous in its untruth, such a round Robin of mere lies, that you knew not which to begin with?—What could you do, but look round with horror and astonishment, pleading silently to human nature itself,—and perhaps (as hath really been the case with me) forget both the slanderer and his slander in the anguish inflicted by the passiveness of your many professed friends, whose characters you had ever been as eager to clear from the least stain of reproach as if a coal of fire had been on your own skin?—But enough of this which would not have occurred to me at all, at this time, had it not been thus suggested.

The feeling, which in point of fact chiefly influenced me in the preceding half apology for the supposition of a divining power in the human mind, arose out of the conviction that an age or nation may become free from certain prejudices, beliefs, and superstitious practices in two ways. It may have really risen above them; or it may have fallen below them, and become too bad for their continuance. The rustic would have little reason to thank the philosopher who should give him true conceptions of ghosts, omens, dreams, and presentiments at the price of abandoning his faith in Providence and in the continued existence of his fellow-creatures after their death. The teeth of the old serpent sowed by the Cadmuses of French literature under Lewis XV. produced a plenteous crop of such philosophers and truth-trumpeters in the reign of his ill-fated successor. They taught many facts, historical, political, physiological, and ecclesiastical, diffusing their notions so widely that the very ladies and hair-dressers of Paris became fluent encyclopedists; and the sole price, which their scholars paid for these treasures of new light, was to believe Christianity an imposture, the Scriptures a forgery, the worship of God superstition, hell a fable, heaven a dream, our life without providence, and our death without hope. What can be conceived more natural than the result, that self-acknowledged beasts should first act, and next suffer themselves to be treated, as beasts?

Thank heaven!—notwithstanding the attempts of Thomas Paine and his compeers, it is not so bad with us. Open infidelity has ceased to be a means even of gratifying vanity: for the leaders of the gang themselves turned apostates to Satan, as soon as the number of their proselytes became so large that atheism ceased to give distinction. Nay, it became a mark of original thinking to defend the Creed and the Ten Commandments: so the strong minds veered round, and religion came again into fashion. But still I exceedingly doubt, whether the superannuation of sundry superstitious fancies be the result of any real diffusion of sound thinking in the nation at large. For instance, there is now no call for a Picus Mirandula to write seven books against astrology. It might seem, indeed, that a single fact like that of the loss of Kempenfeldt and his crew, or the explosion of the ship *L'Orient*, would prove to the common sense of the most ignorant, that even if astrology could be true, the astrologers must be false: for if such a science were possible it could be a science only for gods. Yet Erasmus, the prince of sound common sense, is known to have disapproved of his friend's hardihood, and did not himself venture beyond skepticism; and the immortal Newton, to whom more than to any other human being Europe owes the purification of its general notions concerning the heavenly bodies, studied astrology with much earnestness, and did not reject it till he had demonstrated the falsehood of all its pretended grounds and principles. The exit of two or three superstitions is no more a proof of the entry of good sense, than the strangling of a despot at Algiers or Constantinople is a symptom of freedom. If, therefore, not the mere disbelief, but the grounds of such disbelief must decide the question of our superior illumination, I confess that I could not from my own observations on the books and conversation of the age vote for the affirmative without much hesitation. As many errors are despised by men from ignorance as from knowledge. Whether that be not the case with regard to divination, is a query that rises in my mind (notwithstanding my fullest conviction of the non-existence of such a power) as often as I read the names of the great statesmen and philosophers, which Cicero enumerates in the introductory paragraphs of his work *de Divinatione.—Socrates, omnesque Socratici, * * * plurimisque locis gravis auctor Democritus, * * * Cratippusque, familiaris noster, quem ego parem summis Peripateticis judico, * * * * præsensionem rerum futurarum* *comprobarunt.** Of all the theistic philosophers, Xenophanes was the only one who wholly rejected it. *A stoicis degeneravit Panætius, nec tamen ausus est negare vim esse divinandi, sed dubitare se dixit.*† Nor was this a mere outward assent to the opinions of the State. Many of them subjected the question to the most exquisite arguments, and supported the affirmative not merely by experience, but (especially the Stoics, who of all the sects most cultivated psychology) by a minute analysis of human nature and its faculties: while on the mind of Cicero himself (as on that of Plato with regard to a state of retribution after death) the universality of the faith in all times and countries appears to have made the deepest impression. *Gentem quidem nullam video, neque tam humanam atque doctam, neque tam immanem tamque barbaram, quæ non significari futura, et a quibusdam intelligi prædicique posse censeat.*‡

I fear that the decrease in our feelings of reverence towards mankind at large, and our increasing aversion to every opinion not grounded in some appeal to the senses, have a larger share in this our emancipation from the prejudices of Socrates and Cicero, than reflection, insight, or a fair collation of the facts and arguments. For myself, I would much rather see the English people at large believe somewhat too much than merely just enough, if the latter is to be produced, or must be accompanied, by a contempt or neglect of the faith and intellect of their forefathers. For not to say, what yet is most certain, that a people can not believe just enough, and that there are errors which no wise man will treat with rudeness, while there is a probability that they may be the refraction of some great truth as yet below the horizon; it remains most worthy of our serious consideration, whether a fancied superiority to their ancestors' intellects must not be speedily followed in the popular mind by disrespect for their ancestors' institutions. Assuredly it is not easy to place any confidence in a form of Church or State, of the founders of which we have been taught to believe that their philosophy was jargon, and their feelings and notions rank superstition. Yet are we never to grow wiser?—Are we to be credulous by birthright, and take ghosts, omens, visions, and witchcraft, as an heirloom?—God forbid. A distinction must be made, and such a one as shall be equally availing and profitable to men of all ranks. Is this practicable?—Yes!—it exists. It is found in the study of the Old and New Testament, if only it be combined with a spiritual partaking of the Redeemer's Blood, of which, mysterious as the symbol may be, the sacramental Wine is no mere or arbitrary *memento*. This is the only certain, and this is the universal, preventive of all debasing superstitions; this is the true Hæmony (*αἷμα*, blood, *οἶνος*, wine) which our Milton has beautifully allegorized in a passage strangely overlooked by all his commentators.

* L. i. s. 2.—*Ed.* † Ib.—*Ed.* ‡ L. i. s. 1.—*Ed.*

Bear in mind, reader! the character of a militant Christian, and the results (in this life and the next) of the Redemption by the Blood of Christ; and so peruse the passage:—

> Amongst the rest a small unsightly root,
> But of divine effect, he culled me out:
> The leaf was darkish, and had prickles on it,
> But in another country, as he said,
> Bore a bright golden flower, but not in this soil!
> Unknown and like esteem'd, and the dull swain
> Treads on it daily with his clouted shoon;
> And yet more med'cinal is it than that Moly
> That Hermes once to wise Ulysses gave.
> He called it Hæmony and gave it me,
> And bade me keep it as of sovran use
> 'Gainst all enchantments, mildew, blast, or damp,
> Or ghastly furies' apparition. COMUS.

These lines might be employed as an amulet against delusions: for the man, who is indeed a Christian, will as little think of informing himself concerning the future by dreams or presentiments, as for looking for a distant object at broad noonday with a lighted taper in his hand.

But whatever of good and intellectual our nature worketh in us, it is our appointed task to render gradually our own work. For all things that surround us, and all things that happen unto us, have (each doubtless its own providential purpose, but) all one common final cause: namely, the increase of consciousness in such wise that whatever part of the *terra incognita* of our nature the increased consciousness discovers, our will may conquer and bring into subjection to itself under the sovereignty of reason.

The leading differences between mechanic and vital philosophy may all be drawn from one point: namely, that the former demanding for every mode and act of existence real or possible visibility, knows only of distance and nearness, composition (or rather juxtaposition) and decomposition, in short the relations of unproductive particles to each other; so that in every instance the result is the exact sum of the component quantities, as in arithmetical addition. This is the philosophy of death, and only of a dead nature can it hold good. In life, much more in spirit, and in a living and spiritual philosophy, the two component counter-powers actually interpenetrate each other, and generate a higher third, including both the former, *ita tamen ut sit alia et major.*

To apply this to the subject of this present comment. The elements (the factors, as it were) of religion are reason and understanding. If the composition stopped in itself, an understanding thus rationalized would lead to the admission of the general doctrines of natural religion, the belief of a God, and of immortality; and probably to an acquiescence in the history and ethics of the Gospel. But still it would be a speculative faith, and in the nature of a theory; as if the main object of religion were to solve difficulties for the satisfaction of the intellect. Now this state of mind, which alas! is the state of too many among our self-entitled rational religionists, is a mere balance or compromise of the two powers, not that living and generative interpenetration of both which would give being to essential religion;—to the religion at the birth of which *we receive the spirit of adoption, whereby we cry Abba, Father; the Spirit itself bearing witness with our spirit, that we are the children of God.* (Rom. viii. 15, 16.) In religion there is no abstraction. To the unity and infinity of the Divine Nature, of which it is the partaker, it adds the fulness, and to the fulness, the grace and the creative overflowing. That which intuitively it at once beholds and adores, praying always, and rejoicing always—that doth it tend to become. In all things and in each thing—for the Almighty Goodness doth not create generalities or abide in abstractions—in each, the meanest, object it bears witness to a mystery of infinite solution. Thus *beholding as in a glass the glory of the Lord, it is changed into the same image from glory to glory.* (2 Cor. iii. 18.) For as it is born and not made, so must it grow. As it is the image or symbol of its great object, by the organ of this similitude, as by an eye, it seeth that same image throughout the creation; and from the same cause sympathizeth with all creation in its groans to be redeemed. *For we know that the whole creation groaneth and travaileth in earnest expectation* (Rom. viii. 20–23) of a renewal of its forfeited power, the power, namely, of retiring into that image, which is its substantial form and true life, from the vanity of self, which then only is when for itself it hath ceased to be. Even so doth religion finitely express the unity of the infinite Spirit by being a total act of the soul. And even so doth it represent his fulness by its depth, by its substantiality, and by an all-pervading vital warmth which—relaxing the rigid, consolidating the dissolute, and giving cohesion to that which is about to sink down and fall abroad, as into the dust and crumble of the grave—is a life within life, evermore organizing the soul anew.

Nor doth it express the fulness only of the Spirit. It likewise represents his overflowing by its communicativeness, budding and blossoming forth in all earnestness of persuasion, and in all words of sound doctrine: while, like the citron in a genial soil and climate, it bears a golden fruitage of good-works at the same time, the example waxing in contact with the exhortation, as the ripe orange beside the opening orange-flower. Yea, even his creativeness doth it shadow out by its own powers of impregnation and production (*being such a one as Paul the aged, and also a prisoner for Jesus Christ, who begat to a lively hope his son Onesimus in his bonds*) regenerating in and through the Spirit the slaves of corruption, and fugitives from a far greater and harder master than Philemon. The love of God, and therefore God himself who is love, religion strives to express by love, and measures its growth by the increase and activity of its love. For Christian love is the last and divinest birth, the harmony, unity, and god-like transfiguration of all the vital, intellectual, moral, and spiritual powers. Now it manifests itself as the sparkling and ebullient spring of well-doing in gifts and in labors; and now as a silent fountain of patience and long-suffering, the fulness of which no hatred or persecution can exhaust or diminish; a more than conqueror in the persuasion, *that neither death, nor life, nor angels, nor principalities, nor powers, nor things present, nor things to come, nor height, nor depth, nor any other creature, shall be able to separate it from the love of God which is in Christ Jesus the Lord.* (Rom. viii. 38, 39.)

From God's love through his Son, crucified for us from the beginning of the world, religion begins: and in love towards God and the creatures of God it hath its end and completion. O, how heaven-like it is to sit among brethren at the feet of a minister who speaks under the influence of love and is heard under the same influence! For all abiding and spiritual knowledge, infused into a grateful and affectionate fellow-Christian, is as the child of the mind that infuses it. The delight which he gives he receives; and in that bright and liberal hour the gladdened preacher can scarce gather the ripe produce of to-day without discovering and looking forward to the green fruits and embryons, the heritage and reversionary wealth of the days to come; till he bursts forth in prayer and thanksgiving—*The harvest truly is plenteous, but the laborers few. O gracious Lord of the harvest, send forth laborers into thy harvest! There is no difference between Jew and Greek. Thou, Lord, over all, art rich to all that call upon thee. But how shall they call on him in whom they have not believed? and how shall they believe in him of whom they have not heard? and how shall they hear without a preacher? and how shall they preach except they be sent? And O! how beautiful upon the mountains are the feet of him that bringeth good tidings, that publisheth peace, that bringeth glad tidings of good things, that publisheth salvation; that saith unto the captive soul, Thy God reigneth! God manifested in the flesh hath redeemed thee! O Lord of the harvest, send forth laborers into thy harvest.*

Join with me, reader! in the fervent prayer that we may seek within us what we can never find elsewhere, that we may find within us what no words can put there, that one only true religion, which elevateth knowing into being, which is at once the science of being, and the being and the life of all genuine science.

(C.)

Not without great hesitation should I express a suspicion concerning the genuineness of any the least important passage in the New Testament, unless I could adduce the most conclusive evidence from the earliest manuscripts and commentators, in support of its interpolation: well knowing that such permission has already opened a door to the most fearful license. It is indeed, in its consequences, no less than an assumed right of picking and choosing our religion out of the Scriptures. Most assuredly I would never hazard a suggestion of this kind in any instance in which the retention or the omission of the words could make the slightest difference with regard to fact, miracle, or precept. Still less would I start the question, where the *hypothesis* of their interpolation could be wrested to the discountenancing of any article of doctrine concerning which dissension existed: no, not though the doubt or disbelief of the doctrine had been confined to those, whose faith few but themselves would honor with the name of Christianity; however reluctant we might be, both from the courtesies of social life and the nobler charities of humility, to withhold from the persons themselves the title of Christians.

But as there is nothing in Matthew xii. 40, which would fall within this general rule, I dare permit myself to propose the query, whether there does not exist internal evidence of its being a gloss of some unlearned, though pious, Christian of the first century, which has slipt into the text? The following are my reasons. 1. It is at all events a comment on the words of our Saviour, and no part of his speech. 2. It interrupts the course and breaks down the application of our Lord's argument, as addressed to men who from their unwillingness to sacrifice their vain traditions, gainful hypocrisy, and pride both of heart and of demeanor, demanded a miracle for the confirmation of moral truths that must have borne witness to their own divinity in the consciences of all who had not rendered themselves conscience-proof. 3. The text strictly taken is irreconcilable with the fact as it is afterwards related, and as it is universally accepted. I at least remember no calculation of time, according to which the interspace from Friday evening to the earliest dawn of Sunday morning, could be represented as three days and three nights. As three days our Saviour himself speaks of it (John ii. 19) and so it would be described in common language as well as according to the use of the Jews; but I can find no other part of Scripture which authorizes the phrase of three nights. This gloss is not found either in the repetition of the circumstances by Matthew himself (xvi. 4), nor in Mark (viii. 12), nor in Luke (xii. 54). Mark's narration doth. indeed most strikingly confirm my second reason, drawn from the purpose of our

Saviour's argument: for the allusion to the prophet Jonas is omitted altogether, and the refusal therefore rests on the depravity of the applicants, as proved by the wantonness of the application itself. All signs must have been useless to such men as long as the great sign of the times, the call to repentance, remained without effect. 4. The gloss corresponds with the known fondness of the earlier Jewish converts, and indeed of the Christians in general of the first century, to bring out in detail and into exact square every accommodation of the Old Testament, which they either found in the Gospels, or made for themselves. It is too notorious into what strange fancies (not always at safe distance from dangerous errors) the oldest uninspired writers of the Christian Church were seduced by this passion of transmuting without Scriptural authority incidents, names, and even mere sounds of the Hebrew Scriptures, into Evangelical types and correspondences.

An additional reason may perhaps occur to those who alone would be qualified to appreciate its force: namely, to Biblical scholars familiar with the opinions and arguments of sundry doctors, Rabbinical as well as Christian, respecting the first and second chapter of Jonah.

(D.)

In all ages of the Christian Church, and in the later period of the Jewish (that is, as soon as from their acquaintance first with the Oriental, and afterwards with the Greek, philosophy the precursory and preparative influences of the Gospel began to work) there have existed individuals (Laodiceans in spirit, minims in faith, and nominalists in philosophy) who mistake outlines for substance, and distinct images for clear conceptions; with whom, therefore, not to be a thing is the same as not to be at all. The contempt in which such persons hold the works and doctrines of all theologians before Grotius, and of all philosophers before Locke and Hartley (at least before Bacon and Hobbes), is not accidental, nor yet altogether owing to that epidemic of a proud ignorance occasioned by a diffused sciolism, which gave a sickly and hectic showiness to the latter half of the last century. It is a real instinct of self-defence acting offensively by anticipation. For the authority of all the greatest names of antiquity is full and decisive against them; and man, by the very nature of his birth and growth, is so much the creature of authority, that there is no way of effectually resisting it, but by undermining the reverence for the past *in toto.* Thus, the Jewish Prophets have, forsooth, a certain degree of antiquarian value, as being the only specimens extant of the oracles of a barbarous tribe; the Evangelists are to be interpreted with a due allowance for their superstitious prejudices concerning evil spirits, and St. Paul never suffers them to forget that he had been brought up at the feet of a Jewish Rabbi! The Greeks indeed were a fine people in works of taste; but as to their philosophers—the writings of Plato are smoke and flash from the witch's caldron of a disturbed imagination:—Aristotle's works a quickset hedge of fruitless and thorny distinctions; and all the philosophers before Plato and Aristotle fablers and allegorizers!

But these men have had their day: and there are signs of the times clearly announcing that that day is verging to its close. Even now there are not a few, on whose convictions it will not be uninfluencive to know, that the power, by which men are led to the truth of things, instead of their appearances, was deemed and entitled the living and substantial Word of God by the soundest of the Hebrew Doctors; that the eldest and most profound of the Greek philosophers demanded assent to their doctrine, mainly as *σοφία θεοπαράδοτος*, that is, a traditionary wisdom that had its origin in inspiration; that these men referred the same power to the *πῦρ ἀείζωον ὑπὸ διοικοῦντος Λόγου;* and that they were scarcely less express than their scholar Philo Judæus, in their affirmations of the Logos, as no mere attribute or quality, no mode of abstraction, no personification, but literally and mysteriously *Deus alter et idem.*

When education has disciplined the minds of our gentry for austerer study; when educated men shall be ashamed to look abroad for truths that can be only found within; within themselves they will discover, intuitively will they discover, the distinctions between *the light that lighteth every man that cometh into the world;* and the understanding, which forms the *peculium* of each man, as different in extent and value from another man's understanding, as his estate may be from his neighbor's estate. The words of St. John i. 7–12, are in their whole extent interpretable of the understanding, which derives its rank and mode of being in the human race (that is, as far as it may be contrasted with the instinct of the dog or elephant, in all, which constitutes it human understanding) from the universal light. This light comes therefore as to its own. Being rejected, it leaves the understanding to a world of dreams and darkness: for in it alone is life and the *life is the light of men.* What then but apparitions can remain to a philosophy, which strikes death through all things visible and invisible; satisfies itself then only when it can explain those abstractions of the outward senses, which by an unconscious irony it names indifferently facts and *phænomena*, mechanically—that is, by the laws of death; and brands with the name of mysticism every solution grounded in life, or the powers and intuitions of life?

On the other hand, if the light be received by faith, to such understandings it delegates the privilege (*ἐξουσίαν*) to become sons of God, expanding while it elevates, even as the beams of the sun incorporate with the mist, and make its natural darkness and earthly nature the bearer and interpreter of their own glory. Ἐὰν μὴ πιστεύσητε, οὐ μὴ συνῆτε.

The very same truth is found in a fragment of the Ephesian Heraclitus, preserved by Stobæus. *Ξὺν νόῳ λέγοντας ἰσχυρίζεσθαι χρὴ τῷ ξυνῷ πάντων· τρέφονται γὰρ πάντες οἱ ἀνθρώπινοι νόοι ὑπὸ ἑνὸς τοῦ θείου (Λόγου·) κρατεῖ γὰρ τοσοῦτον ὁκόσον ἐθέλει, καὶ ἐξαρκεῖ πᾶσι καὶ περιγίνεται.** —To discourse rationally (if we would render the discursive understanding discourse of reason) it behooves us to derive strength from that which is common to all men (*the light that lighteth every man*). For all human understandings are nourished by the one Divine Word, whose power is commensurate with his will, and is sufficient for all and overfloweth (*shineth in darkness, and is not contained therein, or comprehended by the darkness*).

This was Heraclitus, whose book is nearly six hundred years older than the Gospel of St. John, and who was proverbially entitled the Dark (*ὁ σκοτεινός*). But it was a darkness which Socrates would not condemn,† and which would probably appear to enlightened Christians the darkness of prophecy, had the work, which he hid in the temple, been preserved to us. But obscurity is a word of many meanings. It may be in the subject; it may be in the author; or it may be in the reader;—and this again may originate in the state of the reader's heart; or in that of his capacity; or in his temper; or in his accidental associations. Two kinds are especially pointed out by the divine Plato in his Sophistes. The beauty of the original is beyond my reach. On my anxiety to give the fulness of the thought, I must ground my excuse for construing rather than translating. The fidelity of the version may well atone for its harshness in a passage that deserves a meditation beyond the ministry of words, even the words of Plato himself, though in them, or nowhere, are to be heard the sweet sounds, that issued from the head of Memnon at the touch of light.—"One thing is the hardness to be understood of the sophist, another that of the philosopher. The former retreating into the obscurity of that which hath not true being (*τοῦ μὴ ὄντος*), and by long intercourse accustomed to the same, is hard to be known on account of the duskiness of the place. But the philosopher by contemplation of pure reason evermore approximating to the idea of true being (*τοῦ ὄντος*) is by no means easy to be seen on account of the splendor of that region. For the intellectual eyes of the many flit, and are incapable of looking fixedly toward the God-like."‡

* Serm. III.—*Ed.*

† Diogenes Laertius has preserved the characteristic criticism of Socrates. *Φασὶ δ' Εὐριπίδην αὐτῷ δόντα τοῦ Ἡρακλείτου σύγγραμμα, ἔρεσθαι, Τί δοκεῖ; τὸν δὲ φάναι, Ἃ μὲν συνῆκα, γενναῖα· οἶμαι δὲ, καὶ ἃ μὴ συνῆκα· πλὴν Δηλίου γέ τινος δεῖται κολυμβητοῦ.* II. v. 7.—*Ed.*

‡ The passage is:—

ΞΕ. *Τὸν μὲν δὴ φιλόσοφον ἐν τοιούτῳ τινὶ τόπῳ καὶ νῦν καὶ ἔπειτα ἀνευ-*

There are, I am aware, persons who willingly admit, that not in articles of faith alone, but in the heights of geometry, and even in the necessary first principles of natural philosophy, there exist truths of apodictic force in reason, which the mere understanding strives in vain to comprehend. Take, as an instance, the descending series of infinites in every finite, a position which involves a contradiction for the understanding, yet follows demonstrably from the very definition of body, as that which fills a space. For wherever there is a space filled, there must be an extension to be divided. When therefore maxims generalized from appearances (*phænomena*) are applied to substances; when rules, abstracted or deduced from forms in time and space, are used as measures of spiritual being, yea even of the Divine Nature which can not be compared or classed (*For my thoughts are not your thoughts, neither are your ways my ways, saith the Lord.* Isaiah lv. 8); such professors can not but protest against the whole process, as grounded on a gross *metabasis* εἰς ἄλλο γένος. Yet still they are disposed to tolerate it as a sort of sanative counter-excitement, that holds in check the more dangerous disease of Methodism. But I more than doubt of both the positions. I do not think Methodism, Calvinistic or Wesleyan, the more dangerous disease; and even if it were, I should deny that it is at all likely to be counteracted by the rational Christianity of our modern Alogi (λόγος πίστεως ἄλογος!) who, mistaking unity for sameness, have been pleased, by a misnomer not less contradictory to their own tenets than intolerant to those of Christians in general, to entitle themselves Unitarians. The two contagions attack each a wholly different class of minds and tempers, and each tends to produce and justify the other, accordingly as the predisposition of the patient may chance to be. If fanaticism be as a fire in the flooring of the Church, the idolism of the unspiritualized understanding is the dry rot in its beams and timbers. *Ὕβριν χρὴ σβεννύειν μᾶλλον ἢ πυρκαϊήν*, says Heraclitus.* It is not the sect of Unitarian Dissenters, but the spirit of Unitarianism in the members of the Church that alarms me. To what open revilings, and to what whispered slanders, I subject my name by this public avowal, I well

ρήσομεν, ἐὰν ζητῶμεν, ἰδεῖν μὲν χαλεπὸν ἐναργῶς καὶ τοῦτον, ἕτερον μὴν τρόπον ἥ τε τοῦ σοφιστοῦ χαλεπότης ἥ τε τούτου.

ΘΕΑΙ. Πῶς;

ΞΕ. Ὁ *μὲν ἀποδιδράσκων εἰς τὴν τοῦ μὴ ὄντος σκοτεινότητα, τριβῇ προσαπτόμενος αὐτῆς, διὰ τὸ σκοτεινὸν τοῦ τόπου κατανοῆσαι χαλεπός. ἦ γάρ;*

ΘΕΑΙ. *Ἔοικεν.*

ΞΕ. Ὁ *δέ γε φιλόσοφος, τῇ τοῦ ὄντος ἀεὶ διὰ λογισμῶν πρόσκείμενος ἰδέᾳ, διὰ τὸ λαμπρὸν αὖ τῆς χώρας οὐδαμῶς εὐπετὴς ὀφθῆναι· τὰ γὰρ τῆς τῶν πολλῶν ψυχῆς ὄμματα καρτερεῖν πρὸς τὸ θεῖον ἀφορῶντα ἀδύνατα.* s. 84. —*Ed.*

Diog. Laert. ix. 1.—*Ed.*

know: *ἀπίστους γὰρ τινὰς εἶναι ἐπιστύφων Ἡράκλειτός, φησιν, ἀκοῦσαι οὐκ ἐπιϛαμένους οὐδ' εἰπεῖν· ἀλλὰ καὶ, κύνες ὥς, βαΰζουσιν ὃν ἂν μὴ γινώσκωσι.*

(E.)

The accomplished author of the Arcadia, the star of serenest brilliance in the glorious constellation of Elizabeth's court, our England's Sir Philip Sidney, the paramount gentleman of Europe, the poet, warrior, and statesman, held high converse with Spenser on the idea of supersensual beauty; on all "earthly fair and amiable," as the symbol of that idea; and on music and poesy as its living educts. With the same genial reverence did the younger Algernon commune with Harrington and Milton on the idea of a perfect State; and in what sense it is true, that the men (that is, the aggregate of the inhabitants of a country at any one time) are made for the State, not the State for the men. But these lights shine no longer, or for a few. *Exeunt:* and enter in their stead Holofernes and Costard, masked as Metaphysics and Common-Sense. And these too have their ideas. The former has an idea that Hume, Hartley, and Condillac, have exploded all ideas, but those of sensation; he has an idea that he was particularly pleased with the fine idea of the last-named philosopher, that there is no absurdity in asking What color virtue is of? inasmuch as the proper philosophic answers would be black, blue, or bottle-green, according as the coat, waistcoat, and small clothes might chance to be of the person, the series of whose motions had excited the sensations, which formed our idea of virtue. The latter has no idea of a better-flavored haunch of venison than he dined off at the Albion. He admits that the French have an excellent idea of cooking in general, but holds that their best cooks have no more idea of dressing a turtle than the gourmands themselves, at Paris, have any real idea of the true taste and color of the fat.

It is not impossible that a portion of the high value attached of late years to the dates and margins of our old folios and quartos may be transferred to their contents. Even now there exists a shrewd suspicion in the minds of reading men, that not only Plato and Aristotle, but even Scotus Erigena,* and the schoolmen from Peter Lombard† to Duns Scotus,‡ are not such mere blockheads, as they pass for with those who have never perused a line of their writings. What the results may be, should this ripen into conviction, I can but guess. But all history seems to favor the persuasion I entertain, that in every age the speculative philosophy in general acceptance, the metaphysical opinions that happen to be predominant, will influence the theology of that age. Whatever is proposed for the belief, as true, must have

* He died at Oxford in 886.—*Ed.*

† He died Bishop of Paris in 1164.—*Ed.*

‡ He died in 1308.—*Ed.*

been previously admitted by reason as possible, as involving no contradiction to the universal forms or laws of thought, no incompatibility in the terms of the proposition; and the determination on this head belongs exclusively to the science of metaphysics. In each article of faith embraced on conviction, the mind determines, first intuitively on its logical possibility; secondly, discursively, on its analogy to doctrines already believed, as well as on its correspondence to the wants and faculties of our nature; and thirdly, historically, on the direct and indirect evidences. But the probability of an event is a part of its historic evidence, and constitutes its presumptive proof, or the evidence *à priori*. Now as the degree of evidence *à posteriori*, requisite in order to a satisfactory proof of the actual occurrence of any fact stands, in an inverse ratio the strength or weakness of the evidence *à priori* (that is, a fact probable in itself may be believed on slight testimony); it is manifest that of the three factors, by which the mind is determined to the admission or rejection of the point in question, the last, the historical, must be greatly influenced by the second, analogy, and that both depend on the first, logical congruity, not indeed as their cause or preconstituent, but as their indispensable condition; so that the very inquiry concerning them is preposterous (*σόφισμα τοῦ ὑςέρου προτέρου*) as long as the first remains undetermined. Again: the history of human opinions (ecclesiastical and philosophical history) confirms by manifold instances, what attentive consideration of the position itself might have authorized us to presume, namely, that on all such subjects as are out of the sphere of the senses, and therefore incapable of a direct proof from outward experience, the question whether any given position is logically impossible (incompatible with reason) or only incomprehensible (that is, not reducible to the forms of sense, namely, time and space, or those of the understanding, namely, quantity, quality, and relation) in other words, the question, whether an assertion be in itself inconceivable, or only by us unimaginable, will be decided by each individual according to the positions assumed as first principles in the metaphysical system which he has previously adopted. Thus the existence of a Supreme Reason, the creator of the material universe, involved a contradiction for a disciple of Epicurus, who had convinced himself that causative thought was tantamount to something out of nothing or substance out of shadow, and incompatible with the axiom, *Nihil ex nihilo:* While on the contrary to a Platonist this position, that thought or mind essentially, *vel sensu eminenti*, is causative, is necessarily pre-supposed in every other truth, as that without which every fact of experience would involve a contradiction in reason. Now it is not denied that the framers of our Church Liturgy, Homilies and Articles, entertained metaphysical opinions irreconcilable in their first principles with the system of speculative philosophy which has been taught in this country, and only not universally received, since the asserted and generally believed defeat of the Bishop of Worcester (the excellent Stillingfleet) in his famous controversy with Mr. Locke. Assuredly therefore it is well worth the consideration of our Clergy whether it is at all probable in itself, or congruous with experience, that the disputed Articles of our Church *de revelatis et credendis* should be adopted with singleness of heart, and in the light of knowledge, when the grounds and first philosophy, on which the framers themselves rested the antecedent credibility (may we not add even the revelability?) of the Articles in question, have been exchanged for principles the most dissimilar, if not contrary? It may be said and truly, that the Scriptures, and not metaphysical systems, are our best and ultimate authority. And doubtless, on Revelation we must rely for the truth of the doctrines. Yet what is considered incapable of being conceived as possible, will be deemed incapable of having been revealed as real: and that philosophy has hitherto had a negative voice, as to the interpretation of the Scriptures in high and doctrinal points, is proved by the course of argument adopted in the controversial volumes of all the orthodox divines from Origen to Bishop Bull, as well as by the very different sense attached to the same texts by the disciples of the modern *metaphysique*, wherever they have been at liberty to form their own creeds according to their own expositions.

I repeat the question then: is it likely, that the faith of our ancestors will be retained when their philosophy is rejected,—rejected *à priori*, as baseless notions not worth inquiring into, as obsolete errors which it would be slaying the slain to confute? Should the answer be in the negative, it would be no strained inference that the Clergy at least, as the conservators of the national faith, and the accredited representatives of learning in general amongst us, might with great advantage to their own peace of mind qualify themselves to judge for themselves concerning the comparative worth and solidity of the two schemes. Let them make the experiment, whether a patient rehearing of their predecessor's cause, with enough of predilection for the men to counterpoise the prejudices against their system, might not induce them to move for a new trial;—a result of no mean importance in my opinion, were it on this account alone, that it would recall certain ex-dignitaries in the book-republic from their long exile on the shelves of our public libraries to their old familiar station on the reading desks of our theological students. However strong the presumption were in favor of principles authorized by names that must needs be so dear and venerable to a minister of the Church in England, as those of Hooker, Whitaker, Field, Donne, Selden, Stillingfleet—(masculine intellects, formed under the robust discipline of an age memorable for keenness of research, and iron industry)—yet no undue preponderance from any previous weight in this scale will be apprehended by minds capable of estimating the counter-weights, which it must first bring to a balance in the scale opposite. The obstinacy of opinions that have always been taken for granted, opinions unassailable even by the remembrance of a doubt, the silent accrescence of belief from the unwatched depositions of a general, never-contradicted, hearsay; the concurring suffrage of modern books, all pre-supposing or re-asserting the same principles with the same confidence, and with the same contempt for all prior systems;—and among these, works of highest authority, appealed to in our Legislature, and lectured on at our Universities; the very books, perhaps, that called forth our own first efforts in thinking; the solutions and confutations in which must therefore have appeared ten-fold more satisfactory from their having given us our first information of the difficulties to be solved, of the opinions to be confuted.—Verily, a clergyman's partiality towards the tenets of his forefathers must be intense beyond all precedent, if it can more than sustain itself against antagonists so strong in themselves, and with such mighty adjuncts.

Nor in this enumeration dare I (though fully aware of the obloquy to which I am exposing myself) omit the noticeable fact, that we have attached a portion even of our national glory (not only to the system itself, that system of disguised and decorous Epicureanism, which has been the only orthodox philosophy of the last hundred years; but also, and more emphatically) to the name of the assumed father of thesystem, whoraised it to its present pride of place, and almost universal acceptance throughout Europe. And how was this effected? Extrinsically, by all the causes, consequences, and accompaniments of the Revolution in 1688: by all the opinions, interests, and passions, which counteracted by the sturdy prejudices of the malcontents with the Revolution; qualified by the compromising character of its chief conductors; not more propelled by the spirit of enterprise and hazard in our commercial towns, than kept in check by the characteristic *vis inertiæ* of the peasantry and landholders; both parties cooled and lessoned by the equal failure of the destruction, and of the restoration, of monarchy;—it was effected extrinsically, I say, by the same influences, which—(not in and of themselves, but with all these and sundry other modifications)—combined under an especial control of Providence to perfect and secure the majestic temple of the British Constitution:—but the very same which in France, without this providential counterpoise, overthrew the motley fabric of feudal oppression to build up in its stead the madhouse of Jacobinism. Intrinsically, and as far as the philosophic scheme itself is alone concerned, it was effected by the mixed policy and *bonhommie*, with which the author contrived to retain in his celebrated work whatever the system possesses of soothing for the indolence, and of flattering for the vanity, of men's average understandings: while he kept out of sight all its darker features which outrage the instinctive faith and moral feelings of mankind, ingeniously threading-on the dried and shrivelled, yet still wholesome and nutritious, fruits plucked from the rich grafts of ancient wisdom, to the barren and worse than barren fig-tree of the mechanic philosophy. Thus, the sensible Christians, *the angels of the church of Laodicea*, with the numerous and mighty sect of their admirers, delighted with the discovery that they could purchase the decencies and the creditableness of religion at so small an expenditure of faith, extolled the work for its pious conclusions: while the infidels, wiser in their generation than the children (at least than these nominal children) of light, eulogized it with no less zeal for the sake of its principles and assumptions, and with the foresight of those obvious and only legitimate conclusions, that might and would be deduced from them. Great at all times and almost incalculable are the influences of party spirit in exaggerating contemporary reputation; but never perhaps from the first syllable of recorded time were they exerted under such a concurrence and conjunction of fortunate accidents, of helping and furthering events and circumstances, as in the instance of Mr. Locke.

I am most fully persuaded, that the principles both of taste, morals, and religion taught in our most popular *compendia* of moral and political philosophy, natural theology, evidences of Christianity, and the like, are false, injurious, and debasing. But I am likewise not less deeply convinced that all the well-meant attacks on the writings of modern infidels and heretics, in support either of the miracles or of the mysteries of the Christian religion, can be of no permanent utility, while the authors themselves join in the vulgar appeal to common sense as the one infallible judge in matters, which become subjects of philosophy only, because they involve a contradiction between this common sense and our moral instincts, and require therefore an arbiter, which containing both *eminenter* must be higher than either. We but mow down the rank misgrowth instead of cleansing the soil, as long as we ourselves protect and manure, as the pride of our garden, a tree of false knowledge, which looks fair and showy and variegated with fruits not its own, that hang from the branches which have at various times been ingrafted on its stem; but from the roots of which under ground the runners are sent off, that shoot up at a distance and bring forth the true and natural crop. I will speak plainly, though in so doing I must bid defiance to all the flatterers of the folly and foolish self-opinion of the half-instructed many. The articles of our Church, and the true principles of government and social order, will never be effectually and consistently maintained against their antagonists till the champions have themselves ceased to worship the same Baal with their enemies, till they have cast out the common idol from the recesses of their own convictions, and with it the whole service and ceremonial of idolism. While all parties agree in their abjuration of Plato and Aristotle, and in their contemptuous neglect of the Schoolmen and the scholastic logic, without which the excellent Selden (that genuine English mind whose erudition, broad, deep, and manifold as it was, is yet less remarkable than his robust healthful common sense) affirms it impossible for a divine thoroughly to comprehend or reputably to defend the whole undiminished and unadulterated scheme of Catholic faith, while all alike preassume, with Mr. Locke, that the mind contains only the reliques of the senses, and therefore proceed with him to explain the substance from the shadow, the voice from the echo,—they can but detect each the other's inconsistencies. The champion of orthodoxy will victoriously expose the bald and staring incongruity of the Socinian scheme with the language of Scripture, and with the final causes of all revealed religion:—the Socinian will retort on the orthodox the incongruity of a belief in mysteries with his own admissions concerning the origin, and nature of all tenable ideas, and as triumphantly expose the pretences of believing in a form of words, to which the believer himself admits that he can attach no consistent meaning. Lastly, the godless materialist, as the only consistent because the only consequent reasoner, will secretly laugh at both. If these sentiments should be just, the consequences are so important that every well-educated man, who has given proofs that he has at least patiently studied the subject, deserves a patient hearing. Had I not the authority of the greatest and noblest intellects for at least two thousand years on my side, yet from the vital interest of the opinions themselves, and their natural, unconstrained, and (as it were) spontaneous coalescence with the faith of the Catholic Church (they being, moreover, the opinions of its most eminent Fathers), I might appeal to all orthodox Christians, whether they adhere to the faith only or both to the faith and forms of the Church, in the words of my motto: *Ad isthæc quæso vos, qualiacunque primo videantur aspectu attendite, ut qui vobis forsan insanire videar, saltem quibus insaniam rationibus cognoscatis.*

There are still a few, however, young men of loftiest minds, and the very stuff out of which the sword and shield of truth and honor are to be made, who will not withdraw all confidence from the writer, although

> 'Tis true, that passionate for ancient truths
> And honoring with religious love the great
> Of elder times, he hated to excess,
> With an unquiet and intolerant scorn,
> The hollow puppets of a hollow age
> Ever idolatrous, and changing ever
> Its worthless idols!*

* Poet. Works, VII. p. 153.—*Ed.*

a few there are, who will still less be indisposed to follow him in his milder mood, whenever their Friend,

> Piercing the long-neglected holy cave,
> The haunt obscure of Old Philosophy,
> Shall bid with lifted torch its starry walls
> Sparkle, as erst they sparkled to the flame
> Of odorous lamps tended by saint and sage!*

I have hinted, above, at the necessity of a glossary, and I will conclude these supplementary remarks with a nomenclature of the principal terms which occur in the elements of speculative philosophy, in their old and rightful sense, according to my belief; at all events the sense in which I have myself employed them. The most general term (*genus summum*) belonging to the speculative intellect, as distinguished from acts of the will, is Representation, or (still better) Presentation.

A conscious Presentation, if it refers exclusively to the subject, as a modification of his own state of being, is = Sensation.

The same if it refers to an Object, is = Perception.

A Perception, immediate and individual, is = an Intuition.

The same, mediate, and by means of a character or mark common to several things, is = a Conception.

A Conception, extrinsic and sensuous, is = a Fact, or a Cognition.

The same, purely mental and abstracted from the forms of the understanding itself = a Notion.

A notion may be realized, and becomes cognition; but that which is neither a sensation nor a perception, that which is neither individual (that is, a sensible intuition) nor general (that is, a conception), which neither refers to outward facts, nor yet is abstracted from the forms of perception contained in the understanding; but which is an educt of the imagination actuated by the pure reason, to which there neither is nor can be an adequate correspondent in the world of the senses;—this and this alone is = an Idea. Whether ideas are regulative only, according to Aristotle and Kant; or likewise constitutive, and one with the power and life of nature, according to Plato, and Plotinus (*ἐν λόγῳ ζωὴ ἦν, καὶ ἡ ζωὴ ἦν τὸ φῶς τῶν ἀνθρώπων*) is the highest problem of philosophy, and not part of its nomenclature.†

* Poetical Works, VII. p. 154.—*Ed.*

† See Table Talk, VI. p. 295.—*Ed.* See also Kant's *Kritik der reinen Vernunft;* conclusion of the chapter *Von den Ideen überhaupt.*—*Am. Ed.*

INDEX TO AIDS TO REFLECTION.

www.ingramcontent.com/pod-product-compliance
Lightning Source LLC
LaVergne TN
LVHW020924110826
845150LV00004B/760

* 9 7 8 1 4 2 5 5 5 3 9 8 2 *